Fundamentals
of Pascal:
Understanding Programming
and Problem Solving

Fundamentals of Pascal:

Understanding Programming and Problem Solving

Douglas W. Nance
CENTRAL MICHIGAN UNIVERSITY

West Publishing Company
ST. PAUL   NEW YORK   LOS ANGELES   SAN FRANCISCO

Dedicated to Bill, Lynda, and Juliann.
We are blessed by their existence.

Copy editor: Janet Hunter
Composition: Auto-Graphics, Inc.
Interior design: Paula Schlosser
Illustrations: Christine Dettner
Cover design: Prism Studios

Library of Congress Cataloging-in-Publication Data

Nance, Douglas W.
    Fundamentals of Pascal.
    Bibliography: p.
    Includes index.
    1. PASCAL (Computer program language)   I. Title.
QA76.73.P2N34   1986   005.13′3   86-11051
ISBN 0-314-93206-2

⊞ Contents

CHAPTER 4 ■ Writing Complete Programs   75

CHAPTER 5 ■ Conditional Statements   123

CHAPTER 6 ■ Looping Statements   179

⊞ Preface

⊞ Those who teach entry-level courses in computer science are familiar with the problems that beginning students encounter. Initially, students can get so involved in learning a language that they may fail to grasp the significance of using the language to solve problems. Conversely, it is possible to emphasize problem solving to the extent that using a particular language to solve problems becomes almost incidental. The intent of this text is to provide a happy medium between these approaches. Students should understand language concepts and subsequently be able to use them to solve problems.

Overview and Organization

The first material (Chapters 1–4) is presented at a deliberate pace. If students in the class have had some computing experience, these chapters may be covered rapidly. Chapters 1 and 4 could be briefly discussed and Chapters 2 and 3 could be covered in one week. However, students must be able to solve problems using top-down design with stepwise refinement.

Throughout the text, I have attempted to explain and carefully develop concepts, which are illustrated by frequent examples and diagrams. New concepts are then used in complete programs to show how they aid in solving problems. An early and consistent emphasis has been placed on good writing habits and on producing neat, attractive output. I firmly believe program documentation and readability are important. Thus, I frequently discuss them in the text, and I offer style tips where appropriate.

This text should provide a complete one-semester course in Pascal. Even if it is introduced at a deliberate pace, records (Chapter 11) and files

(Chapter 12) can still be covered in an 18-week semester. However, it might be difficult to include material from the remaining chapters.

Subprograms are introduced in Chapter 7. By this time, students should be familiar with variables, looping, and selection. A formal development of using parameters is included here. All subsequent work utilizes subprograms in problem solving and program design.

Chapter 8 discusses text files and user-defined data types. Prior to this chapter, all programs were interactive. Since data structures are studied next, students need to be able to get data from a file rather than the keyboard. They also should be aware of the significance of user-defined or enumerated data types. Thus, several sections have been devoted to development of this topic.

Chapters 9 and 10 develop arrays. Due to the significance of this concept, these chapters contain numerous examples, illustrations, and applications. A selection sort and a bubble sort have been used to sort array elements. Records and files are covered in Chapters 11 and 12, respectively. Their placement here is traditional. These chapters, combined with Chapters 9 and 10, present a detailed treatment of static data structures.

Chapter 13, Sets, could be presented any time after Chapter 8. Although a full chapter has been devoted to this topic, a working knowledge could be given to students in one or two days. Dynamic variables and data structures are introduced in Chapter 14. A reasonable discussion and development of pointers, linked lists, and binary trees is included. However, a full development of these concepts would have to come from a second course with a different text.

Pascal statements in this text conform to standard Pascal. Although several other versions can be used, it was felt that standard Pascal was the best choice for an introductory textbook. Only minor modifications would be necessary in order to use this text with other versions of Pascal.

Features

As with any text, several pedagogical features are noteworthy:

- Objectives—concise list of topics and learning objectives in each section
- Self quizzes—short, self-check exercises to allow students to measure their understanding and progress
- Style tips—suggestions for programming style, intended to enhance readability
- Exercises—short-answer questions at the end of each section
- Chapter review exercises—comprehensive and complete lists of review questions for each chapter
- Programming problems—starting with Chapter 4, lengthy lists of suggestions for complete programs given at ends of chapters
- Notes of Interest—tidbits of information intended to create awareness of and interest in various aspects of computer science
- Suggestions for test programs—ideas included in exercises that encourage the student to use the computer to determine answers to questions and to see how to implement concepts in short programs

- Complete programs—when appropriate, a complete program at the end of the chapter that illustrates utilization of concepts developed within the chapter
- Running and debugging hints at the ends of chapters
- New terms are italicized when first introduced

In the back of the book there is a complete glossary, as well as appendixes on reserved words, standard identifiers, syntax diagrams, character sets, compiler error messages, the **GOTO** statement, and assertions. The final two sections of back matter provide answers to self quizzes and selected exercises.

Use of this Text   It is assumed that this text will be used sequentially. There are, however, some possible variations. First, some of the material in Chapters 1–4 can be omitted if an instructor desires a more rapid pace. Second, Chapter 13 could be introduced as early as Chapter 8. Time needed to cover material in an introductory Pascal course varies significantly. Thus, it is difficult to suggest a time frame for presenting sections and chapters from this text. However, there are at least three general scenarios for which this text would be appropriate.

1. A deliberately paced, thorough presentation of concepts would allow you to get to records and/or files in a one-semester course.
2. An accelerated pace with students who have previous computing experience would allow you to get into Chapter 14 in a one-semester course.
3. A deliberate pace with a thorough presentation would allow you to present the material in Chapters 1–14 in a two-quarter sequence.

Ancillaries   Ancillary materials include a separate *Answer Key* and a separate *Teacher's Guide*. The *Answer Key* contains annotated answers to section exercises, answers to chapter review exercises, and three or four complete programs for each chapter from the chapter programming problems.

The *Teacher's Guide* is organized into three sections. The first contains a suggested teaching timeline and also shows how the text material can be organized and presented for students studying for the Advanced Placement examination. The second section contains comments for each chapter. These chapter comments include:

1. Chapter objectives
2. A list of new Pascal commands and statements
3. Chapter outline
4. Teaching remarks and suggestions for each section
5. Chapter test questions
6. Computer games and puzzles (where appropriate)
7. Answer key for chapter test questions

The final section contains transparency masters. About 70 of these illustrate diagrams, examples, charts, and short segments from the text. The rest of them are the chapter summary programs.

All programs and program segments have been run on a computer. Every effort has been made to produce an error-free text, although this is virtually impossible. I assume full responsibility for all errors and omissions. If you detect any, please be tolerant and notify me or West Publishing Company so they can be corrected in subsequent printings and editions.

Acknowledgments

I would like to take this opportunity to thank those who in some way contributed to the completion of this text. Several reviewers contributed significant constructive comments during various phases of manuscript development. They include:

Richard Offerman
Albion High School
Albion, MI

Rev. John Comiskey
Farrell High School
Stratton Island, NY

Robert Caccamo
Chandler High School
Chandler, AZ

Verle Smith
Wilson High School
Portland, OR

Walter Dodge
New Trier East High School
Winnetka, IL

Joan Underwood
Morristown High School
Morristown, NJ

Jim Cowles
Lancaster High School
Lancaster, Ohio

John Parnell
The Hill School
Pottstown, PA

Robert Rodgers
East Brunswick Public Schools
East Brunswick, NJ

Frances Trees
Westfield High School
Westfield, NJ

Jack Knight
Garfield High School
Los Angeles, CA

Linda Lewis
Alief High School
Houston, TX

Bill Ruchte
Wake County School
Raleigh, NC

Jim Aman
St. Pious High School
Houston, TX

Joseph Pescatrice
Cape Coral High School
Cape Coral, FL

Philip Rockfeld
Bronx High School of Science
Bronx, NY

Linda Coyne
Edison High School
Edison, NJ

Adrienne Madura
Curie School
Chicago, IL

John Otterness
Downtown Business Magnet
High School
Los Angeles, CA

Periodic suggestions, ideas, and reactions to questions were appreciated from local Computer Science Department faculty members Richard St. Andre, Sandra Warriner, and James Kelsh. I would also like to thank Shepherd High School for their support and use of computing equipment.

James A. Cowles, reviewer and coauthor, has been instrumental in assisting with the entire project. In addition to reviewing every stage of this text, he prepared the *Teacher's Guide* and *Answer Key*. Copy editor Janet Hunter has been instrumental in making the final copy more readable.

Deanna Quinn, Senior Production Editor for West Publishing Company, supervised the production process. Her leadership and attention to detail have resulted in a timely production schedule. Jerry Westby, Acquisitions Editor for West Publishing Company, deserves special thanks for his commitment to this project. Most of the features that make this text less like a manual are the result of Jerry's suggestions. He has also been instrumental in keeping me on schedule.

My family and friends deserve special mention for their support and patience. Most of my recent spare time and energy have been devoted to this project. This would not have been possible without their encouragement and understanding.

Finally, there is one person without whose help completion of this project would not have been possible. Helen, who was a student in my first Pascal class, has been of tremendous assistance since the inception of this effort. She prepared every part of every stage of the manuscript on her word processor. She served as an "in-house" copy editor and made many helpful suggestions regarding presentation of the material. Her unfailing patience and support were remarkable. Fortunately for me, she has been my wife and best friend for more than a quarter century.

Douglas W. Nance

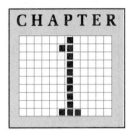

CHAPTER

1

Computer Architecture and Languages

This chapter is intended to provide you with a brief overview of what computers are and how they are used. Although there are various sizes, makes, and models of computers, you will see that they all operate in basically the same straightforward way. Whether you work on a personal computer that costs a few hundred dollars or on a mainframe that costs in the millions, the principles of making the machine work are essentially the same. We will look at components of a computer and the idea of a language for a computer. Also, we will discuss the notion of problem solving, which is independent of any particular language.

As you read this chapter, you will see that certain words are in *italics*; they are defined in the Glossary. But you need not be overly concerned about the introduction and early use of terminology. All terms will be subsequently developed. A good approach to an introductory chapter like this is to reread it periodically. This will help you maintain a good perspective as to how new concepts and techniques fit in the broader picture of using computers. Finally, remember that learning a language that makes a computer work can be exciting.

■ 1.1 Modern Computers

The search for aids to perform calculations is almost as old as number systems. Early devices include the abacus, Napier's bones, and the slide rule. More recently, calculators have changed the nature of personal computing as a result of their availability, low cost, and high speed.

The last few decades have seen the most significant change in computing machines in the world's history resulting from improvements that have led to modern computers. As recently as the 1960s, a computer required several rooms because of its size. However, the advent of silicon chips has reduced the size and increased the availability of computers. It is now possible to purchase personal computers that are more powerful than the early, huge machines.

What is a computer? According to *Webster's New World Dictionary of the American Language* (2nd College Edition), a computer is "an electronic machine which, by means of stored instructions and information, performs rapid, often complex calculations or compiles, correlates, and selects data." Basically, a computer can be thought of as a machine that manipulates information in the form of numbers and characters. This information is referred to as *data*. What makes computers remarkable is the extreme speed and precision with which they can store, retrieve, and manipulate data.

Several types of computers are currently available. An oversimplification is to categorize them as mainframe, minicomputer, or microcomputer. In this grouping, *mainframe* computers are the large machines used by major companies and universities. They have the capability of being used by as many as 100 or more people at the same time and can cost millions of dollars. *Minicomputers*, in a sense, are smaller versions of large computers. They can be used by several people at once but have less storage capacity and cost far less. *Microcomputers* are frequently referred to as personal computers. They have limited storage capacity, are generally used by one person at a time, and can be purchased for as little as a few hundred dollars.

As you begin your work with computers, you will hear people talking about hardware and software. *Hardware* refers to the actual machine and its support devices. *Software* refers to programs that make the machine do something. Many software packages exist for today's computers. They include word processing, data-base programs, spreadsheets, games, operating systems, and compilers. You can (and will!) learn to create your own software. In fact, that is what this book is all about.

A *program* can be thought of as a set of instructions that tells the machine what to do. When you have written a program, the computer will behave exactly as you have instructed it. It will do no more or no less than what is contained in your specific instructions. For example,

```
PROGRAM ComputeAverage (input, output);

VAR
   A,B,C : integer;
   Average : real;

BEGIN
   writeln ('Enter 3 integers separated by spaces');
   writeln ('Press <RETURN> when finished');
   readln (A,B,C);
   Average := (A + B + C) / 3;
   writeln;writeln;
   writeln ('The average is', Average:10:3)
END.
```

is a program that causes a computer to get three integers as input, compute their average, and then print the result. Do not worry about specific parts of this program. It is merely intended to illustrate the idea of a set of instructions. Very soon, you will be able to write significantly more sophisticated programs.

Learning to write programs requires two skills.

1. You need to be able to use specific terminology and punctuation that can be understood by the machine; in other words, you need to learn a programming language.
2. You need to be able to develop a plan for solving a particular problem. Such a plan is often referred to as an *algorithm*. This is a sequence of steps that, when followed, leads to a solution of the problem.

Initially, you may think that learning a language is the more difficult task because your problems will have relatively easy solutions. Nothing could be further from the truth! *The single most important thing you can do as a student of computer science is to develop the skill to solve problems.* Once you have this skill, you can learn to write programs in several different languages.

■ **1.2**
Computer Hardware

Let's take another look at the question: "What is a computer?" Our previous answer indicated it is a machine. Although there are several forms, names, and brands of computers, each consists of a central unit that is somehow hooked to an *input device* and an *output device* as illustrated in Figure 1.1. The central unit can be thought of as containing two parts: a central processing unit (CPU), which is the "brain" of the computer; and memory.

The central processing unit contains an arithmetic/logic unit, which is capable of performing arithmetic operations and evaluating expressions to see if they are true or false. It also contains the control unit, which controls the action of remaining components so your program can be followed step-by-step, or *executed.*

Memory can be thought of as storage similar to mailboxes in a post office. It is a sequence of locations where data representing instructions, numbers, characters, and so on can be stored. Memory contained in the computer is called *main* or *primary memory.* If additional memory is needed, there are *secondary,* or *peripheral, memory* devices. On personal computers, these can be floppy disks or magnetic tapes. On larger computers, these can be hard disks or magnetic tapes. Main memory is used while the computer is turned on and while the program is being executed. Information needed before or after the program is run is stored in secondary memory.

Although it will not affect your learning of Pascal, you might like to know how data are stored in memory. Each memory location has an address and is capable of holding a sequence of *binary* (0 or 1) *digits* or *bits.* Instructions, symbols, letters, numbers, and so on are translated into an appropriate pattern of binary digits and then stored in various mem-

FIGURE 1.1
Computer components

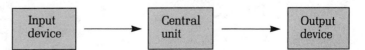

FIGURE 1.2
Main memory

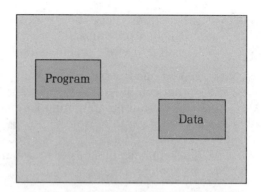

FIGURE 1.3
Central unit

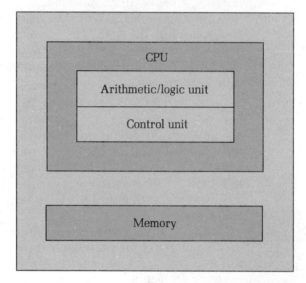

ory locations. These are retrieved, used, and changed according to instructions in your program. In fact, the program itself is similarly translated and stored in part of the main memory. Main memory can be envisioned as in Figure 1.2, and the central unit can be envisioned as in Figure 1.3.

Input devices are necessary so that information can be given to the computer. Typical devices include keyboards and disk drives (Figure 1.4), card readers, tape drives, joysticks, and a mouse. Your program will

FIGURE 1.4
(a) Keyboard and (b)
disk drive

(a)

(b)

A NOTE OF INTEREST

Blaise Pascal

Blaise Pascal was born in 1623 in France. He was acutely ill most of his life and died in 1662 at the age of 39. Mathematics was excluded from his early life for fear that he would overstrain himself by using his head. However, after a belated introduction, he became fascinated with the subject and devoted most of the rest of his life to its study. His major contribution was the development (with Pierre de Fermat) of the theory of probability.

In 1641, at the age of 18, he invented the first calculating machine in history. This machine operated using ten gears (base 10). Values were carried by one gear activating the gear for the next decimal place. Pascal's machine was opposed by tax clerks of the era who viewed it as a threat to their jobs. Pascal presented his machine to Queen Christina of Sweden in 1650; it is not known what she did with it.

be entered through one of these and the program statements will be translated as previously indicated. If floppy disks are used to get or store information, one or more disk drives will be attached to your computer. Output devices are necessary so you can see the results of your programs. These are normally in the form of monitors (CRTs for cathode ray tubes) or printers (Figure 1.5). Input and output devices are frequently referred to as *I/O devices*.

In summary, Figure 1.6 indicates the range of peripheral devices together with the nature of information transmission.

FIGURE 1.5
(a) Monitor and (b) printer

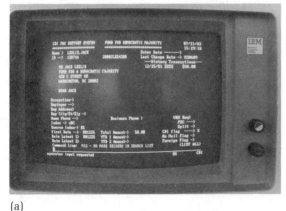

(a)

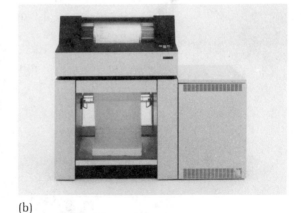

(b)

FIGURE 1.6
Complete computer installation

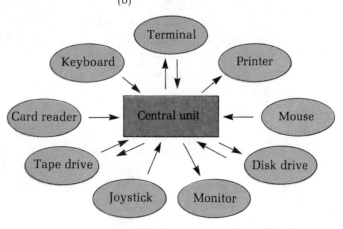

■ **1.3**
Computer Languages

What is a computer language? All data transmission, manipulation, storage, and retrieval is actually done by the machine using sequences of binary digits. Thus, if you want to add two integers, the instruction for this might be

1010010010000000000000001001001101001010000000000000001001010
0111101100010101010011100000000000000001001011100110000000000

Instructions written in this form are referred to as *machine language*. It is possible to write an entire program in machine language. However, this is very time consuming and difficult to read and understand.

The next level of computer language allows words and symbols to be used in an unsophisticated manner to accomplish simple tasks. For example, the previous machine code for adding two integers is replaced by

```
LOAD A
ADD B
STORE C
```

This causes the number in A to be added to the number in B and the result to be stored for later use in C. This kind of computer language is an *assembly language*, which is generally referred to as a *low-level language*. What actually happens is that words and symbols are translated into appropriate binary digits and the machine uses the translated form.

Although assembly language is an improvement on machine language for readability and program development, it is still a bit cumbersome. Consequently, several *high-level languages* have been developed. Some of them are Pascal, PL/I, FORTRAN, BASIC, and COBOL. These languages are intended to simplify even further the terminology and symbolism necessary for directing the machine to perform various manipulations of data. For example, the task of adding two integers can be written as

```
C := A + B;          (Pascal)
C = A + B;           (PL/I)
C = A + B            (FORTRAN)
C = A + B            (BASIC)
ADD A,B GIVING C     (COBOL)
```

Each high-level language makes it easier to read, write, and understand a program. This book develops the concepts, symbolism, and terminology necessary for using Pascal as a programming language for solving problems. After you have become proficient in using Pascal, it will be relatively easy to learn the nuances of other high-level languages.

For a moment, let's consider what happens to a high-level instruction such as

```
C := A + B;
```

This is read by a special program called a *compiler* and translated into machine code whose bit pattern could be

1010010010000000000000001001001101001010000000000000001001010
0111101100010101010011100000000000000001001011100110000000000

A NOTE OF INTEREST

Why Learn Pascal?

From the point of view of many potential users, Pascal's major drawback is that it is a compiled rather than an interpreted language. This means that developing and testing a small Pascal program can take a lot longer and involve many more steps than it would with an interpreted language like BASIC. Most programs written by users of personal computers are small ones designed for quick solutions to particular problems, and the use of Pascal for such programs may be a form of overkill.

Ironically, the characteristics of Pascal that make it relatively unsuited for small programs are a direct consequence of its strengths as a programming language. The discipline imposed by the language makes it easier to understand large programs, but it may be more than a small program demands. For serious development of large programs or for the creation of tools that will be used over and over again (and require modifications from time to time), Pascal is clearly superior.

Experts generally consider Pascal an impor-

tant language for people who are planning to study computer science or to learn programming. Indeed, the College Entrance Examination Board has recently designated Pascal as the required language for advanced-placement courses in computer science for high school students. While it is true that an experienced programmer can write clearly structured programs in any language, learning the principles of structured programming is much easier in Pascal.

Is Pascal difficult to learn? We don't think so, but the question is relative and may depend on which language you learn first. Programmers become accustomed to the first language they learn, making it the standard by which all others are judged. Even the poor features of the familiar language come to be seen as necessities, and a new language seems inferior. Don't let such subjective evaluations bar your way to learning Pascal, a powerful and elegant programming language.

This version is run using some appropriate data. The results are then generated through some form of output device. The special programs that activate the compiler, run the machine-code version, and cause output to be printed are *systems programs*. The program you write is a *source program*, and the machine-code version is an *object program* (also referred to as *object code*).

As you will soon see, the compiler does more than just translate instructions into machine code. It also detects certain errors in your source program and prints appropriate messages. For example, suppose you write the instruction

```
C := 3 * (A + B;
```

where a parenthesis is missing. When the compiler attempts to translate this line into machine code, it will detect that ")" is needed to close the parenthetical expression. It will give you an error message such as

```
ERROR IN VARIABLE
```

You will then need to correct the error (and any others) and recompile your source program before running it with the data.

Before leaving this introductory chapter, let's consider the question: "Why study Pascal?" Various languages have differing strengths and weaknesses. Pascal's strong features include the following:

1. It incorporates program structure in a reasonable approximation of English. For example, if a certain process is to be repeated until some condition is met, this can be written in the program as

REPEAT

   ⎫
   ⎬ (process here)
   ⎭

UNTIL (condition here)

2. It allows the use of descriptive words for variables and data types. Thus, programs for computing payrolls can use words like Hours-Worked, StateTax, FICA, TotalDeductions, and GrossPay.
3. It facilitates good problem-solving habits; in fact, many people consider this to be Pascal's main strength. As previously noted, developing the skill to solve a problem using a computer program is the most important trait to develop as a beginning programmer. Pascal is structured in such a manner that it encourages—indeed, almost requires—good problem-solving skills.

You are now ready to begin a detailed study of Pascal. I hope you find the time spent and frustrations encountered result in an exciting and rewarding learning experience. Good luck.

■ Summary

Key Terms

data	output device	assembly language
mainframe	execute	low-level language
minicomputer	memory	high-level language
microcomputer	main (primary) memory	compiler
hardware	secondary (peripheral)	systems program
software	memory device	source program
program	binary digits or bits	object program (object
algorithm	I/O device	code)
input device	machine language	

Writing Your First Programs

Chapter 1 presented an overview of computers and computer languages. We are now ready to examine problems that computers can solve. First we need to know how to solve a problem and then we need to learn how to use a programming language to implement our solution on the computer.

Before looking at problem solving and writing programs for the computer, some psychological aspects of working in computer science should be considered. Studying computer science can cause a significant amount of frustration for the following reasons:

1. Successful problem solving and programming require extreme precision. Generally, concepts in computer science are not difficult; however, implementation of these concepts allows no room for error. For example, one misplaced semicolon in a 1000-line program would prevent the program from working.
2. Time is a major problem. Writing programs is not like completing other assignments. You cannot expect to complete an assignment by staying up late the night before it is due. You must begin early and expect to make several revisions before your final version will be ready.

In other words, you must be prepared to plan well, start early, be patient, handle frustration, and work hard to succeed in computer science. If you cannot do this, you will probably neither enjoy computer science nor be successful at it.

■ 2.1
Program Development

The key to writing a successful program is planning. Good programs do not just happen; they are the result of careful design and patience. Just as an artist commissioned to paint a portrait would not start out by shading in the lips and eyes, a good computer programmer would not attack a problem by immediately trying to write code for a program to solve the problem. Writing a program is like writing an essay: an overall theme is envisioned, an outline of major ideas is developed, each major idea is subdivided into several parts, and each part is developed using individual sentences.

Five Steps to Good Programming Habits

In developing a program to solve a problem, five steps should be followed: understand the problem, develop an algorithm, write the program, run the program, and test the results. These steps help develop good problem-solving habits and, in turn, solve programming problems correctly. A brief discussion of each of these steps follows.

Step 1. Understand the Problem. This is not a trivial task. Before you can do anything, you must know what it is you are to do. You must be able to formulate a clear and exact statement of what is to be done. You should understand completely what data are available and what may be assumed. You should also know exactly what output is desired and the form it should take.

Step 2. Develop an Algorithm. An *algorithm* is a finite sequence of effective statements that, when applied to the problem, will solve it. An *effective statement* is a clear, unambiguous instruction that can be carried out. Each algorithm you develop should have a specific beginning; at the completion of one step, have the next task uniquely determined; and have an ending that is reached in a reasonable amount of time.

Step 3. Write the Program. When the algorithm correctly solves the problem, you can think about translating your algorithm into the Pascal language. An effective algorithm will significantly reduce the time you need to complete this step.

Step 4. Run the Program. After writing the code, you are ready to run the program. This means submitting your coded version to the computer so it can begin executing your instructions. At this point, you may discover errors that can be as simple as typing errors or that may require a reevaluation of all or parts of your algorithm.

Step 5. Test the Results. After your program has run, you need to be sure that the results are correct, that they are in a form you like, and that your program produces the correct solution in all cases. To be sure the results are correct, you must look at them and compare them with what you expect. In the case of using a program with arithmetic operations, this means checking some results with pencil and paper.

SELF QUIZ 2.1   Explain why "add all the good scores" is not an effective statement.

Developing Algorithms

Algorithms for solving a problem can be developed by stating the problem and then subdividing the problem into major subtasks. Each subtask can then be subdivided into smaller tasks. This process is repeated until each remaining task is one that is easily solved. This process is known as *top-down design*, or *structured programming*, and each successive subdivision is referred to as a *stepwise refinement*. Tasks at each stage of this process are called *modules*. Graphically, this can be represented as shown in Figure 2.1.

More specifically, this can be illustrated by designing a solution to the problem of updating a checkbook after a transaction has been made. A first-level development is shown in Figure 2.2.

Level 1 modules can be further developed. "Get information" could consist of getting the starting balance, type of transaction, and amount of transaction as shown in (a) of Figure 2.3. "Perform computations" will consist of deciding whether to add or subtract the transaction amount. This is illustrated in (b) of Figure 2.3. "Print results" would include

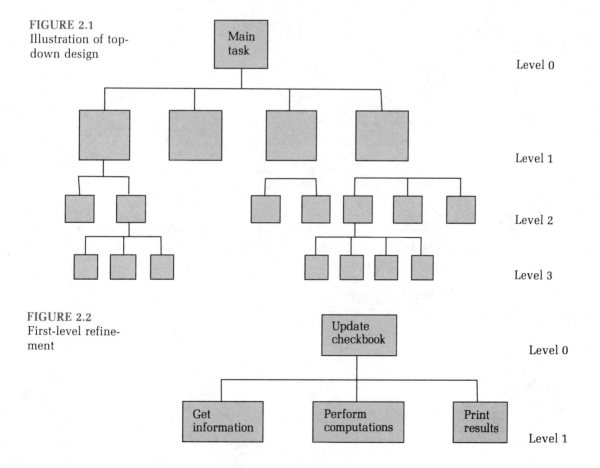

FIGURE 2.1
Illustration of top-down design

FIGURE 2.2
First-level refinement

FIGURE 2.3
Second-level refinements (a), (b), and (c)

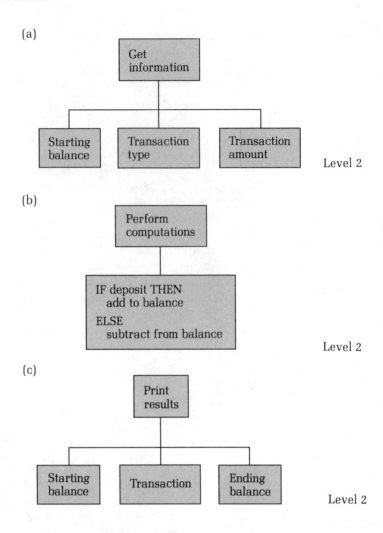

(a)

Get information

Starting balance | Transaction type | Transaction amount

Level 2

(b)

Perform computations

IF deposit THEN
   add to balance

ELSE
   subtract from balance

Level 2

(c)

Print results

Starting balance | Transaction | Ending balance

Level 2

printing the starting balance, the transaction, and the final balance as shown in (c) of Figure 2.3.

Finally, one of the last modules can be developed as shown in Figure 2.4. The complete top-down design can then be envisioned as illustrated in Figure 2.5. Notice that each remaining task can be accomplished in a very direct manner.

At least two comments should be made about top-down design. First, different people can (and probably will) have different designs for the solution of a problem. However, each good design will have well-defined modules with functional subtasks. Second, the graphic method just used

FIGURE 2.4
Third-level refinement

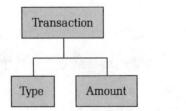

Transaction

Type | Amount

Level 3

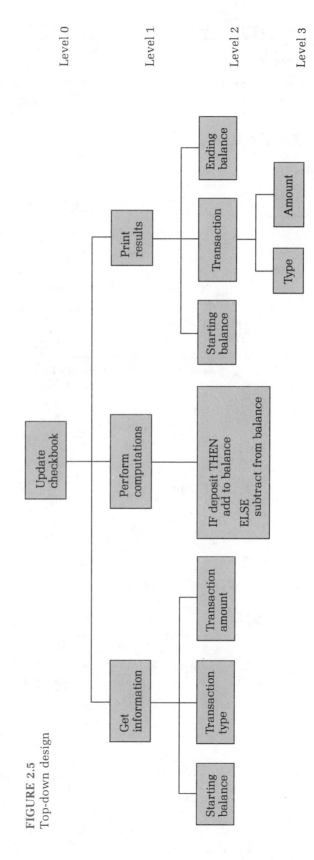

FIGURE 2.5
Top-down design

Microprocessors

The microprocessor and its silicon companion, the memory chip, are the cause of the computer revolution. This revolution started in the 1970s and is far from over. By the mid-1990s, the term microcomputer will be almost synonymous with computer, and all but a very few supercomputers will have silicon chips as their central processing units. There will be nothing small about these microcomputers, however, except their physical size; in computing power they will be as powerful as today's mainframes. And in manufacturing cost, they may be as inexpensive as today's video games.

Since the development of the von Neumann architecture in the late 1940s, every computer has had a central processing unit, or CPU. The CPU pulls information out of a computer's memory, alters it—for example, by adding another number to it—and puts it back into memory.

helps to formulate logic for solving a problem but is somewhat awkward for writing. Thus, we will use a stylized, half-English, half-code method called *pseudocode* to illustrate stepwise refinement in such a design. This will be written in English, but the sentence structure and indentations will suggest Pascal code. Major tasks will be numbered with whole numbers and subtasks with decimal numbers. Stages in the development of the checkbook-balancing problem in pseudocode are

1. Get information
2. Perform computations
3. Print results

A second-level pseudocode development produces

1. Get information
    1.1   get starting balance
    1.2   get transaction type
    1.3   get transaction amount
2. Perform computations
    2.1   **IF** deposit **THEN**
            add to balance
          ELSE
            subtract from balance
3. Print results
    3.1   print starting balance
    3.2   print transaction
    3.3   print ending balance

Finally, step 3.2 of the pseudocode is subdivided as previously indicated into

    3.2   print transaction
        3.2.1   print transaction type
        3.2.2   print transaction amount

Two final comments are in order. First, each module developed should be tested with data for that module. Once you are sure each module does what you want, the whole program should work when the modules are used together. Second, the process of dividing a task into subtasks is especially suitable for writing programs in Pascal. As you will see, the language supports development of subprograms for specific sub-tasks. Thus, learning to think in terms of modular development now will not only aid you in creating algorithms to solve problems, it will also aid you in writing programs to solve problems.

Exercises 2.1

In Exercises 1–5, which statements are effective? Why or why not?

1. Pay the cashier $9.15.
2. Water the plants a day before they die.
3. Determine all positive prime numbers less than 1,000,000.
4. Choose X to be the smallest positive fraction.
5. Invest your money in a stock that will increase in value.

In Exercises 6–8, what assumptions need to be made to understand the problem?

6. Find the largest number of a set of numbers.
7. Alphabetize a list of names.
8. Compute charges for a telephone bill.

In Exercises 9–13, outline the main tasks for solving each problem. Refine the main tasks into a sufficient number of levels so the problem can be solved in a well-defined manner.

9. Write a good term paper.
10. Take a vacation.
11. Choose a college.
12. Get a summer job.
13. Compute the semester average for a student in a computer science course and print all pertinent data.

In Exercises 14 and 15, use pseudocode to write a solution for each problem. Indicate each stage of your development.

14. Compute the wages for two employees of a company. The input information consists of the hourly wage and the number of hours worked in one week. The output should contain a list of all deductions, gross pay, and net pay. For this problem, assume deductions are made for federal withholding taxes, state withholding taxes, social security, and union dues.
15. Compute the average test score for five students in a class. Input for this problem consists of five scores. Output should include each score and the average of these scores.

16. Develop an algorithm to find the total, average, and largest number in a given list of twenty-five numbers.

■ 2.2
Writing Programs

Words in Pascal

Consider the following complete Pascal program.

```
PROGRAM Example (input, output);

CONST
   Skip = ' ';
   LoopLimit = 10;

VAR
   J,Number,Sum : integer;
   Average : real;

BEGIN
   Sum := 0;
   FOR J := 1 TO LoopLimit DO
     BEGIN
        writeln ('Please enter a number and press <RETURN>,');
        readln (Number);
        Sum := Sum + Number
     END;
   Average := Sum/LoopLimit;
   writeln; writeln;
   writeln (Skip:15,'The average is', Average:8:2);
   writeln;
   writeln (Skip:15,'The number of scores is', LoopLimit:3)
END,
```

OBJECTIVES

- to recognize reserved words and predefined standard identifiers
- to recognize and declare valid identifiers
- to know the three basic components of a program
- to understand the basic structure of a Pascal program

As is true of this program, most programming languages require the use of words when writing code. In Pascal, words that have a predefined meaning which cannot be changed are called *reserved words*. Some other predefined words (predefined identifiers) can have their meanings changed if the programmer has strong reasons for doing so. In this text reserved words are capitalized and in bold type, whereas predefined identifiers are lowercase and in bold type. When used in programs, reserved words are capitalized and predefined identifiers are lowercase. Other words (identifiers) must be created according to a well-defined set of rules, but can have any meaning, subject to those rules.

Reserved Words

In Pascal, reserved words are predefined and cannot be used in a program for anything other than the purpose for which they are reserved. Some examples are **AND, OR, NOT, BEGIN, END, IF,** and **FOR.** As you continue in Pascal, you will learn where and how these words are used. At this time, however, you need only become familiar with the reserved words in Figure 2.6; they are also listed in Appendix 1.

FIGURE 2.6
Reserved words

AND	ELSE	IF	OR	THEN
ARRAY	END	IN	PACKED	TO
BEGIN	FILE	LABEL	PROCEDURE	TYPE
CASE	FOR	MOD	PROGRAM	UNTIL
CONST	FORWARD	NIL	RECORD	VAR
DIV	FUNCTION	NOT	REPEAT	WHILE
DO	GOTO	OF	SET	WITH
DOWNTO				

Predefined Identifiers

A second set of words that have been defined are *predefined identifiers*, which can have their meanings changed by the programmer. However, these words should not be used for anything other than their intended use. This list varies somewhat from computer to computer, so you should obtain a list of predefined identifiers used in your local implementation of Pascal. Some predefined identifiers are listed in Figure 2.7 and in Appendix 2. The term *keywords* is used to refer to both reserved words and predefined identifiers in subsequent discussions.

Syntax and Syntax Diagrams

Syntax refers to the rules governing construction of valid statements. This includes the order in which statements occur, together with appropriate punctuation. *Syntax diagramming* is a method to describe formally the legal syntax of language structures. Syntax diagrams show the permissible alternatives for each part of each kind of sentence and where the parts may appear. The symbolism we use is shown in Figure 2.8. A combined listing of syntax diagrams is contained in Appendix 3. Arrows are

FIGURE 2.7
Predefined identifiers

Data Types	Constants	Functions	Procedures	Files
boolean	false	abs	dispose	input
char	maxint	arctan	get	output
integer	true	chr	new	
real		cos	pack	
text		eof	page	
		eoln	put	
		exp	read	
		In	readln	
		odd	reset	
		ord	rewrite	
		pred	unpack	
		round	write	
		sin	writeln	
		sqr		
		sqrt		
		succ		
		trunc		

used to indicate possible alternatives. To illustrate, a syntax diagram for forming words in the English language is

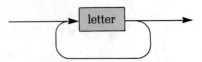

If the word has to start with a vowel, the diagram is

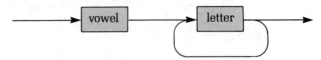

where vowel and letter are defined in a manner consistent with the English alphabet. Syntax diagrams are used throughout the text to illustrate formal constructs. You are encouraged to become familiar with them.

Identifiers

Reserved words and predefined identifiers are restricted in their use; all other words used in a program are referred to as *identifiers,* and most Pascal programs require their use. The more complicated the program, the more identifiers needed. A valid identifier must start with a letter of the alphabet and must consist only of letters and digits. A syntax diagram for forming identifiers is

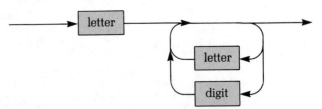

Table 2.1 gives some valid and invalid identifiers along with the reason for those that are invalid. A valid identifier can be of any length. However, some versions of Pascal recognize only the first part of a long iden-

FIGURE 2.8
Symbols used in
syntax diagrams

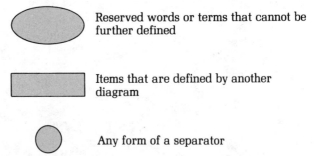

TABLE 2.1
Valid and invalid
identifiers

Identifier	Valid or invalid	Reason
Sum	Valid	
X + Y	Invalid	" + " in not allowed
Average	Valid	
Test1	Valid	
1stNum	Invalid	Must start with a letter
X	Valid	
K mart	Invalid	Spaces are not allowed
ThisIsALongOne	Valid	

tifier, for example, the first eight or the first ten positions. Therefore, identifiers such as MathTestScore1 and MathTestScore2 might be the same identifier to a computer and could not be used as different identifiers in a program. Thus, exercise caution when using long, descriptive identifiers.

The most common use of identifiers is to name the variables to be used in a program. Recall from algebra that variables such as x, y, and z are frequently used in functional relationships; these can also be used as identifiers in a Pascal program. However, we should generally use names that are more descriptive. A detailed explanation of the use of variables is given in Chapter 3.

Another use of identifiers is to name symbolic constants to be used in a program; for example, to identify a certain name or date to be used repeatedly. A third use of identifiers is to name the program. Every program requires a name, and the name must be a valid identifier. Identifiers are also needed to name new data types and subprograms, but don't worry; we'll get to that in later chapters.

SELF QUIZ 2.2

Explain what is wrong with each of the following identifiers.

1. 7Eleven
2. Kentucky Derby
3. ProgramAttempt1

Basic Program Components

A program in Pascal consists of three components: a program heading, a declaration section, and an executable section. These three components are listed and explained in a program as shown in Figure 2.9.

FIGURE 2.9
Components of a
Pascal program

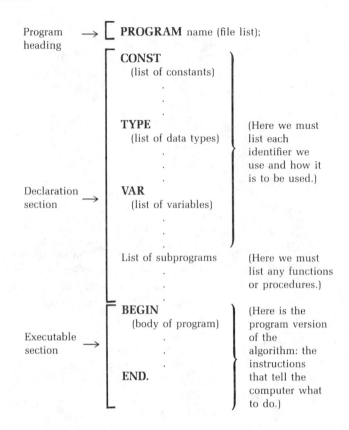

Program heading → **PROGRAM** name (file list);

CONST
(list of constants)
.
.
.

TYPE
(list of data types)   (Here we must
.   list each
.   identifier we
.   use and how it
                          is to be used.)

Declaration → **VAR**
section   (list of variables)
.
.
.

List of subprograms   (Here we must
.   list any functions
.   or procedures.)
.

BEGIN   (Here is the
(body of program)   program version
.   of the
Executable →   algorithm: the
section   .   instructions
.   that tell the
END.   computer what
                          to do.)

The syntax diagram for a program is

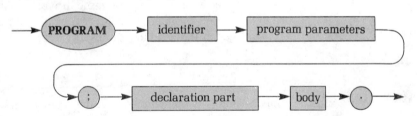

To illustrate, let's reconsider Figure 2.10, the sample program given at the beginning of this section, and indicate the appropriate program parts.

Technically, program comments, which are discussed in Section 4.1, can precede the program heading. But for our purposes, think of the *program heading* as the first statement of any Pascal program. It is usually one line and must contain the reserved word **PROGRAM;** the program name, which must be a valid identifier; a file list of files used; and a semicolon at the end. The respective parts of a program heading are

PROGRAM name (file list);

Program
heading   →   [PROGRAM Example (input, output);

Declaration
section   →
```
CONST
   Skip = ' ';
   LoopLimit = 10;

VAR
   J,Number,Sum : integer;
   Average : real;
```

Executable
section   →
```
BEGIN
   Sum := 0;
   FOR J := 1 TO LoopLimit DO
      BEGIN
         writeln ('Please enter a number and press <RETURN>.');
         readln (Number);
         Sum := Sum + Number
      END;
   Average := Sum/LoopLimit;
   writeln; writeln;
   writeln (Skip:15,'The average is', Average:8:2);
   writeln;
   writeln (Skip:15,'The number of scores is',LoopLimit:3)
END.
```

FIGURE 2.10
A complete Pascal
program

This template or fill-in-the-blanks form is used throughout this book. Reserved words and standard identifiers are shown. The programmer must replace the words in lowercase letters using identifiers. The file list in the program heading contains the names of files used in the program. **input** and **output** are standard files that must be listed in some versions of Pascal. **input** refers to a system input device such as a keyboard or card reader. **output** refers to a system output device such as a monitor or printer.

Examples of program headings include:

```
PROGRAM FirstOne (output);
PROGRAM Rookie (input, output);
PROGRAM FindSum (input, output);
PROGRAM Checkbook (input, output);
PROGRAM Number1 (output);
```

The file **input** is listed whenever data will be entered into the program; **output** is listed whenever something will be written to the screen or printer from the program.

A syntax diagram for a program heading follows.

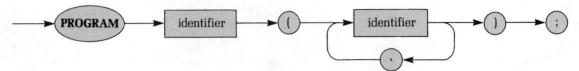

The remainder of the program is sometimes referred to as the main block; major divisions are the declaration section and the executable section. The *declaration section* is used to declare (name) all symbolic constants, data types, variables, and subprograms that are necessary to the program. All constants named in the declaration section are normally referred to as being defined. Thus, we generally say constants are defined and variables are declared.

When constants are defined, they appear in the *constant definition* portion of the declaration section after the reserved word **CONST.** The form for defining a constant is

---

CONST
  identifier 1 = value 1;
  identifier 2 = value 2;
    .
    .
    .
  identifier n = value n;

The syntax diagram for this part is

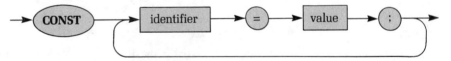

If value is a string of characters, it must be enclosed in single quotation marks (apostrophes). For example,

```
CONST
    Date = 'July 4, 1776';
```

Any number of constants may be defined in this section. Maximum readability is achieved when the constants are listed consecutively and aligned down the page. A typical constant definition portion of the declaration section is

```
CONST
    Skip = ' ';
    Name = 'George Washington';
    Date = 'July 4, 1776';
    Splats = '****************************';
    Line = '_____';
    ClassSize = 35;
    LoopLimit = 10;
```

The **TYPE** portion of the declaration section is explained in Section 8.1. The *variable declaration* portion of the declaration section must be listed after the constant definition portion and must begin with the reserved word **VAR.** This section must contain all identifiers for variables to be used in the program; if a variable is used that has not been declared, an error will occur. As with constants, variables must be valid identifiers and are usually listed down the page to enhance readability.

The form required for declaring variables is somewhat different from that used for defining constants: it requires a colon rather than an equal sign and then specific data types for the variables. The correct form is

> **VAR**
>   identifier 1 : data type 1;
>   .
>   .
>   .
>   identifier n : data type n;

The syntax diagram is

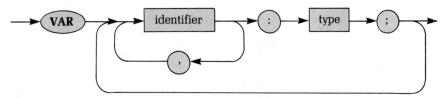

Since data types are not discussed until later in this chapter, assume for now that **real, integer,** and **char** are valid data types. The reserved word **VAR** may appear only once in a program (except when subprograms are developed). If no variables are to be used, a variable declaration section is not needed; however, this seldom happens. A typical variable declaration section is

```
VAR
    Sum : integer;
    Average : real;
    I,J,K : integer;
    Ch : char;
```

Some other examples of permissible methods of writing the declaration section are

```
VAR                         VAR
    I : integer;                I,J,K,Sum: integer;
    J : integer;                Ch : char;
    K : integer;                Average : real;
    Sum : integer;
    Ch : char;
    Average : real;
```

```
VAR                          VAR
   I ,                          I ,J ,
   J ,                          K ,Sum : integer;
   K ,                          Ch : char;
   Sum : integer;              Average : real;
   Ch : char;
   Average : real;
```

The third basic program component is the *executable section*. This section contains the statements that cause the computer to do something. It must start with the reserved word **BEGIN** and conclude with the reserved word **END.** Also, a period must follow the last **END** in the executable section. The syntax diagram is

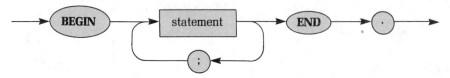

SELF QUIZ 2.3   Find all errors in the following definitions and declaration.

```
CONST
   Edge = '*                        *';
   Speed = '55';
   Christmas = December 25;

VAR
   Price = real;
```

Writing Code in Pascal

We are now ready to examine the use of the executable section of a program. In Pascal, the basic unit of grammar is an *executable statement*, which consists of valid identifiers, predefined identifiers, reserved words, numbers, and/or characters together with appropriate punctuation.

One of the main rules for writing code in Pascal is that a semicolon is used to separate executable statements or program parts. For example, if the statement

```
writeln ('The results are':20, Sum:8, ' and', Aver:6:2)
```

were used in a program, it would (almost always) require a semicolon between it and the next executable statement. Thus, it should be

semicolon ↓

```
writeln ('The results are':20, Sum:8, ' and', Aver:6:2);
```

One instance exists where an executable statement does not need a following semicolon. When a statement is followed by the reserved word **END, END** is not a statement by itself, but part of a **BEGIN ... END** statement; therefore a semicolon is not required. However, as you will see in Section 2.3, if one is included, it will not affect the program.

Video Games

The video game fad is dead and, in a literal way, buried: in August 1983, Atari dumped thousands of unsold *E.T.* cartridges in a trash heap in Arizona and covered them with concrete. Both Atari and Activision reported losses that year, and several video game companies left—or went out of—business.

People have played games for thousands of years, and computer games—or electronic entertainment, as some like to call it—are here to stay. As with other forms of entertainment, such as the movie business, electronic entertainment will have good years and bad years. New technology changes all forms of art and entertainment; color movies are different from those filmed in black and white without sound. Video discs and more powerful home computers may revive the game industry; predicting such trends, however, is as dangerous as saying that 1990 will be a big year for Westerns.

Although you are not currently familiar with many executable statements, you can still visualize the executable section as shown in Figure 2.11. Two comments are now in order. First, Pascal does not require that each statement be on a separate line. Actually, you can write a program as one long line if you want; however, it would be very difficult to read. Compare, for example, the readability of the following two programs.

```
PROGRAM EarlyBird (output); CONST Name = 'George';
Age = 26; VAR J,Sum : integer; BEGIN Sum := 0;
FOR J := 1 TO 10 DO Sum := Sum + J; writeln
('My name is', Name:10); writeln ('My age is', Age:11);
writeln; writeln ('The sum of integers 1 through 10 is',Sum:4) END.
```

```
PROGRAM EarlyBird (output);
CONST
  Name = 'George';
  Age = 26;
VAR
  J,Sum : integer;
BEGIN
  Sum := 0;
  FOR J := 1 TO 10 DO
    Sum := Sum + J;
  writeln ('My name is', Name:10);
  writeln ('My age is', Age:11);
  writeln;
  writeln ('The sum of integers 1 through 10 is', Sum:4)
END.
```

You are not expected to know what the statements mean at this point, but it should be obvious that the second program is much more readable than the first.

Second, Pascal ignores extra spaces and line boundaries. This explains why the two programs above are identical. A good principle to follow is to use spacing to enhance readability. Decide on a style you like (and your instructor can tolerate) and use it consistently.

FIGURE 2.11
Executable section

Executable $\longrightarrow$
section

```
BEGIN
    statement 1;
    statement 2;
         .
         .
         .
    statement n-1;
    statement n
END.
```

Exercises 2.2

1. List the rules for forming valid identifiers.

In Exercises 2–13, which are valid identifiers? Give an explanation for those that are invalid.

2. 7Up
3. Payroll
4. Room222
5. Name List
6. A
7. A1
8. 1A
9. Time&Place
10. CONST
11. X*Y
12. ListOfEmployees
13. Lima,Ohio

In Exercises 14–20, which are valid program headings? Give an explanation for those that are invalid.

14. PROGRAM Rookie (output)
15. PROGRAM Pro (input, output);
16. TestProgram (input, output);
17. PROGRAM (output);
18. PROGRAM GettingBetter (output);
19. PROGRAM Have Fun (input, output);
20. PROGRAM 2ndOne (output);

21. Name the three main sections of a Pascal program.

In Exercises 22–25, write constant definition statements.

22. Your name
23. Your age
24. Your birth date
25. Your birthplace

In Exercises 26–31, find all errors in the definitions and declarations.

```
26. CONST
        Company : 'General Motors';
    VAR
        Salary : real;
27. VAR
        Age = 25;
28. VAR
        Days : integer;
        Ch : char;
    CONST
        Name = 'John Smith';
```

```
29. CONST
       Car : 'Cadillac';
30. CONST
       Score : integer;
31. VAR
       X,Y,Z : real;
       Score,
       Num : integer;
```

32. Discuss the significance of a semicolon when writing Pascal statements.

■ 2.3
Data Types and Output

OBJECTIVES

- to understand and use the data types **integer, real,** and **char**
- to understand the difference between floating-point form and fixed-point form of decimal numbers
- to understand the syntax for and use of **write** and **writeln** for output
- to format output

Type integer

Numbers in some form are used in most computer programs and the kind of number used is referred to as its *type*. We first look at numbers of type **integer,** which are integers that are positive, negative, or zero.

Some rules that must be observed when using integers are

1. Plus " + " signs are not required before a positive integer. For example, + 283 and 283 have the same value and both are allowed.
2. Minus " − " signs are required when using a negative number.
3. Leading zeros are ignored. For example, 00073, + 073, 0073, and 73 all have the same value.
4. Decimal points cannot be used when writing integers. Although 14 and 14.0 have the same value, 14.0 is not of type **integer.**
5. Commas cannot be used when writing integers. 271,362 is not allowed; it must be written as 271362.

The syntax diagram for an integer is

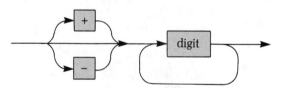

There is a limit on the largest and the smallest integer constant. The largest such constant is **maxint** and the smallest is − **maxint.** Operations with integers are examined in the next section and integer variables are discussed in Chapter 3.

Type real

Working with reals is more complicated than working with integers. When using decimal notation, numbers of type **real** must be written with a decimal point "." with at least one digit on each side of the decimal. Thus, .2 is not a valid **real** but 0.2 is.

Plus " + " and minus " − " signs for data of type **real** are treated exactly as with integers. When working with reals, however, both leading and trailing zeros are ignored. Thus, + 23.45, 23.45, 023.45, 23.450, and 0023.45000 have the same value.

All reals seen thus far have been in *fixed-point form*. The computer will also accept reals in *floating-point* or *exponential form*. Floating-

TABLE 2.2
Forms for equivalent
numbers

Fixed-point	Scientific notation	Floating-point
46.345	4.6345×10^1	4.6345E1
59214.3	5.92143×10^4	5.92143E4
0.00042	4.2×10^{-4}	4.2E-4
36000000000.0	3.6×10^{10}	3.6E10
0.000000005	5.0×10^{-9}	5.0E-9
-341000.0	-3.41×10^5	-3.41E5

point form is an equivalent method for writing numbers in scientific notation to accommodate numbers that may have very large or very small values. The difference is, instead of writing the base decimal times some power of 10, the base decimal is followed by E and the appropriate power of 10. For example, 231.6 in scientific notation is 2.316×10^2 and in floating-point form is 2.316E2. Table 2.2 sets forth several fixed-point decimal numbers with the equivalent scientific notation and floating-point form. Floating-point form for real numbers does not require exactly one digit on the left of the decimal point. In fact, it can be used with no decimal points written. To illustrate, 4.16E1, 416.0E-1, and 416E-1 have the same value and all are permissible. However, it is not a good habit to use floating-point form for decimal numbers unless exactly one digit appears on the left of the decimal. In most cases, fixed-point form is preferable.

The syntax diagram for a real number is

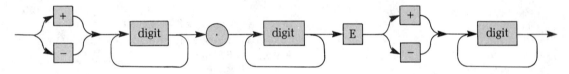

When using reals in a program, either fixed-point or floating-point form may be used, but when the computer prints out reals, it prints the real in floating-point form unless the programmer specifies otherwise. This is discussed later in this section.

SELF QUIZ 2.4   Write the following fixed-point reals in both scientific notation and floating-point form.

1. 568.4391
2. 0.00783

Type char

Another data type available in Pascal is **char,** which is used to represent character data. In standard Pascal, data of type **char** can be only a single character. These characters come from an available character set that differs somewhat from computer to computer, but always includes

1. the letters of the alphabet;
2. the digits 0, 1, 2, 3, 4, 5, 6, 7, 8, and 9; and
3. special symbols such as #, &, !, +, −, *, /, and so on. Two common character sets are given in Appendix 4.

Character constants of type **char** must be enclosed in single quotation marks when used in a program. Thus, to use the letter A as a constant, you type 'A'. The use of digits and standard operation symbols as characters is also permitted; for example, '7' is considered a character, but 7 is an integer.

If a word of one or more characters is used as a constant in a program, it is referred to as a *string constant*. String constants, are defined in the **CONST** portion of the declaration section. The entire string must be enclosed in single quotation marks. Some sample definitions are

```
CONST
   Name = 'John Q, Public';
   Date = 'July 4, 1776';
   Splats = '************************';
```

When a single quotation mark is needed within a string, this is represented by two single quotation marks. For example, if the name desired is O'Malley, it is represented by

```
'O''MALLEY',
```

When a single quotation mark is needed as a single character, it can be represented by placing two single quotation marks within single quotation marks. When typed, this appears as ''''. Note that these are all single quotation marks; use of the double quotation mark character here does not produce the desired result.

Output

The goal of almost every program is to print something. What gets printed (either on paper or on a screen) is referred to as *output*. The two program statements that produce output are **write** and **writeln** (pronounced "write line"). They are usually followed by character strings, numbers, or numerical expressions enclosed in parentheses. The general form is

> **write** (expression 1, expression 2, . . . , expression n)
>
> or
>
> **writeln** (expression 1, expression 2, . . . , expression n)

A syntax diagram for **write** (and **writeln**) is

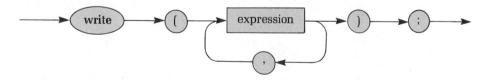

write statements cause output to be all on one line. **writeln** causes the next output to be on the next line.

```
write ('This is a test,');
writeln ('How many lines are printed?');
```

causes the output

```
This is a test,How many lines are printed?
```

whereas,

```
writeln ('This is a test,');
writeln ('How many lines are printed?');
```

causes the output

```
This is a test,
How many lines are printed?
```

If you are working on a system where output goes to the screen, you may have to specify an output device as part of your **write** or **writeln** statement when you want output directed to a printer. For example, in Apple Pascal you would declare

```
VAR
   Out : interactive;
```

and then have program statements

```
rewrite (Out, 'Printer:');
writeln (Out, expression);
```

In Turbo Pascal you would use the statement

```
writeln (Lst, expression);
```

You should check with your teacher or see your system reference manual for details.

As indicated, character strings can be printed by enclosing the string in single quotation marks within the parentheses. Numerical data can be printed by including the desired number within the parentheses. Thus,

```
writeln (100);
```

produces

```
100
```

EXAMPLE 2.1   Let's write a complete Pascal program to print the address

```
1403 South Drive
Apartment 3B
Pittsburgh, PA 15238
```

A complete program to print this is

```
PROGRAM Address (output);

BEGIN
   writeln ('1403 South Drive');
   writeln ('Apartment 3B');
   writeln ('Pittsburgh, PA', 15238);
END,
```

writeln can also be used to produce blank lines in output. When **writeln** is used without a following expression, it causes the next line of output to begin on the next line (the output skips a line). This technique is frequently used to produce more readable output.

STYLE TIP

▪ ▪ ▪ ▪ ▪ ▪ ▪

writelns at the beginning and end of the executable section separate desired output from other messages. The initial ones separate output from the program listing and the final ones create blank lines between output and computer messages. Thus, the previous program for printing an address can be

```
PROGRAM Address (output);

BEGIN
  writeln; writeln;
  writeln ('1403 South Drive');
  writeln ('Apartment 3B');
  writeln ('Pittsburgh, PA', 15238);
  writeln; writeln
END.
```

When designing a program to solve a problem, you should constantly be aware of how the output should appear. The spacing of output on a line can be controlled by formatting expressions in **write** and **writeln** statements.

Formatting Integers

If the programmer does not control the output, integers may be printed adjacent to each other; or they may be printed in a predetermined field width depending upon the machine and version of Pascal being used. Spacing of integers in output can be controlled by *formatting*. It is relatively easy to format output for integers. Using a **writeln** statement, the desired field width is designated by placing a colon ":" after the integer and then an integer specifying the field width. The integer printed will be printed at the right side (right justified) in the specified field. The general form for formatting integers is

> **writeln** (integer:n);

Some illustrations for formatting integer output are

Program Statement	Output
writeln (123:6);	123
writeln (15, 10:5);	15 10
writeln (-263:7, 21:3);	-263 21
writeln (+5062:6);	5062
writeln (65221:3);	65221

Note that in line five an attempt is made to specify a field width smaller than the number of digits contained in the integer. Most versions of Pascal automatically print the entire integer; however, some versions print only in the specified width. The following program enables you to find out exactly what your machine does.

```
PROGRAM FieldWidth (output);

BEGIN
   writeln; writeln;
   writeln ('This program will check field width');
   writeln ('_____');
   writeln;
   writeln (12345:3, 123:5, -67:4);
   writeln; writeln
END.
```

Formatting Reals

As with data of type **integer,** data of type **real** can be used in **writeln** statements. If no formatting is used, the output will be in floating-point form. Different machines and different versions of Pascal produce a variety of default field widths. For example, some use a standard field width of 10 columns, some use 16, and some even use 22 columns. To check field width on your computer, write and run the following program.

```
PROGRAM UnformattedReals (output);

BEGIN
   writeln; writeln;
   writeln (231.45);
   writeln (0.00456);
   writeln (4.0);
   writeln (-526.1E5);
   writeln (0.91E-8);
   writeln (-0.052);
   writeln; writeln
END.
```

Most programs using data of type **real** require a neater method of expressing the output. This can be accomplished by formatting. To format reals you must specify both the field width and the number of decimal places to the right of the decimal. This is done by writing the number, followed by a colon ":", followed by an integer, followed by a colon and another integer. For example, if you are writing a program that prints wages of workers, you can get a field width of eight with two places to the right of the decimal as follows:

```
writeln (231.45:8:2);
```

231.45 is the computed wage, 8 specifies the field width, and 2 specifies how many digits appear to the right of the decimal. The output for this statement is

```
  231.45
```

The general form for formatting reals is

```
writeln (real:n1:n2);
```

Use of this formatting procedure causes the following to happen.

1. The decimal uses one position in the specified field width.
2. Leading zeros are not printed.
3. Trailing zeros are printed to the specified number of positions to the right of the decimal.
4. Leading plus " + " signs are omitted.
5. Leading minus " − " signs are printed and use one position of the specified field.
6. Digits appearing to the right of the decimal have been rounded rather than truncated.

As with integers, if a field width is specified that is too small, most versions of Pascal default to the minimum width required to present all digits to the left of the decimal as well as the specified digits to the right of the decimal. The following table illustrates how output using data of type **real** can be formatted.

Program Statement	Output
writeln (765.432:10:3);	765.432
writeln (023.14:10:2);	23.14
writeln (65.50:10:2);	65.50
writeln (+341.2:10:2);	341.20
writeln (-341.2:10:2);	-341.20
writeln (16.458:10:2);	16.46
writeln (0.00456:10:4);	0.0046

Floating-point form can also be used in a formatted **writeln** statement. Output from

```
PROGRAM FormatReals (output);

BEGIN
  writeln; writeln;
  writeln (1.234E2:10:2);
  writeln (-723.4E-3:10:5);
  writeln (-723.4E-3:10:3);
  writeln (6.435E2:10:2, 2.3145E2:10:2);
  writeln; writeln
END.
```

is

```
  123.40
0.72340
 -0.723
643.50     231.45
```

Formatting Strings

Strings and string constants can be formatted using a single colon ":" followed by a positive integer "n" to specify field width. The general form for formatting strings is

---

writeln ('string':n);

A NOTE OF INTEREST

Laser Printers

The print quality of an ink-jet printer is slightly fuzzy because of the difficulty of precisely controlling the trajectory of the drops of ink. Laser printers use a laser beam, which can be controlled precisely, and direct it at photographic film or paper, as in a conventional phototypesetting machine. In 1982, Canon, the Japanese camera maker, introduced a low-cost, computer-controlled typesetting machine that uses laser technology. Minolta, another Japanese cam-

era maker, introduced its SP-50B laser printer in 1983. It prints in eight type styles at 20 pages per minute.

Laser printers are used with mainframes for billing, bank statements, and in other high-volume applications. These printers are made by such companies as IBM and Burroughs. Storage Technology Corp. (STC) introduced in 1983 its 6100, which prints at speeds up to 103 pages a minute.

The string is right justified in the field. The following program illustrates such formatting.

```
PROGRAM StringFormat (output);

CONST
   Indent = ' ';

BEGIN
    writeln; writeln;
    writeln (Indent:10, 'Note the strings below.');
    writeln (Indent:10, '_____');
    writeln;
    writeln ('This is a sample string.':35);
    writeln ('This is a sample string.':30);
    writeln ('This is a sample string.':25);
    writeln ('This is a sample string.':20);
    writeln; writeln
END.
```

The output from this program is

```
         Note the strings below.
         _____

                 This is a sample string.
             This is a sample string.
         This is a sample string.
         This is a sample string.
```

STYLE TIP
■ ■ ■ ■ ■ ■ ■ ■

Note the use of the constant Indent above. This is used to control indented output. You can also define

```
Skip = ' ';
```

and use Skip:n to control blank spaces on a line of output.

EXAMPLE 2.2   Write a complete Pascal program to produce the following output.

```
COMPUTER SCIENCE
Test Scores:
       100      98      93
        89      82      76
        73      64
```

Assuming a field width of seven for the scores, we have

```
PROGRAM PrintScores (output);

BEGIN
  writeln; writeln;
  writeln ('COMPUTER SCIENCE ');
  writeln ('_____');
  writeln ('Test Scores:');
  writeln (100:7, 98:7, 93:7);
  writeln (89:7, 82:7, 76:7);
  writeln (73:7, 64:7);
  writeln; writeln
END.
```

Test Programs

Programmers should develop the habit of using test programs to improve their knowledge and programming skills. Test programs should be relatively short and written to provide an answer to a specific question. For example, **maxint** was discussed earlier in this section. It was mentioned that the value of **maxint** depended upon the machine being used. You can use a test program to discover what your computer uses for **maxint.** A complete program that accomplishes this is

```
PROGRAM TestMax (output);

BEGIN
  writeln ('Maxint is ', maxint)
END.
```

Notice that a brief message, 'Maxint is ', is included to explain the output. Always include some kind of descriptive message when you have numerical output. This makes it easier to identify what the numbers represent.

Exercises 2.3   In Exercises 1–7, which are valid **integers?** Explain why the others are invalid.

1. 521
2. −32.0
3. 5,621
4. +00784
5. +65
6. 6521492183
7. −0

In Exercises 8–17, which are valid **reals**? Explain why the others are invalid.

  8. 26.3
  9. +181.0
  10. −.14
  11. 492.
  12. +017.400

  13. 43E2
  14. −0.2E−3
  15. 43,162.3E5
  16. −176.52E+1
  17. 1.43000E+2

In Exercises 18–22, change the fixed-point decimals to floating-point decimals with exactly one nonzero digit to the left of the decimal.

  18. 173.0
  19. 743927000000.0
  20. −0.000000023

  21. +014.768
  22. −5.2

In Exercises 23–27, change the floating-point decimals to fixed-point decimals.

  23. −1.0046E+3
  24. 4.2E−8
  25. 9.020E10

  26. −4.615230E3
  27. −8.02E−3

In Exercises 28–34, indicate the data type.

  28. −720
  29. −720.0
  30. 150E3
  31. 150

  32. '150'
  33. '23.4E2'
  34. 23.4E−2

35. Write and run test programs for each of the following:
  a. Examine the output for a decimal number
```
writeln (2.31);
```
  b. Try to print a message without using quotation marks for a character string
```
writeln (Hello);
```

In Exercises 36 and 37, write a program that produces the indicated output.

36. SCORE

SCORE
86
82
79

where "S" is in column 10.

37. PRICE

PRICE
$ 19.94
$100.00
$ 58.95

where "P" is in column 50.

38. Assume the hourly wages of five student employees are

    3.65
    4.10
    2.89
    5.00
    4.50

Write a program that produces this output.

```
 ----------------------
 Employee   Hourly Wage
 ----------------------
     1         $ 3.65
     2         $ 4.10
     3         $ 2.89
     4         $ 5.00
     5         $ 4.50
 ----------------------
```

39. What is the output from the following segment of code?

```
writeln ('My test average is', 87.5);
writeln ('My test average is':20, 87.5:10);
writeln ('My test average is':25, 87.5:10:2);
writeln ('My test average is':25, 87.5:6:2);
```

40. Write a program that produces the following output. Start "Student" in column 20 and "Test" in column 40.

```
Student Name          Test Score

Adams, Mike            73
Conley, Theresa        86
Samson, Ron            92
O'Malley, Colleen      81
```

41. The Great Lakes Shipping Company wants a computer program to generate billing statements for their customers. The heading of each bill should be

```
      GREAT LAKES SHIPPING COMPANY
        SAULT STE. MARIE, MICHIGAN
---------------------------------------------------
     Thank you for doing business with our company.
     The information listed below was used to
     determine your total cargo fee. We hope you
     were satisfied with our service.
---------------------------------------------------
CARGO        TONNAGE         RATE/TON        TOTAL DUE
```

Write a complete Pascal program to produce this heading.

In Exercises 42–44, what output is produced by the statements or sequence of statements when executed by the computer?

42. `writeln (1234, 1234:8, 1234:6);`
43. `writeln (12:4, -21:4, 120:4);`
44.
```
writeln ('FIGURE   AREA   PERIMETER');
writeln ('_____');
writeln;
writeln ('Square', 16:7, 16:12);
writeln;
writeln ('Rect  ', 24:7, 20:12);
```

45. Write a complete program to produce the following table.

```
WIDTH          LENGTH          AREA
  4              2              8
 21              5             105
```

In Exercises 46–51, what output is produced when each is executed?

46. `writeln (2.134:15:2);`
47. `writeln (423.73:5:2);`
48. `writeln (-42.1:8:3);`
49. `writeln (-4.21E3:6:2);`
50. `writeln (10.25);`
51. `writeln (1.25, 1.25:6:2, 1.25:6:1);`

52. Write a complete program that produces the following output.

Hourly Wage	Hours Worked	Total
5.0	20.0	100.00
7.50	15.25	114.375

Basic Operations for Integers

In the last section, we examined some types of data that can be used when writing programs in Pascal: in particular, you can use data of type **real, integer** or **char.** Now we need to examine how these data types can be used. Since we must be able to use numeric data in arithmetic expressions, there must be a specific set of rules that governs operations and distinguishes between reals and integers. This section shows you how arithmetic operations are performed in Pascal and what restrictions are necessary when working with reals and integers.

Integer arithmetic in Pascal allows the operations of addition, subtraction, and multiplication to be performed. Raising to a power is not allowed in standard Pascal; however, an alternative is discussed in Chapter 7. The notation for the integer operations is

Symbol	Operation	Example	Value
+	Addition	3 + 5	8
−	Subtraction	43 − 25	18
*	Multiplication	4 * 7	28

Noticeably absent from this list is a division operation. This is because *integer arithmetic operations* are expected to produce integer answers. Since division problems might not produce integers, Pascal provides two operations, **MOD** and **DIV,** to use instead of division to produce integer answers.

In a standard division problem, there is a quotient and remainder. In Pascal, **DIV** produces the quotient and **MOD** produces the remainder. For example, in the problem 17 divided by 3, 17 **DIV** 3 produces 5, and 17 **MOD** 3 produces 2. When using **DIV,** care should be taken to avoid division by zero. Several integer expressions and their values are shown in Table 2.3. Notice that when 3 is multiplied by −2, the expression is written as 3 * (−2) rather than 3 * −2. This is because consecutive operators cannot appear in an arithmetic expression. However, this expression can be written as −2 * 3.

Order of Operations for Integers

Expressions involving more than one operation are frequently used when writing programs. When this happens, it is important to know the order in which these operations are performed. The priorities for these are

1. All expressions within a set of parentheses are evaluated first. If there are parentheses within parentheses (the parentheses are nested), the innermost expressions are evaluated first.

TABLE 2.3
Integer arithmetic

Expression	Value
−3 + 2	−1
2 − 3	−1
−3 * 2	−6
3 * (−2)	−6
−3 * (−2)	6
17 **DIV** 3	5
17 **MOD** 3	2
17 **DIV** (−3)	−5
17 **MOD** (−3)	2
−17 **DIV** 3	−5
−17 **MOD** 3	−2
−17 **DIV** (−3)	5
−17 **MOD** (−3)	−2

2. The operations *, **MOD,** and **DIV** are evaluated next in order from left to right.

3. The operations + and − are evaluated last from left to right.

These operations are summarized in Table 2.4.

Some examples of values of arithmetic expressions using data of type **integer** are

Expression	Value
3 − 4 * 5	−17
3 − (4 * 5)	−17
(3 − 4) * 5	−5
3 * 4 − 5	7
3 * (4 − 5)	−3
17 − 10 − 3	4
17 − (10 − 3)	10
(17 − 10) − 3	4
−42 + 50 **MOD** 17	−26

As expressions get more elaborate, it can be helpful to list partial evaluations in a manner similar to the order in which the computer performs the evaluations. For example, suppose the expression

(3 − 4) + 18 **DIV** 5 + 2

is to be evaluated. If we consider the order in which subexpressions are evaluated, we get

$$
\begin{array}{l}
\underline{(3 - 4)} + 18\ \textbf{DIV}\ 5 + 2 \\
\quad\downarrow \\
\ -1\quad + \underline{18\ \textbf{DIV}\ 5} + 2 \\
\qquad\qquad\downarrow \\
\underline{-1\quad +\qquad 3}\qquad + 2 \\
\quad\downarrow \\
\qquad 2\qquad\qquad + 2 \\
\qquad\qquad\downarrow \\
\qquad\quad 4
\end{array}
$$

TABLE 2.4
Integer arithmetic
priority

Expression or Operation	Priority
( )	1. Evaluate from inside out
* , **MOD, DIV**	2. Evaluate from left to right
+ , –	3. Evaluate from left to right

What is the value of the following expression?

8 **MOD** 3 – 15 * (5 + 1)

Basic Operations for Reals

The operations of addition, subtraction, and multiplication are the same for data of type **real** as for integers. Additionally, division is now permitted. Since **MOD** and **DIV** are restricted to data of type **integer,** the symbol for division of data of type **real** is "/". The *real arithmetic operations* are as follows:

Symbol	Operation	Example	Value
+	Addition	4.2 + 19.36	23.56
–	Subtraction	19.36 – 4.2	15.16
*	Multiplication	3.1 * 2.0	6.2
/	Division	54.6 / 2.0	27.3

Division is given the same priority as multiplication when arithmetic expressions are evaluated by the computer. The rules for order of operation are the same as those for evaluating integer arithmetic expressions. A summary of these operations is shown in Table 2.5.

Some examples of values of arithmetic expressions using data of type **real** are

Expression	Value
2.0 * (1.2 – 4.3)	– 6.2
2.0 * 1.2 – 4.3	– 1.9
– 12.6 / 3.0 + 3.0	– 1.2
– 12.6 / (3.0 + 3.0)	– 2.1

As with integers, consecutive operation signs are not allowed. Thus, if you want to multiply 4.3 by – 2.0, you can use – 2.0 * 4.3 or 4.3 * (– 2.0), but you cannot use 4.3 * – 2.0. As expressions get a bit more

TABLE 2.5
Real arithmetic
priority

Expression or Operation	Priority
( )	1. Evaluate from inside out
* , /	2. Evaluate from left to right
+ , –	3. Evaluate from left to right

complicated, it is again helpful to write out the expression and evaluate it step by step. For example,

$$-4.3 * (10.1 + (\underline{72.3 / 3.0} - 4.5)) + 18.2$$
$$\downarrow$$
$$-4.3 * (10.1 + (\underline{24.1 - 4.5})) + 18.2$$
$$\downarrow$$
$$-4.3 * (\underline{10.1 + 19.6}) + 18.2$$
$$\downarrow$$
$$\underline{-4.3 * 29.7} + 18.2$$
$$\downarrow$$
$$\underline{-127.71 + 18.2}$$
$$\downarrow$$
$$-109.51$$

Overflow and Underflow

Arithmetic operations with computers have some limitations. One of these is the problem of *overflow*. Integer overflow occurs when an integer expression exceeds the value of **maxint.** Real overflow occurs when the absolute value of a real is too large to fit into a memory location (discussed further in Section 3.1). Ideally, an error message should be given when overflow occurs. Unfortunately, that is not always the case. Some systems just assign a meaningless value and keep on computing. You should check the limitations for your system.

A second problem occurs when working with reals. If a real number is too small to be represented, it is replaced by zero. This is called *underflow*. Thus, your computations may produce a real of the magnitude 1.0×10^{-100}, but your system could replace this with a zero.

In general, underflow is less of a problem than overflow. You should, however, always guard against both possibilities when performing numerical computations.

Mixed Expressions

We have seen examples of arithmetic expressions using data of types **integer** and **real.** What happens if both **integer** and **real** data types are used in the same expression?

It is possible for some expressions to contain data of both types. These are called *mixed-mode expressions*. All operations studied thus far except **MOD** and **DIV** allow operands of both types. However, when any operand in a simple arithmetic expression is of type **real,** the value of the expression is given as a real and not as an integer. For example, 4 + 3.0 is the real 7.0 rather than the integer 7. It is permissible to use data of type **integer** with the real number operation division "/"; when this happens, the answer is given as a real number. For example, 6 / 3 is the real 2.0 rather than the integer 2. However, when data of type **real** are used with either **MOD** or **DIV,** an error message occurs. Several examples of valid and invalid mixed-mode expressions are shown in Table 2.6.

Evaluation of mixed-mode expressions is similar to evaluating either real or integer arithmetic expressions. If an expression is valid, the order of operations for evaluating the expression is the same as that used for the data type of the value of the expression. As an example, consider the evaluation of the expression $(-4.2 + 17$ **DIV** $3 * 2.1) / 2$. Within the parentheses, 17 **DIV** 3 has first priority, hence the operation is valid. The sequential evaluation is given by

$$(-4.2 + \underline{17 \textbf{ DIV } 3} * 2.1) / 2$$
$$\downarrow$$
$$(-4.2 + \underline{\quad 5 \quad * 2.1)} / 2$$
$$\downarrow$$
$$\underline{(-4.2 + \quad\quad 10.5)} \quad / 2$$
$$\downarrow$$
$$\underline{6.3 \quad\quad\quad\quad\quad / 2}$$
$$\downarrow$$
$$3.15$$

Mixed-mode expressions can be used in **writeln** statements. The programmer must be careful, however, when formatting output. Only data of type **real** can be formatted using two colons (:8:3). If this method of formatting is used on other data types, an error results. However, reals can be formatted with a single colon. For example,

```
writeln (18.5:8);
```

is a valid statement. This produces 18.5 in floating-point form in a total field width of eight columns, as 1.850E+1. However, this is usually not a desirable practice.

Some valid and invalid statements using formatted output are

Statement	Valid	Output
writeln (14.0/(-2):8:2);	Yes	-7.00
writeln (17*(3+8):6);	Yes	187
writeln (17*(3+8):6:2);	No	
writeln (-27/3:8);	Yes	-9.00E+0
writeln (-27/3:6:2);	Yes	-9.00
writeln (-5*16:8:3);	No	

Now that you have some degree of familiarity with mixed-mode expressions, you should know that, if possible, you should avoid them.

TABLE 2.6
Mixed mode expressions

Expression	Valid	Data Type
-2.0 * 17	Yes	**real**
13.1 - 22	Yes	**real**
14 / 7	Yes	**real**
14 / 7.0	Yes	**real**
10.0 **MOD** 2	No	
10 **MOD** 2.0	No	
-15 **DIV** 3	Yes	**integer**
-15 **DIV** 3.0	No	
32.0 **DIV** 4.0	No	
7 + 5.0	Yes	**real**

There are at least three good reasons for not using mixed-mode expressions:

    1. invalid expressions may be obtained (10 **MOD** 2.0);

    2. improper formatting can result; and

    3. improper assignment statements can result (see Section 3.1).

Exercises 2.4

In Exercises 1–10, find the value of expression.

1. $17 - 3 * 2$
2. $-15 * 3 + 4$
3. 123 **MOD** 5
4. 123 **DIV** 5
5. $5 * 123$ **DIV** $5 + 123$ **MOD** 5

6. $-21 * 3 * (-1)$
7. $14 * (3 + 18$ **DIV** $4) - 50$
8. $100 - (4 * (3 + 2)) * (-2)$
9. -56 **MOD** 3
10. $14 * 8$ **MOD** $5 - 23$ **DIV** (-4)

In Exercises 11–17, find the value of the expression.

11. $3.21 + 5.02 - 6.1$
12. $6.0 / 2.0 * 3.0$
13. $6.0 / (2.0 + 3.0)$
14. $-20.5 * (2.1 + 2.0)$

15. $-2.0 * ((56.8 / 4.0 + 0.8) + 5.0)$
16. $1.04E2 * 0.02E3$
17. $800.0E-2 / 4.0 + 15.3$

In Exercises 18–27, which are valid expressions? For those that are, indicate whether they are of type **integer** or **real**. Evaluate each of the valid expressions.

18. $18 - (5 * 2)$
19. $(18 - 5) * 2$
20. $18 - 5 * 2.0$
21. $25 * (14$ **MOD** $7.0)$
22. $1.4E3 * 5$

23. $28 / 7$
24. $28.0 / 4$
25. $-5.21 + 16$
26. 24 **DIV** $6 / 3$
27. 24 **DIV** $(6 / 3)$

28. What output is produced by the following program?

```
PROGRAM MixedMode (output);

BEGIN
   writeln; writeln;
   writeln ('    Expression    Value');
   writeln ('    ----------    -----');
   writeln;
   writeln ('    10/5', 10/5:12:3);
   writeln ('    2.0+7*(-1)', 2.0 + 7 * (-1));
   writeln; writeln
END.
```

In Exercises 29–34, indicate which are executable Pascal statements. Explain why the others are not executable.

29. writeln (-20 DIV 4.0 :8:3);
30. writeln (-20 DIV 4 :8:3);
31. writeln (-20 DIV 4 :8);
32. writeln (8 - 3.0 * 5 :6);
33. writeln (7 * 6 DIV 3 / 2 :6:2);
34. writeln (-17.1 +5 * 20.0 :8:3);

■ Summary

Key Terms

algorithm
effective statement
top-down design
structured programming
stepwise refinement
module
pseudocode
reserved word
predefined identifier
keyword
syntax
syntax diagramming

identifier
program heading
declaration section
constant definition
   section
variable declaration
   section
executable section
executable statement
type
fixed point form
floating point form

string constant
output
formatting
integer arithmetic
   operations: +, −, *,
   MOD, DIV
real arithmetic
   operations: +, −, *, /
overflow
underflow
mixed-mode expression

Keywords

PROGRAM
input
output
CONST
VAR

BEGIN
END
integer
maxint
real

char
write
writeln
MOD
DIV

Key Concepts

- Five steps in problem solving include: understand the problem, develop an algorithm, write the program, run the program, and test the results against answers manually computed with paper and pencil.
- Top-down design is a process of dividing tasks into subtasks until each subtask can be readily accomplished.
- Stepwise refinement refers to refinements of tasks into subtasks.
- The rules for forming valid identifiers are: they must begin with a letter, and they can contain only letters and digits.
- The three components of a Pascal program are program heading, declaration section, and executable section.
- Semicolons are used to separate executable statements.
- Extra spaces are ignored in Pascal.
- **write** and **writeln** are used to cause a program to produce some output.
- Test programs are short programs used to help you become familiar with concepts in Pascal or local implementation features.
- Output is generated by using **write** or **writeln.**
- Numerical data must be of type **real** or **integer.**
- Character data **(char)** must be enclosed in single quotation marks ('A').
- Integer output is formatted using a single colon followed by a positive integer, for example
  ```
  writeln (25:6);
  ```
- Reals are formatted using two colons, each followed by a positive integer; the first controls the total field width and the second controls the number of positions to the right of the decimal, for example
  ```
  writeln (1234.5:8:2);
  ```
- Strings are formatted using a single colon followed by a positive integer that specifies the total field width; for example
  ```
  writeln ('This is a string.':30);
  ```
- Operations on integers are addition "+", subtraction "−", multiplication "*"; division is accomplished by **MOD** and **DIV.**

- Priority for order of operations on integers is
  1. *, **MOD, DIV** in order from left to right
  2. +, − in order from left to right.
- Operations on reals are addition " + ", subtraction " − ", multiplication " * ", and division "/".
- Priority for order of operations on reals is
  1. *, / in order from left to right
  2. +, − in order from left to right
- Mixed-mode expressions return values of type **real.**
- Priority for order of operations on mixed-mode expressions is
  1. *, /, **MOD, DIV** in order from left to right
  2. +, − in order from left to right
- Overflow is caused by a value too large for computing on a particular machine.
- Underflow is caused by a value too small (close to zero) for computing. These numbers are replaced by zero.

■ Chapter Review Exercises

1. List the five steps in developing a program.

For Exercises 2–6, write pseudocode showing the tasks needed for solving each problem.

2. Determine the weekly salary of a worker.
3. Find the batting average of a baseball player.
4. Find the slope of a line. (Remember that the slope can be undefined.)
5. Determine the letter grade earned on a test.
6. Find the smallest number from a set of 50 numbers.

For Exercises 7–12, state whether or not the identifiers are valid. If not, explain why.

7. C
8. Chapter2
9. For
10. Alpha
11. 6weeks
12. Here-and-there

For Exercises 13–16, explain why the program headings are invalid.

13. PROGRAM test,
14. PROGRAM (input, output):
15. PROGRAM 1test (input, output);
16. PROGRAM-One (output);

For Exercises 17–20, write constant definition statements.

17. Your city
18. The year
19. Your school name
20. Your grade number

For Exercises 21–23, write variable definitions.

21. An integer called A.
22. Real numbers named Number1, Number2, and Number3.
23. A character variable called First and a real number called Second.

In Exercises 24–29, tell whether the number is an integer or a real.

24. 7
25. 0.0
26. 403.0
27. 4.8
28. 2E8
29. −3954

In Exercises 30–36, find the value of the expression.

30. 12 * 4 + 7

31. 7 + 4 * 12

32. 8 − 7 **DIV** 3

33. 12 **MOD** 5 * 6 − 7

34. 14 + 75 * (18 − 5 **MOD** 2)

35. 3.5 + 8.7 / 2.1

36. 3.03E5 * 2.1E8

In Exercises 37–40, if the expression is valid, tell whether it is of type **integer** or **real** and evaluate it. If the expression is invalid, explain why.

37. 4 * 8.0 − 3

38. 4.2 **MOD** 9.1

39. '12' * '6' − '4'

40. 5 / 3

For Exercises 41–44, show the exact output produced.

```
41. writeln (-10:5, 3.0 / 2.0:8:2);
42. writeln (10.0 / 2.0:10:2, 10.0 / 2.0:6:2);
43. writeln (7 DIV 3:2, 'r':3, 7 MOD 3:2);
44. writeln ('test':5, 'test':7, 'test':10);
```

■ Programming Problems

Write and run a short program for each of the following.

1. A program to print your initials in block letters. Your output could look like:

```
JJJJJ              A             CC
    J             A A          C    C
    J            A   A        C
    J           AAAAA        C
 J  J           A   A         C    C
  JJ            A   A          CC
```

2. Design a simple picture and print it out using **writeln** statements. It will help to plan the picture using a sheet of graph paper to make spacing easier.

3. Susan purchases a computer for $985. The sales tax on the purchase is 5.5 percent. Compute and print the total purchase price.

4. Find and print the area and perimeter of a rectangle that is 4.5 feet long and 2.3 feet wide. Print both rounded to the nearest tenth of a foot.

5. Compute the number of minutes in a year.

6. Light travels at 3 × 10 meters per second. Compute the distance that a light beam would travel in one year. (This is called a light year.)

7. The 1927 New York Yankees won 110 games and lost 44. Compute their winning percentage and print it rounded to three decimal places.

8. A 10 kilogram object is travelling at 12 meters per second. Compute its momentum and velocity.

9. Convert 98.0 degrees Fahrenheit to degrees Celsius.

Variables, Input, Constants, and Standard Functions

In this chapter we discuss how to use data in a program and how to use constants and variables. We also discuss the use of functions to perform standard operations such as finding the square root or absolute value of a number.

OBJECTIVES

- to understand use of computer storage
- to distinguish between name of a memory location and value of a memory location
- to use variables in assignment statements, expressions, and output statements

Memory Locations

It is frequently necessary to store values for later use. This is done by putting the value into a *memory location* and using a symbolic name to refer to this location. If the contents of the location are to be changed during a program, the symbolic name is referred to as a *variable*; if the contents cannot be changed, it is referred to as a *constant*.

A simple way to think about memory locations is to picture them as boxes; each box is named and a value is stored inside the box. For example, suppose a program is written to add a sequence of numbers. If we name the memory location to be used Sum, initially we have

```
┌──────┐
│      │
└──────┘
  Sum
```

which depicts a memory location that has been reserved and can be accessed by a reference to Sum. If we then add the integers 10, 20, and 30 and store them in Sum, we have

```
┌──────┐
│  60  │
└──────┘
  Sum
```

It is important to distinguish between the name of a memory location (Sum) and the value or contents of a memory location (60). The name does not change during a program, but the contents can be changed as often as necessary. If 30 is added to the contents in the previous example, the new value stored in Sum can be depicted as

90

Sum

Prior to their use, variable names must be declared in the variable declaration section of the program as indicated in Section 2.2. For example,

```
VAR
   Sum : integer;
```

Assignment Statements

Let's now examine how the contents of variables are manipulated. A value may be put into a memory location with an *assignment statement* in the form of

```
Variable name := value;
```

where "variable name" is the name of the memory location. For example,

```
Sum := 30;
```

changes

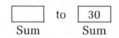

to | 30 |

Sum   Sum

The syntax diagram for this is

Some important rules concerning assignment statements are

1. The assignment is always made from right to left (←).
2. The syntax for assigning requires a colon followed immediately by an equal sign (:=).
3. Only one variable can be on the left of the assignment symbol (:=).
4. The assigned value may be a constant, a constant expression, the value of a variable, or the value of an arithmetic expression.
5. Any values on the right side of the assignment symbol are not changed by the assignment.

Two common errors that beginners make are trying to assign from left to right and forgetting the colon when using an assignment statement.

Repeated assignments can be made, but the only value kept is the last value assigned. For example, if Sum is an integer variable, the statements

```
Sum := 50;
Sum := 70;
Sum := 100;
```

produce first 50, then 70, and finally 100 as shown.

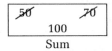

Sum

Data types must match when using assignment statements: reals must be assigned to **real** variables, integers to **integer** variables, and characters to **char** variables. An exception is that an integer can be assigned to a **real** variable; however, the integer is then converted to a real. If, for example, Average is a **real** variable and the assignment statement

```
Average := 21;
```

is made, the value is stored as the real 21.0.

Assignments to a character variable require that the value be enclosed in single quotation marks. For example, if Letter is of type **char** and you want to store the letter C in Letter, use the assignment statement

```
Letter := 'C';
```

This can be pictured as

```
+-----+
|  C  |
+-----+
Letter
```

Furthermore, only one character can be assigned or stored in a character variable at a time.

To illustrate working with assignment statements, assume that the variable declaration portion of the program is

```
VAR
    Sum : integer;
    Average : real;
    Letter : char;
```

Examples of valid and invalid assignment statements are shown in Table 3.1.

TABLE 3.1
Assignment
statements

Statement	Valid	Reason
Sum := 50;	Yes	
Sum := 10.5;	No	Data types do not match
Average := 15.6;	Yes	
Average := 33;	Yes	
Letter := 'A';	Yes	
Letter := 'HI';	No	Not a single character
Letter := 20;	No	Data types do not match
Letter := 'Z';	Yes	
Letter := A;	?	Depends on A

Expressions

Actual use of variables in a program is usually more elaborate than what we have just seen. Variables may be used in any manner that does not violate their type declarations. This includes both arithmetic operations and assignment statements. For example, if X, Y, Z, and Average are **real** variables,

```
X := 72.3;
Y := 89.4;
Z := 95.6;
Average := (X + Y + Z)/3.0;
```

is a valid fragment of code.

Let's now consider the problem of accumulating a total. Assuming A and Total are **integer** variables, the following code is valid.

```
Total := 0;
A := 5;
Total := Total + A;
A := 7;
Total := Total + A;
```

This sequence can be depicted as

```
Total := 0;            [ 0 ]
                       Total

A := 5;                [ 5 ]
                         A

Total := Total + A;    [ 5 ]
                       Total

A := 7;                [ 7 ]
                         A

Total := Total + A;    [ 12 ]
                       Total
```

Notice here that Total was initially assigned the value zero by

```
Total := 0;
```

This is necessary in Pascal because variables are not automatically initialized to zero (set to a starting value of zero) as they are in most versions of BASIC.

SELF QUIZ 3.1

Assume A, B, and Sum have been declared as variables of type **integer**. What is the value of Sum after the following statements are executed?

```
A := -8;
B := 3;
Sum := A + B;
A := 3 * B;
B := A;
Sum := Sum + A + B;
```

Output

Variables and expressions can also be used when creating output. When used in a **writeln** statement, they perform the same function as a constant. For example, if the assignment statement

```
A := 5;
```

is made, the two statements

```
writeln (5);
writeln (A);
```

produce the same output. If A, B, C, and Sum are integer variables and the assignments

```
A := 21;
B := 30;
C := 12;
Sum := A + B + C;
```

are made,

```
writeln ('The sum is ', 21 + 30 + 12);
writeln ('The sum is ', A + B + C);
writeln ('The sum is ', Sum);
```

each produces the same output.

Formatting variables and expressions in **writeln** statements follows the same rules that were presented in Chapter 2 for formatting constants. The statements needed to write the sum of the problem we just saw in a field width of four are

```
writeln ('The sum is ', (21 + 30 + 12):4);
writeln ('The sum is ', (A + B + C):4);
writeln ('The sum is ', Sum:4);
```

EXAMPLE 3.1

Suppose you want a program to print data about the cost of three pairs of pants and the average price of the pants. The variable declaration section might include:

```
VAR
    JeansPrice, CordsPrice,
    SlacksPrice,
    Total, Average : real;
```

A portion of the program can be

```
JeansPrice := 17.95;
CordsPrice := 15.95;
SlacksPrice := 20.95;
Total := JeansPrice + CordsPrice + SlacksPrice;
Average := Total/3;
```

The output can be created by

```
writeln; writeln;
writeln ('Pants                    Price');
writeln ('_____                    _____');
writeln;
writeln ('Jeans', JeansPrice:13:2);
writeln ('Cords', CordsPrice:13:2);
writeln ('Slacks', SlacksPrice:12:2);
writeln;
writeln ('Total', Total:13:2);
writeln;
writeln ('The average price is', Average:8:2);
```

and the output is

```
Pants           Price
_____           _____

Jeans           17,95
Cords           15,95
Slacks          20,95

Total           54,85

The average price is    18,28
```

Exercises 3.1

In Exercises 1–8, assume the variable declaration section of a program is

```
VAR
   Age, IQ : integer;
   Income : real;
```

Indicate which of the following are valid assignment statements. Give the reason for each that is invalid.

1. Age := 21;
2. IQ := Age + 100;
3. IQ := 120,5;
4. Age + IQ := 150;
5. Income := 22000;
6. Income := 100 * (Age + IQ);
7. Age := IQ/3;
8. IQ := 3 * Age;

9. Write a test program to illustrate what happens when values of one data type are assigned to variables of another type.

In Exercises 10–12, suppose A, B, and Temp are declared as **integer** variables. Indicate the contents of A and B at the end of each sequence of statements.

```
10. A := 5;
    B := -2;
    A := A + B;
    B := B - A;
11. A := 31;
    B := 26;
    Temp := A;
    A := B;
    B := Temp;
12. A := 0;
    B := 7;
    A := A + B MOD 2 * (-3);
    B := B + 4 * A;
```

13. Suppose X and Y are **real** variables and the assignments

    ```
    X := 121.3;
    Y := 98.6;
    ```

    are made. What **writeln** statements cause the following output?

    ```
    a. The value of X is    121.3
    b. The sum of X and Y is    219.9
    c. X =        121.3
       Y =         98.6
                   -----
       Total = 219.9
    ```

14. Assume the variable declaration section of a program is

    ```
    VAR
        Age, Height : integer;
        Weight : real;
        Sex : char;
    ```

    What output is created by the following program fragment?

    ```
    Age := 18;
    Height := 73;
    Weight := 186.5;
    Sex := 'M';
    writeln ('Sex', Sex:13);
    writeln ('Age', Age:14);
    writeln ('Height', Height:9, ' inches');
    writeln ('Weight', Weight:12:1, ' lbs');
    ```

15. Write a complete program that allows you to add five integers and then print out

    a. The integers   b. Their sum   c. Their average

16. Assume Ch and Age are appropriately declared. What output is produced by the following?

    ```
    Ch := 'M';
    Age := 21;
    writeln ('******************************':40);
    writeln ('*':11, '*':29);
    write ('*':11, 'Name':7, 'Age':9);
    writeln ('Sex':9, '*':4);
    writeln ('*':11, '____':7, '___':9, '___':9, '*':4);
    writeln; writeln;
    write ('*':11, 'Jones':8, Age:8, Ch:9, '*':4);
    writeln;
    writeln ('*':11, '*':29);
    writeln ('******************************':40);
    ```

For Exercises 17 and 18, assume the variable declaration section of a program is

```
VAR
    Weight1, Weight2 : integer;
    AverageWeight : real;
```

and the following assignment statements are made.

```
Weight1 := 165;
Weight2 := 174;
AverageWeight := (Weight1 + Weight2)/2;
```

17. What output is produced by the following section of code?

```
writeln ('Weight');
writeln ('_____');
writeln;
writeln (Weight1);
writeln (Weight2);
writeln;
writeln ('The average weight is', (Weight1 + Weight2)/2);
```

18. Write a segment of code to produce this output (use AverageWeight).

```
        Weight
        _____

          165
          174
          ___
Total     339

The average weight is 169.5 pounds.
```

19. Assume the variable declaration section of a program is

```
VAR
    Letter : char;
```

and the following assignment statement is made.

```
Letter := 'A';
```

What output is produced from the following section of code?

```
writeln ('This reviews string formatting.':40);
writeln ('When a letter', Letter, 'is used.');
writeln ('Oops!':14, 'I forgot to format.':20);
writeln ('When a letter':22, Letter:2, 'is used.':9);
writeln ('it is a string of length one.':38);
```

■ 3.2
Input

OBJECTIVES

- to use **read** and **readln** to get data for a program
- to understand the difference between interactive input and batch input

Earlier, "running a program" was subdivided into the three general categories of getting the data, manipulating it appropriately, and printing the results. Our work thus far has centered on creating output and manipulating data. We are now going to focus on how to get data for a program.

Input Statements

Data for a program are referred to as *input* and are obtained from an input device, which can be a terminal, keyboard, card reader, disk, or tape. When such data are obtained, typically the standard file **input** must be included in the file list of the program heading. Some interactive systems use a different method; check with your teacher. Your program heading will (probably) have the form

> **PROGRAM** program name **(input, output);**

The Pascal statements used to get data are **read** and **readln;** they are analogous to **write** and **writeln** for output. General forms for these input statements are

> **read** (variable name);
> **read** (variable 1, variable 2, . . . , variable n);
> **readln** (variable name);
> **readln** (variable 1, variable 2, . . . , variable n);

A syntax diagram for **read** statements is

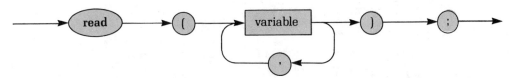

When **read** or **readln** is used to get data, the value of the data item is stored in the indicated memory location. (The difference between **read** and **readln** will be explained in Chapter 8.) Data read into a program must match the type of variable in the variable list. To illustrate, if a variable declaration section includes

```
VAR
    Age : integer;
    Wage : real;
```

and the data items are

      21   5.25

then

```
    readln (Age, Wage);
```

results in

      | 21 | | 5.25 |
      Age   Wage

Interactive Input

Interactive input refers to entering values from the keyboard while the program is running. In this case, **read** or **readln** causes the program to halt and wait for data items to be typed. A *prompt* may appear on the screen. For example, if you want to enter three scores at some point in a program, you can use

```
    readln (Score1, Score2, Score3);
```

as a program statement. At this point, you must enter at least three integers and press <RETURN> (or some sequence of integers and <RETURN> until at least three numbers are read as data items). The remaining part of the program is then executed. To illustrate, the following program reads in three integers and prints them and their average as output.

```
PROGRAM Average (input, output);

CONST
   Skin = ' ';

VAR
   Score1, Score2, Score3 : integer;
   Average : real;

BEGIN
   readln (Score1, Score2, Score3);
   Average := (Score1 + Score2 + Score3)/3;
   writeln; writeln;
   writeln (Skip:10, 'The numbers are', Score1:5, Score2:5,
                        Score 3:5);
   writeln ('Their average is', Average:8:2);
   writeln; writeln
END.
```

When the program halts, if you type in 89, 90, and 91 and press <RE-TURN>, output is

```
The numbers are   89   90   91
Their average is   90.00
```

Interactive programs require a prompting message to the user so the user knows what to do when a prompt appears. For example, the problem in the previous example can be modified by the line

```
writeln ('Please enter 3 scores and press <RETURN>.');
```

before the line

```
readln (Score1, Score2, Score3);
```

The screen will display the message

```
Please enter 3 scores and press <RETURN>.
```

when the program is run.

Clearly stated screen messages to the person running a program are what make a program *user-friendly*. For long messages or several lines of output, you might wish to use **readln** as a complete statement to halt execution. When you press <RETURN>, the program will continue. When **read** or **readln** is used for input, <RETURN> must be pressed before program execution will continue.

Reading Numeric Data

Reading numeric data into a program is a reasonably straightforward process. At least one blank must be used to separate numbers. The <RE-TURN> character is read as a blank, so any sequence of numbers and spaces or <RETURN> can be used to enter the required data.

Since the type of data items entered must match the data types for variables in an input statement, exercise some caution when using both reals and integers as input. To illustrate, suppose a variable declaration section is

```
VAR
  A : integer;
  X : real;
```

and you wish to enter the data items 97.5 and 86 respectively. **readln** (X,A) achieves the desired result. However, **readln** (A,X) results in an error. Since A is of type **integer,** only the 97 is read into A. The next character is a period and when an attempt is made to read this period into the memory location for X, a type mismatch error occurs. One exception is that an integer can be read into a variable of type **real.** However, it is stored as a real and must be used accordingly.

Data items can be entered using various combination of **read** and **readln.** For example,

```
readln (Score1, Score2, Score3);
```

can be replaced by any of the following:

1. ```
   readln (Score1);
   readln (Score2, Score3);
   ```
2. ```
   read (Score1, Score2);
   readln (Score3);
   ```
3. ```
   read (Score1);
   read (Score2);
   readln (Score3);
   ```

Note that in each case, three integers are to be entered in such a manner that the first one is stored in Score1, the second in Score2, and the third in Score3.

Reading Character Data

Reading characters is much different from reading numeric data. When using standard Pascal, the following features apply to reading data of type **char.**

1. Only one character can be read at a time.
2. Each blank is a separate character.
3. The <RETURN> character is read as a blank.
4. Each digit of a number is read as a separate character.

If you want to read in a student's initials followed by three test scores,

```
read (FirstInitial, MiddleInitial, LastInitial;
readln (Score1, Score2, Score3);
```

accomplishes this. When program execution is halted, you would type in something like

JDK 89 90 91

and press <RETURN>.
```

Some errors are caused by not being careful with character data. For example, suppose you want to enter three test scores followed by a student's initials. Appropriate program statements are

```
read (Score1, Score2, Score3);
readln (FirstInitial, MiddleInitial, LastInitial);
```

When program execution halts for expected input, if you enter

89 90 91 JDK

when you try to print these values using

```
writeln (Score1, Score2:5, Score3:5);
writeln (FirstInitial, MiddleInitial, LastInitial);
```

the output is

```
89    90    91
   JD
```

because the blank following 91 is read as a character when an attempt is made to read FirstInitial. Note that the first three characters following 91 are a blank followed by 'J' and 'D'. This problem can be avoided by entering the data as

89 90 91JDK

However, it probably would be better to enter the initials first and then the scores. The topic of reading character data is expanded when text files are introduced in Chapter 8.

Batch Input

Batch input refers to a program getting data from cards or from a file that has previously been created. Since this text is written assuming the reader will use an interactive mode, development of batch input is deferred until Chapter 8. If you are working in a batch mode, you should read Chapter 8 at this time and check with your teacher.

Exercises 3.2

1. Discuss the difference between using **read** and **readln** to get data for a program.

For Exercises 2–13, assume a variable declaration section is

```
VAR
  Num1, Num2 : integer;
  Num3 : real;
  Ch : char;
```

and you wish to enter the data

15 65.3 -20

Explain what results from each statement. Also indicate what values are assigned to appropriate variables.

```
2. readln (Num1, Num3, Num2);
3. readln (Num1, Num2, Num3);
4. readln (Num1, Num2, Ch, Num3);
5. readln (Num2, Num3, Ch, Num2);
6. readln (Num2, Num3, Ch, Ch, Num2);
```

```
 7. readln (Num3, Num2);
 8. readln (Num1, Num3);
 9. readln (Num1, Ch, Num3);
10. read (Num1, Num3, Num2);
11. read (Num1, Num3, Ch, Num2);
12. read (Num1, Num3, Ch, Ch, Num2);
13. read (Num2, Num1, Ch, Num2);
```

14. Write a program statement to be used to print a message to the screen directing the user to enter data in the form used for Exercises 2–13.

For Exercises 15–19, write an appropriate program statement (or statements) to produce a screen message and write an appropriate input statement.

15. Desired input is number of hours worked and hourly pay rate.
16. Desired input is three positive integers followed by −999.
17. Desired input is price of an automobile and the state sales tax rate.
18. Desired input is the game statistics for one basketball player (check with a coach to see what must be entered).
19. Desired input is a student's initials, age, height, weight, and sex.

For Exercises 20–27, assume variables are declared as in Exercises 2–13. If an input statement is

```
readln (Num1, Num2, Ch, Num3);
```

indicate which lines of data do not result in an error message. For those that do not, indicate the values of the variables. For those that produce an error, explain what the error is.

20. 83 95 100
21. 83 95.0 100
22. 83-72 93.5
23. 83-72   93.5
24. 83.5
25. 70 73-80.5
26. 91 92 93 94
27. -76-81-16.5

28. Why is it a good idea to print out values of variables that have been read into a program?

29. Suppose Price is a variable of type **real** and you have a program statement

```
read (Price);
```

a. What happens if you enter 17.95?
b. How does this input statement compare to **readln** (Price)?

3.3
Using
Constants

OBJECTIVES

- to be aware of appropriate use of constants
- to use constants in programs
- to format constants

The word "constant" has several interpretations. In this section, it refers to values defined in the **CONST** definition subsection of a program. Recall that a Pascal program consists of a program heading, a declaration section, and an executable section. The declaration section contains a variable declaration part (discussed in Section 3.1) and a constant definition part. We now examine uses for constants defined in the **CONST** subsection.

Rationale for Uses

There are many reasons to use constants in a program. If a number is to be used frequently, the programmer may wish to give it a descriptive name in the **CONST** definition subsection and then use the descriptive name in the executable section, thus making the program easier to read. For example, if a program included a segment that computed a person's state income tax, and the state tax rate was 6.25 percent of taxable income, the **CONST** section might include:

```
CONST
     StateTaxRate = 0.0625;
```

In the executable portion of the program, the statement

```
StateTax := Income * StateTaxRate;
```

computes the state tax owed. Or suppose you want a program to compute areas of circles. Depending upon the accuracy desired, you can define pi "π" as

```
CONST
     Pi = 3.14159;
```

You can then have a statement in the executable section such as

```
Area := Pi * Radius * Radius;
```

where Area and Radius are appropriately declared variables.

Another use of constants is for values that are currently fixed but subject to change for subsequent runs of the program. If these are defined in the **CONST** section, they can be used throughout the program. If the value changes later, only one change need be made to keep the program current. These constants might be

```
CONST
     MinimumWage = 3.75;
     SpeedLimit = 55;
     Price = 0.75;
     StateTaxRate = 0.0625;
     ClassSize = 25;
     LoopLimit = 15;
```

Constants can also be used to name character strings that are used frequently as output in a program. Suppose a program needs to print two different company names. Instead of typing the names each time they are needed, the following definition can be used.

```
CONST
     Company1 = 'First National Bank of America';
     Company2 = 'Metropolitan Bank of New York';
```

Company1 and Company2 can then be used in **writeln** statements.

Another situation might call for a constant defined for later repeated use in making output more attractive. Included could be constants for underlining and for separating sections of output. Some definitions can be

```
CONST
     Underline = '_____';
     Splats = '**********************************';
```

To separate the output with asterisks the statement

```
writeln (Splats, Splats);
```

can be used. In a similar fashion

```
writeln (Underline);
```

can be used for underlining.

Defined Constants and Space Shuttle Computing

An excellent illustration of the utilization of defined constants in a program was given by J. F. ("Jack") Clemons, manager of avionics flight software development and verification for the space shuttle on-board computers. In an interview with David Gifford, editor for *Communications of the ACM*, Clemons was asked: "Have you tried to restructure the software so that it can be changed easily?"

His response was, "By changing certain data constants, we can change relatively large portions of the software on a mission-to-mission basis. For example, we've designed the software so that characteristics like atmospheric conditions on launch day or different lift-off weights can be loaded as initial constants into the code. This is important when there are postponements or last-minute payload changes that invalidate the original inputs."

Formatting Constants

Formatting of numerical constants is identical to formatting reals and integers as discussed in Section 2.3. If the constant definition section contains

```
CONST
    Pi = 3.14159;
    SpeedLimit = 55;
```

then

```
writeln ('Pi is used as', Pi:10:5);
writeln ('Speed limit is', SpeedLimit:4);
```

produces

```
Pi is used as   3.14159
Speed limit is  55
```

When character strings are defined as constants, a single positive integer can be used for formatting. This integer establishes the field width for the character string and places the string at the right side of the field (called right justification). For example, suppose the constant definition section includes

```
CONST
    Company1 = 'First National Bank of America';
    Company2 = 'Metropolitan Bank of New York';
    Underline = '_____';
    Splats = '*******************************************';
```

If the program contains the program fragment

```
writeln; writeln;
writeln (Splats:50);
writeln;
writeln (Company1:45);
writeln (Underline:45);
writeln;
writeln (Company2:44);
writeln (Underline:45);
writeln;
writeln (Splats:50);
```

these statements produce the output

```
********************************************

     First National Bank of America
     ------------------------------------

     Metropolitan Bank of New York
     -----------------------------------

********************************************
```

Exercises 3.3

1. One use of constants is for values that are used throughout a program but are subject to change over time (minimum wage, speed limit, and so on). List at least five items in this category that were not mentioned in this section.

2. Assume the **CONST** definition section of a program is

```
CONST
   CourseName = 'Computer Science';
   TotalPts = 100;
   Underline = '_____';
```

Fill in the appropriate formatting positions in the following **writeln** statements to produce the output below.

```
writeln ('Course:':17, CourseName:    , 'Test #1':   );
writeln (Underline:   );
writeln; writeln;
writeln ('Total Points':22, TotalPts:   );
```

We want output as follows:

```
Course:            Computer Science      Test #1
-------            ----------------       -------

Total Points     100
```

3. Using the same **CONST** definition section as in Exercise 2, what output is produced by the following segment of code?

```
writeln; writeln;
writeln (CourseName:20, 'Test #2':20);
writeln (Underline:40);
writeln; writeln;
writeln ('Total points':16, TotalPts:15);
writeln ('My score':12, 93:19);
writeln ('Class average':17, 82.3:14:1);
```

For Exercises 4–12, use the constant definition section to define appropriate constants.

4. Your name
5. Today's date
6. Your social security number
7. Your age
8. The name of your school
9. The number of students in your class
10. The average age of students in your class
11. The average hourly wage of steelworkers
12. The price of a new car

■ 3.4
Standard
Functions

- to understand reasons for having standard functions
- to use standard functions in a program
- to use appropriate data types for arguments of standard functions

Some standard operations required by programmers are squaring numbers, finding square roots of numbers, rounding numbers, and truncating numbers. Because these operations are so basic, Pascal provides *standard (built-in) functions* for them. Different versions of Pascal and other programming languages have differing standard functions available, so you should always check which functions can be used. Appendix 2 sets forth those available in most versions of Pascal.

The standard form for *invoking* (or *calling*) a function is

> function name (argument)

where function name is any valid identifier and *argument* is a list of values or expressions having values. A function is invoked by using it in a program. If, for example, you want to square the integer 5,

    sqr(5)

produces the desired value.

The syntax diagram for this is

Many functions operate on numbers, starting with a given number and returning some associated value. Table 3.2 shows five standard functions together with their argument type, data type of return, and an explanation of the value returned.

Several examples of specific function expressions together with the value returned by each expression are depicted in Table 3.3.

TABLE 3.2
Numeric function calls and return types

Function Call	Argument Type	Type of Return	Function Value
sqr(argument)	**real** or **integer**	Same as argument	Returns the square of the argument
sqrt(argument)	**real** or **integer** (nonnegative)	**real**	Returns the square root of the argument
abs(argument)	**real** or **integer**	Same as argument	Returns absolute value of the argument
round(argument)	**real**	**integer**	Returns value rounded to the nearest integer
trunc(argument)	**real**	**integer**	Returns value truncated to an integer

Herman Hollerith

Herman Hollerith (1860–1929) was hired by the United States Census Bureau in 1879 at the age of 19. Since the 1880 census was predicted to take a long time to complete (it actually took until 1887), Hollerith was assigned the task of developing a mechanical method of tabulating census data. He introduced his census machine in 1887. It consisted of four parts:

1. a punched paper card that represented data using a special code (Hollerith code),
2. a card punch apparatus,
3. a tabulator that read the punched cards, and
4. a sorting machine with 24 compartments.

The punched cards used by Hollerith were the same size as cards still in use today.

Using Hollerith's techniques and equipment, the 1890 census tabulation was completed in one-third the time required for the previous census tabulation. This included working with data for twelve million additional people.

Hollerith proceeded to form the Tabulating Machine Company (1896), which supplied equipment to census bureaus in the United States, Canada, and western Europe. After a disagreement with the census director, Hollerith began marketing his equipment in other commercial areas. Hollerith sold his company in 1911. It was later combined with twelve others to form the Computing-Tabulating-Recording Company, a direct ancestor of International Business Machines Corp.

In the meantime, Hollerith's successor at the census bureau, James Powers, redesigned the census machine. He then formed his own company, which subsequently became Remington Rand and Sperry Univac.

Using Functions

When a function is invoked, it produces a value in much the same way that 3 + 3 produces 6. Thus, use of a function should be treated similarly to using constants or values of an expression. Since function calls are not Pascal statements, they may only be used as a part of other statements. Typical uses are in assignment statements,

```
X := sqrt(16.0);
```

output statements,

```
writeln (abs(-8):20);
```

TABLE 3.3
Function values

Expression	Value
sqr(2)	4
sqr(2.0)	4.0
sqr(-3)	9
sqrt(25.0)	5.0
sqrt(25)	5.0
sqrt(0.0)	0.0
sqrt(-2.0)	Not permissible
abs(5.2)	5.2
abs(-3.4)	3.4
abs(-5)	5
round(3.78)	4
round(8.50)	9
round(-4.2)	-4
trunc(3.78)	3
trunc(8.5)	8
trunc(-4.2)	-4

or arithmetic expressions

```
X := round(3.78) + trunc(-4.1);
```

Arguments of functions can be expressions, variables, or constants. Be careful, however, that the argument is always appropriate. For example,

```
X := sqrt(trunc(3.2));
```

is appropriate, but

```
X := sqrt(trunc(-3.2));
```

produces an error since **trunc**(−3.2) has the value −3 and **sqrt**(−3) is not a valid expression.

The following example illustrates how functions can be used in expressions.

EXAMPLE 3.2   Find the value of the following expression.

$$4.2 + \textbf{round}(\textbf{trunc}(2.0 * 3.1) + 5.3) - \textbf{sqrt}(\textbf{sqr}(-4.1));$$

The solution is

$$4.2 + \textbf{round}(\textbf{trunc}(\underline{2.0 * 3.1}) + 5.3) - \textbf{sqrt}(\textbf{sqr}(-4.1))$$
$$\swarrow$$
$$4.2 + \textbf{round}(\underline{\textbf{trunc}(6.2)} + 5.3) - \underline{\textbf{sqrt}(16.81)}$$
$$\swarrow \qquad\qquad\qquad \searrow$$
$$4.2 + \textbf{round}(\underline{6.0 + 5.3}) \qquad - \qquad 4.1$$
$$\swarrow$$
$$4.2 + \underline{\textbf{round}(11.3)} \qquad - \qquad 4.1$$
$$\searrow$$
$$\underline{4.2 + \qquad 11.0} \qquad - \qquad 4.1$$
$$\searrow$$
$$\underline{15.2 \qquad\qquad\qquad\qquad - \qquad 4.1}$$
$$\downarrow$$
$$11.1$$

SELF QUIZ 3.2   Find the value of the following expression.

$$\textbf{sqr}(\textbf{trunc}(\textbf{sqrt}(\textbf{abs}(-14.5))))$$

Character Sets

In addition to the numeric functions just examined, other functions can have characters as arguments. Some of these return a character when called and some return an integer.

Before we look at functions dealing with characters, we need to examine the way in which character data are stored. In the **char** data type, each character is associated with an integer. Thus, the sequence of characters is associated with a sequence of integers. The particular sequence used by a machine for this purpose is referred to as the *collating sequence* for that *character set*. Two such sequences currently in use are

1. American Standard Code for Information Exchange (ASCII) and
2. Extended Binary Coded Decimal Interchange Code (EBCDIC).

TABLE 3.4
ASCII code

ƀ ! " # $ % & ' ( ) * + , - . / 0 1 2 3 4 5 6 7 8 9 : ; < = > ? @
A B C D E F G H I J K L M N O P Q R S T U V W X Y Z [\ ] ↑ _ '
a b c d e f g h i j k l m n o p q r s t u v w x y z { | } ~

Note: Of the special characters, ƀ is the symbol to denote a blank.

Each collating sequence contains an ordering of the characters in a character set and is listed in Appendix 4. For programs in this text, we use the ASCII code. As shown in Table 3.4, fifty-two of these characters are letters, ten are digits, and the rest are special characters.

TABLE 3.5
ASCII ordering of
a character set

Ordinal	Character	Ordinal	Character	Ordinal	Character
32	ƀ	64	@	96	'
33	!	65	A	97	a
34	"	66	B	98	b
35	#	67	C	99	c
36	$	68	D	100	d
37	%	69	E	101	e
38	&	70	F	102	f
39	'	71	G	103	g
40	(	72	H	104	h
41	)	73	I	105	i
42	*	74	J	106	j
43	+	75	K	107	k
44	,	76	L	108	l
45	-	77	M	109	m
46	.	78	N	110	n
47	/	79	O	111	o
48	0	80	P	112	p
49	1	81	Q	113	q
50	2	82	R	114	r
51	3	83	S	115	s
52	4	84	T	116	t
53	5	85	U	117	u
54	6	86	V	118	v
55	7	87	W	119	w
56	8	88	X	120	x
57	9	89	Y	121	y
58	:	90	Z	122	z
59	;	91	[	123	{
60	<	92	\	124		
61	=	93	]	125	}
62	>	94	↑	126	~
63	?	95	_		

Note: Codes 00–31 and 127 are nonprintable control characters.

	Function Call	Argument Type	Type of Result	Function Value
TABLE 3.6 Function calls with ordinal arguments or character values	**ord**(argument)	Any ordinal type	**integer**	Ordinal corresponding to argument
	pred(argument)	Any ordinal type	Same as argument	Predecessor of the argument
	succ(argument)	Any ordinal type	Same as argument	Successor of the argument
	chr(argument)	**integer**	**char**	Character associated with the ordinal of the argument

Character Functions

Ordering a character set requires associating an integer with each character. Data types ordered in some association with the integers are known as *ordinal data types*. Each integer is the ordinal of its associated character. Integers are therefore considered to be an ordinal data type. Character sets are also considered to be an ordinal data type, as shown in Table 3.5. In each case, the ordinal of the character appears to the left of the character.

Using ASCII, as shown in Table 3.5, the ordinal of a capital a (A) is 65, the ordinal of the arabic number one (1) is 49, the ordinal of a blank (b̸) is 32, and the ordinal of a lowercase a (a) is 97.

Pascal provides several standard functions that have arguments of ordinal type. These are listed in Table 3.6 together with a related function **chr** that returns a character when called.

Again, using the ASCII collating sequence shown in Table 3.5, the use of these functions is shown in Table 3.7.

TABLE 3.7
Values of character
functions

Expression	Value
ord('E')	69
ord('9')	57
ord(9)	9
ord('>')	62
pred('N')	M
pred('A')	@
succ('(')	)
succ('!')	"
chr(74)	J
chr(32)	b̸
chr(59)	;
chr(114)	r

Variables and variable expressions can be used as arguments for functions. For example, if Ch is a **char** variable and the assignment statement

```
Ch := 'D';
```

is made, then **ord**(Ch) has the value 68.

Let's now consider a short program that allows the use of standard functions **ord, pred, succ,** and **chr.**

```
PROGRAM FunctionTest (output);

VAR
   Ch : char;

BEGIN
   Ch := 'C';
   writeln ('Ord of C is', ord(Ch):4);
   writeln ('Succ of C is', succ(Ch):3);
   writeln ('Pred of C is', pred(Ch):3);
   writeln ('Chr of 67 is', chr(67):4)
END.
```

When this program is run, the output is

```
Ord of C is    67
Succ of C is   D
Pred of C is   B
Chr of 67 is    C
```

You should obtain a complete list of characters available and their respective ordinals for your local system. Note particular features such as when using EBCDIC, **succ**('R') is not 'S'; and when using ASCII, **chr**(n) is nonprintable for n < 32 or n > 126.

Exercises 3.4

In Exercises 1–6, find the value of each expression.

1. **abs**(−11.2) + **sqrt**(**round**(15.51))
2. **trunc**(**abs**(−14.2))
3. 4 * 11 **MOD** (**trunc**(**trunc**(8.9)/**sqrt**(16)))
4. **sqr**(17 **DIV** 5 * 2)
5. −5.0 + **sqrt**(5 * 5 − 4 * 6)/2.0
6. 3.1 * 0.2 − **abs**(−4.2 * 9.0 / 3.0)

7. Write a test program that illustrates what happens when an inappropriate argument is used with a function. Be sure to include something like **ord**(15.3) and **chr**(30).

8. Two standard algebraic problems come from the Pythagorean theorem and the quadratic formula. Assume variables A, B, and C are declared in a program. Write Pascal expressions that allow you to evaluate

   a. the length of the hypotenuse of a right triangle $(\sqrt{a^2 + b^2})$
   b. one solution to an equation solved by using the quadratic formula

   $$\frac{-b \pm \sqrt{b^2 - 4ac}}{2a}$$

In Exercises 9–15, indicate whether the expression is valid or invalid. Find the value of those that are valid; explain why the others are invalid.

9. -6 **MOD** (**sqrt**(16))
10. 8 **DIV** (**trunc**(**sqrt**(65)))
11. **sqrt**(63 **MOD** (-2))
12. **abs**($-$**sqrt**(**sqr**(3) + 7))
13. **sqrt**(16 **DIV** (-3))
14. **sqrt**(**sqr** -4))
15. **round**(14.38 * 10)/10

16. The standard function **round** permits you to round to the nearest integer. Write an expression that permits you to round the real number X to the nearest tenth.

In Exercises 17–23, find the value of the expression.

17. **ord**(13 + 4 **MOD** 3)
18. **pred**(**succ**('E'))
19. **succ**(**pred**('E'))
20. **ord**(5)
21. **ord**('5')
22. **chr**(**ord**(' + '))
23. **ord**(**chr**(40))

For Exercises 24–26, assume the variable declaration section of a program is

```
VAR
   X : real;
   A : integer;
   Ch : char;
```

What output is produced by the program fragment?

24. ```
X := -4.3;
writeln (X:6:2, abs(X):6:2, trunc(X):6, round(X):6);
```
25. ```
X := -4.3;
A := abs(round(X));
writeln (ord(A));
writeln (ord('A'));
```
26. ```
Ch := chr(26);
writeln (Ch:5, pred(Ch):5, succ(Ch):5);
```

27. Write a complete program to print each letter of the alphabet and its ordinal in the collating sequence used by your machine's version of Pascal.

---

## Style Tip Summary

Writing styles and suggestions are gathered for quick reference in the style tip summary. These tips are intended to stimulate rather than terminate your imagination.
```

STYLE TIP
■ ■ ■ ■ ■ ■ ■ ■

1. Use descriptive identifiers. The words Sum, Score, Average are more meaningful than the letters A,B,C or X,Y,Z.
2. Use constants to create neat, attractive output.
   For example,

```
CONST
  Splats = '*******************************';
  Underline = '_____';
  Border = '*                              *';
```

3. Use the constant definition section to define an appropriately named blank and use it to control line spacing for output. Thus, you can have

```
CONST
  Skip = ' ';
  Indent = '   ';
```

and then output statements can be

```
writeln (Skip:20, message, Skip:10, message);
```

or

```
writeln (Indent:20, message, Skip:10, message);
```

4. Insert blanks for line spacing within the program. Spacing between words and expressions should resemble typical English usage. Thus,

```
PROGRAM EarlyBird (input, output);
```

is preferable to

```
PROGRAM    EarlyBird   (     input,       output    );
```

5. Line up decimal points in a column of reals.

```
 14.32
181.50
 93.63
```

6. Make output attractive by using columns, left and right margins, under-lining, and blank lines.
7. Insert **writelns** at the beginning and end of the executable section to separate desired output from other messages. For example,

```
BEGIN
  writeln; writeln;
        .
        .   (program body here)
        .
  writeln; writeln
END.
```

■ Summary

Key Terms

memory location	prompt	argument
variable	user-friendly	collating sequence:
constant	batch input	ASCII and EBCDIC
assignment statement	standard (built-in)	character set
input	function	ordinal data type
interactive input	invoke (call)	

Keywords

read   **readln**

Key Concepts

- Each memory location has a name which refers to the contents of the location.
- The name of a memory location is different from the contents of the memory location.
- Assignment statements are used to assign values to memory locations; for example,

```
Sum := 30 + 60;
```

- Variables and variable expressions can be used in output statements.
- **read** is used to get data. Correct form is
  read (variable name);
  read (variable 1, variable 2, . . . , variable n);
- **readln** is used similarly to **read**
- **readln** (variable name) causes a value to be stored in the appropriate memory location.
- Interactive input expects data items to be entered from the keyboard at appropriate times during execution of the program.
- Batch input expects data to be read from a card reader or file previously created.
- Data types for variables in a **read** or **readln** statement should match data items entered as input.
- User-friendly refers to a program which provides clear, unambiguous instructions to the user.
- Appropriate uses for constants in the **CONST** definition section include frequently used numbers; current values subject to change over time, for example, (MinimumWage = 3.75); and character strings for output.
- Character strings are formatted using a single colon.
- Five standard numeric functions available in Pascal are **sqr, sqrt, abs, round,** and **trunc.**
- Functions can be used in assignment statements,

```
X := sqrt(16.0);
```

in output statements,

```
writeln (abs(-8):20);
```

and in arithmetic expressions,

```
X := round(3.78) + trunc(-4.1);
```

- Four standard character functions available in Pascal are **ord, pred, succ,** and **chr.**

■ **Chapter Review Exercises**

For Exercises 1–10, if A is an **integer,** B is a **real,** and C is a **char,** which assignment statements are valid? If they are invalid, explain why.

1. A := round(A);
2. B := sqr(abs(B));
3. B := ord(c);
4. C := A + B;
5. A := A + B;
6. B :+ A + 1;
7. A + 1 := b;
8. C := 'Chapter 3';
9. A := 8 / 3;
10. B = 3.0 * 3.2;

Write constant definitions for Exercises 11–15.

11. The name of your favorite football team.
12. The number of miles you live from your school.
13. The number of ounces in a pound.
14. The capital of your state.
15. The room number of your computer class.

16. Explain the difference between reading numeric and character data.

For Exercises 17–20, suppose the data line

```
AB 5 6.7 C
```

is entered into a program which uses the variables

```
X, Y : integer;
J, K : real;
M, N, P : char;
```

Explain what happens when each statement is executed.

17. readln (M,N,X,J,P);
18. readln (M,N,A,B);
19. readln (M,N,J,P);
20. read (M,N,P,J,K);

For Exercises 21–25, find the value of the expression.

21. **sqr**(4) − **abs**(−12) ∗ **round**(0.6)
22. **sqrt**(**abs**(−25)) − **sqr**(5.2)
23. **pred**(34) **MOD succ**(10)
24. **chr**(**sqr**(**ord**('Y')) + **abs**(**pred**(−57)))
25. **succ**(**chr**(**ord**(**pred**('J'))))

■ Programming Problems

Write a complete Pascal program for each of the following problems. Each program should use one or more **read** or **readln** statements to obtain necessary values. Each **read** or **readln** should be preceded by an appropriate prompting message.

1. Given a positive number, print its square and square root.

2. The Golden Sales Company pays its salespeople $.27 for each item they sell. Given the number of items sold by a salesperson, print the amount of pay due.

3. Given the length and width of a rectangle, print its area and perimeter.

4. The kinetic energy of a moving object is given by the formula:

KE = (1/2) mv²

Given the mass (m) and the speed (v) of an object, find its kinetic energy.

5. Miss Lovelace wants a program to enable her to balance her checkbook. She wishes to enter a beginning balance, five letters for an abbreviation for the recipient of the check, and the amount of the check. Given this information, write a program that will find the new balance in the account.

6. A supermarket wants to install a computerized weighing system in its produce department. Input to this system will consist of a three-letter identifier for the type of produce, the weight of the produce purchase (in pounds), and the cost per pound of the produce. Print a label showing the input information along with the cost of the purchase. The label should appear as follows:

```
%%%%%%%%%%%%%%%%%%%%%%%%%%%%%%%%%%%%%%%%%%%

         Penny Spender Supermarket
            Produce Department

   ITEM       WEIGHT       COST/lb      COST
    ABC       2.0 lb        $1.98      $1.96

              Thank you!


%%%%%%%%%%%%%%%%%%%%%%%%%%%%%%%%%%%%%%%%%%%
```

7. The New-Wave Computer Company sells its product, the NW-PC for $675. In addition, they sell memory expansion cards for $69.95, disk drives for $198.50, and software for $34.98 each. Given the number of memory cards, disk drives, and software packages desired by a customer purchasing an NW-PC, print out a bill of sale that appears as follows:

```
***************************
      New Wave Computers

   ITEM                COST
1  NW-PC            $675.00
2  Memory card       139.90
1  Disk Drive        198.50
4  Software          139.92
                   -------
      TOTAL       $1153.32
```

8. Write a test program that allows you to see the characters contained within the character set of your computer. Given a positive integer, you can use the **chr** function to determine the corresponding character. On most computers only integers less than 255 are valid for this. Also, remember that most character sets contain some unprintable characters such as ASCII values less than 32. Print your output in the form:

```
Character number nn is x.
```

Writing Complete Programs

We are now at the stage where we can begin a thorough look at writing more complete programs. Chapter 2 gave us the three basic components of a program: program heading, declaration section, and executable section. Chapter 3 provided some additional tools for use in constructing programs, specifically, the use of variables, input, constants, and standard functions. Before using these ideas to write programs to solve problems, however, we need to look at the method in which programs should be constructed. Oversimplified, but absolutely essential, the idea is to design the program and write code for the program. You should never start writing code to solve a problem until you have an adequately designed solution. In this chapter, we will see how the writing of code follows in a natural fashion from a carefully designed algorithm. We will then look at typical errors. These will include both mechanical errors (syntax, declaration, assignment, and so on) and design errors (why your program doesn't solve the problem).

OBJECTIVES

■ to write code from pseudocode
■ to use program comments
■ to use indenting and blank lines to enhance readability

Writing Code from Pseudocode

The process of writing statements that are part of a program to solve a problem is referred to as *writing code*. This expression is commonly used and we will use it throughout the text. To illustrate the idea of writing actual code to solve a problem from an algorithm developed using pseudocode, consider the problem of computing your bowling score for an evening. Assume you are to read in three integer scores, compute their average, and print out the scores together with the average. A design for this problem is shown in Figure 4.1.

FIGURE 4.1
Top-down design

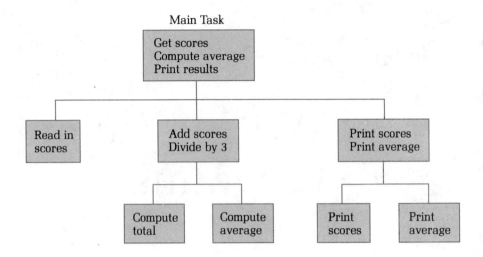

Corresponding pseudocode is

1. Read in Score1, Score2, and Score3
2. Perform computations
    2.1   let Sum = Score1 + Score2 + Score3
    2.2   let Average = Sum divided by 3
3. Print results
    3.1   print scores
    3.2   print average

Assuming Score1, Score2, and Score3 are declared as **integer** variables, then

1. Read in Score1, Score2, and Score3

is coded as

```
read (Score1, Score2, Score3);
```

Assuming Sum and Average are declared as **integer** and **real** variables, respectively, then

2.1   let Sum = Score1 + Score2 + Score3
2.2   let Average = Sum divided by 3

is coded as

```
Sum := Score1 + Score2 + Score3;
Average := Sum/3.0;
```

The third line of pseudocode,

3.   Print results

requires us to know the desired form for the output. Before writing code for this you need to be aware of the significance of being able to produce attractive output. Many students feel that just getting the desired information printed is a sufficient accomplishment. This is not true! It is extremely important that you develop good habits with respect to producing clear, attractive output. Some ideas to consider include:

1. Use **writeln** to produce blank lines where appropriate.

2. Use **writeln** ('_____') with the appropriate number of dashes for underlining.
3. Move the output in from the left margin of the page.
4. Use appropriate left margins and columns for various sections of the output.
5. Use descriptive headings and messages.

EXAMPLE 4.1

Assume we want the following output produced.

```
Game        Score
____        _____

 1          150
 2          178
 3          162


Your series total is      490
The average score is   163.33
```

If the constant definition section includes

```
CONST
   Skip = ' ';
```

this can be accomplished by using **writeln** statements as follows:

```
writeln (Skip:19, 'Game', Skip:6, 'Score');
writeln (Skip:19, '____', Skip:6, '_____');
writeln;
writeln (1:22, Score1:12);
writeln (2:22, Score2:12);
writeln (3:22, Score3:12);
writeln;
writeln (Skip:19, 'Your series total is', Sum:8);
writeln (Skip:19, 'The average score is', Average:8:2);
writeln; writeln;
```

Each line of pseudocode has now been translated into Pascal statements, so we can write a complete program using five variables (Sum, Score1, Score2, Score3, and Average) to solve the problem.

```
PROGRAM Bowling (input,output);

CONST
   Skip = ' ';

VAR
   Score1,Score2,Score3 : integer;
   Sum : integer;
   Average : real;

BEGIN
   writeln('Please enter 3 scores and press <RETURN>.');
   read(Score1,Score2,Score3);
   Sum := Score1 + Score2 + Score3;
   Average := Sum/3.0;
   writeln; writeln;
   writeln(Skip:19, 'Game', Skip:6, 'Score');
   writeln(Skip:19, '____', Skip:6, '_____');
   writeln;
```

```
      writeln(1:22, Score1:12);
      writeln(2:22, Score2:12);
      writeln(3:22, Score3:12);
      writeln;
      writeln(Skip:19, 'Your series total is', Sum:8);
      writeln(Skip:19, 'The average score is', Average:8:2);
      writeln; writeln
END.
```

When this program is run on the computer, we obtain the following output.

```
   Please enter 3 scores and press <RETURN>.

   150  178  162

   Game           Score

    1              150
    2              178
    3              162

   Your series total is      490
   The average score is  163.33
```

Program Comments

Programming languages typically include some provision for putting *comments* in a program. These comments are nonexecutable and are used to document and explain various parts of the program. In Pascal, the form for including comments in a program is either

> (* ... comment ... *)
>
> or
>
> { ... comment ... }

depending on local implementation.

A major use of comments is for program documentation. For example, suppose your teacher wants you to include the following as part of a program but not as part of the output.

```
Course
Assignment number
Due date
Author
Teacher
```

This documentation is frequently included immediately after (or before) the program heading and can be written as either a single comment or can a series of comments. A sample documentation section is

```
(*********************************************************
          Course              Pascal
          Assignment          One
          Due Date            Sept 20
          Author              Mary Smith
          Teacher             Mr. Jones

          *********************************************************)
```

These comments do not appear as output when the program is run; they merely make the program more readable. You should try several ways to include comments within a program. Other than the fact that you must begin with "(*" or "{" and end with "*)" or "}," you are limited only by your imagination and your teacher's wishes. Let's now rewrite our previous example program using a documentation section and other comments within the program.

```
PROGRAM Bowling (input,output);
(*********************************************************************

          Course              Pascal
          Assignment          One
          Due Date            Sept 20
          Author              Mary Smith
          Teacher             Mr. Jones


   *********************************************************************)
CONST
   Skip = ' ';

VAR
   Score1,Score2,Score3 : integer;
   Sum : integer;
   Average : real;

BEGIN
   writeln('Please enter 3 scores and press <RETURN>.');
   read(Score1,Score2,Score3);                    (*  Get the scores   *)
   Sum := Score1 + Score2 + Score3;               (*  Compute the values  *)
   Average := Sum/3.0;
   writeln; writeln;
   writeln(Skip:19, 'Game', Skip:6, 'Score');     (*  Print a heading  *)
   writeln(Skip:19, '____', Skip:6, '_____');
   writeln;
   writeln(1:22, Score1:12);                       (*  Print the results  *)
   writeln(2:22, Score2:12);
   writeln(3:22, Score3:12);
   writeln;
   writeln(Skip:19, 'Your series total is', Sum:8);
   writeln(Skip:19, 'The average score is', Average:8:2);
   writeln; writeln
END.
```

Program Style

When writing a program, a major point to remember is to make your program easy to read. Three commonly used methods for doing this are indenting, using blank lines, and using program comments. Indenting is used to show sections of a program and should roughly correspond to the indenting used in writing pseudocode. No standard exists regarding the number of spaces to use for indenting. However, we find that using only one space makes programs difficult to read, and four or more spaces sometimes does not leave sufficient room on a line for complicated statements. All sample programs in this text will use two spaces for indenting.

Many programmers use the leftmost column for the reserved words **PROGRAM, CONST, VAR, BEGIN,** and **END** where **BEGIN** and **END** denote the start and finish of the executable section of the program. Other statements are indented at least two spaces. This does not affect the program; it simply makes it easier to read.

A second technique is to use blank lines to separate sections of code. The use of blank lines is not standardized; it depends on your preference for readability. A note of caution, however; too many blank lines can be distracting. To illustrate how blank lines may be used, consider the following version of the program to compute bowling scores.

```
PROGRAM Bowling (input,output);

(*************************************************************************

              Course                Pascal
              Assignment            One
              Due Date              Sept 20
              Author                Mary Smith
              Teacher               Mr. Jones


     *********************************************************************)

CONST
  Skip = ' ';

VAR
  Score1,Score2,Score3 : integer;
  Sum : integer;
  Average : real;

BEGIN
  writeln('Please enter 3 scores and press <RETURN>.');

  (*  Get the scores  *)

  read(Score1,Score2,Score3);

  (*  Perform the computations  *)

  Sum := Score1 + Score2 + Score3;
  Average := Sum/3.0;
  writeln;writeln;
```

```
(*  Print a heading  *)

writeln(Skip:19, 'Game', Skip:6, 'Score');
writeln(Skip:19, '____', Skip:6, '_____');
writeln;

(*  Print the results  *)

writeln(1:22, Score1:12);
writeln(2:22, Score2:12);
writeln(3:22, Score3:12);
writeln;
writeln(Skip:19, 'Your series total is', Sum:8);
writeln(Skip:19, 'The average score is', Average:8:2);
writeln; writeln

END.
```

Since this is such a short program, you may not see much difference in readability between this and the version before it, but blank lines have been used to separate sections of the program and parts within the executable section.

Comments can also be used so that each program contains a description of what the program does. The program description generally follows the program heading. You will realize the necessity for such descriptions as you accumulate a group of programs. Using our bowling problem, a program description can be

```
(***********************************************

     This is one of our early complete Pascal
     programs.  It solves the problem of
     listing bowling scores and computing the
     total and average.  In addition to this,
     the final version will contain an initial
     effort to develop a programming style
     using
          1.   Indenting
          2.   Blank lines
          3.   Program comments

************************************************)
```

Another relatively standard use of program comments is to establish a *variable dictionary*. In short programs, the need for this is not obvious; however, it is essential for longer programs.

Several styles are used for describing variables. One method is to use comments on the same line as the variables in the variable declaration section. For example, for the bowling problem, you might use

```
VAR

  Score1, Score2, Score3 : integer;   (* Scores for games *)
  Sum : integer;                      (* Sum of the scores *)
  Average : real;                  (* Average of game scores *)
```

A second method is to use a separate comment section preceding the variable declaration section, such as

```
(*********************************************

               Variable Dictionary

     Average      Average game score
     Score1       Score for game one
     Score2       Score for game two
     Score3       Score for game three
     Sum          Sum of the scores


 *********************************************)
```

You are encouraged to try both styles of describing variables as well as any variation you might like.

Another use of program comments is to describe what a section of code is to do. In the bowling example, the executable section consists of three sections: get data, perform computations, and produce output. A comment was used to describe what happens in each portion of the program.

```
(*   Get the scores   *)
             .
             .
             .
(*   Perform the computations   *)
             .
             .
             .
(*   Print the heading   *)
             .
             .
             .
(*   Print the results   *)
             .
             .
             .
```

At this stage, you may think that developing a style for writing programs was the subject of Shakespeare's play *Much Ado About Nothing* since none of these suggestions has anything to do with whether or not a program runs. Nothing could be further from the truth! It is fairly easy to learn to write short programs. As you continue your study of computer science, you will accumulate programs that are progressively longer and more complex. Thus, you should begin now to develop a concise, consistent style for writing programs.

Now we will incorporate all the previous suggestions for writing style into our earlier bowling problem example.

EXAMPLE 4.2

```
PROGRAM Bowling (input,output);

(*************************************************************************

        Course                     Pascal
        Assignment                 One
        Due Date                   Sept 20
        Author                     Mary Smith
        Teacher                    Mr. Jones


   *********************************************************************)

(*************************************************************************

     This is one of our early complete Pascal programs. It
     solves the problem of listing bowling scores and computing
     the total and average. In addition to this, the final
     version will contain an initial effort to develop a programming
     style using

        1. Indenting
        2. Blank lines
        3. Program comments


   *********************************************************************)

CONST
  Skip = ' ';

VAR
  Score1,Score2,Score3 : integer;          (*  Scores for games  *)
  Sum : integer;                        (*  Sum of the three scores  *)
  Average : real;                         (*  Average game score  *)

BEGIN

  writeln('Please enter 3 scores and press <RETURN>.');

(*   Get the scores   *)

  read(Score1,Score2,Score3);

(*   Perform the computations   *)

  Sum := Score1 + Score2 + Score3;
  Average := Sum/3.0;
  writeln;writeln;
```

```
(*    Print the heading    *)

  writeln(Skip:19, 'Game', Skip:6, 'Score');
  writeln(Skip:19, '____', Skip:6, '_____');
  writeln;

(*    Print the results    *)

  writeln(1:22, Score1:12);
  writeln(2:22, Score2:12);
  writeln(3:22, Score3:12);
  writeln;
  writeln(Skip:19, 'Your series total is', Sum:8);
  writeln(Skip:19, 'The average score is', Average:8:2);
  writeln; writeln

END.
```

We conclude this section by considering the problem of writing a program to be used by a company to compute the wages for an employee. The following questions will need to be answered:

1. Is the employee salaried or hourly?
2. What is the wage rate?
3. How many units (hours, weeks, and so on) in a pay period?
4. What deductions need to be taken from the total wage?
5. What information needs to be included as part of the output?

We assume these questions are answered as follows:

1. Hourly
2. $12.75 per hour
3. 40 hours
4. Union dues, social security (FICA), federal withholding tax, and state withholding tax
5. Hours worked, wage rate, list of deductions, total deductions, gross pay, and net pay

You cannot yet start solving this problem because you need to know more. What are the union dues? What are the rates for the other three deductions? This information will be provided later.

Algorithm Development

Now that the problem is sufficiently defined, we can develop an algorithm for its solution. We continue using pseudocode with stepwise refinement in developing our algorithms. An initial algorithm for this problem is

1. Get information from the company
2. Compute gross pay
3. Compute deductions
4. Compute net pay
5. Print check

Documentation Employment

The rapidly growing use of software and user-friendly systems has created a new job market. A need for user-friendly documentation has created a group of specialists referred to as technical writers or documentation teams. These writers must have a good background in computer science or management information systems as well as the ability to write clearly and concisely. Their responsibilities include writing instructions, descriptions, and explanations for user's manuals.

The need for these writers is growing because of customer demands concerning usability of products. Major companies that employ such writers include IBM, DEC, and Bell Laboratories.

A refined version of this is

1. Get information from the company
   1.1 number of hours
   1.2 hourly rate
2. Compute gross pay
3. Compute deductions
   3.1 union dues
   3.2 social security (FICA)
   3.3 federal withholding tax
   3.4 state withholding tax
   3.5 get total deductions
4. Compute net pay
5. Print check
   5.1 list gross pay
   5.2 list deductions
   5.3 list total deductions
   5.4 list net pay

We now need to decide if further refinement is needed. Since each pseudocode line can be implemented in a relatively direct fashion, some programmers might choose to make no further refinements. However, we further refine step 5.2 to obtain

5.2 list deductions
    5.2.1 union dues
    5.2.2 social security (FICA)
    5.2.3 federal withholding tax
    5.2.4 state withholding tax

The data for this problem are

Number of hours	= 40
Hourly rate	= $12.75
Union dues	= $6.50
Social security rate (FICA)	= 5%
Federal withholding rate	= 17%
State withholding rate	= 4.3%

The pseudocode is translated into lines of code by

1. Get information from company

```
readln (NumHours, HourlyRate);
```

2. Compute gross pay

```
GrossPay := NumHours * HourlyRate;
```

3. Compute deductions

```
UnionDues := 6.50;
FICA := GrossPay * 0.05;
FederalTax := GrossPay * 0.17;
StateTax := GrossPay * 0.043;
TotalDeduc := UnionDues + FICA + FederalTax + StateTax;
```

4. Compute net pay

```
NetPay := GrossPay - TotalDeduc;
```

5. Print check
several **writeln** statements here with suitable formatting

A program to solve this problem can now be written incorporating previous suggestions of writing style.

EXAMPLE 4.3

```
PROGRAM ComputeWage (input,output);

(***************************************************************

     This program is designed to compute the wage for
     an hourly worker. Information for the employee will
     be obtained, deductions computed and totaled,
     the net pay computed, and all information printed in a
     reasonable manner.

     ***********************************************************)

CONST
     CompanyName = 'Tite Packing Company';
     EmployeeName = 'Frederick Adamson';
     Underline = '_____';
     Indent = ' ';
     UnionDues = 6.50;
     FICARate = 0.05;
     StateTaxRate = 0.043;
     FedTaxRate = 0.17;
```

```
VAR
  FederalTax,        (*   Withholding for federal tax      *)
  FICA,              (*   Withholding for social security   *)
  GrossPay,          (*   Pay before deductions            *)
  HourlyRate,        (*   Hourly wage rate                 *)
  NetPay,            (*   Amount due employee              *)
  StateTax,          (*   Withholding for state tax        *)
  TotalDeduc,        (*   Sum of deductions                *)
  UnionDues: real;   (*   Withholding for union dues       *)
  NumHours: integer; (*   Hours worked by employee         *)

BEGIN

(*   Get data    *)

  writeln('Please enter hours worked and hourly rate,');
  writeln('Press <RETURN> when finished,');
  readln(NumHours,HourlyRate);

(*    Compute gross pay    *)

  GrossPay := NumHours * HourlyRate;

(*    Compute deductions    *)

  FICA := GrossPay * FICARate;
  FederalTax := GrossPay * FedTaxRate;
  StateTax := GrossPay * StateTaxRate;
  TotalDeduc := UnionDues + FICA + FederalTax + StateTax;

(*    Compute net pay    *)

  NetPay := GrossPay - TotalDeduc;

(*    Now print all information    *)

  writeln;writeln;
  writeln(Indent:30,CompanyName);
  writeln(Indent:30,Underline,Underline);
  writeln;
  writeln(Indent:19,'Employee name:',EmployeeName:20);
  writeln;
  writeln(Indent:19,'Hours worked:',NumHours:17);
  writeln(Indent:19,'Hourly wage:',HourlyRate:21:2);
  writeln;
  writeln(Indent:19,'Gross pay:',GrossPay:33:2);
  writeln;
  writeln(Indent:19,'Deductions:');
  writeln;
  writeln(Indent:21,'Union dues',UnionDues:21:2);
```

```
        writeln(Indent:21,'FICA',FICA:27:2);
        writeln(Indent:21,'Federal tax',FederalTax:20:2);
        writeln(Indent:21,'State tax',StateTax:22:2);
        writeln('_____':52);
        writeln;
        writeln(Indent:21,'Total deductions',TotalDeduc:15:2);
        writeln;
        writeln(Indent:19,'Net pay','$':28,NetPay:8:2);
        writeln('_____':62)
   END.
```

The output from this program is

```
        Please enter hours worked and hourly rate.
        Press <RETURN> when finished.
        40    12.75


              Tite Packing Company
              --------------------

        Employee name:   Frederick Adamson

        Hours worked:           40
        Hourly wage:            12.75

        Gross pay:                          510.00

        Deductions:

           Union dues          6.50
           FICA               25.50
           Federal tax        86.70
           State tax          21.93
                              ------

           Total deductions  140.63

        Net pay                      $   369.37
                                         ------
```

Exercises 4.1

In Exercises 1–7, assume that each is a line of pseudocode. Write Pascal statements for each.

1. Add the scores from Test1, Test2, Test3, and Test4
2. Let Average = Total divided by 4
3. Let TotalIncome = Salary plus Tips
4. Let Time = Distance divided by Rate
5. Let Grade = TotalPoints divided by 6
6. Write out your name, TotalPoints, and Grade
7. Write out NumberAttending, TicketPrice, and TotalReceipts

8. Assume the output for a program to compute parking lot fees is to contain

   a. Vehicle type (car or truck)   d. Total time
   b. Time in   e. Parking fee
   c. Time out

   Use **writeln** statements to produce a suitable heading for this output.

9. Given the following algorithm in pseudocode form, write a complete program to compute the volume of a box.

    1. Assign dimensions
    2. Compute volume
    3. Print results
       3.1 dimensions
       3.2 volume

10. List four uses for program comments.

11. Discuss variations in program writing styles for each of the following:

    a. Using blank lines
    b. Using program comments
    c. Writing variable dictionaries

12. Use program comments to create a program description block that might be used to solve the problem of computing semester grades for a class.

In Exercises 13–20, which are valid forms for program comments?

```
13. (*         message here         *)

14. (*                             *)
    (*         message here         *)
    (*                             *)

15. (*
              message here
                                    *)

16.  *         message here         *)

17. (*************************
     *                       *
     *         message here   *
     *                       *
     *************************)

18. (*                       *
    (*         message here   *
    (*                       *)

19. (*                       *)
     *                       *)
     *         message here   *)
     *                       *)
     *                       *)

20. (*************************)
    (*                       *)
    (*         message here   *)
    (*                       *)
    (*************************)
```

With this chapter we hope to help you avoid problems when first working with Pascal. You are now aware of the significance of carefully designing an algorithm to solve a problem before you attempt to write a program. Also, you are now able to write code to implement an algorithm via a Pascal program. Therefore, to help you avoid frustration, we will examine some typical errors made when writing code.

Syntax

In Section 2.2, it was stated that syntax refers to the rules governing construction of valid statements. This includes spelling, punctuation, and placement of certain key symbols. Errors made by improper use of syntax (*syntax errors*) are usually easy to identify and correct.

For our first example of a syntax error, let's examine uses of the semicolon. This is the fundamental punctuation mark in Pascal: it is used to separate statements. It first appears after the program heading statement and then between complete statements throughout the program. However, there are some exceptions.

1. Certain keywords appear on a line but are not complete statements.
2. Semicolons are not required between a statement and **END**.
3. A semicolon is not used immediately before an **ELSE** (Section 5.3).

To see how semicolons are needed, consider the following:

Incorrect Program		Correct Program
`PROGRAM CheckSemi (output)`	1.	`PROGRAM CheckSemi (output);`
`VAR`		`VAR`
` A,B : real`	2.	` A,B : real;`
`BEGIN`		`BEGIN`
` A := 3.0`	3.	` A := 3.0;`
` B := 2 * A`	4.	` B := 2 * A;`
` writeln (A:5:2, B:5:2)`		` writeln (A:5:2, B:5:2)`
`END.`		`END.`

The program on the left has no semicolons; the one on the right has the minimum number of semicolons required to make the program run: four. These are explained as follows:

1. A semicolon must appear after the program heading.

   `PROGRAM CheckSemi (output);`

2. A semicolon must appear after each declaration list in the variable declaration section.

   `A,B : real;`

3. and **4.** A semicolon must appear between complete statements in the executable portion of the program.

   `A := 3.0;`
   `B := 2 * A;`

Two comments are in order. First, since Pascal ignores extra blanks and line boundaries, the semicolons do not have to be written directly after the statements. Second, as we've seen before, the semicolon at the end of the last statement preceding the reserved word **END** is unnecessary.

Insert the minimum number of semicolons required to make the following program correct.

```
PROGRAM Sample (output)

VAR
   A : integer

BEGIN
   A := 4
   writeln (A)
END.
```

A second syntax error results from using the symbol for equality "=" instead of the symbol for an assignment statement ":=". This is compounded by the fact that several programming languages use the equal sign to assign values to variables, and the equal sign is used to define values in the **CONST** section.

A third type of syntax error occurs when writing program comments. As discussed in Section 4.1, a comment begins with "(*" and ends with "*)". As comments get longer and you attempt to produce attractive, readable programs, you may produce some of the following errors.

1. Improper beginning

(instead of (*

2. Improper ending

) instead of *)
* instead of *)
$) instead of *)

3. Extra blanks

(*   comment   *   ) instead of (*   comment   *)

4. No close for a long comment (no ending parenthesis)

```
(**********************************

    This is a long comment with
    improper closing punctuation.


**********************************
```

A fourth type of syntax error results from omitting the period after **END** at the end of the executable portion of the program. This error will be detected by the compiler.

A fifth type of error that some computer programmers consider a syntax error is misspelling keywords. Table 4.1 sets forth a program with seven misspelled keywords. You may think the identifiers Inital and Scre

TABLE 4.1
Identifying keywords
and identifiers

	Incorrect Spelling	Correct Spelling
PROGRM Spelling (output);		PROGRAM
VR		VAR
Wage : reale;		real
Inital : chr;		char
Scre : interger;		integer
BEGN		BEGIN
Wage := 5.0;		
Inital := 'D';		
Scre := 75;		
writln (Wage:10:2, Inital:3, Scre:5)		writeln
END.		

are also misspelled keywords. But remember: they are not keywords and can be used as spelled in the program. It is not good practice to use identifiers like this, however, since you could easily spell them differently throughout the program and they would not be recognized as variables by the compiler.

SELF QUIZ 4.2

Find three syntax errors in the following program.

```
PROGRAM Syntax (output);

VAR
   A : interger;
        (Executable section)

BEGIN
   A := 5;
   A = 2 * A;
   writeln (A)
END.
```

Declarations

Errors sometimes made when defining constants in the **CONST** section include:

1. Using an assignment statement rather than an equal sign

   Incorrect
   ```
   CONST
      MaxScore := 100;
   ```
   Correct
   ```
   CONST
      MaxScore = 100;
   ```

2. Omitting single quotation marks from string constants

   Incorrect
   ```
   CONST
      Name = Mary Smith;
      Letter = Z;
   ```
   Correct
   ```
   CONST
      Name = 'Mary Smith';
      Letter = 'Z';
   ```

3. Using double quotation marks rather than single quotation marks

   Incorrect
   ```
   CONST
      Name = "Mary Smith";
   ```
   Correct
   ```
   CONST
      Name = 'Mary Smith';
   ```

TABLE 4.2
Errors in declaration
sections

Incorrect	Correct

VAR
  A;B;C : real
	VAR
	  A,B,C : real;

VAR
  Age ; integer;
	VAR
	  Age : integer;

VAR
  Initial = char;
	VAR
	  Initial : char;

VAR
  Wage : real;
  Score
  Hours : integer;
	VAR
	  Wage : real;
	  Score,
	  Hours : integer;

4. Using single quotation marks around numerical constants

Incorrect	*Correct*
CONST	CONST
MaxScore = '100';	MaxScore = 100;

The declaration

```
MaxScore = '100';
```

will not result in an error during compilation. Technically, it is not an error. However, this declaration makes MaxScore a string rather than the integer constant 100. Consequently, you could not assign MaxScore to an integer variable or use it in any arithmetic computation.

More errors are usually made in the variable declaration section than in the constant definition section. Several illustrations of incorrect variable declarations and the corrected versions are shown in Table 4.2.

Assignment Statements

In Section 3.1 you learned to assign a value to a variable with a statement such as

```
Score := 87;
```

Some common mistakes in assignment statements are:

1. Trying to put more than one variable on the left of an assignment statement

Incorrect	*Correct*
X + Y := Z;	Z := X + Y;
A + 3 := B;	B := A + 3;

2. Trying to make an assignment from left to right

Incorrect	*Correct*
87 := Score;	Score := 87;

3. Trying to assign the value of one identifier (A) to another identifier (B) from left to right

Incorrect	*Correct*
A := B;	B := A;

(This statement will not be detected as an error during compilation; thus, your program will run, but you will probably get incorrect results.)

4. Attempting to assign a value of one data type to a variable of another data type. If, for example, Score were declared as an **integer** variable, each of the following would produce an error.

```
Score := 77.3;
Score := 150/3;
A := 18.6;
Score := A;
```

There is an exception to this rule. The value of an **integer** data type can be assigned to a variable of type **real**. For example, if Average is a **real**,

```
Average := 43;
```

is a valid assignment statement. However, 43 is then stored as the **real** 43.0 rather than the **integer** 43.

5. Attempting to use undeclared variables and constants. This error often results from listing the variables used in the program in the variable declarations section after the program has been written, and inadvertently omitting some variable from the list. During compilation, you will get the error message "Identifier not declared" when the variable first appears in a line of code. This is easily corrected by adding the variable to the **VAR** section.

This same error results from misspelling identifiers. For example, if the **VAR** section has

```
VAR
    Initial : char;
```

and you use the statement

```
Inital := 'D';
```

in the executable section, you will get an error message. The error message will be the same as that for an undeclared identifier because the compiler did not find Inital in its list of previously declared identifiers. Misspellings are not obvious and are difficult to detect. This is another reason for using descriptive identifiers; they are common words and you are less likely to misspell them.

SELF QUIZ 4.3   Suppose the variable declaration section of a program is

```
VAR
    A,B : integer;
    X : real;
```

Which of the following program statements produce an error?

```
A := 5 * 3;
B := A DIV 3;
B := A/3;
X := A DIV 3;
X := A/3;
```

Using writeln

The last general category of errors concerns statements used to create output. Section 2.3 discussed the use of **writeln** for creating a line of output. We have subsequently used this as part of executable statements in several examples. In an attempt to help you avoid making certain errors, we will examine common incorrect uses of **writeln.**

1. Format errors. When using format control with **writeln** statements, the following three errors are typical.

    a. Attempting to format an **integer** as a **real**

    Incorrect   *Correct*
    ```
    writeln (Score:20:2);           writeln (Score:20);
    ```

    b. Attempting to use a noninteger as a format control number

    Incorrect   *Correct*
    ```
    writeln (Average:20:2.0);     writeln (Average:20:2);
    ```

    (where Average is a **real** variable).

    c. Attempting to format a **real** as an **integer.** This will not cause a compilation error; your program will run, but you will get unexpected output. For example, suppose Average is a **real** variable whose value is 83.42 and you want a line of output to be

    ```
    The average score is:     83.42
    ```

    If you use the statement

    ```
    writeln ('The average score is:', Average:10);
    ```

    the output is

    ```
    The average score is:   8.3420E+01
    ```

    Note that floating-point form is used for the real but the total field width is controlled by the use of ":10". This statement should be written

    ```
    writeln ('The average score is:':30, Average:10:2);
    ```

2. Inappropriate use of quotation marks. Errors of this type result from omitting needed single quotation marks or putting quotation marks where they are not needed. Remember that character strings must be enclosed in single quotation marks. For example, assume you want the output Hello.

    Incorrect   *Correct*
    ```
    writeln (Hello:20);             writeln ('Hello':20);
    ```

    A more subtle problem arises when constants and variables are declared in the **CONST** and **VAR** declaration sections. Assume these sections are as follows:

    ```
    CONST
       Name = 'Mary Smith';
       Age = 18;

    VAR
       A : integer;
    ```

    and consider the following program fragments.

a. `writeln ('My name is':20, Name:15);`

This is correct and produces

`My name is      Mary Smith`

b. `writeln ('My name is':20, 'Name':15);`

This is also correct but produces

`My name is                Name`

This program runs, but you get incorrect output.

c. `writeln ('My age is':20, Age:4);`

This is correct and produces

`My age is   18`

d. Assume the assignment

`A := 10;`

is made in the program and consider

`writeln ('A':5, A:5);`

This produces

`    A   10`

Note that using 'A' creates a character string of one character, but using A causes the contents of A to be printed. This suggests a method of obtaining descriptive output. If you want both the name of a variable and the value of a variable, you can use

`writeln ('A =':5, A:5);`

to obtain

`A =      10`

3. Attempting to have an executable statement within the parentheses.

Incorrect	Correct
`writeln (A := B + C);`	`A := B + C;`
	`writeln (A);`

Attempts to do this probably result from the fact that expressions can be used in a **writeln** statement. Assuming suitable declarations of variables, each of the following is correct.

```
writeln (A + B:15);
writeln ('Her IQ is':10, Age + 100:5);
writeln ('The total is':20, Average * 12:6:2);
```

In summary, you should now be aware of some errors you may make at some time during your programming career. They are easily corrected and you will make fewer of them as you write more programs.

Exercises 4.2

1. Find two syntax errors in the following program fragment.

```
X := 3 * Y
Y = 4 - 2 * Z;
writeln (X,Y);
```

2. Write a test program to illustrate what happens when extra semicolons are used in a program.

3. Add the minimum number of semicolons required to make the following program syntactically correct.

```
PROGRAM ExerciseThree (output)

CONST
  Name = 'Jim Jones'
  Age = 18

VAR
  Score : integer

BEGIN
  Score := 93
  writeln ('Name':13, Name:15)
  writeln ('Age':12, Age:16)
  writeln ('Score':14, Score:14)
END.
```

4. Find all incorrect uses of "=" and ":=" in the following program.

```
PROGRAM ExerciseFour (output);

CONST
  Name := 'Jim Jones';
  Age := 18;

VAR
  Score = integer;

BEGIN
  Score = 93;
  writeln (Name:10, Age:10, Score:10)
END.
```

5. Find and correct all misspelled keywords in the following program.

```
PROGRRAM ExercseFiv (output);
VAR
  X,Y : reals;
  Nam : chr;
  Scor : interger;

BEGIN
  X := 3.0;
  Y := X * 4.2;
  Nam := 'S';
  Scor := X + Y;
  writln (X:4:2, Y:4:2, Nam:3, Scor:4)
END.
```

For Exercises 6–15, assume the variable declaration section of a program is

```
VAR
    A, Score : integer;
    X : real;
    Init : char;
```

Indicate which assignment statements are valid and which are invalid. Give a reason for each that is invalid.

```
6. A := 4 * (-3);          11. A := X + A;
7. Score := 1 * 2.0;       12. Init := 'M';
8. A := Score MOD 8;       13. Init := A;
9. X := Score/6;           14. Init := 'A';
10. X := X + A;            15. X := Init;
```

In Exercises 16–24, assume the declaration section of a program is

```
CONST
    Name = 'John Harris';

VAR
    A,B : integer;
    Wages : real;
    CourseName : char;
```

Indicate which statements are valid and which are invalid. Explain those that are invalid.

```
16. A := A + B;            21. Wages := Hours * 6.0;
17. A + B := A;            22. CourseName := Name;
18. C := A - 2;            23. Name := 'John Harris';
19. Wage := 5.75;          24. A := 2 * Wages;
20. CourseName := 'C';
```

For Exercises 25–34, assume the declaration section of a program is the same as in Exercises 16–24. Label each as valid or invalid. Correct those that are invalid.

```
25. writeln (Name);
26. writeln (Name:20);
27. writeln ('Name':20);
28. writeln (A,B);
29. writeln ('A', 'B');
30. writeln ('A = ', A);
31. writeln ('A = ':10, A:3, B = :10, B:3);
32. writeln ('A = ':10, 'A':3);
33. writeln (Wages, ' are wages');
34. writeln (' Wages are', Wages);
```

35. Find all errors in the following program.

```
PROGRAM Errors (output(;

(*****************************************)

(*   There are at least ten errors.        $)

(*****************************************
VAR
    Day : char;
    Percent : real
    A,B ; int;
```

```
BEGIN
  Day = 'M';
  Percentage := 72/10;
  A := 5;
  B := A * 3.2;
  writln (A,B:20);
  writeln (Day:10:2);
  writeln (A + B:8, Percent:8)
END
```

■ 4.3
Making a
Program Run

OBJECTIVES

- to understand the difference between compilation errors, run-time errors, and design errors
- to use the following error-correcting techniques: debugging, program walk-throughs, echo checking, using short programs, and design-error checking

Now that we have examined some typical errors, you may think all programs should run on the first try. Unfortunately, this is not true. All programmers eventually encounter problems when trying to make a program run. Although some short programs may run the first time and produce the desired output, you should always plan time for correcting your program. This is a normal part of a programmer's life and you should not get discouraged when you have to rework a program.

In an ideal situation, you would submit your program to the computer and it would run with no errors and produce exactly what you desire for output on the first attempt. Since this probably will not happen, you need to be aware of the kinds of errors that can occur. These fall into three general categories: compilation errors, run-time errors, and design errors.

Compilation Errors

Compilation errors (for example, syntax errors) are errors detected when the program is being compiled. The printed error messages usually are sufficient to enable you to correct your program. As you gain experience, you will make fewer errors of this type. Your program will not run until all compilation errors are removed, so you must develop the ability to correct these errors.

Run-Time Errors

Run-time errors occur after your program has all compilation errors corrected, but when you run your program, you get error messages instead of output. A run-time error occurs in the following incorrect program.

Incorrect Program

```
PROGRAM RunError (output);

VAR
  A,B : integer;

BEGIN
  A := 3;
  B := 0;
  A := A DIV B;
  writeln (A,B)
END.
```

The compiler will not detect any errors, but when this is run, you get a message something like the following (depending on your computer and version of Pascal).

```
Program terminated   at line 9 in program RunError.
Division by zero.
                             ___ RunError ___
           A =      3                            B =     0
```

As you develop more programming skills, you may encounter run-time errors involving the logical flow of your program which are generally more difficult to locate and correct.

Design Errors

Design errors occur after you have eliminated both compilation errors and run-time errors. At this stage, your program runs and produces output; however, when you examine the output, it is not what you want. The problems can include having columns incorrectly lined up, having incorrect values for the output, or not getting all of the output.

```
PROGRAM DesignError (output);

VAR
   Score : integer;

BEGIN
   writeln; writeln;
   writeln ('Scores':20);
   writeln ('_____':25);
   Score := 87;
   writeln (Score);
   Score := 92;
   writeln (Score);
   writeln; writeln
END.
```

produces the output

```
        Scores
             _____
87
92
```

instead of

```
        Scores
        _____

             87
             92
```

Therefore, the program should be modified as follows:

```
PROGRAM DesignError (output);

CONST
   LabelWidth = 20;

VAR
   Score : integer;
```

```
BEGIN
  writeln; writeln;
  writeln ('Scores':LabelWidth);
  writeln ('_____':LabelWidth);
  writeln;
  Score := 87;
  writeln (Score:18);
  Score := 92;
  writeln (Score:18);
  writeln; writeln
END.
```

STYLE TIP

■ ■ ■ ■ ■ ■ ■

We have been using constants Skip and Indent to control spacing of output. If some strings are to be right justified (abutting the right-hand margin), we can define a constant as in **PROGRAM** DesignError

```
CONST
  LabelWidth = 20;
```

and use it to format strings. For example,

```
writeln ('Score':LabelWidth);
writeln ('_____':LabelWidth);
```

The remainder of this section covers techniques to help you detect and correct program errors. Programmers use many different techniques for doing this. We will examine some of the more common, helpful practices, which include debugging, program walk-throughs, echo checking, short programs, and design error checking.

Debugging

Debugging is a term loosely used to refer to the process of eliminating errors or "bugs" from a program. The term refers to compilation errors, run-time errors, and design errors.

When trying to debug a program, you can do several things. First, carefully reading the code will help you identify and eliminate many of the errors mentioned in the previous section, such as syntax errors, invalid identifiers, incorrect spelling, and incorrect use of **writeln** statements. This technique requires patience and thoroughness, but will save you time in the end by making your programs run sooner.

Second, compiler error messages can help you to correct errors you missed during your careful reading of code. Since these messages vary from machine to machine, you will have to learn to interpret the messages printed by your machine. A list of typical messages is included in Appendix 5.

Errors causing compiler error messages are not always easy to find. Sometimes an error message on one line is the result of a previous error several lines earlier. For example, the program

```
PROGRAM CompileError (output);

(*  This will detect a compilation error  $)

CONST
  Name = 'Mary Smith';
  Indent = ' ';

VAR
  Age : integer;

BEGIN
  Age := 18;
  writeln (Indent:10, 'My name is', Name:15);
  writeln (Indent:10, 'My age is', Age:3)
END.
```

when compiled, may produce

```
PROGRAM CompileError (output);

(*  This will detect a compilation error  $)

CONST
  Name = 'Mary Smith';
  Indent = ' ';

VAR
  Age : integer;

BEGIN
  Age := 18;
  writeln (Indent:10, 'My name is', Name:15);
  writeln (Indent:10, 'My age is', Age:3)
END.
*** Incomplete program.
Compiler error message(s).
```

This can be corrected by changing the comment line

```
(*  This will detect a compilation error  $)
```
                                              ↑ Syntax error

to

```
(*  This will detect a compilation error  *)
```

By removing the syntax error ($), you should have an error-free compilation and be ready to run the program.

It is possible that, if a number of compilation errors occur, correcting the first one may result in some of the others being eliminated. Thus, you should eliminate compilation errors starting with the first one listed.

A third debugging technique can be used after you get an error-free compilation. Run the program and get a list of run-time error messages. (If you have been very careful, you may not have any run-time errors.)

A NOTE OF INTEREST

Debugging

Do you wonder why the term *debugging* is used when referring to the process of eliminating errors from a program? In 1945, computer scientists were working on the Mark II. Suddenly, something went wrong with the machine. During a check of the machine, someone found that a moth had been caught in one of the relays. It was removed and the first computer had been debugged. The term caught on and is now used in a somewhat broader sense.

Consider the program

```
PROGRAM RunTimeError (output);

VAR
  A,B : integer;
  Average : real;

BEGIN
  A := 10;
  Average := (A+B)/2.0;
  writeln ('The average is':20, Average:10:2)
END.
```

There are no compilation errors in the program, but the output is something equivalent to

```
Program terminated at line 9 in program RunTimeErr.
Integer larger than maxint.
                        ___ RunTimeErr ___
    Average =    Undef                                    A =    10
          B =    Undef
```

and not the desired output because B has not been assigned a value.

Use these messages to analyze and correct your program. Remember, these messages are machine dependent and it will take time before you can understand them.

Program Walk-Through

Program walk-through, sometimes referred to as a *trace*, is used to describe the process of playing computer with pencil and paper. Two types of walk-throughs are used by programmers. First, you trace the logical flow of your program. During this check, you are not looking for syntax errors; you are merely making sure that the order in which things are done is correct. This type of checking will be more efficient after you have written more programs. A second type of program walk-through is to keep track of values of the variables on paper. The following example illustrates this idea.

EXAMPLE 4.4 Let's walk through the following program.

```
PROGRAM WalkThru (output);

VAR
  A,B : integer;

BEGIN
  A := 5;
  B := A + 4;
  A := B - 2;
  B := A * 5;
  B := B DIV 3;
  writeln (A:5, B:5)
END.
```

To walk through this program, we list the variables and then proceed through the program one line at a time.

Statement	Value of A	Value of B
A := 5;	5	Undefined
B := A + 4;	5	9
A := B - 2;	7	9
B := A * 5;	7	35
B := B DIV 3;	7	11

At the end of the program, A has the value 7 and B has the value 11. ◼

SELF QUIZ 4.4 Walk through the values of the variables in the following program.

```
PROGRAM Switch (output);

VAR
  A,B,Temp : integer;

BEGIN
  A := -6;
  B := 10;
  writeln (A,B);
  Temp := A;
  A := B;
  B := Temp;
  writeln (A,B)
END.
```

Echo Checking

Echo checking is a technique whereby you let the computer check the values of your variables and the data used in your program. When reading values or changing the value of a variable, you use a **writeln** statement to immediately print out the new value with a short, descriptive message. To illustrate, consider the short program WalkThru in Example 4.4. An echo check can be implemented by inserting **writeln** statements as follows:

```
PROGRAM WalkThru (output);

VAR
   A,B : integer;

BEGIN
   A := 5;
   writeln ('A =', A:3);
   B := A + 4;
   writeln ('B =', B:3);
   A := B - 2;
   writeln ('A =', A:3);
   B := A * 5;
   writeln ('B =', B:3);
   B := B DIV 3;
   writeln ('B =', B:3);
   writeln ('A =', A:3, ' B =', B:3)
END.
```

The output for this program is

```
A =   5
B =   9
A =   7
B =  35
B =  11
A =   7 B =  11
```

You can echo check input data similarly. For example, if an input statement is

```
readln (A,B,C);
```

the values can be checked by inserting an output statement such as

```
writeln ('A=', A, ' B=', B, ' C=', C);
```

You probably will not want to print each variable value in the final program. Therefore, once your program produces the desired output, remove the **writeln** statements used for checking and you have a working program.

Short Programs

Using short programs is another technique for error checking. It is particularly effective on longer, more complex programs, but to illustrate, we will consider the following short example.

EXAMPLE 4.5

Suppose you are writing a program and you want to exchange the values of variables A and B. You think this can be accomplished by

```
A := B;
B := A;
```

You can write a short program to check this as follows:

```
PROGRAM ExchangeCheck (output);

VAR
  A,B : integer;

BEGIN
  A := 5;
  B := 10;
  writeln ('A =', A:3, ' B =', B:3);

(*  Now exchange  *)

  A := B;
  B := A;
  writeln ('A =', A:3, ' B =', B:3)
END.
```

When you run this short program, the output

```
A =   5 B =  10
A =  10 B =  10
```

indicates your method of exchanging values did not work and you have to redesign your program. The exchange can be accomplished by declaring a third variable Temp and then using the code:

```
Temp := A;
A := B;
B := Temp;
```
■

The example given is quite simple, but as you start writing programs to solve complex problems, you will find that using short programs is a very effective technique.

Exercises 4.3

1. Perform a program walk-through for the following program segment to determine the values of A, B, and C at the end of the segment.

```
A := 33;
B := -2;
A := A - 5;
B := A;
C := B + 2;
A := B;
C := A - B + 1;
A := A + 1;
```

2. Write test programs to illustrate what error messages appear for each of the following:

a. division by zero
b. printing a variable that has not been assigned a value
c. using a variable that has not been assigned a value

For Exercises 3 and 4, correct all compilation errors. Check your results by running the program exactly as it is written here and examining the compilation error messages.

3. ```
PROGRAM CompileErrors (output);
CONST
  Max = 100.0 : real;
VAR
  A,Sum : integer

BEGIN
  A := 86.0;
  Sum := A + 0;
  A + Sum := Sum
  writeln (Sum:15:2)
END.
```

4. ```
PROGRAM Compile Errors (output);

VAR
  A : integer;
  Ch : char;

BEGIN
  Ch := 'M';
  A := 83;
  B := A - 10;
  writeln (' The value of A is :20, A:6);
  writeln (Ch:20)
END.
```

5. Suppose the output from a program is as follows.

```
NameJohn    JohnsAge    18
  Test Scores

-----
73               82               96
```

Indicate a more desirable form for the output and describe what changes should be made in the program to achieve the desired results.

6. Consider the program

```
PROGRAM Donations (output);

VAR
  Amount1,Amount2,
  Amount3,Amount4,
  Sum : real;

BEGIN
  Amount1 := 100.0;
  Amount2 := 150.0;
  Amount3 := 75.0;
  Amount4 := 200.50;
  Sum := Amount1 + Amount2 + Amount3 + Amount4;
  writeln ('Donations':30);
  writeln (Amount1:28:2);
  writeln (Amount2:28:2);
  writeln (Amount3:28:2);
  writeln (Amount4:28:2);
  writeln ('_____':28);
  writeln (Sum:28:2)
END.
```

The output for this program is

```
Donations
  100.00
  150.00
   75.00
  200.50
  -------
  525.50
```

Change the program so the output is

```
        Donations
        ---------

        $ 100.00
        $ 150.00
        $  75.00
        $ 200.50
        ---------

Total    $ 525.50
```

7. The following program has no compilation errors. However, there are some run-time errors. Find them and indicate what can be done to correct them.

```
PROGRAM RunErrors (output);

VAR
   A  : integer;
   X  : real;
   Ch : char;

BEGIN
   A := 4;
   X := 100.0;
   Ch := 'F';
   X := X / (4 MOD 2);
   X := 3 * X;
   writeln (Ch:5, X:8:2, A:5)
END.
```

8. List three types of errors made by computer programmers. Discuss their differences and what methods may be used to correct them.

9. Utilize **writeln** statements in the following program to echo check the values of each of the variables. Indicate what the output is when you run the echo-check version.

```
PROGRAM EchoCheck (output);

VAR
   Sum, Score, Count : integer;
   Average : real;

BEGIN
   Count := 0;
   Sum := 0;
   Score := 86;
```

```
Sum := Sum + Score;
Count := Count + 1;
Score := 89;
Sum := Sum + Score;
Count := Count + 1;
Average := Sum/Count;
writeln; writeln;
writeln ('There are':20, Count:3, ' Scores.');
writeln;
writeln ('The average is':24, Average:6:2)
END.
```

■ 4.4
Writing a Complete Pascal Program

■ to write a complete Pascal program to solve a problem

We end this chapter with one complete program in which five steps in problem solving, program documentation and writing style, getting data from the keyboard, and neat, attractive output are featured. It is important to be able to write complete programs that include these features. With the ability to do this, you can incorporate new programming skills within this framework.

Mr. Lae Z. Programmer, teacher of computer science, wants a program that allows him to give an individual progress report to each student in his class. The report for each student should include the student's initials, three test scores, test average, five quiz scores, weighted quiz total, and final percentage. We will develop a program for this problem and test it by running it for one student. In Chapter 6, we will see how this program can be conveniently used for the entire class.

The first step in problem solving is to understand the problem. For this particular problem, we need to know the following:

1. What the input will look like.
2. How the quizzes are to be weighted.
3. How "final percent" is to be computed.
4. What form is desired for the output.

Let's assume these questions are answered as follows:

1. The data for a student consist of the student's three initials followed by three test scores and five quiz scores. Scores are integers and are separated by blanks. The test scores are based on 100 points each and the quiz scores are based on 10 points each. Thus, data for one student looks like

   MJS 91 87 79 8 10 10 9 7

2. The quizzes are to be counted as the equivalent of one 100-point test. Thus, their total should be multiplied by two when computing the weighted total.
3. Final percent is to be computed based on a total of 400 points: 100 for each test and 100 for the quiz total.

4. The interim report should look like

```
*********************
*                   *
*   Interim Report  *
*   -------------   *
*                   *
*********************
```

```
Class:          Computer Science
Date:           October 15
Teacher:        Mr. Lae Z. Programmer
```

Initials	Test Scores	Test Average	Quiz Scores	Quiz Total
MJS	91 87 79	85.67	8 10 10 9 7	88

```
Final percent =   86.25
```

The second step in problem solving is to develop an algorithm. This is done using stepwise refinement. As a first level of pseudocode, we have

1. Get the data
2. Perform computations
3. Print student report

A refinement of step 1 is

1. Get the data
    1.1 get initials
    1.2 get test scores
    1.3 get quiz scores

Each of these lines can be refined further. For example, step 1.1 can be divided into

    1.1 get initials
        1.1.1 get first initial
        1.1.2 get second initial
        1.1.3 get third initial

At some stage, you have to decide what is a sufficient refinement when developing an algorithm. This will vary according to students and teachers. In general, when you have a clearly defined statement that can be accomplished by a single line of code, there is no need for subsequent refinement. In fact, a single line of pseudocode may require several lines of written code in a program. The important thing to remember is that algorithm development via pseudocode is only a step in helping solve a problem; it is not the solution itself.

Refining step 2, we have

2. Perform computations
    2.1 compute test average

2.2   compute quiz total
2.3   compute final percentage

This can be further refined to

2.   Perform computations
2.1   compute test average
2.1.1   add test scores
2.1.2   divide by three
2.2   compute quiz total
2.2.1   add quiz scores
2.2.2   multiply by two
2.3   compute final percentage
2.3.1   add test totals to quiz total
2.3.2   divide by four

Refining step 3 might result in

3.   Print student report
3.1   print report heading
3.2   print student information

This can be further refined to

3.   Print student report
3.1   print report heading
3.1.1   print title
3.1.2   print class information
3.1.3   print column headings
3.2   print student information
3.2.1   print initials
3.2.2   print test scores
3.2.3   print test average
3.2.4   print quiz scores
3.2.5   print quiz total
3.2.6   print final percentage

The complete algorithm is

1. Get the data
   1.1   get initials
         1.1.1   get first initial
         1.1.2   get second initial
         1.1.3   get third initial
   1.2   get test scores
   1.3   get quiz scores
2. Perform computations
   2.1   compute test average
         2.1.1   add test scores
         2.1.2   divide by three
   2.2   compute quiz total
         2.2.1   add quiz scores
         2.2.2   multiply by two
   2.3   compute final percentage
         2.3.1   add test totals to quiz total
         2.3.2   divide by four
3. Print student report
   3.1   print report heading
         3.1.1   print title
         3.1.2   print class information
         3.1.3   print column headings
   3.2   print student information
         3.2.1   print initials
         3.2.2   print test scores
         3.2.3   print test average
         3.2.4   print quiz scores
         3.2.5   print quiz total
         3.2.6   print final percentage

You may now write code for the algorithm. In the following version, an attempt to create presentable output includes boxed descriptions of headings, centering on the page when appropriate, underlining, skipping lines, and carefully created columns.

```
PROGRAM StudentReport (input,output);

(*******************************************************************

    This program is written for Mr. Lae Z. Programmer.
    It will produce an interim progress report. The
    following features have been included:

              1. Program documentation
              2. Writing style
              3. Descriptive variables
              4. Neat, attractive output


    *************************************************************)
```

```
CONST
  Splats = '***********************';
  Edge =    '*                     *';
  Line = '_____';
  Skip = ' ';
VAR
  FinalPercent : real;                 (*   Final percentage score  *)
  Init1, Init2, Init3 : char;          (*   Student's initials       *)
  Quiz1, Quiz2, Quiz3, Quiz4,
  Quiz5 : integer;                     (*   Quiz scores              *)
  QuizTotal : integer;                 (*   Sum of quizzes           *)
  Test1, Test2, Test3 : integer;       (*   Three test scores        *)
  TestAverage : real;                  (*   Average of test scores   *)
  TestTotal : integer;                 (*   Sum of test scores       *)

(***************************************************************

            Now begin the report.

***************************************************************)

BEGIN

(*  Get data  *)

  writeln ('Please enter student's initials and press <RETURN>.');
  readln (Init1, Init2, Init3);
  writeln ('Now enter 3 test scores and press <RETURN>.');
  readln (Test1, Test2, Test3);
  writeln ('Enter 5 quiz scores and press <RETURN>.');
  readln (Quiz1, Quiz2, Quiz3, Quiz4, Quiz5);

(*  Perform necessary computations  *)

  TestTotal := Test1 + Test2 + Test3;
  TestAverage := TestTotal/3.0;
  QuizTotal := (Quiz1 + Quiz2 + Quiz3 + Quiz4 + Quiz5)*2;
  FinalPercent := (TestTotal + QuizTotal)/4.0;

(***************************************************************

            Print a heading for the report.

***************************************************************)

(*  Print the title  *)

  writeln (Skip:30, Splats);
  writeln (Skip:30, Edge);
  writeln (Skip:30, '*    Interim Report    *');
  writeln (Skip:30, '*    _____    *');
  writeln (Skip:30, Edge);
  writeln (Skip:30, Splats);
```

```
(*  Print the class information  *)

    writeln;
    writeln (Skip:15, 'Class:        Computer Science');
    writeln (Skip:15, 'Date:         October 15');
    writeln (Skip:15, 'Instructor:   Mr. Lae Z Programmer');
    writeln; writeln; writeln;

(*  Print the column headings  *)

    writeln (Skip:27, 'Test', 'Test':10, 'Quiz':13, 'Quiz':14);
    writeln (Skip:15, 'Initials', 'Scores':9, 'Average':11,
                      'Scores':12, 'Total':13);
    writeln (Skip:15, Line);
    writeln;

(*  Print the student's information  *)

    write (Init1:18, Init2, Init3);
    write (Test1:7, Test2:3, Test3:3);
    write (TestAverage:8:2);
    write (Quiz1:7, Quiz2:3, Quiz3:3, Quiz4:3, Quiz5:3);
    writeln (QuizTotal:7);
    writeln;
    writeln (Skip:15, 'Final percent =', FinalPercent:7:2);
    writeln (Skip:15, '_____');
    writeln; writeln
END.
```

■ Summary

Key Terms

writing code	compilation error	program walk-through
comment	run-time error	(trace)
variable dictionary	design error	echo checking
syntax error	debugging	

Key Concepts

- It is not sufficient to produce correct output; your output should also be clear, neat, and attractive.
- Attractive output is produced by using blank lines, underlining, right- and left-hand margins, columns, and descriptive headings and messages as appropriate.
- Program comments are nonexecutable statements that can be included in a program using the form

  ```
  (*  ... comment ...  *)
  ```

  or

  ```
  {  ... comment ...  }
  ```

- Program readability is enhanced by indenting, using blank lines, and using program comments.

A NOTE OF INTEREST

Debugging or Sleuthing: Answers

1. "The problem was in the terminal's keyboard: the tops of two keys were switched. When the programmer was seated, he was a touch-typist and the problem went unnoticed, but when he stood, he was led astray by hunting and pecking."

2. "When [the programmers] observed the behavior more closely, they found that the problem occurred as they entered data for the country of Ecuador: when the user typed the name of the capital city (Quito), the program interpreted that as a request to quit the run!"

- Programs should be documented by using a comment block to describe the program and a variable dictionary.
- Common syntax errors result from inappropriate use of the semicolon, using "=" for assigning rather than ":=", incorrectly starting or ending comments, forgetting the period "." at the end of the program, or misspelling keywords.
- Other sources of errors for beginners include errors made in declarations or assignment statements, or in using **writeln.**
- Program errors can be detected and eliminated by debugging, program walk-throughs, echo checking, using short programs, and design error checking.
- When writing a complete program, make sure all questions concerning input, processing, and output are answered before attempting to design the solution.
- After all questions are answered, design a solution to the problem; refine steps in the solution until you can easily write code for the program.
- When writing the program, use a neat, consistent, readable writing style. Your style should include documentation, including a program description section, a variable dictionary and, when appropriate, comment sections and line comments. You should use consistent indenting and blank lines to separate code.
- The output for your program should be neat and readable; features should include the use of the middle of the output page, suitable titles and headings, columns where appropriate, blank lines, and underlining.

■ **Chapter Review Exercises**

1. Explain the importance of the use of frequent comments and the use of writing styles such as blank lines and variable dictionaries in Pascal programming.

In Exercises 2–17, correct any errors in the Pascal statements.

```
 2. X := 3Y + 4;
 3. Z = 2 + T
 4. writeln ("The answer is ":5, A:3);
 5. readln (sqrt(G));
 6. D := 'This is a list of characters.';
 7. VAR
       var1 = real;
       var2; var3 = integer;
 8. A := abst(-5.2);
 9. X := ord(7.2);
10. writeln ('Question 10':12:5);
11. PROGRAM 4Chapter (input; output)
```

12. CONST
```
    A := 15;
```
13. T := 5.3 MOD 1.8;
14. readln (A:5);
15. writeln (Pascal Programming:18);
16. VAR
```
    a : real,
    b ; integer,
    c ; char.
```

17. (&   This is a comment,   &)

18. Explain the difference between a compilation error, a run-time error, and a design error.

19. What output is produced from the following program?

```
PROGRAM Exercise (output);

CONST
    A = 5;

VAR
    B: real;
    C, D : integer;

BEGIN
    B := 4.5;
    C := sqr(A);
    D := C + 5;
    B := abs(B);
    C := succ(C);
    B := B + C * A;
    writeln (B:5:2, A:6, B:4)
END.
```

20. Correct all errors in the following program.

```
PROG Test (output)

VAR
    A, B : integer
    C : real;

BEGIN
    writeln (Enter an integer and a real number);
    readln (A,C);
    B = A + B;
    C := pred(C) + 4;
    D := sqr(C);
    A := 0;
    B := B DIV A;
    writeln (A:5, B:5:2, C:5)
END
```

■ Programming Problems

Before going on, you should test your knowledge of the material by writing a complete program for some of the following problems.

1. The Roll-Em Lanes bowling team wants a computer program to print the team results for one series of games. The team consists of four members whose names are Weber, Fazio, Martin, and Patterson. Each person on the team bowls three games during the series; thus, typical input is

181	179	210	155
192	201	190	160
175	180	200	180

   where each line represents the respective scores for one game. Your output should include all input data, individual series totals, game average for each member, team series, and team average.

2. The Natural Pine Furniture Company has recently hired you to help them convert their antiquated payroll system to a computer-based model. They know you are still learning, so all they want right now is a program to print a one-week pay report for three employees. You should use the constant definition section for the following:

a. Federal withholding tax rate	18%
b. State withholding tax rate	4.5%
c. Hospitalization	$25.65
d. Union dues	$ 7.85

   Input for each employee is

   a. Employee's initials
   b. Number of hours worked
   c. Hourly rate

   Your output should include a report for each employee and a summary report for the company files.

3. The Child-Growth Encyclopedia Company wants a computer program to print a monthly sales chart. Products produced by the company, prices, and sales commissions for each are

a. Basic encyclopedia	$325.00	22%
b. Child educational supplement	$127.50	15%
c. Annual update book	$ 18.95	20%

   Write a program to get the monthly sales data for two sales regions and produce the desired company chart. Data for a region contain a two-letter code for the region followed by three integers representing number of products a, b, and c sold, respectively. The prices may vary from month to month and should be defined in the constant definition section. The commissions are not subject to change.

4. The Village Variety Store is having its annual Christmas sale. They want you to write a program to produce a daily report for the store. Each item sold is identified by a code consisting of one letter followed by one digit. Your report should include data for three items. Input for each item consists of item code, number of items sold, original item price, and reduction percentage. Your report should include a chart with the input data, sale price per item, and total amount of sales per item. You should also print a daily summary.

5. The Holiday-Out Motel Company, Inc., wants a program to print a statement for each overnight customer. Input for each customer is a room number (integer), number of nights (integer), room rate (real), telephone charges (real), and restaurant charges (real). You should use the constant definition section for the date and current tax rate. Each customer statement should include all input data, the date, tax rate and amount, total due, appropriate heading, and appropriate closing message. Test your program by running it for two customers.

6. As a part-time job this semester, you are working for the Family Budget Assistance Center. Your boss has asked you to write and execute a Pascal program to analyze data for a family. Input for each family consists of

Name	(2 single characters)
Number in family	(integer)
Income	(real)
Total debts	(real)

Your program should output the following:

a. An appropriate header
b. The family's name, number in family, income, and total debts
c. Predicted family living expenses ($3000 times the size of the family)
d. The monthly payment necessary to pay off the debt in one year
e. The amount the family should save (the family size times 2 percent of the income minus debt)
f. Your service fee (.5 percent of the income)

Run your program for the following two families:

Name	Size	Income	Debts
Anderson	4	18000.00	2000.00
Sherrell	7	26000.00	4800.00

7. The Caswell Catering and Convention Service has asked you to write a computer program to produce customers' bills. The program should read in the following data.

a. The number of adults to be served
b. The number of children to be served
c. The cost per adult meal
d. The cost per child's meal (60 percent of the cost of the adult's meal)
e. The cost for dessert (same for adults and children)
f. The room fee (no room fee if catered at the person's home)
g. A percentage for tip and tax (not applied to the room fee)
h. Any deposit should be deducted from the bill

Write a program and test it using data sets 2, 3, and 4.

Test Data	Child Count	Adult Count	Adult Cost	Dessert Cost	Room Rate	Tip/ Tax	Deposit
1	7	23	12.75	1.00	45.00	18%	50.00
2	3	54	13.50	1.25	65.00	19%	40.00
3	15	24	12.00	0.00	45.00	18%	75.00
4	2	71	11.15	1.50	0.00	6%	0.00

Note that data set 1 was used to produce the following sample output.

```
Caswell Catering and Convention Service
               Final Bill

              Number of adults:          23
              Number of children:         7
Cost per adult without dessert:    $   12.75
Cost per child without dessert:    $    7.65
              Cost per dessert:    $    1.00
                     Room fee:    $   45.00
              Tip and tax rate:    $    0.18

     Total cost for adult meals:   $  293.25
     Total cost for child meals:   $   53.55
        Total cost for dessert:    $   30.00
             Total food cost:      $  376.80
            Plus tip and tax:      $   67.82
                Plus room fee:     $   45.00
                 Less deposit:     $   50.00

                 Balance due:      $  439.62
```

8. The Maripot Carpet Store has asked you to write a computer program to calculate the amount a customer should be charged. The president of the company has given you the following information to help in writing the program.

a. The carpet charge is equal to the number of square yards purchased times the labor cost per square yard.

b. The labor cost is equal to the number of square yards purchased times the labor cost per square yard. A fixed fee for floor preparation is added to some customers' bills.

c. Large volume customers are given a percentage discount but the discount applies only tq the carpet charge, not the labor costs.

d. All customers are charged 4 percent sales tax on the carpet; there is no sales tax on the labor cost.

Write the program and test it for customers 2, 3, and 4. Note that the data for customer 1 were used to produce the sample output.

Customer	Sq. yds.	Cost per sq. yd.	Labor per sq. yd.	Prep. Cost	Discount
1	17	18.50	3.50	38.50	2%
2	40	24.95	2.95	0.00	14%
3	23	16.80	3.25	57.95	0%
4	26	21.25	0.00	80.00	0%

```
Square yards purchased:          17
   Cost per square yard:   $    18.50
  Labor per square yard:   $     3.50
Floor preparation cost:    $    38.50

        Cost for carpet:   $   314.50
         Cost for labor:   $    98.00
    Discount on carpet:    $     6.29
         Tax on carpet:    $    12.33
    Charge to customer:    $   418.54
```

9. The manager of the Croswell Carpet Store has asked you to write a program to print customers' bills. The manager has given you the following information.

a. The store expresses the length and width of a room in terms of feet and tenths of a foot. For example, the length might be reported as 16.7 feet.

b. The amount of carpet purchased is expressed as square yards. It is found by dividing the area of the room (in square feet) by nine.

c. The store does not sell a fraction of a square yard. Thus, square yards must always be rounded up.

d. The carpet charge is equal to the number of square yards purchased times the carpet cost per square yard. Sales tax equal to 4 percent of the carpet cost must be added to the bill.

e. All customers are sold a carpet pad at $2.25 per square yard. Sales tax equal to 4 percent of the pad cost must be added to the bill.

f. The labor cost is equal to the number of square yards purchased times $2.40, which is the labor cost per square yard. No tax is charged on labor.

g. Large volume customers may be given a discount. The discount may apply only to the carpet cost (before sales tax is added), only to the pad cost (before sales tax is added), only to the labor cost, or to any combination of the three charges.

h. Each customer is identified by a five-digit number and that number should appear on the bill.

The sample output follows:

```
        Croswell Carpet Store
              Invoice

Customer number:    26817

        Carpet :    574.20
           Pad :     81.00
         Labor :     86.40

      Subtotal :    741.60
 Less discount :     65.52

      Subtotal :   676.08
      Plus tax :    23.59
         Total :   699.67
```

Write the program and test it for the following three customers.

a. Mr. Wilson (customer 81429) ordered carpet for his family room, which measures 25 feet long and 18 feet wide. The carpet sells for $12.95 per square yard and the manager agreed to give him a discount of 8 percent on the carpet and 6 percent on the labor.

b. Mr. and Mrs. Adams (customer 04246) ordered carpet for their bedroom which measures 16.5 feet by 15.4 feet. The carpet sells for $18.90 per square yard and the manager granted a discount of 12 percent of everything.

c. Ms. Logan (customer 39050) ordered carpet that cost $8.95 per square yard for her daughter's bedroom. The room measures 13.1 by 12.5 feet. No discounts were given.

10. Each month Abduhl's Flying Carpets pays its salespeople a base salary plus a bonus for each carpet they sell. In addition, they pay a commission calculated as a percentage of thousands of dollars of sales per salesperson plus one-half the commission on the remaining fraction of $1000.

Write a program to compute a salesperson's salary for the month by inputting Base, Bonus, Quantity, and Sales, and making the necessary calculations. Use the following test data:

Salesperson	Base	Bonus	Quantity	Commission	Sales
1	250.00	15.00	20	20	1543.69
2	280.00	19.50	36	20	2375.90

The commission figure is 20 percent. Be sure you can change this easily if necessary. Sample (incomplete) output follows:

Sales-person	Base	Bonus	Quantity	Total Bonus	Commission	Sales	Total Commission	Pay
1	$250.00	$15.00	20		20%	$1543.69		

Conditional Statements

The previous four chapters set the stage for using computers. You saw how programs in Pascal can be used to get data, perform computations, and print results. You should be able to write complete, short programs, so it is time to examine other aspects of programming.

A major feature of a computer is its ability to make decisions; that is, a condition is examined and a decision is then made as to which program statement is next executed. Statements that permit a computer to make decisions are called *conditional statements*. Conditional statements are examples of *control structures* because they allow the programmer to control the flow of execution of program statements. Before we see how decisions are made, we need to examine the logical constructs in Pascal.

■ 5.1
boolean
Expressions

- to use the data type **boolean**
- to use relational operators
- to understand the hierarchy for simple **boolean** expressions
- to use the logical connectives **AND, OR,** and **NOT**

The logical constructs in Pascal include a new data type called **boolean,** which allows you to determine if something is **true** or **false.** Although this sounds relatively simple (and it is), this is a very significant feature of computers.

The boolean Data Type

Thus far we have used only the three data types **integer, real,** and **char;** a fourth data type is **boolean.** There are only two values for variables of the **boolean** data type: **true** and **false.** These are constant predefined identifiers and can only be used as **boolean** values. A typical declaration of a **boolean** variable is

```
VAR
   Flag : boolean;
```

123

- to use compound **boolean** expressions
- to understand the hierarchy for compound **boolean** expressions

In general, **boolean** variables are declared by

```
VAR
      variable 1,
      variable 2,
              .
              .
              .
      variable n : boolean;
```

When these assignments are made, the contents of the designated memory locations are the assigned values. For example, if the declaration

```
VAR
    Flag1, Flag2 : boolean;
```

is made,

```
Flag1 := true;
Flag2 := false;
```

produces

true		false
Flag1		Flag2

As with other data types, if two variables are of type **boolean,** the value of one variable can be assigned to another variable as

```
Flag1 := true;
Flag2 := Flag1;
```

and can be envisioned as

true		true
Flag1		Flag2

Note that quotation marks are not used when assigning the values **true** or **false** since these are **boolean** constants, not strings.

Output of boolean

In most versions of standard Pascal, **boolean** variables can be used as arguments for **write** and **writeln.** Thus,

```
Flag := true;
writeln (Flag);
```

produces

```
true
```

You will need to check your version. For example, the version first developed at the University of California at San Diego, UCSD Pascal, will not support output of **boolean** variables.

The field width for **boolean** output varies with the machine being used. However, it can be controlled by formatting with a colon followed by a positive integer to designate the field width. The **boolean** value will appear right justified in the field. To illustrate, if Flag is a **boolean** variable with the value **false,** the segment of code

```
writeln (Flag:6);
writeln (Flag:8);
```

produces the output

```
false
    false
```

boolean constants **true** and **false** can also be used in **writeln** statements. For example,

```
writeln (true);
writeln (false);
writeln (true:6, false:6);
```

produces

```
true
false
    true false
```

Although **boolean** variables and constants can be assigned and used in output statements, they cannot be used in input statements. Thus, if Flag is a **boolean** variable, a statement such as

```
read(Flag);
```

produces an error. Instead, one would typically read some value and then assign an appropriate **boolean** value to a **boolean** variable. This technique will be illustrated later.

Relational Operators and Simple boolean Expressions

In arithmetic, integers and reals can be compared using equalities ($=$) and inequalities ($<$, $>$, $\neq$, and so on). Pascal also provides for the comparison of numbers or values of variables. The operators used for comparison are called *relational operators* and there are six of them. Their arithmetic notation, Pascal notation, and meaning are given in Table 5.1.

When two numbers or variable values are compared using a single relational operator, the expression is referred to as a *simple* **boolean** *expression.* Each simple **boolean** expression has the **boolean** value **true** or **false** according to the arithmetic validity of the expression. In general, only data of the same type can be compared; thus, integers must be compared to integers, reals must be compared to reals, and characters must

TABLE 5.1
Relational operators

Arithmetic Operation	Relational Operator	Meaning
$=$	$=$	Is equal to
$<$	$<$	Is less than
$>$	$>$	Is greater than
$\leq$	$<=$	Is less than or equal to
$\geq$	$>=$	Is greater than or equal to
$\neq$	$<>$	Is not equal to

TABLE 5.2
Values of simple
boolean expressions

Simple boolean Expression	boolean Value
7 = 7	true
−3.0 = 0.0	false
4.2 > 3.7	true
−18 < −15	true
13 < 100	true
13 <= 100	true
13 <= 13	true
0.012 > 0.013	false
−17.32 <> −17.32	false
A <= B	true
B > A	true

be compared to characters. The usual exception can be applied here; that is, reals can be compared to integers.

Table 5.2 sets forth several **boolean** expressions and their respective **boolean** values, assuming the assignment statements

```
A := 3;
```

and

```
B := 4;
```

are made.

Arithmetic expressions can also be used in simple **boolean** expressions. Thus,

```
4 < (3 + 2)
```

has the value **true.** When the computer evaluates this expression, the parentheses dictate that (3 + 2) be evaluated first and then the relational operator. Sequentially, this becomes

```
4 < (3 + 2)
4 <     5
true
```

What if the parentheses had not been used? Could the expression

```
4 < 3 + 2
```

be evaluated? This type of expression necessitates a priority level for the relational operators and the arithmetic operators. A summary for the priority of these operations is

Expression	Priority
*, /, **MOD**, **DIV**	1
+, −	2
=, <, >, <=, >=, <>	3

Thus, we see that the relational operators are evaluated last. As with arithmetic operators, these are evaluated in order from left to right. Thus, the expression

```
4 < 3 + 2
```

can be evaluated without parentheses and would have the same **boolean** value.

The following example illustrates the evaluation of a somewhat more complex simple **boolean** expression.

EXAMPLE 5.1

Indicate the successive steps in the evaluation of the **boolean** expression

10 **MOD** 4 * 3 − 8 <= 18 + 30 **DIV** 4 − 20

The steps in this evaluation are

Even though, as shown in this example, parentheses are not required when using arithmetic expressions with relational operators, it is usually a good idea to use them to enhance the readability of the expression and to avoid using an incorrect expression.

SELF QUIZ 5.1

What is the **boolean** value of the following expression?

− 3 * 4 + 5 >= 10 **DIV** 2 * (− 1)

Logical Connectives and Compound boolean Expressions

boolean values may also be generated by using *logical connectives* and *negation* with simple **boolean** expressions. The logical connectives used by Pascal are **AND** and **OR;** they are used to connect two **boolean** expressions. Negation is represented by **NOT;** it is used to negate (reverse) the **boolean** value of an expression. When these connectives or negation are used to generate **boolean** values, the complete expression is referred to as a *compound* **boolean** *expression*.

If **AND** is used to join two simple **boolean** expressions, the resulting compound expression is **true** only when both simple expressions are **true.** If **OR** is used, the result is **true** if either or both of the expressions are **true.** This is summarized as follows:

Expression 1 (E1)	Expression 2 (E2)	E1 AND E2	E1 OR E2
true	true	true	true
true	false	false	true
false	true	false	true
false	false	false	false

As previously indicated, **NOT** merely produces the logical negation of an expression as follows:

Expression (E)	NOT E
true	false
false	true

The three reserved words **AND, OR,** and **NOT** are called *logical operators*. When using these operators with relational expressions, parentheses are required. Illustrations of the **boolean** values generated using logical operators are given in Table 5.3.

Complex **boolean** expressions can be generated by using several logical operators in an expression. The priority for evaluating these operators is

Operator	Priority
NOT	1
AND	2
OR	3

When complex expressions are being evaluated, the logical operators, arithmetic expressions, and relational operators are evaluated during successive passes through the expression. The priority list is now complete as follows:

Expression or Operation	Priority
( )	1. Evaluate from inside out
NOT	2. Evaluate from left to right
*, /, **MOD, DIV, AND**	3. Evaluate from left to right
+, —, **OR**	4. Evaluate from left to right
<, <=, >, >=, =, <>	5. Evaluate from left to right

As expressions become more complex, be sure to use parentheses for clarity. The following examples illustrate evaluation of some complex **boolean** expressions.

TABLE 5.3
Values of compound **boolean** expressions

Expression	boolean Value
(4.2 >= 5.0) **AND** (8 = (3 + 5))	false
(4.2 >= 5.0) **OR** (8 = (3 + 5))	true
(−2 < 0) **AND** (18 >= 10)	true
(−2 < 0) **OR** (18 >= 10)	true
(3 > 5) **AND** (14.1 = 0.0)	false
(3 > 5) **OR** (14.1 = 0.0)	false
NOT (18 = (10 + 8))	false
NOT (−4 > 0)	true

A NOTE OF INTEREST

George Boole

George Boole was a self-taught mathematician who knew only hard work and deprivation during his early years. He was born in England in 1815 and until 1849, when he was appointed professor of mathematics at Queen's College in Cork, Ireland, a major portion of his time was spent teaching so he could support his parents. After the appointment, he could devote more time to mathematics and subsequently pub-

lished "An Investigation of the Laws of Thought, on which are founded the Mathematical Theories of Logic and Probabilities" at the relatively advanced age of thirty-nine. The data type, Boolean, is named in honor of George Boole because he is credited with laying the foundation for what is currently studied as formal logic.

EXAMPLE 5.2

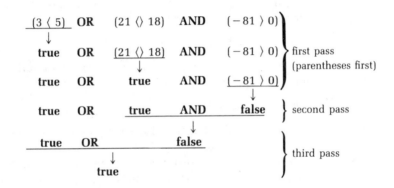

EXAMPLE 5.3

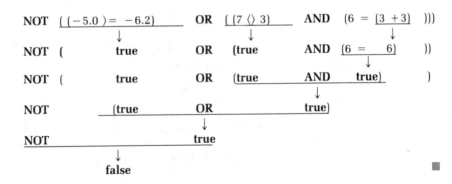

EXAMPLE 5.4   Assume X and Y are real variables, Flag is a **boolean** variable, and the assignment statements

```
X := 12.5;
Y := -100;
Flag := true;
```

are made.

$$(X <> 7 / 3) \textbf{ OR NOT } ((X >= 4) \textbf{ AND } (\textbf{NOT } Flag))$$

can be evaluated as:

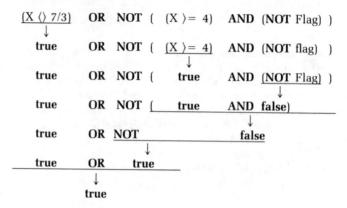

Extra care should be taken with the syntax of **boolean** expressions. For example, the expression

3 < 4 **AND** 100 > 80

in a program produces an error. Since relational expressions are evaluated last, the first pass through this expression attempts to evaluate

4 **AND** 100

This is not valid because logical operators can only operate on **boolean** values **true** and **false.**

If an expression produces a **boolean** value and is evaluated before a connective, then that expression need not be in parentheses. For example,

(3 < 5) **AND NOT** (0 >= −2)

is a valid expression, and is evaluated as follows:

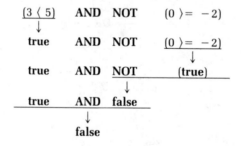

1. Assume the variable declaration section of a program is

```
VAR
    Flag1, Flag2 : boolean;
```

What output is produced by the following segments of code?

```
Flag1 := true;
Flag2 := false;
writeln (Flag1, true:6, Flag2:8);
Flag1 := Flag2;
writeln (Flag2:20);
```

2. Write a test program that illustrates what happens when **boolean** expressions are not enclosed in parentheses. For example,

3 < 5 **AND** 8.0 <> 4 * 3

For Exercises 3–8, assume the variable declaration section of a program is

```
VAR
    Ch : char;
    Flag : boolean;
```

Indicate if the assignment statement is valid or invalid.

3. `Flag := 'true';`   6. `Ch := Flag;`
4. `Flag := T;`   7. `Ch := true;`
5. `Flag := true;`   8. `Ch := 'T';`

In Exercises 9–15, indicate whether the expression is valid or invalid. Evaluate those that are valid.

9. 3 < 4 **OR** 5 <> 6
10. **NOT** 3.0 = 6 / 2
11. **NOT** (true **OR** false)
12. **NOT** true **OR** false
13. **NOT** true **OR NOT** false
14. **NOT** (18 < 25) **AND OR** (-3 < 0)
15. 8 * 3 < 20 + 10

For Exercises 16–22, indicate if the simple **boolean** expression is **true, false,** or invalid.

16. $-3.01 <= -3.001$
17. $-3.0 = -3$
18. 25 − 10 <> 3 * 5
19. 42 **MOD** 5 < 42 **DIV** 5
20. $-5 * (3 + 2) > 2 * (-10)$
21. 10 / 5 < 1 + 1
22. 3 + 8 **MOD** 5 >= 6 − 12 **MOD** 2

In Exercises 23–27, evaluate the expression.

23. (3 > 7) **AND** (2 < 0) **OR** (6 = 3 + 3)
24. ((3 > 7) **AND** (2 < 0)) **OR** (6 = 3 + 3)
25. (3 > 7) **AND** ((2 < 0) **OR** (6 = 3 + 3))
26. **NOT** ((−4.2 <> 3.0) **AND** (10 < 20))
27. (**NOT** (−4.2 <> 3.0)) **OR** (**NOT** (10 < 20))

For Exercises 28–32, assume the variable declaration section of a program is

```
VAR
    Int1, Int2 : integer;
    Real1, Real2 : real;
    Flag1, Flag2 : boolean;
```

and the values of the variables are

0	8	−15.2	−20.0	false	true
Int1	Int2	Real1	Real2	Flag1	Flag2

Evaluate each expression.

28. (Int1 <= Int2) **OR NOT** (Real2 = Real1)
29. **NOT** (Flag1) **OR NOT** (Flag2)
30. **NOT** (Flag1 **AND** Flag2)
31. ((Real1-Real2) < 100/Int2) **AND** ((Int1 < 1) **AND NOT** (Flag2))
32. **NOT** ((Int2 − 16 **DIV** 2) = Int1) **AND** Flag1

■ 5.2
IF ... THEN Statements

- to learn the form and syntax required for using an **IF ... THEN** statement
- to understand the flow of control when using an **IF ... THEN** statement
- to use an **IF ... THEN** statement in a program
- to understand why compound statements are needed
- to understand how **BEGIN ... END** are used to write compound statements
- to use correct syntax in writing a compound statement
- to design programs using **IF ... THEN** statements

The first decision-making statement we examine is the **IF ... THEN** statement. **IF ... THEN** is used to make a program do something only when certain conditions are **true.** The form and syntax for an **IF ... THEN** statement are

> **IF boolean** expression **THEN**
>   statement;

The **boolean** expression can be any valid expression that is either **true** or **false** at the time of evaluation. If it is **true,** the statement following the reserved word **THEN** is executed. If it is **false,** control is transferred to the first program statement following the complete **IF ... THEN** statement. A structure diagram is given in Figure 5.1.

As a further illustration of how an **IF ... THEN** statement works, consider the program fragment

```
Sum := 0.0;
read (Num);
IF Num > 0.0 THEN
   Sum := Sum + Num;
writeln (Sum:10:2);
```

If the value read is 75.85, prior to execution of the **IF ... THEN** statement, the contents of Num and Sum are

| 75.85 | | 0.0 |
| Num | | Sum |

The **boolean** expression Num > 0.0 is now evaluated and, since it is **true,** the statement

```
Sum := Sum + Num;
```

is executed and we have

| 75.85 | | 75.85 |
| Num | | Sum |

The next program statement is executed and produces the output

```
75.85
```

However, if the value read is −25.5, the variable values are

| −25.5 | | 0.0 |
| Num | | Sum |

The **boolean** expression Num > 0.0 is **false** and control is transferred to the line

```
writeln (Sum);
```

Thus, the output is

```
0.00
```

Now, let's suppose you are writing a program in which one of the objectives is to count the periods encountered in the line of input. As-

FIGURE 5.1
IF . . . THEN struc-
ture diagram

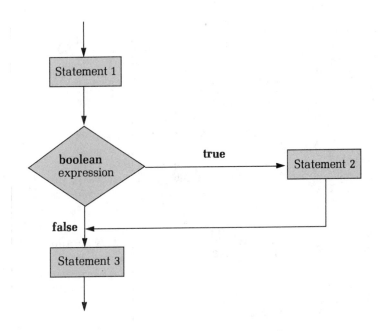

suming suitable initialization and declaration, a program fragment for this task is

```
read (Ch);
IF Ch = ',' THEN
   Count := Count + 1;
```

One writing style for using an **IF . . . THEN** statement calls for indenting the program statement to be executed if the **boolean** expression is **true.** This, of course, is not required as

```
IF Ch = ',' THEN
   Count := Count + 1;
```

can be written

```
IF Ch = ',' THEN Count := Count + 1;
```

However, the indenting style for simple **IF . . . THEN** statements is consistent with the style used with more elaborate conditional statements.

SELF QUIZ 5.2   Assuming variables are appropriately declared, indicate the contents of each variable after the following program fragment is executed.

```
Flag := false;
A := 0;
B := 10;
IF A <> 0 THEN
   Flag := true;
   B := A + B;
   A := 1;
```

Compound Statements

The last concept needed before looking at selection in Pascal is a *compound statement*. Simple statements are single commands separated by semicolons. Thus,

```
readln (A,B);
A := 3 * B;
writeln (A);
```

are three simple statements.

In some instances, it is necessary to perform several simple statements when some condition is **true.** For example, you may want the program to do certain things if a condition is **true** (say A < 0). In this situation, several simple statements that can be written as a single compound statement would be very helpful. A compound statement is created by using the reserved words **BEGIN** and **END** at the beginning and end of a sequence of simple statements. Correct syntax for a compound statement is

> **BEGIN**
>   statement 1;
>   statement 2;
>   .
>   .
>   .
>   statement n
> **END**;

Statements within a compound statement are followed by a semicolon. The last statement before **END,** however, does not require a semicolon, but if a semicolon is used here, it will not affect the program. Finally, a semicolon is used after the **END,** because it completes the compound statement.

When a compound statement is executed within a program, the entire segment of code between **BEGIN** and **END** is treated as a single statement. It is important that you develop a consistent, acceptable writing style for writing compound statements. What you use will vary according to your teacher's wishes and your personal preferences. Examples in this text indent each simple statement within a compound statement two spaces. Thus,

```
BEGIN
  read (A,B);
  A := 3 * B;
  writeln (A)
END;
```

is a compound statement in a program; what it does is easily identified.

Some examples of compound statements follow. Although the concept, syntax, and writing style do not appear to be difficult at this point, one of the most frequent errors for beginning programmers is incorrect use of compound statements.

EXAMPLE 5.5

Let's write a compound statement that allows you to read a real, print the real, and add it to a total. Assuming variables are suitably declared and initialized, a compound statement to do this is

```
BEGIN
  writeln('Enter a real number and press <RETURN>.');
  readln(Num);
  writeln(Num:8:2);
  Total := Total + Num
END;
```
■

EXAMPLE 5.6

Suppose you are writing a program to enable your teacher to compute grades for your class. For each student you need to read three scores from a line of data, add the scores, compute the average score, and print the scores and the test average. Again, assuming variables are suitably declared, a compound statement for this is

```
BEGIN
  writeln('Enter three scores and press <RETURN>.');
  readln(Score1, Score2, Score3);
  Total := Score1 + Score2 + Score3;
  Average := Total/3.0;
  write(Score1:6, Score2:6, Score3:6);
  writeln(Average:12:2)
END;
```
■

Using Compound Statements

As you might expect, compound statements can be (and frequently are) used as part of an **IF ... THEN** statement. The form and syntax for this are:

```
IF boolean expression THEN
  BEGIN
     statement 1;
     statement 2;
          .
          .
          .
     statement n
  END;
```

Program control is exactly as before depending on the value of the **boolean** expression. For example, suppose you want to determine how many positive numbers are being entered and also compute their sum. This can be accomplished by the program fragment

```
Sum := 0.0;
Count := 0;
read (Num);
IF Num > 0.0 THEN
  BEGIN
    Sum := Sum + Num;
    Count := Count + 1
  END; (* of IF ... THEN *)
```

The next example designs a program to solve a problem using an **IF** . . . **THEN** statement.

EXAMPLE 5.7

Let's write a program that reads two integers and prints them in the order larger first, smaller second. The first-level pseudocode solution is

1. Read numbers
2. Determine larger
3. Print results

Step 1 is a single line of code, and step 3 is some **writeln** statements. However, step 2 requires some refinement. A second-level solution is

1. Read numbers
2. **IF** Num1 < Num2 **THEN**
   2.1 exchange numbers
3. Print results
   3.1 print Num1
   3.2 print Num2

Step 2.1, is further refined to produce

   2.1 exchange numbers
      2.1.1 Temp gets Num1
      2.1.2 Num1 gets Num2
      2.1.3 Num2 gets Temp

We can now write code for the program to solve this problem.

```
writeln('Enter two integers and press <RETURN>.');
readln (Num1, Num2);
IF Num1 < Num2 THEN
   BEGIN
      Temp := Num1;
      Num1 := Num2;
      Num2 := Temp
   END;   (* of IF ... THEN *)
writeln (Num1:15, Num2:15);
```

Before writing a complete program for this example, let's look at the "exchange" in step 2.1 since this is an important concept. Suppose Num1, Num2, and Temp are initially

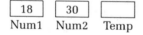

18	30	
Num1	Num2	Temp

Since Num1 is less than Num2, the exchange proceeds as follows:

```
Temp := Num1;
```

produces

18	30	18
Num1	Num2	Temp

```
Num1 := Num2;
```

produces

30	30	18
Num1	Num2	Temp

```
Num2 := Temp;
```

produces

30	18	18
Num1	Num2	Temp

Thus, you see that the values have been exchanged. Let's now write a complete program for this example.

```
PROGRAM UseIFTHEN (input,output);

(****************************************************************

     This short program is designed to illustrate using an
     IF ... THEN statement. Two numbers are read and
     then printed in order, larger first.

 ****************************************************************)

CONST
  Skip = ' ';


VAR
  Num1, Num2 : integer;        (*  Numbers to be compared  *)
  Temp : integer;     (*  Variable for temporary storage  *)


BEGIN
  writeln ('Enter two integers and press <RETURN>.');
  readln (Num1, Num2);

  (*  Print a heading  *)

  writeln;
  writeln (Skip:19, 'Larger Number', Skip:10, 'Smaller Number');
  writeln (Skip:19, '_____', Skip:10, '_____');
  IF Num1 < Num2 THEN
    BEGIN
      Temp := Num1;
      Num1 := Num2;
      Num2 := Temp
    END;
  writeln;
  writeln(Num1:26, Num2:23);
  writeln
END.
```

If you enter 18 and 30, the output for this program is

```
Enter two integers and press <RETURN>.
18 30

Larger number          Smaller number
_____          _____

      30                     18
```

Exercises 5.2

In Exercises 1–6, what output is produced from the program fragment? Assume the following assignment statements precede each fragment.

```
A := 10;
B := 5;
```

1. IF A <= B THEN
       B := A;
    writeln (A,B);
2. IF A <= B THEN
       BEGIN
          B := A;
          writeln (A,B)
       END;
3. IF A < B THEN
       Temp := A;
    A := B;
    B := Temp;
    writeln (A,B);
4. IF A < B THEN
       BEGIN
          Temp := A;
          A := B;
          B := Temp
       END;
    writeln (A,B);

5. IF (A < B) OR (B - A < 0) THEN
       BEGIN
          A := A + B;
          B := B - 1;
          writeln (A,B)
       END;
    writeln (A,B);
6. IF (A < B) AND (B - A < 0) THEN
       BEGIN
          A := A + B;
          B := B - 1;
          writeln (A,B)
       END;
    writeln (A,B);

7. Write a test program to illustrate what happens when a semicolon is inadvertently inserted after **THEN** in an **IF** ... **THEN** statement. For example,

```
IF A > 0 THEN;
   Sum := Sum + A;
```

In Exercises 8–11, find and explain the errors in the program fragment. You may assume all variables are suitably declared.

8. IF A := 10 THEN
       writeln (A);
9. X := 7;
    IF 3 < X < 10 THEN
       BEGIN
          X := X + 1;
          writeln (X)
       END;

10. Count := 0;
     Sum := 0;
     A := 50;
     IF A > 0 THEN
         Count := Count + 1;
         Sum := Sum + A;
11. read (Ch);
     IF Ch = 'A' OR 'B' THEN
         writeln (Ch:10);

In Exercises 12 and 13, what output is produced from the program fragment? Assume variables are suitably declared.

12. J := 18;
     IF J MOD 5 = 0 THEN
        writeln (J);
13. A := 5;
     B := 90;
     B := B DIV A - 5;
     IF B > A THEN
        B := A * 30;
     writeln (A,B);

14. Can a simple statement be written as a compound statement using **BEGIN** ... **END**? Write a short program that allows you to verify your answer.

15. Discuss the differences in the following programs. Predict the output for each program using sample values for Num.

```pascal
PROGRAM Exercise15a (input, output);
VAR
  Num : real;
BEGIN
  writeln('Enter a number and press <RETURN>.');
  readln(Num);
  IF Num > 0 THEN
    writeln; writeln;
    writeln('The number is':22, Num:6:2);
    writeln;
    writeln('The number squared is':30, Num * Num:6:2);
    writeln('The number cubed is':28, Num * Num * Num:6:2);
    writeln; writeln
END.
```

```pascal
PROGRAM Exercise15b (input, output);
VAR
  Num : real;
BEGIN
  writeln('Enter a number and press <RETURN>.');
  readln(Num);
  If Num > 0 THEN
    BEGIN  (*  Start output  *)
      writeln; writeln;
      writeln('The number is':22, Num:6:2);
      writeln;
      writeln('The number squared is':30, Num * Num:6:2);
      writeln('The number cubed is':28, Num * Num * Num:6:2);
      writeln; writeln
    END  (*  Output for one number  *)
END.
```

16. Discuss writing style and readability of compound statements.

In Exercises 17–20, find all errors in each compound statement.

17.
```pascal
BEGIN
  read(A)
  writeln(A)
END;
```

18.
```pascal
BEGIN
  Sum := Sum + Num
END;
```

19.
```pascal
BEGIN
  read(Size1, Size2);
  writeln(Size1:8, Size2:8)
END.
```

20.
```pascal
BEGIN
  readln(Age, Weight);
  TotalAge := TotalAge + Age;
  TotalWeight := TotalWeight + Weight;
  writeln(Age:8, Weight:8)
```

21. Write a single compound statement that will:
    a. Read three integers from a data line
    b. Add them to a previous total
    c. Print the numbers on one line
    d. Skip a line (output)
    e. Print the new total

22. Write a program fragment that reads three reals as input, counts the number of positive reals, and accumulates the sum of positive reals.

23. Write a program fragment that reads three characters as input and then prints them only if they are read in alphabetical order (for example, it prints "boy" but not "dog").

24. Given two integers, A and B, A is a divisor of B if B **MOD** A = 0. Write a complete program that reads two positive integers A and B and then, if A is a divisor of B,
    a. Print A
    b. Print B
    c. Print the result of B divided by A

    For example, the output could be

    ```
    A is 14
    B is 42
    B divided by A is 3
    ```

■ 5.3 IF ... THEN ... ELSE Statements

OBJECTIVES

- to learn the form and syntax required for using an **IF... THEN ... ELSE** statement
- to understand the flow of control when using an **IF... THEN ... ELSE** statement
- to use an **IF ... THEN ... ELSE** statement in a program
- to design programs using **IF ... THEN ... ELSE** statements

Form and Syntax

The previous section discussed the one-way control statement **IF ... THEN.** The second conditional control statement we examine is the two-way control statement **IF ... THEN ... ELSE.** Correct form and syntax for **IF ... THEN ... ELSE** are

> **IF boolean** expression **THEN**
>   statement
> **ELSE**
>   statement;

Flow of control when using an **IF ... THEN ... ELSE** statement is as follows:

1. The **boolean** expression is evaluated.
2. If the **boolean** expression is **true,** the statement following **THEN** is executed and control transfers to the first program statement following the complete **IF ... THEN ... ELSE** statement.
3. If the **boolean** expression is **false,** the statement following **ELSE** is executed and control transfers to the first program statement following the **IF ... THEN ... ELSE** statement.

A structure diagram is given in Figure 5.2.

FIGURE 5.2
**IF ... THEN ...
ELSE** structure dia-
gram

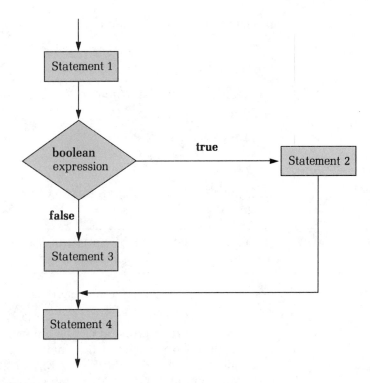

To illustrate this flow of control, let's consider the problem of printing the larger of two numbers using an **IF ... THEN ... ELSE** statement. A program segment for this is

```
readln (Num1, Num2);
IF Num1 > Num2 THEN
    writeln (Num1)
ELSE
    writeln (Num2);
writeln ('All done':16);
```

If the values read are

80		15
Num1		Num2

the **boolean** expression Num1 > Num2 is **true** and the statement

```
writeln (Num1)
```

is executed to produce

```
80
```

Control is then transferred to the next program statement,

```
writeln ('All done':16);
```

and the output is

```
80
All done
```

However, if the values read are

| 10 | 75 |
| Num1 | Num2 |

the **boolean** expression Num1 > Num2 is **false,** control is transferred to

```
writeln (Num2);
```

and the output is

```
75
All done
```

with the 75 printed from the **ELSE** option of the **IF** ... **THEN** ... **ELSE** statement.

SELF QUIZ 5.3

Use an **IF** ... **THEN** ... **ELSE** statement as part of a program fragment to read two numbers and then print them in order, larger first.

And now, a few points to remember concerning **IF** ... **THEN** ... **ELSE** statements.

1. The **boolean** expression can be any valid expression having a value of **true** or **false** at the time it is evaluated.
2. The complete **IF** ... **THEN** ... **ELSE** statement is one program statement and is separated from other complete statements by a semicolon whenever appropriate.
3. There is no semicolon preceding the reserved word **ELSE.** A semicolon preceding the reserved word **ELSE** causes the compiler to treat the **IF** ... **THEN** portion as a complete program statement and the **ELSE** portion as a separate statement. This produces an error message indicating that **ELSE** is being used without an **IF** ... **THEN.**
4. Writing style should include indenting within the **ELSE** option in a manner consistent with indenting in the **IF** ... **THEN** option.

Example 5.8 illustrates the use of an **IF** ... **THEN** ... **ELSE** statement.

EXAMPLE 5.8

Let's write a program fragment to keep separate counts of the negative and non-negative numbers entered as input. Assuming all variables are suitably declared, an **IF** ... **THEN** ... **ELSE** statement can be used as follows:

```
read (Num);
IF Num < 0 THEN
  NegCount := NegCount + 1
ELSE
  NonNegCount := NonNegCount + 1;
```

Using Compound Statements

Program statements in both the **IF** ... **THEN** option and the **ELSE** option can be compound statements. When using compound statements in these options, you should use a consistent, readable indenting style; remember to use **BEGIN** ... **END** for each compound statement; and remember to not put a semicolon before **ELSE**.

EXAMPLE 5.9

Suppose you want a program to read a number, count it as negative or nonnegative, and print it in either a column of positive numbers or a column of negative numbers. Assuming all variables are suitably declared and initialized, the fragment might be

```
writeln('Please enter a number and press <RETURN>,');
readln (Num);
IF Num < 0 THEN
   BEGIN
      NegCount := NegCount + 1;
      writeln (Num:15)
   END  (*  of IF ... THEN option  *)
ELSE
   BEGIN
      NonNegCount := NonNegCount + 1;
      writeln (Num:30)
   END;  (*  of ELSE option  *)
```

We conclude this section with an example of a program fragment that requires the use of compound statements within an **IF** ... **THEN** ... **ELSE** statement.

EXAMPLE 5.10

Let's write a program fragment that computes gross wages for an employee of the Florida OJ Canning Company. A line of input consists of three initials, the total hours worked, and the hourly rate. Thus a typical data line is

JHA 44.5 12.75

Overtime (more than 40 hours) is computed as time-and-a-half. The output should include all input data and the gross wages. A first-level pseudocode for this problem is

1. Get the data
2. Perform computation
3. Print results

Step 1 can be accomplished by a single **readln** statement. Step 2 can be refined to

2. Perform computation
   2.1 **IF** Hours $<=$ 40.0 **THEN**
       compute regular time
     ELSE
       compute time-and-a-half

Step 2.1 can be coded as

```
IF Hours <= 40.0 THEN
   TotalWage := Hours * PayRate
ELSE
   BEGIN
      Overtime := 1.5 * (Hours - 40.0) * PayRate;
      TotalWage := 40 * PayRate + Overtime
   END;
```

Step 3 can be refined to

3.   Print results
    3.1   print initials
    3.2   print Hours and PayRate
    3.3   print TotalWage

The program fragment for this problem is

```
writeln('Please enter three initials and press <RETURN>.');
readln (Init1, Init2, Init3);
writeln('Now enter hours worked and pay rate.');
writeln('Press <RETURN> when finished.');
readln (Hours, PayRate);
IF Hours <= 40.0 THEN
  TotalWage := Hours * PayRate
ELSE
  BEGIN
    Overtime := 1.5 * (Hours - 40.0) * PayRate;
    TotalWage := 40 * PayRate + Overtime
  END;
write (Init1:5, Init2, Init3);
write (Hours:10:2, PayRate:10:2);
writeln ('$':10, TotalWage:7:2);
```

If this fragment is run on the data line given at the beginning of this example, we get

    JHA   44.50   12.75 $ 596.06   ■

Program Protection

As you have seen by now, in order to work properly, a program must be given correct data and the proper formulas for processing. **IF ... THEN ... ELSE** statements can be used to help protect programs from bad data or unreasonable computed values. For example, if a program fragment is

```
readln (Score);
     .
     . (process Score here)
     .
```

you can guard against an erroneous entry by

```
readln (Score);
IF (Score >= 0) AND (Score <= 100) THEN
     .
     . (process Score here)
     .
ELSE
     writeln ('There is an input error. Score is ', Score);
```

In a similar manner, when you are performing computations in a program, you can guard against unreasonable values by

1. Compute value
2. **IF** unreasonable value **THEN**
    error message
    ELSE
    proceed with program

Exercises 5.3

In Exercises 1–3, what output is produced from the program fragment? Assume all variables are suitably declared.

1. ```
   A := -14;
   B := 0;
   IF A < B THEN
      writeln (A, abs(A))
   ELSE
      writeln (A * B);
   ```

2. ```
   A := 50;
   B := 25;
   Count := 0;
   Sum := 0;
   IF A = B THEN
      writeln (A,B)
   ELSE
      BEGIN
         Count := Count + 1;
         Sum := Sum + A + B;
         writeln (A,B)
      END;
   writeln (Count, Sum);
   ```

3. ```
   Temp := 0;
   A := 10;
   B := 5;
   IF A > B THEN
      writeln (A,B)
   ELSE
      Temp := A;
      A := B;
      B := Temp;
   writeln (A,B);
   ```

4. Write a test program that illustrates what error message occurs when a semicolon precedes **ELSE** in an **IF . . . THEN . . . ELSE** statement. For example,

   ```
   PROGRAM SyntaxError (output);

   VAR
      A,B : integer;

   BEGIN
      A := 10;
      B := 5;
      IF A < B THEN
         writeln (A);
      ELSE
         writeln (B)
   END.
   ```

In Exercises 5–7, find all errors in the program fragment.

5. ```
   IF Ch <> '.' THEN
      CharCount := CharCount + 1;
      writeln (Ch)
   ELSE
      PeriodCount := PeriodCount + 1;
   ```

```
6. IF Age < 20 THEN
     BEGIN
       YoungCount := YoungCount + 1;
       YoungAge := YoungAge + Age
     END;
   ELSE
     BEGIN
       OldCount := OldCount + 1;
       OldAge := OldAge + Age
     END;
7. IF Age < 20 THEN
     BEGIN
       YoungCount := YoungCount + 1;
       YoungAge := YoungAge + Age
     END
   ELSE
     OldCount := OldCount + 1;
     OldAge := OldAge + Age;
```

8. Write a program fragment to help balance your checkbook. Your fragment should read an entry from the data, keep track of the number of deposits and checks, and keep a running balance. Each line of input consists of a character, D (deposit) or C (check), followed by an amount.

■ 5.4 Nested IF Statements

Multiway Selection

Sections 5.2 and 5.3 examined one-way (**IF ... THEN**) and two-way (**IF ... THEN ... ELSE**) selection. Since each of these is a single Pascal statement, either can be used as part of a selection statement to achieve multiple selection. In this case, the multiple selection statement is referred to as a *nested IF statement*. These nested statements can be any combination of **IF ... THEN** or **IF ... THEN ... ELSE** statements.

To illustrate, let's write a program fragment to issue interim progress reports for students in a class. If a student's score is below 50, the student is failing. If the score is between 50 and 69 inclusive, the progress is unsatisfactory. If the score is 70 or above, the progress is satisfactory. The first decision to be made is based on whether the score is below 50 or not; the design is

```
IF Score >= 50 THEN
   •
   •  (progress report here)
   •
ELSE
   writeln ('You are currently failing.');
```

We now use a nested **IF ... THEN ... ELSE** statement for the progress report for students who are not failing. The complete fragment is

```
IF Score >= 50 THEN
   IF Score > 69 THEN
      writeln ('Your progress is satisfactory.')
   ELSE
      writeln ('Your progress is unsatisfactory.')
ELSE
   writeln ('You are currently failing.');
```

This fragment can be designed differently and the decisions made in the following order.

```
IF Score > 69 THEN
   writeln ('Your progress is satisfactory.')
ELSE
   IF Score >= 50 THEN
      writeln ('Your progress is unsatisfactory.')
   ELSE
      writeln ('You are currently failing.');
```

If you trace through both fragments with scores of 40, 60, and 80, you will see they produce identical output.

Another method of writing the nested fragment is to use sequential conditional statements as follows:

```
IF Score > 69 THEN
   writeln ('Your progress is satisfactory.');
IF (Score <= 69) AND (Score >= 50) THEN
   writeln ('Your progress is unsatisfactory.');
IF Score < 50 THEN
   writeln ('You are currently failing.');
```

However, this is less efficient because each **IF ... THEN** statement is executed each time through the program. You should generally avoid using sequential **IF ... THEN** statements if a nested statement can be used; this reduces execution time for a program.

Tracing the flow of logic through nested **IF** statements can be tedious. However, it is essential that you develop this ability. For practice, let's trace through the following example.

EXAMPLE 5.11   Consider the nested statement

```
IF A > 0 THEN
   IF A MOD 2 = 0 THEN
      Sum1 := Sum1 + A
   ELSE
      Sum2 := Sum2 + A
ELSE
   IF A = 0 THEN
      writeln('A is zero')
   ELSE
      NegSum := NegSum + A;
writeln('All done');
```

Let's trace through this statement and discover what action is taken when A is assigned 20, 15, 0, and -30, respectively. For A := 20, the statement $A > 0$ is **true,** hence

```
A MOD 2 = 0
```

is evaluated. This is **true,** so

```
Sum1 := Sum1 + A
```

is executed and control is transferred to

```
writeln ('All done');
```

For A := 15, $A > 0$ is **true** and

```
A MOD 2 = 0
```

is evaluated. This is **false**, so

```
Sum2 := Sum2 + A
```

is executed and control is again transferred out of the nested statement to

```
writeln ('All done');
```

For A := 0, A > 0 is **false**, thus

```
A = 0
```

is evaluated. Since this is **true**, the statement

```
writeln ('A is zero')
```

is executed and control is transferred to

```
writeln ('All done');
```

Finally, for A := −30, A > 0 is **false**, thus

```
A = 0
```

is evaluated. This is **false**, so

```
NegSum := NegSum + A;
```

is executed and then control is transferred to

```
writeln ('All done');
```

∎

Note that this example traces through all possibilities involved in the nested statement. This is essential to guarantee your statement is properly constructed. Our next example illustrates several layers of nesting.

EXAMPLE 5.12

Write a program fragment that allows you to assign letter grades based on students' semester averages. Grades are to be assigned according to the scale

100 >= X >= 90	A
90 > X >= 80	B
80 > X >= 70	C
70 > X >= 55	D
55 > X	E

Nested **IF**s can be used to accomplish this as follows:

```
IF Average >= 90 THEN
  Grade := 'A'
ELSE
  IF Average >= 80 THEN
    Grade := 'B'
  ELSE
    IF Average >= 70 THEN
      Grade := 'C'
    ELSE
      IF Average >= 55 THEN
        Grade := 'D'
      ELSE
        Grade := 'E';
```

Since any Average over 100 or less than zero is a sign of some data or program error, this example can be protected with a statement as follows:

```
IF (Average <= 100) AND (Average >= 0) THEN
   .
   .    (compute letter grade)
   .
ELSE
    writeln ('There is an error. Average is', Average:8:2);  ■
```

<table>
<tr><td>

SELF QUIZ 5.4

</td><td>

What are the values of A, B, and C after the following program fragment is executed?

</td></tr>
</table>

```
A := -8;
B := 21;
C := A + B;
IF A > B THEN
  BEGIN
    A := B;
    C := A * B
  END
ELSE
  IF A < 0 THEN
    BEGIN
      A := abs(A);
      B := B - A;
      C := A * B
    END
  ELSE
    C := 0;
```

<table>
<tr><td>

STYLE TIP

■ ■ ■ ■ ■ ■ ■

</td><td>

It is very important to use a consistent, readable writing style when using nested **IF** statements. The style used here is to indent each nested statement two spaces. Also, each **ELSE** of an **IF** . . . **THEN** . . . **ELSE** statement is in the same column as the **IF** of that statement. This allows you to see at a glance where the **ELSE**s match with the **IF** . . . **THEN**s. For example,

```
IF...THEN
  IF...THEN
    IF...THEN
      IF...THEN
      ELSE
    ELSE
  ELSE
ELSE
```

</td></tr>
</table>

Form and Syntax

The rule for matching **ELSE**s in nested selection statements is

> When an **ELSE** is encountered, it is matched with the most recent **THEN** that has not yet been matched.

Matching **IF** . . . **THEN**s with **ELSE**s is a common source of errors. When designing programs, you should be very careful to match them correctly.

To illustrate, suppose you want to write a program fragment that reads two numbers, X and Y. If X is less than zero, you want to examine Y. If Y is less than zero, you want to increment a negative counter. If X is not less than zero, you want to increment a positive counter. The design is

```
IF  X  <  0  THEN
    ,
    ,    (examine Y)
    ,    (increment  negative  counter)
ELSE
    ,
    ,    (increment  positive  counter)
    ,
```

The code for "examine Y" is

```
IF  Y  <  0  THEN
    NegCount  :=  NegCount  +  1;
```

At this stage, you may naively write the incorrect fragment

```
IF  X  <  0  THEN
    IF  Y  <  0  THEN
        NegCount  :=  NegCount  +  1
ELSE
    PosCount  :=  PosCount  +  1;
```

Although you want the **ELSE** to be matched with the statement

```
IF  X  <  0  THEN
```

the computer will match it with the most recent **THEN,** which is

```
IF  Y  <  0  THEN
```

Thus, the fragment is really

```
IF  X  <  0  THEN
    IF  Y  <  0  THEN
        NegCount  :=  NegCount  +  1
    ELSE
        PosCount  :=  PosCount  +  1;
```

which is not the correct fragment to solve the problem. You may resolve this in one of two ways. First, you can make the option "examine Y" a compound statement by using a **BEGIN ... END** as follows:

```
IF  X  <  0  THEN
    BEGIN
        IF  Y  <  0  THEN
            NegCount  :=  NegCount  +  1
    END
ELSE
    PosCount  :=  PosCount  +  1;
```

Or you can redesign the fragment as follows:

```
IF  X  >=  0  THEN
    PosCount  :=  PosCount  +  1
ELSE
    IF  Y  <  0  THEN
        NegCount  :=  NegCount  +  1;
```

SELF QUIZ 5.5   What output is produced when the following fragment of code is executed?

```
A := 15;
IF A > 0 THEN
   IF A MOD 2 = 0 THEN
      writeln (A + 100)
ELSE
   writeln (A - 100);
```

Using semicolons before **ELSE**s becomes more of a problem as you nest to several layers and use compound statements within the nesting. In some cases, it may be wise to redesign a complex, deeply nested fragment to enhance readability.

We conclude this section with an example that uses a complete program with nested **IF** statements.

EXAMPLE 5.13   Let's write a program that computes the gross pay for an employee of the Clean Products Corporation of America. The corporation produces three products: A, B, and C. Supervisors earn a commission of 7 percent of sales and representatives earn 5 percent. Bonuses of $100 are paid to supervisors whose commission exceeds $300 and to representatives whose commission exceeds $200. Each input line is in the form

S 18 15 10

where the first position contains an 'S' or 'R' for supervisor or representative, respectively. The next three integers indicate the number of units of each of the products sold. Since product prices may vary over time, the constant definition section is used to indicate the current prices as follows:

```
CONST
   SuperRate = 0.07;
   RepRate = 0.05;
   APrice = 13.95;
   BPrice = 17.95;
   CPrice = 29.95;
```

A first-level pseudocode development for this problem might be

1. Get a line of data
2. Process the data
3. Print a heading
4. Print a summary

Step 1 is a message and a **readln** statement. Step 2 is further developed as

2. Process the data
   IF employee is supervisor **THEN**
      compute supervisor's wage
   ELSE
      compute representative's wage

where "compute supervisor's wage" is refined to

    2.1.1. compute commission from sales of A
    2.1.2. compute commission from sales of B
    2.1.3. compute commission from sales of C
    2.1.4. compute total commission

2.1.5.   compute supervisor's bonus
    2.1.5.1 **IF** total commission > 300 **THEN**
         bonus is 100.00
      ELSE
         bonus is 0.00

A similar development follows for computing a representative's wage. Step 3 includes appropriate **writeln** statements for a heading. Step 4 contains appropriate output, including at least the number of sales, amount of sales, commissions, bonuses, and total compensation.

A complete pseudocode solution to this problem is

1. Get a line of data
2. Process the data
   2.1 **IF** employee is a supervisor **THEN**
      2.1.1   compute commission from sales of A
      2.1.2   compute commission from sales of B
      2.1.3   compute commission from sales of C
      2.1.4   compute total commission
      2.1.5   compute supervisor's bonus
         2.1.5.1 **IF** total commission > 300 **THEN**
            bonus is 100.00
          ELSE
            bonus is 0.00
    ELSE
      2.1.6   compute commission from sales of A
      2.1.7   compute commission from sales of B
      2.1.8   compute commission from sales of C
      2.1.9   compute total commission
      2.1.10   compute representative's bonus
         2.1.10.1 **IF** total commission > 200 **THEN**
            bonus is 100.00
          ELSE
            bonus is 0.00
3. Print a heading
4. Print a summary
   4.1   print input data
   4.2   print sales data
   4.3   print commission
   4.4   print total wage

A complete program to solve this problem is

```
PROGRAM ComputeWage (input,output);

(*******************************************************************

      This program uses nested selection to determine
      total compensation for an employee of Clean
      Products Corporation of America.

   *****************************************************************)
```

```
CONST
  CompanyName = 'Clean Products Corporation of America';
  Underline  = '_____';
  SuperRate = 0.07;
  RepRate = 0.05;
  APrice = 13.95;
  BPrice = 17.95;
  CPrice = 29.95;
  Month = 'June';
  Skip = ' ';

VAR
  ASales,BSales,
  CSales : integer;           (*  Sales for A, B, and C            *)
  AComm,BComm,CComm : real;   (*  Commission for A, B, and C       *)
  TotalComm,                  (*  Total commission due             *)
  Bonus : real;               (*  Bonus due                        *)
  Classification : char;      (*  Employee classification (S or R) *)

BEGIN

(*  Get the data  *)

  writeln ('Enter S or R for classification, ASales, BSales, CSales.');
  writeln ('Press <RETURN> when finished.');
  readln (Classification,ASales,BSales,CSales);

(*  Now compute compensation due  *)

  IF Classification = 'S' THEN                    (*  Supervisor  *)
    BEGIN
      AComm := ASales * APrice * SuperRate;
      BComm := BSales * BPrice * SuperRate;
      CComm := CSales * CPrice * SuperRate;
      TotalComm := AComm + BComm + CComm;
      IF TotalComm > 300.0 THEN
        Bonus := 100.0
      ELSE
        Bonus := 0.0
    END  (*  of IF ... THEN block for supervisor  *)
  ELSE
    BEGIN                                         (*  Representative  *)
      AComm := ASales * APrice * RepRate;
      BComm := BSales * BPrice * RepRate;
      CComm := CSales * CPrice * RepRate;
      TotalComm := AComm + BComm + CComm;
      IF TotalComm > 200.0 THEN
        Bonus := 100.0
      ELSE
        Bonus := 0.0
    END; (*  of ELSE block for representative  *)
```

```
(*    Print a heading    *)

  writeln;
  writeln (Skip:10, CompanyName);
  writeln (Skip:10, Underline);
  writeln;
  writeln (Skip:10, 'Sales report for', Month:10);
  writeln;

(*   Now print the results   *)

  write(Skip:10,'Classification');
  IF Classification = 'S' THEN
    writeln(Skip:12,('Supervisor')
  ELSE
    writeln(Skip:12,'Representative');
  writeln;
  writeln(Skip:12,'Product      Sales      Commission');
  writeln(Skip:12,'_____      _____      _____');
  writeln;
  writeln(Skip:15,'A',ASales:11,AComm:16:2);
  writeln(Skip:15,'B',BSales:11,BComm:16:2);
  writeln(Skip:15,'C',CSales:11,CComm:16:2);
  writeln;
  writeln('Subtotal':31,'$':3,TotalComm:9:2);
  writeln('Your bonus is:':31,'$':3,Bonus:9:2);
  writeln('_____':43);
  writeln;
  writeln('Total Due':31,'$':3,(TotalComm + Bonus):9:2);
  writeln;writeln
END.
```

If this is run with the data   S 18 15 20   the output is

```
Enter S or R for classification, ASales, BSales, CSales.
Press <RETURN> when finished.
S    18    15    20

Clean Products Corporation of America
_____

Sales Report for        June

Classification              Supervisor

       Product      Sales      Commission
       _____      _____      _____

          A          18          17.58
          B          15          18.85
          C          20          41.93

                  Subtotal   $    78.36
           Your bonus is:    $     0.00
                                 _____

                  Total Due  $    78.36
```

Exercises 5.4   For Exercises 1–4, consider the program fragment

```
IF X >= 0.0 THEN
  IF X < 1000.0 THEN
    BEGIN
      Y := 2 * X;
      IF X <= 500 THEN
        X := X/10
    END
  ELSE
    Y := 3 * X
ELSE
  Y := abs(X);
```

Indicate the values of X and Y after this fragment is executed for the initial values of X.

1. X := 381.5;

2. X := -21.0;

3. X := 600.0;

4. X := 3000.0;

5. Write a test program that illustrates the checking of all branches of nested **IF** ... **THEN** ... **ELSE** statements.

For Exercises 6–9, rewrite the fragment using nested **IFS** without compound conditions. (You may assume the values for Ch are M or F.)

```
6. IF (Ch = 'M') AND (Sum > 1000) THEN
     X := X + 1;
   IF (Ch = 'M') AND (Sum <= 1000) THEN
     X := X + 2;
   IF (Ch = 'F') AND (Sum > 1000) THEN
     X := X + 3;
   IF (Ch = 'F') AND (Sum <= 1000) THEN
     X := X + 4;
```

```
7. read (Num);
   IF (Num > 0) AND (Num <= 10000) THEN
     BEGIN
       Count := Count + 1;
       Sum := Sum + Num
     END
   ELSE
     writeln ('Value out of range':27);
```

```
8. IF (A > 0) AND (B > 0) THEN
     writeln ('Both positive':22)
   ELSE
     writeln ('Some negative':22);
```

```
9. IF ((A > 0) AND (B > 0)) OR (C > 0) THEN
     writeln ('Option one':19)
   ELSE
     writeln ('Option two':19);
```

For each of the fragments given in Exercises 10–13, indicate the output of the following assignment statements.

```
a. A := -5;
   B := 5;
b. A := -5;
   B := -3;
c. A := 10;
   B := 8;
d. A := 10;
   B := -4;
```

```
10. IF A < 0 THEN
       IF B < 0 THEN
          A := B
    ELSE
       A := B + 10;
    writeln (A,B);
```

```
11. IF A < 0 THEN
       BEGIN
          IF B < 0 THEN
             A := B
       END
    ELSE
       A := B + 10;
    writeln (A,B);
```

```
12. IF A >= 0 THEN
       A := B + 10
    ELSE
       IF B < 0 THEN
          A := B;
    writeln (A,B);
```

```
13. IF A >= 0 THEN
       A := B + 10;
    IF B < 0 THEN
       A := B;
    writeln (A,B);
```

14. In Example 5.12, we assigned grades to students. Rewrite the grade assignment fragment using a different nesting. Can you rewrite it without using any nesting? Should you?

15. Many nationally based tests report scores and indicate in which quartile the score lies. Assuming the following quartile designation,

Score	Quartile
100–75	1
74–50	2
49–25	3
24–0	4

write a program fragment to read a score as input and report in which quartile the score lies.

■ 5.5
**CASE
Statements**

OBJECTIVES

■ to know the form
and syntax required
for using **CASE**
statements
■ to understand how
CASE statements
can be used as an
alternate method for
multiway selection
■ to use **CASE** state-
ments in designing
programs to solve
problems

Thus far, this chapter has dealt with the topic of selection in Pascal. We have examined one-way selection, two-way selection, and multiway selection. Section 5.4 illustrated how multiple selection can be achieved using nested **IF** statements. Since multiple selection can sometimes be difficult to follow, Pascal provides an alternative method of handling this concept. It is through the use of a **CASE** statement.

Form and Syntax

CASE statements can be used when there are several options that depend on the value of a variable or expression. The general structure for a **CASE** statement is

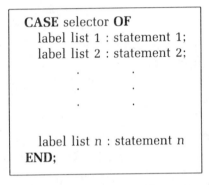

```
CASE selector OF
    label list 1 : statement 1;
    label list 2 : statement 2;
                .        .
                .        .
                .        .

    label list n : statement n
END;
```

and is shown graphically in Figure 5.3.

FIGURE 5.3
CASE structure
diagram

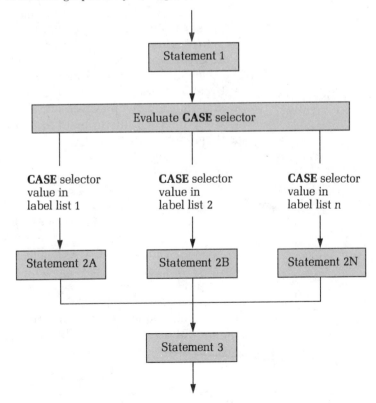

The selector can be any variable or expression whose value is any data type we have studied previously except **real**. Only ordinal data types can be used. Values of the selector constitute the label list. Thus, if Age is a variable whose values are restricted to 16, 17, and 18, we can have

```
CASE Age OF
    16 : statement 1;
    17 : statement 2;
    18 : statement 3
END;
```

When this program statement is executed, the value of Age determines to which statement control is transferred. More specifically, the program fragment

```
Age := 17;
CASE Age OF
    16 : writeln ('Soon I'll get my driver's permit.');
    17 : writeln ('I just got my driver's license.');
    18 : writeln ('This is my second year of driving.')
END;
```

produces the output

```
I just got my driver's license.
```

Before considering more examples, several comments are in order.

1. The flow of logic within a **CASE** statement is as follows:
   a. The value of the selector is determined
   b. The value is found in the label list
   c. The statement following the value in the list is executed
   d. Control is transferred to the first program statement following the **CASE** statement
2. The selector can have a value of any type previously studied except **real**. Only ordinal data types may be used.
3. Several values may appear on one line. For example, if Age can have any integer value from 15 to 25 inclusive, the **CASE** statement can appear as

```
CASE Age OF
    15, 16, 17      : statement 1;
    18, 19, 20, 21  : statement 2;
    22, 23, 24      : statement 3;
    25              : statement 4
END;
```

4. All possible values of the **CASE** selector do not have to be listed. However, if a value is used that is not listed, some versions of Pascal produce an error message and execution is terminated. Consequently, it is preferable to list all values of the **CASE** selector. If certain values require no action, list them on the same option and follow the colon with a semicolon; for example,

```
CASE Age OF
    16 : statement 1;
    17 : ;
    18 : statement 2
END;
```

5. Values for the selector can appear only once in the list. Thus,

```
CASE Age OF
   16       : statement 1;
   16, 17 : statement 2;
   18       : statement 3
END;
```

produces an error since it is not clear which statement should be executed when the value of Age is 18.

6. Proper syntax for using **CASE** statements includes:

   a. a colon ":" separates each label from its respective statement;

   b. a semicolon follows each statement option except the statement preceding **END**;

   c. commas are placed between labels on the same option.

7. **END** is used without a **BEGIN**. This is our first instance of this happening. An appropriate program comment should indicate the end of a **CASE** statement. Therefore, our examples will include

```
END;  (*  of CASE  *)
```

8. Statements for each option can be compound; if they are, they must be in a **BEGIN** . . . **END** statement.

STYLE TIP

■ ■ ■ ■ ■ ■ ■ ■

Writing style for a **CASE** statement should be consistent with your previously developed style. The lines containing options should be indented, the colons should be lined up, and **END** should start in the same column as **CASE**. Thus, a typical **CASE** statement is

```
CASE Score OF
   10,9,8     : writeln ('Excellent');
   7,6,5      : writeln ('Fair');
   4,3,2,1,0 : writeln ('Failing')
END;  (*  of CASE  *)
```

SELF QUIZ 5.6

Assume Score is an **integer** variable. What is wrong with the following **CASE** statement?

```
CASE Score OF
   9,10   : Grade := 'A';
   7,8    ; Grade := 'B';
   5,6,7 : Grade := 'C';
   3,4    : Grade := 'D';
   0,1,2 : Grade := 'E'
```

At this stage, let's consider several examples that illustrate various uses of **CASE** statements. Since our purpose is for illustration, the examples are somewhat contrived. Later examples illustrate how these statements are used in solving problems.

EXAMPLE 5.14 The selector can have a value of type **char,** and the ordinal of the character determines the option. Thus, the label list must contain the appropriate characters in single quotation marks. If Grade has values 'A', 'B', 'C', 'D', or 'E', a **CASE** statement can be

```
CASE Grade OF
   'A' : Points := 4.0;
   'B' : Points := 3.0;
   'C' : Points := 2.0;
   'D' : Points := 1.0;
   'E' : Points := 0.0
END;  (*  of CASE  *)
```

EXAMPLE 5.15 To avoid inappropriate values for the **CASE** selector, the entire **CASE** statement may be protected by using an **IF ... THEN ... ELSE** statement. For example, suppose you are using a **CASE** statement for number of days worked. You expect the values to be 1, 2, 3, 4, or 5, so you can protect the statement by

```
IF (NumDays > 0) AND (NumDays < 6) THEN
   CASE NumDays OF
      1 : statement 1;
      2 : statement 2;
      3 : statement 3;
      4 : statement 4;
      5 : statement 5
   END  (*  of CASE  *)
ELSE
   writeln ('Value of NumDays', NumDays,
            'is out of range,');
```

A good debugging technique is to print the value of the selector in your **ELSE** statement.

Compound statements can be used with any or all of the options in the following form.

```
CASE Age OF
   16 : BEGIN
          .
          .
          .
        END;
   17 : BEGIN
          .
          .
          .
        END;
   18 : BEGIN
          .
          .
          .
        END
END;  (*  of CASE  *)
```

FIGURE 5.4
CASE statement with
OTHERWISE option

```
CASE selector OF
    label 1 : statement 1;
              .
              .
              .
    label n : statement n
OTHERWISE
    statement 1;
    statement 2;
         .
         .
         .
    statement n
END; (* of CASE *)
```

OTHERWISE Option

Some versions of Pascal provide an additional option to be used with **CASE** statements. It is the **OTHERWISE** option and is used in the form shown in Figure 5.4. This option can be used for program protection if the same action is to be taken for several values of the **CASE** selector. Note that the statements following **OTHERWISE** are executed sequentially and do not require a **BEGIN** . . . **END** statement. You should check your version of Pascal to see if this option is available to you.

Equivalent of Nested IFs

As previously indicated, **CASE** statements can sometimes (ordinal data types) be used instead of nested **IFs** when multiple selection is required for solving a problem. Program readability is usually enhanced by listing possible values of the selector together with the action to be taken for the respective values. The following example illustrates how **CASE** statements are related to nested **IFs**.

EXAMPLE 5.16

Let's rewrite the following program fragment using a **CASE** statement.

```
IF (Score = 10) OR (Score = 9) THEN
  Grade := 'A'
ELSE
  IF (Score = 8) OR (Score = 7) THEN
    Grade := 'B'
  ELSE
    IF (Score = 6) OR (Score = 5) THEN
      Grade := 'C'
    ELSE
      Grade := 'E';
```

If we assume Score is an **integer** variable with values 0, 1, 2, . . . , 10, we can use a **CASE** statement as follows:

```
CASE Score OF
   10, 9           : Grade := 'A';
    8, 7           : Grade := 'B';
    6, 5           : Grade := 'C';
    4, 3, 2, 1, 0 : Grade := 'E'
END;  (*  of CASE  *)
```

Use in Problems

We close this section with some examples that illustrate how **CASE** statements can be used in solving problems. In each instance, a program fragment is developed.

EXAMPLE 5.17

Suppose you are writing a program for a gasoline station owner who sells four grades of gasoline: regular, regular unleaded, premium unleaded, and diesel. Your program reads a character (R, U, P, D) that designates which kind of gasoline is purchased and then takes subsequent action. The outline for this fragment is

```
read (GasType);

CASE GasType OF
   'R' : action for regular;
   'U' : action for regular unleaded;
   'P' : action for premium unleaded;
   'D' : action for diesel
END;  (*  of CASE  *)
```

EXAMPLE 5.18

An alternative method of assigning letter grades based on integer scores between 0 and 100 inclusive is to divide the score by 10 and assign grades according to some scale. This idea can be used in conjunction with a **CASE** statement as follows:

```
NewScore := Score DIV 10;

CASE NewScore OF
   10, 9           : Grade := 'A';
    8              : Grade := 'B';
    7              : Grade := 'C';
    6, 5           : Grade := 'D';
    4, 3, 2, 1, 0 : Grade := 'E'
END;  (*  of CASE  *)
```

Exercises 5.5

1. Discuss the need for program protection when using a **CASE** statement.

2. Write a test program to see whether or not the **OTHERWISE** option is available on your system.

3. Show how the following **CASE** statement can be protected against unexpected values.

```
CASE Age DIV 10 OF
   10,9,8,7 : writeln ('These are retirement years.');
     6,5,4 : writeln ('These are middle age years.');
       3,2 : writeln ('These are mobile years.');
         1 : writeln ('These are school years.')
END;  (*  of CASE  *)
```

In Exercises 4–9, find all the errors.

```
4. CASE A OF
     1          :  ;
     2          : A := 2 * A
     3          ; A := 3 * A;
     4; 5; 6 : A := 4 * A
   END; (*  of CASE  *)
5. CASE Num OF
     5              : Num := Num + 5;
     6, 7           ; Num := Num + 6;
     7, 8, 9, 10 : Num := Num + 10
   END; (*  of CASE  *)
6. CASE Age OF
     15, 16, 17 : YCount := YCount + 1;
                  writeln (Age, YCount);
     18, 19, 20 : MCount := MCount + 1;
     21         : writeln (Age)
   END; (*  of CASE  *)
7. CASE Ch OF
     A : Points := 4.0;
     B : Points := 3.0;
     C : Points := 2.0;
     D : Points := 1.0;
     E : Points := 0.0
   END; (*  of CASE  *)
8. CASE Score OF
     5         : Grade := 'A';
     4         : Grade := 'B';
     3         : Grade := 'C';
     2, 1, 0 : Grade := 'E';
9. CASE Num / 10 OF
     1 : Num := Num + 1;
     2 : Num := Num + 2;
     3 : Num := Num + 3
   END; (*  of CASE  *)
```

In Exercises 10–13, what output is produced from the program fragment?

```
10. A := 5;
    Power := 3;
    CASE Power OF
      0 : B := 1;
      1 : B := A;
      2 : B := A * A;
      3 : B := A * A * A
    END; (*  of CASE  *)
    writeln (A, Power, B);
11. write ('You have purchased    ');
    GasType := 'U';
    CASE GasType OF
       'R' : write ('regular');
       'U' : write ('regular unleaded');
       'P' : write ('premium unleaded');
       'D' : write ('diesel')
    END; (*  of CASE  *)
    writeln (' gasoline');
```

```
12. A := 6;
    B := -3;
    CASE A OF
       10, 9, 8 : CASE B OF
                     -3, -4, -5 : A := A * B;
                      0, -1, -2 : A := A + B
                  END;
        7, 6, 5 : CASE B OF
                     -5, -4 : A := A * B;
                     -3, -2 : A := A + B;
                     -1,  0 : A := A - B
                  END
    END; (*  of CASE  *)
    writeln (A, B);
13. Symbol := '-';
    A := 5;
    B := 10;
    CASE Symbol OF
       '+' : Num := A + B;
       '-' : Num := A - B;
       '*' : Num := A * B
    END; (*  of CASE  *)
    writeln (A, B, Num);
```

For Exercises 14–16, rewrite the program fragment using a **CASE** statement.

```
14. IF Power = 1 THEN
       Num := A;
    IF Power = 2 THEN
       Num := A * A;
    IF Power = 3 THEN
       Num := A * A * A;
```

15. Assume Score is an integer between 0 and 10.

```
    IF Score < 9 THEN
      IF Score < 8 THEN
        IF Score < 7 THEN
          IF Score < 5 THEN
            Grade := 'E'
          ELSE
            Grade := 'D'
        ELSE
          Grade := 'C'
      ELSE
        Grade := 'B'
    ELSE
      Grade := 'A';
```

16. Assume Measurement is either M or N.

```
    IF Measurement = 'M' THEN
      BEGIN
        writeln ('This is a metric measurement.');
        writeln ('It will be converted to nonmetric.');
        Length: = Num * CMToInches
      END
    ELSE
```

```
BEGIN
  writeln ('This is a nonmetric measurement.');
  writeln ('It will be converted to metric.');
  Length := Num * InchesToCM
END;
```

17. Show how a **CASE** statement can be used in a program to compute college tuition fees. Assume there are different fee rates for each of undergraduates (U), graduates (G), foreign students (F), and special students (S).

18. Use nested **CASE** statements to design a program fragment to compute postage for domestic (nonforeign) mail. The design should provide for minimal weights only for both letters and packages. Each can be sent first, second, third, or fourth class.

RUNNING AND DEBUGGING TIPS

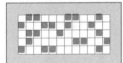

1. **IF ... THEN ... ELSE** is a single statement in Pascal. Thus, a semicolon before the **ELSE** creates an **IF ... THEN** statement and **ELSE** appears incorrectly as a reserved word.

2. A misplaced semicolon used with an **IF ... THEN** statement can also be a problem. For example,

Incorrect
```
IF A > 0 THEN;
  writeln (A);
```

Correct
```
IF A > 0 THEN
  writeln (A);
```

3. Be careful with compound statements as options in an **IF ... THEN ... ELSE** statement. They must be in a **BEGIN ... END** block.

Incorrect
```
IF A >= 0 THEN
  writeln (A);
  A := A + 10
ELSE
  writeln ('A is negative');
```

Correct
```
IF A >= 0 THEN
  BEGIN
    writeln (A);
    A := A + 10
  END
ELSE
  writeln ('A is negative');
```

4. Your test data should include values that check both options of an **IF ... THEN ... ELSE** statement.

5. **IF** ... **THEN** ... **ELSE** can be used to check for other program errors. In particular,
   a. Check for bad data by
   ```
   read (data);
   IF (bad data) THEN
       .
       . (error message)
       .
   ELSE
       .
       . (proceed with program)
       .
   ```
   b. Check for reasonable computed values by
   ```
   IF (unreasonable values) THEN
       .
       . (error message)
       .
   ELSE
       .
       . (proceed with program)
       .
   ```

   For example, if you were computing a student's test average, you can have
   ```
   IF (TestAverage > 100) OR (TestAverage < 0) THEN
       .
       . (error message)
       .
   ELSE
       .
       . (proceed with program)
       .
   ```

6. Be careful with **boolean** expressions. You should always keep expressions reasonably simple, use parentheses, and minimize use of **NOT**.

7. Be careful to properly match **ELSE**s with **IF**s in nested **IF** ... **THEN** ... **ELSE** statements. Indenting levels for writing code are very helpful.
   ```
   IF condition 1 THEN
       IF condition 2 THEN
           .
           . (action here)
           .
       ELSE
           .
           . (action here)
           .
   ELSE
       .
       . (action here)
       .
   ```

■ Summary

Key Terms

conditional statement	logical connective	logical operators
control structure	negation	compound statement
relational operator	compound **boolean**	nested **IF** statement
simple **boolean**	expression	
expression		

Keywords

boolean	AND, OR	IF ... THEN ... ELSE
true	NOT	CASE
false	IF ... THEN	OTHERWISE

Key Concepts

- Logical connectives **AND** and **OR** are used to connect **boolean** expressions.
- Relational operators are $=, >, <, >=, <=, <>$.
- Priority for evaluating relational operators is last.
- Logical operators **AND, OR,** and **NOT** are used as operators on **boolean** expressions.
- Variables of type **boolean** may only have values **true** or **false.**
- A complete priority listing of arithmetic operators, relational operators, and logical operators is

Expression or Operation	Priority
( )	1. Evaluate from inside out
NOT	2. Evaluate from left to right
$*$, /, **MOD, DIV, AND**	3. Evaluate from left to right
$+$, $-$, **OR**	4. Evaluate from left to right
$<, <=, >, >=, =, <>$	5. Evaluate from left to right

- A conditional statement is a program statement that transfers control to various branches of the program.
- Control structures are statements that allow the programmer to control the flow of execution of program statements.
- A compound statement is sometimes referred to as a **BEGIN ... END** statement; when it is executed, the entire segment of code between the **BEGIN** and **END** is treated like a single statement.
- **IF ... THEN ... ELSE** is a two-way conditional statement.
- A semicolon should not precede the **ELSE** portion of an **IF ... THEN ... ELSE** statement.
- If the **boolean** expression in an **IF ... THEN ... ELSE** statement is **true,** the command following **THEN** is executed; if the expression is **false,** the command following **ELSE** is executed.
- Multiple selections can be achieved by using decision statements within decision statements; this is termed multiway selection.
- **CASE** statements can be used as alternatives to multiple selection.
- **CASE** statements use an **END** without any **BEGIN.**
- **OTHERWISE,** in some versions of Pascal, can be used to handle values not listed in the **CASE** statement.

■ Chapter Review Exercises

In Exercises 1–8, indicate if the **boolean** expressions are **true, false,** or invalid.

1. $5 < (7 - 2)$
2. $((8 + 7) < 12)$ **OR** $((12 + 6) > 10)$
3. $((8 + 7) < 12)$ **AND** $((12 + 6) > 10)$
4. $8 + 7 > 4$ **OR** $6 + 3 > 5$
5. **NOT** $(12 > (5 + 9))$
6. $(18 <> (4 + 5 * 2))$ **AND** (**NOT** $(16 = (5 * 4)))$
7. 15 **MOD** $8 > 6$ **MOD** 3
8. **NOT** $(8.3 < 5.4)$ **OR** $(4.5 > -3.5)$

In Exercises 9–13, assume that C is of **char** type and B is of **boolean** type. State if the assignment statements are valid or invalid and, if invalid, explain why.

9. `B  :=  'false';`
10. `C  :=  'false';`
11. `B  :=  C;`
12. `B  :=  'T';`
13. `C  :=  'T';`

For Exercises 14–20, write a valid Pascal statement.

14. Add 4 to the value of the integer variable A if C is greater than 5.4.
15. Print the value of H if the **boolean** G is **true.**
16. Print either the word "Zero" or "Non-Zero" based upon the value of the real variable D.
17. Add 5 to the value of A and print out this new value if the integer H is negative.
18. Print the letter "A" if G > 90, "B" if G is between 80 and 90, or "C" if G is less than 80.
19. Read new values for A or B if either of them is less than 0.0.
20. Skip three lines if the value of the integer variable LineCnt is greater than 64.

Write Exercises 21 and 22 with nested **IF** statements.

21. If the value of the integer variable A is 2, square it. If it is 3, read in a new value for A. If it is 4 or 5, multiply it by 3 and print out the new value.
22. G is a character variable. If it contains either "A" or "D", print the letter. If it contains "B", print the value of the **real** variable H using a ten-character field with three places after the decimal. If it is "C", print the value of G.

23. Rewrite Exercise 21 using a **CASE** statement.

24. Rewrite Exercise 22 using a **CASE** statement.

25. Rewrite the program fragment in Example 5.13 using a **CASE** statement.

■ **Chapter Summary Program**

The Gas-N-Clean Service Station sells gasoline and has a car wash. Fees for the car wash are $1.25 with a gasoline purchase of $10.00 or more and $3.00 otherwise. Three kinds of gasoline are available: regular at $1.149, unleaded at $1.199, and super unleaded at $1.289 per gallon. Let's write a program that prints a statement for a customer. Input consists of number of gallons purchased, kind of gasoline purchased (R, U, S, or—for no purchase—N), and car wash desired (Y or N). A typical input line is

   9.7 UY

Use the constant definition section for gasoline prices. Your output should include appropriate messages. A first-level pseudocode development is

1. Get information
2. Compute charges
3. Print results

A refinement of this is

1. Get information
   1.1 read number of gallons
   1.2 read kind of gas purchased
   1.3 read car wash option
2. Compute charges
   2.1 compute gasoline charge
   2.2 compute car wash charge
   2.3 compute total

3. Print results
    3.1   print heading
    3.2   print amount due
    3.3   print closing meassage

A further refinement is

1. Get information
    1.1   read number of gallons
    1.2   read kind of gas purchased
    1.3   read car wash option
2. Compute charges
    2.1   compute gasoline charge
        2.1.1   **CASE** GasType **OF**
            'R'
            'U'
            'S'
            'N'
    2.2   compute car wash charge
        2.2.1   **IF** WashOption is yes **THEN**
            2.2.1.1   compute charge
            ELSE
            2.2.1.2   charge is 0
    2.3   compute total
        2.3.1   Total is GasCost plus WashCost
3. Print results
    3.1   print heading
    3.2   print amount due
        3.2.1   print gasoline results
        3.2.2   print car wash results
        3.2.3   print total
    3.3   print closing message

A complete program for this problem is

```
PROGRAM GasNClean (input,output);
(****************************************************************

     This program prints a statement for customers
     of Gas-N-Clean Service Station. It computes the
     amount due for gasoline and car wash. Features used
     include defined constants, CASE statements,
     and nested selection (IF ... THEN ... ELSE).


****************************************************************)

CONST
  Skip = ' ';
  Date = 'July 25, 1986';
  RegularPrice = 1.149;
  UnleadedPrice = 1.199;
  SuperUnleadedPrice = 1.289;
```

```
VAR
  Blank,                  (*  Read blanks from input                *)
  GasType,                (*  Type of gasoline purchased (R,U,S,N)  *)
  WashOption : char;      (*  Character designating option (Y,N)    *)
  NumGallons,             (*  Number of gallons purchased           *)
  GasCost,                (*  Computed cost for gasoline            *)
  WashCost,               (*  Car wash cost                         *)
  Total : real;           (*  Total amount due                      *)

BEGIN

(*  Get the data  *)

  writeln ('Enter number of gallons, and gas type (R,U,S, or N).');
  writeln ('Enter space, Y or N for car wash, and press <RETURN>.');
  readln (NumGallons, Blank, GasType, WashOption);

(*   Compute gas cost   *)

  CASE GasType OF
    'R': GasCost := NumGallons * RegularPrice;
    'U': GasCost := NumGallons * UnleadedPrice;
    'S': GasCost := NumGallons * SuperUnleadedPrice;
    'N': GasCost := 0.0
  END;   (*   of CASE   *)

(*   Compute carwash cost   *)

  IF WashOption = 'Y' THEN
    IF GasCost >= 10.0 THEN
      WashCost := 1.25
    ELSE
      WashCost := 3.0
  ELSE
    WashCost := 0.0;

  Total := GasCost + WashCost;

(*   Now print the results   *)

  writeln; writeln;
  writeln(Skip:20,'******************************************');
  writeln(Skip:20,'*                                        *');
  writeln(Skip:20,'*      Gas-N-Clean Service Station       *');
  writeln(Skip:20,'*                                        *');
  writeln(Skip:20,'*',Skip:10,Date,Skip:11,'*');
  writeln(Skip:20,'*                                        *');
  writeln(Skip:20,'******************************************');
  writeln;

  writeln(Skip:10,'Amount of gasoline purchased',Skip:12,
          NumGallons:6:3,' Gallons');
  write(Skip:10,'Price per gallon',Skip:22,'$');
```

```
CASE  GasType OF
  'R': writeln(RegularPrice:7:3);
  'U': writeln(UnleadedPrice:7:3);
  'S': writeln(SuperUnleadedPrice:7:3);
  'N': writeln(0.0:7:3)
END;   (*  of CASE  *)
writeln(Skip:10,'Total gasoline cost',Skip:19,'$',GasCost:6:2);
writeln(Skip:10,'Car wash cost',Skip:25,'$',WashCost:6:2);
writeln(Skip:50,'_____');
writeln(Skip:25,'Total due',Skip:14,'$',Total:6:2);
writeln;
writeln(Skip:28,,'Thank you for stopping.');
writeln;
writeln(Skip:30,'Please come again.');
writeln;
writeln(Skip:20,'Remember to buckle up and drive safely.');
writeln;writeln
END.
```

Output for the data line

```
9.7 UY
```

is

```
*****************************************
*                                       *
*      Gas-N-Clean Service Station      *
*                                       *
*          July 25, 1986                *
*                                       *
*****************************************


Amount of gasoline purchased        9.700   Gallons
Price per gallon                $   1.199
Total gasoline cost             $  11.63
Car wash cost                   $   1.25
                                    ------
              Total due         $  12.88

            Thank you for stopping.

              Please come again.

        Remember to buckle up and drive safely.
```

■ **Programming Problems**

The first 13 problems listed here are relatively short, but to complete them you must use concepts presented in this chapter.

The remaining programming problems are used as the basis for writing programs for Chapters 6 and 7 as well as for this chapter. In this chapter, each program is run on a very limited set of data. Material in Chapter 6 permits us to run the programs on larger data bases. In Chapter 7 we develop the programs using subprograms for various parts. Since these problems are referred to and used repeatedly, carefully choose which ones you work on and then develop them completely.

1. A three-minute telephone call to Scio, N.Y., costs $1.15. Each additional minute costs $0.26. Given the total length of a call in minutes, print the cost.

2. When you first learned to divide, you expressed answers using a quotient and a remainder rather than a fraction or decimal quotient. For example, if you divided 7 by 2, your answer would have been given as 3 r. 1. Given two integers, divide the larger by the smaller and print the answer in this form. Do not assume that the numbers are entered in any order.

3. Revise Problem 2 so that, if there is no remainder, you print only the quotient without a remainder or the letter r.

4. Given the coordinates of two points on a graph, find and print the slope of a line passing through them. Remember that the slope of a line can be undefined.

5. Mr. Lae Z. Programmer wishes to change his grading system. He gives five tests, then averages only the four highest scores. An average of 90 or better earns a grade of A, 80–89 a grade of B, and so on. Write a program that accepts five test scores and prints the average and grade according to this method.

6. Given the lengths of three sides of a triangle, print whether the triangle is scalene, isosceles, or equilateral.

7. Given the lengths of three sides of a triangle, determine whether or not the triangle is a right triangle using the Pythagorean theorem. Do not assume that the sides are entered in any order.

8. Given three integers, print only the largest.

9. The island nation of Babbage charges its citizens an income tax each year. The tax rate is based upon the following table:

Income	Tax Rate
$ 0 - 5,000	0
5,001 - 10,000	3%
10,001 - 20,000	5.5%
20,001 - 40,000	10.8%
over $40,000	23.7%

Write a program which, given a person's income, prints the tax owed rounded to the nearest dollar.

10. Many states base the cost of car registration on the weight of the vehicle. Suppose the fees are as follows:

Weight	Cost
up to 1500 pounds	$23.75
1500 to 2500 pounds	27.95
2500 to 3000 pounds	30.25
over 3000 pounds	37.00

Given the weight of a car, find and print the cost of registration.

11. The Mapes Railroad Corporation pays an annual bonus as a part of its profit sharing plan. This year all employees who have been with the company for more than ten years receive a bonus of 12 percent of their annual salary, and those who have worked at Mapes between five and nine years receive a bonus of 5.75 percent. Those who have been with the company less than five years receive no bonus.

Given the initials of an employee, the employee's annual salary, and the number of years employed with the company, find and print the bonus. All bonuses are rounded to the nearest dollar. Output should be in the following form.

```
MAPES RAILROAD CORP.

Employee xxx          Years of service nn
     Bonus earned: $ yyyy
```

12. A substance floats in water if its density (mass/volume) is less than 1 g/cc. It sinks if it is 1 or more. Given the mass and volume of an object, print whether it will sink or float.

13. Mr. Arthur Einstein, your school's physics teacher, wants a program for English to metric conversions. You are given a letter indicating whether the measurement is in pounds (P), feet (F), or miles (M). Such measures are to be converted to newtons, meters, and kilometers respectively. (There are 4.9 newtons in a pound, 3.28 feet in a meter, and 1.61 kilometers in a mile.)

Given an appropriate identifying letter and the size of the measurement, convert it to metric units. Print the answer in the following form.

```
3.0 miles = 4.83 kilometers.
```

14. The Caswell Catering and Convention Service has decided to revise its billing practices and is in need of a new program to prepare bills. The changes Caswell wishes to make follow.

a. For adults, the deluxe meals cost $15.80 per person and the standard meals cost $11.75 per person, dessert included. Children's meals cost 60 percent of adult meals. Everyone within a given party must be served the same meal type.

b. There are five banquet halls. Room A rents for $55.00, room B rents for $75.00, room C rents for $85.00, room D rents for $100,00, and room E rents for $130.00. The Caswells are considering increasing the room fees in about six months and this should be taken into account.

c. A surcharge, currently 7 percent, is added to the total bill if the catering is to be done on the weekend (Friday, Saturday, or Sunday).

d. All customers are charged the same rate for tip and tax, currently 18 percent. It is applied only to the cost of food.

e. To induce customers to pay promptly, a discount is offered if payment is made within ten days. This discount depends on the amount of the total bill. If the bill is less than $100.00, the discount is .5 percent; if the bill is at least $100.00 but less than $200.00, the discount is 1.5 percent; if the bill is at least $200.00 but less than $400.00, the discount is 3 percent; if the bill is at least $400.00 but less than $800.00, the discount is 4 percent; and, if the bill is at least $800.00, the discount is 5 percent.

Test your program on each of the following three customers.

a. Customer A is using room C on Tuesday night. The party includes 80 adults and 6 children. The standard meal is being served. The customer paid a $60.00 deposit.

b. Customer B is using room A on Saturday night. Deluxe meals are being served to 15 adults. A deposit of $50.00 was paid.

c. Customer C is using room D on Sunday afternoon. The party includes 30 children and 2 adults, all of whom are served the standard meal.

15. State University charges $90.00 for each semester hour of credit, $200.00 per semester for a regular room, $250.00 per semester for an air-conditioned room, and $400.00 per semester for food. All students are charged a $30.00 matriculation fee. Graduating students must also pay a $35.00 diploma fee. Write a program to compute the fees that must be paid by a student. Your program should include an appropriate warning message if a student is taking more than 21 credit hours or fewer than 12 credit hours. A typical line of data for one student would include room type (R or A), student number (in four digits), credit hours, and graduating (T or F).

16. Write a program to determine the day of the week a person was born given his or her birth date. Following are the steps you should use to find the day of the week corresponding to any date in this century.

 a. Divide the last two digits of the birth year by 4. Put the quotient (ignoring the remainder) in Total. For example, if the person was born in 1983, divide 83 by 4 and store 20 in Total.

 b. Add the last two digits of the birth year to Total.

 c. Using the following table, find the "month number" and add it to Total.

January = 1	July = 0
February = 4	August = 3
March = 4	September = 6
April = 0	October = 1
May = 2	November = 4
June = 5	December = 6

 d. If the year is a leap year (the last two digits of the year divide by four with zero remainder) and, if the month you are working with is either January or February, then subtract one from the Total.

 e. Find the remainder when Total is divided by seven. Look up the remainder in the following table to determine the day of the week the person was born. Note that you should not use this procedure if the person's year of birth is earlier than 1901.

1 = Sunday	5 = Thursday
2 = Monday	6 = Friday
3 = Tuesday	0 = Saturday
4 = Wednesday	

A typical line of data is

5 – 15 78

where the first entry (5 – 15) represents the birthdate (May 15) and the second entry (78) represents the birth year. If a person's birthday corresponds to the day the program is being run, the age is increased by one. An appropriate error message should be printed if a person's year of birth is before 1901.

17. Community Hospital needs a program to compute and print a statement for each patient. Charges for each day are as follows:

a. room charges
  ▪ private room—$125.00

- semiprivate room—$95.00
- ward—$75.00

b. television charge—$3.50
c. telephone charge—$1.75

Write a program to get a line of data, compute the patient's bill, and print an appropriate statement. A typical line of data is

5PYN

where "5" indicates the number of days spent in the hospital, "P" represents the room type (P, S, or W), "Y" represents the television option (Y or N), and "N" represents the telephone option (Y or N).

18. Write a program that converts degrees Fahrenheit to degrees Celsius and degrees Celsius to degrees Fahrenheit. In a typical data line, the temperature is followed by a designator (F or C) indicating whether the given temperature is Fahrenheit or Celsius.

19. The city of Mt. Pleasant bills its residents for sewage, water, and sanitation every three months. The sewer and water charge is figured according to how much water is used by the resident. The scale is

Amount (gallons)	Rate (per gallon)
Less than 1000	$0.03
1000 to 2000	$30 + $0.02 for each gallon over 1000
Greater than 2000	$50 + $0.015 for each gallon over 2000

The sanitation charge is $7.50 per month.

Write a program to read the number of months for which a resident is being billed (1, 2, or 3), how much water was used, and print out a statement with appropriate charges and messages. Use the constant definition section for all rates and include an error check for incorrect number of months. A typical line of data is

3 2175

20. Al Derrick, owner of the Lucky Wildcat Well Corporation, wants a program to help him decide whether or not a well is making money. Data for a well are on one line. It contains a single character (D for a dry well, O for oil found, and G for gas found) followed by a real number for the cost of the well. If an "O" or "G" is detected, the cost is followed by an integer indicating the volume of oil or gas found. In this case, there is also an "N" or "S" indicating whether or not sulfur is present. If there is sulfur, the "S" is followed by the percentage of sulfur present in the oil or gas

Unit prices are $5.50 for oil and $2.20 for gas. These should be defined as constants. Your program should compute the total revenue for a well (reduce output for sulfur present) and print out all pertinent information with an appropriate message to Mr. Derrick. A gusher is defined as a well with profit in excess of $50,000. A typical line of data is

S 0.15

21. The Mathematical Association of America hosts an annual summer meeting. Each state sends one official delegate to the section officer's meeting at this

summer session. The national organization reimburses the official state delegates according to the following scale:

Round-trip Mileage	Rate
Up to 500 miles	15 cents per mile
500 to 1000 miles	$75.00 plus 12 cents for each mile over 500
1000 to 1500 miles	$135.00 plus 10 cents for each mile over 1000
1500 to 2000 miles	$185.00 plus 8 cents for each mile over 1500
2000 to 3000 miles	$225.00 plus 6 cents for each mile over 2000
Over 3000 miles	$285.00 plus 5 cents for each mile over 3000

Write a program that accepts as input the number of round-trip miles for a delegate and computes the amount of reimbursement.

22. Mr. Lae Z. Programmer wants you to write a program to compute and print out the grade for a student in his class. The grade is based on three examinations (100 points possible on each), five quizzes (10 points each), and a 200-point final examination. Your output should include all scores, the percentage grade, and the letter grade. The grading scale is

$90 <= $ average $<= 100$ A
$80 <= $ average < 90 B
$70 <= $ average < 80 C
$60 <= $ average < 70 D
$\ 0 <= $ average < 60 E

Typical input is

80 93 85   (examination scores)

9 10 8 7 10   (quiz scores)

175   (final examination)

23. Mr. Lae Z. Progammer now wants you to modify Problem 22 by adding a check for bad data. Any time an unexpected score occurs, you are to print an appropriate error message and terminate the program.

24. A quadratic equation is one of the form

$ax^2 + bx + c = 0$

where $a \neq 0$. Solutions to this equation are given by

$$x = \frac{-b \pm \sqrt{b^2 - 4ac}}{2a}$$

where the quantity $(b^2 - 4ac)$ is referred to as the discriminant of the equation. Write a program to read three integers as the respective coefficients (a, b, and c), compute the discriminant, and print out the solutions. Use the following rules.

a. discriminant $= 0 \rightarrow$ single root
b. discriminant $< 0 \rightarrow$ no real number solution
c. discriminant $> 0 \rightarrow$ two distinct real solutions

25. The sign on the attendant's booth at the Pentagon parking lot is

PENTAGON VISITOR PARKING

Cars:

First 2 hours	Free
Next 3 hours	0.50/hour
Next 10 hours	0.25/hour

Trucks:

First 1 hour	Free
Next 2 hours	1.00/hour
Next 12 hours	0.75/hour

Senior Citizens: No charge

Write a program that accepts as input a one-character designator (C, T, or S) followed by the number of minutes a vehicle has been in the lot. The program should then compute the appropriate charge and print a ticket for the customer. Any part of an hour is to be counted as a full hour.

26. Milt Walker, the chief of advertising for the Isabella Potato Industry, wants you to write a program to compute an itemized bill and total cost of his "This Spud's for You!" ad campaign. The standard black and white full-page ads have base prices as follows:

Drillers' News (code D)	$ 400
Playperson (code P)	$2000
Meadow and Creek (code M)	$ 900
Independent News (code I)	$1200

Each ad is allowed 15 lines of print with a rate of $20.00 for each line in excess of 15 lines. Each ad is either black and white (code B) and subject to the base prices, or is in color (code C) and subject to the following rates:

| Three color (code T) | 40 percent increase over base |
| Full color (code F) | 60 percent increase over base |

Write a program to input Milt's choice of magazine (D, P, M, or I), the number of lines of print (integer), and either black and white (B) or color (C) with a choice of three colors (T) or full color (F). Output should include an appropriate title, all the information and costs used to compute the price of an ad, the total price of the ad, and finally the total price of all ads.

27. Write a program to add, subtract, multiply and divide fractions. Input consists of a single line representing a fraction arithmetic problem. Your program should

a. check for division by zero
b. check for proper operation symbols
c. print the problem in its original form
d. print the answer
e. print all fractions in horizontal form

For the sample input

2/3 + 1/2

sample output is

```
              2   1
Problem:      - + -
              3   2

              7
Answer:       -
              6
```

CHAPTER 6

Looping Statements

The previous chapter on selection introduced you to a programming concept that takes advantage of a computer's speed. A second major concept utilizing this feature of a computer is repetition.

This chapter examines the different methods Pascal permits for performing some process repeatedly. For example, as yet we cannot conveniently write a program that solves the simple problem of adding the integers from 1 to 100. By the end of this chapter, you will be able to solve this problem three different ways. The three forms of repetition (loops) are **FOR . . . TO . . . DO, WHILE . . . DO**, and **REPEAT . . . UNTIL**.

FOR . . . TO . . . DO is a *fixed repetition* loop: it causes a fragment of code to be executed a predetermined number of times. **WHILE . . . DO** is a *pretest loop:* it examines a **boolean** expression before executing a fragment. **REPEAT . . . UNTIL** is a *posttest loop:* it examines a **boolean** expression after a fragment is executed.

■ 6.1
Fixed
Repetition
Loops

OBJECTIVES

- to understand when fixed repetition loops should be used in a program
- to understand how the loop control variable is used in a loop

Fixed repetition or *iterated loops* are used when you know in advance how often a segment of code needs to be repeated. For instance, you might have a known number of repetitions of a segment of code for: (1) a program to add the integers from 1 to 100; (2) programs that use a fixed number of data lines, for example, game statistics for a team of twelve basketball players; or (3) attractive output, such as a diamond of asterisks.

```
            *
          *   *
        *       *
      *           *
    *               *
      *           *
        *       *
          *   *
            *
```

179

- to understand the flow of control when using a fixed repetition loop in a program
- to use a **FOR ... TO ... DO** loop in a program
- to use a **FOR ... DOWNTO ... DO** loop in a program

FOR ... TO ... DO Loops

Fixed repetition of a segment of code in Pascal is accomplished by using a **FOR ... TO ... DO** loop. The form necessary for using such a loop is

> **FOR** index := initial value **TO** final value **DO**
>   statement;
>
> or
>
> **FOR** index := initial value **TO** final value **DO**
>   **BEGIN**
>   statement 1;
>   statement 2;
>   .
>   .
>   .
>   statement n
>   **END**;

A **FOR ... TO ... DO** loop is considered to be a single executable statement. It begins with the reserved word **FOR** and ends with a semicolon. The actions performed in the loop are referred to as the body of the loop. A structure diagram is given in Figure 6.1. The problem of adding the integers from 1 to 100 needs only one statement in the body of the loop. This problem can be solved by

```
Sum := 0;
FOR J := 1 TO 100 DO
   Sum := Sum + J;
```

FIGURE 6.1
FOR ... TO ... DO
structure diagram

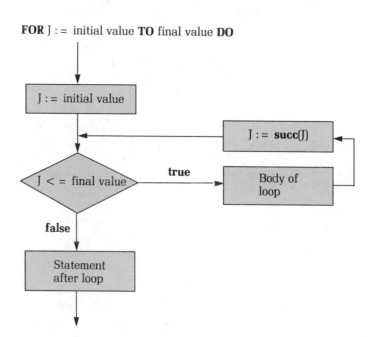

For another example using this type of loop, assume you are writing a program that requires thirty test scores to be read as input. Furthermore, each score is to be added to Total. The code for this is

```
Total := 0;
FOR J := 1 TO 30 DO
   BEGIN
      writeln ('Enter a score and press <RETURN>.');
      readln (Score);
      Total := Total + Score
   END;
```

Some comments concerning the syntax and form of **FOR ... TO ... DO** loops are now necessary.

1. The words **FOR, TO,** and **DO** are reserved and must be used only in the order **FOR ... TO ... DO.**
2. The *index* must be declared as a variable. Although it can be any ordinal data type, we will use mostly integer examples.
3. The index variable can be any valid identifier. Many texts and programmers use I, J, and K for these variables. However, since I is easily misread as a 1, we will usually not use it.
4. Within the loop, the index can be used in computations, comparisons, or output. However, never use the index variable on the left of an assignment statement within a loop.
5. The initial and final values may be constants or variable expressions with appropriate values.
6. Never change the final value for the loop while in the body of the loop.
7. The loop is repeated for each value of the index in the range indicated by the initial and final values.
8. The first time through the loop, the index is assigned the initial value. Each successive time through the loop, the index assumes the next value in the specified range.
9. The index may not retain the last value it had during the last time through the loop. When the loop is finished, the index variable may no longer have an assigned value.
10. The internal logic of a **FOR ... TO ... DO** loop is
    a. the index is assigned the initial value
    b. the index value is compared to the final value
    c. if the index value is less than or equal to the final value
       - the body of the loop is executed
       - the index value is incremented by one
       - another check with the final value is made
    d. if the index value exceeds the final value
       - the index may revert to an unassigned status
       - control of the program is transferred to the first statement following the loop
11. Do not put a semicolon after the **DO** in a **FOR ... TO ... DO** loop.

Let's now consider some examples that illustrate these features of **FOR ... TO ... DO** loops.

EXAMPLE 6.1

Let's write a segment of code to list the integers from 1 to 10 together with their squares and cubes. This can be done by

```
FOR J := 1 TO 10 DO
    writeln (J:10, J * J:10, J * J * J:10);
```

This segment produces

```
 1           1            1
 2           4            8
 3           9           27
 4          16           64
 5          25          125
 6          36          216
 7          49          343
 8          64          512
 9          81          729
10         100         1000
```

Initial and final values for the loop control variable for a **FOR ... TO ... DO** loop can be values in expressions. Example 6.2 illustrates how you can allow such a limit to be entered from the keyboard.

EXAMPLE 6.2

The following segment of code prints a chart of integers together with their squares and cubes as illustrated in Example 6.1. However, this segment allows the size of the chart to be entered from the keyboard.

```
writeln ('Please enter the final value and press <RETURN>.');
readln (ChartSize);
writeln; writeln;
FOR J := 1 TO ChartSize DO
    writeln (J:10, J * J:10, J * J * J:10);
```

EXAMPLE 6.3

Construct a **FOR ... TO ... DO** loop that shows what happens when the initial value is greater than the final value.

```
writeln ('This is before the loop.');
writeln;
FOR J := 10 TO 1 DO
    writeln (J);
writeln ('This is after the loop.');
```

This segment of code produces the output

```
This is before the loop.

This is after the loop.
```

Because the initial value of the index exceeded the ending value originally, control of the program was transferred to the first executable statement following the loop.

EXAMPLE 6.4

Let's use a **FOR** ... **TO** ... **DO** loop to produce the following design.

```
****************************
*                          *
*                          *
*                          *
*                          *
*                          *
****************************
```

This problem requires a bit of development. A first-level pseudocode development is

1. Produce the top line
2. Produce the center lines
3. Produce the bottom line

and a second-level development of step 2 is

2. Produce the center lines
   2.1 **FOR** J := 1 **TO** 5 **DO**
       produce a middle line

We can now code the algorithm as follows:

```
PROGRAM DesignBox (output);

CONST
  Splats = '****************************';
  Edge =   '*                          *';
  Skip = ' ';

VAR
  J : integer;

BEGIN
  writeln (Skip:10, Splats);
  FOR J := 1 TO 5 DO
    writeln (Skip:10, Edge);
  writeln (Skip:10, Splats)
END.
```

The index of a loop can also be used for formatting. This is particularly useful when the output is in the form of a design. The next example illustrates this.

EXAMPLE 6.5

Let's write a **FOR** ... **TO** ... **DO** loop to produce the following design.

```
    **
   *  *
  *    *
 *      *
*        *
```

Assuming the first asterisk is in column 20, the following loop produces the desired result. Note carefully how the output is formatted.

```
FOR J := 1 TO 5 DO
  writeln ('*':21-J, '*': 2*J-1);
```

EXAMPLE 6.6

Let's use a **FOR** ... **TO** ... **DO** loop to print the letters of the alphabet on a diagonal. Since **char** is an ordinal data type, this can be accomplished by

```
Indent := 1;
FOR Ch := 'A' TO 'Z' DO
  BEGIN
     writeln (Ch:Indent);
     Indent := Indent + 1
  END;
```

which produces

```
A
 B
  C
   D
    E
     F
      G
       H
        I
         J
          K
           L
            M
             N
              O
               P
                Q
                 R
                  S
                   T
                    U
                     V
                      W
                       X
                        Y
                         Z
```

■

SELF QUIZ 6.1

Write a segment of code to print a diamond of asterisks as illustrated.

EXAMPLE 6.7

When computing compound interest, it is necessary to evaluate the quantity $(1 + R)^N$ where R is the interest rate for one time period and N is the number of time periods. A **FOR** ... **TO** ... **DO** loop can be used to perform this computation. If we declare a variable Base, this can be solved by

```
Base := 1;
FOR J := 1 TO N DO
   Base := Base * (1 + R);
```

A **FOR** ... **TO** ... **DO** loop can also be used to temporarily halt messages being printed to the screen. This is necessary because long messages may be difficult to read. At the point in your program where such a pause is desired, a loop such as

```
FOR J := 1 TO 1000 DO;
```

produces the desired effect. This causes the loop (which does nothing) to be executed 1000 times before the program continues. The length of the pause can be varied by changing the loop limit.

FOR ... DOWNTO ... DO Loops

A second fixed repetition loop is the **FOR** ... **DOWNTO** ... **DO** loop. This loop does exactly what you expect; it is identical to a **FOR** ... **TO** ... **DO** loop except the index variable is decreased by one instead of increased by one each time through the loop. Proper form and syntax for a loop of this type are

> **FOR** index := initial value **DOWNTO** final value **DO**
>   statement;
>
> or
>
> **FOR** index := initial value **DOWNTO** final value **DO**
>   **BEGIN**
>   statement 1;
>   statement 2;
>   .
>   .
>   .
>   statement *n*
>   **END**;

The conditions on **FOR** ... **DOWNTO** ... **DO** loops are the same as **FOR** ... **TO** ... **DO** loops. We now consider some examples of **FOR** ... **DOWNTO** ... **DO** loops.

EXAMPLE 6.8

Illustrate the index values of a **FOR** ... **DOWNTO** ... **DO** loop by writing the index value during each pass through the loop. The segment of code for this is

```
FOR K := 20 DOWNTO 15 DO
   writeln ('K =', K:4);
```

and the output is

```
K =   20
K =   19
K =   18
K =   17
K =   16
K =   15
```

EXAMPLE 6.9

Let's use a **FOR** ... **DOWNTO** ... **DO** loop to produce the design

```
***
 ***
  ***
   ***
    ***
```

If we assume the first line of output ends in column 20, the code for this is

```
FOR J: = 20 DOWNTO 16 DO
    writeln ('***':J);
```

■

Both **FOR** ... **TO** ... **DO** and **FOR** ... **DOWN TO** ... **DO** loops are generally referred to as **FOR** loops. The form intended should be clear from the context.

Determine the output from the following fragment of code.

```
Sum := 0;
FOR J := 3 DOWNTO -2 DO
    BEGIN
        Sum := Sum + J;
        writeln ('*':10+abs(J))
    END;
writeln (Sum:15);
```

Writing Style for Loops

As you can see, writing style is an important consideration when writing code using loops. There are three features to consider. First, the body of the loop should be indented. For example, compare the following:

```
FOR J := 1 TO 10 DO
    BEGIN
        read (Num, Amt);
        Total1 := Total1 + Amt;
        Total2 := Total2 + Num;
        writeln ('The number is', Num:6:2)
    END;
writeln ('The total amount is', Total1:8:2);
Average := Total2/10;
```

```
FOR J := 1 TO 10 DO
BEGIN
read (Num, Amt);
Total1 := Total1 + Amt;
Total2 := Total2 + Num;
writeln ('The number is', Num:6:2)
END;
writeln ('The total amount is', Total1:8:2);
Average := Total2/10;
```

Because of the indenting in the first segment, it is easier to determine what is contained in the body of the loop than it is in the second segment.

Second, blank lines can be used before and after a loop for better readability. Compare the following:

```
readln (X,Y);
writeln (X:6:2, Y:6:2);
writeln;

FOR J := -3 TO 5 DO
  writeln (J:3, '*':5);

Sum := Sum + X;
writeln (Sum:10:2);


readln (X,Y);
writeln (X:6:2, Y:6:2);
writeln;
FOR J := -3 TO 5 DO
  writeln (J:3, '*':5);
Sum := Sum + X;
writeln (Sum:10:2);
```

Again, the first segment is clearer because it emphasizes that the entire loop is a single executable statement and makes it easy to locate the loop.

Third, comments before, during, and after loops make them more readable. In particular, a comment should always accompany the **END** of a compound statement that is the body of a loop. The general form for this is

```
(*  Beginning of a loop  *)

FOR J := 1 TO 50 DO
  BEGIN
    .
    .  (body of the loop)
    .
  END;  (*  of FOR loop  *)

(*  Now continue with the program  *)
```

There are two features you may wish to incorporate as you work with **FOR** loops. First, the loop limit can be defined as a constant or declared as a variable and then have an assigned value. Thus, you can have

```
CONST
  LoopLimit = 50;
```

Second, the loop control variable can be declared as

```
VAR
  LCV : integer;
```

The loop can then be written as

```
FOR LCV := 1 TO LoopLimit DO
    .
    .  (body of the loop here)
    .
```

A NOTE OF INTEREST

Ada Augusta Byron

Ada Augusta Byron (1815–1852), Countess of Lovelace, sister of the poet, Lord Byron, became familiar with the work of Charles Babbage when she was translating a paper from French to English. Eventually, she became a full collaborator with Babbage, who was the first to propose the concept on which today's computers are based. Her most significant contribution was the concept of a loop. She noted that a single calcula-tion could be performed by a repetition of a sequence of instructions. By using a conditional jump, her method could perform calculations with a fraction of the effort previously required.

Because of her work, she is recognized as the first programmer. In honor of her work, a state-of-the-art programming language (Ada) has been named after her.

We close this section with an example that uses a **FOR** loop to solve a problem.

EXAMPLE 6.10

Suppose you have been asked to write a program to compute the test average for each of thirty students in a class and the overall class average. Assume each student has taken four tests. A first-level pseudocode development is

1. Print a heading
2. Initialize Total
3. Process data for each of thirty students
4. Compute class average
5. Print a summary

A **FOR** loop can be used to implement step 3. The step can first be refined to

3. Process data for each student
   3.1 get data for a student
   3.2 compute average
   3.3 add to Total
   3.4 print student data

The code for this step is

```
FOR J := 1 TO ClassSize DO
   BEGIN
      writeln ('Enter four scores and press <RETURN>.');
      readln (Score1, Score2, Score3, Score4);
      Average := (Score1 + Score2 + Score3 + Score4)/4;
      Total := Total + Average;
      writeln;
      writeln ('Your average is', Average:8:2)
   END;
```

■

Exercises 6.1

In Exercises 1–4, what output is produced from each segment of code?

```
1. FOR K := 3 TO 8 DO
      writeln ('*':K);
2. FOR J := 1 TO 10 DO
      writeln (J:4, ' :', (10-J):5);
3. A := 2;
   FOR J := (3 * 2 - 4) TO 10 * A DO
      writeln ('**', J:4);
```

```
4. FOR J := 50 DOWNTO 30 DO
      writeln (51 - J:5);
```

For Exercises 5 and 6, write test programs.

5. Assign a value to the loop control variable inside the loop.
6. Examine the value of the loop control variable before the loop and after the loop.

In Exercises 7–10, write segments of code using **FOR ... TO ... DO** or **FOR ... DOWNTO ... DO** loops to produce the design indicated.

```
7. *        8. ***              9.      *           10. *********
   *           ***                   *  *                *******
   *           ***                 *      *              *****
   *           ***               *          *            ***
               ***             **** ****                  *
               ***                *  *
               ***                *  *
               ***                ***
```

In Exercises 11–14, find all the errors.

```
11. FOR K := 1 TO 5 DO;
       writeln (K);
       Sum := 0;
12. FOR J := 1 TO 10 DO
       read (A);
       Sum := Sum + A;
    writeln (Sum:15);
13. Sum := 0;
    FOR J = -3 TO 3 DO
       Sum := Sum + J;
14. A := 0;
    FOR K := 1 TO 10 DO
       BEGIN
          A := A + K;
          writeln (K:5, A:5, A + K:5)
       END;
    writeln (K:5, A:5, A + K:5);
```

In Exercises 15 and 16, produce the output using both a **FOR ... TO ... DO** loop and a **FOR ... DOWNTO ... DO** loop.

```
15. 1   2   3   4   5
16. *
       *
          *
             *
                *
```

17. Rewrite the following segment of code using a **FOR ... DOWNTO ... DO** loop to produce the same result.

```
Sum := 0;
FOR K := 1 TO 4 DO
   BEGIN
      writeln ('*':21+K);
      Sum := Sum + K
   END;
```

18. Rewrite the following segment of code using a **FOR** ... **TO** ... **DO** loop to produce the same result.

```
FOR J := 10 DOWNTO 2 DO
  writeln (J:J);
```

19. Write a complete program that produces a table showing the temperature equivalents in degrees Fahrenheit and degrees Celsius.

20. Write a complete program that produces a chart consisting of the multiples of 5 from −50 to 50 together with the squares and cubes of these numbers.

21. The formula $A = P(1 + R)^N$ can be used to compute the amount due (A) when a principal (P) has been borrowed at a monthly rate (R) for a period of N months. Write a complete program to read in the principal, annual interest rate (divide by 12 for monthly rate), and number of months. Produce a chart that shows how much is due at the end of each month.

■ 6.2
Pretest Loops

In Section 6.1, **FOR** loops, loops in which the body of the loop is repeated a fixed number of times, were presented. There are problems in which this loop is inappropriate, since a segment of code may need to be repeated a variable number of times. For example, if you are working with an unknown number of items, you will need to continue reading data until you reach some special value. These special values are called *sentinel values*. Typically, they are values that are obviously not part of the data; for example, when you are working with test scores, −999 could be used as a sentinel value. The condition controlling the loop must be a variable rather than a constant. Pascal provides two looping statements with variable control conditions, one with a pretest condition and one with a posttest condition (posttest loops are examined in the next section).

Pretest Condition

The first type of variable control loop we examine is a pretest or *entrance controlled loop*. In this type of loop, a condition is checked before going through the loop. The condition controls whether or not the body of the loop is executed. If the condition is **true,** the body of the loop is executed. If the condition is **false,** the program skips to the first line of code following the loop.

Variable condition loops are needed to solve problems where conditions change within the body of the loop. These conditions involve sentinal values, **boolean** flags, or arithmetic expressions with changing values. A pretest loop is useful if, for example, you wish to keep entering values from the keyboard until a special value is entered to denote there are no more data. You could also have a message appear on the screen to specifically ask whether the operator wants to continue. Such a message could be

```
Any more data?  Y or N
```

Loops controlled by these conditions must be able to be terminated whenever the operator desires.

WHILE . . . DO Loops

The pretest loop in Pascal is a **WHILE** . . . **DO** loop. The condition controlling the loop is a **boolean** expression written between the reserved words **WHILE** and **DO.** Correct form and syntax for such a loop are

```
WHILE boolean expression DO
   statement;
or
WHILE boolean expression DO
   BEGIN
      statement 1;
      statement 2;
          .
          .
          .
      statement n
   END;
```

The structure diagram for a **WHILE** . . . **DO** loop is given in Figure 6.2.

Before analyzing the components of this statement, let's consider two short examples.

FIGURE 6.2
WHILE . . . **DO** structure diagram

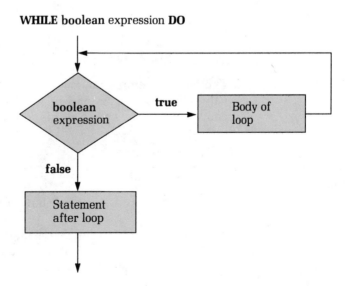

WHILE boolean expression **DO**

EXAMPLE 6.11

This example allows you to find the total of scores to be entered from a keyboard. A sentinel value is used.

```
Sum := 0;
writeln ('Enter a score; -999 to stop.');
readln (Score);
WHILE Score <> -999 DO
   BEGIN
      Sum := Sum + Score;
      writeln ('Enter a score; -999 to stop.');
      readln (Score)
   END;
```

Note that one value is read outside the loop so that the **boolean** expression

```
Score <> -999
```

is valid the first time it is evaluated.   ■

EXAMPLE 6.12

This example prints some powers of two.

```
PowerOf2 := 1;
WHILE PowerOf2 < 100 DO
   BEGIN
      writeln (PowerOf2);
      PowerOf2 := PowerOf2 * 2
   END;
```

The output from this segment of code is

```
    1
    2
    4
    8
   16
   32
   64
```
■

With these examples in mind, let's examine the general form for using a **WHILE** ... **DO** loop.

1. The **boolean** expression can be any expression that has **boolean** values. Standard examples include relational operators and **boolean** variables; thus, each of the following is appropriate.

```
WHILE J < 10 DO
WHILE A <> B DO
WHILE Flag = true DO
WHILE Flag DO
```

2. The **boolean** expression must have a value prior to entering the loop.
3. The body of the loop can be a single statement or a compound statement.
4. Program control when using a **WHILE** ... **DO** loop follows in order as shown.
   a. The loop condition is examined.

A NOTE OF INTEREST

Debugging Space Flight Programs

J. F. ("Jack") Clemons, manager of avionics flight software development and verification for the space shuttle on-board computers, was recently interviewed by Alfred Spector, editor for *Communications of the ACM*. In response to a question about checking software, Clemons stated: "One of the abort simulations they chose to test is called a 'TransAtlantic abort,' which supposes that the crew can neither return to the launch site nor go into orbit. The objective is to land in Spain after dumping some fuel. The crew was about to go into this dump sequence when all four of our flight computer machines locked up and went 'catatonic.' Had this been the real thing, the shuttle would probably have had difficulty landing. This kind of scenario could only occur under a very specific and unlikely combination of physical and aerodynamic conditions; but there it was: Our machines all stopped. Our greatest fear had materialized—a generic software problem.

"We pulled four or five of our best people together, and they spent two days trying to understand what had happened. It was a very subtle problem.

"We started outside the module with the bad branch and worked our way backward until we found the code that was responsible. The module at fault was a multipurpose piece of code that could be used to dump fuel at several points of the trajectory. In this particular case, it had been invoked the first time during ascent, had gone through part of its process, and was then stopped by the crew. It had stopped properly. Later on, it was invoked again from a different point in the software, when it was supposed to open the tanks and dump some additional fuel. There were some counters in the code, however, that had not been reinitialized. The module restarted, thinking it was on its first pass. One variable that was not reinitialized was a counter that was being used as the basis for a **GOTO**. The code was expecting this counter to have a value between 1 and x, say, but because the counter was not reinitialized, it started out with a high value. Eventually the code encountered a value beyond the expected range, say x + 1, which caused it to branch out of its logic. It was an 'uncomputed' **GOTO**. Until we realized that the code had been called a second time, we couldn't figure out how the counter could return a value so high."

b. If the loop condition is **true,** the entire body of the loop is executed before another check is made.

c. If the loop condition is **false,** control is transferred to the first line following the loop. For example,

```
A := 1;
WHILE A < 0 DO
   BEGIN
      Num := 5;
      writeln (Num);
      A := A + 10
   END;
writeln (A);
```

produces the single line of output

1

5. Provision must be made for appropriately changing the loop control condition in the body of the loop. If no such changes are made, several things can happen.

a. If the loop condition is **true** and no changes are made, a condition called an *infinite loop* is caused. For example,

```
A := 1;
WHILE A > 0 DO
   BEGIN
      Num := 5;
      writeln (Num)
   END;
writeln (A);
```

The condition A > 0 is **true,** the body is executed, and the condition is retested. However, since the condition is not changed within the loop body, it is always **true** and causes an infinite loop. It does not produce a compilation error, but when you run the program, the output will be a list of 5s. The length of this list depends on the time limit your machine sets for a program.

b. If the loop condition is **true** and changes are made, but the condition never becomes **false,** you again have an infinite loop. An example of this is

```
PowerOf3 := 1;
WHILE PowerOf3 <> 100 DO
   BEGIN
      writeln (PowerOf3);
      PowerOf3 := PowerOf3 * 3
   END;
```

Since the variable PowerOf3 is never assigned the value 100, the condition PowerOf3 <> 100 is always **true** and you never get out of the loop.

Writing Style

Writing style for **WHILE . . . DO** loops should be similar to that adopted for **FOR** loops; that is, indenting, skipping lines, and comments should all be used to enhance readability.

Using Counters

Since **WHILE . . . DO** loops may be repeated a variable number of times, it is a common practice to count the number of times the loop body is executed. This is accomplished by declaring an appropriately named integer variable, initializing it to zero before the loop, and then incrementing it by one each time through the loop. For example, if you use Count for your variable name, Example 6.12 (in which we printed some powers of two) can be modified to

```
Count := 0;
PowerOf2 := 1;
```

```
WHILE PowerOf2 < 100 DO
   BEGIN
      writeln (PowerOf2);
      PowerOf2 := PowerOf2 * 2;
      Count := Count + 1
   END;  (*  of WHILE ... DO  *)

writeln;
writeln ('There are',Count:4,
         'powers of 2 less than 100.');
```

The output from this segment of code is

```
   1
   2
   4
   8
  16
  32
  64
```

```
There are    7 powers of 2 less than 100.
```

Although the process is tedious, it is instructive to trace the values of variables through a loop where a *counter* is used. Therefore, let's consider the segment of code we have just seen. Before the loop is entered, we have

0		1
Count		PowerOf2

The loop control is PowerOf2 < 100 or 1 < 100. Since this is **true,** the loop body is executed and the new values become

1		2
Count		PowerOf2

Prior to each successive time through the loop, the condition PowerOf2 < 100 is checked. Thus, the loop produces the sequence of values

Count	PowerOf2
1	2
2	4
3	8
4	16
5	32
6	64
7	128

Since 128 < 100 is **false,** control is transferred to the line following the loop. Although PowerOf2 is 128, the remainder of the loop is executed before checking the loop condition. Once a loop is entered, it is executed completely before the loop control condition is reexamined.

EXAMPLE 6.13

If a counter is added to Example 6.11, the class average can be computed. This is accomplished by

```
Sum := 0;
Count := 0;
writeln ('Enter a score; -999 to stop.');
readln (Score);
WHILE Score <> -999 DO
   BEGIN
      Count := Count + 1;
      Sum := Sum + Score;
      writeln ('Enter a score; -999 to stop.');
      readln (Score)
   END;
Average := Sum/Count;
```

■

SELF QUIZ 6.3

What output is produced from the following segment of code?

```
Count := 0;
Sum := 0;
Num := 1;

WHILE Num < 100 DO
   BEGIN
      Count := Count + 1;
      Sum := Sum + Num;
      Num := Num * 3
   END;

writeln ('Count is', Count:5);
writeln ('Sum is', Sum:5);
writeln ('Num is', Num:5);
```

The next example illustrates the use of a **WHILE ... DO** loop where the **boolean** condition is controlled by message from the person entering values from the keyboard.

EXAMPLE 6.14

Write a segment of code to compute the wages for several employees. Assume each line of data consists of information about one employee. It contains three initials, the hourly rate (real), and the number of hours worked (integer). There are blanks before each number; thus, a data line can be

```
MTM 14.60 40
```

The person running the program can be allowed to control termination of the process by

```
Continue := 'Y';
WHILE Continue = 'Y' DO
   BEGIN
      .
      . (process here)
      .
      writeln ('Any more?  Y to continue, N to stop.');
      read(Continue)
   END; (* of WHILE ... DO *)
```

If GrossWage is computed by

```
GrossWage := HourRate * Hours;
```

and you wish to print out information for each employee, you can have

```
Continue := 'Y';
WHILE Continue = 'Y' DO
   BEGIN
      write ('Enter three initials, hourly rate,');
      writeln ('and hours worked.');
      readln (Init1, Init2, Init3, HourRate, Hours);
      GrossWage := HourRate * Hours;
      writeln;
      writeln ('Employee initials are:', Skip:8, Init1,
               Init2, Init3);
      writeln ('The hourly rate is:', Skip:11, HourRate:5:2);
      writeln ('Hours worked:', Skip:17, Hours);
      writeln ('Gross wages are:', Skip:14, GrossWage:6:2);
      writeln; writeln;
      writeln ('Any more? Y to continue, N to stop.');
      readln (Continue)
   END; (*  of WHILE ... DO  *)
```

A typical run of this segment using data for two employees produces

```
Enter three initials, hourly rate, and hours worked.
MTM 14.60 40

Employee initials are:      MTM
The hourly rate is:         14.60
Hours worked:               40
Gross wages are:            584.00

Any more?  Y to conintue, N to stop.
Y
Enter three initials, hourly rate, and hours worked.
MJB 21.0 35

Employee initials are:      MJB
The hourly rate is:         21.00
Hours worked:               35
Gross wages are:            735.00

Any more?  Y to conintue, N to stop.
N
```

Multiple Conditions

All previous examples and illustrations of **WHILE** ... **DO** loops used simple **boolean** expressions. However, since any **boolean** expression can be used as a loop control condition, compound **boolean** expressions can also be used. For example,

```
read (A,B);
WHILE (A > 0) AND (B > 0) DO
```

```
BEGIN
  writeln (A:10,B:10);
  A := A-5;
  B := B-3
END;
```

goes through the body of the loop only when the **boolean** expression (A > 0) **AND** (B > 0) is **true.** Thus, if the values of A and B are

17 8

the output from this segment of code is

```
 17          8
 12          5
  7          2
```

Compound **boolean** expressions can be as complex as you wish to make them. However, if several conditions are involved, the program can become difficult to read and debug; therefore, you may wish to redesign your solution to avoid this problem.

Exercises 6.2

1. Compare and contrast **FOR** loops with **WHILE** ... **DO** loops.

2. Write a test program that illustrates what happens when you have an infinite loop.

In Exercises 3–7, what output is produced from the segment of code?

```
3. K := 1;
   WHILE K <= 10 DO
     BEGIN
       writeln (K);
       K := K + 1
     END;
4. A := 1;
   WHILE 17 MOD A <> 5 DO
     BEGIN
       writeln (A, 17 MOD A);
       A := A + 1
     END;
5. A := 2;
   B := 50;
   WHILE A < B DO
     A := A * 3;
   writeln (A,B);
6. Count := 0;
   Sum := 0;
   WHILE Count < 5 DO
     BEGIN
       Count := Count + 1;
       Sum := Sum + Count;
       writeln ('The partial sum is', Sum:4)
     END;
   writeln ('The count is', Count:4);
```

```
7. X := 3.0;
   Y := 2.0;
   WHILE X * Y < 100 DO
     X := X * Y;
   writeln (X:10:2, Y:10:2);
```

In Exercises 8–11, indicate which are infinite loops and explain why they are infinite.

```
8. J := 1;
   WHILE J < 10 DO
     writeln (J);
     J := J + 1;

9. A := 2;
   WHILE A < 20 DO
     BEGIN
       writeln (A);
       A := A * 2
     END;

10. A := 2;
    WHILE A <> 20 DO
      BEGIN
        writeln (A);
        A := A * 2
      END;

11. B := 15;
    WHILE B DIV 3 = 5 DO
      BEGIN
        writeln (B, B DIV 5);
        B := B - 1
      END;
```

In Exercises 12–15, write a segment of code that uses a **WHILE . . . DO** loop.

12. Read three values and print their sum as long as they are all positive.
13. Read three values and print their sum as long as one of them is positive.
14. Print a table of cubes of integers from 1 to N where the value of N is entered from the keyboard.
15. Print a table of squares of integers starting with 1 and continuing until the difference of consecutive squares exceeds 25.

16. Write a complete program that will find the smallest positive integer N such that the sum $1 + 2 + \ldots + N$ exceeds some value entered from the keyboard.

17. Write a segment of code that reads a positive integer and prints a list of powers of that integer that are less than 10,000.

18. Modify the code of Example 6.14 to incorporate a counter to count the number of employees and computations of total hours worked, total wages paid, and the average wage paid.

■ 6.3
Posttest Loops

OBJECTIVES

- to understand what is meant by a posttest loop
- to understand the flow of control using a posttest loop
- to use posttest loops in a program
- to use posttest loops with multiple conditions

The previous two sections discussed two kinds of repetition. We looked at fixed repetition using **FOR** loops and variable repetition using **WHILE** ... **DO** loops. Pascal provides a second form of variable repetition, a **REPEAT** ... **UNTIL** loop. The difference between the two forms of variable repetitions is that the **WHILE** ... **DO** loop is an entrance controlled (pretest) loop and the **REPEAT** ... **UNTIL** loop is an *exit controlled* (posttest) loop. We now examine the **REPEAT** ... **UNTIL** loop.

REPEAT ... UNTIL Loops

The basic form and syntax for a **REPEAT** ... **UNTIL** loop is

```
REPEAT
    statement 1;
    statement 2;
         .
         .
         .
    statement n
UNTIL boolean expression;
```

A structure diagram for a **REPEAT** ... **UNTIL** loop is given in Figure 6.3. Prior to examining this form, let's consider the fragment of code

```
Count := 0;
REPEAT
   Count := Count + 1;
   writeln (Count)
UNTIL Count = 5;
writeln ('All done');
```

The output for this fragment is

```
1
2
3
4
5
All done
```

With this example in mind, the following comments concerning the use of a **REPEAT** ... **UNTIL** loop are in order.

1. The program statements between **REPEAT** and **UNTIL** are executed in order as they appear. Thus, a **BEGIN** ... **END** block is not necessary.
2. A semicolon is not required between the last statement in the body of the loop and the reserved word **UNTIL**.
3. The **boolean** expression must have a value before the loop.
4. The loop must be executed at least once because the **boolean** expression is not evaluated until after the loop body has been executed.

5. When the **boolean** expression is evaluated, if it is **false,** control is transferred back to the top of the loop; if it is **true,** control is transferred to the next program statement.

6. Provision must be made for changing values inside the loop so that the **boolean** expression used to control the loop will eventually be **true.** If this is not done, you have an infinite loop, as shown.

```
J := 0;
REPEAT
   J := J + 2;
   writeln (J)
UNTIL J = 5;
```

7. Writing style for using **REPEAT** ... **UNTIL** loops should be consistent with your style for using other loop structures.

There are two important differences between **WHILE** ... **DO** and **REPEAT** ... **UNTIL** loops. First, a **REPEAT** ... **UNTIL** loop must be executed at least once, but a **WHILE** ... **DO** loop can be skipped if the initial value of the **boolean** expression is **false.** Second, the initial value of the **boolean** expression in a **REPEAT** ... **UNTIL** loop is usually **false** and the loop is repeated until the value becomes **true;** in a **WHILE** ... **DO** loop, the initial value is usually **true** and the loop is repeated until the value becomes **false.**

FIGURE 6.3
REPEAT ... **UNTIL**
structure diagram

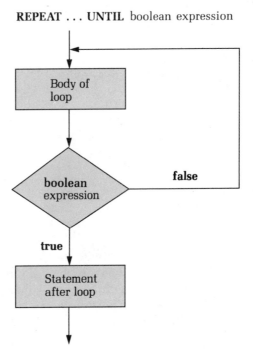

REPEAT ... **UNTIL** boolean expression

A NOTE OF INTEREST

Charles Babbage

Charles Babbage (1791–1871) was a mathematician intrigued with the idea of building a machine that could compute properties of numbers accurate to 20 digits. His first machine was a difference engine; however, technology prevented him from making a good working model. Discouraged by this, he worked on a general purpose problem-solving machine called the analytical engine. His design for this is considered to be the forerunner of modern computers. It consisted of four components:

1. a "mill" for manipulating and computing
2. a "store" for storing data
3. an "operator" for carrying out instructions
4. a device for receiving information and entering data

After several years designing variations and improvements for his analytical engine, he received assistance from Countess Ada Augusta Byron.

SELF QUIZ 6.4

What output is produced from the following program fragment?

```
A := 0;
B := 5;
REPEAT
  A := A + 1;
  writeln (A, B)
UNTIL A > B;
```

EXAMPLE 6.15

Let's use a **REPEAT** ... **UNTIL** loop to print powers of two which are less than 100. This can be done by

```
PowerOf2 := 1;
REPEAT
  writeln (PowerOf2);
  PowerOf2 := PowerOf2 * 2
UNTIL PowerOf2 > 100;
```

When run, this segment produces

```
1
2
4
8
16
32
64
```

As was the case with **WHILE** ... **DO** loops, sentinel values can be used to determine when a process should terminate. These can be in the form of some predetermined data value (for example, -999) or the result of a response to a question on the screen asking whether or not the person running the program wishes to continue. This is illustrated in Example 6.16.

EXAMPLE 6.16

Write a segment of code to allow a positive integer to be entered from the keyboard and then print a table of squares less than or equal to the indicated value. Code for this is

```
N := 0;
writeln ('Enter a positive integer and press <RETURN>.');
readln (UpperLimit);
writeln ('The squares less than or equal to ',
         UpperLimit,' are:');
writeln;
REPEAT
   writeln (N * N);
   N := N + 1
UNTIL N * N > UpperLimit;
```

A sample run for this segment is

```
Enter a positive integer and press <RETURN>.
200
The squares less than or equal to 200 are:

0
1
4
16
25
36
49
64
81
100
121
144
169
196
```

Multiple Conditions

The **boolean** expression used with a **REPEAT** ... **UNTIL** loop can be as complex as you choose to make it. However, if the expression gets too complicated, you might enhance program readability and design by changing the algorithm to use simpler expressions.

EXAMPLE 6.17

Let's show how multiple conditions can be used to read in and total at most twenty-five scores. This can be achieved by

```
writeln ('Please enter scores, -999 when done.');
Total := 0;
Count := 0;
REPEAT
   readln (Score);
   Total := Total + Score;
   Count := Count + 1
UNTIL (Count > 25) OR (Score = -999);
```

Exercises 6.3

1. Explain the difference between a pretest loop and a posttest loop.

2. Write a test program that illustrates what happens when the initial condition for a **REPEAT ... UNTIL** loop is **false.** Compare this with a similar condition for a **WHILE ... DO** loop.

In Exercises 3–6, indicate what output is produced.

```
 3. A := 0;
    B := 10;
    REPEAT
      A := A + 1;
      B := B - 1;
      writeln (A,B)
    UNTIL A > B;
 4. Power := 1;
    REPEAT
      Power := Power * 2;
      writeln (Power)
    UNTIL Power > 100;
```

```
 5. J := 1;
    REPEAT
      writeln (J);
      J := J + 1
    UNTIL J > 10;
 6. A := 1;
    REPEAT
      writeln (A, 17 MOD A);
      A := A + 1
    UNTIL 17 MOD A = 5;
```

In Exercises 7–10, indicate which are infinite loops and give an explanation for those that are infinite.

```
 7. J := 1;
    REPEAT
      writeln (J)
    UNTIL J > 10;
    J := J + 1;
 8. A := 2;
    REPEAT
      writeln (A);
      A := A * 2
    UNTIL A > 20;
 9. A := 2;
    REPEAT
      writeln (A);
      A := A * 2
    UNTIL A = 20;
10. B := 15;
    REPEAT
      writeln (B, B DIV 5);
      B := B - 1
    UNTIL B DIV 3 <> 5;
```

In Exercises 11–14, write a segment of code that uses a **REPEAT ... UNTIL** loop.

11. Print a table of squares of integers starting with 1 and continuing until the difference of consecutive squares exceeds 25.

12. Print a table of cubes of integers from 1 to N where the value of N is entered from the keyboard.

13. Read three values and print their sum as long as one of them is positive.

14. Read three values and print their sum as long as they are all positive.

15. Use a **REPEAT ... UNTIL** loop in a program to find the smallest positive integer N such that the sum 1 + 2 + ... + N exceeds some value entered from the keyboard.

16. Write a segment of code that reads a positive integer and then prints a list of powers of the integer that are less than 10,000.

■ **6.4**
Comparison of Loops

OBJECTIVES

- to understand the similarities and differences between any two types of loops
- to understand why variable loops cannot, in general, be converted to fixed loops
- to convert (when possible) from one type of loop to another

The last three sections presented three types of loops used in Pascal: one fixed loop (**FOR ... TO ... DO**) and two variable loops (**WHILE ... DO** and **REPEAT ... UNTIL**). It is natural to wonder if any of these can replace any other. As you will see in this section, we could get by with only one type of loop. However, program situations and personal preference make it convenient to have all three loops available. This section examines the similarities and differences among loops and shows how some of the loops can be rewritten as another type of loop.

Similarities and Differences

You probably have noticed by now that the three types of loops have some similarities and differences; for easy reference, these are summarized in Table 6.1.

Conversion of Loops

It is an interesting exercise to rewrite a loop using a different type of loop. In some cases, this can always be done; in others, it can only be accomplished when certain conditions are present. There are six possibilities for such rewriting; we will examine four and leave two for the Exercises at the end of this section.

Let's first rewrite a **FOR** loop as a **WHILE ... DO** loop. Both are pretest loops, but the **WHILE ... DO** structure is a form of variable repetition. To accomplish our objective, we must use a counter in the **WHILE ... DO** loop in a manner similar to the index in a **FOR** loop. Thus, we initialize the counter outside the loop and change it accordingly inside the loop. The **boolean** expression in the **WHILE ... DO** loop is written so that the last index value produces the final time through the loop.

EXAMPLE 6.18

Let's rewrite the following **FOR** loop using a **WHILE ... DO** loop.

```
Sum := 0;
FOR K := 5 TO 10 DO
  BEGIN
    Sum := Sum + K;
    writeln (K)
  END;
writeln (Sum);
```

The initialization must correspond to K := 5 and the **boolean** expression that causes the loop to be exited must correspond to K > 10. With these requirements in mind, the revision becomes

```
K := 5;
Sum := 0;
WHILE K < 11 DO
  BEGIN
    Sum := Sum + K;
    writeln (K);
    K := K + 1
  END;
writeln (Sum);
```

■

TABLE 6.1
Comparing and contrasting loops

Traits of Loops	FOR Loop	WHILE . . . DO Loop	REPEAT . . . UNTIL Loop
Pretest loop	yes	yes	no
Posttest loop	no	no	yes
BEGIN . . . END for compound statements	required	required	not required
Repetition	fixed	variable	variable
Loop index	yes	no	no
Index automatically incremented	yes	no	no
boolean expression used	no	yes	yes

The changes illustrated in this example can always be made; any **FOR** loop can be rewritten as a **WHILE . . . DO** loop. The only other type of loop that can always be rewritten as another type is a **REPEAT . . . UNTIL** loop; it can always be converted to a **WHILE . . . DO** loop. In this revision, the **boolean** expression of the **WHILE . . . DO** loop is the logical complement (opposite) of that used in the **REPEAT . . . UNTIL** loop. A revision of this type is illustrated in the following example.

EXAMPLE 6.19

Let's rewrite the **REPEAT . . . UNTIL** loop using a **WHILE . . . DO** loop.

```
read (A);
REPEAT
   writeln (A);
   A := A * A
UNTIL A > 100;
```

The **boolean** expression A > 100 is replaced by A <= 100 in the new loop.

```
read (A);
WHILE A <= 100 DO
   BEGIN
      writeln (A);
      A := A * A
   END;
```

As demonstrated by the last two examples, Pascal programmers could use only the **WHILE . . . DO** loop structure. However, since there are cases in which one of the other two may be preferred, beginning courses in Pascal typically present and use all three types of loops.

SELF QUIZ 6.5

Rewrite the following **REPEAT . . . UNTIL** loop as an equivalent **WHILE . . . DO** loop.

```
REPEAT
   readln (Num);
   Sum := Sum + Num;
   Count := Count + 1
UNTIL Num < 0;
```

Some conversions require special circumstances to be true before the conversions can be made. Let's consider the problem of rewriting a **WHILE . . . DO** loop as a **FOR** loop. Since a **WHILE . . . DO** loop is a variable repetition loop and uses a **boolean** expression for loop control, both of these must be suitable for conversion before the loop can be rewritten as an indexed loop. For example,

```
K := 1;
WHILE K < 10 DO
   BEGIN
      writeln (K);
      K := K + 1
   END;
```

can be rewritten as

```
FOR K := 1 TO 9 DO
   writeln (K);
```

This form requires less code and is certainly preferable.

Now let's consider the problem of rewriting a **WHILE** ... **DO** loop as a **REPEAT** ... **UNTIL** loop. Since both loops use **boolean** expressions for loop control, logical complements can be used for the transition. However, **WHILE** ... **DO** is a pretest loop and **REPEAT** ... **UNTIL** is a posttest loop. Since a posttest loop must be executed at least once before the exit condition is checked, a pretest loop that is not entered cannot be written as a posttest loop. Thus,

```
A := 10;
WHILE A < 5 DO
   BEGIN
      writeln (A);
      A := A * 2
   END;
```

cannot be rewritten as a **REPEAT** ... **UNTIL** loop. However, if the **WHILE** ... **DO** loop is executed at least once, it can be revised into a **REPEAT** ... **UNTIL** loop. The next example illustrates this.

EXAMPLE 6.20

Let's rewrite the following using a **REPEAT** ... **UNTIL** loop.

```
A := 1;
Power := 3;
WHILE A < 100 DO
   BEGIN
      writeln (A);
      A := A * Power
   END;
```

The **boolean** expression for a **REPEAT** ... **UNTIL** loop becomes A >= 100 and the revision is

```
A := 1;
Power := 3;
REPEAT
   writeln (A);
   A := A * Power
UNTIL A >= 100;
```                                                                      ■

When considering the remaining loop conversions in the Exercises, carefully note fixed repetition versus variable repetition and pretest versus posttest conditions.

Exercises 6.4

1. Compare and contrast the three looping structures discussed in this section.

In Exercises 2–4, determine whether or not the conversions indicated can be made.

2.
```
Sum := 0;
FOR K := 1 TO 100 DO
   Sum := Sum + K;
```
a. convert to **REPEAT . . . UNTIL?**
b. convert to **WHILE . . . DO?**

3.
```
Count := 0;
Sum := 0;
readln (A);
WHILE A <> 0 DO
   BEGIN
      Sum := Sum + A;
      Count := Count + 1;
      readln (A)
   END;
```
a. convert to **REPEAT . . . UNTIL?**
b. convert to **FOR . . . TO . . . DO?**
c. convert to **FOR . . . DOWNTO . . . DO?**

4.
```
X := 0.0;
REPEAT
   writeln (X:20:2);
   X := X + 0.5
UNTIL X = 4.0;
```
a. convert to **WHILE . . . DO?**
b. convert to **FOR . . . TO . . . DO?**
c. convert to **FOR . . . DOWNTO . . . DO?**

5. For each of the conversions you indicated was possible in Exercises 2 through 4, write the revised loop.

6. Explain completely the problems encountered when trying to make the following loop conversions.
   - **FOR . . . TO . . . DO** to **REPEAT . . . UNTIL**
   - **REPEAT . . . UNTIL** to **FOR . . . TO . . . DO**

7. Explain why the following cannot be rewritten as a **REPEAT . . . UNTIL** loop.
```
WHILE 6 < 5 DO
   BEGIN
      .
      .  (loop body)
      .
   END;
```

■ **6.5**
Using Loops

In this chapter, we examined three loop structures. Each was discussed with respect to syntax, form, writing style, and use in programs. But remember that each loop is treated as a single Pascal statement. In this sense, it is possible to have a loop as one of the statements in the body of another loop. When this happens, the loops are said to be *nested*.

Loops can be nested to any depth. That is, a loop within a loop within a loop, and so on. Also, any of the three types of loops can be nested within any loop. However, a programmer should be careful not to design a program with nesting that is too complex. If program logic becomes too difficult to follow, you might redesign the program.

Flow of Control

To illustrate using a loop within a loop, consider

```
FOR K := 1 TO 5 DO
    FOR J := 1 TO 3 DO
        writeln (K + J);
```

When this fragment is executed, the following happens:

1. K is assigned a value.
2. For each value of K, the following loop is executed.

```
FOR J := 1 TO 3 DO
    writeln (K + J);
```

Thus, for K := 1, the "inside" or nested loop produces the output

```
2
3
4
```

At this point, K := 2 and the next portion of the output produced by the nested loop is

```
3
4
5
```

The complete output from these nested loops is

$$\left.\begin{array}{l} 2 \\ 3 \\ 4 \end{array}\right\} \text{from K := 1}$$

$$\left.\begin{array}{l} 3 \\ 4 \\ 5 \end{array}\right\} \text{from K := 2}$$

$$\left.\begin{array}{l} 4 \\ 5 \\ 6 \end{array}\right\} \text{from K := 3}$$

$$\left.\begin{array}{l} 5 \\ 6 \\ 7 \end{array}\right\} \text{from K := 4}$$

$$\left.\begin{array}{l} 6 \\ 7 \\ 8 \end{array}\right\} \text{from K := 5}$$

As you can see, for each value assigned to the index of the outside loop, the inside loop is executed completely. Suppose you want the output to be printed in the form of a chart as follows:

2	3	4
3	4	5
4	5	6
5	6	7
6	7	8

The pseudocode design to produce this output is

1. **FOR** K := 1 **TO** 5 **DO**
   produce a line

A refinement of this is

1. **FOR** K := 1 **TO** 5 **DO**
   1.1 print on one line
   1.2 advance the printer

The Pascal code for this development becomes

```
FOR K := 1 TO 5 DO
   BEGIN
     FOR J := 1 TO 3 DO
        write ((K + J):4);
     writeln
   END;
```

Our next example shows how nested loops can be used to produce a design.

EXAMPLE 6.21

Let's use nested **FOR** loops to produce the output

```
*
**
***
****
*****
```

where the left asterisks are in column 10.

The first-level pseudocode to solve this problem is

1. **FOR** K := 1 **TO** 5 **DO**
   produce a line

A refinement of this can be

1. **FOR** K := 1 **TO** 5 **DO**
   1.1 print on one line
   1.2 advance the printer

Step 1.1 is not yet sufficiently refined, so our next level can be

1. **FOR** K := 1 **TO** 5 **DO**
   1.1 print on one line
        1.1.1 put a blank in column 9
        1.1.2 print the asterisks
   1.2 advance the printer

We can now write a program fragment to produce the desired output as follows:

```
FOR K := 1 TO 5 DO
   BEGIN
     write (' ':9);
     FOR J := 1 TO K DO
        write ('*');
     writeln
   END;  (* of outer loop *)
```

A significant feature has been added to this program fragment. Note that the loop control for the inner loop is the index of the outer loop. ■

Use nested **FOR** loops to write a fragment of code to produce the chart

0	0	0
1	2	3
·2	4	6
3	6	9
4	8	12

STYLE TIP
■ ■ ■ ■ ■ ■ ■

When working with nested loops, use line comments to indicate the effect of each loop control variable. For example,

```
FOR K := 1 TO 50 DO (* Each value produces a line *)
  BEGIN
    write (' ':9);
    FOR J := 1 TO K DO  (* This moves across one line *)
      write ('*');
    writeln
  END;  (* of outer loop  *)
```

Thus far, nested loops were used only with **FOR** loops, but any of the loop structures may be used in nesting. Our next example illustrates a **REPEAT ... UNTIL** loop nested within a **WHILE ... DO** loop.

EXAMPLE 6.22

Let's trace the flow of control and indicate the output for the following program fragment.

```
A := 10;
B := 0;
WHILE A > B DO
  BEGIN
    writeln (A:5);
    REPEAT
      writeln (A:5, B:5, (A + B):5);
      A := A - 2
    UNTIL A <= 6;
    B := B + 2
  END;  (* of WHILE ... DO  *)
writeln;
writeln ('All done':20);
```

The assignment statements produce

10	0
A	B

and A > B is **true**; thus, the **WHILE ... DO** loop is entered. The first time through this loop the **REPEAT ... UNTIL** loop is used. Output for the first pass is

```
10
10   0    10
```

and the values for A and B are

8	0
A	B

The **boolean** expression A <= 6 is **false** and the **REPEAT** ... **UNTIL** loop is executed again to produce the next line of output

```
8     0     8
```

and the values for A and B become

```
  6       0
  A       B
```

At this point, A <= 6 is **true** and control transfers to the line of code

```
B := B + 2;
```

Thus, the variable values are

```
  6       2
  A       B
```

and the **boolean** expression A > B is **true**. This means the **WHILE** ... **DO** loop is repeated. The output for the second time through this loop is

```
6
6     2     8
```

and the values for the variables are

```
  4       4
  A       B
```

Now A > B is **false** and control is transferred to the line following the **WHILE** ... **DO** loop. Output for the complete fragment is

```
10
10     0    15
 8     0     8
 6
 6     2     8
```

Example 6.22 is a bit contrived and tracing the flow of control somewhat tedious. However, it is important for you to be able to follow the logic involved in using nested loops.

SELF QUIZ 6.7

Trace the values of the variables and indicate the output from the following:

```
Count := 0;
Stop := 4;
WHILE Count < Stop DO
  BEGIN
    FOR K := 1 TO Count DO
      write (K:3);
    writeln;
    Count := Count + 1
  END;
writeln ('All done');
```

Writing Style

As usual, you should be aware of the significance of using a consistent, readable style of writing when using nested loops. There are at least three features you should consider.

1. Indenting. Each loop should have its own level of indenting. This makes it easier to identify the body of the loop. If the loop body consists of a compound statement, the **BEGIN** and **END** should start in the same column. Using our previous indenting style, a typical nesting might be

```
FOR K := 1 TO 10 DO
   BEGIN
      WHILE A > 0 DO
         BEGIN
            REPEAT
                  .
                  .
                  .
            UNTIL condition  (*  End of REPEAT loop  *)
         END;
      statement;
      statement
END;    (*  of FOR loop  *)
```

If the body of a loop becomes very long, it is sometimes difficult to match the **BEGIN**s with the proper **END**s. In this case, you should either redesign the program or be especially careful.

2. Using comments. Comments can precede a loop and explain what the loop will do, or they can be used with statements inside the loop to explain what the statement does. They should be used to indicate the end of a loop where the loop body is a compound statement.

3. Skipping lines. This is an effective way of isolating loops within a program and making nested loops easier to identify.

A note of caution is in order with respect to writing style. Program documentation is important; however, excessive use of comments and skipped lines can detract from readability. You should develop a happy medium.

We close this section with two more examples of nested loops. The first one analyzes a program fragment with nested loops, and the second asks you to write a program to produce a certain output.

EXAMPLE 6.23

Let's find the output produced by the following program fragment of nested loops. Assume A and B have been declared as integer variables and the data entered are

4 7

The fragment

```
readln (A,B);
REPEAT    (*  Produce one block of output   *)
   FOR K := A TO B DO
      BEGIN
         Num := A;

(*  Print one line  *)

         WHILE Num <= B DO
            BEGIN
               write (Num:4);
               Num := Num + 1
            END;   (*  of WHILE ... DO loop  *)
         writeln

      END;   (*  of FOR loop  *)

   A := A + 1;
   writeln; writeln

UNTIL A = B;  (*  End of REPEAT ... UNTIL loop  *)
```

produces the output

```
4    5    6    7
4    5    6    7
4    5    6    7
4    5    6    7

5    6    7
5    6    7
5    6    7

6    7
6    7
```

EXAMPLE 6.24   Let's write a complete program whose output is the multiplication table from 1 × 1 to 10 × 10. A suitable heading should be part of the output. A program to do this is as follows:

```
PROGRAM MultiplicationTable (output);

(****************************************************************

        This program prints a multiplication table
        from 1 * 1 to 10 * 10.

 ****************************************************************)

CONST
   Indent = ' ';

VAR
   J,K : integer;
```

```
BEGIN

(*  Print a heading  *)

  writeln; writeln;
  writeln (Indent:19, 'Multiplication Table');
  writeln (Indent:19, '_____');
  writeln;
  writeln (Indent:15, '( Generated by nested FOR loops )');
  writeln;

(*  Now print the multiplication table  *)

  writeln (Indent:11,'!  1   2   3   4   5   6   7   8   9  10');
  writeln (Indent:8,'___!_____');

(*  Now start the loop  *)

  FOR K := 1 TO 10 DO
    BEGIN  (*  Print one row  *)
      write (K:10, ' !');
      FOR J := 1 TO 10 DO
        write (K * J:4);
      writeln;
      writeln (Indent:11, '!')
    END;  (*  of each row  *)
  writeln; writeln
END.
```

The output from this program is

<u>Multiplication Table</u>

(Generated by nested FOR loops)

```
         1   2   3   4   5   6   7   8   9  10
   ___!_____
    1 !  1   2   3   4   5   6   7   8   9  10
      !
    2 !  2   4   6   8  10  12  14  16  18  20
      !
    3 !  3   6   9  12  15  18  21  24  27  30
      !
    4 !  4   8  12  16  20  24  28  32  36  40
      !
    5 !  5  10  15  20  25  30  35  40  45  50
      !
    6 !  6  12  18  24  30  36  42  48  54  60
      !
    7 !  7  14  21  28  35  42  49  56  63  70
      !
    8 !  8  16  24  32  40  48  56  64  72  80
      !
    9 !  9  18  27  36  45  54  63  72  81  90
      !
   10 ! 10  20  30  40  50  60  70  80  90 100
      !
```

A NOTE OF INTEREST

Structured Programming

From 1950 to the early 1970s programs were designed and written on a linear basis. A program written and designed on such a basis can be called an unstructured program. Structured programming, on the other hand, organizes a program around separate semi-independent modules that are linked together by a single sequence of simple commands.

In 1964, mathematicians Corrado Bohm and Guiseppe Jacopini proved that any program logic, regardless of complexity, can be expressed by using sequence, selection, and iteration. This result is termed the structure theorem. This re-sult, combined with the efforts of Edger W. Dijkstra, led to a significant move toward structured programming and away from the use of **GOTO** statements (see Appendix 6).

The first time structured programming concepts were applied to a large-scale data processing application was the IBM Corporation "New York Times Project" from 1969 to 1971. Using these techniques, programmers posted productivity figures from four to six times higher than those of the average programmer. In addition, the error rate was a phenomenally low 0.0004 per line of coding.

Conditionals Within Loops

In Chapter 5 we discussed the use of conditional statements. In this chapter we discussed the use of three different types of loops. It is now time to see how they are used together. We first examine conditional statements contained within the body of a loop and then loops within conditional statements.

EXAMPLE 6.25

Let's write a program fragment that counts all the blanks in a line of text. For this problem, we assume the line of text ends with a period. A first-level pseudocode solution is

1. Initialize counter
2. Read a character
3. **WHILE** character not a period **DO**
   3.1   process a character

Step 3.1 can be refined to

   3.1   process a character
         3.1.1   IF Ch = ' ' **THEN**
                 add 1 to BlankCount
         3.1.2   read a character

The code for this fragment is

```
BlankCount := 0;
read (Ch);
WHILE Ch <> '.' DO
  BEGIN
    IF Ch = ' ' THEN
      BlankCount := BlankCount + 1;
    read (Ch)
  END;  (* of WHILE ... DO loop *)
```

Just as **IF ... THEN** statements can be used with loops, **IF ... THEN ... ELSE** statements can be similarly used. The next example illustrates such a use.

EXAMPLE 6.26

Let's write a program fragment that computes gross wages for an employee of the Florida OJ Canning Company. Data for an employee consist of an employee number, the total hours worked, and the hourly rate. Thus, a typical data line is

    156 44.5 12.75

Overtime (more than 40 hours) is computed as time-and-a-half. The output should include all input data and an employee's gross wages.

A first-level pseudocode development for this program is

1. **WHILE** more employees **DO**
    1.1 process a line of data
    1.2 print results

This can be refined to

1. **WHILE** more employees **DO**
    1.1 process a line of data
        1.1.1 get data
        1.1.2 compute wage
    1.2 print results

Step 1.1.2 can be refined to

    1.1.2 compute wage
        1.1.2.1 **IF** Hours $<=$ 40.0 **THEN**
                    compute regular time
                ELSE
                    compute time-and-a-half

and the final algorithm for the fragment is

1. **WHILE** more employees **DO**
    1.1 process a line of data
        1.1.1 get data
        1.1.2 compute wage
            1.1.2.1 **IF** Hours $<=$ 40.0 **THEN**
                        compute regular time
                    ELSE
                        compute time-and-a-half
    1.2 print results

The code for this fragment is

```
writeln ('Do you wish to continue?');
writeln ('Enter Y or N and press <RETURN>.');
readln (MoreEmployees);
WHILE MoreEmployees = 'Y' DO
   BEGIN
      writeln ('Enter employee #, hours, and pay rate.');
      readln (IdentificationNumber, Hours, PayRate);

      IF Hours <= 40.0 THEN
         TotalWage := Hours * PayRate
      ELSE
```

```
    BEGIN
      Overtime := 1.5 * (Hours - 40.0) * PayRate;
      TotalWage := 40 * PayRate + Overtime
    END;      (*   of ELSE option    *)
  writeln;
  write (IdentificationNumber, Hours:10:2);
  writeln (PayRate:10:2, '$':10, TotalWage:7:2);
  writeln;
  writeln ('Do you wish to continue?');
  writeln ('Enter Y or N and press <RETURN>.');
  readln (MoreEmployees)
END; (*  of WHILE ... DO loop  *)
```

A typical run of this program for three employees using the data

```
    156 44.5 12.75
    024 40.0 9.80
    081 37.5 11.50
```

generates

```
    Do you wish to continue?
    Enter Y or N and press <RETURN>.
    Y
    Enter employee #, hours and pay rate.
    156 44.5 12.75

    156      44.50      12.75            $596.06

    Do you wish to continue?
    Enter Y or N and press <RETURN>.
    Y
    Enter employee #, hours and pay rate.
    0.24 40.0 9.80

    024      40.00       9.80            $392.00

    Do you wish to continue?
    Enter Y or N and press <RETURN>.
    Y
    Enter employee #, hours and pay rate.
    081 37.5 11.50

    081      37.50      11.50            $431.25

    Do you wish to continue?
    Enter Y or N and press <RETURN>.
    N
```

Loops Within Conditionals

The next example illustrates the use of a loop within an **IF ... THEN** statement.

EXAMPLE 6.27   Let's write a program fragment that allows you to read an integer as input. If the integer is between 0 and 50, you are to print a chart containing all positive integers less than the integer, their squares and cubes. Thus, if 4 is read, the chart is

```
1     1     1
2     4     8
3     9    27
```

The design for this problem has a first-level pseudocode development of

1. **read** Num
2. **IF** (Num > 0) **AND** (Num < 50) **THEN**
   2.1 print the chart

Step 2.1 can be refined to

   2.1 print the chart
     2.1.1 **FOR** K := 1 **TO** Num − 1 **DO**
        2.1.1.1 print each line

We can now write the code for this fragment as follows:

```
read (Num);
IF (Num > 0) AND (Num < 50) THEN
  FOR K := 1 TO Num - 1 DO
    writeln (K, K * K, K * K * K);
```

Exercises 6.5   1. Write a program that allows the size of a multiplication table to be entered from the keyboard. The requested table should then be printed as output. For example, if you enter 2 3, output is

```
1 * 1 = 1
1 * 2 = 2
1 * 3 = 3
2 * 1 = 2
2 * 2 = 4
2 * 3 = 6
```

In Exercises 2–5, what output is produced from the fragment?

```
2. FOR K := 2 TO 6 DO
     BEGIN
       FOR J := 5 TO 10 DO
         write (K + J);
       writeln
     END;
3. FOR K := 2 TO 6 DO
     BEGIN
       FOR J := 5 TO 10 DO
         write (K * J);
       writeln
     END;
```

```
4. Sum := 0;
   A := 7;
   WHILE A < 10 DO
      BEGIN
         FOR K := A TO 10 DO
            Sum := Sum + K;
         A := A + 1
      END;
   writeln (Sum);
5. Sum := 0;
   FOR K := 1 TO 10 DO
      FOR J := (10*K-9) TO (10*K) DO
         Sum := Sum + J;
   writeln (Sum);
```

In Exercises 6–8, write a program fragment using nested loops to produce the design.

```
6. *****      7.      *        8. ***
   ****              ***          ***
   ***             *****          ***
   **             *******         ***
   *               *****        ******
                    ***         ******
                     *          ******
```

9. Write a program fragment that uses nested loops to produce the output

```
2      4      6      8      10
3      6      9     12      15
4      8     12     16      20
5     10     15     20      25
```

In Exercises 10 and 11, find and explain the errors in the program fragment. You may assume all variables are suitably declared.

```
10. A := 25;
    Flag := true;
    WHILE Flag = true DO
       IF A >= 100 THEN
          BEGIN
             writeln (A);
             Flag := false
          END;
11. FOR K := 1 TO 10 DO
       writeln (K, K * K);
       IF K MOD 3 = 0 THEN
          BEGIN
             write (K);
             writeln (' is a multiple of three')
          END;
```

In Exercises 12–17, what output is produced from the program fragment? Assume variables are suitably declared.

```
12. FOR K := 1 TO 100 DO
       IF K MOD 5 = 0 THEN
          writeln (K);
```

```
13. J := 20;
    IF J MOD 5 = 0 THEN
      FOR K := 1 TO 100 DO
        writeln (K);
14. A := 5;
    B := 90;
    REPEAT
      B := B DIV A - 5;
      IF B > A THEN
        B := A + 30
    UNTIL B < 0;
    writeln (A, B);
15. Count := 0;
    FOR K := -5 TO 5 DO
      IF K MOD 3 = 0 THEN
        BEGIN
          WHILE Count < 10 DO
            BEGIN
              Count := Count + 1;
              writeln (Count)
            END;
          Count := 0
        END;
16. A := 50;
    B := 25;
    IF A < B THEN
      FOR K := A TO B DO
        writeln (K)
    ELSE
      FOR K := A DOWNTO B DO
        writeln (K);
17. FOR K := -5 TO 5 DO
      BEGIN
        A := K;
        IF K < 0 THEN
          REPEAT
            writeln (2 * A);
            A := A + 1
          UNTIL A > 0
        ELSE
          WHILE (A MOD 2 = 0) DO
            BEGIN
              writeln (A);
              A := A + 1
            END
      END;
```

18. Write a program fragment that reads reals from a data file, counts the number of positive reals, and accumulates their sum.

19. Write a program that counts all the periods in several lines of data. The keyboard operator will indicate when there are no more lines.

20. Write a program that reproduces a data line, omitting all blanks.

21. Given two integers, A and B, A is a *divisor* of B if B **MOD** A = 0. Write a complete program that reads a positive integer B as input and then prints all the positive divisors of B.

RUNNING AND DEBUGGING TIPS

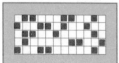

1. Most errors involving loops are not compilation errors. Thus, it is when you try to run the program that you detect most errors.
2. A syntax error that is not detected by the compiler is a semicolon after a **WHILE ... DO**. The fragment

```
WHILE more data DO;
    BEGIN
        readln (A);
        writeln (A)
    END;
```

is incorrect and will not get past

```
WHILE more data DO;
```

Also, note that this is an infinite loop.
3. Carefully check your data file when using loops to input data. Be sure that your lines are correctly and consistently formatted.
4. Carefully check entry conditions for each loop.
5. Carefully check exit conditions for each loop. Make sure the loop is exited (not infinite) and that you have the correct number of repetitions.
6. Loop entry, execution, and exit can be checked by
   a. pencil and paper check on initial and final values
   b. count of the number of repetitions
   c. use of debugging **writeln**s
      - **boolean** condition prior to loop
      - variables inside loop
      - values of the counter in loop
      - **boolean** values inside the loop
      - values after loop is exited

■ **Summary**

Key Terms

fixed repetition (iterated) loop	index	exit controlled (posttest) loop
pretest loop	entrance controlled (pretest) loop	nested loops
posttest loop	infinite loop	
sentinel value	counter	

Keywords

FOR ... TO ... DO	WHILE ... DO
FOR ... DOWNTO ... DO	REPEAT ... UNTIL

Key Concepts

- A fixed repetition loop **(FOR ... TO ... DO)** is used when you know exactly how many times something is to be repeated. The basic form for a **FOR** ... **TO** ... **DO** loop is

```
FOR J := 1 TO 5 DO
   program statement;
```

or

```
FOR J := 1 TO 5 DO
   BEGIN
      statement 1;
      statement 2;
            .
            .
            .
      statement n
   END;
```

- After a fixed repetition loop is finished, program control is transferred to the first executable statement following the loop. The value of the index variable may become unassigned.
- A sentinel value is a special value which signifies the end of a set of data. These are typically used for variable repetition loops.
- A **WHILE** ... **DO** loop is a pretest loop that can have a variable loop control; a typical loop is

```
WHILE NOT sentinel value DO
   BEGIN
      readln (Score);
      Sum := Sum + Score;
      Count := Count + 1
   END;
```

- A counter is a variable whose purpose is to indicate how often the body of a loop is executed.
- An infinite **WHILE** ... **DO** loop is caused by having a **true** loop control condition that is never changed to **false.**
- A posttest loop has a **boolean** condition checked after the loop body has been completed.
- A **REPEAT** ... **UNTIL** loop is a posttest loop; a typical loop is

```
Count := 0;
Sum := 0;
read(Num);
REPEAT
   Sum := Sum + Num;
   Count := Count + 1;
   read(Num)
UNTIL Num < 0;
```

- **FOR** loops can always be rewritten as equivalent **REPEAT** ... **UNTIL** or **WHILE** ... **DO** loops.
- **REPEAT** ... **UNTIL** loops can always be rewritten as **WHILE** ... **DO** loops.
- **REPEAT** ... **UNTIL** and **WHILE** ... **DO** are variable control loops and **FOR** is a fixed control loop.

- **WHILE** ... **DO** and **FOR** are pretest loops; **REPEAT** ... **UNTIL** is a posttest loop.
- Any one of these loops can be nested within any other of the loops.
- Indenting each loop is important for program readability.
- Several levels of nesting make the logic of a program difficult to follow.
- Loops and conditionals are frequently used together. Careful program design facilitates writing code in which these concepts are integrated; typical forms are

```
WHILE condition1 DO
   BEGIN
      .
      .
      .
      IF condition2 THEN
         .
         .
         .
      ELSE
         .
         .
         .
      .
      .
      .
   END;
```

and

```
IF conditional THEN
   BEGIN
      .
      .
      .
      FOR J := value1 TO valueN DO
         BEGIN
            .
            .
         END;
      .
      .
      .
   END
ELSE
   .
   .
   .
```

■ Chapter
Review
Exercises

In Exercises 1–12, indicate if the statement is valid or invalid. If invalid, explain why.

1. FOR K := 1 TO 10 DO
2. FOR J = 1 TO 5 STEP 2 DO
3. FOR J := 10 TO 1 DO
4. FOR X := 1.0 TO 3.0 DO
5. FOR C := 'A' TO 'Z' DO

```
 6. FOR K := A DOWNTO B DO
 7. J := 1 TO 10 DO
 8. WHILE J := 1 DO
 9. WHILE M = 1.5 DO
10. WHILE X <> 'A' DO
11. WHILE K := 1 TO 10 DO
12. WHILE BooleanVariable DO
```

For Exercises 13–16, write a program to print a table of integers, their squares, and their square roots using integers running from 1 to 25.

13. Use a **FOR** ... **TO** ... **DO** loop.
14. Use a **FOR** ... **DOWNTO** ... **DO** loop.
15. Use a **WHILE** ... **DO** loop.
16. Use a **REPEAT** ... **UNTIL** loop.

17. Write a program that uses **FOR** loops to produce the following pattern.

18. Use nested loops to produce the following numbering on the screen or page.

```
1


1
2


1
2
3


1
2
3
4
```

19. Is it possible to execute a **FOR** loop without ever continuing into the statements that are inside the loop? Is this also true of **WHILE** ... **DO** loops? **REPEAT** ... **UNTIL** loops?

20. Brian wants the following program segment to print a list of numbers and their cubes. What happens when it is executed? Can you correct it for him (if necessary)?

```
FOR K := 1 TO 10 DO;
   Z := K * K * K;
   writeln (K:10, Z:10);
```

21. Rewrite Example 6.2 from Section 6.1 using a **WHILE** ... **DO**

22. Rewrite Example 6.2 from Section 6.1 using a **REPEAT** ... **UNTIL** loop.

23. Explain why it is important to use proper indentation, blank lines, and comments when writing programs that involve loops.

■ **Chapter Summary Program**

This program illustrates the use of loops. A loop with an interactive message is used to input and a **WHILE ... DO** loop is nested within a **FOR ... TO ... DO** loop.

The problem is to read a positive integer as input and print the prime numbers less than or equal to the number read. The process continues until a message is given from the keyboard. You should note the mathematical property that a number K is prime if it has no divisors (other than 1) less than its square root. Thus, when we check for divisors, it is only necessary to check up to **sqrt**(K). Also note that 1 is not prime by definition.

A first-level pseudocode development for this problem is
WHILE more data **DO**
1. Get a number
2. **IF** Number is 1 **THEN**
    2.1 print a message for one
    ELSE
    2.2 process the number

Step 2.2 can be refined to
2.2 process the number
    2.2.1 print message
    2.2.2 check for primes less than or equal to number

Step 2.2.2 is then refined to
2.2.2 **FOR** K := 2 **TO** Number **DO**
    2.2.2.1 check K for prime
    2.2.2.2 **IF** K is prime **THEN**
            print K in list of primes

A complete pseudocode solution for this problem is
WHILE more data **DO**
1. Get a number
2. **IF** Number is 1 **THEN**
    2.1 print a message for one
    ELSE
    2.2 process the number
        2.2.1 print message
        2.2.2 **FOR** K := 2 **TO** Number **DO**
            2.2.2.1 check K for prime
            2.2.2.2 **IF** K is prime **THEN**
                    print K in list of primes

A complete program for this problem follows. This has been run using the input

10 17 1 25 2

```
PROGRAM ListPrimes (input,output);
(***********************************************************

     This program reads positive integers from an
     input file and then lists prime numbers less than or
     equal to each number read. Note how loops are featured.

  ***********************************************************)
CONST
  Skip = ' ';
  Dashes = '_____';

VAR
  Candidate,             (*  Possible divisors of a number        *)
  K,                     (*  Loop index variable                  *)
  Number : integer;      (*  Integer read from input; primes less
                             than or equal to this will be listed *)
  Prime : boolean;       (*  boolean variable used in prime check  *)


BEGIN
  writeln ('Enter a positive integer; 0 to quit.');
  readln (Number);
  WHILE Number > 0 DO
    BEGIN
      IF Number = 1 THEN
        BEGIN
          writeln;
          writeln (Skip:10, Dashes);
          writeln (Skip:20, '1 is not prime by definition.');
          writeln
        END
      ELSE
        BEGIN

          (*   Print a message   *)

          writeln;
          writeln(Skip:10,Dashes);
          writeln(Skip:20,'The number is',Number:5,
                  '. The prime numbers');
          writeln(Skip:20,'less than or equal to',Number:5,' are:');
          writeln;

  (*   Check each positive integer less than or equal to Number   *)
```

```
        FOR K := 2 TO Number DO
          BEGIN
            Prime := true;
            Candidate := 2;
            WHILE (Candidate <= sqrt(K)) AND ( Prime = true ) DO
              BEGIN
                IF K MOD Candidate = 0 THEN
                  Prime := false;     (*  K has a divisor  *)
                Candidate := Candidate + 1
              END; (*  of prime check  *)
            IF Prime THEN              (*  print in list of primes  *)
              writeln(K:35)
          END (*  of processing K  *)
      END   (*  of ELSE option  *)
      writeln;
      writeln ('Enter a positive integer; 0 to quit.');
      readln(Number)
    END  (*  of WHILE ... DO  *)
END.
```

A sample run for this program produces the following:

```
    Enter a positive integer; 0 to quit.
    10


                          ------------------------------------------------------
                          The number is    10. The prime numbers
                          less than or equal to    10 are:


                                   2
                                   3
                                   5
                                   7


    Enter a positive integer; 0 to quit.
    17

                          ------------------------------------------------------
                          The number is    17. The prime numbers
                          less than or equal to    17 are:


                                   2
                                   3
                                   5
                                   7
                                  11
                                  13
                                  17


    Enter a positive integer; 0 to quit.
    1

                          ------------------------------------------------------
                          1 is not prime by definition.


    Enter a positive integer; 0 to quit;
    25
```

```
-------------------------------------------------------
            The number is    25. The Prime numbers
            less than or equal to    25 are:

                    2
                    3
                    5
                    7
                    11
                    13
                    17
                    19
                    23

Enter a positive integer; 0 to quit.
2
          -------------------------------------------------------
            The number is    2. The Prime numbers
            less than or equal to    2 are:

                    2

Enter a positive integer; 0 to quit.
0
```

■ **Programming Problems**

1. The Caswell Catering and Convention Service (Problem 7, Chapter 4 and Problem 14, Chapter 5) wants you to upgrade their program so they can use it for all of their customers. Modify it to run with an unknown number of customers.

2. A prime number is a positive integer that can be divided evenly only by 1 and the number itself (for example, 17). Write a program that determines whether or not a given positive integer is prime. (Hint: You only have to check for divisors less than or equal to the square root of the number being tested. Thus, if 79 is the positive integer being examined, the check of divisors is 2, 3, 5, 7.)

3. Now that you have a "prime number checker," write a program that reads an integer and prints all primes less than or equal to the integer read. Include checks for negative integers, zero, and one.

4. Modify the Gas-N-Clean Service Station program (Chapter Summary Program, Chapter 5) so that it can be used for an unknown number of customers. Your output should include the number of customers and all other pertinent items in a daily summary.

5. Modify the Community Hospital program (Problem 17, Chapter 5) so that it can be run with information for all patients leaving the hospital in one day. Include appropriate bad data checks and daily summary items.

6. The greatest common divisor (GCD) of two integers a and b is a positive integer c such that c divides a, c divides b, and for any other common divisor d of a and b, d is less than or equal to c. (For example, the GCD of 18 and 45 is 9.) Write a program that reads an unknown number of pairs of integers and finds the GCD of each pair.

7. In these days of increased awareness of automobile mileage, more motorists are computing their miles per gallon (mpg) than ever before. Write a program that performs these computations for a traveler. Data for the program are entered on lines indicated by the following table.

Odometer Reading	Gallons of Fuel Purchased
18828(start)	—
19240	9.7
19616	10.2
19944	8.8
20329	10.1
20769(finish)	10.3

The program should compute the mpg for each tank and the cumulative mpg each time the tank is filled up. Your output should produce a table with the following headings:

Odometer (begin)	Odometer (end)	Fuel (tank)	Miles (tank)	Fuel (trip)	Miles (trip)	Mpg (tank)	Mpg (trip)

8. Parkside's Other Triangle is generated from two positive integers, one for the size and one for the seed. For example,

Size 6, Seed 1

```
1  2  4  7  2  7
   3  5  8  3  8
      6  9  4  9
         1  5  1
            6  2
               3
```

Size 5, Seed 3

```
3  4  6  9  4
   5  7  1  5
      8  2  6
         3  7
            8
```

Write a program that reads pairs of positive integers and produces Parkside's Other Triangle for each pair. The check for bad data should include checking for seeds between one and nine inclusive.

9. Modify the sewage, water, and sanitation problem (Problem 19, Chapter 5) so that it can be used with data containing appropriate information for all residents of the community.

10. Modify the program for the Lucky Wildcat Well Corporation (Problem 20, Chapter 5) so that it can be run with data containing information about all of Al Derrick's wells. The first line of data consists of a positive integer that represents the total number of wells drilled.

11. Modify the program concerning the Mathematical Association of America (Problem 21, Chapter 5). Fifty official state delegates attend the summer national meeting. The new data contain the two-letter state abbreviation for each delegate.

12. In Fibonacci's sequence,

1, 1, 2, 3, 5, 8, 13, . . .

the first two terms are 1 and each successive term is formed by adding the previous two terms. Write a program that reads a positive integer and then prints the number of terms indicated by each integer read. Be sure to test your program with a data file that includes the integers 1 and 2.

13. Mr. Lae Z. Programmer is at it again. Now that you have written a program to compute the grade for one student in his class (Problem 22, Chapter 5), he wants you to modify this program so it can be used for the entire class. He will help you by making the first line of data be a positive integer representing the number of students in the class. Your new version should compute an overall class average and the number of students receiving each letter grade.

14. Modify the Pentagon Parking Lot problem (Problem 25, Chapter 5) so that it can be used for all customers in one day. In the new data, time should be entered in military style as a four-digit integer. The lot opens at 0600 (6:00 A.M.) and closes at 2200 (10:00 P.M.). Your program should include appropriate summary information.

15. The Natural Pine Furniture Company (Problem 2, Chapter 4) now wants you to refine your program so that it prints a one-week pay report for each employee. You do not know how many employees there are, but you do know that all information for each employee is on a separate line. Each line of input contains the employee's initials, the number of hours worked, and the hourly rate. You are to use the constant definition section for the following:

federal withholding tax rate	18%
state withholding tax rate	4.5%
hospitalization	$25.65
union dues	$ 7.85

Your output should include a report for each employee and a summary report for the company files.

16. Orlando Tree Service, Incorporated, offers the following services and rates to its customers:

tree removal	$300 per tree
tree trimming	$50 per hour
stump grinding	$20 plus $2 per inch for each stump whose diameter exceeds ten inches. The $2 charge is only for the diameter inches in excess of ten.

Write a complete program to allow the manager, Mr. Sorwind, to provide an estimate when he bids on a job. Your output should include a listing of each separate charge and a total. A 10 percent discount is given for any job whose total exceeds $1,000. Typical input for one customer is

R 7   T 6.5   G 8
8 10 12 14 15 15 20 25

where R, T, and G are codes for removal, trimming, and grinding, respectively. The integer following G represents the number of stumps to be ground. The next line of integers represents the diameters of stumps to be ground.

17. Write a program that prints a calendar for one month. Input consists of an integer specifying the first day of the month (1 = Sunday) and an integer specifying how many days are in a month.

18. An amortization table shows the rate at which a loan is paid off. It contains monthly entries showing the interest paid that month, the principal paid, and the remaining balance. Given the amount of money borrowed (the principal), the annual interest rate, and the amount the person wishes to repay each month, print an amortization table. (Be certain that the payment desired is

larger than the first month's interest.) Your table should stop when the loan is paid off, and should be printed with the following heads.

MONTH NUMBER   INTEREST PAID   PRINCIPAL PAID   BALANCE

19. Computers work in the binary system, which is based upon powers of 2. Write a program that prints out the first fifteen powers of 2 beginning with 2 to the zero power. Print your output in headed columns.

20. Print a list of the positive integers less than 500 that are divisible by either 5 or 7. When the list is complete, print a count of the number of integers that were found.

21. Write a program that reads in twenty real numbers, then prints the average of the positive numbers and the average of the negative numbers.

22. In 1626, the Dutch settlers purchased Manhattan Island from the Indians. According to legend, the purchase price was $24. Suppose that the Indians had invested this amount at 3 percent annual interest compounded quarterly. If the money had earned interest from the start of 1626 to the end of last year, how much money would the Indians have in the bank today? (Hint: Use nested loops for the compounding.

23. Write a program to print the sum of the odd integers from 1 to 99.

24. The theory of relativity holds that as an object moves, it gets smaller. The new length of the object can be determined from the formula:

New Length = Original Length $* \sqrt{1 - B^2}$

B^2 is the percentage of the speed of light at which the object is moving, entered in decimal form. Given the length of an object, print its new length for speeds ranging from 0 to 99 percent of the speed of light. Print the output in the following columns:

Percent of Light Speed   Length

25. Mr. Christian uses a 90 percent, 80 percent, 70 percent, 60 percent grading scale on his tests. Given a list of test scores, print out the number of As, Bs, Cs, Ds, and Fs on the test. Terminate the list of scores with a sentinel value.

26. The mathematician Gottfried Leibniz determined a formula for estimating the value of pi.

$$\frac{Pi}{4} = 1 - \frac{1}{3} + \frac{1}{5} - \frac{1}{7} + \frac{1}{9} - \frac{1}{11} + \cdots$$

Evaluate the first 200 terms of this formula and print its approximation of pi.

27. In a biology experiment, Cory finds that a sample of an organism doubles in population every twelve hours. If he starts with one thousand organisms, in how many hours will he have one million?

28. Pascal does not have a mathematical operator that permits raising a number to a power. We can easily write a program to perform this function, however. Given an integer to represent the base number and a positive integer to represent the power desired, write a program that prints the number raised to that power.

29. Mr. Thomas has negotiated a salary schedule for his new job. He will be paid one cent the first day, with the daily rate doubling each day. Write a program

that will find his total earnings for thirty days. Print your results in a table set up as follows:

```
Day Number          Daily Salary          Total Salary
     1                    .01                   .01
     2                    .02                   .03
     3
     .
     .
     .
    30
```

30. Write a program to print the perimeter and area of rectangles using all combinations of lengths and widths running from 1 foot to 10 feet in increments of 1 foot. Print the output in headed columns.

31. Teachers in most school districts are paid on a salary schedule that provides a salary based on their number of years of teaching experience. Suppose that a beginning teacher in the Babbage School District is paid $16,000 the first year. For each year of experience after this up to twelve years, a 4 percent increase over the preceding value is received. Write a program that prints a salary schedule for teachers in this district. The output should appear as follows:

```
Years Experience         Salary
----------------         ------
       0                $16,000
       1                $16,640
       2                $17,305
       3                $17,997
       .
       .
       .
      12
```

(Actually, most teacher's salary schedules are more complex than this. As an additional problem, you might like to find out how the salary schedule is determined in your school district and write a program to print the salary schedule.)

Procedures and Functions

This chapter could be entitled "All You Ever Wanted to Know About Subprograms." A *subprogram* is a program within a program and is provided for in most programming languages.

Each subprogram should complete some task. The nature of that task can range from simple to complex. You could have a subprogram that prints only a line of data, or you could write an entire program as a subprogram. The main idea is that a subprogram is used to perform some task.

Subprograms are particularly useful for facilitating program design. If a task has to be performed more than once, an appropriate subprogram can be written and then used whenever it is needed. More important, each task in a program can be assigned to a subprogram and the subprogram can be used whenever the task is to be performed. The main part of the program would then consist of calling the subprograms appropriately.

■ 7.1
Procedures for Output

- to understand the idea of a subprogram
- to be aware of some uses for procedures

Pascal provides two kinds of subprograms: *procedures* and functions. You already used some built-in functions in Chapter 3. In Section 7.4 you will learn how to write your own functions. First, however, you must learn to use procedures.

Kinds of Procedures

There are several kinds of procedures. Generally, they can be categorized into two types: those that get data from the main program or send data to it, and those that do not. In this section, we examine only those procedures that do not get data from the main program.

235

- to be aware of differences in procedures
- to understand the form for a procedure
- to use a procedure in a program

Form for a Procedure

Let's now see how a procedure is written. Basically, a procedure is a program and, as such, it has the same divisions as a complete program.

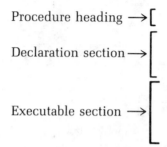

Procedure heading →

Declaration section →

Executable section →

The procedure heading must contain the reserved word **PROCEDURE** followed by the procedure name, which can be any valid identifier. Since no parameters are used at this point, the form for a procedure heading is

PROCEDURE procedure name;

When we expand the use of procedures, the procedure name will be followed by a list of parameters and the procedure heading will be

PROCEDURE procedure name (parameter list);

It is important to develop the habit of using descriptive names for procedures. For example, if you are going to write a procedure to print a heading for the output, PrintHeader might be a good choice. This allows you to recognize the task the procedure is supposed to accomplish and makes the program more readable. Each of the following is a reasonable, descriptive procedure heading.

```
PROCEDURE PrintHeader;
PROCEDURE GetData;
PROCEDURE ComputeTax;
PROCEDURE TotalPoints;
PROCEDURE PrintScores;
PROCEDURE PrintCourseInfo;
```

The declaration section of a procedure is identical to the declaration section of a program containing **CONST** and **VAR** subsections. The executable section of a procedure resembles the executable section of a program in that it must start with the reserved word **BEGIN,** but it differs in a significant way: the **END** of a procedure is followed by a semicolon instead of a period. Thus, a procedure has the following basic form:

```
PROCEDURE procedure name;
    CONST
        (list of constants)
    VAR
        (list of variables)
    BEGIN
        (body of procedure)
    END;  (*  of PROCEDURE name  *)
```

The syntax diagram for this is

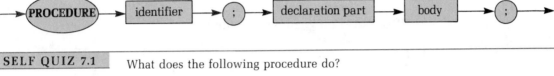

SELF QUIZ 7.1   What does the following procedure do?

```
PROCEDURE Skip3;
    BEGIN
       writeln; writeln; writeln
    END;
```

EXAMPLE 7.1   Suppose you are writing a program for Our Lady of Mercy Hospital. The program is to print a billing statement for each patient as the patient leaves the hospital. Let's write a procedure that prints a heading for each statement as follows:

```
/////////////////////////////////////////////
/                                           /
/          Our Lady of Mercy Hospital       /
/          --------------------------       /
/                                           /
/                1306 Central City          /
/                Phone (416)-333-5555       /
/                                           /
/////////////////////////////////////////////
```

The procedure to do this is

```
PROCEDURE StatementHeading;
  CONST
    Marks = '/////////////////////////////////////////////';
    Edge = '/                                           /';
    Skip = ' ';
  BEGIN
    writeln;writeln;    (*  Skip two lines  *)
    writeln(Skip:10,Marks);
    writeln(Skip:10,Edge);
    writeln(Skip:10, '/', Skip:7, 'Our Lady of Mercy Hospital', Skip:6, '/');
    writeln(Skip:10, '/', Skip:7, '--------------------------', Skip:6, '/');
```

```
     writeln(Skip:10,Edge);
     writeln(Skip:10, '/', Skip:11, '1306 Central City', Skip:11, '/');
     writeln(Skip:10, '/', Skip:10, 'Phone (416)-333-5555', Skip:9, '/');
     writeln(Skip:10,Edge);
     writeln(Skip:10,Marks);
     writeln; writeln              (*   Skip two lines   *)
END;   (*   of PROCEDURE StatementHeading   *)
```

Placement in a Program

Procedures are placed in the declaration section after the variable declaration subsection in a program. Thus, a full program with a procedure has the following form.

PROGRAM program name (**output**);

CONST

.

.

.

VAR

.

.

.

PROCEDURE procedure name;
  CONST

.

.

.

  VAR

.

.

.

  BEGIN

.

. (body of procedure)

.

  END; (* of **PROCEDURE** name *)

BEGIN (* Main program *)

.

. (body of program)

.

END. (* of main program *)

Using procedures in a program can make a program harder to read unless you enhance the readability by using comments, blank lines, and indenting. You should develop a style with which you are comfortable. The examples in this text use the following style:

1. A comment section separated by blank lines precedes most procedures.
2. Lines are skipped at the end of each procedure.
3. A comment section generally precedes the main program.

Therefore, our general form for putting a procedure in a program is

```
PROGRAM program name (output);
CONST

VAR

(************************************************

        A brief description of the procedure.

 ********************************************** )
PROCEDURE procedure name;
  CONST

  VAR

  BEGIN

    (body of procedure)

  END;  (*  of PROCEDURE name  *)


(************************************************

           Now start the main program.

 ********************************************** )
BEGIN  (*  Main program  *)

  .  (body of main program)
  .
  .
END.  (*  of main program  *)
```

What is wrong with the following program?

```
PROGRAM Quiz (output);

BEGIN

   PROCEDURE Message;
   BEGIN
      writeln ('There is an error.':50)
   END;

   Message;
   writeln ('Can you find it?')
END.
```

Calling a Procedure

Now that you know how to write a procedure and where it belongs in a program, you need to know how to call the procedure from the main program. Since no parameters are used in procedures at this point, the procedure name as a statement in the main program causes a procedure to be executed by the computer. For example, if PrintHeader is the name of a procedure,

```
BEGIN (*  Main program  *)
   PrintHeader;
      .
      .    (remainder of program)
      .
END.  (*  of main program  *)
```

causes the procedure PrintHeader to be executed in the main program before anything else is done.

When a procedure name is encountered as a program statement, control of execution is transferred to the procedure. At that time, the procedure is run as a separate program and, when the procedure is complete, control returns to the next statement in the main program following the call to the procedure. The following illustrates this control.

```
PROGRAM FirstProcedure (output);

(************************************************

      This procedure prints a line of output.

 ************************************************)
```

```
PROCEDURE PrintMessage;
  BEGIN
    writeln ('This is written from the procedure.')
  END;  (*  of PROCEDURE PrintMessage  *)


(***************************************************

          Now begin the main program.

***************************************************)

BEGIN  (*  Main program  *)
  writeln; writeln;
  writeln ('This is written from the main program.');
  writeln;
  PrintMessage;
  writeln; writeln
END.  (*  of main program  *)
```

The output from this program is

```
This is written from the main program.

This is written from the procedure.
```

EXAMPLE 7.2

Let's construct a short program that calls a procedure several times and have the procedure print the message

```
This is written by a procedure.
Now return to the main program.
```

Furthermore, let's have the main program print a message that includes a count of how often the procedure is called. A pseudocode design is

1. Initialize counter
2. Print message from the main program
3. Call procedure
4. Increment counter
5. Print message from the main program
6. Call procedure
7. Increment counter
8. Print message from the main program
9. Call procedure

The program for this design is

```
PROGRAM ProcedurePractice (output);

(********************************************************

    This program illustrates multiple calls to a
    procedure for printing a message.

********************************************************)

CONST
  Indent = '  ';
```

```
VAR
  Count : integer;

(**********************************************************

    This procedure prints a two-line message
    every time it is called.

 **********************************************************)
PROCEDURE PrintMessage;
  BEGIN
    writeln;
    writeln(Indent:20,'This is written by a procedure.');
    writeln(Indent:20,'Now return to the main program.');
    writeln
  END;    (*  of PROCEDURE PrintMessage  *)


(**********************************************************

          Now start the main program.

 **********************************************************)
BEGIN    (*  Main program  *)

  Count := 1;
  writeln(Indent:10,'This is written from the main program.');
  writeln(Indent:10,'It is call #',Count:3,' to the procedure.');
  PrintMessage;

  Count := Count + 1;
  writeln(Indent:10,'This is written from the main program.');
  writeln(Indent:10,'It is call #',Count:3,' to the procedure.');
  PrintMessage;

  Count := Count + 1;
  writeln(Indent:10,'This is written from the main program.');
  writeln(Indent:10,'It is call #',Count:3,' to the procedure.');
  PrintMessage

END.    (*  of main program  *)
```

The output from this program is

```
        This is written from the main program.
        It is call #  1 to the procedure.

                  This is written by a procedure.
                  Now return to the main program.

        This is written from the main program.
        It is call #  2 to the procedure.

                  This is written by a procedure.
                  Now return to the main program.
```

```
This is written from the main program,
It is call #  3 to the procedure,

       This is written by a procedure,
       Now return to the main program,                      ▨
```

Multiple Procedures

You should now be able to write a procedure with no parameters, know where it belongs in a program, and be able to call it from the main body of the program. The next step is to use more than one procedure in a program. Each procedure is developed separately and listed sequentially after the variable declaration subsection of the main program. Thus, the basic program with multiple procedures appears as follows:

PROGRAM program name (**output**);

CONST

.

.

.

VAR

.

.

.

PROCEDURE procedure name 1;

PROCEDURE procedure name 2;

.

.

.

PROCEDURE procedure name n;

BEGIN   (*   Main program   *)

.

.

.

END.   (*   of main program   *)

These procedures can be called in any order and as often as needed. Just remember that when a procedure is called from the main program, control is transferred to the procedure, the procedure is executed, and control returns to the next program statement in the main program.

STYLE TIP

■ ■ ■ ■ ■ ■ ■ ■

If a constant is to be used in several procedures, it can be declared in the constant definition section of the main program and then used by each subprogram. For example,

```
CONST
  Indent = '  ';
```

The following program illustrates the use of multiple procedures.

```
PROGRAM MultipleProcedures (output);

CONST
  Indent = ' ';

(******************************************************

            This is procedure one.

 *****************************************************)
PROCEDURE Message1;
  BEGIN
    writeln;
    writeln(Indent:10,'This is from procedure #1.')
  END;

(******************************************************

            This is procedure two.

 *****************************************************)
PROCEDURE Message2;
  BEGIN
    writeln;
    writeln(Indent:10,'This is from procedure #2.')
  END;

(******************************************************

            This is procedure three.

 *****************************************************)
PROCEDURE Message3;
  BEGIN
    writeln;
    writeln(Indent:10,'This is from procedure #3.')
  END;

(******************************************************

            Now begin the main program.

 *****************************************************)
BEGIN     (*  Main program  *)
  Message1;
  Message2;
  Message3;
  Message2;
  Message1;
  writeln;writeln
END.    (*  of main program  *)
```

The output from this program is

```
This is from procedure #1,

This is from procedure #2,

This is from procedure #3,

This is from procedure #2,

This is from procedure #1,
```

Examples of Using Procedures for Output

We close this section with some examples using procedures to produce output. By learning how to write and use procedures in this very limited fashion, you should be better able to work with them when they become more complicated.

EXAMPLE 7.3

Your computer science teacher wants course and program information included as part of the output of a program. Consequently, you are to write a procedure that can be used to print this information. Sample output is

```
*************************************************
*                                               *
*       Author:        Mary Smith               *
*       Course:        Pascal                    *
*       Assignment:    Program #3                *
*       Due Date:      September 18              *
*       Teacher:       Mr. Samson               *
*                                               *
*************************************************
```

The procedure to do this is

```
PROCEDURE PrintInfo;
   CONST
      Indent = ' ';
   BEGIN
      writeln(Indent:30,'*************************************************');
      writeln(Indent:30,'*                                               *');
      writeln(Indent:30,'*       Author:        Mary Smith               *');
      writeln(Indent:30,'*       Course:        Pascal                    *');
      writeln(Indent:30,'*       Assignment:    Program #3                *');
      writeln(Indent:30,'*       Due Date:      September 18              *');
      writeln(Indent:30,'*       Teacher:       Mr. Samson               *');
      writeln(Indent:30,'*                                               *');
      writeln(Indent:30,'*************************************************')
   END;    (*  of PROCEDURE PrintInfo  *)
```

EXAMPLE 7.4

As part of a program that computes and prints grades for each student in your class, you have been asked to write a procedure that produces a heading for each student report. Assume the columns for the various headings are as follows:

- The border for the class name starts in column 30
- Student Name starts in column 20
- Test Average starts in column 40
- Grade starts in column 55

The heading should appear as

```
                       ************************
                       *                      *
                       *         Pascal        *
                       *                      *
                       ************************


          Student Name          Test Average    Grade
          _____          _____    _____
```

A descriptive name for this procedure can be PrintHeader. With this information, the procedure can be written as follows:

```
PROCEDURE PrintHeader;
  CONST
    Skip = ' ';
  BEGIN
    writeln; writeln;
    writeln(Skip:29,'************************');
    writeln(Skip:29,'*                      *');
    writeln(Skip:29,'*         Pascal        *');
    writeln(Skip:29,'*                      *');
    writeln(Skip:29,'************************');
    writeln;
    writeln(Skip:19,'Student Name', Skip:8,'Test Average', Skip:3,'Grade');
    writeln(Skip:19,'_____', Skip:8,'_____', Skip:3,'_____');
    writeln
  END;    (*   of PROCEDURE PrintHeader   *)
```

EXAMPLE 7.5

The Greater Metro Airport has hired you to write a program to print a ticket for each parking lot customer. The parking lot authorities want each ticket to contain a suitable message and the amount to be paid upon leaving the parking lot. You should test the program for three customers. A pseudocode design for this problem is

1. **WHILE** more customers **DO**
   1.1 read amount due
   1.2 print heading
   1.3 print amount due
   1.4 print closing message

Let's write procedures for steps 1.2 and 1.4 of this design.
Each ticket has the following heading.

```
     Greater Metro Airport

          Parking Lot
          April 15
```

A procedure to print the heading is

```
(**************************************************************

    This procedure prints a ticket heading.

 *************************************************************)
PROCEDURE PrintHeader;
  CONST
    Date = 'April 15';
BEGIN
  writeln;
  writeln(Indent:20,'Greater Metro Airport');
  writeln;
  writeln(Indent:25,'Parking Lot');
  writeln(Indent:27,Date);
  writeln
END;    (*  of PROCEDURE PrintHeader  *)
```

Each ticket contains the following closing message.

```
    Thank you for using the
    Greater Metro Airport

    Please drive carefully
    _____
```

A procedure to print this message is

```
(**************************************************************

    This procedure prints a closing message.

 *************************************************************)
PROCEDURE PrintMessage;
  BEGIN
    writeln;
    writeln(Indent:20,'Thank you for using the');
    writeln(Indent:20,'Greater Metro Airport');
    writeln;
    writeln(Indent:20,'Please drive carefully');
    writeln(Indent:15,'_____')
  END;    (*  of PROCEDURE PrintMessage  *)
```

Each ticket contains the following message concerning the charge for parking:

```
    Your charge is        $ amount
```

A complete program for this problem follows.

```
    PROGRAM ParkingLot (input,output);

    CONST
      Indent = ' ';
    VAR
      Fee : real;
```

```
(*************************************************************

      This procedure prints a ticket heading.

**************************************************************)
PROCEDURE PrintHeader;
  CONST
    Date = 'April 15';
  BEGIN
    writeln;
    writeln(Indent:20,'Greater Metro Airport');
    writeln;
    writeln(Indent:25,'Parking Lot');
    writeln(Indent:27,Date);
    writeln
  END;    (*  of PROCEDURE PrintHeader  *)


(*************************************************************

      This procedure prints a closing message.

**************************************************************)
PROCEDURE PrintMessage;
  BEGIN
    writeln;
    writeln(Indent:20,'Thank you for using the');
    writeln(Indent:20,'Greater Metro Airport');
    writeln;
    writeln(Indent:20,'Please drive carefully');
    writeln(Indent:15,'_____')
  END;    (*  of PROCEDURE PrintMessage  *)


(*************************************************************

            Now start the main program.

**************************************************************)
BEGIN  (*  Main program  *)
  writeln ('Enter amount due; -999 to quit.');
  readln (Fee);
  WHILE Fee <> -999 DO
    BEGIN
      PrintHeader;
      writeln (Indent:20, 'Your charge is   $', Fee:6:2);
      PrintMessage;
      writeln;
      writeln ('Enter amount due; -999 to quit.');
      readln (Fee)
    END (*  of WHILE ... DO loop  *)
END. (*  of main program  *)
```

A sample run of this program for three customers is

```
Enter amount due; -999 to quit.
5.75

        Greater Metro Airport

            Parking Lot
            April 15

    Your charge is    $   5.75

    Thank you for using the
    Greater Metro Airport

    Please drive carefully
------------------------------------------

Enter amount due; -999 to quit.
8.00

        Greater Metro Airport

            Parking Lot
            April 15

    Your charge is    $   8.00

    Thank you for using the
    Greater Metro Airport

    Please drive carefully
------------------------------------------

Enter amount due; -999 to quit.
4.25

        Greater Metro Airport

            Parking Lot
            April 15

    Your charge is    $   4.25

    Thank you for using the
    Greater Metro Airport

    Please drive carefully
------------------------------------------
Enter amount due; -999 to quit.
-999
```

1. Explain the difference between a procedure and a program.

2. What output is produced when the following procedure is called from the main program?

```
PROCEDURE ExerciseTwo;
  CONST
    Splats = '*****************************';
    Underline = '_____';
    Skip = ' ';
  BEGIN
    writeln (Skip:4, Splats);
    writeln (Skip:9, '*', Skip:19, '*');
    write (Skip:9, '   Sample Output');
    writeln ('*':5);
    writeln (Skip:9, '*', Underline:15, '*':5);
    writeln (Skip:9, '*', Skip:19, '*');
    writeln (Skip:4, Splats)
END;
```

3. Write a procedure to produce the following:

```
******************************
*                            *
*        your name here      *
*        today's date here   *
*                            *
******************************
```

4. Write a program that calls the procedure in Exercise 3 five times.

In Exercises 5–8, create a suitable message for the heading of a billing statement for the business and write a procedure to print the heading when called from the main program.

5. R & R Produce Company   7. Sleep E-Z-E Motel
6. Atlas Athletic Equipment   8. Pump-Your-Own Service Station

9. Consider the output

```
//////////////////////////////
/                            /
/        Special Olympics     /
/        _____ _____     /
//////////////////////////////

//////////////////////////////
/                            /
/        Special Olympics     /
/        _____ _____     /
//////////////////////////////

//////////////////////////////
/                            /
/        Special Olympics     /
/        _____ _____     /
//////////////////////////////
```

   a. Write a program that produces this output without using procedures.
   b. Write a program that produces this output using a procedure.

10. Consider the following program

```
PROGRAM Exercise10 (output);

CONST
  Splats = '*************************';
  Edge = '*                       *';
  Skip = ' ';
VAR
  Interest : real;

BEGIN     (*  Main program  *)
  writeln;writeln;
  writeln(Skip:15,Splats);
  writeln(Skip:15,Edge);
  writeln(Skip:15,'*     Federal Savings     *');
  writeln(Skip:15,'*     Monthly Report      *');
  writeln(Skip:15,Edge);
  writeln(Skip:15,Splats);
  writeln;writeln;
  Interest := 114.53;
  writeln(Skip:10,'Thank you for banking with Federal Savings.');
  writeln(Skip:10,'Your current interest payment is below.');
  writeln('$':20,Interest:8:2);
  writeln;
  Interest := 87.93;
  writeln(Skip:10,'Thank you for banking with Federal Savings.');
  writeln(Skip:10,'Your current interest payment is below.');
  writeln('$':20,Interest:8:2);
  writeln;writeln
END.    (*  of main program  *)
```

and its output.

```
            *************************
            *                       *
            *     Federal Savings    *
            *     Monthly Report     *
            *                       *
            *************************


       Thank you for banking with Federal Savings.
       Your current interest payment is below.
            $   114.53

       Thank you for banking with Federal Savings.
       Your current interest payment is below.
            $    87.93
```

Rewrite this program using
a. a procedure for the heading
b. a procedure for the customer message

11. What is the output from the following program?

```
PROGRAM Exercise11 (output);

CONST
  Skip = ' ';

PROCEDURE Number1;
  BEGIN
    writeln (Skip:10, 'She loves me,')
  END;  (*  of PROCEDURE Number1  *)

PROCEDURE Number2;
  BEGIN
    writeln (Skip:10, 'She loves me not,')
  END;  (*  of PROCEDURE Number2  *)

BEGIN  (*  Main program  *)
  Number1;
  Number2;
  Number1;
  Number2;
  Number1
END.  (*  of main program  *)
```

12. Rewrite the following program using indenting, blank lines, comments, and comment sections to enhance readability.

```
PROGRAM Plain (output);
VAR
Score1, Score2 : integer;
Average : real;
PROCEDURE PrintHeader;
BEGIN
writeln; writeln;
writeln ('Your test results are below,');
writeln;
writeln ('Keep up the good work!');
writeln; writeln
END;
BEGIN
PrintHeader;
Score1 := 89;
Score2 := 95;
Average := (Score1 + Score2)/2.0;
writeln ('Score1':15, Score1:6);
writeln ('Score2':15, Score2:6);
writeln;
writeln ('Your average is':24, Average8:2)
END.
```

■ 7.2
Procedures

- to use correct form and syntax for writing a procedure
- to understand the difference between variable and value parameters
- to understand the difference between formal parameters and actual parameters
- to use a procedure in a program

Parameters

The significant change between our previous use of procedures for headings only and procedures in general is the use of parameters. As shown in Section 7.1, the heading for a procedure is

> **PROCEDURE** procedure name (parameter list);

Parameters are used so that values of variables may be transmitted (passed) from the main program to the procedure and from the procedure to the main program. If values are to be passed only from the main program to the procedure, the parameters are called *value parameters*. If values are to be passed from the main program to the procedure and from the procedure to the main program, they are called *variable parameters*.

When using parameters with procedures, the following should be noted.

1. *Parameter list* is a list of *formal parameters* which can be thought of as blanks waiting to receive values from *actual parameters* in a calling program. Actual parameters are variables used in the calling program. The formal parameter list must match the number and corresponding types of actual parameters used when the procedure is called from the main program.
2. The number of parameters in the parameter list must match the number of variables used when calling the procedure from the main program.
3. The type of parameters must match the corresponding type of variables used when calling the procedure from the main program.
4. The parameter types are declared in the procedure heading.

To illustrate formal and actual parameters used with procedures, consider the following complete program.

```
PROGRAM ProcDemo1 (output);

VAR
  Num1, Num2 : integer;
  Num3 : real;

(********************************************************

    This procedure demonstrates the
    use of formal and actual parameters.

    It is called by PrintNum (Num1, Num2, Num3);

*********************************************************)
PROCEDURE PrintNum (N1, N2 : integer; N3 : real);
  BEGIN
    writeln;
    writeln (N1:10, N2:10, N3:10:2);
    writeln
  END; (*  of PROCEDURE PrintNum  *)
```

```
(*  Now start the main program  *)

BEGIN  (*  Main program  *)
  Num1 := 5;
  Num2 := 8;
  Num3 := Num2/Num1;
  PrintNum (Num1, Num2, Num3)
END. (*  of main program  *)
```

When this program is run, the output is

```
5       8      1.60
```

In this program, N1, N2, and N3 are formal parameters; Num1, Num2, and Num3 are actual parameters. Let's now examine the relationship between the parameter list in the procedure

```
PROCEDURE PrintNum (N1, N2 : integer; N3 : real);
```

and the procedure call in the main program.

```
PrintNum (Num1, Num2, Num3);
```

In this case, Num1 corresponds to N1, Num2 corresponds to N2, and Num3 corresponds to N3. Notice that both the number and type of variables in the parameter list correspond with the number and type of variables listed in the procedure call.

STYLE TIP

Identifiers used in subprograms should not be the same as identifiers used in the main program. However, use of similar or related identifiers can help in identifying program logic and tracing values through a program. Thus, if a procedure call is

```
PrintData (Initial1,Initial2,Score1,Score2,Score3);
```

the procedure heading can be

```
PROCEDURE PrintData (Init1,Init2:char;
                     Sc1,Sc2,Sc3:integer);
```

Value Parameters

The preceding procedure demonstrated the use of value parameters or of one-way transmission of values. Different memory areas have been set aside for the variables Num1, Num2, and Num3 and for N1, N2, and N3. Thus, initially we have

Main Program   Procedure

Num1   N1

Num2   N2

Num3   N3

The assignment statements

```
Num1 := 5;
Num2 := 8;
Num3 := Num2/Num1;
```

produce

Main Program	Procedure
5	
Num1	N1
8	
Num2	N2
1.6	
Num3	N3

When the procedure PrintNum is called from the main program by

```
PrintNum (Num1, Num2, Num3);
```

the values are transmitted to N1, N2, and N3, respectively, as follows:

Main Program	Procedure
5	5
Num1	N1
8	8
Num2	N2
1.6	1.6
Num3	N3

At this stage, the procedure PrintNum can use N1, N2, and N3 in any appropriate manner.

It is important to note that since the passing of values is from the main program to the procedure only, we are using value parameters.

If the procedure changes the value of N1, N2, or N3, the values of Num1, Num2, and Num3 are not changed. For example, suppose the procedure is changed to

```
PROCEDURE PrintNum (N1, N2 : integer; N3 : real);
  BEGIN
    writeln (N1:10, N2:10, N3:10:2);
    N1 := 2 * N1;
    N2 := 2 * N2;
    N3 := 2 * N3;
    writeln (N1:10, N2:10, N3:10:2);
  END; (* of PROCEDURE PrintNum *)
```

Furthermore, suppose the main program is changed to

```
BEGIN  (*  Main  Program  *)
  Num1 := 5;
  Num2 := 8;
  Num3 := Num2/Num1;
  writeln;
  writeln (Num1:10, Num2:10, Num3:10:2);
  PrintNum (Num1, Num2, Num3);
  writeln (Num1:10, Num2:10, Num3:10:2);
  writeln
END.  (*  of main Program  *)
```

When this program is run, the output is

```
  5           8          1.60      (from  main  program)
  5           8          1.60      (from  procedure)
 10          16          3.20      (from  procedure)
  5           8          1.60      (from  main  program)
```

The first line of this output is produced by the first

```
  writeln (Num1:10, Num2:10, Num3:10:2);
```

of the main program. The next two lines of output come from the procedure. The last line of output is produced by the second

```
  writeln (Num1:10, Num2:10, Num3:10:2);
```

of the main program. You should carefully note that after the procedure changes the values of N1, N2, and N3, the values of Num1, Num2, and Num3 are not changed. Thus, we have

Main Program	Procedure
5	10
Num1	N1
8	16
Num2	N2
1.6	3.2
Num3	N3

Before considering two-way passing of values (variable parameters), let's look at another example of a procedure using value parameters by writing a procedure to find the average of three scores, print the scores, and print the average. Since the procedure receives three integer values from the main program, a suitable procedure heading is

```
  PROCEDURE FindAverage (S1, S2, S3 : integer);
```

In this case, an additional variable must be used, so the declaration section of the procedure is

```
  VAR
    Av : real;
```

Now the complete procedure is

```
PROCEDURE FindAverage (S1, S2, S3 : integer);
  CONST
    Indent = ' ';
  VAR
    Av : real;
  BEGIN
    Av := (S1 + S2 + S3) / 3;
    writeln;
    writeln (Indent:9, 'The scores are');
    writeln;
    writeln (S1:15, S2:5, S3:5);
    writeln;
    writeln (Indent:9, 'Their average is', Av:10:2)
  END;  (*  of PROCEDURE FindAverage  *)
```

Assume Score1, Score2, and Score3 are the corresponding variables in the main program. If the data entered are

89 92 85

the statements from the main program

```
readln (Score1, Score2, Score3);
FindAverage (Score1, Score2, Score3);
```

produce

```
The scores are

    89    92    85

Their average is      88.66
```

<hr>

SELF QUIZ 7.3

Consider the procedure

```
PROCEDURE Switch (X1, Y1 : real);
  VAR
    Temp : real;
  BEGIN
    writeln (X1:10:2, Y1:10:2);
    Temp := X1;
    X1 := Y1;
    Y1 := Temp;
    writeln (X1:10:2, Y1:10:2)
  END;  (*  of PROCEDURE Switch  *)
```

1. How is this called from the main program?
2. What happens when it is called?

<hr>

Variable Parameters

It is frequently the case that you want a procedure to change several values in the main program. This can be accomplished by using variable parameters in the parameter list. Variable parameters are declared by using the reserved word **VAR** to precede appropriate formal parameters in the procedure heading. When variable parameters are declared, transmission of values is two-way rather than one-way. Thus, any change of values in the procedure produces a corresponding change of values in the main program.

To illustrate the declaration of variable parameters, consider the procedure heading

```
PROCEDURE PrintNum (VAR N1, N2 : integer; N3 : real);
```

In this case, N1 and N2 are variable parameters corresponding to integer variables in the main program. N3 is a value parameter corresponding to a real variable. This procedure can be called from the main program by

```
PrintNum (Num1, Num2, Num3);
```

To illustrate the passing of values, assume the procedure is

```
PROCEDURE PrintNum (VAR N1, N2 : integer; N3 : real);
  BEGIN
    writeln (N1, N2, N3:10:2);
    N1 := 2 * N1;
    N2 := 2 * N2;
    N3 := 2 * N3;
    writeln (N1, N2, N3:10:2)
  END; (* of PROCEDURE PrintNum *)
```

If the corresponding variables in the main program are Num1, Num2, and Num3, respectively, initially we have

Main Program   Procedure

```
┌──────────┐                ┌──────────┐
│          │                │          │
└──────────┘                └──────────┘
   Num1                         N1

┌──────────┐                ┌──────────┐
│          │                │          │
└──────────┘                └──────────┘
   Num2                         N2

┌──────────┐                ┌──────────┐
│          │                │          │
└──────────┘                └──────────┘
   Num3                         N3
```

Remember: Technically, N1 and N2 do not exist. They are merely aliases for Num1 and Num2. The figures here are designed to help you understand the difference between value and variable parameters.

If the main program makes the assignment statements

```
Num1 := 5;
Num2 := 8;
Num3 := Num2/Num1;
```

we have

Main Program   Procedure

```
┌──────────┐                ┌──────────┐
│    5     │                │    5     │
└──────────┘                └──────────┘
   Num1                         N1

┌──────────┐                ┌──────────┐
│    8     │                │    8     │
└──────────┘                └──────────┘
   Num2                         N2

┌──────────┐                ┌──────────┐
│   1.6    │                │   1.6    │
└──────────┘                └──────────┘
   Num3                         N3
```

When the following statements from the procedure

```
N1 := 2 * N1;
N2 := 2 * N2;
N3 := 2 * N3;
```

are executed, we have

Main Program   Procedure

| 10 | | 10 |
Num1   N1

| 16 | | 16 |
Num2   N2

| 1.6 | | 3.2 |
Num3   N3

Notice that the variable parameters N1 and N2 produce changes in the corresponding variables in the main program, but the value parameter N3 does not.

Let's now consider a short, complete program that illustrates the difference between variable and value parameters.

```
PROGRAM ProcDemo2 (output);

VAR
  X, Y : real;
  Ch : char;

(**************************************************************

  Procedure to demonstrate variable versus value parameters.

  **************************************************************)

PROCEDURE VarDemo (VAR X1:real; Y1:real; VAR Ch1:char);
  BEGIN
    writeln (X1:10:2, Y1:10:2, Ch1:5);
    X1 := 2 * X1;
    Y1 := 2 * Y1;
    Ch1 := '*';
    writeln (X1:10:2, Y1:10:2, Ch1:5)
  END;  (* of PROCEDURE VarDemo  *)

BEGIN (*  Main program  *)
  X := 3.6;
  Y := 5.2;
  Ch := 'A';
  writeln (X:10:2, Y:10:2, Ch:5);
  VarDemo (X, Y, Ch);
  writeln (X:10:2, Y:10:2, Ch:5)
END.  (*  of main program  *)
```

The output from the program is

```
3.60        5.20        A        (from  main  program)
3.60        5.20        A        (from  procedure)
7.20       10.40        *        (from  procedure)
7.20        5.20        *        (from  main  program)
```

The variables when declared can be depicted as

Main Program   Procedure

| | | |
|---| |---|
| X | | X1 |

| | | |
|---| |---|
| Y | | Y1 |

| | | |
|----| |-----|
| Ch | | Ch1 |

The assignment statements

```
X  := 3.6;
Y  := 5.2;
Ch := 'A';
```

produce

Main Program   Procedure

| 3.6 | | 3.6 |
|-----| |-----|
| X | | X1 |

| 5.2 | | 5.2 |
|-----| |-----|
| Y | | Y1 |

| A | | A |
|-----| |-----|
| Ch | | Ch1 |

When the assignment statements

```
X1  := 2 * X1;
Y1  := 2 * Y1;
Ch1 := '*';
```

are made and the program is executed, the variables are

Main Program   Procedure

| 7.2 | | 7.2 |
|-----| |-----|
| X | | X1 |

| 5.2 | | 10.4 |
|-----| |------|
| Y | | Y1 |

| * | | * |
|-----| |-----|
| Ch | | Ch1 |

A NOTE OF INTEREST

Ada

Of the many programming languages available other than Pascal, Ada deserves special mention. As you learned in an earlier Note of Interest, Ada is not an acronym, but is named after Ada Augusta Byron.

Ada was developed in the 1970s and was sponsored by the United States Department of Defense. It was developed as a language to be used in embedded applications, that is, applications that use a computer as part of a larger complex of electronics and mechanics. Generally, this is the role of a control system. These applications require reliability, complexity, and host and target computers.

Ada's main features are the same as those of Pascal. In addition, it has separate compilation of modules, concurrent execution of several modules, powerful features for error handling, and provisions for machine-independent operating system linkages. Because of these characteristics and the strong support of the Department of Defense, it is anticipated that Ada will be the primary language used by professional programmers by the year 2000.

Notice that changes in the variable parameters X1 and Ch1 produce corresponding changes in X and Ch, but a change in the value parameter Y1 does not produce a change in Y.

SELF QUIZ 7.4   Consider the procedure

```
PROCEDURE Switch (VAR X1, Y1 : real);
   VAR
     Temp : real;
   BEGIN
     Temp := X1;
     X1 := Y1;
     Y1 := Temp
   END;  (*  of PROCEDURE Switch  *)
```

What output is produced by the following main program fragment?

```
BEGIN (*  Main program  *)
  X := 2.0;
  Y := 3.0;
  writeln (X:10:2, Y:10:2);
  Switch (X,Y);
  writeln (X:10:2, Y:10:2)
END.  (*  of main program  *)
```

We close this section with a sample program using four procedures. The program reads three reals as input, computes their average, and then prints the results. A first-level pseudocode development for this program is

1. Get data
2. Process data
3. Print header
4. Print results

We can write a procedure for each of these pseudocode steps.

1. Get data

becomes

```
PROCEDURE GetData (VAR S1, S2, S3 : real);
  BEGIN
    writeln ('Enter three reals and press <RETURN>.');
    readln (S1, S2, S3)
  END;  (*  of PROCEDURE GetData  *)
```

Note that this procedure uses variable parameters so that values from the procedure are transmitted back to the program.

2. Process data

becomes

```
PROCEDURE FindAverage (S1, S2, S3 : real;
                            VAR Aver : real);
  BEGIN
    Aver := (S1 + S2 + S3) / 3
  END;  (*  of PROCEDURE FindAverage  *)
```

Note that S1, S2, and S3 are value parameters and Aver is a variable parameter. When this procedure is called from the main program, it returns the computed average. (In Section 7.4 we will see how this can be written as a function.)

3. Print header

becomes

```
PROCEDURE PrintHeader;
  CONST
    Indent = '  ';
  BEGIN
    writeln;
    writeln (Indent:30, 'Scores');
    writeln (Indent:30, '_____');
    writeln
  END;  (*  of PROCEDURE PrintHeader  *)
```

4. Print results

becomes

```
PROCEDURE PrintResults (S1, S2, S3, Av : real);
  BEGIN
    writeln (S1:36:2);
    writeln (S2:36:2);
    writeln (S3:36:2);
    writeln ('_____':36);
    writeln (Av:36:2)
  END;  (*  of PROCEDURE PrintResults  *)
```

Now that procedures are written for each part of the program, the main part of the program is

```
BEGIN  (*  Main Program  *)
  GetData (Score1, Score2, Score3);
  FindAverage (Score1, Score2, Score3, Average);
  PrintHeader;
  PrintResults (Score1, Score2, Score3, Average)
END.  (*  of main program  *)
```

The complete program is

```
PROGRAM ProcDemo (input, output);
(***********************************************************

   This Program demonstrates the use of Procedures. Both
   value and variable Parameters are featured. Notice
   how the main Program merely consists of calling
   appropriate Procedures.


************************************************************)

VAR
  Average : real;        (*  The average of three reals  *)
  Score1,                (*  First score read            *)
  Score2,                (*  Second score read           *)
  Score3 : real;         (*  Third score read            *)


(***********************************************************

           This Procedure gets the data.

************************************************************)
PROCEDURE GetData (VAR S1, S2, S3 : real);
  BEGIN
    writeln ('Enter three reals and Press <RETURN>.');
    readln (S1, S2, S3)
  END; (*  of PROCEDURE GetData  *)


(***********************************************************

           This Procedure computes the average.

************************************************************)
PROCEDURE FindAverage (S1, S2, S3 : real; VAR Aver:real);
  BEGIN
    Aver := (S1 + S2 + S3)/3
  END; (*  of PROCEDURE FindAvease  *)


(***********************************************************

          This Procedure Prints a heading.

************************************************************)
```

```
PROCEDURE PrintHeader;
  CONST
    Indent = ' ';
  BEGIN
    writeln;
    writeln (Indent:30, 'Scores');
    writeln (Indent:30, '_____');
    writeln
  END;  (*  of PROCEDURE PrintHeader  *)

(*************************************************************

          This procedure prints the results.

  *************************************************************)
PROCEDURE PrintResults (S1, S2, S3, Av : real);
  BEGIN
    writeln (S1:36:2);
    writeln (S2:36:2);
    writeln (S3:36:2);
    writeln ('_____':36);
    writeln (Av:36:2)
  END;  (*  of PROCEDURE PrintResults  *)

(*************************************************************

    All procedures are written.  Now start the main
    program.

  *************************************************************)
BEGIN  (*  Main program  *)
  GetData (Score1, Score2, Score3);
  FindAverage (Score1, Score2, Score3, Average);
  PrintHeading;
  PrintResults (Score1, Score2, Score3, Average)
END.  (*  of main program  *)
```

If the data entered are

```
89.3 92.4 84.6
```

A sample run of this program is

```
Enter three reals and press <RETURN>.
89.3 92.4 84.6


                              Scores

                              89.30
                              92.40
                              84.60
                              _____
                              88.77
```

STYLE TIP

Occasionally you may wish to have a program pause during execution. Pauses of varying length can be achieved by

```
PROCEDURE Pause (PauseLength : integer);
  VAR
    J : integer;
  BEGIN
    FOR J := 1 TO PauseLength DO
  END;  (*  of PROCEDURE Pause  *)
```

This procedure can be called by

```
Pause (1000);
```

where the value used in the procedure call can be changed to cause varying length pauses.

Exercises 7.2

1. Explain the difference between value parameters and variable parameters. Also explain the difference between actual parameters and formal parameters.

2. Write a test program to find what happens if the parameter lists do not match when a procedure is called from the main program. Investigate each of the following:

   a. Correct number of parameters, wrong order
   b. Incorrect number of parameters

In Exercises 3–5, indicate which parameters are value parameters and which are variable parameters.

```
3. PROCEDURE Demo1 (VAR A,B : integer;
                        X : real);
4. PROCEDURE Demo2 (VAR A : integer;
                        B : integer;
                        VAR X : real;
                        Ch : char);
5. PROCEDURE Demo3 (A,B : integer;
                        VAR X,Y,Z : real;
                        Ch : char);
```

In Exercises 6–10, indicate which are appropriate procedure headings. Explain the problem with those that are inappropriate.

```
6. PROCEDURE Prac1 (A : integer : Y : real);
7. PROCEDURE Error? (Ch1, Ch2 : char);
8. PROCEDURE Prac2 (A, VAR B : integer);
9. PROCEDURE Prac3 (A,B,C : integer
                        VAR X,Y : real
                        Ch : char
                        Flag : boolean);
10. PROCEDURE Prac4 (VAR A : integer, X : real);
```

In Exercises 11–15, indicate how the procedures are called from the main program.

```
11. PROCEDURE Exercise11 (A,B : integer; Ch : char);
12. PROCEDURE PrintHeader;
```

```
13. PROCEDURE FindMax (N1, N2 : integer;
                          VAR NewMax : integer);
14. PROCEDURE Switch (VAR X,Y : real);
15. PROCEDURE SwitchAndTest (VAR X,Y : real;
                               VAR F1 : boolean);
```

In Exercises 16–19, using the following procedure,

```
PROCEDURE Switch (VAR A,B : integer);
  VAR
     Temp : integer;
  BEGIN
     Temp := A;
     A := B;
     B := Temp
  END;  (*  of PROCEDURE Switch  *)
```

indicate the output produced by the fragment of code in the main program.

```
16. Num1 := 5;
    Num2 := 10;
    writeln (Num1, Num2);
    Switch (Num1, Num2);
    writeln (Num1, Num2);
    Switch (Num1, Num2);
    writeln (Num1, Num2);
17. Num1 := -3;
    Num2 := 2;
    IF Num1 > Num2 THEN
       Switch (Num1, Num2)
    ELSE
       Switch (Num2, Num1);
    writeln (Num2, Num1);
18. N := 3;
    M := 20;
    Switch (M,N);
    writeln (M,N);
    Switch (N,M);
    writeln (N,M);
19. Count := 0;
    Max := 10;
    WHILE Count < Max DO
       BEGIN
          Switch (Count, Max);
          writeln (Count, Max);
          Count := Count + 1
       END;  (*  of WHILE ... DO  *)
```

In Exercises 20–24, write a procedure and indicate how it is called from the main program.

20. Print the heading for the output.

```
Acme National Electronics
   Board of Directors
     Annual Meeting
```

21. Find the maximum and average of three reals. Both values are to be returned to the main program.

22. Count the number of occurrences of the letter *A* in a line of character data. The count should be returned to the main program.
23. Convert Fahrenheit temperature to Celsius.
24. Find and print all divisors of a positive integer.

In Exercises 25–32, assume a program contains the variable declaration section

```
VAR
   Num1, Num2 : integer;
   X, Y : real;
   Ch1, Ch2 : char;
```

Furthermore, suppose the same program contains a procedure whose heading is

```
PROCEDURE Demo (VAR N1, N2 : integer;
                    X1 :  real;
                    Ch :  char);
```

Indicate which are appropriate calls to the procedure Demo. Explain those that are inappropriate.

25. `Demo (Num1, Num2);`
26. `Demo (Num1, Num2, X);`
27. `Demo (Num1, Num2, X, Ch1);`
28. `Demo (X, Y, Num1, Ch2);`
29. `Demo (Num2, X, Y, Ch1);`
30. `Demo (Num1, Num2, Ch2);`
31. `Demo;`
32. `Demo (Num2, Num1, Y, Ch1);`

■ 7.3
Scope of Identifiers

Local and Global Variables

Variables declared in the declaration section of a program can be used throughout the entire program. For purposes of this section, we will think of the program as a heading and a *block* and envision it as in Figure 7.1. Furthermore, if X1 is a variable in Scope, we indicate this as shown in Figure 7.2, where an area in memory is set aside for X1. When a program contains a subprogram, a separate memory area within the memory area for the program is set aside for the subprogram. This is sometimes referred to as the block for the subprogram. Thus, if Scope contains a procedure named Subprog1, we can envision this as shown in Figure 7.3. If Subprog1 contains the variable X2, we have the program shown in Figure 7.4. This can all be indicated in a program by

```
PROGRAM Scope (input, output);

VAR
   X1 : real;

PROCEDURE Subprog1 (X2 : real);
```

We now must consider which variables are available to the various parts of the program. When subprograms are used, each variable is available to the block in which it is declared; this includes all subprograms

FIGURE 7.1
Program heading and
main block

PROGRAM Scope

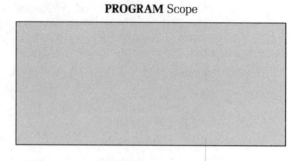

FIGURE 7.2
Variable location in
main block

PROGRAM Scope

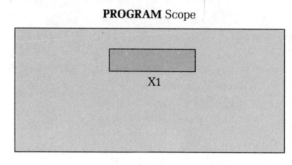

FIGURE 7.3
Illustration of a sub-
block

PROGRAM Scope

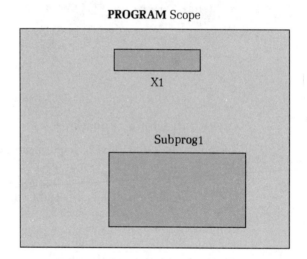

contained within its block. In addition, variables are not available outside their blocks.

Variables that can be used by all subprograms in a program are called
global variables; variables that are restricted to use within a block are
called *local variables.* Variable X1 in the previous illustration can be
used in the main program and in **PROCEDURE** Subprog1; therefore it is
a global variable. On the other hand, X2 can only be used within the
procedure where it is declared; it is a local variable. Any attempt to
reference X2 outside the procedure results in an error.

As you can see, global and local are relative terms. If a subprogram

FIGURE 7.4
Variable location
within a subblock

PROGRAM Scope

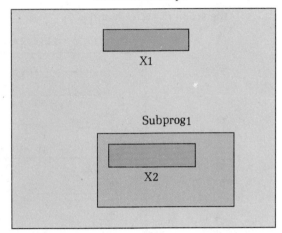

FIGURE 7.5
Local and global
variables

PROGRAM Scope

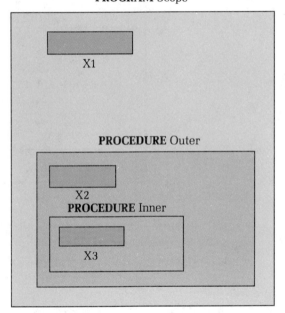

contains a subprogram (see Section 7.5), as in Figure 7.5, with variables
X1, X2, and X3 as indicated, X2 is local with respect to **PROCEDURE**
Outer but global with respect to **PROCEDURE** Inner. The only nonrela-
tive uses of these terms are that variables declared in the main program
are always global and variables declared in the innermost subprogram are
always local.

The *scope of an identifier* refers to the largest block in which the variable is available. Hence, in the previous illustration, the scope of X3 is
PROCEDURE Inner, the scope of X2 is **PROCEDURE** Outer, and the
scope of X1 is **PROGRAM** Scope.

Given the following schematic representation of a program's identifiers, indicate the scope of each identifier.

PROGRAM Main

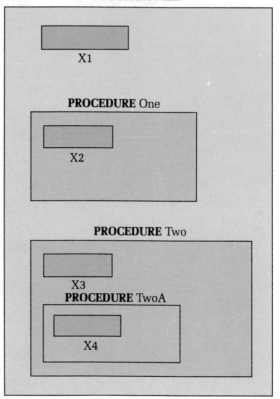

Let's now examine an illustration of local and global variables. Consider the program and procedure declaration

```
PROGRAM ScopePrac (output);

VAR
   A,B : integer;

PROCEDURE Subprog (A1 : integer);
   VAR
      X : real;
```

Memory area for this program can be envisioned as shown in Figure 7.6. Since A and B are global, the statement

```
writeln (A, B, A1, X:10:2);
```

can be used in **PROCEDURE** Subprog although A and B were not specifically declared there. However,

```
writeln (A, B, A1, X:10:2);
```

cannot be used in the main program because A1 and X are local to **PRO-CEDURE** Subprog.

FIGURE 7.6
Scope of variables

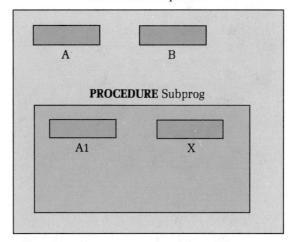

Using Global Variables

In general, it is not good practice to refer to global variables within procedures. Using locally defined variables enables you to avoid unexpected side effects and protect your program. In addition, locally defined variables facilitate debugging and top-down design, and they enhance the portability of procedures.

There are, however, at least two instances in which using global variables is appropriate. First, you may wish to save some value from one call of a subprogram until the next call to that subprogram. If all variables are local, this is not done because values of the local variables are not retained when a subprogram is exited. Second, you may have a program with several functions and procedures that all work with some large data structure (see Chapters 9 and 10). In this case, you can leave the large structure as a global variable but work with it from various procedures and functions.

STYLE TIP

■ ■ ■ ■ ■ ■ ■ ■

Global constants can be declared in the main program. In particular, constants for output such as

```
CONST
    Indent = ' ';
    Skip = ' ';
    Splats = '********************';
    Underline = '_____';
```

can be defined for subsequent use by several procedures.

Names of Identifiers

Since separate areas in memory are set aside when subprograms are used, it is possible to have identifiers with the same name in both the main program and a subprogram. Thus,

```
PROGRAM Demo (input, output);

VAR
  A : integer;

PROCEDURE Subprog (A : integer);
```

can be envisioned as shown in Figure 7.7 and is a valid method for declaring variables. By doing so, however, you create two separate variables called A. These two values are not necessarily the same. When the same name is used in this manner, any reference to this name results in action being taken on the most local form of the variable. Thus, the assignment statement

```
A := 20;
```

made in **PROCEDURE** Subprog assigns 20 to A in the procedure but not in the main program (see Figure 7.8). Now that you know you can use the same name for an identifier in a subprogram and the main program, it is time for a warning: Using the same identifiers can create problems. First, a reference to such identifiers may not be clear. For example, suppose Age is declared as a variable in both the main program and a procedure. If an assignment statement such as

```
Age := 21;
```

is made in either the subprogram or the main program, it is not easy to find exactly where this statement applies. Second, programs that contain the same name at various levels can present problems in debugging; it is more difficult to trace values of variables and flow of logic. Therefore, you should avoid using the same variable name.

A reasonable alternative to using the same name for identifiers is to use identifiers with similar or related names. For example, if the main program contains variables Age1 and Age2 to be used as parameters in a procedure call, the formal parameters A1 and A2 can be used in the procedure heading to correspond to Age1 and Age2. It is then relatively clear which values are transferred to which variables and which variables are used in expressions and assignment statements.

FIGURE 7.7
Using identifiers in
subprograms

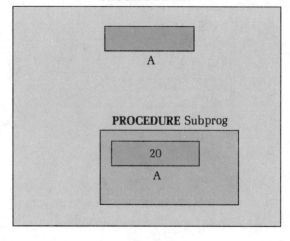

PROGRAM Demo

FIGURE 7.8
Assigning values in
subprograms

PROGRAM Demo

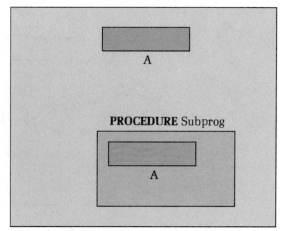

What output is produced from the following program?

```
PROGRAM VarPrac (output);

VAR
   A : integer;

PROCEDURE Subprog (A : integer);
   BEGIN
     A := 30;
     writeln (A)
   END; (* of PROCEDURE Subprog *)

BEGIN (* Main program *)
   A := 20;
   writeln (A);
   Subprog (A);
   writeln (A)
END. (* of main program *)
```

Procedure Names as Identifiers

The name of a procedure is also an identifier. Thus, variable identifiers
cannot use these names if they are on the same level. That is,

```
PROGRAM Demo2 (output);

VAR
   Prac : integer;

PROCEDURE Prac (A : integer);
```

produces an error because Prac is an identifier declared twice on the
same level. This can be envisioned as shown in Figure 7.9. Even where
permitted, this practice should be avoided.

FIGURE 7.9
Procedure name as
an identifier

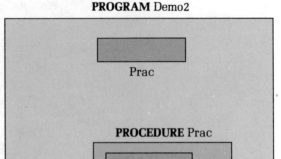

Multiple Procedures

As we learned in Section 7.2, more than one procedure can be used in a
program. When this occurs, all the previous uses and restrictions of identifiers apply to each procedure. Blocks for multiple procedures can be
depicted as shown in Figure 7.10. Identifiers in the main program can be
accessed by each procedure. However, local identifiers in the procedures
cannot be accessed by the main program or by other procedures.

The same names for identifiers can be used in different procedures.
Thus, if the main program uses variables Wage and Hours, and both of
these are used as arguments in calls to different procedures, you have the
situation shown in Figure 7.11. Using the same names for identifiers in
different procedures makes it easier to keep track of the relationship between variables in the main program and their associated parameters in
each subprogram. For example, if Wage and Hours are used in the main
program, W and H can be used as corresponding parameters in all procedures.

FIGURE 7.10
Blocks for multiple
subprograms

PROCEDURE A

PROCEDURE B

PROCEDURE C

FIGURE 7.11
Identifiers in multiple subprograms

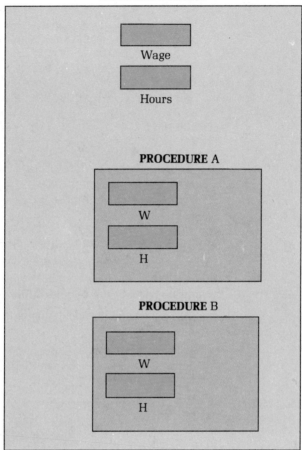

Exercises 7.3

1. Explain the difference between local and global variables.

2. State the advantages of using local variables.

3. Discuss some appropriate uses for global variables. List several constants that would be appropriate global definitions.

4. What is meant by the scope of an identifier?

5. Write a test program to enable you to see

   a. what happens when an attempt is made to access an identifier outside of its scope; and

   b. how the values change as a result of assignments in the subprogram and the main program when the same identifier is used in the main program and a procedure.

6. Review the following program.

```
PROGRAM Practice (input, output);

VAR
   A,B : integer;
   X : real;
   Ch : char;
```

```
PROCEDURE Sub1 (A1 : integer);
  VAR
    B1 : integer;
  BEGIN  (*  PROCEDURE Sub1  *)
    .
    .
    .
  END;  (*  of PROCEDURE Sub1  *)

PROCEDURE Sub2 (A1 : integer; VAR B1 : integer);
  VAR
    X1 : real;
    Ch1 : char;
  BEGIN  (*  PROCEDURE Sub2  *)
    .
    .
    .
  END;  (*  of PROCEDURE Sub2  *)
```

a. List all global variables.
b. List all local variables.
c. Indicate the scope of each identifier.

7. Provide a schematic representation of the program and all subprograms and variables in Exercise 6.

8. Using the program with variables and subprograms as depicted in Figure 7.12, state the scope of each identifier.

FIGURE 7.12
Program structure for
Exercise 8

PROGRAM Exercise8

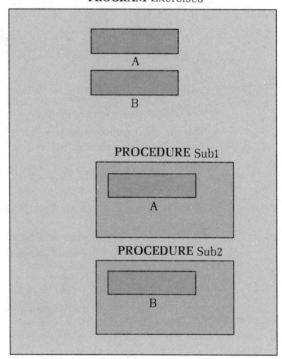

9. What output is produced from the following program?

```
PROGRAM Exercise9 (output);

VAR
  A : integer;

PROCEDURE Sub1 (A : integer);
  BEGIN
    A := 20;
    writeln (A)
  END;  (*  of PROCEDURE Sub1  *)

PROCEDURE Sub2 (VAR A : integer);
  BEGIN
    A := 30;
    writeln (A)
  END;  (*  of PROCEDURE Sub2  *)

BEGIN  (*  Main program  *)
  A := 10;
  writeln (A);
  Sub1 (A);
  writeln (A);
  Sub2 (A);
  writeln (A)
END.  (*  of main program  *)
```

For Exercises 10–12, assume the variable declaration section of a program is

```
VAR
  Age, Hours : integer;
  Average : real;
  Initial : char;
```

Furthermore, assume that procedure headings and declaration sections for procedures in this program are as follows. Find all errors.

10. PROCEDURE Average (Age1, Hrs : integer;
                       VAR Aver : real);

11. PROCEDURE Sub1 (Hours : integer;
                    VAR Average : real);

    VAR
      Age : integer;
      Init : char;

12. PROCEDURE Compute (Hrs : integer;
                       VAR Aver : real);

    VAR
      Age : real;

13. Discuss the advantages and disadvantages of using the same names for identifiers in a subprogram and the main program.

14. Write appropriate headings and declaration sections for the program and subprograms illustrated in Figure 7.13.

FIGURE 7.13
Program structure for
Exercise 14

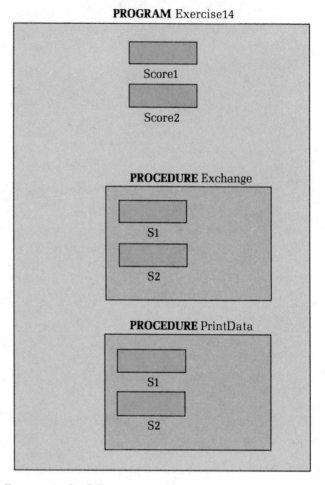

15. Find all errors in the following program.

```
PROGRAM Exercise15 (output);

VAR
  X, Y : real;

PROCEDURE Sub1 (VAR X1 : real);
  BEGIN
    writeln (X1:20:2);
    writeln (X:20:2);
    writeln (Y:20:2)
  END;  (*  of PROCEDURE Sub1  *)

BEGIN  (*  Main program  *)
  X := 10.0;
  Y := 2 * X;
  writeln (X:20:2, Y:20:2);
  Sub1 (X);
  writeln (X1:20:2);
  writeln (X:20:2);
  writeln (Y:20:2)
END.  (*  of main program  *)
```

OBJECTIVES

■ to use the correct
form and syntax for
writing a function
■ to call a function
from the main pro-
gram
■ to write a function
to perform a specific
task

You have seen some standard functions, specifically, **sqr, sqrt, abs, round,** and **trunc.** To briefly review, some concepts using these functions are

1. An argument is required for each; thus, **sqrt**(Y) and **abs**(−21) are appropriate.
2. They can be used in assignment statements; for example,

```
X := sqrt(Y);
```

3. They can be used in output statements; for example,

```
writeln (sqr(3):8);
```

Need for User-Defined Functions

It is relatively easy to envision the need for functions that are not on the list of standard functions available in Pascal. For example, if you must frequently cube numbers, it would be convenient to have a function Cube so you can make an assignment such as

```
X := Cube (Y);
```

Other examples from mathematics include exponential function (x^Y), factorial ($n!$), computing a discriminant ($b^2 - 4ac$), and roots of a quadratic equation

$$\left(\frac{-b \pm \sqrt{b^2 - 4ac}}{2a} \right)$$

In business, a motel might like to have available a function to determine a customer's bill given the number in the party, the length of stay, and any telephone charges. Similarly, a hospital might like a function to compute the room charge for a patient given the type of room (private, ward, and so on) and various other options, including telephone (yes or no) and television (yes or no). Functions such as these are not standard functions. However, in Pascal, we can create *user-defined functions* to perform these tasks.

Form for User-Defined Functions

A user-defined function is a subprogram and has the components

Heading → [

Declaration section → [

Executable section → [

The general form for a function heading is

FUNCTION function name (parameter list) : return type;

A syntax diagram for this is

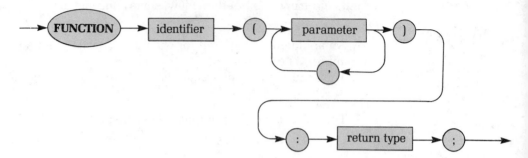

The heading for a function to compute the cube of an integer can therefore be

```
FUNCTION Cube (X:integer):integer;
```

Several comments on the general form for a function heading are now in order.

1. **FUNCTION** is a reserved word and must be used only as indicated.
2. "Function name" is any valid identifier.
   a. It should be descriptive.
   b. It serves as a variable with some restrictions.
   c. Some value must be assigned to the function name in the executable section of the function. The last assigned value is the value returned to the main program; for example, in FUNCTION Cube, we have

   Cube := X * X * X;

   d. The function name cannot be used on the right side of an assignment statement within the function. For example,

   Cube := Cube + 1;

   produces an error. (An exception to this rule involves recursion and is discussed in Section 7.6.)
   e. In the calling program, the function name cannot be used on the left of an assignment statement.
3. As with procedures, the formal parameter list (variables in the function heading) must match the number and corresponding types of actual parameters (variables in the function call) used when the function is called from the main program. Thus, if you are writing a function to compute the area of a rectangle and you want to call the function from the main program by

```
RectArea := Area (Width, Length);
```

the function Area might have the heading

```
FUNCTION Area (W,L:integer):integer;
```

The two formal parameters, W and L, correspond to the actual parameters, Width and Length, assuming that Width and Length are of type **integer.** In general, you should make sure the formal parameter list and actual parameter list match up as indicated.

```
(W,L:integer)
(Width, Length)
```

4. "Return type" declares the data type for the function name. This indicates what type is returned to the main program.

SELF QUIZ 7.7   Write a function heading that is appropriate for a function to compute the average of three real numbers.

As in the main program, there does not have to be a declaration section for a function, but when there is one, only variables needed in the function are declared. Further, the section is usually not very elaborate because the purpose of a function is normally a small, single task.

Finally, the executable section for a function must perform the desired task, assign a value to the function name, terminate with a semicolon rather than a period, and have the general form

```
BEGIN
    .
    .   (work of function here)
    .

END;
```

We now illustrate user-defined functions with several examples.

EXAMPLE 7.6   Write a function to compute the cube of an integer. Since the actual parameter from the main program is of **integer** type, we can have

```
FUNCTION Cube (X:integer):integer;
   BEGIN
     Cube := X * X * X
   END;
```

A typical call to this function from the main program is

```
A := Cube(8);
```

EXAMPLE 7.7   Write a function to compute the average of three reals. From the answer to Self Quiz 7.7, we know the actual parameters are three reals, so our function can be written as

```
FUNCTION Average (N1, N2, N3 : real) : real;
   BEGIN
     Average := (N1 + N2 + N3)/3
   END;
```

and called from the main program by

```
X := Average (Num1, Num2, Num3);
```

EXAMPLE 7.8

Given two positive integers, m and n, write a function to compute m^n (m to the power of n). Since there are two actual parameters, the formal parameter list requires two variables of type **integer**. The function returns an integer, so the return type is **integer**. The desired function is

```
FUNCTION Power (M1, N1 : integer): integer;
   VAR
     Temp, K : integer;
   BEGIN
     Temp := M1;
     FOR K := 2 TO N1 DO
        Temp := Temp * M1;
     Power := Temp
   END;
```

This can be called from the main program by

```
A := Power (3,5);
```

■

Since the function in Example 7.8 is more elaborate than previous examples, let's examine it more closely. First, note that we need additional variables, Temp and K. Next, let's trace what happens to the various values and variables.

When Power (3,5) is encountered in the main program, control is transferred to Power and M1 and N1 receive their respective values. At this stage, the variables can be depicted as

Power	M1	N1	Temp	K
	3	5		

The first executable statement in the function causes

Power	M1	N1	Temp	K
	3	5	3	

The first pass through the loop produces

Power	M1	N1	Temp	K
	3	5	9	2

At the completion of the loop, K becomes unassigned and Power is assigned the final value of Temp to produce

Power	M1	N1	Temp	K
243	3	5	243	

At this point, control is transferred back to the main program and the value in Power is assigned accordingly. Thus

```
A := Power (3,5);
```

yields

A
243

EXAMPLE 7.9

Let's now write a function to compute the total charge for a hospital room. Actual parameters are the number of days **(integer)** and room type **(char)**. We may assume rates for private (P), semiprivate (S), and ward (W) are defined in the **CONST** definition section of the main program. A typical function is

```
FUNCTION RoomCharge (ND:integer; RT:char):real;
  BEGIN
    CASE RT OF
      'P' : RoomCharge := ND * PrivateRate;
      'S' : RoomCharge := ND * SemiprivateRate;
      'W' : RoomCharge := ND * WardRate
    END  (*  of CASE  *)
  END;  (*  of FUNCTION RoomCharge  *)
```

This function can be called from the main program by

```
RoomAmount := RoomCharge (NumDays, RoomType);
```
■

Using the function RoomCharge given in Example 7.9, what is wrong with the following function call from the main program?

```
RoomAmount := RoomCharge (RoomType, NumDays);
```

Use in a Program

Now that you have seen several examples of user-defined functions, let's consider their use in a program. Once they are written, they can be used in the same manner as standard functions. This usually means in one of the following forms.

1. Assignment statements

```
A := 5;
B := Cube(A);
```

2. Arithmetic expressions

```
A := 5;
B := 3 * Cube(A) + 2;
```

3. Output statements

```
A := 5;
writeln (Cube(A):17);
```

4. Relational statements

```
IF Cube(A) < B THEN
          .
          .
          .
```

Position in a Program

All subprograms are placed after the variable declaration section for the main program. Program execution begins with the first statement of the main program. Execution of the function occurs only when it is called from the main program or from some subprogram. Writing style for functions is consistent with that used for procedures. We now illustrate with a complete program that prints a chart of the integers 1 to 10 together with their squares and cubes. The function Cube is used as previously written.

```
PROGRAM Table (output);

VAR
  J : integer;

(*****************************************************************

              This procedure will print a heading.

 ****************************************************************)
PROCEDURE PrintHeading;
  BEGIN
    writeln;writeln;
    writeln('Number':28,'Number Squared':18,'Number Cubed':16);
    writeln('_____':28,'_____':18,'_____':16);
    writeln
  END;  (*  of PROCEDURE PrintHeading  *)


(*****************************************************************

              This function cubes an integer.

 ****************************************************************)
FUNCTION Cube (X : integer):integer;
  BEGIN
    Cube := X * X * X
  END;  (*  of FUNCTION Cube  *)


(*****************************************************************

              Now start the main program.

 ****************************************************************)
BEGIN (*   Main program   *)
  PrintHeading;
  FOR J := 1 TO 10 DO
    writeln(J:25,sqr(J):14,Cube(J):17);
  writeln
END.  (*   of main program  *)
```

The output from this program is

Number	Number Squared	Number Cubed
1	1	1
2	4	8
3	9	27
4	16	64
5	25	125
6	36	216
7	49	343
8	64	512
9	81	729
10	100	1000

Multiple Functions

Programs can contain more than one function. When several user-defined functions are needed in a program, each should be developed and positioned in the program as previously indicated. For readability, be sure to use blank lines and comment sections to separate and explain each function.

When a program contains several functions, they can be called from the main part of the program in any order. However, if one function contains a call to another function, the function being called must appear before the function from which it is called. (We will examine an exception to this when we consider forward reference in Section 7.6.)

Exercises 7.4

1. Discuss the difference between actual parameters and formal parameters.

2. Write a test program to see what happens when the function name is used on the right side of an assignment statement. For example,

```
FUNCTION Total (OldSum,NewNum : integer) : integer;
  BEGIN
    Total := OldSum;
    Total := Total + NewNum
  END;
```

In Exercises 3–7, indicate which are valid function headings. Explain what is wrong with those that are invalid.

```
3. FUNCTION RoundTenth (X:real);
4. FUNCTION MakeChange (X,Y) : real;
5. FUNCTION Max (M1, M2, M3 : integer) : integer;
6. FUNCTION Sign (Num : real) : char;
7. FUNCTION Truth (Ch:char, Num:real) : boolean;
```

In Exercises 8–10, find all errors in the function.

```
8. FUNCTION MaxOf2 (N1, N2 : integer) : integer;
   BEGIN
     IF N1 > N2 THEN
       MaxOf2 := N1
   END;
9. FUNCTION AvOf2 (N1, N2 : integer) : integer;
   BEGIN
     AvOf2 := (N1 + N2)/2
   END;
10. FUNCTION Total (L:integer) : integer;
    VAR
      J : integer;
    BEGIN
      Total := 0;
      FOR J := 1 TO L DO
        Total := Total + J
    END;
```

In Exercises 11–17, write a function for each.

11. Find the maximum of two reals.
12. Find the maximum of three reals.
13. Round a real to the nearest tenth.
14. Convert degrees Fahrenheit to degrees Celsius.

15. Determine the sign of a real number.

16. Examine an integer to see if it is a multiple of five; if so, return the **boolean** value **true;** if not, return the **boolean** value **false.**

17. Compute the charge for cars at a parking lot; the rate is 75 cents per hour or fraction thereof.

18. Write a program that uses the function you wrote for Exercise 17 to print a ticket for a customer who parks in the parking lot. Assume the input is in minutes.

19. The factorial of a positive integer *n* is

$$n! = n * (n-1) * \ldots * 2 * 1$$

Write a function (Factorial) that computes and returns *n*!.

20. Write a complete program using Cube and Factorial that produces a table of the integers 1 to 10 together with their squares, cubes, and factorials.

21. Write a function, Arithmetic, that receives a sign (+ or *) and two integers, N1 and N2, and then computes and returns either N1 + N2 or N1 * N2 depending on the sign received.

■ 7.5
Using Subprograms

OBJECTIVES

- to understand how subprograms can be used in designing programs
- to use procedures to get data for programs
- to use subprograms to perform tasks required in programs
- to use procedures for output

Program Design

Throughout this text you have seen examples of problems solved by the development of a sequence of tasks. In general, tasks are stated in the order in which they are to be performed and then each task is refined according to its level of complexity. Now that you are capable of using procedures and functions in a program, you should see how they can be used to design a program for solving a problem. After the algorithm for solving the problem has been developed in pseudocode, subprograms can be written for the various tasks and then called from the main program as needed.

To illustrate, let's consider how a program can be designed using subprograms. We will not write the subprograms at this point; we will only indicate how they will be used in designing the program. Our problem is to compute grades for a class. A first-level pseudocode development is

1. Initialize variables
2. Process each student
3. Print a summary

This can be refined to

1. Initialize variables
2. **WHILE** more students **DO**
   2.1 get data
   2.2 compute average
   2.3 compute letter grade
   2.4 print data
   2.5 compute totals
3. Print a summary
   3.1 print class average
   3.2 print number receiving each grade

TABLE 7.1
Using subprograms

Pseudocode Statement	Subprogram
1. Initialize variables	**PROCEDURE** Initialize
2. **WHILE** more students **DO**	
2.1 get data	**PROCEDURE** GetData
2.2 compute average	**FUNCTION** Average
2.3 compute letter grade	**FUNCTION** LetterGrade
2.4 print data	**PROCEDURE** PrintData
2.5 compute totals	**PROCEDURE** ComputeTotals
3. Print a summary	
3.1 print class average	**PROCEDURE** PrintAverage
3.2 print number receiving each grade	**PROCEDURE** PrintNumGrades

Subprograms can now be used to design a program consistent with this algorithm as illustrated in Table 7.1. Note that this particular choice of procedures and functions is not the only solution available to us; there are many other ways to use subprograms in a program to solve our problem.

Now that we have identified procedures and functions for various tasks in this problem, we can write the program design. Since we are relatively early in the design stage, we will not include parameters for the subprograms, but as we develop each subprogram, we will indicate appropriate value and variable parameters.

The main program can be

```
BEGIN  (*  Main Program  *)
  Initialize (            );
  writeln('Any more students? Y or N');
  read(Response);
  WHILE Response = 'Y' DO
    BEGIN
      GetData (            );
      Aver := Average (            );
      LetGrade := LetterGrade (            );
      PrintData (            );
      ComputeTotals (            );
      writeln ('Any more students? Y or N');
      read(Response)
    END;
  PrintAverage (            );
  PrintNumGrades (            )
END.
```

Now we take a closer look at how subprograms are used to complete tasks in a program.

Procedures for Initializing Variables

Programs may require variables to be initialized at the beginning of the program. This initialization can be done in the main program or in a procedure; it is generally the first step in developing an algorithm. Thus,

    1. Initialize variables

frequently is listed as a line of pseudocode and, when a procedure is written to implement this task, the program design becomes

```
BEGIN  (*  Main Program  *)
  Initialize (            );
```

Procedures for initializing require variable parameters because variables in the main program must get their values from those assigned in the procedure.

The program for our grading problem requires initialization of variables Count, ClassTotal, NumA, NumB, NumC, NumD, and NumE. Appropriate initialization can be accomplished by the following procedure.

```
PROCEDURE Initialize (VAR Ct : integer;
                      VAR ClTot : real;
                      VAR NA, NB, NC, ND, NE : integer);
  BEGIN
    Ct : 0;
    ClTot := 0.0;
    NA := 0;
    NB := 0;
    NC := 0;
    ND := 0;
    NE := 0
  END;  (*  of PROCEDURE Initialize  *)
```

This procedure can be called from the main program by

```
Initialize (Count, ClassTotal, NumA, NumB,
            NumC, NumD, NumE);
```

Procedures for Input

As noted earlier, a simplified pseudocode version of most programs is

1. Get the data
2. Process the data
3. Print results

Let's now take a closer look at procedures for input. Since the data obtained will be used in the program as well as the procedure, you will need variable parameters declared in the procedure heading. Thus, if each line of data contains three integer test scores, a reasonable procedure heading is

```
PROCEDURE GetData (VAR Sc1, Sc2, Sc3 : integer);
```

The procedure can be called from the main program by

```
GetData (Score1, Score2, Score3);
```

Note that the identifiers are selected so the program will be easier to read and debug. The following example demonstrates a procedure to get data for a program.

EXAMPLE 7.10 Let's write a procedure to get data for a program to print payroll checks for a company. Each line of data contains one employee's initials, the hours worked (integer), and the hourly rate (real). Thus, one line can be depicted as

> RJS 38 11.50

A complete procedure for getting a line of data is

```
PROCEDURE GetData (VAR Init1, Init2, Init3 : char;
                   VAR Hrs : integer;
                   VAR HRate : real);
   BEGIN
      writeln ('Enter three initials, hours worked, and pay rate.');
      readln (Init1, Init2, Init3, Hrs, HRate)
   END; (* of PROCEDURE GetData *)
```

This procedure can be called from the main program by

```
GetData (Initial1, Initial2, Initial3, Hours, HourlyRate;  ■
```

Write a procedure to get data for a customer of the Gas-N-Clean Service Station. Each line of data contains a letter designating the type of gasoline purchased, a real indicating how many gallons of gasoline were purchased, and a letter indicating whether or not a car wash is desired. Thus, typical data are

> P 11.3 Y

Show how this procedure is called from the main program.

Subprograms for Tasks

The second step of pseudocode "Process the data," can be quite complex. When an algorithm is developed to solve a problem, this step usually requires several levels of refinement. When these levels have been sufficiently refined, subprograms can be developed to implement each level. Then the main program calls the appropriate subprograms as needed.

When writing procedures for various tasks, you need to be careful with the use of value and variable parameters. Remember, if the main program needs a different value of the variable for later use in the program, you must use a variable parameter; for instance, if a count is being made in a procedure or if a running total is being kept. On the other hand, if the procedure merely performs some computation with the values received and the results are not needed in the calling program, then the values may be passed with value parameters.

To illustrate, let's consider some of the tasks from our earlier problem of computing grades for a class. One task is to print the data for one student. The initials, three test scores, test average, and letter grade are available for each student. Since the procedure only prints the data, all values can be passed by value parameters. Assuming all data should be printed on one line in appropriate columns, the procedure is

```
PROCEDURE PrintData (Init1, Init2, Init3 : char;
                     Sc1, Sc2, Sc3 : integer;
                     TestAv : real;
                     LGrade : char);
```

```
BEGIN
  write (Init1:20, Init2, Init3);
  write (Sc1:10, Sc2:5, Sc3:5);
  writeln (TestAv:10:2, LGrade:5)
END;  (*  of PROCEDURE PrintData  *)
```

This procedure can be called from the main program by

```
PrintData (Initial1, Initial2, Initial3, Score1, Score2,
           Score3, Aver, LetGrade);
```

Another task from the same problem is to compute running totals for the class. Therefore, we need to count the number of students, accumulate averages so we can compute a class average, and count the number of students receiving each letter grade. In this case, both value and variable parameters are needed. Formal variable parameters are used for the actual parameters,

```
Count
ClassTotal
NumA, NumB, NumC, NumD, NumE
```

and formal value parameters are used for the actual parameters

```
Aver
LetGrade
```

With the variables thus identified, the procedure is

```
PROCEDURE ComputeTotals (Av : real; LGrade : char;
                         VAR Ct : integer;
                         VAR ClTot : real;
                         VAR NA, NB, NC, ND, NE : integer);
  BEGIN
    Ct := Ct + 1;
    ClTot := ClTot + Av;
    CASE LGrade OF
      'A' : NA := NA + 1;
      'B' : NB := NB + 1;
      'C' : NC := NC + 1;
      'D' : ND := ND + 1;
      'E' : NE := NE + 1
    END    (*  of CASE  *)
  END;  (*  of PROCEDURE ComputeTotals  *)
```

This procedure can be called from the main program by

```
ComputeTotals (Aver, LetGrade, Count, ClassTotal,
               NumA, NumB, NumC, NumD, NumE);
```

Finally, let's consider the function Average. This function receives three integer test scores, computes their average, and returns a real to the main program. The function is

```
FUNCTION Average (Sc1, Sc2, Sc3 : integer) : real;
  BEGIN
    Average := (Sc1 + Sc2 + Sc3) / 3
  END;  (*  of FUNCTION Average  *)
```

This can be called from the main program by

```
Aver := Average (Score1, Score2, Score3);
```

A NOTE OF INTEREST

Niklaus Wirth: Pascal to Modula-2

Niklaus Wirth began his work in the computing field by taking a course in numerical analysis at Laval University in Quebec, Canada. However, the computer (Alvac III E) was frequently out of order and the hexadecimal code programming exercises went untested. He received his doctorate from the University of California, Berkeley, in 1963.

After other early experiences in programming, it became apparent to Wirth that computers of the future had to be more effectively programmable. Consequently, he joined a research group that worked on developing a compiler for an IBM 704. This language was NELIAC, a dialect of ALGOL 58. In rapid succession, he developed or contributed to the development of *Euler*, ALGOL W, and PL360. In 1967, he returned to Switzerland and established a team of three assistants with whom he developed and implemented the language Pascal.

One of the main purposes of Pascal was its use as a language for teaching. This was particularly successful because it allowed the teacher to focus on structures and concepts rather than features and peculiarities.

A decade later, Wirth's attention turned to hardware design. In order to continue his work and incorporate advances in technology, he developed yet another language, Modula-2. This was an offspring of Pascal and Modula. It was developed for use with the Lilith, a computer designed with all systems written in a single language. Modula-2 compilers have been in use since 1979. Recent versions are so efficient that their code is approximately five thousand lines long compared to Ada compilers of several hundred thousand lines.

Procedures for Output

A standard part of every program is to generate some output. Thus, when designing a program, the third step of pseudocode in the problem solution, "Print results," can either have a single procedure written for it or it can be refined into subtasks and have a procedure written for each subtask. When writing procedures for output, only value parameters are needed. Since you are only printing results, it is not necessary to pass values back to the main program.

Writing procedures for output can be tedious because of the need for neat, attractive output. Be careful to use columns when appropriate, the center of the page, underlining, blank lines, spacing within a line (formatting), and appropriate messages.

Using Stubs

As programs get longer and incorporate more subprograms, a technique frequently used to get the program running is *stub programming*. A stub program is a no-frills, simple version of what will be a final program. It does not contain details of output and full algorithm development. It does contain a rough version of each subprogram and all parameter lists. When the stub version runs, you know your logic is correct and values are appropriately being passed to and from subprograms. Then you can fill in necessary details to get a complete program.

Using Drivers

The main program is sometimes referred to as the *main driver*. When subprograms are used in a program, this driver can be modified to check subprograms in a sequential fashion. For example, suppose a main driver is

```
BEGIN  (*  Main driver  *)
  Initialize (Count, Sum);
  MoreData := true;
  WHILE MoreData DO
    GetData (Sum, Count, MoreData);
  PrintResults (Sum, Count)
END.  (*  of main driver  *)
```

The first procedure can be checked by putting comment indicators around the rest of the program and temporarily adding a statement to print values of variables. Thus, you can run the following version:

```
BEGIN  (*  Main driver  *)
  Initialize (Count, Sum);
  writeln ('Count is', Count; ' Sum is', Sum);
(*MoreData := true;
  WHILE MoreData DO
    GetData (Sum, Count, MoreData);
  PrintResults (Sum, Count)  *)
END.  (*  of main driver  *)
```

Once you are sure the first subprogram is running, you can remove the comment indicators and continue through the main driver to check successive subprograms.

Exercises 7.5

1. Discuss whether value parameters or variable parameters should be used in procedure to
   a. initialize variables
   b. get data
   c. print results

2. Write a test program that utilizes subprograms for solving the problem of reading integers, computing their sum and average, and printing results. The main program should include

```
Initialize (Count, Total);
WHILE MoreData DO
  GetData (Count, Total);
Average := FindAverage (Count, Total);
PrintHeading;
PrintResults (Count, Total, Average);
```

3. Suppose the pseudocode for solving a problem is
   1. Initialize variables
   2. Print a heading
   3. **WHILE** Flag = **true DO**
      3.1 get new data
      3.2 perform computations
      3.3 increment counter
      3.4 check Flag condition
   4. Print results

   Show how subprograms can be used to design a program to implement this algorithm.

In Exercises 4 and 5, write a function for the task.

4. Given positive integer a and any integer b (positive, negative, or zero), compute a^b.

5. Given real numbers a, b, and c, compute the discriminant $(b^2 - 4ac)$.

6. You have been asked to write a program for the Sleep Cheap motel chain. Each line of data contains information for one customer. This information consists of number of nights occupancy (integer), room rate (real), and telephone charges (real). Your program should print a statement for each customer and keep totals for the number of customers served, total room charges, and total telephone charges.
   Assume the pseudocode for solving this problem is
   1. Initialize variables
   2. **WHILE** More Customers **DO**
        2.1 get customer data
        2.2 perform computations
        2.3 print statement
        2.4 add totals
   3. Print summary
        a. Design a program to implement this algorithm.
        b. Write a procedure or function for each statement of the algorithm.

7. Write a complete program to solve the grading problem posed at the beginning of this section.

■ 7.6
Forward Reference, Nesting, and Recursion

By now you should be familiar with the important concepts of procedures and functions, and relatively comfortable with using them for the modular design of a program. As you examined material in the first five sections of this chapter, you may have noticed that use of subprograms was restricted to the main program calling procedures or functions and procedures or functions calling previously declared subprograms. In this section we examine more sophisticated uses of subprograms, specifically, forward reference, nesting, and recursion.

Subprograms That Call Other Subprograms

Sections 7.1 and 7.4 included brief discussions concerning the use of multiple procedures and functions. In review, suppose a program has two functions **(FUNCTION** A and **FUNCTION** B) and a procedure **(PROCEDURE** C). This can be envisioned as shown in Figure 7.14. Thus far we have only been able to have a subprogram call another subprogram that was previously declared. For example, in the diagram, **FUNCTION** B can call **FUNCTION** A and **PROCEDURE** C can call either **FUNCTION** A or **FUNCTION** B. Any other calls result in errors.

Forward Reference

These restrictions on function and procedure calls impose limitations on program development. There may be times when it is either desirable or necessary for a subprogram to call another subprogram that appears later in the declaration section. This can be accomplished by a *forward reference*.

FIGURE 7.14
Multiple subpro-
grams

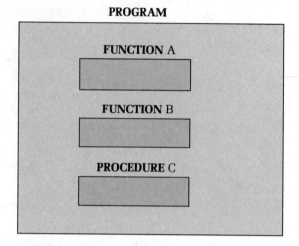

A forward reference is achieved by listing the function or procedure heading with all parameters followed by the reserved word **FORWARD**. If a function is to be forward referenced, the function type should be included as part of the heading listed; for example,

```
FUNCTION B (X : real) : real; FORWARD;
```

When used this way, **FORWARD** is an executable statement.

When the function or procedure is declared later in the program, the parameter list and function type are omitted. To illustrate, consider

```
FUNCTION B (X : real) : real; FORWARD;

FUNCTION A (Ch : char) : char;
   BEGIN
      .
      .
      .
   END;   (*  of FUNCTION A  *)

FUNCTION B;
   BEGIN
      .
      .
      .
   END;   (*  of FUNCTION B  *)
```

In this case, **FUNCTION** A can call **FUNCTION** B because **FUNCTION** B has been forward referenced. **FUNCTION** B can call **FUNCTION** A because **FUNCTION** A is declared before **FUNCTION** B.

Forward reference is necessary to list subprograms in a particular order to make a program more readable. A programmer may, for instance, choose to list functions in order of complexity from least complex to most complex or from most complex to least complex. Either listing might necessitate a forward reference. Also, a program design may require a forward reference for some subprograms. If **FUNCTION** A has an option that calls **FUNCTION** B and **FUNCTION** B has an option that calls **FUNCTION** A, one of them must have a forward reference. It can even be such that **FUNCTION** A always calls **FUNCTION** B and **FUNCTION** B always calls **FUNCTION** A. This situation is referred to as mutual recursion and is discussed later in this section.

When using a forward reference, use a line comment to indicate parameters when the subprogram is developed.

```
FUNCTION First (S1,S2,S3:integer):integer;FORWARD;
    .
    .
    .


FUNCTION Second (parameter  list):return type;
   BEGIN
    .
    .
    .
   END;  (*  of FUNCTION Second  *)

FUNCTION First; (*  (S1,S2,S3:integer):integer  *)
                 ─────────────────────────────────
                            comment here
```

In summary, when using forward reference, you should

1. List all parameters and function types when the forward reference is made.
2. Use the reserved word **FORWARD** as a statement when the forward reference is made.
3. Omit the parameter list when the forward-referenced subprogram is written.
4. Use a comment to indicate what the parameter list is for the forward-referenced subprogram.

Nesting

Since a subprogram can contain the same sections as the main program, the declaration section of a function or procedure can contain a function or procedure. When this occurs, the subprograms are said to be *nested*. Subprograms can be nested to any level desired by the programmer. However, as we have seen, several levels of nesting tend to make programs difficult to follow and debug. If the nesting is too complicated, you should redesign the program.

Nested subprograms may be represented as shown in Figure 7.15. This schematic representation of nesting assists us in understanding the scope of various identifiers. Recall, identifiers are restricted to the block (and all subblocks) in which they are declared. To illustrate, suppose variables are declared in a program as shown in Figure 7.16. X, which is declared in the main program, can be accessed by any subprogram in this program. In particular, even the nested function, **FUNCTION** B, can use values in X from the main program. However, X1 can only be used by **PROCEDURE** A and **FUNCTION** B. The variables used in this illustration and their scope are shown in Table 7.2.

FIGURE 7.15
Nested subprograms

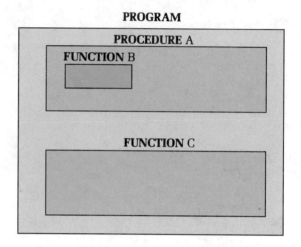

FIGURE 7.16
Variables in nested subprograms

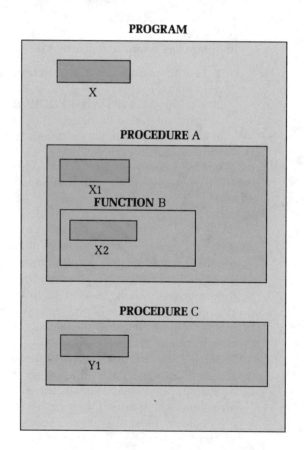

TABLE 7.2
Scope of variables

Variable	Scope (can be accessed by)
X	main program **PROCEDURE** A **FUNCTION** B **PROCEDURE** C
X1	**PROCEDURE** A **FUNCTION** B
X2	**FUNCTION** B
Y1	**PROCEDURE** C

SELF QUIZ 7.10

Using the illustration of Figure 7.16, state if each of the following indicated calls to a subprogram is valid or invalid.

1. A statement in **PROCEDURE** A calling **PROCEDURE** C
2. A statement in **PROCEDURE** C calling **PROCEDURE** A
3. A statement in **PROCEDURE** A calling **FUNCTION** B
4. A statement in the main program calling **FUNCTION** B
5. A statement in **FUNCTION** B calling **PROCEDURE** C

We conclude the discussion on nesting subprograms with an example that illustrates only nested functions. However, the principles behind it apply to any combination of nested programs and to any level of nesting.

EXAMPLE 7.11

Let's write a function TotalCharge to compute the total charge for guests of a motel chain. You may assume that RoomRate and TaxRate are defined in the **CONST** section of the main program and that NumNights is assigned an appropriate value. The function is called by

```
AmountDue := TotalCharge (NumNights);
```

For purposes of this example, the tax is computed by a nested function Tax. Thus, we have

```
FUNCTION TotalCharge (NumNts : integer) : real;
   VAR
      RoomCharge, RoomTax : real;
   FUNCTION Tax (RmCharge : real) : real;
      BEGIN  (*  FUNCTION Tax  *)
         Tax := RmCharge * TaxRate
      END;  (*  of FUNCTION Tax  *)

   BEGIN  (*  FUNCTION TotalCharge  *)
      RoomCharge := NumNts * RoomRate;
      RoomTax := Tax (RoomCharge);
      TotalCharge := RoomCharge + RoomTax
   END;  (*  of FUNCTION TotalCharge  *)
```

Figure 7.17 is a schematic representation of the constants, variables, and functions used in Example 7.11.

FIGURE 7.17
Variables in nested
functions

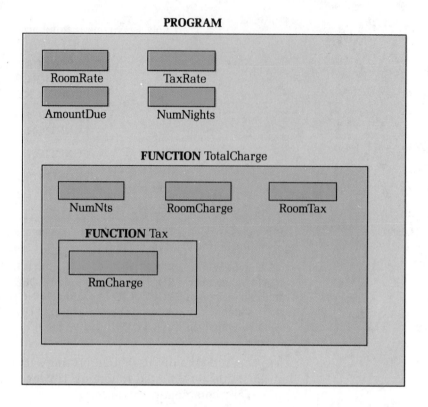

SELF QUIZ 7.11   Rewrite Example 7.11 without using nested functions.

Recursion

At this point, you should be comfortable with the idea of one subprogram calling another subprogram. Let's now consider the situation in which a subprogram calls itself; this is called *recursion* or is referred to as a *recursive subprogram*. As an example of a recursive function, consider the sigma function (denoted by $\sum_{i=1}^{n} i$) which computes the sum of intergers from 1 to n.

```
FUNCTION Sigma (N : integer) : integer;
  BEGIN
    IF N <= 1 THEN
      Sigma := N
    ELSE
      Sigma := N + Sigma(N-1)
  END;  (*  of FUNCTION Sigma  *)
```

To illustrate how this recursive function works, suppose it is called from the main program by a statement such as

```
Sum := Sigma(5);
```

In the function, we first have

```
Sigma := 5 + Sigma(4);
```

At this stage, note that Sigma(4) must be computed. This call produces

```
Sigma := 4 + Sigma(3);
```

If we envision these recursive calls as occurring on levels, we have

```
1. Sigma := 5 + Sigma(4);
   2. Sigma := 4 + Sigma(3);
      3. Sigma := 3 + Sigma(2);
         4. Sigma := 2 + Sigma(1);
            5. Sigma := 1;
```

Now the end of the recursion has been reached and the steps are reversed for assigning values. Thus, we have

```
            5. Sigma := 1;
         4. Sigma := 2 + 1;
      3. Sigma := 3 + 3;
   2. Sigma := 4 + 6;
1. Sigma := 5 + 10;
```

Before analyzing what happens in memory when recursive subprograms are used, some comments about recursion are in order.

1. The recursive process must have a well-defined termination. This termination is referred to as a *stopping state*. In the previous example, the stopping state was

```
IF N <= 1 THEN SIGMA := N;
```

2. The recursive process must have well-defined steps that lead to the stopping state. These steps are usually called *recursive steps*. In the previous example, these steps were

```
Sigma := N + Sigma(N-1);
```

Let's now examine what happens when recursion is used. The first call creates a level of recursion that contains a partially complete assignment statement such as

```
Sigma := 5 + Sigma(4);
```

At this level, operation is temporarily suspended until a value is returned for Sigma(4). However, this call produces

```
Sigma := 4 + Sigma(3);
```

This creates a second level of recursion that again contains a partially complete assignment statement. At this level, operation is temporarily suspended until Sigma(3) is computed. This process is repeated until finally the last call, Sigma(1), returns a value. At this stage, the levels of recursion that were temporarily suspended can now be completed in reverse order. Thus, since the assignment

```
Sigma(1) := 1;
```

is made, then

```
Sigma(2) := 2 + Sigma(1);
```

becomes

```
Sigma(2) := 2 + 1;
```

This then permits

```
Sigma(3) := 3 + Sigma(2);
```

to become

```
Sigma(3) := 3 + 3;
```

Continuing until the first level of recursion is reached, we obtain

```
Sigma := 5 + 10;
```

Let's now consider a second example of a recursive function. Recall, the factorial of a nonnegative integer, n, is defined to be

$$1 * 2 * 3 * \ldots * (n-1) * n$$

and is denoted by $n!$. Thus,

$$4! = 1 * 2 * 3 * 4$$

For the sake of completing this definition, $1! = 1$ and $0! = 1$. A recursive function to compute $n!$ is

```
FUNCTION Factorial (N : integer) : integer;
  BEGIN
    IF N = 0 THEN
      Factorial := 1
    ELSE
      Factorial := N * Factorial(N-1)
  END; (* of FUNCTION Factorial *)
```

If this function is called from the main program by the statement

```
Product := Factorial(4);
```

we can envision the levels of recursion as

```
1. Factorial := 4 * Factorial(3);
  2. Factorial := 3 * Factorial(2);
    3. Factorial := 2 * Factorial(1);
      4. Factorial := 1 * Factorial(0);
        5. Factorial(0) := 1;
```

Successive values are then assigned in reverse order to produce

```
        5. Factorial(0) := 1;
      4. Factorial := 1 * 1;
    3. Factorial := 2 * 1;
  2. Factorial := 3 * 2;
1. Factorial := 4 * 6;
```

SELF QUIZ 7.12 What is wrong with the following recursive function?

```
FUNCTION Recur (Num : integer) : integer;
  BEGIN
    Recur := 1 + Recur (Num)
  END;
```

If you carefully examined the previous two examples of recursion, you may have noticed that each of them can be replaced by a function that uses repetition (also called iteration) instead of recursion. For example, we can write

```
FUNCTION RepeSigma (N : integer) : integer;
  VAR
    J, Sum : integer;
  BEGIN
    Sum := 0;
    FOR J := 1 TO N DO
      Sum := Sum + J;
    RepeSigma := Sum
  END;  (*  of FUNCTION RepeSigma  *)
```

It is not coincidental that the recursive function Sigma can be rewritten using the repetitive function RepeSigma. In fact, any recursive subprogram can be rewritten using repetition. Furthermore, recursion generally requires more memory than equivalent repetition and is usually difficult for beginning programmers to comprehend. Why then do we use recursion? Some reasons include:

1. Sometimes it is the best way to solve a problem.
2. Some recursive solutions can be very short compared to repetition.
3. Implementation of recursive algorithms can be very simple.
4. Subsequent work in Pascal can be aided by using recursive data structures.

You should therefore become familiar with using recursive subprograms, be able to recognize when a recursive algorithm is appropriate, and be able to implement a recursive subprogram.

Mutual Recursion

There is one additional type of recursion we have not yet discussed. If two subprograms call each other, this is referred to as *mutual recursion*. Logically, if **PROCEDURE** A contains a call to **PROCEDURE** B and **PROCEDURE** B contains a call to **PROCEDURE** A, one of them must be declared using a forward reference. To illustrate, you can have a situation such as

```
PROCEDURE B (parameter list); FORWARD;

PROCEDURE A (parameter list);
  BEGIN
    .
    .  (call PROCEDURE B)
    .
  END;

PROCEDURE B;
  BEGIN
    .
    .  (call PROCEDURE A)
    .
  END;
```

If you use a mutually recursive algorithm, you must make sure that a well-defined stopping state is always reached.

Computer Science Myths

Discussing the issue of computer science myths, Twila Slesnick, senior editor for *Classroom Computer Learning*, stated, "Many people fear what might become of youngsters who spend a lot of time alone with a computer. The mythical computer freak is an idiot savant with rounded shoulders, glazed eyes, and no friends. The source of this fear is hard to trace. It can't really be the solitude that is objectionable. Reading, for example, is a highly respected solitary activity—one nurtured incessantly by schools. And besides, computing is no longer the isolated activity it was, as is evidenced by the rising popularity of electronic bulletin boards, through which computer users communicate with fellow students, subject-matter experts, and potential friends and sweethearts.

"We must also discount monomania as soci-

ety's true objection to avid computing. After all, we greatly esteem scientists, musicians, and artists who devote their entire lives to one discipline (and sometimes to one project). But computing for many people is just a hobby—an infatuation like coin collecting, Monopoly, or chess—that is intense for awhile and then abates or fades away.

I think the real source of the fear is simply ignorance of computers. Many adults remember spending hours (days? years?) playing chess or poring over coins and know that these passing infatuations left them unscathed. But since they have not experienced a childhood love affair with computers, today's adults don't know that kids will survive this particular obsession. As computers become more familiar, this fear will no doubt subside.

Exercises 7.6

1. Explain why forward reference can be necessary in a program.

2. Write a test program to illustrate what happens when one subprogram calls another subprogram that is listed later and a forward reference is not made.

3. Write a test program to see what happens when a stopping state is not included in a recursive subprogram.

4. Discuss the advantages and disadvantages of using recursion instead of repetition.

5. Discuss the scope of identifiers in nested subprograms.

In Exercises 6–10, find and correct all errors.

```
6. FUNCTION AddOne (A : integer) : integer;
     BEGIN
        AddOne := A + 1
     END;   (*  of FUNCTION AddOne  *)
   PROCEDURE AddTwo (VAR B : integer);
     BEGIN
        B := AddOne(B);
        B := AddOne(B)
     END;   (*  of PROCEDURE AddTwo  *)
7. PROCEDURE AddTwo (VAR B : integer);
     BEGIN
        B := AddOne(B);
        B := AddOne(B)
     END;   (*  of PROCEDURE AddTwo  *)
   FUNCTION AddOne (A : integer): integer;
     BEGIN
        AddOne := A + 1
     END;   (*of FUNCTION AddOne  *)
```

8. ```
FUNCTION AddOne (A: integer) : integer; FORWARD;
PROCEDURE AddTwo (VAR B: integer);
  BEGIN
    B := AddOne(B);
    B := AddOne(B)
  END; (* of PROCEDURE AddTwo *)
FUNCTION AddOne (A : integer) : integer;
  BEGIN
    AddOne := A + 1
  END; (* of FUNCTION AddOne *)
```

9. ```
FUNCTION AddOne (A : integer) : integer; FORWARD;
PROCEDURE AddTwo (VAR B : integer);
  BEGIN
    B := AddOne(B);
    B := AddOne(B)
  END; (* of PROCEDURE AddTwo *)
FUNCTION AddOne;
  BEGIN
    AddOne := A + 1
  END; (* of FUNCTION AddOne *)
```

10. ```
FUNCTION AddOne (A: integer) : integer; FORWARD;
PROCEDURE AddTwo (VAR B : integer);
  BEGIN
    B := AddOne(B);
    B := AddOne(B)
  END; (* of PROCEDURE AddTwo *)
FUNCTION AddOne; (* (A : integer) : integer *)
  BEGIN
    AddOne := A + 1
  END; (* of FUNCTION AddOne *)
```

11. Give a schematic representation and indicate the scope of identifiers for the following subprograms contained in **PROGRAM** Exercise11.

```
PROGRAM Exercise11 (input, output);

VAR
 X, Y : real;
 Ch : char;

PROCEDURE A (VAR X1:real; Ch1:char);
  VAR
    J : integer;
  FUNCTION Inner (M:integer; Y1:real) : real;
    BEGIN

      .
      .
      .

    END; (* of FUNCTION Inner *)
  BEGIN (* PROCEDURE A *)
    .
    .
  END; (* of PROCEDURE A *)
```
```

```
PROCEDURE B (X1:real; VAR Ch2:char);
  BEGIN  (* PROCEDURE B  *)
     .
     .
     .
  END;  (*  of PROCEDURE B   *)
```

12. Consider the block structure shown in Figure 7.18 for **PROGRAM** Exercise12.

   a. Indicate which subprograms can be called from the main program.
   b. Indicate all appropriate calls from one subprogram to another subprogram.
   c. List three inappropriate calls and explain why they cannot be made.

13. Consider the following program.

```
PROGRAM Exercise13 (input, output);

VAR
  A, B, Num : integer;

FUNCTION MaxPower (A1, B1 : integer) : integer;
  VAR
    Prod, K : integer;
  PROCEDURE Sort (VAR A2, B2 : integer);
    VAR
      Temp : integer;
    BEGIN  (*  PROCEDURE Sort  *)
      IF B2 < A2 THEN
        BEGIN
          Temp := A2;
          A2 := B2;
          B2 := Temp
          END  (*  of IF ... THEN  *)
    END;  (*  of PROCEDURE Sort  *)
  BEGIN  (*  FUNCTION MaxPower  *)
    Sort (A1, B1);
    Prod := A1;
    FOR K := 1 TO B1-1 DO
      Prod := Prod * A1;
    MaxPower := Prod
  END;  (*  of FUNCTION MaxPower  *)

BEGIN  (* Main program  *)
  read (A,B);
  Num := MaxPower (A,B);
  writeln(Num)
END.  (*  of main program  *)
```

   a. Give a schematic representation and indicate the scope of identifiers.
   b. What is the output if the numbers read for A and B are 5 and 3, respectively?
   c. Explain what this program does for positive integers A and B.
   d. Rewrite **FUNCTION** MaxPower using recursion rather than

```
Prod := A1;
FOR K := 1 TO B-1 DO
Prod := Prod * A1;
```

FIGURE 7.18
Block with subblocks

PROGRAM Exercise12

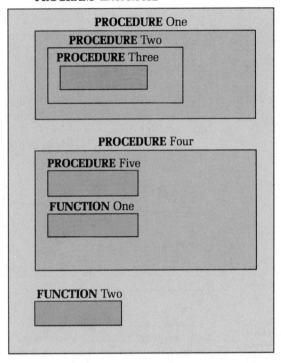

14. Explain what is wrong with the following recursive function.

```
FUNCTION Recur (X : real) : real;
   BEGIN
      Recur := Recur(X/2)
   END;  (*  of FUNCTION Recur  *)
```

For Exercises 15–17, consider the following recursive function.

```
FUNCTION A (X:real; N:integer) : real;
   BEGIN
      IF N = 0 THEN
         A := 1.0
      ELSE
         A1 := X * A(X, N-1)
   END;  (*  of FUNCTION A  *)
```

15. What is the value of Y for each of the following:
   a. Y := A(3.0, 2);
   b. Y := A(2.0, 3);
   c. Y := A(4.0, 4);
   d. Y := A(1.0, 6);
16. Explain what standard computation is performed by **FUNCTION** A.
17. Rewrite **FUNCTION** A using repetition rather than recursion.
18. Write a recursive procedure to write a line of character data in the reverse order from which it is read. That is, if the input is

   This is line one

   the output from the procedure is

   eno enil si sihT

19. Recall the Fibonacci sequence

    1, 1, 2, 3, 5, 8, 13, 21, . . .

    where for $n > 2$ the nth term is the sum of the previous two. Write a recursive function to compute the nth term in the Fibonacci sequence.

20. The Tower of Hanoi is a classic problem that can be solved by a recursive process. The problem involves three pegs and disks as depicted in Figure 7.19. The objective is to move the disks from peg 1 to peg 3. The rules are that only one disk may be moved at a time and a larger disk can never be placed on a smaller disk.

    Write a recursive procedure to print out step-by-step instructions for solving this problem.

FIGURE 7.19
Tower of Hanoi

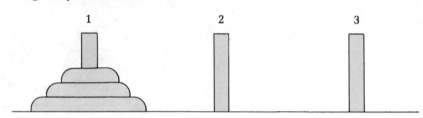

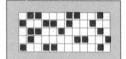

1. Each subprogram can be tested separately to see if it is producing the desired result. This is accomplished by a main program that calls and tests only the subprogram in question.

2. Use related but not identical variable names in the parameter lists. For example,

   ```
   PROCEDURE Compute (N1,N2:integer; VAR Av:real);
   ```

   can be called by

   ```
   Compute (Number1, Number2, Average);
   ```

3. Be sure the type and order of actual parameters and formal parameters agree. You can do this by listing them one below the other. For example,

   ```
   PROCEDURE GetData (VAR Init1,Init2:char; Sc:integer);
                GetData (Initial1, Initial2, Score);
   ```

4. Carefully distinguish between value parameters and variable parameters. If a value is to be returned to the main program, it must be passed through a variable parameter. This means it must be declared with **VAR** in the procedure heading.

■ **Summary**

Key Terms

subprogram	block	forward reference
procedure	global variable	nested subprogram
value parameter	local variable	recursion
variable parameter	scope of an identifier	recursive subprogram
parameter list	user-defined function	stopping state
formal parameter	stub programming	recursive step
actual parameter	main driver	mutual recursion

Keywords

PROCEDURE   **FUNCTION**   **FORWARD**

Key Concepts

- A subprogram is a program within a program; procedures and functions are subprograms.
- Subprograms are generally written to accomplish specific tasks.
- A typical procedure heading which could be used when writing a procedure to produce the heading for the output is

```
PROCEDURE PrintHeader;
```

- A procedure is called, or invoked, from the main program by a reference to the procedure name.

```
BEGIN  (*  Main program  *)
  PrintHeader;
END.  (*  of main program  *)
```

- Procedures are placed in a program after the variable declaration section and before the start of the main program.

```
PROGRAM Practice (input, output);

VAR

PROCEDURE PrintTitle;
  BEGIN
     .
     .
     .
    END;  (*  of PROCEDURE PrintTitle  *)

BEGIN  (*  Main program  *)
     .
     .
     .
END.  (*  of main program  *)
```

- The general form for a procedure heading is

PROCEDURE name (parameter list);

- Value parameters are used when values are passed only from the main program to the procedure; a typical parameter list is

```
PROCEDURE PrintData (N1,N2:integer; X,Y:real);
```

- Variable parameters are used when values are passed from the main program to the procedure and from the procedure to the main program; a typical parameter list is

```
PROCEDURE GetData (VAR Init1,Init2:char;
                   VAR N1:integer);
```

- Procedures are often used to initialize variables (variable parameters), get data (variable parameters), print headings (no variables needed), perform computations (value and/or variable parameters), and print data (value parameters).
- Global variables can be used by the main program and all subprograms.

- Local variables are available only to the subprogram in which they are declared.
- Each variable is available to the block in which it is declared; this includes all subprograms contained within the block.
- Variables are not available outside their blocks.
- The scope of an identifier refers to the blocks in which the identifier is available.
- Understanding scope of identifiers is aided by graphic illustration of blocks in a program; thus,

```
PROGRAM Practice (input, output);
VAR
   X,Y,Z : real;
PROCEDURE Sub1 (X1 : real);
   VAR
     X2 : real;
   BEGIN
     .
     .
     .
   END;

PROCEDURE Sub2 (X1 : real);
   VAR
     Z2 : real;
```

can be visualized as shown in Figure 7.20.

FIGURE 7.20
Scope of identifiers

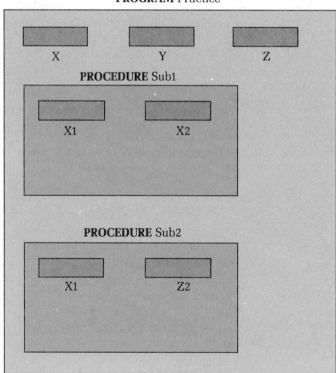

PROGRAM Practice

- A user-defined function is a subprogram that performs a specific task.
- The form for a user-defined function is

    FUNCTION function name (parameter list) : return type;
      VAR
      BEGIN

        $\left.\begin{array}{c} . \\ . \\ . \end{array}\right\}$ (work of function here)

      END;

- A formal parameter is one listed in the function heading; it is like a blank waiting to receive a value from the calling program.

    formal parameters

    ```
    FUNCTION Arithmetic (Sym:char; N1,N2:integer):integer;
    ```

- An actual parameter is a variable listed in the function call in the calling program.

    actual parameters

    ```
    Arithmetic (Symbol, Num1, Num2);
    ```

- The formal parameter list in the function heading must match the number and types of actual parameters used in the main program when the function is called.

    ```
    FUNCTION Arithmetic (Sym:char; N1,N2:integer):integer;
    Arithmetic (Symbol, Num1, Num2);
    ```

- An assignment must be made to the function name in the body of the function.
- The function name cannot be used on the right of an assignment statement.
- Forward reference of a subprogram can be achieved by listing the function or procedure heading with all parameters and following that with the reserved word **FORWARD,** as

    ```
    FUNCTION B(X:real) : real; FORWARD;
    ```

- A recursive process must have well-defined steps that lead to a stopping state.
- Any recursive subprogram can always be rewritten using repetition.
- Mutual recursion occurs when each of two subprograms calls the other; stopping states must be carefully built in.

■ **Chapter Review Exercises**

1. Explain the difference between a value parameter and a variable parameter. Give an example of how each is used.

2. Explain the difference between an actual parameter and a formal parameter.

3. A procedure is defined as

    ```
    PROCEDURE SampleProc (A:integer; VAR B:real; C:char);
    ```

    Which parameters in this definition are variable parameters and which are value parameters?

In Exercises 4–12, which procedure calls are valid? (Int1 represents an integer variable, Real1 represents a real, and Ch1 represents a character.) If it is invalid, explain why.

```
 4. SampleProc (Int1, Real1, Ch1);
 5. SampleProc;
 6. SampleProc (Int1; VAR Real1; Ch1);
 7. SampleProc (Int1; Real1; Ch1);
 8. SampleProc (Int1, Ch1);
 9. SampleProc (3, 5.0, 'X');
10. SampleProc (Real1, Int1, Ch1);
11. SampleProc (Int1, Int2, Int3);
12. SampleProc (Real1, Int1, Ch1);
```

13. Write a procedure to print the following:

```
<<<<<<<<<<<<<<<<<<<<<<<<<<<>>>>>>>>>>>>>>>>>>>>>>>>>>>

            Programming in Pascal

                 is GREAT !!

<<<<<<<<<<<<<<<<<<<<<<<<<<<>>>>>>>>>>>>>>>>>>>>>>>>>>>
```

14. Write a main program to print the message from Exercise 13 five times.

In Exercises 15–21, indicate if the statement is a valid procedure declaration. Explain the problem for those that are invalid.

```
15. PROCEDURE Exercise15 (A:integer, Y:real);
16. PROCEDURE Exercise16 (VAR A; X:integer);
17. PROCEDURE Exercise17 (VAR A:integer; VAR B:integer);
18. PROCEDURE (VAR A:integer; B:char);
19. PROCEDURE Exercise19 ((VAR A:integer : VAR B:integer);
20. PROCEDURE Exercise20 (A:integer; VAR B:char);
21. PROCEDURE Exercise21 (VAR A:integer; VAR c:char);
```

For Exercises 22–26, write a statement that can be used to call the procedure or function.

```
22. PROCEDURE Exercise22 (VAR A,B:integer, C:real);
23. PROCEDURE Exercise23 (VAR A:integer; B:real);
24. FUNCTION Exercise24 (A:integer; B:real) : real;
25. PROCEDURE Exercise25;
26. FUNCTION Exercise26 (A:real) : char;
```

For Exercises 27–33, indicate which are valid function headings. Explain the problem with those that are invalid.

```
27. FUNCTION Exercise27 (X:real);
28. FUNCTION Exercise28;
29. FUNCTION Exercise29 (VAR A:integer) : integer;
30. FUNCTION Exercise30 (X:real) : char;
31. FUNCTION Exercise31 (A:integer; B:real) : boolean;
32. FUNCTION Exercise32 (A:integer; B:real) : integer;
33. FUNCTION Exercise33 (A, B:real; C:integer) ; integer;
```

34. Write a statement that can be used to call the valid functions in Exercises 27–33.

35. Why are variable parameters used in a procedure designed to initialize variables?

36. Write a program containing a recursive routine that prints the integers from 1 to a value input by the program user. All values should be printed in the recursive routine.

For Exercises 37–40, examine the following program.

```
PROGRAM Exercise37To40 (output);

VAR
  A, B : integer;

PROCEDURE ProcOne (A:integer; VAR B:integer);
  BEGIN
    A := 2;
    B := B + 1;
    writeln (A,B)
  END;  (*  of PROCEDURE ProcOne  *)

PROCEDURE ProcTwo (VAR A:integer; B:integer);
  PROCEDURE ProcThree (A,B : integer);
    BEGIN
      A := 10;
      B := 11;
      writeln (A,B)
    END;  of PROCEDURE ProcThree  *)
  BEGIN  (*  PROCEDURE ProcTwo  *)
    ProcOne;
    A := A + 1;
    B := B * 2;
    writeln (A,B);
    ProcOne;
    ProcThree;
    writeln (A,B)
  END;  (*  of PROCEDURE ProcTwo  *)

FUNCTION Funct1 (A:integer) : integer;
  VAR
    B : integer;
  BEGIN
    B := 3;
    Funct1 := A + B
  END;  (*  of FUNCTION Funct1  *)

BEGIN  (*  Main program  *)
  A := 4;
  B := 5;
  writeln (A,B);
  ProcOne (A,B);
  writeln (A,B);
  ProcTwo (A,B);
  writeln (A,B);
  B := Funct1 (B);
  writeln (A,B);
  ProcOne (B,A);
  writeln (A,B)
END.  (*  of main program  *)
```

37. What output is produced by the program?

38. Draw a diagram showing the block structure of the program.

39. What is the scope of each variable?

40. Make a table showing the permissible procedure and function calls in the program.

■ **Chapter Summary Program**

This program solves the same problem and has the same program design and output as the Chapter Summary Program in Chapter 6. However, this version uses subprograms. A procedure with no parameters prints a message for the integer 1. A procedure with a value parameter prints a message for integers other than 1. A function is used to determine whether or not a specific integer is prime. A complete program for this problem follows.

```
PROGRAM ListPrimes2 (input,output);
(*****************************************************************

       This program is an improved version of the one
       presented at the end of Chapter 6. In this version,
       subprograms are used to facilitate program
       design. Specifically, the following subprograms
       are used.
           1.    Get Another         Reads a number as input
           2.    PrintOneMessage     Prints message for 1
           3.    PrintMessage        Prints heading for number
           4.    PrimeCheck          Function to check for prime


       ******************************************************************)
CONST
  Skip = ' ';
  Dashes = '_____';


VAR
  K ,                        (*  Loop index variable                   *)
  Number: integer;           (*  Integer read from input; primes less  *)
                             (*  than or equal to this are listed       *)
  Prime: boolean;            (*  boolean variable used in prime check   *)


(*****************************************************************

       This procedure gets a number.

       ******************************************************************)
PROCEDURE GetAnother (VAR Num : integer);
  BEGIN
    writeln ('Enter a positive integer; 0 to quit.');
    readln (Num)
  END; (*  of PROCEDURE GetAnother  *)
```

```
(******************************************************************

                This procedure prints a message for 1.

 *****************************************************************)
PROCEDURE PrintOneMessage;
  BEGIN
    writeln; writeln;
    writeln(Skip:10,Dashes);
    writeln;
    writeln(Skip:20,'1 is not prime by definition.')
  END;  (*    of PROCEDURE PrintOneMessage     *)

(******************************************************************

    This procedure prints a short message for each
    number read other than 1.

 *****************************************************************)
PROCEDURE PrintMessage (Num : integer);
  BEGIN
    writeln; writeln;
    writeln(Skip:10,Dashes);
    writeln;
    writeln(Skip:20,'The number is',Num:5,
             '. The prime numbers');
    writeln(Skip:20,'less than or equal to',Num:5,' are:');
    writeln
  END;  (*    of PROCEDURE PrintMessage    *)

(******************************************************************

    This function checks to see if an integer is prime.
    A boolean value is returned.

 *****************************************************************)
FUNCTION PrimeCheck (K1 : integer):boolean;
  VAR
    Candidate : integer;
    PrimeFlag : boolean;
  BEGIN
    PrimeFlag := true;
    Candidate := 2;
    WHILE (Candidate <= sqrt(K1)) AND (PrimeFlag = true) DO
      BEGIN
        If K1 MOD Candidate = 0 THEN
          PrimeFlag := false;
        Candidate := Candidate + 1
      END;  (*    of WHILE ... DO loop     *)
    PrimeCheck := PrimeFlag
  END;       (*    of FUNCTION PrimeCheck    *)
```

```
(****************************************************************

            All subprograms are written.    Begin main program.

  ****************************************************************)
BEGIN    (*    Main program    *)
  GetAnother (Number);
  WHILE Number > 0 DO
    BEGIN
      IF Number = 1 THEN
        PrintOneMessage
      ELSE
        BEGIN
          PrintMessage(Number);
          writeln (1:35); (*  Put 1 in the list  *)
          FOR K := 2 TO Number DO
            BEGIN
              Prime := PrimeCheck(K);
              IF Prime THEN
                writeln(K:35)
            END  (*   of processing K  *)
        END;  (*   of ELSE option  *)
      GetAnother(Number)
    END  (*   of WHILE ... DO loop  *)
END.  (*   of main program  *)
```

■ **Programming Problems**

In order to facilitate the use of subprograms in writing programs to solve problems, the programming problems for this chapter consist of redesigning previous programs. Table 7.3 refers to programming problems from earlier chapters and indicates which subprograms should be used in the new version.

TABLE 7.3
Programming
problems using
subprograms

Problem	Chapter	Subprograms	
1	6	a. Compute meal cost.	(procedure)
		b. Compute room rate.	(procedure)
		c. Compute surcharge.	(procedure)
		d. Compute tax and tip.	(function)
		e. Compute discount.	(procedure)
		f. Print statement.	(procedure)
2	6	a. Write a function that returns a **boolean** value: **true** for a prime number **false** otherwise (composite number).	
3	6	a. Read and check data.	(procedure)
		b. Print primes.	(procedure)
		(This procedure should call the function developed in your redesign of Problem 2, Chapter 6.)	
17	5	a. Compute room charge.	(function)
		b. Compute television charge.	(function)
		c. Compute telephone charge.	(function)
7	6	a. Get a line of data.	(procedure)
		b. Compute per-tank mileage.	(function)
		c. Print a line of output.	(procedure)
		d. Compute total mileage.	(function)
8	6	a. Get data.	(procedure)
		b. Check for bad data.	(procedure)
		c. Print triangle.	(procedure)
13	6	a. Get a student's data.	(procedure)
		b. Compute grade.	(function)
		c. Print results.	(procedure)
14	6	a. Get data.	(procedure)
		b. Convert to hours.	(function)
		c. Compute charge.	(function)
		d. Print ticket.	(procedure)

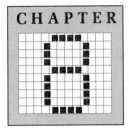
Text Files and User-Defined Data Types

Thus far data for programs were entered interactively. In this chapter we learn to use files which allow us to solve problems with larger data bases in a more sophisticated manner. We also learn how Pascal permits data types other than **integer, real, char,** and **boolean** to be defined and subsequently used in a program.

■ 8.1 Text Files

OBJECTIVES

- to understand what a text file is
- to get data from a text file
- to store data in a text file

The ability to work with *text files* permits us to write programs for large sets of data and to write them without using an interactive mode for input. When data are entered using the interactive mode, a message is displayed on the screen, and the desired information is appropriately entered. However, writing clear screen messages to prompt the user becomes tedious. Also, it is difficult to use interactive programs with large sets of data. Most important, however, is that it is frequently desirable to save information between runs of a program for later use.

To avoid these problems, we can store data in some secondary storage device, usually magnetic tapes or disks. Data can be created separately from a program, stored on these devices, and then accessed by programs when necessary. It is also possible to modify and save this information for other runs of the same program or for running another program using this same data. For now we will store all data in text files (other kinds of files are examined in Chapter 12).

Text files can be created by a text editor or by a program. Often the editor you use to create your program can be used to create a text file. The use of text editors varies significantly from machine to machine and you should consult your teacher and/or manual to use this method. This, however, is how your teacher may create data files for you to use with subsequent programming problems. A text file created from a program is declared by

```
VAR
   file name : text;
```

where file name is any valid identifier. Thus,

```
VAR
   ClassList : text;
```

provides a text file whose name is ClassList.

Text files that exist before or after a program is run are called *external files* and must be listed in the program heading. Thus, if a program named ClassRecordBook uses the text file ClassList, the program heading is

```
PROGRAM ClassRecordBook (input, output, ClassList);
```

The listing here is required so the operating system can connect the file name ClassList to the text file.

Data in a text file can be thought of as a sequence of characters stored in a sequence of lines. Each line has an *end-of-line* (**eoln**) *marker* (▮) after it. Each file has an *end-of-file* (**eof**) *marker* (■) after the last end-of-line marker. For example, suppose a text file is used to store data for students in a class. If each line consists of an identification number for each student followed by three scores, a typical file can be envisioned as

```
00723 85 93 100 ▮
```

```
00131 78 91 85 ▮
```

```
00458 82 75 86 ▮ ■
```

Technically these lines are stored as one continuous stream with end-of-line markers used to differentiate between lines and the end-of-file marker to signify the end of one file.

```
00723 85 93 100 ▮ 00131 78 91 85 ▮ 00458 82 75 86 ▮ ■
```

However, we frequently use separate lines to illustrate lines in a text file. Both end-of-line and end-of-file markers are appropriately placed by the computer at the time a file is created. When characters are read, these markers are read as blanks.

Reading from a Text File

Reading from a text file is very similar to getting input interactively. Standard procedures **read** and **readln** are used with appropriate variables as arguments in either format as shown.

```
      read (file name, input list);

or
      readln (file name, input list);
```

If the file name is not specified, the standard file **input** is assumed. Thus, data from one line of the file of student test scores, ClassList, can be obtained by

```
read (ClassList, IdNumber, Score1, Score2, Score3);
```

or

```
readln (ClassList, IdNumber, Score1, Score2, Score3);
```

Before data can be read from a file, the file must be *opened for reading*. This is done by the statement

reset (file name);

This statement moves a data pointer to the first position of the first line of the data file to be read. Thus,

```
reset (ClassList);
```

positions the pointer as follows:

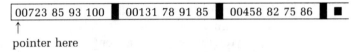

pointer here

As data items are read (using **read**), the pointer moves to the first position past the last data item read. Thus, the statement

```
read (ClassList, IdNumber, Score1);
```

results in the following:

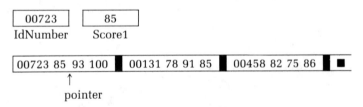

pointer

readln works the same as **read** except that it causes the pointer to skip over the data items remaining on that line and go to the first position past the end-of-line marker. Thus,

```
reset (ClassList);
readln (ClassList, IdNumber, Score1);
```

results in

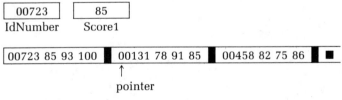

pointer

Variables in the variable list of **read** and **readln** can be listed one at a time or in any combination that does not result in a type conflict. For example,

```
read (CLassList, IdNumber, Score1);
```

can be replaced by

```
read (ClassList, IdNumber);
read (CLassList, Score1);
```

Only if the data pointer is at an end-of-line or end-of-file marker is the **boolean** function **eoln**(file name) **true.** Similarly, **eof**(file name) is **true** only when the data pointer is positioned at the end-of-file marker. This allows both **eoln**(file name) and **eof**(file name) to be used as **boolean** conditions when designing problem solutions. Thus, part of a solution might be

WHILE NOT eof(file name) **DO**
    process a line of data

where "process a line of data" is appropriately refined.

Text files can contain any character available in the character set being used. When numeric data are stored, the system converts a number to an appropriate character representation. When this number is retrieved from the file, another conversion takes place to change the character representation to a number. Since each conversion introduces the possibility of an error, you should be careful to check output for erroneous results. In Chapter 12 we will see how to avoid this problem by using other kinds of files.

EXAMPLE 8.1

Let's now write a short program that uses the text file ClassList and the end-of-file (**eof**) condition. If the problem is to print a listing of student identification numbers, test scores, and test averages, a first-level pseudocode development is

1. Print a heading
2. **WHILE NOT eof**(text file) **DO**
    2.1 process a line of data

Step 2.1 can be refined to

    2.1 process a line of data
        2.1.1 get the data
        2.1.2 compute test average
        2.1.3 print the data

A short program to accomplish this task is

```
PROGRAM ClassRecordBook (input, output, ClassList);
(*************************************************************

        This program uses data from a text file. Data
        for each student are on a separate line in the
        file. Lines are processed until there are no
        more.

 *************************************************************)

VAR
        Score1, Score2, Score3,        (*  Test scores             *)
        IdNumber : integer;            (*  Student number          *)
        TestAverage : real;            (*  Average of three tests  *)
        ClassList : text;              (*  External file           *)
```

```
FUNCTION Average (S1, S2, S3 : integer) : real;
  BEGIN
    Average := (S1 + S2 + S3) / 3
  END; (* of FUNCTION Average *)

PROCEDURE PrintHeading;
  CONST
    Skip = ' ';
  BEGIN
    writeln; writeln;
    writeln ('Identification Number', Skip:5, ' Test Scores',
            Skip:5, 'Average');
    writeln ('_____', Skip:5, ' _____',
            Skip:5, '_____');
    writeln
  END; (* of PROCEDURE PrintHeading *)

BEGIN (* Main Program *)
  PrintHeading;
  reset (ClassList);
  WHILE NOT eof(ClassList) DO
    BEGIN
      readln (ClassList, IdNumber, Score1, Score2, Score3);
      TestAverage := Average (Score1, Score2, Score3);
      writeln (IdNumber:10, Score1:19, Score2:4,
                          Score3:4, TestAverage:11:2)
    END (* of WHILE NOT eof DO loop *)
END. (* of main program *)
```

When this program is run using the text file ClassList with values

```
00123 85 93 100
```

```
00131 78 91 85
```

```
00458 82 75 86 ■
```

the output produced is

```
Identification Number    Test Scores    Average
_____    _____    _____

      00123              85  93 100      92.67
      00131              78  91  85      84.67
      00458              82  78  86      81.00
```

A note of caution is in order. Any attempt to **read** beyond the end of a file results in an error. To illustrate, if

```
read (ClassList, IdNumber, Score1, Score2, Score3);
```

had been used in the previous example instead of

```
readln (ClassList, IdNumber, Score1, Score2, Score3);
```

an error would have occurred because, when **read** is used with the last line of data, the data pointer is positioned as

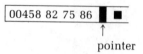

pointer

At this point, **eof**(ClassList) is still **false** and the loop for processing a line of data is entered one more time. Using **readln,** however, positions the data pointer as

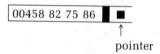

pointer

and this causes the end-of-file condition to be **true** when expected.

SELF QUIZ 8.1   Assume a text file, InFile, consists of the data line

| This is a practice file. ▮ |

| It contains three lines ▮ |

| of data. ▮ ■ |

and that a variable Ch of type **char** has been declared. What output is produced from the following segment of code?

```
reset (InFile);
WHILE NOT eof(InFile) DO
   BEGIN
      WHILE NOT eoln(InFile) DO
         BEGIN
            read (InFile, Ch);
            write (InFile, Ch)
         END;   (*  of one line  *)
      writeln
   END;   (*  of the data file  *)
```

Writing to a Text File

As stated, when you are working with an external file, it must be listed in the program heading as well as declared in the declaration section. If the file has not been previously created and you do not wish to save the file when you are through with the program, it does not have to be included in the file list part of the program heading. It is then an *internal file.* Before writing to an internal or external text file, the file must be *opened for writing* by

    rewrite (file name);

This standard procedure creates an empty file with the specified name. If there were any values previously in the file, they are erased by this statement. Data are then written to the file by using standard procedures **write** and **writeln.** The general form is

> **write** (file name, list of values);
>
> or
>
> **writeln** (file name, list of values);

These both cause the list of values to be written on one line in the file. The difference is that **writeln** causes an end-of-line marker to be placed after the last data item. Using **write** allows you to continue entering data items on the same line with subsequent **write** or **writeln** statements. If you wish,

```
writeln (file name);
```

can be used to place an end-of-line marker at the end of a data line.

Formatting can be used to control spacing of data items in a line of text. For example, since numeric items must be separated, you might choose to put test scores in a file by

```
writeln (ClassList, Score1:4, Score2:4, Score3:4);
```

If the scores are 85, 72, and 95, the line of data created is

```
85  72  95
```

Let's now illustrate writing to a file with two examples.

EXAMPLE 8.2

Let's write a program that allows you to create a text file which will contain data for students in a class. Each line in the file is to contain a student identification number followed by three test scores. A first-level pseudocode development is

1. Open the file
2. **WHILE** more data **DO**
   2.1 process a line

Step 2.1 can be refined to

2.1 process a line
   2.1.1 get data from keyboard
   2.1.2 write data to text file

A complete program for this is

```
PROGRAM CreateFile (input, output, ClassList);
(*************************************************************

   This program creates a text file. Each line of
   the file contains data for one student. Data are
   entered interactively from the keyboard
   and then written to the file.

*************************************************************)

VAR
   Score1, Score2, Score3,  (*  Scores for three tests      *)
   IdNumber : integer;      (*  Student number              *)
   Response : char;         (*  Indicator for continuation  *)
   MoreData : boolean;      (*  Loop control variable       *)
   ClassList : text;        (*  External text file          *)
```

```
BEGIN   (*  Main Program  *)
   rewrite (ClassList);           (*  Open for writing  *)
   MoreData := true;
   WHILE MoreData DO
     BEGIN
       write ('Please enter a student ID number');
       writeln ('and three test scores.');
       writeln ('Separate entries by a space.');
       writeln;
       readln (IdNumber, Score1, Score2, Score3);
       writeln (ClassList, IdNumber, Score1:4, Score2:4,
                  Score3:4);

(*  Check for more data  *)

       writeln;
       writeln ('Any more students?  Y or N');
       readln (Response);
       IF Response = 'N' THEN
         MoreData := false
     END  (*  of WHILE . . . DO loop  *)
END.  (*  of main program  *)
```

At this point we have an external file ClassList which contains a line of data for each student in a class. ∎

STYLE TIP

■ ■ ■ ■ ■ ■ ■ ■

> The program given in Example 8.2 used the **boolean** variable MoreData as a loop control. Values were assigned to MoreData by
>
> ```
> readln (Response);
> IF Response = 'N' THEN
>   MoreData := false;
> ```
>
> This code is used because it is easy to read. However, the same task can be accomplished by
>
> ```
> readln (Response);
> MoreData := (Response <> 'N');
> ```

For our next example, we will modify an existing external file.

EXAMPLE 8.3

Let's write a program that allows you to update the text file ClassList by adding one more test score to each line of data. We need two text files in this program: ClassList (external) and TempFile (internal). With these two files, we can copy contents of ClassList to TempFile, open ClassList for writing (erase old contents), and update ClassList one line at a time by using lines from TempFile. A first-level pseudocode solution for this problem is

1. Open files
2. Copy contents of ClassList to TempFile
3. Open files
4. **WHILE NOT eof**(TempFile) **DO**
   4.1   update a line of data

A complete program for this problem is

```
PROGRAM UpdateClassList (input, output, ClassList);
(******************************************************

     This program updates an existing text file.
     The process requires a second file. Contents of
     the external file are copied to a temporary
     internal file and the external file is then
     updated one line at a time.

******************************************************)
VAR
    Score1, Score2,               (*   Scores for four tests  *)
    Score3, Score4,
    IdNumber : integer;               (*   Student number  *)
    ClassList, TempFile : text;       (*   Text files  *)

BEGIN (*  Main program  *)
   reset (ClassList);                    (*    Open files  *)
   rewrite (TempFile);
   WHILE NOT eof(ClassList) DO        (*   Copy to TempFile  *)
      BEGIN
         readln (CLassList, IdNumber, Score1, Score2, Score3);
         writeln (TempFile, IdNumber, Score1:4, Score2:4,
                   Score3:4)
      END;  (* of copying ClassList to TempFile *)
   reset (TempFile);                        (*   Open files  *)
   rewrite (ClassList); (*  Note: Contents of old ClassList
                                         are erased.  *)

   WHILE NOT eof(TempFile) DO
      BEGIN
         readln (TempFile, IdNumber, Score1, Score2, Score3);
         writeln ('Enter a new test score for student ', IdNumber);
         readln (Score4);            (*  Get the new score  *)
         writeln (ClassList, IdNumber, Score1:4, Score2:4,
                   Score3:4, Score4:4)
      END (*  of lines in TempFile  *)
END. (*  of main program  *)
```

The material in this section allows us to make a substantial change in our approach to writing programs. We are no longer dependent upon an interactive mode and we can now proceed assuming data files exist for a program. This somewhat simplifies program design and also allows us to design programs for large sets of data. Consequently, most programs developed in the remainder of this text use text files for input. If you wish to continue with interactive programs, previous work should allow you to make appropriate modifications.

Exercises 8.1

1. Explain the difference between an external file and an internal file. Give appropriate uses for each.

2. Write a test program that allows you to reproduce a line of text from a text file.

3. Explain what is wrong with

   ```
   writeln (ClassList, Score1, Score2, Score3);
   ```

   when trying to write three scores to the text file ClassList.

4. Write a program that allows you to print a text file line by line.

For Exercises 5–8, assume that a text file, InFile, is as illustrated.

```
18 19M  -14.3 JO 142.1F  ■
```

The pointer is positioned at the beginning of the file, and the variable declaration section of a program is

```
VAR
  A,B : integer:
  X,Y : real;
  CH : char;
  InFile : text;
```

What output is produced from each segment of code?

5. ```
   read (InFile, A);
   read (InFile, B, Ch);
   writeln (A:5, B:5, Ch:5);
   ```
6. ```
   read (InFile, Ch);
   write (Ch:10);
   readln (InFile, Ch);
   writeln (Ch);
   read (InFile, Ch);
   writeln (Ch:10);
   ```
7. ```
   read (InFile, A, B, Ch, X);
   writeln (A, B, Ch, X);
   writeln (A:5, B:5, Ch:5, X:10:2);
   read (InFile, Ch);
   writeln (Ch:5);
   ```
8. ```
   readln (InFile);
   read (InFile, Ch, Ch);
   readln (InFile, Y);
   writeln (Ch:5, Y:10:2);
   ```

For Exercises 9–16, use the same stream input and variable declaration section as in Exercises 5–8. Indicate the contents of each variable location and the position of the pointer after the segment of code is executed. Assume the pointer is positioned at the beginning for each problem.

9. ```
   read (InFile, Ch, A);
   ```
10. ```
    readln (InFile, Ch, A);
    ```
11. ```
    readln (InFile);
    ```
12. ```
    readln (InFile);
    readln (InFile);
    ```
13. ```
    readln (InFile, A, B, Ch, X);
    ```
14. ```
    read (InFile, A, B, Ch, Y);
    ```
15. ```
    readln (InFile, A, Ch);
    readln (InFile, Ch, Ch, B);
    ```
    ```

16. `read (InFile, A, B, Ch, X, Ch);`

For Exercises 17–21, again use the same stream input and variable declaration section as in Exercises 5–8. Indicate if the exercise produces an error and, if so, explain why an error occurs.

17. `read (InFile, X, Y);`
18. `readln (InFile, A);`
    `read (InFile, B);`
19. `readln (InFile, Ch);`
    `readln (InFile, Ch);`
    `readln (InFile, Ch);`
20. `read (InFile, X, A, Ch, B, Ch);`
21. `readln (InFile);`
    `read (InFile, Ch, Ch, A, Ch, B);`

22. Write a complete Pascal program that reads your initials and five test scores from a text file. Your program should then compute your test average and print out all information in a reasonable form with suitable messages.

23. Write a program that allows you to create a text file that contains your name, address, social security number, and age. **reset** the file and have the information printed as output. Save the file in secondary storage for later use.

24. Show what output is produced from the following program. Also indicate the contents of each file after the program is run.

```
PROGRAM Exercise24 (input, output, F2);

VAR
  F1, F2 : text;
  Ch : char;

BEGIN
  rewrite (F1);
  rewrite (F2);
  writeln (F1, 'This is a test.');
  writeln (F1, 'This is another line.');
  reset (F1);
  WHILE NOT eof (F1) DO
    BEGIN
      read (F1,Ch);
      IF Ch = ' ' THEN
        writeln ('*')
      ELSE
        write (F2, Ch);
      IF eoln (F1) THEN
        readln (F1)
    END
END.
```

25. Write a program that deletes all blanks from a text file. Your program should save the revised file for later use.

26. Write a program to scramble a text file by replacing all blanks with an asterisk (*), and interchanging all As with Us and Es with Is. Your program should print out the scrambled file and save it for subsequent use.

27. Write a program to update a text file by numbering the lines consecutively as 1, 2, 3, ...

28. Write a program to count the number of words in a text file. Assume that each word is followed by a blank or a period.

29. Write a program to find the longest word in a text file. Output should include the word and its length.

30. Write a program to compute the average length of words in a text file.

■ 8.2
TYPE Definitions in Pascal

- to understand what is meant by ordinal data type
- to declare user-defined data types
- to use user-defined data types in a program
- to understand why user-defined data types are of value in writing programs

Ordinal Data Types

Of the four data types we have previously used, **integer, char,** and **boolean** are called *ordinal data types.* This means the data are countable, each has a unique predecessor and successor, and they can be ordered and compared. The **real** type is not an ordinal data type because reals are not countable. Furthermore, a real does not have a unique predecessor or successor. Permissible values for data of these three ordinal data types are as follows:

Data Type	Values
integer	−**maxint** to **maxint**
char	Character set in a collating sequence
boolean	**true, false**

The four data types used thus far are standard data types. We are now ready to see how Pascal allows us to define new data types called *user-defined data types.*

User-Defined Data Types

The declaration section of a program may contain a **TYPE** definition section that can be used to define a data type. For example,

```
TYPE
    Weekday = (Mon, Tues, Wed, Thur, Fri);
```

After such a definition is made, the variable declaration section can contain identifiers of the type Weekday. Thus, we can have

```
VAR
    Day : Weekday;
```

Several comments are now in order concerning the **TYPE** definition.

1. User-defined data types are frequently referred to as *enumerated* types.
2. A newly defined type is an ordinal data type with the first defined constant having ordinal zero. Ordinal values increase by one in order from left to right.
3. Variables can be declared to be of the new type.
4. The values declared in the **TYPE** definition section are constants that can be used in the program.

5. No value can belong to more than one user-defined data type.
6. Defined values cannot be used as operands in arithmetic expressions.
7. Identifiers used as data types cannot be used as variable or subprogram names.

Thus, given the previous **TYPE** definition of Weekday and the variable declaration of Day, each of the following is an appropriate program statement.

```
1. Day := Tues;
2. IF Day = Mon THEN
      .
      .
      .
   ELSE
      .
      .
      .
3. FOR Day := Mon TO Fri DO
      BEGIN
         .
         .
         .
      END.
```

Now that you have seen an example of a user-defined data type and some typical related program statements, let's look at a more formal method of definition. In general, we have

TYPE
    type identifier = (constant1, constant2, . . . , constantn);

VAR
    identifier : type identifier;

The **TYPE** definition section is part of the declaration section of a program. It follows the constant definition section **(CONST)** and precedes the variable declaration section **(VAR)** as shown in Figure 8.1.

The following short program illustrates the placement and use of user-defined data types.

```
PROGRAM TypePrac (output);

CONST
   Skip = ' ';
TYPE
   Weekday = (Mon, Tues, Wed, Thur, Fri);
VAR
   Day : Weekday;
```

```
BEGIN
  Day := Wed;
  IF Day < Fri THEN
    writeln (Skip, 'Not near the weekend.')
  ELSE
    writeln (Skip, 'The weekend starts tomorrow.')
END.
```

The output from this program is

```
Not near the weekend.
```

SELF QUIZ 8.2   Define a data type whose constants are the four seasons. Indicate how a variable of this type would be declared.

Reasons for Using User-Defined Types

At first it may seem like a lot of trouble to define new types for use in a Pascal program, but there are several reasons for using them. In fact, being able to create user-defined types is one of the advantages of using Pascal as a programming language. Why? With user-defined data types, you can express clearly the logical structure of data, enhance the readability of your program, provide program protection against bad data values, and declare parameters in subprograms.

FIGURE 8.1
Placement of **TYPE**
definition section

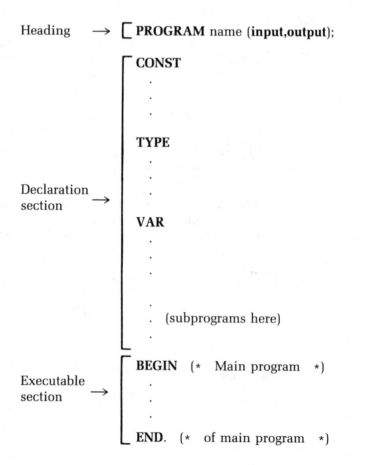

Heading → [**PROGRAM** name (**input,output**);

Declaration → section

 ⌈ **CONST**
  .
  .
  .

 TYPE
  .
  .
  .

 VAR
  .
  .
  .

  .
  . (subprograms here)
  .

Executable → section

 ⌈ **BEGIN** (* Main program *)
  .
  .
  .
 ⌊ **END**. (* of main program *)

How Girls Lose Interest: A Summary of the Research

We should not expect educational researchers to tell us whether boys or girls are overall "better" computer learners—the question is too subjective to answer. Research can, however, reveal sex-related tendencies that educators may wish to address. Listed here, for example, are some results of surveys of computer use in and out of school. When examined by age and sex, these results point to a disturbing trend.

Elementary school boys and girls generally like computers equally well.

> —*Charlotte Beyers, "Bridging the Gender Gap," Family Computing (August 1984)*

In the sixth grade (and usually before), there are no sex differences in self-confidence about, attitude toward or perceived utility of computers.

> —*Marlaine Lockheed and Steven Frakt, "Sex Equity: Increasing Girls' Use of Computers," The Computing Teacher (April 1984)*

By high school, girls have less confidence than boys do in their ability to learn computer skills.

> —*Dennis Cole and Michael Hanuafin, "An Analysis of Why Students Select Introductory High School Computer Coursework," Educational Technology (April 1983)*

There is little difference in achievement among teenage girls and boys who take required computer courses.

> —*Charlotte Beyers, above*

After one course, 52 percent of girls are interested in taking more word processing or business applications courses; 59 percent of boys want more programming courses.

> —*I. Miura and R. Hess, Sex Differences in Computer Access, Interest and Use, Stanford University (1983)*

Elective programming courses in high school have a two-to-one ratio of boys to girls.

> —*National Assessment in Science, 1982*

Among teenage girls, 7 percent use computers outside of class; 40 percent of boys do.

> —*Charlotte Beyers, above*

Twenty-five percent more boys than girls come home to a computer.

> —*Charlotte Beyers, above*

There are three times more boys than girls in summer computer camps.

> —*R. Hess and I. Miura, Gender and Socioeconomic Differences in Enrollment in Computer Camps and Classes, Stanford University (1982)*

Suppose you are working on a program to count the number of days in some month of a certain year. User-defined data types allow you to use the following definition and subsequent declaration.

```
TYPE
    AllMonths = (Jan, Feb, March, April, May, June, July,
                 Aug, Sept, Oct, Nov, Dec);
VAR
    Month : AllMonths;
    Year, NumDays : integer;
```

With this definition, the readability of your program is enhanced; it can contain a statement such as

```
IF (Month = Feb) AND (Year MOD 4 = 0) THEN
    NumDays := 29;
```

which clearly indicates that you are counting the extra day in February for a leap year.

Once a user-defined data type has been defined in a program, it is available to all subprograms. Thus, if you have a function for counting the days, a typical function heading might be

```
FUNCTION NumDays (Mth:AllMonths; Yr:integer):integer;
```

This aspect of user-defined data types will become more significant when we examine structured data types, including arrays and records.

You need to be aware of a limitation imposed on variables that are of a user-defined type. They are for internal use only; you cannot **read** or **write** values of these variables. Thus, in the earlier example using months of the year, you can have the following statement

```
Month := June;
```

but not

```
writeln (Month);
```

We close this section with some typical definitions for user-defined data types. These are intended to improve program readability. You are encouraged to incorporate user-defined data types in your subsequent programs. In general, you are limited only by your imagination.

```
TYPE
    SoftDrinks = (Pepsi, Coke, SevenUp, Orange, RootBeer);
    Seasons = (Winter, Spring, Summer, Fall);
    Colors = (Red, Orange, Yellow, Green, Blue, Indigo, Violet);
    ClassStanding = (Freshman, Sophomore, Junior, Senior);
    Ranks = (Sarg, Lieut, Cptn, Major, Corp);
    Fruits = (Apple, Orange, Banana);
    Vegetables = (Corn, Peas, Broccoli, Spinach);
```

With these type definitions, each of the following is a reasonable variable declaration.

```
VAR
    Pop, Soda : SoftDrinks;
    Season : Seasons;
    Hue : Colors;
    Class : ClassStanding;
    Rank : Ranks;
    Appetizer : Fruits;
    SideDish : Vegetables;
```

Exercises 8.2

1. Explain what is meant by ordinal data type.

2. Write a test program to see what happens when you try to **write** the value of a variable that is a user-defined data type.

In Exercises 3–5, find all errors in the definitions.

```
3. TYPE
    Names = (John, Joe, Mary, Jane);
    People = (Henry, Sue, Jane, Bill);
4. TYPE
    Colors = (Red, Blue, Red, Orange);
5. TYPE
    Letters = A, C, E;
```

6. Assume the **TYPE** definition

```
TYPE
   Colors = (Red, Orange, Yellow, Blue, Green);
```

is given. Indicate whether each of the following is **true** or **false.**

a. Orange < Blue
b. (Green <> Red) AND (Blue > Green)
c. (Yellow < Orange) OR (Blue >= Red)

For Exercises 7–14, assume the **TYPE** definition and variable declaration

```
TYPE
   AllDays = (Sun, Mon, Tues, Wed, Thur, Fri, Sat);
VAR
   Day, Weekday, Weekend: AllDays;
```

are given. Indicate which are valid program statements and, for those that are invalid, explain why.

```
 7. Day := Tues;
 8. Day := Tues + Wed;
 9. Weekday := Sun;
10. IF Day = Sat THEN
       writeln ('Clean the garage.':30);
11. IF (Day < Sat) AND (Day > Sun) THEN
       writeln ('It is a workday.':30)
    ELSE
       writeln ('It is the weekend.':30);
12. FOR Day := Mon TO Fri DO
       writeln (Day);
13. read (Day);
    IF Day < Sat THEN
       Weekday := Day;
14. Wed := Tues + 1;
```

15. Assume the following definitions and declarations are made in a program.

```
TYPE
   Cloth = (Flannel, Cotton, Rayon, Orlon);
VAR
   Material : Cloth;
   NumberOfYards,Price : real;
```

What output is produced from the following segment of code?

```
Material := Cotton;
NumberOfYards := 3.5;
IF (Material = Rayon) OR (Material = Orlon) THEN
   Price := NumberOfYards * 4.5
ELSE
   IF Material = Cotton THEN
      Price := NumberOfYards * 2.75
   ELSE
      Price := NumberOfYards * 2.5;
writeln (Price:30:2);
```

■ 8.3
Subrange as a Data Type

- to define a subrange as a data type
- to use subrange data types in a program
- to understand compatibility of data types
- to understand why subrange data types are used in a program

Defining Subranges

In the previous section, we learned how to define new data types using the **TYPE** definition section. Now we will investigate yet another way to define new data types.

A *subrange* of an existing ordinal data type may be defined as a data type by

> **TYPE**
>   identifier = initial value .. final value;

For example, we can have a subrange of the integers defined by

```
TYPE
    USYears = 1776 . . 1986;
```

When defining a subrange, the following items should be noted.

1. The original data type must be an ordinal type.
2. Any valid identifier may be used for the name of the type.
3. The initial and final values must be of the original data type.
4. Exactly two periods, "..", separate the initial and final value.
5. Since the underlying data type is ordinal, it is ordered. In this ordering, the initial value of a defined subrange must occur before the final value. For example,

```
TYPE
    BadType = 1000 . . 1;
```

is not valid.

6. Only values in the indicated subrange (endpoints included) may be assigned to a variable of the type defined by the subrange.
7. The same value may appear in different subranges.

We illustrate some of these points in Example 8.4.

Consider the subranges Weekdays and Midweek of the user-defined ordinal Days.

```
TYPE
    Days = (Sun, Mon, Tues, Wed, Thur, Fri, Sat);  (* User-Defined *)
    Weekdays = Mon . . Fri;                         (* Subrange     *)
    Midweek = Tues . . Thur;                        (* Subrange     *)
VAR
    SchoolDay : Weekdays;
    Workday : Midweek;
```

In this case, Days is defined first and we can then define appropriate subranges. With the variable SchoolDay declared as of type Weekdays, you can use any of the values Mon, Tues, Wed, Thur, or Fri with SchoolDay. However, you cannot assign either Sat or Sun to SchoolDay.

Notice that Tues, Wed, and Thur are values that appear in different type definitions. However, since they appear in subranges, this will not produce an error. Furthermore,

```
        SchoolDay := Tues;
        Workday := Tues;
```

are both acceptable statements.

■

Some other subrange definitions are

```
TYPE
  Grades = 'A' . . 'E';
  Alphabet = 'A' . . 'Z';
  ScoreRange = 0 . . 100;
  Months = (Jan, Feb, Mar, Apr, May, June, July, Aug, Sept,
            Oct, Nov, Dec);
  Summer = June . . Aug;
```

In this definition, months is not a subrange. However, once it is defined, an appropriate subrange such as Summer may be defined. With these subranges defined, each of the following declarations is appropriate.

```
VAR
  FinalGrade : Grades;
  Letter : Alphabet;
  TestScore : ScoreRange;
  SumMonth : Summer;
```

Suppose a computer science course is being taught on a pass/fail basis; a score of 70 or greater is needed to pass. Show how a user-defined subrange of the integers and subsequent declaration can be used to reflect this.

Compatible and Identical Types

Now that we know how to define subranges of existing ordinal data types, we need to look carefully at compatibility. Data types are *compatible* if they have the same base type; that is, they are of the same type, one is a subrange of the other, or they both are subranges of the same type. Variables are compatible if they are of compatible type. Thus, in

```
TYPE
  AgeRange = 0 . . 110;

VAR
  Age : AgeRange;
  Year : integer;
```

the variables Age and Year are compatible because they both have **integer** as the base type (AgeRange is a subrange of integers). If variables are compatible, assignments may be made between them or they may be manipulated in any manner that variables of that base type may be manipulated.

Even when variables are compatible, you should exercise caution when making assignment statements. To illustrate, using Age and Year as previously declared, consider the statements

```
Age := Year;
Year := Age;
```

Since Age is of type AgeRange and AgeRange is a subrange of **integer,** any value in Age is acceptable as a value that can be assigned to Year. Thus,

```
Year := Age;
```

is permissible. However, since values for Age are restricted to the defined subrange, it is possible that

```
Age := Year;
```

will produce a run-time error. Since they are compatible, there is not a compilation error, but consider

```
Year := 150;
Age := Year;
```

Since 150 is not in the subrange for Age, execution would be halted and an error message printed.

Two variables are said to be of *identical type* if—and only if—they are declared with the same type identifier. It is important to distinguish between compatible and identical types for variables when using subprograms. A value parameter and its argument must be of compatible type; a variable parameter and its argument must be of identical type. **TYPE** definitions must be used in the main program since they cannot be defined in a subrpogram heading. To illustrate, consider

```
TYPE
   GoodScore = 60 . . 100;
VAR
   Score1, Score2 : GoodScore;

PROCEDURE Compute (S1:integer; VAR S2:GoodScore);
```

This procedure may be called by

```
Compute (Score1, Score2);
```

Note that S1 is a value parameter and need only be compatible with Score1. S2 is a variable parameter and must be identical in type to Score2.

SELF QUIZ 8.4   Consider the following definitions and declarations.

```
TYPE
   HighTemp = 80 . . 100;
   LowTemp = 0 . . 30;
VAR
   HotDay : HighTemp;
   ColdDay : LowTemp;
   AMTemp, PMTemp : integer;
```

Indicate whether the following pairs of variables are compatible or identical and why.

```
HotDay, AMTemp
ColdDay, HotDay
AMTemp, PMTemp
ColdDay, PMTemp
```

Using Subranges

There are several good reasons for using subranges. Although extra time and thought are required when you are writing a program, the long-range benefits far outweigh these minor inconveniences. One major benefit is program protection. By carefully defining subranges, you avoid the possibility of working with bad data or data out of the expected range. Although such data are not detected during compilation, an inappropriate assignment will halt execution. This makes it easier to locate the source of an error. It also avoids the possibility of producing incorrect results. If, for example, a keypunch operator inadvertently types in 400 rather than 40 for the hours worked by an employee, a definition and declaration such as

```
TYPE
   TotalHours = 0 , , 60;
VAR
   Hours : TotalHours;
```

causes execution to be stopped with the statement

```
read (Hours);
```

since 400 is not in the defined subrange. (Some versions of Pascal continue the program but may assign meaningless values to the variable.)

Another benefit of using subranges is increased program readability. Descriptive identifiers with clearly stated subranges make it easier to follow a program. For example, if a chemical reaction normally occurs around 180 degrees Fahrenheit, you can have

```
TYPE
   ReactRange = 150 , , 210;
VAR
   ReactTemp : ReactRange;
```

STYLE TIP

The **CONST** and **TYPE** definition sections can be used together to enhance readability and facilitate program design. For example, rather than use the subrange

```
TYPE
   USYears = 1776 , , 1986;
```

you can define an ending constant and then use it as indicated.

```
CONST
   CurrentYear = 1986;


TYPE
   USYears = 1776 , , CurrentYear;
```

Exercises 8.3

In Exercises 1–5, indicate whether the **TYPE** definitions, subsequent declarations, and uses are valid or invalid. Explain what is wrong with those that are invalid.

```
1. TYPE
      Reverse = 10 , , 1;
2. TYPE
      Bases = (Home, First, Second, Third);
      Double = Home , , Second;
      Score = Second , , Home;
```

```
3. TYPE
     Colors = (Red, White, Blue);
     Stripes = Red . . White;
   VAR
     Hue : Stripes;
   BEGIN
     Hue := Blue;
4. TYPE
     Weekdays = Mon . . Fri;
     Days = (Sun, Mon, Tues, Wed, Thur, Fri, Sat);
5. TYPE
     ScoreRange = 0 . . 100;
     HighScores = 70 . . 100;
     Midscores = 50 . . 70;
     LowScores = 20 . . 60;
   VAR
     Score1 : Midscores;
     Score2 : HighScores;
   BEGIN
     Score1 := 60;
     Score2 := Score1 + 5;
```

6. Write a test program to see what happens when you try to assign or read a value for a variable that is not in the defined subrange.

In Exercises 7–10, explain why each subrange definition might be used in a program.

7. `Dependents = 0 . . 20;`   9. `QuizScores = 0 . . 10;`

8. `HoursWorked = 0 . . 60;`   10. `TotalPoints = 0 . . 700;`

In Exercises 11–15, indicate a reasonable subrange and explain your answer.

11. `TwentiethCentury =`
12. `Digits =`
13. `JuneTemp =`
14. `WinterRange =`
15. `Colors = (Black, Brown, Red, Pink, Yellow, White);`
    `LightColors =`

For Exercises 16–21, assume the declaration section of a program contains

```
TYPE
  ChessPieces = (Pawn, Knight, Bishop, Rook, King, Queen);
  Expendable = Pawn . . Rook;
  Valuable = King . . Queen;
  LowRange = 0 . . 20;
  Midrange = 40 . . 80;
VAR
  Piece1 : Valuable;
  Piece2 : Expendable;
  Piece3 : ChessPieces;
  Score1 : LowRange;
  Score2 : Midrange;
  Score3 : integer;
```

Indicate which pairs of variables are of compatible type.

16. `Piece1 and Piece2`   19. `Score1 and Score2`

17. `Piece2 and Piece3`   20. `Score1 and Score3`

18. `Piece3 and Score1`   21. `Piece2 and Score3`

For Exercises 22–26, assume the declaration section of a program contains

```
TYPE
   PointRange = 400 . . 700;
   FlowerList = (Rose, Iris, Tulip, Begonia);
   Sublist = Rose . . Tulip;
VAR
   TotalPts : PointRange;
   Total : integer;
   Flower : Sublist;
   OldFlower : FlowerList;
```

and the procedure heading is

```
PROCEDURE TypePrac (A:PointRange;
                    VAR B:integer;
                    FL:Sublist);
```

Indicate which are valid calls to this procedure.

22. `TypePrac (TotalPts, Total, Flower);`
23. `TypePrac (Total, TotalPts, Flower);`
24. `TypePrac (TotalPts, Total, OldFlower);`
25. `TypePrac (Total, Total, Flower);`
26. `TypePrac (Total, Total, OldFlower);`

■ 8.4
Operations on Ordinal Data Types

OBJECTIVES

- to use functions **ord, pred,** and **succ** with user-defined data types
- to use ordinal data types in **boolean** expressions
- to use ordinal data types in **CASE** statements
- to use ordinal data types as loop indices

Functions for Ordinal Data Types

Earlier we discussed the meaning of ordinal data types. Data of ordinal type are countable, each element has a unique predecessor and successor, and can be ordered and compared. Of the standard data types, only **real** is not ordinal. User-defined data types are ordinal. Until now, in discussing functions on ordinal data types, we have used only standard data types. The functions **ord, pred,** and **succ** may also be used on user-defined ordinal data types. When this happens, they return values in a manner consistent with their use on standard ordinal data. Thus, if we have the definition

```
TYPE
   Days = (Sun, Mon, Tues, Wed, Thur, Fri, Sat);
   Weekdays = Mon . . Fri;
```

the following function calls have the indicated values.

Function Call	Value
ord(Sun)	0
ord(Wed)	3
pred(Thur)	Wed
succ(Fri)	Sat
ord(**pred**(Fri))	4

When using functions on user-defined ordinals, the following should be noted.

1. The first-listed value has ordinal zero.
2. Successive ordinals are consistent with the manner in which values are listed.

3. You cannot use **pred** on the first value or **succ** on the final value.

4. If a subrange data type is defined, the functions return values consistent with the underlying base type; for example,

ord(Wed) = 3

Consider the following definitions.

```
TYPE
   Color = (Red, Orange, Yellow, Green, Blue, Indigo, Violet);
   Hue = Yellow . . Indigo;
```

Indicate what values are produced by each of the following function calls and why.

ord(Yellow)
pred(Yellow)
pred(Red)
succ(Indigo)

Using Ordinal Values of User-Defined Ordinals

Now that you have some familiarity with ordinal data types and functions that use them as arguments, let's consider some ways they can be incorporated into programs. One typical use is in **boolean** expressions. Suppose you are writing a program to compute the payroll for a company that pays time-and-a-half for working on Saturday. Assume the definition and declaration

```
TYPE
   Workdays = (Mon, Tues, Wed, Thur, Fri, Sat);
VAR
   Day : Workdays;
```

are made. A typical segment of code is

```
Day := some value;
IF Day = Sat THEN
   Compute overtime
ELSE
   Compute regular pay
```

A second use is with **CASE** statements. As previously noted, one limitation of user-defined ordinals is that they have no external representation (that is, you cannot **read** or **write** their values). However, you can circumvent this limitation by appropriate use of a **CASE** statement. For example, suppose we have the definition and declaration

```
TYPE
   Colors = (Red, White, Blue);
VAR
   Hue : Colors;
```

If you wish to print the value of Hue, you can do so by

```
CASE Hue OF
    Red   : writeln ('Red':20);
    White : writeln ('White':20);
    Blue  : writeln ('Blue':20)
END;   (*   of CASE   *)
```

This statement has the same effect as

```
writeln (Hue:20);
```

which is not allowed.

A third use is as a loop index. We now know that user-defined ordinals can be used in a manner consistent with most uses of standard ordinal data types. Thus, it should come as no surprise that user-defined ordinals can be used as loop indices. For example, consider

```
TYPE
    AllDays = (Sun, Mon, Tues, Wed, Thur, Fri, Sat);
VAR
    Day : AllDays;
```

Each of the following is an appropriate loop.

```
1. FOR Day := Mon TO Fri DO
      BEGIN
         .
         .
         .
      END;
```

```
2. Day := Mon;
   WHILE Day < Sat DO
     BEGIN
       Day := succ(Day);
              .
              .
              .
     END;
3. Day := Sun;
   REPEAT
     Day := succ(Day);
          .
          .
          .
   UNTIL Day = Fri;
```

The loop control in a **FOR** loop is based on the ordinals of the values of the loop index. Thus, the statement

```
FOR Day := Mon TO Fri DO
```

is treated like the statement

```
FOR J := 1 TO 5 DO
```

because **ord**(Mon) is 1 and **ord**(Fri) is 5.

In the **WHILE ... DO** and **REPEAT ... UNTIL** loops, you must be sure to increment—increase the ordinal of—the variable. One method of doing this is to use the function **succ** as indicated.

Exercises 8.4

For Exercises 1–7, suppose the following **TYPE** definition is given.

```
TYPE
  Trees = (Oak, Ash, Maple, Pine);
  SlackType = (Denim, Cotton, Polyester);
```

Give the value of the expression or indicate if the expression is invalid.

1. **pred**(Ash)
2. **succ**(Denim)
3. **ord**(Polyester)
4. **ord(pred**(Oak))
5. **ord(succ**(Maple)
6. **succ**(Polyester)
7. **ord(pred(succ**(Oak)))

8. Write a test program that lists the ordinals of values in a subrange of a user-defined data type.

The character set for some computers is such that **ord**('A') = 1 and **ord**('Z') = 26. For Exercises 9–14, assuming such a sequence, what is the value of the expression? Indicate if the expression is invalid.

9. **chr(ord**(‘D’)**)**
10. **ord(chr**(10)**)**
11. **chr(3 ∗ ord**(‘E’)**)**
12. **ord(chr**(10 **MOD** 3) + **chr**(20)**)**
13. **ord(pred**(‘K’) + 3**)**
14. **succ(chr(ord**(‘Z’) − 1)**)**

15. Write a program to list the characters and their respective ordinals for the character set used with your machine.

For Exercises 16–19, assume the **TYPE** definition and variable declaration

```
TYPE
    AllDays = (Sun, Mon, Tues, Wed, Thur, Fri, Sat);
VAR
    Day : AllDays;
```

are made.

16. What output is produced from the following **REPEAT ... UNTIL** loop?

```
Day := Sun;
REPEAT
   CASE Day OF
      Sat, Sun                    : writeln ('Weekend':20);
      Mon, Tues, Wed, Thur, Fri : writeln ('Weekday':20)
   END; (* of CASE *)
   Day := succ(Day)
UNTIL Day = Sat;
```

17. Rewrite the loop in Exercise 16 as both a **WHILE ... DO** loop and a **FOR** loop.

18. Find another method to control the loop variable in Exercise 16. For example, replace

```
Day := succ(Day)
```

and make any other necessary changes.

19. Revise the loop in Exercise 16 so that all seven days are considered.

For Exercises 20 and 21, convert an integer character to its corresponding numerical value, for example, the character ‘2’ to the number 2. Since the digits are listed sequentially in every character set, this can be accomplished by

```
ord('2') - ord('0')
```

20. Write a function to convert a single character digit (‘0’, ‘1’, . . ., ‘9’) to its corresponding numerical value.

21. Write a function to convert a two-digit number read as consecutive characters into the corresponding numerical value.

22. Suppose you are working with a program that reads an integer representing a month of the year (Jan = 1). Write a function to convert the integer into the appropriate month.

RUNNING AND DEBUGGING TIPS

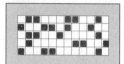

1. An end-of-line marker is read as a blank. When reading numeric data, this is not a problem. However, when reading data of type **char,** you may forget to advance the pointer to the next line.
2. Permanent text files must be listed in the program heading file list as well as in the variable declaration section.
3. Subranges should be used if the bounds of a variable are known.
4. User-defined data types should be used to enhance readability.
5. Be careful not to use **pred** on the first element in a list or **succ** on the last element.
6. Make sure parameters passed to subprograms are of identical type. For example, using the following declaration

```
TYPE
   Weekdays = (Mon, Tues, Wed, Thur, Fri);
VAR
   Day : Weekdays;
```

if a procedure call is

```
PrintChart (Day);
```

a procedure heading can be

```
PROCEDURE PrintChart (Wkday : Weekdays);
```

■ Summary

Key Terms

text file	opened for reading	enumerated type
external file	internal file	subrange
end-of-line (**eoln**) marker	opened for writing	compatible
	ordinal data type	identical type
end-of-file (**eof**) marker	user-defined data type	

Keywords

text	**eof**	**rewrite**
eoln	**reset**	**TYPE**

Key Concepts

- Text files can be used to store data between runs of a program.
- A text file can be declared by

```
VAR
   file name : text;
```

- An external file exists outside the program block in secondary storage. When used, it must be included in the file list as part of the program heading.
- An internal file exists within the program block. Values stored there will be lost when the program is no longer running.
- Text files must be opened before they can be written to or read from. Before reading from a file, it can be opened by

reset (file name);

Before writing to a file, it can be opened by

rewrite (file name);

- An end-of-line marker (█) is placed at the end of each line in a text file.
- An end-of-file marker (■) is placed after the last line in a text file.
- Reading from a text file can be accomplished by

  read (file name, list of variables);
  or
  readln (file name, list of variables);

- Writing to a text file can be accomplished by

  write (file name, list of values);
  or
  writeln (file name, list of values);

- A data type is ordinal if data of that type are countable and can be ordered and compared.
- User-defined data types can be defined by using the **TYPE** definition section; typical syntax and form are

  ```
  TYPE
      Weekdays = (Mon, Tue, Wed, Thur, Fri);
  ```

- When a user-defined data type has been defined,
  1. The newly defined type is an ordinal data type.
  2. Variables can be declared to be of the new type.
  3. The values declared in the **TYPE** definition section are constants that can be used in the program.
  4. No value can belong to more than one data type.
  5. Defined values cannot be used as operands in expressions.
- You cannot **read** or **write** values of a user-defined data type.
- A subrange of an existing ordinal data type can be defined by

  TYPE
  identifier = initial value .. final value;

  For example;

  ```
  TYPE
      ScoreRange = 0 .. 100;
      Alphabet = 'A' .. 'Z';
  ```

- Type compatible variables have the same base type.
- Type identical variables must have the same type identifier.
- Two significant reasons for using subranges are program protection and program readability.
- The functions **pred, succ,** and **ord** can be used on user-defined data types and subranges of existing ordinal data types.
- When one of the functions **pred, succ,** or **ord** is used with an argument whose value is in a subrange, reference is to the base data type, not the subrange; thus, in

  ```
  TYPE
      Letters = 'J' .. 'O';
  ```

  ord('J') does not have the value O. Rather, it yields the appropriate ordinal for the collating sequence being used. In the ASCII collating sequence, **ord**('J') yields 74, and in EBCDIC it yields 209.

■ Chapter
Review
Exercises

1. Show all definitions and declarations necessary to create a text file named Exercise1Text. Show how to put values into the file so that it looks like

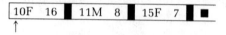

| 10F   16 | 11M   8 | 15F   7 | ■ |

For Exercises 2–7, use the text file from Exercise 1. Assume the variables are declared as follows:

```
A, B : integer;
C, D : char;
E : real;
```

Indicate if the statements are valid. If so, indicate what values are read and where the pointer is after the statement is executed. Assume the pointer is at the beginning for each exercise.

```
2. read (Exercise1Text, A, C, B);
3. readln (Exercise1Text, A, C, B);
4. read (Exercise1Text, A, B, C);
5. read (Exercise1Text, A, C, D);
6. read (Exercise1Text, A, C, E);
7. readln (Exercise1Text);
```

8. Write a segment of code to write the integers 1 through 10 to a text file.

9. Explain the difference between **read** and **readln** statements.

10. What is the purpose of a **reset** statement?

11. Write a segment of code to count the number of lines in a text file.

Exercises 12–19, find all the errors in the type declarations.

```
12. Exercise12 = (Red; Blue; Yellow);
13. Exercise13 = 10 . . 1;
14. Exercise14 = 'A', 'B', 'C', 'D';
15. Exercise15 = 'A' . . 'E';
16. Exercise16 = 'E' . . 'A';
17. Exercise17 = (Red, Orange, Yellow);
18. Exercise18 = ('Red', 'Orange', 'Yellow');
19. Exercise19 = 1.0 . . 2.5;
```

For Exercises 20–29, assume the following type and variable declarations are made.

```
TYPE
  Month = (Jan,Feb,Mar,Apr,May,Jun,Jul,Aug,Sep,Oct,Nov,Dec);
  Summer = Jun . . Sep;
  LastCentury = 1801 . . 1900;
VAR
  Date, Start : Month;
  Season : Summer;
  Year : LastCentury;
  J : integer;
```

Indicate if the statement is valid or invalid. If invalid, explain why.

```
20. J := Date;              25. Summer := succ(May);
21. read (Year);            26. Start := pred(Jan);
22. Year := 1986;          27. J := ord(pred(Jun);
23. J := Year + 2;          28. read (Season);
24. Summer := Aug;          29. Start := Start + 1;
```

For Exercises 30–36, using the same declarations as in Exercises 20–29, indicate if the statement is valid or invalid. If invalid, explain why.

```
30. writeln (Date, J);
31. writeln (Year);
32. writeln (ord(succ(Aug)));
33. writeln (Summer);
34. writeln (succ(Year));
35. writeln (pred(ord(Jan)));
36. writeln (Start);
```

Using the same declarations as in Exercises 20–29, indicate if Exercises 37–42 are **true, false,** or invalid.

37. Jan < Feb
38. **ord**(Mar) = 3
39. **ord**(Jan = 0

40. **pred**(Mar) > **succ**(Jan)
41. Apr = Mar + 1
42. 2000 = Year

For Exercises 43 and 44, consider the following type and variable declarations.

```
TYPE
    Hours = 1 . . 40;
    Letters = 'A' . . 'Z';
    Scores = 0 . . 100;
    Passing = 60 . . 100;
VAR
    HoursWorked, Overtime : Hours;
    Grades : Letters;
    Test1, Test2 : Scores;
    GoodGrade : Passing;
    J, K : integer;
    Average : real;
    Names : char;
```

43. Which of the variables are of identical type?
44. Which of the variables are of compatible type?

For Exercises 45–49, use the declarations from Exercises 43 and 44 and the procedure:

```
PROCEDURE Demo (VAR A:Hours; B:Scores; VAR C:Letters);
```

Which of the following procedure calls are valid? If invalid, explain why.

```
45. Demo (Overtime, J, Names);
46. Demo (J, K, Grades);
47. Demo (HoursWorked, Test1, Grades);
48. Demo (GoodGrade, GoodGrade, Grades);
49. Demo (Overtime, Average, Grades);
```

■ Chapter Summary Program

Let's write a program to compute the number of days in your birth year from your birthday to the end of the year. Sample input (if your birth date was March 16, 1965) is the line of data

```
3 16 65
```

We want the output to be

```
During your birth year, 1965,
you were alive 291 days.
```

A reasonable first-level pseudocode design for this program is

1. Get data
2. Assign the month
3. Compute days
4. Print results

The program includes procedures for steps 1, 2, and 4 and a function for step 3. Since the procedures are relatively short, we will only look at a refinement of the function that is used to do the computing. A first refinement is

3. Compute days
   3.1 compute days alive during birth month
   3.2 compute total of days in remaining months

This can be refined to

3. Compute days
   3.1 compute days alive during birth month
      3.1.1 compute for months with 31 days
      3.1.2 compute for months with 30 days
      3.1.3 compute for February
        IF leap year **THEN**
          use 29 days
        ELSE
          use 28 days
   3.2 compute total of days in remaining months
      IF not December **THEN**
        FOR rest of months **DO**
          add number of days in month

The complete program to solve this problem is

```
PROGRAM Birthday (input,output);
(******************************************************************

      This program tells how many days you were
      alive during your birth year. Input your
      birth date. Later, you can use this program as the
      basis for a biorhythm program.

      Pay special attention to the use of user-defined
      data types and subranges.

  ******************************************************************)

TYPE
  AllMonths = (Jan,Feb,March,April,May,June,
               July,Aug,Sept,Oct,Nov,Dec);
  DayRange = 1 . . 31;
  MonthRange = 1 . . 12;
  YearRange = 0 . . 99;
```

```
VAR
  BirthMonth : AllMonths; (*   Literal form of birth month           *)
  DayNum : DayRange;       (*  Number representing day you were born  *)
  Month : MonthRange;      (*  Numerical representation of birth month *)
  TotalDays : integer;     (*  Days alive in birth year          .    *)
  Year : YearRange;        (*  Representation of birth year           *)
```

```
(*****************************************************************
                 This procedure gets the data.
*******************************************************************)
PROCEDURE GetData (VAR Mon:MonthRange; VAR Day:DayRange;
                   VAR Yr:YearRange);
  BEGIN
    writeln('Enter your birth date in the form 2 23 65');
    readln(Mon,Day,Yr)
  END; (*   of PROCEDURE GetData   *)
```

```
(*****************************************************************
     This procedure converts the numerical representation
     of a month to the month name. This is to enhance
     readability.
*******************************************************************)
PROCEDURE AssignMonth (Mon:MonthRange; VAR BMonth:AllMonths);
  BEGIN
    CASE Mon OF
       1 : BMonth := Jan;
       2 : BMonth := Feb;
       3 : BMonth := March;
       4 : BMonth := April;
       5 : BMonth := May;
       6 : BMonth := June;
       7 : BMonth := July;
       8 : BMonth := Aug;
       9 : BMonth := Sept;
      10 : BMonth := Oct;
      11 : BMonth := Nov;
      12 : BMonth := Dec
    END    (*   of CASE statement   *)
  END; (*   of PROCEDURE AssignMonth   *)
```

```
(*******************************************************************

     This function computes the number of days alive
     during your birth year.

*******************************************************************)
FUNCTION ComputeDays (BMonth : AllMonths; Day : DayRange;
                        Yr : YearRange) : integer;
  VAR
    Days : integer;
    Mon : AllMonths;
  BEGIN

  (*   Compute days alive in birth month   *)

    CASE BMonth OF
      Jan,March,May,July,Aug,Oct,Dec : Days := 31-Day+1;
      April,June,Sept,Nov            : Days := 30-Day+1;
      Feb                            : IF Yr MOD 4 = 0 THEN
                                         Days := 29-Day+1
                                       ELSE
                                         Days := 28-Day+1
    END;   (*   of CASE statement   *)

  (*   Now compute days in remaining months   *)

    IF BMonth <> Dec THEN
      FOR Mon := succ(BMonth) TO Dec DO
        CASE Mon OF
          Jan,March,May,July,Aug,Oct,Dec : Days := Days+31;
          April,June,Sept,Nov            : Days := Days+30;
          Feb                            : IF Yr MOD 4 = 0 THEN
                                             Days := Days+29
                                           ELSE
                                             Days := Days+28
        END;   (*   of CASE statement   *)

  (*   Assign total days to function name   *)

    ComputeDays := Days

  END;   (*   of FUNCTION ComputeDays   *)

(*******************************************************************

             This procedure prints the results.

*******************************************************************)
PROCEDURE PrintResults (TDays : integer; Yr : YearRange);
  BEGIN
    writeln; writeln;
    writeln('During your birth year,':62,(Yr+1900):6,',');
    writeln('you were alive':53,TDays:5, ' days.');
    writeln; writeln
  END;   (*   of PROCEDURE PrintResults   *)
```

```
(********************************************************************

      All subprograms are now written.  The main program
      can now begin,

      ********************************************************************)
BEGIN      (*    Main program    *)
  GetData(Month,DayNum,Year);
  AssignMonth(Month,BirthMonth);
  TotalDays := ComputeDays(BirthMonth,DayNum,Year);
  PrintResults(TotalDays,Year)
END,       (*    of main program    *)
```

The output from this program is

```
During your birth year,  1965,
you were alive  291 days,
```

■ Programming Problems

Each of these programming problems should be written for use with a data file. You may either be provided with one or asked to create your own data file.

1. Write a program to compute the payroll for a company. Data for each employee are on two lines. Line 1 contains an employee number followed by the hourly wage rate. Line 2 contains seven integer entries indicating the hours worked each day. Wages are to be computed at time-and-a-half for anything over eight hours on a weekday and double time for any weekend work. Deductions should be withheld as follows:
   a. state income tax   4.6%
   b. federal income tax   21.0%
   c. social security (FICA)   6.8%

   ₋mployee numbers are the subrange 0001 .. 9999. You should define and use a data type for the days of the week.

2. The Caswell Catering and Convention Service (Problem 7, Chapter 4; Problem 14, Chapter 5; and Problem 1, Chapter 6) wants to upgrade their existing computer program. Use the **TYPE** definition section for each of the following and revise the program you developed previously as appropriate.
   a. The room names are changed to a color-coded scheme as follows:

Room A	RedRoom
Room B	BlueRoom
Room C	YellowRoom
Room D	GreenRoom
Room E	BrownRoom

   b. Use a subrange for the room rents.
   c. Use defined constants for the low value and high value of the room rents.

3. State University (Problem 15, Chapter 5) wants you to upgrade their computer program by using the **TYPE** definition section for each of the following:
   a. The room types are Regular or AirConditioned.
   b. Students' numbers are between 0001 and 9999 (use **CONST** for end values).
   c. Credit hours taken must be between 1 and 25.
   d. The GoodRange for credit hours is 12 to 21.

   Your new version should be used on a data file with several students' information.

4. Al Derrick (Problem 20, Chapter 5, and Problem 10, Chapter 6) wants you to revise his program by using the **TYPE** definition section to enhance readability and ensure protection against bad data. Your new version should run for several wells and include: types of wells (Dry, Oil, and Gas), volume for gas (between 10,000 and 100,000), and volume for oil (between 2,000 and 50,-000).

5. Mr. Lae Z. Programmer is relentless. He wants you to modify your latest version of the grading program by using the **TYPE** definition section. Your new version should include a range for test scores (from 0 to 100), a range for quiz scores (from 0 to 10), and a range for the final examination (from 0 to 200).

6. Upgrade your most recent version of the Pentagon Parking Lot program by using the **TYPE** definition section. Time in and time out are between 0600 and 2200 (6:00 A.M. and 10:00 P.M.). Vehicle type should be denoted by Car, Truck, or Senior.

7. Read a text file containing a paragraph of text. Count the number of words in the paragraph.

8. Write a program to print the contents of a text file omitting any occurrences of the letter "e" from the output.

9. A text file contains a list of integers in order from lowest to highest. Write a program to read and print the text file with all duplications eliminated.

10. Mr. John Napier, Principal of Lancaster High School, wants a program to compute grade point averages. Each line of a text file contains three initials followed by an unknown number of letter grades. These grades are A, B, C, D, or F. Write a program that reads the file and prints a list of the students' initials and their grade point averages. (Assume an A is 4 points, a B is 3 points, and so on.) Print an asterisk next to any grade point average that is greater than 3.75.

11. Revise the amortization table (Problem 18, Chapter 6) by employing a user-defined data type for the month number. Limit this to require that the loan be paid back within 60 months.

12. Revise the Manhattan Island problem (Problem 22, Chapter 6) with a user-defined data type for the range of years (1626 to last year) that will be used.

13. Update the grading program (Problem 25, Chapter 6) written for Mr. Christian to use a subrange of the integers for the input grades.

14. Revise the rectangle perimeter and area problem (Problem 30, Chapter 6) to restrict the lengths and widths to a subrange of the integers from 1 to 10.

CHAPTER

One-Dimensional Arrays

This chapter begins a significant new stage of programming. Thus far, we have been unable to manipulate and store large amounts of data in a convenient way. For example, if we wanted to work with a long list of numbers or names, we had to declare a separate variable for each number or name. Fortunately, Pascal (and all other programming languages) provides several structured variables to facilitate solving problems that require large amounts of data. Simply put, a structured variable uses one identifier to reserve a large amount of memory. This memory is capable of holding several individual values. Structured variables included in this text are arrays, records, sets, and files.

Arrays, the topic of this chapter, are designed to handle data of the same type. Some very standard applications for array variables include creating tabular output (tables), alphabetizing a list of names, analyzing a list of test scores, manipulating character data, and keeping an inventory.

■ 9.1
Basic Ideas and Notation

OBJECTIVES

- to understand the basic concept of an array
- to use correct notation for arrays

As previously mentioned, there are many instances in which several variables of the same data type are required. Let's, at this point, work with a list of five integers: 18, 17, 21, 18, and 19. Prior to this chapter, we would have declared five variables—A, B, C, D, and E—and assigned them appropriate values, or read them from an input file. This would have produced five values in memory each accessed by a separate identifier.

18	17	21	18	19
A	B	C	D	E

- to declare arrays with both variable declarations and type definitions
- to use array components with appropriate arithmetic operations
- to use array components with appropriate **read** and **write** statements

If the list was very long, this would be an inefficient way to work with this data; an alternative is to use an array. In Pascal, we declare a variable as an array variable using either of the following methods:

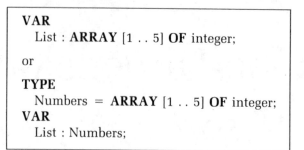

```
VAR
    List : ARRAY [1 .. 5] OF integer;

or

TYPE
    Numbers = ARRAY [1 .. 5] OF integer;
VAR
    List : Numbers;
```

With either of these declarations, we now have five integer variables with which to work. They are denoted by

List[1]	List[2]	List[3]	List[4]	List[5]

and each is referred to as a *component of the array*. A good method of visualizing these variables is to assume that memory locations are stacked on top of each other and the name of the stack is List. If we then assign the five values of our list to these five variables, we have the following in memory.

List

18	List[1]
17	List[2]
21	List[3]
18	List[4]
19	List[5]

The components of an array are referred to by their relative position in the array. This relative position is called the *index* or *subscript* of the component. In the array of our five values, the component List[3] has an index of 3 and value of 21. It is important to remember that each array component is a variable and can be treated exactly as any other declared variable in the program. Notice that when declaring an array and referring to specific elements, the subscripts are enclosed in brackets.

Declaring an Array

An array can be declared by reference to a user-defined type or by defining the type in the variable declaration section. An earlier declaration was given as

```
VAR
    List : ARRAY [1 . . 5] OF integer;
```

Let's now examine this declaration more closely. Several comments are in order.

1. List can be any valid identifier. As always, it is good practice to use descriptive names to enhance readability.

2. **ARRAY** is a reserved word and is used to indicate that an array variable is being declared.
3. [1 .. 5] is the syntax that indicates the array consists of five memory locations accessed by specifying each of the numbers, 1, 2, 3, 4, and 5. We frequently say the array is of length five. The information inside the brackets is the *index type* and is used to refer to components of an array. This index type can be any ordinal data type that specifies a beginning value and an ending value. However, subranges of integer data type are the most easily read and frequently used index types.
4. The reserved word **OF** refers to the data type for the components of the array.
5. The keyword **integer** indicates the data type for the components. This can, of course, be any valid data type.

The general form for declaring an array in the variable declaration section is

> **VAR**
>   name : **ARRAY** [index type] **OF** data type;

where "name" is any valid identifier, "index type" is any ordinal data type that specifies both an initial value and a final value, and "data type" is any predefined or user-defined data type. The syntax diagram for this is

The following example illustrates another declaration of an array variable.

EXAMPLE 9.1

Suppose you want to create a list of ten integer variables for the hours worked by ten employees as follows:

Employee Number	Hours Worked
1	35
2	40
3	20
4	38
5	25
6	40
7	25
8	40
9	20
10	45

Let's declare an array that has ten components of type **integer** and show how it can be visualized. A descriptive name can be Hours. There are ten items, so we will use **ARRAY** [1 .. 10] in the declaration. Since the data consist of integers, the data type is **integer**. An appropriate declaration is

```
VAR
    Hours : ARRAY [1 .. 10] of integer;
```

At this stage, the components can be visualized as

Hours

	Hours[1]
	Hours[2]
	Hours[3]
	Hours[4]
	Hours[5]
	Hours[6]
	Hours[7]
	Hours[8]
	Hours[9]
	Hours[10]

After making appropriate assignment statements, Hours can be visualized as

Hours

35	Hours[1]
40	Hours[2]
20	Hours[3]
38	Hours[4]
25	Hours[5]
40	Hours[6]
25	Hours[7]
40	Hours[8]
20	Hours[9]
45	Hours[10]

SELF QUIZ 9.1

Show how the following array could be depicted. How many variables are available for use?

```
VAR
    A : ARRAY [-2 . . 3] OF real;
```

Give an example illustrating an assignment to a component.

Other Indices and Data Types

The previous two arrays used index types that were subranges of the **integer** data type. Although this a common method of specifying the length of an array, one could use subranges of any ordinal type for this declaration. The following examples illustrate some array declarations with other indices and data types.

EXAMPLE 9.2

Let's declare an array to allow you to store the hourly price for a share of IBM stock. A descriptive name is StockPrice. A price is quoted at each hour from 9:00 A.M. to 3:00 P.M., so we will use **ARRAY** [9 .. 15] in the declaration section. Since the data consist of reals, the data type must be **real.** A possible declaration is

```
VAR
    StockPrice : ARRAY [9 . . 15] of real;
```

This then allows us to store the 9:00 A.M. price in StockPrice[9], the 1:00 P.M. price in StockPrice[13], and so on.

EXAMPLE 9.3

The declaration

```
VAR
    Alpha : ARRAY [-2 , , 3] OF char;
```

reserves components, which can be depicted as

Alpha

	Alpha[− 2]
	Alpha[− 1]
	Alpha[0]
	Alpha[1]
	Alpha[2]
	Alpha[3]

Each component is a character variable.   ■

EXAMPLE 9.4

The declaration

```
VAR
    Grade : ARRAY ['A' , , 'E'] OF real;
```

reserves components, which can be depicted as

Grade

	Grade['A']
	Grade['B']
	Grade['C']
	Grade['D']
	Grade['E']

Components of this array are real variables.   ■

EXAMPLE 9.5

The declaration

```
VAR
    Flag : ARRAY [1 , , 4] of boolean;
```

reserves components, which can be depicted as

Flag

	Flag[1]
	Flag[2]
	Flag[3]
	Flag[4]

Components of the array are **boolean** variables.   ■

It is important to note that in each example, the array components have no values assigned until the program specifically makes some kind of assignment. Declaring an array does not assign values to any of the components.

Declarations like those just illustrated are sufficient for the student who is trying to understand the concept of an array. However, there are at least three good reasons to use the **TYPE** definition section when declaring arrays.

1. Several arrays may have the same data type.
2. Passing arrays to procedures and functions requires a **TYPE** definition.
3. Using the **TYPE** definition facilitates use of descriptive names.

Descriptive constants and type identifiers should be utilized when working with arrays. For example, if you are working with an array of test scores for a class of 35 students, you could have

```
CONST
   ClassSize = 35;
TYPE
   TestScores = 0 .. 100;
   ScoreList = ARRAY [1 .. ClassSize] OF TestScores;
VAR
   Score: ScoreList;
```

Two additional array declarations follow.

1.
```
TYPE
   Days = (Mon, Tues, Wed, Thur, Fri, Sat, Sun);
   Workdays = ARRAY [Mon .. Fri] OF real;
VAR
   HoursWorked : Workdays;
```

2.
```
TYPE
   List50 = ARRAY [1 .. 50] OF real;
   List25 = ARRAY [1 .. 25] OF integer;
   String20 = ARRAY [1 .. 20] OF char;
VAR
   PhoneCharge : List50;
   Score : List25;
   Word : String20;
   A, B, C, D : List50;
```

A more efficient method of manipulating character data than the strings just used is presented in Section 9.5 when we discuss packed arrays.

Assignment Statements

Suppose we have declared an array

```
A : ARRAY [1 .. 5] OF integer;
```

and we want to put the values 1, 4, 9, 16, and 25 into the respective components. We can accomplish this with the assignment statements

```
A[1] := 1;
A[2] := 4;
A[3] := 9;
A[4] := 16;
A[5] := 25;
```

If variables B and C of type **integer** are declared in the program, the following are also appropriate assignment statements.

```
A[3] := 8;
C := A[2];
A[2] := A[5];
```

If you want to interchange values of two components (for example, exchange A[2] with A[3]), you can use a third integer variable.

```
Temp := A[2];
A[2] := A[3];
A[3] := Temp;
```

This exchange is frequently used in sorting algorithms, so let's examine it more closely. Assume Temp contains no previously assigned value, and A[2] and A[3] contain 4 and 9, respectively.

```
        ┌─────┐   ┌─────┐
        │     │   │  4  │  A[2]
        └─────┘   └─────┘
         Temp     ┌─────┐
                  │  9  │  A[3]
                  └─────┘
```

The assignment statement

```
Temp := A[2];
```

produces

```
        ┌─────┐   ┌─────┐
        │  4  │   │  4  │  A[2]
        └─────┘   └─────┘
         Temp     ┌─────┐
                  │  9  │  A[3]
                  └─────┘
```

The assignment statement

```
A[2] := A[3];
```

produces

```
        ┌─────┐   ┌─────┐
        │  4  │   │  9  │  A[2]
        └─────┘   └─────┘
         Temp     ┌─────┐
                  │  9  │  A[3]
                  └─────┘
```

and finally the assignment statement

```
A[3] := Temp;
```

produces

```
        ┌─────┐   ┌─────┐
        │  4  │   │  9  │  A[2]
        └─────┘   └─────┘
         Temp     ┌─────┐
                  │  4  │  A[3]
                  └─────┘
```

With the next example, we illustrate the use of a **TYPE** definition and a subsequent assignment statement.

EXAMPLE 9.6

```
TYPE
    Seasons = (Fall, Winter, Spring, Summer);
    TemperatureList = ARRAY [Seasons] OF real;
VAR
    AvTemp : TemperatureList;
```

An assignment statement such as

```
AvTemp[Fall] := 53.2;
```

is appropriate.

Arithmetic

Array variables can also be used in any appropriate arithmetic operation. For example, suppose A is an array of five integer components as declared earlier in the section. Values of the components are

A	
1	A[1]
4	A[2]
9	A[3]
16	A[4]
25	A[5]

and the values of the components of the array are to be added. This can be accomplished by the statement

```
Sum := A[1] + A[2] + A[3] + A[4] +A[5];
```

Each of the following is also a valid use of an array variable

```
B := 3 * A[2];
C := A[4] MOD 3;
D := A[2] * A[5];
```

For the array A given, these assignment statements produce

55	12	1	100
Sum	B	C	D

Some invalid assignment statements and the reasons they are invalid follow.

```
A[0] := 7;          (0 is not a valid subscript.)
A[2] := 3.5;        (Component A[2] is not of type real.)
A[2.0] := 3;        (A subscript of type real is not allowed.)
```

Reading and Writing

Since array components are names for variables, they can be used with **read, readln, write,** and **writeln.** For example, if Score is an array of five integers and you want to input the scores 65, 43, 98, 75, and 83 from a data line, you can use the code

```
readln (Score[1], Score[2], Score[3], Score[4], Score[5]);
```

This produces the array

Score

65	Score[1]
43	Score[2]
98	Score[3]
75	Score[4]
83	Score[5]

If you want to print the scores above 80, you can use the code

```
writeln (Score[3]:10, Score[5]:10);
```

to produce

```
    98          83
```

It is important to note that you cannot **read** or **write** values into or from an entire array by a reference to the array name (an exception will be explained later). Statements such as

```
read(Score),
writeln(Score)
```

are invalid.

Exercises 9.1

In Exercises 1–4, declare an array variable using descriptive names.

1. A list of 35 test scores
2. The prices of 20 automobiles
3. The answers to 50 true or false questions
4. A list of letter grades for the classes you are taking this semester
5. Write a test program in which you declare an array of three components, read values into each component, sum the components, and print out the sum and value of each component.

For Exercises 6–11, find all errors in the declaration of array variables.

```
6. VAR
       Time : ARRAY [1 . . 12] OF Hours;
7. VAR
       Scores : ARRAY [1 . . 30] OF integer;
8. VAR
       Alphabet : ARRAY OF char;
9. VAR
       List : ARRAY [1 TO 10] OF real;
10. VAR
       Answers: ARRAY [OF boolean];
11. VAR
       X : ARRAY [1 . . . 5] OF real;
```

For Exercises 12–23, assume the array List is declared as

```
CONST
  Max = 100;
TYPE
  Scores = ARRAY [1 , , Max] OF integer;
VAR
  List : Scores;
```

and that all other variables are appropriately declared. Label each as valid or invalid. Include an explanation for any that are invalid.

12. `read (List[3]);`
13. `A := List[3] + List[4];`
14. `writeln (List);`
15. `List[10] := 3.2;`
16. `Max := List[50];`
17. `Average := (List[1] + List[8])/2;`
18. `write (List[25, 50, 75, 100]);`
19. `write ((List[10] + List[90]):25);`
20. `read (List);`
21. `List[36] := List[102];`
22. `Scores[47] := 92;`
23. `List[40] := List[41]/2;`

In Exercises 24–26, change each so that the **TYPE** definition section is used to define the array type.

24.
```
VAR
  LetterList : ARRAY [1 , , 100] OF 'A' , , 'Z';
```
25.
```
VAR
  CompanyName : ARRAY [1 , , 30] OF char;
```
26.
```
VAR
  ScoreList : ARRAY [30 , , 59] OF real;
```

27. Consider the array declared by

```
VAR
  WaistSize : ARRAY [1 , , 5] OF integer;
```

a. Sketch how the array can be envisioned in memory.
b. After assignments

```
WaistSize[1] := 34;
WaistSize[3] := 36;
WaistSize[5] := 32;
WaistSize[2] := 2 * 15;
WaistSize[4] := (WaistSize[1] + WaistSize[3]) DIV 2;
```

are made, sketch the array and indicate the contents of each component.

For Exercises 28–30, let the array Money be declared by

```
TYPE
  List3 = ARRAY [1 , , 3] OF real;
VAR
  Money : List3;
```

Let Temp, X, and Y be real variables and assume Money has the indicated values

Money

19.26	Money[1]
10.04	Money[2]
17.32	Money[3]

Indicate what the array contains after each section of code.

28. ```
Temp := 173.21;
X := Temp + Money[2];
Money[1] := X;
```
29. ```
IF Money[2] < Money[1] THEN
    BEGIN
        Temp := Money[2];
        Money[2] := Money[1];
        Money[1] := Temp
    END;
```
30. ```
Money[3] := 20 - Money[3];
```
31. Let the array List be declared by

```
CONST
  Max = 5;
TYPE
  Scores = ARRAY [1 . . Max] OF real;
VAR
  List : Scores;
```

Write a program segment to initialize all components of List to 0.0.

■ **9.2**
Using Arrays

Loops for Input and Output

One advantage of using arrays is the small amount of code needed when loops are used to manipulate array components. For example, suppose a list of 100 scores stored in a text file named Data is to be used in a program. If an array is declared by

```
TYPE
  List100 = ARRAY [1 . . 100] OF integer;
VAR
  Score : List100;
  Data : text;
```

the data file can be read into the array using a **FOR** loop as follows:

```
reset (Data);
FOR J := 1 TO 100 DO
  read (Data, Score[J]);
```

Remember, a statement such as **read** (Data, Score) is invalid. You may only read data into individual components of the array.

Loops can be similarly used to produce output of array components. For example, if the array of test scores just given is to be printed in a column,

```
FOR J := 1 TO 100 DO
  writeln (Score[J]);
```
```

accomplishes this. If the components of Score contain the values

Score

78	Score[1]
93	Score[2]
.	.
.	.
.	.
82	Score[100]

the loop for writing produces

```
78
93
.
.
.
82
```

Note that you cannot cause the array components to be printed by a statement such as **write** (Score) or **writeln** (Score). These are invalid. You must refer to the individual components.

Loops for output are seldom this simple. Usually we are required to format the output in some manner. For example, suppose the array Score is as declared and we wish to print these scores ten to a line, each with a field width of five spaces. The following segment of code accomplishes this.

```
FOR J := 1 TO 100 DO
   BEGIN
      write (Score[J]:5);
      IF J MOD 10 = 0 THEN
         writeln
   END;
```

Loops for Assigning

Loops can also be used to assign values to array components. In certain instances, you might wish to have an array contain values that are not read from an input file. The following examples show how loops can be used to solve such instances.

EXAMPLE 9.7

Recall the array A in Section 9.1 in which we made the following assignments.

```
A[1] := 1;
A[2] := 4;
A[3] := 9;
A[4] := 16;
A[5] := 25;
```

These assignments can be made with the loop

```
FOR J := 1 TO 5 DO
   A[J] := J * J;
```

EXAMPLE 9.8

Suppose an array is needed whose components contain the letters of the alphabet in order from A to Z. The desired array can be declared by

```
TYPE
   Letters = ARRAY [1 . . 26] OF char;
VAR
   Alphabet : Letters;
```

The array Alphabet can then be assigned the desired characters by the statement

```
FOR J := 1 TO 26 DO
   Alphabet[J] := chr(J-1 + ord('A'));
```

If

```
J := 1;
```

we have

```
Alphabet[1] := chr(ord('A'));
```

Thus,

```
Alphabet[1] := 'A';
```

Similarly,

```
FOR J := 2;
```

we have

```
Alphabet[2] := chr(1 + ord('A'));
```

Eventually we obtain

Alphabet

'A'	Alphabet[1]
'B'	Alphabet[2]
'C'	Alphabet[3]
.	.
.	.
.	.
'Z'	Alphabet[26]

■

Assignment of values from components of one array to corresponding components of another array is a frequently encountered problem. For example, suppose the arrays A and B are declared as

```
TYPE
   List50 = ARRAY [1 . . 50] OF real;
VAR
   A, B : List50;
```

If B has been assigned values and you want to put the contents of B into A component by component, you can use the loop

```
FOR J := 1 TO 50 DO
   A[J] := B[J];
```

However, for problems of this type, Pascal allows the entire array to be assigned by

```
A := B;
```

This aggregate assignment actually causes 50 assignments to be made at the component level. The arrays must be of the same type to do this. If the arrays are not of the same type, then an appropriate loop for assigning is needed.

Processing with Loops

The array structure makes using loops especially suitable for reading, writing, and assigning array components. Loops can also be used in conjunction with arrays to process data. For example, suppose A and B are declared as

```
TYPE
   List100 = ARRAY [1 . . 100] OF real;
VAR
   A, B : List100;
```

and you want to add the values of components of B to the respective values of components of A. You can use the loop

```
FOR J := 1 TO 100 DO
   A[J] := A[J] + B[J];
```

It appears that since

```
A := B;
```

is valid,

```
A := A + B;
```

would accomplish this. Not true. Pascal does not allow the aggregate addition of A + B.

The following examples illustrate additional uses of loops for processing data contained in array variables.

EXAMPLE 9.9

Recall the problem earlier in this section in which we read 100 test scores into an array. Assume the scores are read and you now wish to find the average score and the largest score. Assume variables Sum, Max, and Average are appropriately declared. The following segment computes the average.

```
Sum := 0;
FOR J := 1 TO 100 DO
   Sum := Sum + Score[J];
Average := Sum/100;
```

The maximum score can be found by using the following segment of code.

```
Max := Score[1];
FOR J := 2 TO 100 DO
   IF Score[J] > Max THEN
      Max := Score[J];
```
Of course, these two tasks can be accomplished in the same loop. ∎

EXAMPLE 9.10

Let's write a segment of code to find the smallest value of array A and the index of the smallest value. Assume the variables are declared as

```
TYPE
   Column100 = ARRAY [1 . . 100] OF real;
VAR
   A : Column100;
   Min : real;
   Index : integer;
```

and the values are read into components of A. The following pseudocode solves the problem.

1. Assign the initial value of A to Min;
2. Assign 1 to Index;
3. **FOR** J := 2 **TO** 100 **DO**
   IF A[J] < Min **THEN**
       assign A[J] to Min and J to Index.

The segment of code is

```
Min := A[1];
Index := 1;
FOR J := 2 TO 100 DO
  IF A[J] < Min THEN
    BEGIN
      Min := A[J];
      Index := J
    END;
```

SELF QUIZ 9.2

Let List be an array consisting of 20 real numbers. Write a segment of code to count the number of times zero is in the list.

EXAMPLE 9.11

Suppose arrays A, B, and C are declared as

```
TYPE
   List100 = ARRAY [1 . . 100] OF real;
   List50 = ARRAY [1 . . 50] OF real;
VAR
   A : List100;
   B, C : List50;
```

and we want to assign B to the top half of A, and C to the bottom half. The loop

```
FOR J := 1 TO 50 DO
  A[J] := B[J];
```

accomplishes the first part of the task. To assign C to the bottom half of A we can use these 50 assignment statements:

```
A[51] := C[1];
A[52] := C[2];
     .          .
     .          .
     .          .
A[100] := C[50];
```

However, by examining the indices, we see this can be done more efficiently by

```
FOR J := 1 TO 50 DO
   A[50+J] := C[J];
```

These two assignment loops can be visualized as

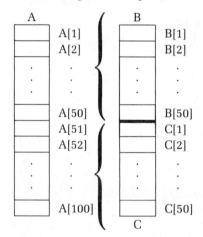

The next example illustrates a very standard problem encountered when working with arrays: What do you do when you don't know exactly how many components of an array are needed?

EXAMPLE 9.12   Suppose you wish to enter an unknown number of dollar amounts from personal checks. Write a segment of code to read them into an array and output the number of checks. Since the data are in dollars, we use real components and the identifier Check.

```
TYPE
   List = ARRAY [1 . . ?] OF real;
VAR
   Check : List;
```

At this stage, we must decide some upper limit for the length of the array (that is, the number of checks). A standard procedure is to declare a reasonable limit keeping two points in mind.

1. The length must be sufficient to store all the data.
2. The amount of storage space must not be excessive; do not set aside excessive amounts of space that will not be used.

If we know there are fewer than 50 checks, we can define a constant by

```
CONST
   MaxChecks = 50;
```

and then define List by

```
List = ARRAY [1 . . MaxChecks] OF real;
```

The data can then be accessed using a **WHILE** . . . **DO** loop.

```
J := 1;
writeln ('Enter amount of check,  -999 to quit.');
readln (Check[1]);
```

```
WHILE (Check[J] <> -999) AND J < MaxChecks) DO
   BEGIN
      J := J + 1;
      writeln ('Enter amount of check, -999 to quit.');
      readln (Check[J]
   END;  (*  of WHILE . . . DO  *)
IF J = MaxChecks THEN
   BEGIN
      writeln ('You have entered ', MaxChecks, ' checks.');
      writeln ('Redefine MaxChecks for more data.')
   END;  (*  of IF . . . THEN  *)
```

We have used two **readln** (Check[ ]) statements, one above the loop and the other in the loop. The first one is used to initialize Check[1] before the **WHILE ... DO** statement. This statement is only executed once. All remaining input is done through the second **readln** statement.

The value of the index at the end of the loop is the number of checks in the list, so we can preserve it for later use by adding the line

```
NumberOfChecks := J-1;
```

to the code. Now we have the data in the array, we know the number of data items, and NumberOfChecks can be used as a loop limit. The loop

```
FOR J := 1 TO NumberOfChecks DO
   BEGIN
      writeln;
      writeln('Check number':20,J:4,'$':5,Checks[J]:7:2)
   END;
```

prints the checks on every other line.   ■

We close this section with a final example using more elaborate **TYPE** definitions, loops, and arrays. Input is read from the permanent file, GNPFile.

EXAMPLE 9.13

```
PROGRAM Economy (input,output,GNPFile);

(*******************************************************************

    This program illustrates the use of TYPE definitions
    loops, and arrays, Values are read into an array
    and the maximum is found, Then the array
    contents and maximum are printed,

*******************************************************************)
TYPE
   RecentYears = 1970 . . 1986;
   EconIndicator = ARRAY [RecentYears] OF real;
VAR
GrossNatlProd : EconIndicator;    (*  Array of Gross National Product   *)
Max : real;                       (*  Maximum value from the array      *)
Year : RecentYears;               (*  Variable for year from 1970 . . 1986  *)
GNPFile : text;                   (*  External data file                *)
```

```
BEGIN  (*   Main program   *)
(*   Get data   *)

  reset (GNPFile);
  FOR Year := 1970 TO 1986 DO
    read(GNPFile,GrossNatlProd[Year]);

(*   Find maximum   *)

  Max := GrossNatlProd[1970];          (*   Get initial value   *)
  FOR Year := 1971 TO 1986 DO
    IF GrossNatlProd[Year] > Max THEN (*   Check for larger value   *)
      Max := GrossNatlProd[Year];

(*   Now print all data   *)

  writeln('Year':20,'Gross National Product':30);
  writeln('____':20,'_____':30);
  writeln;
  FOR Year := 1970 TO 1986 DO
    writeln(Year:20, GrossNatlProd[Year]:25:2);

(*   Now print the maximum   *)

  writeln;
  writeln('The greatest GNP in recent years was':40,Max:20:2);
  writeln; writeln

END.   (*   of main program   *)
```

The output for this program is

Year	Gross National Product
1970	670000000000.00
1971	675000000000.00
1972	680000000000.00
1973	690000000000.00
1974	700000000000.00
1975	706000000000.00
1976	710000000000.00
1977	720000000000.00
1978	724000000000.00
1979	734400000000.00
1980	756000000000.00
1981	810000000000.00
1982	876700000000.00
1983	887000000000.00
1984	912000000000.00
1985	980000000000.00
1986	123000000000.00

```
The greatest GNP in recent years was    123000000000.00
```

STYLE TIP

Indices with semantic meaning can be useful when working with arrays. For example, suppose you are writing a program that includes the inventory for shoe styles in a shoe store. If the styles are loafer, wing tip, docksider, high pump, low pump, and plain tie, you would define

```
TYPE
   Style = (Loafer, WingTip, Docksider, HighPump,
            LowPump, PlainTie);
   ShoeInventory = ARRAY [Loafer . . PlainTie] OF
                                             integer;
VAR
   Stock : ShoeInventory;
   ShoeType : Style;
```

A typical program statement is

```
Stock[WingTip] := 25;
Stock[Loafer] := Stock[Loafer] - 3;
FOR ShoeType := Loafer . . PlainTie DO
   writeln (Stock[ShoeType]);
```

Exercises 9.2

For Exercises 1–4, assume the following array declarations.

```
VAR
   List, Score : ARRAY [1 . . 5] OF integer;
   Answer : ARRAY [1 . . 10] OF boolean;
   Name: ARRAY [1 . . 20] OF char;
```

Indicate the contents of the array after each segment of code.

```
1. FOR J := 1 TO 5 DO
      List[J] := J DIV 3;
2. FOR J := 2 TO 6 DO
      BEGIN
         List[J-1] := J + 3;
         Score[J-1] := List[J-1] DIV 3
      END;
3. FOR J := 1 TO 10 DO
      Answer[J] := (J MOD 2 = 0);
4. FOR J := 1 TO 20 DO
      Name[J] := chr(J + 6);
```

5. Write a test program to illustrate what happens when you try to use an index that is not in the defined subrange for an array; for example, try to use the loop

```
FOR J := 1 TO 10 DO
   read (A[J]);
```

when A has been declared as

```
VAR
   A : ARRAY[1 . . 5] OF integer;
```

6. Let the array Best be declared by

```
TYPE
   List30 = ARRAY [1 . . 30] OF integer;
VAR
   Best : List30;
```

and assume that test scores are read into Best. What does the following section of code do?

```
Count := 0;
FOR J := 1 TO 30 DO
   IF Best[J] > 90 THEN
      Count := Count + 1;
```

7. Declare an array and write a segment of code to
   a. Read 20 integer test scores into the array.
   b. Count the number of scores greater than or equal to 55.

8. Declare an array using the **TYPE** definition section and write a section of code to read a name of 20 characters from a line of input.

9. Let the array List be declared by

```
CONST
   Max = 17;
TYPE
   Numbers = ARRAY [11 . . Max] OF integer;
VAR
   List : Numbers;
```

and assume the components have values of

List

− 2	List[11]
3	List[12]
0	List[13]
− 8	List[14]
20	List[15]
14	List[16]
− 121	List[17]

Show what the array components are after the following program segment is executed.

```
FOR J := 11 TO Max DO
   IF List[J] < 0 THEN
      List[J] := 0;
```

10. Assume the array A is declared as

```
CONST
   Max = 100;
TYPE
   List = ARRAY [1 . . Max] OF real;
VAR
   A : List;
```

Write a segment of code that uses a loop to initialize all components to zero.

For Exercises 11–13, let the array N be declared as

```
TYPE
   String10 = ARRAY [1 , , 10] OF char;
VAR
   N : String10;
```

and assume the array components are assigned the values

J	O	H	N		S	M	I	T	H
N[1]	N[2]	N[3]	N[4]	N[5]	N[6]	N[7]	N[8]	N[9]	N[10]

What output is produced by the following?

11.
```
FOR J := 1 TO 10 DO
   write (N[J]);
writeln;
```
12.
```
FOR J := 1 TO 5 DO
   write (N[J+5]);
write (', ');
FOR J := 1 TO 4 DO
   write (N[J]);
writeln;
```
13.
```
FOR J := 10 DOWNTO 1 DO
   writeln (N[J]);
```

For Exercises 14–18, let arrays A, B, and C be declared as

```
TYPE
   FirstList = ARRAY [21 , , 40] OF real;
   SecondList = ARRAY [-4 , , 15] OF real;
VAR
   A, B : FirstList;
   C : SecondList;
```

Indicate if the exercise is valid or invalid. Include an explanation for those that are invalid.

14.
```
FOR J := 21 TO 40 DO
   A[J] := C[J-25];
```
15.
```
A := B;
```
16.
```
A := C;
```
17.
```
FOR J := 1 TO 10 DO
   B[J+20] := C[J-5];
```
18.
```
FOR J := 11 TO 20 DO
   B[J+20] := A[J+20];
```

19. Assume an array has been declared as

```
TYPE
   List50 = ARRAY [1 , , 50] OF integer;
VAR
   TestScore : List50;
```

Write a segment of code to print a suitable heading (assume this is a list of test scores) and then output a numbered list of the array components.

20. Write a program segment to read 100 real numbers from a data file, compute the average, and find both the largest and smallest values.

■ 9.3
Selection Sort and Bubble Sort

A common problem involving arrays is sorting the components of the array in either ascending or descending order. Let's now consider one of the easier methods, the *selection sort*.

OBJECTIVE

■ to sort arrays using the selection sort
■ to sort arrays using the bubble sort

Selection Sort

Suppose we have an array A of five integers that we wish to sort from smallest to largest. The values currently in A are as depicted on the left; we wish to sort A to produce the values on the right.

A			A	
6	A[1]		1	A[1]
4	A[2]		4	A[2]
8	A[3]		6	A[3]
10	A[4]		8	A[4]
1	A[5]		10	A[5]

The basic idea of a selection sort is

1. Find the smallest number in the array and exchange it with A[1].
2. Find the smallest number among A[2] through A[5] and exchange it with A[2].
3. Continue this process until the array is sorted.

The first step produces

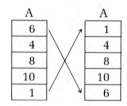

The second step produces

A		A
1		1
4	→	4
8		8
10		10
6		6

Notice that since the second smallest number is already in place, we do not exchange anything. The third step produces

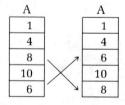

The fourth and final step yields the sorted list.

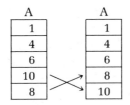

Before writing the pseudocode for this sorting procedure, note the following:

1. If the array is of length n, we need $n - 1$ steps.
2. We must be able to find the smallest number.
3. We need to exchange appropriate array components.

If two or more values in the list are equal, an exchange is not made when finding the smallest number. Thus, rather than find the smallest numbers, we must be able to find one of the remaining smallest numbers.

When the code is written for this sort, note that strict inequality ($<$) rather than weak inequality ($<=$) is used when looking for the smallest remaining value. This is because there is no need to exchange equal values. The pseudocode to sort by selection is:

1. **FOR** J := 1 **TO** N − 1 **DO**
    1.1   find the smallest value among A[J], A[J + 1], . . . A[N];
    1.2   store the smallest value in Temp and the index of the smallest value in Index;
    1.3   exchange the values of A[J] and A[Index].

In Section 9.2 (Example 9.10) we saw a segment of code required to find the smallest value of array A. With suitable changes, we incorporate this in the segment of code for a selection sort.

```
Temp := A[1];
Index := 1;
FOR J := 2 TO ArrayLength DO
  IF A[J] < Temp THEN
     BEGIN
        Temp := A[J];
        Index := J
     END;
```

Let A be an array of length n and assume all variables are appropriately declared. The following selection sort sorts A from low to high.

```
FOR J := 1 TO N−1 DO       (*   Number of passes   *)
  BEGIN
     Temp := A[J];
     Index := J;
     FOR K := J+1 TO N DO
       IF A[K] < Temp THEN
          BEGIN                 (*   Find smallest number   *)
             Temp := A[K];
             Index := K
          END;
       A[Index] := A[J]; (*   Exchange smallest number   *)
       A[J] := Temp
  END; (*   of one pass   *)
```

Let's now trace this sort for the five integers in the array we sorted in the beginning of this section.

A

6	A[1]
4	A[2]
8	A[3]
10	A[4]
1	A[5]

FOR J := 1, Temp := A[1], and Index := 1 produce

6		1
Temp		Index

For the loop **FOR** K := 2 **TO** 5, we get successive assignments

K	Temp	Index
2	4	2
3	4	2
4	4	2
5	1	5

The statements A[Index] := A[J] and A[J] := Temp produce the partially sorted array

A

1	A[1]
4	A[2]
8	A[3]
10	A[4]
6	A[5]

Each successive value of J continues to partially sort the array until J := 4. This pass produces a completely sorted array.

EXAMPLE 9.14

Our concluding example inputs 20 real numbers from an input file; echo prints the numbers in a column of width six with two places to the right of the decimal (:6:2); sorts the array from low to high; and prints the sorted array using the same output format.

An expanded pseudocode development for this is

1. Print header—prints a suitable explanation of the program and includes a heading for the unsorted list.
2. Get data (echo print)—uses a **FOR** loop to read the data and print it in the same order in which it is read.
3. Sort list—uses the selection sort to sort the array from low to high.
4. Output sorted list—uses a **FOR** loop to output the sorted list.

```
PROGRAM ArraySample (input,output,DataFile);

(***************************************************************

     This program illustrates the use of a selection
     sort with an array of reals. Output
     includes data in both an unsorted and a sorted list.
     The data is formatted and numbered to enhance
     readability.

 ***************************************************************)
CONST
  Skip = ' ';
  ListMax = 20;
TYPE
  NumList = ARRAY[1 . . ListMax] OF real;
```

```
VAR
   Index : integer;        (*   Stores position of an element        *)
   J,K : integer;          (*   Indices                              *)
   Temp : real;            (*   Temporary storage for array element  *)
   List : NumList;         (*   Array of reals                       *)
   DataFile : text;        (*   Data for program                     *)

(*     This procedure prints a heading.       *)

PROCEDURE PrintHeading;
  BEGIN
    writeln; writeln;
    writeln(Skip:10, 'This sample program does the following:');
    writeln;
    writeln(Skip:12, '<1> Get ListMax reals from a data file');
    writeln(Skip:12, '<2> Echo print the data');
    writeln(Skip:12, '<3> Sort the data from low to high');
    writeln(Skip:12, '<4> Print a sorted list of the data');
    writeln; writeln    (*   Skip two lines    *)
  END;      (*    of PROCEDURE PrintHeading    *)

BEGIN      (*    Main program    *)

(*    Print the heading    *)

  PrintHeading;

(*    Now get data and echo print    *)

  writeln(Skip:10, 'The original data are as follows:');
  writeln;
  J := 0;
  reset(DataFile);
  WHILE NOT eof (DataFile) AND (J < ListMax) DO
    BEGIN
      J := J + 1;
      readln(DataFile, List[J]);
      writeln(Skip:12, '<', J:2, '>', List[J]:6:2)
    END;      (*  of WHILE NOT eof  *)
  IF NOT eof THEN
    writeln('Too much data');

(*    Now sort the list    *)

  For J := 1 TO ListMax-1 DO
    BEGIN
      Temp := List[J];
      Index := J;
      FOR K := J+1 TO ListMax DO
        IF List[K] < Temp THEN
```

```
        BEGIN
          Temp := List[K];
          Index := K
        END;
   List[Index] := List[J];
   List[J] := Temp
  END;   (*  of selection sort   *)

(*   Now print the sorted list   *)

  writeln; writeln;
  writeln(Skip:10, 'The sorted list is as follows:');
  writeln;
  FOR J := 1 TO ListMax DO
    writeln(Skip:12, '<',J:2, '>', List[J]:6:2)

END.   (*   of main program   *)
```

The output for this program is

```
This sample program does the following:

    <1> Get ListMax reals from a data file
    <2> Echo print the data
    <3> Sort the data from low to high
    <4> Print a sorted list of the data

The original data are as follows:

    < 1> 34.56
    < 2> 78.21
    < 3> 23.30
    < 4> 89.90
    < 5> 45.00
    < 6> 56.80
    < 7> 39.01
    < 8> 45.56
    < 9> 34.40
    <10> 45.10
    <11> 98.20
    <12>  5.60
    <13>  8.00
    <14> 45.00
    <15> 99.00
    <16> 56.78
    <17> 56.78
    <18> 45.00
    <19> 89.80
    <20> 95.60
```

```
The  sorted  list  is  as  follows:

    < 1>   5.60
    < 2>   8.00
    < 3>  23.30
    < 4>  34.40
    < 5>  34.56
    < 6>  39.01
    < 7>  45.00
    < 8>  45.00
    < 9>  45.00
    <10>  45.10
    <11>  45.56
    <12>  56.78
    <13>  56.78
    <14>  56.80
    <15>  78.21
    <16>  89.80
    <17>  89.90
    <18>  95.60
    <19>  98.20
    <20>  99.00
```

Bubble Sort

The sorting algorithm commonly referred to as a *bubble sort* rearranges the elements of an array until they are in either ascending or descending order. Like the selection sort, an extra array is not used. Basically, a bubble sort starts at the top of an array and compares two consecutive elements of the array. If they are in the correct order, the next pair of elements are compared. If they are not in the correct order, they are switched and the next pair compared. When this has been done for the entire array, the largest (or smallest) element will be in the last position.

Starting at the top each time, successive passes through the array are made until the array is sorted. Two points should be noted here.

1. For efficiency, a flag is needed to indicate whether or not an exchange was made during the pass through the array. If none was made, the array is sorted.
2. Since each pass filters the largest (or smallest) element to the bottom, the length of what remains to be sorted can be decreased by one after each pass.

To illustrate how this algorithm works, assume the array is

A

12
0
3
2
8

The first pass through the array produces

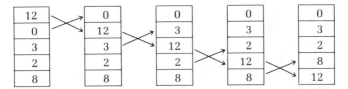

Since an exchange was made, we need to make at least one more pass through the array. However, the length is decreased by one because there is no need to compare the last two elements.

A second pass produces

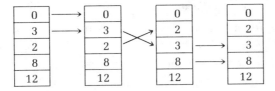

At this stage, the array is sorted, but since an exchange is made, the length is decreased by one and another pass is made. Since no exchange is made during this third pass, the sorting process is terminated.

Assuming the variable declaration section includes

```
VAR
   ExchangeMade : boolean;
   J, Length, Temp : integer;
```

values to be sorted are in the array A, and Length has been assigned a value, the algorithm for a bubble sort can be in the following form.

```
ExchangeMade := true;
Length := Length − 1;
WHILE ExhangeMade DO
  BEGIN
    ExchangeMade := false;
    FOR J := 1 TO Length DO
      IF A[J] > A[J + 1] THEN
        BEGIN (*   Exchange values   *)
          Temp := A[J];
          A[J] := A[J + 1];
          A[J + 1] := Temp;
          ExchangeMade := true
        END;
    Length := Length − 1 (*   Decrement length   *)
  END (*   of one pass   *)
```

Exercises 9.3

1. Assume the array Column is to be sorted from low to high using the selection sort.

   Column

− 20
10
0
10
8
30
− 2

   a. Sketch the contents of the array after each of the first two passes.
   b. How many exchanges are made during the sort?

2. Write a test program that prints the partially sorted arrays after each pass during a selection sort.

3. Change the code for the selection sort so it sorts an array from high to low.

4. Write a complete program to
   a. Read ten reals into an array from an input file.
   b. Sort the array from high to low if the first real is positive; if it is negative, sort the array from low to high.
   c. Print a numbered column containing the sorted reals with the format :10: 2.

5. The array

17
0
3
2
8

   requires five exchanges of elements when sorted using a bubble sort. Since each exchange requires three assignment statements, there are 15 assignments for elements in the array. Sort the same array using the selection sort and determine the number of assignments made.

6. Modify the selection sort by including a counter that counts the number of assignments of array elements made during a sort.

7. Using the modification in Exercise 3, sort list of differing lengths which contain randomly generated numbers. Display the results of how many assignments were made for each sort on a graph similar to that below. Use lists whose lengths are multiples of ten.

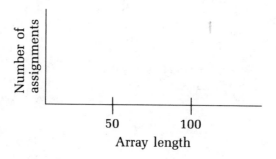

8. Modify the bubble sort to include a counter for the number of assignments made during a sort.

9. Use the modified versions of both sorts to examine their relative efficiency; that is, run them on arrays of varying lengths and plot the results on a graph. What are your conclusions?

10. Modify both sorts to sort from high to low rather than low to high.

11. Sorting parallel arrays is a common practice (for example, an array of names and a corresponding array of scores on a test). Modify both sorts so that you can sort a list of initials and associated test scores.

■ 9.4
Arrays and Subprograms

OBJECTIVE

■ to use arrays correctly with subprograms

Procedures and functions should be used with arrays to maintain the top-down design philosophy. Before we look at specific examples, let's examine the method and syntax necessary for passing an array to a procedure. Recall that to pass either a value or variable parameter to a procedure, we must declare a variable of exactly the same type as the parameter in the procedure heading and use **VAR** for a variable parameter. There must be a one-for-one ordered matching of the parameters with the variables in the heading of the procedure.

Let's consider a program to read two integer test scores, compute their average in a procedure called GetMean, and output the results.

EXAMPLE 9.15

```
PROGRAM AverageOfTwo (input, output);

VAR
   Num1, Num2 : integer;
   Ave : real;

PROCEDURE GetMean (X, Y : integer; VAR Mean : real);
   VAR
      Sum : integer;
   BEGIN
      Sum := X + Y;
      Mean := Sum/2.0
   END;   (*  of PROCEDURE GetMean  *)

BEGIN  (* Main program *)
   writeln ('Enter two numbers and press <RETURN>.');
   readln (Num1, Num2);
   GetMean (Num1, Num2, Ave);
   writeln ('The average of ', Num1:5, ' and ', Num2:5, ' is ',
            Ave:6:2)
END.   (*  of Main program  *)
```

The procedure call

```
   GetMean (Num1, Num2, Ave);
```

and the procedure heading

```
   PROCEDURE GetMean (X, Y : integer; VAR Mean : real);
```

have the desired matching of variables.   ■

Let's now modify the program so it determines the average of 100 test scores in the array Scores. The procedure call in the program is

```
GetMean (Scores, Ave);
```

and the procedure heading must match these variables. If Marks is the variable name to be used in the procedure heading, we have

```
PROCEDURE GetMean (Marks : ???; VAR Mean : real);
```

where Marks must have the same declaration as Scores. To accomplish this, Pascal requires that a **TYPE** definition be given for both variables, Scores and Marks. For example, if we have

```
CONST
  MaxLength = 100;
TYPE
  List = ARRAY [1 . . MaxLength] OF integer;
VAR
  Scores : List;
```

the procedure heading is

```
PROCEDURE GetMean (Marks : List; VAR Mean : real);
```

This is consistent with allowing only identifiers of identical types to be associated. A common mistake is to attempt to build a data type inside the procedure heading. This will not work. The statement

```
PROCEDURE GetMean (Marks : ARRAY [1 . . MaxLength] OF integer;
                   VAR Mean : real);
```

produces an error message because Pascal compilers check for name equivalence rather than structure equivalence. To illustrate, you can have two arrays

```
Position : ARRAY [1 . . 3] OF real;
Nutrition : ARRAY [1 . . 3] OF real;
```

where Position is used to represent coordinates of a point in space and Nutrition is used to represent the volume, weight, and caloric content of a serving of food. Although Position and Nutrition have the same structure, they have significantly different meanings. Thus, by insisting on name equivalence, the chances of inadvertent or meaningless uses of structured variables are decreased.

We can now write a revised version of the program in Example 9.15 to find the average and include a procedure that requires passing an array. Since many items are to be entered, we assume data for input are stored in a permanent file called ScoreFile.

EXAMPLE 9.16

```
PROGRAM Average (input, output, ScoreFile);

CONST
  MaxLength = 100;
TYPE
  List = ARRAY [1 . . MaxLength] OF integer;
```

```
VAR
  Scores : List;
  Ave : real;
  J,ListSize : integer;
  ScoreFile : text;

PROCEDURE GetMean (Marks : List; VAR Mean : real;
                   Length : integer);
  VAR
    J, Sum : integer;
  BEGIN
    Sum := 0;
    FOR J := 1 TO Length DO
      Sum := Sum + Marks[J];
    Mean := Sum/Length
  END; (*  of PROCEDURE GetMean  *)

BEGIN  (* Main Program *)
  ListSize := 0;
  reset (ScoreFile);
  WHILE NOT eof (ScoreFile) AND (ListSize < MaxLength) DO
    BEGIN
      ListSize := ListSize +1;
      readln (ScoreFile,Scores[ListSize])
    END;
  GetMean (Scores, Ave, ListSize);
  writeln ('The average of':20);
  writeln;
  FOR J := 1 TO ListSize DO
    writeln (Score[J]:12);
  writeln;
  writeln ('is':10, Ave:8:2)
END. (*  of main program  *)
```

Before we consider more procedures with arrays, we restate a rule: To pass an array to a procedure or function, the array must be declared with an identifier that uses a **TYPE** definition; the matching variable in the procedure must use the same **TYPE** definition.

SELF QUIZ 9.3   Write a procedure that allows you to enter 30 reals into an array from the keyboard.

Now that we know how to pass an array, let's rewrite our last example using a completely modular development. In this version, GetMean is a function instead of a procedure. The first-level pseudocode development is

1. Get the scores (**PROCEDURE** GetData)
2. Compute the average (**FUNCTION** GetMean)
3. Print a header (**PROCEDURE** PrintHeader)
4. Print the results (**PROCEDURE** PrintResults)

The procedure to get the scores requires a **VAR** declaration in the procedure heading for the array. If List has been defined as a data type, we have

```
PROCEDURE GetData (VAR Marks : List; VAR ListSize : integer);
  BEGIN
    ListSize := 0;
    reset (ScoreFile);
    WHILE NOT eof (ScoreFile) AND (ListSize < MaxLength) DO
      BEGIN
        ListSize := ListSize + 1;
        readln (ScoreFile, Mark[ListSize])
      END
END;
```

The average score can be computed by the function GetMean.

```
FUNCTION GetMean (X : List; ListSize : integer) : real;
  VAR
    J, Sum : integer;
  BEGIN
    Sum := 0;
    FOR J := 1 TO ListSize DO
      Sum := Sum + X[J];
    GetMean := Sum/ListSize
  END;
```

A procedure to print a heading would be written in a manner similar to that we have used previously. Suppose we want the output to be

```
Test Scores
____ _____

    Score 1
    Score 2
        .
        .
        .
    Score 100

The average score on the test was . . .
```

The procedure for the heading is

```
PROCEDURE PrintHeader;
  BEGIN
    writeln; writeln;
    writeln ('Test Scores':20);
    writeln ('____ _____ :20);
    writeln
  END;  (*  of PROCEDURE PrintHeader  *)
```

A procedure to print the results is

```
PROCEDURE PrintResults (X:List; Av:real; ListSize:integer);
  VAR
    J : integer;
```

```
BEGIN
  FOR J := 1 TO ListSize DO
    writeln (X[J]:25);
  writeln; writeln;
  writeln    ('The average score on this test was':43,
               Av:6:2, '.')
END;
```

This procedure can be called by

```
PrintResults (Scores, Ave, Length);
```

where Ave is found by

```
Ave := GetMean (Scores, Length);
```

We now use these procedures and a function to write a complete program.

EXAMPLE 9.17

```
PROGRAM TestScores (input, output, ScoreFile);

CONST
  MaxLength = 100;
TYPE
  List = ARRAY [1 . . MaxLength] OF integer;
VAR
  Scores : List;
  Ave : real;
  Length : integer;
  ScoreFile : text;

(*  Function to figure average score  *)

FUNCTION GetMean (X : List; ListSize : integer) : real;
  VAR
    J, Sum : integer;
  BEGIN
    Sum := 0;
    FOR J := 1 TO ListSize DO
      Sum := Sum + X[J];
    GetMean := Sum/ListSize
  END;  (*  of FUNCTION GetMean  *)

(*  Procedure to get data  *)

PROCEDURE GetData (VAR Marks:List; VAR ListSize:integer);
  BEGIN
    ListSize := 0;
    reset (ScoreFile);
```

```
      WHILE NOT eof (ScoreFile) AND (ListSize < MaxLength) DO
        BEGIN
          ListSize := ListSize + 1;
          readln (ScoreFile,Marks[ListSize])
        END
    END; (*  of PROCEDURE GetData  *)


(*  Procedure to print header  *)

PROCEDURE PrintHeader;
  BEGIN
    writeln; writeln;
    writeln ('Test Scores':20);
    writeln ('____ _____':20);
    writeln
  END; (*  of PROCEDURE PrintHeader  *)


(*  Procedure to print results  *)

PROCEDURE PrintResults (X:List; Av:real; ListSize:integer);
  VAR
    J : integer;
  BEGIN
    FOR J := 1 TO ListSize DO
      writeln (X[J]:25);
    writeln; writeln;
    writeln  ('The average score on this test was':43,
               Av:6:2,'.')
  END; (*  of PROCEDURE PrintResults  *)


(*  Now start main program  *)

BEGIN  (* Main program *)
  GetData (Scores, Length);
  Ave := GetMean (Scores, Length);
  PrintHeader;
  PrintResults (Scores, Ave, Length)
END. (*  of main program  *)
```

As previously mentioned, sorting arrays is a standard problem for programmers. Now that we can pass arrays to procedures and functions, let's consider a problem in which an unknown number of reals are to be read from an input file and a sorted list (high to low) is to be printed as output. A first-level pseudocode design is

1. Get data (**PROCEDURE** GetData)
2. Sort list (**PROCEDURE** Sort)
3. Print header (**PROCEDURE** PrintHeader)
4. Print sorted list (**PROCEDURE** PrintData)

Since the number of data items is unknown, we must declare an array that is of sufficient length to store all the data but that does not use an unreasonable amount of memory. The nature of the problem will provide sufficient information for this declaration. For now, assume we know there are at most 50 data items. Then the following declaration will be sufficient.

```
CONST
  MaxLength = 50;
TYPE
  NumList = ARRAY [1 .. MaxLength] OF real;
VAR
  List : NumList;
```

The procedure to sort the array uses a version of the selection sort from Section 9.3. Both the array and the number of data items need to be passed to the procedure. An appropriate procedure is

```
PROCEDURE Sort (VAR X : NumList; ListSize : integer);
  VAR
    J, K, Index : integer;
    Temp : real;
  BEGIN
    FOR J := 1 TO ListSize-1 DO
      BEGIN
        Temp := X[J];
        Index := J;
        FOR K := J+1 TO ListSize DO
          IF X[K] > Temp THEN
            BEGIN
              Temp := X[K];
              Index := K
            END;
        X[Index] := X[J];
        X[J] := Temp
      END   (*  of FOR loop  *)
  END; (*  of PROCEDURE Sort  *)
```

This procedure can be called by the statement

```
Sort (List, Length);
```

After suitable procedures are written for a header and printing the data, the main body of the program is

```
BEGIN  (* Main program *)
  GetData (List, Length);
  Sort (List, Length);
  PrintHeader;
  PrintData (List, Length)
END.  (* of main program *)
```

Exercises 9.4

For Exercises 1–10, assume the following declarations are made in a program.

```
TYPE
  Row = ARRAY [1 .. 10] OF integer;
  Column = ARRAY [1 .. 30] OF real;
  String20 = ARRAY [1 .. 20] OF char;
  Week = (Sun, Mon, Tues, Wed, Thur, Fri, Sat);
VAR
  List1, List2 : Row;
  Aray : Column;
  Name1, Name2 : String20;
  Day : Week;
  A, B : ARRAY [1 .. 10] OF integer;
```

Indicate which are valid **PROCEDURE** declarations and write an appropriate line of code to call each. Include an explanation for those that are invalid.

```
1. PROCEDURE NewList (X : Row; Y : Column);
2. PROCEDURE NewList (VAR X : Row: VAR Y : Column);
3. PROCEDURE NewList (X : ARRAY [1 .. 10] OF integer);
4. PROCEDURE NewList (VAR X, Y : Row);
5. PROCEDURE NewList (VAR Column : Column);
6. PROCEDURE WorkWeek (Days : ARRAY [Mon .. Fri] OF Week)
7. PROCEDURE Surname (X : Name);
8. PROCEDURE Surnames (X, Y : String20);
9. PROCEDURE GetData (X : Week; VAR Y : Name);
10. PROCEDURE Table (VAR X : Row; VAR Y : Row);
```

11. Write a test program that illustrates what happens when you define an array structure in a procedure heading. For example,

```
PROCEDURE Sort (List:ARRAY [1 .. 20] OF real);
```

For Exercises 12–15, when possible, use the **TYPE** and **VAR** declaration sections from Exercises 1–10 to write **PROCEDURE** declarations so that the statement in the main program is an appropriate call to a procedure. Explain any inappropriate calls.

```
12. OldList (List1, Aray);
13. ChangeList (List1, Name1, Day);
14. Scores (A, B);
15. Surname (String20);
```

For Exercises 16–19, write an appropriate **PROCEDURE** declaration and a line of code to call the procedure.

16. A procedure to **read** 20 test scores into an array and save them for later use.
17. A procedure to count the number of occurrences of the letter A in an array of 50 characters.
18. A procedure to take two arrays of 10 integers each and produce a sorted array of 20 integers for later use.
19. A procedure to **read** integer test scores from a data file, count the number of scores, count the number of scores greater than or equal to 90, and save this information for later use.

For Exercises 20–22, assume the following declarations are made.

```
TYPE
  Column10 : ARRAY [1 .. 10] OF integer;
VAR
  List1, List2 : Column10;
  K : integer;
```

Indicate the contents of the array after the call to the corresponding procedure.

```
20. PROCEDURE Sample (VAR A : Column10; B : Column10);
    VAR
      J : integer;
    BEGIN
      FOR J := 1 TO 10 DO
        BEGIN
          A[J] := J * J;
          B[J] := A[J] MOD 2
        END
    END; (* of PROCEDURE Sample *)
```

```
BEGIN  (*  Main program  *)
  .
  .
  .
  FOR K := 1 TO 10 DO
    BEGIN
      List1[K] := 0;
      List2[K] := 0
    END;
  Sample (List1, List2);
```

21. Replace the procedure call in Exercise 20 with

    ```
    Sample (List2, List1);
    ```

22. Replace the procedure call in Exercise 20 with consecutive calls.

    ```
    Sample (List1, List2);
    Sample (List2, List1);
    ```

For Exercises 23–25, declare appropriate variables, write the indicated procedures, and call the procedures from the main program.

23. **read** a line of text from an input file that contains 30 characters.
24. Count the number of blanks in the line of text.
25. Print the line of text in reverse order and print the number of blanks.

26. Write a procedure to examine an array of integers and then return the maximum value, minimum value, and number of negative values to the main program.

27. Write **PROCEDURE** SelectionSort for the selection sort of Section 9.3. Show how it would be called from the main program.

28. Write **PROCEDURE** BubbleSort for the bubble sort of Section 9.3. Show how it would be called from the main program.

29. Write **PROCEDURE** Exchange for the bubble sort that will exchange values of array components. Then rewrite the bubble sort using **PROCEDURE** Exchange.

■ 9.5
Packed Arrays

Basic Idea and Notation

Arrays are useful for handling large amounts of data. One of the disadvantages of using arrays, however, is that they require large amounts of memory. In particular, arrays of character data use much more memory than is necesary. To illustrate, let's take a closer look at an array declared by

```
VAR
  Examine : ARRAY [1 . . 5] OF char;
```

When this structured variable is declared, the following variables are reserved.

■ to use string vari-
  ables

Examine

Examine[1]
Examine[2]
Examine[3]
Examine[4]
Examine[5]

Each component of the array Examine is one *word* in memory and each word consists of several *bytes*. Let's consider the array Examine in which each word consists of ten bytes. The array would be pictured as

Examine

Examine[1]
Examine[2]
Examine[3]
Examine[4]
Examine[5]

We can assign the word "HELLO" to the array Examine by either

```
Examine[1] := 'H';
Examine[2] := 'E';
Examine[3] := 'L';
Examine[4] := 'L';
Examine[5] := 'O';
```

or

```
Examine := 'HELLO';
```

depending on which version of Pascal is being used. In either case, after the assignment, the array would look like

Examine

H									
E									
L									
L									
O									

Examine[1]
Examine[2]
Examine[3]
Examine[4]
Examine[5]

because a byte is the unit of storage necessary for storing a character variable.

As you can see, 50 bytes of storage have been reserved, but only 5 have been used. Pascal provides a more efficient way of defining arrays that does not use unnecessary amounts of storage space. Instead of declaring a variable as an array, we can declare a variable as a *packed array*. With this declaration, the computer then packs the data in consecutive bytes.

Packed arrays can be used with any data type **(char, real, integer, boolean,** and so on). However, it is not always wise to do so because it takes longer to access individual components of a packed array than it does to access individual components of an unpacked array. Storage space is saved, but time is lost.

Let's now consider the declaration

```
TYPE
   String5 = PACKED ARRAY [1 . . 5] OF char;
VAR
   Examine : String5;
```

and the assignment of the word "HELLO" as before. Using a packed array, we then have the following in memory.

Examine

H	E	L	L	O				

Notice that less than one word (5 bytes) is used to store what previously required five words (50 bytes). We can still access the individual components as before. For example,

```
writeln (Examine[2]);
```

produces

```
E
```

as a line of output.

Character Strings

Every programming language needs to be able to handle character data. Names, words, phrases, and sentences are frequently used as part of some information that must be analyzed. In standard Pascal, character strings are formed by declaring packed arrays of character variables. For example, if the first 20 spaces of an input line are reserved for a customer's name, an appropriate character string can be declared by

```
TYPE
   String20 = PACKED ARRAY [1 . . 20] OF char;
VAR
   Name : String20;
```

If the line of input is

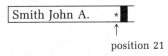

position 21

we can read the name into the packed array by the code

```
FOR J := 1 TO 20 DO
   read (DataFile, Name[J]);
```

Now when we refer to the array Name, we can envision the string

```
'Smith John A.'
```

But since we declared a fixed length string, the actual string is

```
'Smith John A.
```

There are at least three important uses for string variables.

1. String variables of the same length can be compared (**boolean** values); this permits alphabetizing.
2. String variables can be written using a single **write** or **writeln** statement; they cannot be read using a single **read** statement.
3. A single assignment statement can assign text to a string variable.

Let's examine these uses individually.

Comparing String Variables. Strings of the same length can be compared using the standard relational operators: $=$, $<$, $>$, $<>$, $<=$, and $>=$. For example, if 'Smith' and 'Jones' are strings, then 'Smith' $<$ 'Jones', 'Smith' $<>$ 'Jones', and so on are all valid **boolean** expressions. The **boolean** value is determined by the collating sequence. Using the collating sequence for the ASCII character set, the following comparisons yield the indicated values.

Comparison	boolean Value
'Smith' $<$ 'Jones'	false
'Jake' $<$ 'John'	true
'ABC' $=$ 'ABA'	false
'Smith Doug' $<$ 'Smith John'	true

What would happen if 'William Joe' were compared ($<$) to 'Williams Bo'? Since a character-by-character comparison is implemented by the computer, no decision is made until the blank following m is compared to s. Using the full ASCII character code or EBCDIC, this is **true;** but using some other character sets, this may be **false.** Thus, there is a need for caution when trying to alphabetize a list of names.

Writing String Variables. Recall the declaration

```
TYPE
   String20 = PACKED ARRAY [1 . . 20] OF char;
VAR
   Name : String20;
```

When data are read from an input file, a loop is used to get the data one character at a time.

```
FOR J := 1 TO 20 DO
   read (DataFile, Name[J]);
```

If we now wish to write the string Name, we can use a similar loop and write it one character at a time.

```
FOR J := 1 TO 20 DO
   write (Name[J]);
```

However, Pascal provides a more convenient method for writing strings. The write loop can be replaced by

```
write (Name);
```

Assigning Text to a String. The third feature of string variables is that a single assignment statement can be used to assign text to a string. If Name is a string of length 20, then

```
Name := 'Smith John A.          ';
```

is a valid statement. Note that there must be exactly 20 characters in the text string in order for this assignment to be valid. The statements

```
Name := 'Smith John A.';
Name := 'Theodore Allen Washington';
```

are both invalid because the text strings are not exactly 20 characters long.

SELF QUIZ 9.4 Write a fragment of code to read two strings of ten characters each where each string is on a separate line in an input file called NameFile.

There are some standard problems that are encountered when trying to read data into a packed array. First, assume we have to read a line of data that consists of a company name. Furthermore, assume we do not know the length of the name. The input line can be

```
Prudent Investors Company
```

or

```
Com Mfg. Co.
```

If we know the company name is no more than 30 characters, we can declare a fixed length array in the following manner.

```
TYPE
   String30 = PACKED ARRAY [1 . . 30] OF char;
VAR
   CompanyName : String30;
```

and then read the name with the segment of code

```
FOR J := 1 TO 30 DO
   IF NOT eoln (CompanyFile) THEN
      read (CompanyFile,CompanyName[J])
   ELSE
      CompanyName[J] := ' ';
readln; (* Advance the pointer *)
```

This reads the name as desired and then fills the array with blanks to the desired length. Applied to the two data lines just mentioned, this segment of code produces the following character strings.

```
'Prudent Investors Company     '
'Com Mfg. Co.                  '
```

Second, we may want to read data from an input file in which a field of fixed length is used for some character data. For example, suppose the first 30 columns of an input line are reserved for the company name and then some other information is on the same line. We can have

Prudent Investors Company   1905 South Drive

↑

column 31

A NOTE OF INTEREST

Computer Music

Computer music, like computer graphics, is a field whose maturity those alive today may not live long enough to see. Computer-synthesized instruments may well be the norm of the twenty-first century, just as electrically amplified instruments are the norm of the twentieth.

Computers can be involved in music either as *performance instruments* or as *compositional tools*. The second type of system uses a computer as a kind of musical word processor that gives composers the convenience of writing, playing back, and printing their scores by computer, even if the result is intended to be per-

formed on traditional acoustic instruments, not synthesizers. Writers who work on word processors—but don't care to see their work published on dot-matrix printers—are in a similar situation.

Chips can, however, create sounds. Microcomputers tend to sound like reedy organs when they play music—which is a reason some composers dislike them. Progress in chip technology promises to change this situation only slowly: musical sound is complicated and not entirely understood.

This data can be accessed by the loop

```
FOR J := 1 TO 30 DO
   read (CompanyFile,CompanyName[J]);
```

Although the second format for an input file is easier to use, it is sometimes difficult to obtain data in such a precise format. Hence, we must be able to read data both ways.

We are now ready to write a short program using packed arrays. Suppose the problem is to get two names from a data file, arrange them alphabetically, and then print the alphabetized list. A first-level pseudocode development is

1. Get the data (**PROCEDURE** GetData)
2. Arrange alphabetically (**PROCEDURE** Alphabetize)
3. Print the data (**PROCEDURE** PrintData)

A procedure to get one name is

```
PROCEDURE GetData (VAR Name : String25);
   VAR
      J, StringLength : integer;
   BEGIN
      StringLength := 0;
      writeln ('Enter a name.  Press <RETURN> when done.');
      WHILE NOT eoln DO
        BEGIN
          StringLength := StringLength + 1;
          read (Name[StringLength])
        END;  (*  of WHILE NOT eoln DO  *)
      readln;
      FOR J := (StringLength+1) TO 25 DO
        Name[J] := ' '  (*  blank fill rest of name  *)
   END;  (*  of PROCEDURE GetData  *)
```

Computer "Scores" for Composers

STANFORD, Calif. (UPI)—Beethoven and Bach never had it so good—a computer that listens to the piano and writes down the notes on paper.

They say it works well with classical music, but doesn't deal real well with rock.

Researchers at Stanford's Center for Computer Research in Music and Acoustics developed the computer program that hears music and produces a written score, complete with correct note value, tempo and in key.

The program works best with such composers as Mozart, whose rhythms are more conventional, said Bernard Mont-Reynaud, one of its developers.

"Much contemporary music avoids all conventional patterns," Mont-Reynaud said. "We can't deal with such pieces very well."

The machine hears music that is either played into a keyboard or is recorded. When music is analyzed from records, the computer scans the sound 30,000 times a second, then "writes a book" on the piece and prints it out.

Mont-Reynaud said the National Science Foundation, which partially funded the research, was not so much interested in producing musical scores mechanically as it was in integrating analysis of sound with artificial intelligence.

But he said the developments, if they are marketed, will enable composers and performers to play music and instantly have a score that they can change as they work.

Mont-Reynaud thinks it will be particularly useful in composing scores for films.

After the two names are read, they can be arranged alphabetically by

```
PROCEDURE Alphabetize (VAR N1, N2 : String25);
   VAR
     Temp : String25;
   BEGIN
     IF N2 < N1 THEN
       BEGIN (*  Exchange when necessary  *)
         Temp := N1;
         N1 := N2;
         N2 := Temp
     END
   END; (*  of PROCEDURE Alphabetize  *)
```

The procedure for printing the name should include some header and some formatting of the names. For example, suppose you want to say

        The alphabetized list is below.

and then print the list indented four spaces after skipping two lines. A procedure to do this is

```
PROCEDURE PrintData (N1, N2 : String25);
   CONST
     Skip = ' ';
   BEGIN
     writeln; writeln; (*  Skip two lines  *)
     writeln (Skip:10, 'The alphabetized list is below.');
     writeln (Skip:10, '___ _____ ____ __ _____');
     writeln; writeln; (*  Skip two lines  *)
     writeln (Skip:4, N1); (*  Indent four spaces  *)
     writeln (Skip:4, N2)
   END; (* of PROCEDURE PrintData  *)
```

We can now write the complete program.

```pascal
PROGRAM SampleNames (input, output);
CONST
  Skip = ' ';
  MaxLength = 25;
TYPE
  String = PACKED ARRAY [1 .. MaxLength] OF char;
VAR
  Name1, Name2 : String;

(*  Procedure to get data  *)

PROCEDURE GetData (VAR Name : String);
  VAR
    J, StringLength : integer;
  BEGIN
    StringLength := 0;
    writeln ('Enter a name.  Press <RETURN> when done.');
    WHILE NOT eoln DO
      BEGIN
        StringLength := StringLength + 1;
        read (Name[StringLength])
      END;  (*  of WHILE NOT eoln DO  *)
    readln;
    FOR J := (StringLength+1) TO MaxLength DO
      Name[J] := ' '
  END;  (*  of PROCEDURE GetData  *)

(*  Procedure to alphabetize data  *)

PROCEDURE Alphabetize (VAR N1, N2 : String);
  VAR
    Temp : String;
  BEGIN
    IF N2 < N1 THEN
      BEGIN  (*  Exchange when necessary *)
        Temp := N1;
        N1 := N2;
        N2 := Temp
      END
  END;  (*  of PROCEDURE Alphabetize  *)

(*  Procedure to print data  *)

PROCEDURE PrintData (N1, N2 : String);
  CONST
    Skip = ' ';
  BEGIN
    writeln; writeln; (*  Skip two lines  *)
    writeln (Skip:10, 'The alphabetized list is below.');
    writeln (Skip:10, '___ _____ ____ __ _____');
    writeln; writeln; (*  Skip two lines  *)
    writeln (Skip:4, N1); (*  Indent four spaces  *)
    writeln (Skip:4, N2)
  END;  (*  of PROCEDURE PrintData  *)
```

```
(*  Now start main program  *)

BEGIN  (*  Main program  *)
  GetData (Name1);
  GetData (Name2);
  Alphabetize (Name1, Name2);
  PrintData (Name1, Name2)
END,  (*  of main program  *)
```

Exercises 9.5

For Exercises 1–6, indicate which string comparisons are valid. For those that are, indicate whether they are **true** or **false** using the full ASCII character set.

1. `'Mathematics' <> 'ComputerScience'`
2. `'Jefferson' < 'Jeffersonian'`
3. `'Smith Karen' < 'Smithsonian'`
4. `'#45' <= '$45'`
5. `'Hoof in mouth' = 'Foot in door'`
6. `'453012' > '200000'`

7. Write a test program that allows you to examine the **boolean** expression

```
'William Joe' < 'Williams Bo'
```

For Exercises 8–11, suppose Message is declared as

```
TYPE
  String75 = PACKED ARRAY [1 , , 75] OF char;
VAR
  Message : String75;
```

and the input consists of the line

```
To err is human, To forgive is not the province of the
computer,
```

What output is produced by each segment?

```
8. FOR J := 1 TO 75 DO
     IF NOT eoln THEN
       read (Message[J])
     ELSE
       Message[J] := ' ';
   writeln (Message);
9. FOR J := 1 TO 75 DO
     IF NOT eoln THEN
       read (Message[J])
     ELSE
       Message[J] := ' ';
   Count := 0;
   FOR J := 1 TO 75 DO
     IF Message[J] := ' ' THEN
       Count := Count + 1;
   writeln (Message);
   writeln ('There are', Count:3, 'blanks,':8);
10. FOR J := 1 TO 30 DO
      read (Message[2+J]);
    FOR J := 31 TO 60 DO
      Message[J] := ' ';
    FOR J := 61 TO 75 DO
      Message[J] := '*';
    writeln (Message);
```

```
11. FOR J := 1 TO 75 DO
       IF NOT eoln THEN
          read (Message[J])
       ELSE
          Message[J] := ' ';
    writeln (Message);
    FOR J := 75 DOWNTO 1 DO
       write (Message[J]);
```

For Exercises 12–15, assume the following declarations.

```
TYPE
   String10 = PACKED ARRAY [1 .. 10] OF char;
   String20 = PACKED ARRAY [1 .. 20] OF char;
VAR
   A, B : String10;
   C : String20;
```

Indicate if the exercise is valid or invalid.

```
12. A := B;
13. C := A + B;
14. FOR J := 1 TO 20 DO
       C[J] :=A[J] + B[J];
15. FOR J := 1 TO 20 DO
       IF J <= 10 THEN
          A[J] := C[J]
       ELSE
          B[J-10] := C[J]);
```

16. Using the declarations as in Exercises 12–15, write a segment of code to make the string C consist of the strings A and B where the lesser (alphabetically) of A and B is the first half of C.

17. Assume a packed array Message of length 100 has been declared and data are read into it from an input file. Write a segment of the code to count the number of occurrences of the letter M in the string Message.

18. Write a test program to see what happens if you try to read in an entire packed array with one **read** or **readln** statement.

■ 9.6
Searching Algorithms

OBJECTIVES

- to use a sequential (linear) search to find the first occurrence of a value
- to use a sequential search to find all occurrences of a value
- to use a binary search to find a value

The need to search an array for a value is a common problem. For example, you might wish to replace a test score for a student, delete a name from a directory or mailing list, or upgrade the pay scale for certain employees. These and other problems require you to be able to examine elements in some list until the desired value is located. When it is found, some action is taken. The lists, of course, could be either arrays or files.

Sequential Search

The first searching algorithm we examine is a *sequential search*. This process is accomplished by examining the first element in some list and then proceeding to examine the elements in the order they appear until a match is found. Variations of this basic process include searching an ordered list for the first occurrence of a value, searching an ordered list for all occurrences of a value, and searching an unordered list for the first occurrence of a value.

to understand the relative efficiency of a binary search compared to a sequential search

To illustrate a sequential search, suppose you have an array A of integers and you want to find the first occurrence of some particular value (Num). As you search the array, if the desired value is located, you want to print its position. If the value is not in the array, you want an appropriate message to be printed. The code for such a search is

```
Index := 1;
WHILE (Num <> A[Index]) AND (Index < Length) DO
   Index := Index + 1;
```

A reasonable message for output is

```
IF Num = A[Index] THEN
   writeln (Num, ' is in position', Index:5, '.')
ELSE
   writeln (Num, ' is not in the list.');
```

Let's now consider some variations of this problem. Our code works for both a sorted and an unsorted list. However, if we are searching an ordered list, the algorithm can be improved. For example, if the array components are sorted from low to high, we need to continue the search only until the value in an array component exceeds the value of Num. At that point, there is no need to examine the remaining components. The only change required in the loop for searching is to replace

```
Num <> A[Index]
```

with

```
Num < A[Index]
```

Thus, we have

```
Index := 1;
WHILE (Num < A[Index]) AND (Index < Length) DO
   Index := Index + 1;
```

A relatively easy modification of the sequential search is to examine a list for all occurrences of some value. If you are searching an array, you generally print the positions and values when a match is found. To illustrate, if A is an array of integers and Num has an integer value, we can search A for the number of occurrences of Num by

```
Count := 0;
FOR Index := 1 TO Length DO
   BEGIN
     IF Num = A[Index] THEN
       BEGIN
         Count := Count + 1;
         writeln (Num, ' is in position', Index:5, '.')
       END
   END;
```

As before, this code works for an unsorted list. A modification of the code for working with a sorted list is included in the Exercises.

Binary Search

Searching relatively small lists sequentially does not require much computer time. However, when the lists get longer (as, for example, telephone directories and lists of credit card customers), sequential searches are inefficient. In a sense, they correspond to looking up a word in the dictionary by starting at the first word and proceeding word by word until the desired word is found. Since extra computer time means extra expense for most companies, a more efficient way of searching is needed.

If the list to be searched has been sorted, it can be searched for a particular value by a method referred to as a *binary search*. Essentially, a binary search consists of examining a middle value of an array to see which half contains the desired value. The middle value of this half is then examined to see which half of the half contains the value in question. This halving process is continued until the value is located or it has been determined that the value is not in the list. In order to use a binary search, the list must be sorted.

The code for this process is relatively short. Suppose A is the array to be searched for Num, and First, Mid, and Last are integer variables such that First contains the index of the first possible position to be searched and Last contains the index of the last possible position. The code for a list in ascending order is

```
Found := false;
WHILE NOT Found AND (First <= Last) DO
   BEGIN
      Mid := (First + Last) DIV 2;
      IF Num < A[Mid] THEN
        Last := Mid - 1
      ELSE
        IF Num > A[Mid] THEN
          First := Mid + 1
        ELSE
          Found := true
   END;
```

When this loop is executed, it is exited when the value is located or it is determined that the value is not in the list. Depending on what you want done with the value being looked for, you can modify action at the bottom of the loop or use the values in Found and Mid outside the loop. For example, if you just want to know where the value is, you can change

```
Found := true
```

to

```
BEGIN
  Found := true;
  writeln (Num, ' is in position', Mid:5, '.')
END;
```

Before continuing, let's walk through this search to better understand how it works. Assume A is the array

4	7	19	25	36	37	50	100	101	205	220	271	306	321

A[1]   A[14]

with values as indicated. Furthermore, assume Num contains the value 25. Then initially, First, Last, and Num have the values

1	14	25
First	Last	Num

A listing of values by each pass through the loop produces

	First	Last	Mid	A[Mid]	Found
Before loop	1	14	Undefined	Undefined	**false**
After first pass	1	6	7	50	**false**
After second pass	4	6	3	19	**false**
After third pass	4	4	5	36	**false**
After fourth pass	4	4	4	25	**true**

To illustrate what happens when the value being looked for is not in the array, suppose Num contains 210. The listing of values then produces

	First	Last	Mid	A[Mid]	Found
Before loop	1	14	Undefined	Undefined	**false**
After first pass	8	14	7	50	**false**
After second pass	8	10	11	220	**false**
After third pass	10	10	9	101	**false**
After fourth pass	11	10	10	205	**false**

At this stage, First > Last and the loop is exited.

SELF QUIZ 9.5

Would a binary search work if the condition of the **WHILE** ... **DO** loop is

```
WHILE NOT Found AND (First < Last) DO
```

Relative Efficiency of Searches

Let's now examine briefly the efficiency of a binary search compared to a sequential search. For purposes of this discussion, assume a sequential search on a list of 15 items requires at most 15 microseconds. The nature of a sequential search is such that every time you double the list length, the maximum searching time is also doubled. Figure 9.1 illustrates this increase.

Next, assume a list of 15 items requires a maximum of 60 microseconds when searched by a binary search. Since this process consists of successively halving the list, at most four passes are required to locate the value. This means each pass uses 15 microseconds. When the list length is doubled, it only requires one more pass. Thus, a list of 30 items requires 75 microseconds and a list of 60 items requires 90 microseconds. This is shown graphically in Figure 9.2.

The comparison of these two searches is shown on the same graph in Figure 9.3.

FIGURE 9.1
Sequential search

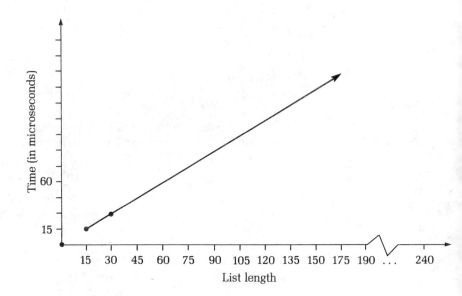

FIGURE 9.2
Binary search

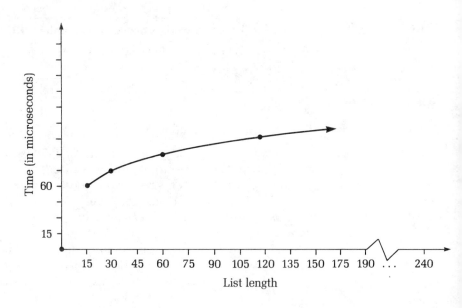

FIGURE 9.3
Sequential search
versus binary search

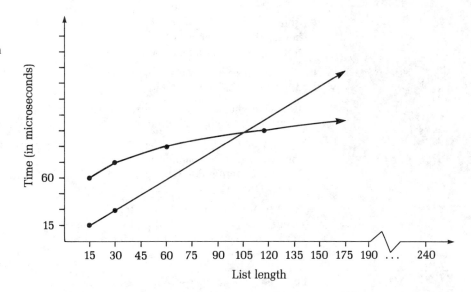

Exercises 9.6

1. Modify the sequential search in the beginning of this section to locate and print all occurrences of the same value.

2. Write a procedure for the sequential search and show how it can be called from the main program.

3. Modify the sequential search by putting a counter in the loop to count how many passes are made when searching a sorted array for a value. Write and run a program that uses this version on lists of length 15, 30, 60, 120, and 240. In each case, search for a value as listed below and plot your results on a graph.

   a. In the first half
   b. In the second half
   c. That is not there

4. Repeat Exercise 3 for a binary search.

5. Suppose the array A is

18	25	37	92	104
A[1]				A[5]

   Trace the values using a binary search to look for

   a. 18
   b. 92
   c. 76

For Exercises 6–9, suppose a sorted list of social security numbers is in secondary storage in a file named StudentNum.

6. Show how this file can be searched for a certain number using a sequential search.

7. Show how this file can be searched for a certain number using a binary search.

8. Show how a binary search can be used to indicate where a new number can be inserted in proper order.

9. Show how a number can be deleted from the file.

10. Write a procedure to read text from an input file and determine the number of occurrences of each vowel.

11. Using a binary search on an array of length 35, what is the maximum number of passes through the loop that can be made when searching for a value?

12. Using worst-case possibilities of 3 seconds for a sequential search of a list of ten items and 25 seconds for a binary search of the same list, construct a graph illustrating relative efficiency for these two methods applied to lists of longer lengths.

13. Modify the sequential search that you developed in Exercise 1 to list all occurrences of a value so that it can be used on a sorted list. That is, have it stop after the desired value is passed in the list.

RUNNING AND DEBUGGING TIPS

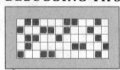

1. Be careful not to misuse type identifiers. For example, in

```
TYPE
   String = PACKED ARRAY [1 .. 10] OF char;
VAR
   Word : String;
```

String is a data type; hence, a reference such as String := 'Firstname' is incorrect.

2. Do not attempt to use a subscript that is out of range. Suppose we have

```
VAR
   List : ARRAY [1 .. 6] OF integer;
```

An inadvertent reference such as

```
FOR J := 1 TO 10 DO
   writeln (List[J]);
```

produces an error message indicating that the subscript is out of range.

3. Counters are frequently used with loops and arrays. Be careful to make the final value the correct value. For example,

```
Count := 1;
WHILE NOT eof (file name) DO
   BEGIN
      readln (file name, A[Count]);
      Count := Count + 1
   END;
```

used on the data file

```
18   21   33   ■
```

has a value of 4 in Count when this loop is exited. This can be corrected by rewriting the segment as

```
Count := 0;
WHILE NOT eof (file name) DO
   BEGIN
      Count := Count + 1;
      readln (file name, A[Count])
   END;
```

4. Comparing array components to each other can lead to errors in using subscripts. Two common misuses are shown.
   a. Attempting to compare A[J] to A[J + 1]. If this does not stop at array length − 1, then J + 1 will be out of range.
   b. Attempting to compare A[J − 1] to A[J]. This presents the same problem at the beginning of an array. Remember, J − 1 cannot have a value less than the initial index value.
5. Make sure the array index is correctly initialized. For example,

```
WHILE NOT eof (file name) DO
  BEGIN
    readln (file name, A[J]);
    J := J + 1
  END;
```

must be preceded by a statement that initializes the index. Such a statement is

```
J := 1;
```

6. After using a sequential search, make sure you check to see if the value has been found. For example, if Num contains the value 3 and A is the array

1	4	5	10

A

the search

```
Index := 1;
WHILE (Num <> A[Index]) AND (Index < Length) DO
  Index := Index + 1;
```

yields values

Depending on program use, you should check for Num = A[Index] or use a **boolean** flag to indicate if a match has been found.

■ Summary

Key Terms

array	selection sort	packed array
component of an array	bubble sort	sequential search
index (subscript)	word	binary search
index type	byte	

Keywords

ARRAY . . . OF
PACKED

Key Concepts

- An array is a structured variable; a single declaration can reserve several variables.
- It is good practice to define array types in the **TYPE** declaration section and then declare a variable of that type; for example,

```
TYPE
  List10 = ARRAY [1 . . 10] OF real;
VAR
  X : List10;
```

▪ Arrays can be visualized as lists; thus, the previous array can be envisioned as

```
   X
┌──────┐  X[1]
├──────┤  X[2]
├──────┤  X[3]
├──────┤  X[4]
├──────┤  X[5]
├──────┤  X[6]
├──────┤  X[7]
├──────┤  X[8]
├──────┤  X[9]
├──────┤  X[10]
└──────┘
```

▪ Each component of an array is a variable of the declared type and can be used in the same manner as any other variable of that type.
▪ Loops can be used to read data into arrays; for example,

```
J := 0;
WHILE NOT eof (file name) AND (J < MaxLength) DO
  BEGIN
    J := J + 1;
    readln (file name, List[J])
  END;
```

▪ Loops can be used to print data from arrays; for example, if Score is an array of 20 test scores, they can be printed by

```
FOR J := 1 TO 20 DO
  writeln (Score[J]);
```

▪ Manipulating components of an array is generally accomplished by using the index as a loop variable; for example, assuming the previous Score, to find the smallest value in the array we can use

```
Small := Score[1];
FOR J := 2 TO 20 DO
  IF Score[J] < Small THEN
    Small := Score[J];
```

▪ A selection sort is one method of sorting elements in an array from high to low or low to high; for example, if A is an array of length n, a low-to-high sort is

```
FOR J := 1 TO N-1 DO
  BEGIN
    Temp := A[J];
    Index := J;
    FOR K := J+1 TO N DO
      IF A[K] < Temp THEN
        BEGIN
          Temp := A[K];
          Index := K
        END;
    A[Index] := A[J];
    A[J] := Temp
  END; (* of selection sort *)
```

- A bubble sort sorts an array by comparing consecutive elements in the array and exchanging them if they are out of order; several passes through the array are made until the list is sorted.
- When arrays are to be passed to subprograms, the type should be defined in the **TYPE** section; thus, we can have

```
TYPE
   List200 = ARRAY [1 , , 200] OF real;
PROCEDURE Practice (X : List200);
```

- If the array being passed is a variable parameter, it should be declared accordingly; for example,

```
PROCEDURE GetData (VAR X : List200);
```

- Sorting arrays is conveniently done using procedures; such procedures facilitate program design.
- Packed arrays are used for character strings to reduce memory required for string storage and manipulation; a typical packed array declaration is

```
TYPE
   String20 = PACKED ARRAY [1 , , 20] OF char;
VAR
   Name : String20;
```

- Character strings (packed arrays of characters) can be compared; this can eventually lead to alphabetizing a list of names.
- Character strings can be printed using a single **write** or **writeln** statement; thus, if Name is a packed array of characters, it can be printed by

```
writeln (Name:30);
```

- Packed arrays of characters must still be read one character at a time.
- A single assignment statement can be used to assign a string to a packed array of the same length; for example,

```
Name := 'Smith John';
```

- A sequential search of a list consists of examining the first item in a list and then proceeding through the list in sequence until the desired value is found or the end of the list is reached; code for this search is

```
Index := 1;
WHILE (Num <> A[Index]) AND (Index < Length) DO
   Index := Index + 1;
```

- A binary search of a list consists of deciding which half of the list contains the value in question and then which half of that half, and so on; code for this search is

```
Found := false;
WHILE NOT Found AND (First <= Last) DO
   BEGIN
     Mid := (First + Last) DIV 2;
     IF Num < A[Mid] THEN
       Last := MID-1
     ELSE
       IF Num > A[Mid] THEN
         First := Mid + 1
       ELSE
         Found := true
   END;
```

■ **Chapter**
Review
Exercises

For Exercises 1–15, assume the following declarations are made.

```
VAR
    A : ARRAY [1 . . 10] OF integer;
    B : ARRAY ['A' . . 'F'] OF char;
    C : ARRAY [1 . . 5] OF real;
    X, Y : integer;
    Z : real;
```

Which of the following are valid subscripted variables? Rewrite the variable declarations for Exercises 1–15 using type declarations.

1. A[1]
2. B[1]
3. C[1]
4. C[1.0]
5. B['A']
6. B[A]
7. A[X + Y]
8. A[X **MOD** Y]
9. B[X + Y]
10. A[10]
11. C[10]
12. A(5)
13. A[X/Z]
14. C[0]
15. A[A[4]]

For Exercises 16–21, assume the array A defined as in Exercises 1–15 contains the following values:

1	4	6	8	9	3	7	10	2	9

Indicate if the following are valid subscripts of A and, if so, find the value of the subscript. If invalid, explain why.

16. A[2]
17. A[5]
18. A[A[2]]
19. A[4 + 7]
20. A[A[5] + A[2]]
21. A[**pred**(A[3])]

For Exercises 22–26, write array declarations. Define the arrays as data types.

22. X, an array of **integer** with subscripts from 0 to 5.
23. Z, an array of **char** with subscripts from 1 to 10.
24. M, an array of **real** with subscripts from 5 to 10.
25. T, an array of **boolean** with subscripts from −5 to 5.
26. D, an array of **char** with subscripts from 'A' to 'Z'.

For Exercises 27–33, list the errors in the array declarations.

```
27. C : ARRAY [1 . . 10];
28. D : ARRAY [-5 . . 5] OF boolean;
29. E = ARRAY [1 . . 3] OF integer;
30. F : ARRAY [1.0 . . 5.0] OF real;
31. G : ARRAY 1 . . 10 [OF integer];
32. ARRAY [0 . . 100] OF char;
33. H : ARRAY [10 . . 1] OF integer;
```

34. Write a segment of code to store the first ten even positive numbers into subscripts 1 through 10 of the array Even.

35. Write a segment of code that reads 20 integers and then prints the numbers in reverse order from the way in which they were read.

36. Write a segment of code to perform a selection sort to put an array of 20 real numbers into ascending order.

37. Rewrite Exercise 36 using a bubble sort.

38. Write a procedure which reads 20 characters from a data file called CharFile and returns these characters to the main program.

39. Write an appropriate call to the procedure in Problem 38.

40. Rewrite the procedure in Exercise 38 to count the number of blanks read.

41. Declare a packed array to hold 20 characters. Write a procedure to read the characters and print the array contents.

42. What condition must be true before a binary search can be used on a list?

43. Write a function that counts the number of occurrences of the letter "A" in an array of 100 characters.

44. Write a sequential search that returns the position of the number 5 in an array of 20 integers.

45. Rewrite Exercise 44 using a binary search. Assume the list is sorted from low to high.

■ Chapter Summary Program

The sample program for this chapter features the use of arrays and sub-programs. Since sorting an array is a common practice, it has been included as part of the program. Specifically, suppose the Home Sales, Inc. Realty Company wants to print a list of their sales for a month. Each sale is recorded on a separate line of input and the number of homes sold is less than 20. Write a program to do the following:

1. Read the data from the input file.
2. Print the data in the order in which it is read with a suitable header and format.
3. Print a sorted list (high to low) of sales with a suitable header and format.
4. Print the total number of sales for the month, the total amount of sales, the average sale price, and the company commission (7 percent).

A first-level pseudocode development is

1. Get data (**PROCEDURE** GetData)
2. Print header (**PROCEDURE** PrintH1)
3. Print list (**PROCEDURE** PrintList)
4. Sort list (**PROCEDURE** Sort)
5. Print header (**PROCEDURE** PrintH2)
6. Print sorted list (**PROCEDURE** PrintList)
7. Compute data (**FUNCTION** Total and **FUNCTION** Average)
8. Print data (**PROCEDURE** PrintData)

Notice that **PROCEDURE** PrintList is called twice and **PROCEDURE** PrintData includes output for number of sales, total of sales, average sale price, and company commission. These are printed with suitable headings.

```
PROGRAM MonthlyList (input,output,SalesList);
(**************************************************************

      This program illustrates the use of arrays with
      procedures and functions. Note the use of both value
      and variable parameters. Also note that a procedure
      is used to sort the array.

  ***********************************************************)
CONST
  Skip = ' ';
  ComRate = 0.07;
  MaxLength = 20;
TYPE
  List = ARRAY [1 . . MaxLength] OF real;
VAR
  JuneSales : List;              (*   Number of June Sales       *)
  Tot,                           (*   Total of June Sales        *)
  Av,                            (*   Amount of average sale     *)
  CompanyCom : real;             (*   Commission for the company *)
  SalesList : text;              (*   Data for program           *)

  (**************************************************************

            This procedure gets the data.

  ***********************************************************)
PROCEDURE GetData (VAR Sales : List; VAR ListSize : integer);
  BEGIN
    reset (SalesList);
    ListSize := 0;
    WHILE NOT eof (SalesList) AND (ListSize < MaxLength) DO
      BEGIN
        ListSize := ListSize + 1;
        readln(SalesList,Sales[ListSize])
      END
  END;      (*   of PROCEDURE GetData   *)

  (**************************************************************

            This procedure prints a heading.

  ***********************************************************)
PROCEDURE PrintH1;
  BEGIN
    writeln; writeln;
    writeln(Skip:10,'An unsorted list of sales for the');
    writeln(Skip:10,'month of June is as follows:');
    writeln(Skip:10,'_____');
    writeln
  END;      (*   of PROCEDURE PrintH1   *)
```

```
(*********************************************************************

              This procedure prints the list.

 *********************************************************************)
PROCEDURE PrintList (S : List; ListSize : integer);
  VAR
    J : integer;
  BEGIN
    FOR J := 1 TO ListSize DO
      writeln(Skip:12,'<', J:2, '>', '$':2, S[J]:11:2)
  END;    (*   of PROCEDURE PrintList   *)


(*********************************************************************

              This procedure sorts the list.

 *********************************************************************)
PROCEDURE Sort (VAR S : List; ListSize : integer);
  VAR
    J,K,Index : integer;
    Temp : real;
  BEGIN
    FOR J := 1 TO ListSize-1 DO
      BEGIN
        Temp := S[J];
        Index := J;
        FOR K := J+1 TO ListSize DO
          IF S[K] > Temp THEN
            BEGIN
              Temp := S[K];
              Index := K
            END;
        S[Index] := S[J];
        S[J] := Temp
      END
  END;       (*   of PROCEDURE Sort   *)


(*********************************************************************

       This procedure prints a second heading.

 *********************************************************************)
PROCEDURE PrintH2;
  BEGIN
    writeln; writeln;
    writeln(Skip:10,'Sales for the month of June');
    writeln(Skip:10,'sorted from high to low are:');
    writeln(Skip:10,'_____');
    writeln
  END;      (*   of PROCEDURE PrintH2   *)
```

```
(******************************************************************

          This function computes a total.

 ******************************************************************)
FUNCTION Total (S : List; ListSize : integer):real;
  VAR
    J : integer;
    Sum : real;
  BEGIN
    Sum := 0;
    FOR J := 1 TO ListSize DO
      Sum := Sum + S[J];
    Total := Sum
  END;        (*     of FUNCTION Total    *)


(******************************************************************

          This function computes the average.

 ******************************************************************)
FUNCTION Average (Sum : real; ListSize : integer):real;
  BEGIN
    Average := Sum/ListSize
  END;        (*     of FUNCTION Average    *)


(******************************************************************

       Now all procedures and functions are written.
       We are ready to start the main program.

 ******************************************************************)

BEGIN     (*     Main program     *)
  GetData(JuneSales,Length);
  PrintH1;
  PrintList(JuneSales,Length);
  Sort(JuneSales,Length);
  PrintH2;
  PrintList(JuneSales,Length);
  writeln; writeln;

(*    Now perform computations    *)

  Tot := Total(JuneSales,Length);
  Av := Average(Tot,Length);
  CompanyCom := Tot * ComRate;

(*    Now print last data    *)

  writeln; writeln;
  writeln(Skip:10,'There were',Length:3,' sales during June.');
  writeln; writeln;
  writeln(Skip:10,'The total sales were', '$':2, Tot:12:2);
  writeln; writeln;
  writeln(Skip:10,'The average sale was', '$':2, Av:12:2);
```

```
writeln; writeln;
writeln(Skip:10,'The company commission was', '$':2,
        CompanyCom:11:2);
writeln; writeln
END,    (*    of main program    *)
```

The output for this program is

```
An unsorted list of sales for the
month of June is as follows:_____

        < 1> $    65000,00
        < 2> $    56234,00
        < 3> $    95100,00
        < 4> $    78200,00
        < 5> $   101750,00
        < 6> $    56700,00


Sales for the month of June
sorted from high to low are:

        < 1> $   101750,00
        < 2> $    95100,00
        < 3> $    78200,00
        < 4> $    65000,00
        < 5> $    56700,00
        < 6> $    56234,00


There were  6 sales during June,

The total sales were $    452984,00

The average sale was $    75497,33

The company commission was $    31708,88
```

■ **Programming Problems**

1. Write a program to read an unknown number of integer test scores from an input file. Print out the original list of scores, the scores sorted from low to high, the scores sorted from high to low, the highest score, the lowest score, and the average score.

2. Write a program to help you balance your checkbook. The input consists of the beginning balance and then a sequence of transactions, each followed by a transaction code. Deposits are followed by a "D" and withdrawals are followed by a "W." The output should consist of a list of transactions, a running balance, an ending balance, the number of withdrawals, and the number of deposits. Include an appropriate message for overdrawn accounts.

3. Write a program to read a line of text as input. Print out the original line of text, the line of text in reverse order, and the number of vowels contained in the line.

4. Write a program that sorts data of type **real** as it is read from the input file. Do this by putting the first data item in the first component of an array and then inserting each subsequent number in the array in order from high to low. Print out the sorted array.

5. A palindrome is a word that is spelled the same forwards and backwards. Write a program to read several lines of text as input. Inspect each word to see if it is a palindrome. The output should list all palindromes and a count of the number of palindromes in the message.

6. One of the problems faced by designers of word processors is that of printing text without separating a word at the end of a line. Write a program to read several lines of text as input. Then print the message with each line starting in column 10 and no line exceeding column 70. No word should be separated at the end of a line.

7. Your local state university wants to raise funds for an art center. As a first step, they are going to approach 20 previously identified donors and ask for additional donations. Because the donors wish to remain anonymous, only the respective totals of their previous donations are listed in a data file. After they are contacted, the additional donations are listed at the end of the data file in the same order as the first 20 entries. Write a computer program to read the first 20 entries into one array and the second 20 entries into a second array. Compute the previous total donations and the new donations for the art center. Print the following:

   a. The list of previous donations
   b. The list of new donations
   c. An unsorted list of total donations
   d. A sorted list of total donations
   e. Total donations before the fund drive
   f. Total donations for the art center
   g. The maximum donation for the art center

8. Write a program that can be used as a text analyzer. Your program should be capable of reading an input file and keeping track of the frequency of occurrence of each letter of the alphabet. There should also be a count of all characters (including blanks) encountered that are not in the alphabet. Your output should be the data file printed line-by-line followed by a histogram reflecting the frequency of occurrence of each letter in the alphabet. For example, the following histogram indicates five occurrences of a, two of b, and three of c.

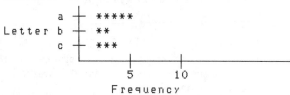

9. The Third Interdenominational Church has on file a list of all its benefactors (a maximum of 20 names, each up to 30 characters) along with an unknown number of amounts that each has donated to the church. You have been asked to write a program that does the following:

   a. Print the name of each donor and the amount (in descending order) of any donations given by each.
   b. Print the total amounts in ascending order.
   c. Print the grand total of all donations.
   d. Print the largest single amount donated and the name of the benefactor who made this donation.

10. Read in a list of 50 integers from the data file NumberList. Place the even numbers into an array called Even, the odd numbers into an array called

Odd, and the negatives into an array called Negative. Print all three arrays after all numbers have been read.

11. Read in 300 real numbers. Print the average of the numbers followed by all the numbers that are greater than the average.

12. Read in the names of five candidates in a class election and the number of votes received by each. Print the list of candidates, the number of votes they received, and the percentage of the total vote they received sorted into order from the winner to the person with the fewest votes. You may assume that all names are 20 characters in length.

13. In many sports events, contestants are rated by judges with an average score being determined by discarding the highest and lowest scores and averaging the remaining scores. Write a program in which eight scores are entered, computing the average score for the contestant.

14. Given a list of 20 test scores (integers), print the score that is nearest to the average.

15. The Game of Nim is played with three piles of stones. There are three stones in the first pile, five stones in the second, and eight stones in the third. Two players alternate taking as many stones as they like from any one pile. Play continues until someone is forced to take the last stone. The person taking the last stone loses. Write a program which permits two people to play the game of Nim using an array to keep track of the number of stones in each pile.

16. There is an effective strategy that can virtually guarantee victory in the game of Nim. Devise a strategy and modify the program in Problem 15 so that the computer plays against a person. Your program should be virtually unbeatable if the proper strategy is developed.

17. The median of a set of numbers is the value in the middle of the set if the set is arranged in order. Given a list of 21 numbers, print the median of the list.

18. Rewrite Problem 17 to permit the use of any length list of numbers.

19. The standard deviation is a statistic frequently used in education measurement. Write a program that, given a list of test scores, will find and print the standard deviation of the numbers. The standard deviation formula can be found in most statistics books.

20. Revise Problem 19 so that after the standard deviation is printed, you can print a list of test scores that are more than one standard deviation below the average and a list of the scores more than one standard deviation above the average.

21. The z-score is defined as the score earned on a test divided by the standard deviation. Given a data file containing an unknown number of test scores (maximum of 100), print a list showing each test score (from highest to lowest) and the corresponding z-score.

22. Salespeople for the Wellsville Wholesale Company earn a commission based up their sales. The commission rates are as follows.

Sales	Commission
$0–1000	3%
1001–5000	4.5%
5001–10000	5.25%
over 10000	6%

In addition, any salesperson who sells above the average of all salespeople receives a $50 bonus, and the top salesperson receives an addition $75 bonus.

Given the names and amounts sold by each of 20 salespeople, write a program which prints a table showing the salesperson's name, the amount sold, the commission rate, and the total amount earned. The average sales should also be printed.

23. Ms. Alicia Citizen, your school's Student Council advisor, has come to you for help. She wants a program to total votes for the next Student Council election. Fifteen candidates will be in the election with five positions to be filled. Each person can vote for up to five candidates. The five highest vote getters will be the winners.

    A data file called VoteList contains a list of candidates (by candidate number) voted for by each student. Any line of the file may contain up to five numbers, but if it contains more than five numbers, it is discarded as a void ballot. Write a program to read the file and print a list of the total votes received by each candidate. Also, print the five highest vote getters in order from highest to lowest vote totals.

24. The data file TeacherList contains a list of the teachers in your school along with the room number to which each is assigned. Write a program which, given the name of the teacher, does a linear search to find and print the room to which the teacher is assigned.

25. Rewrite Problem 24 so that when given a room number, the name of the teacher assigned to that room is found using a binary search. Assume the file is arranged in order of room numbers.

26. Write a language translation program which permits the entry of a word in English, with the corresponding word of another language being printed. The dictionary words can be stored in parallel arrays, with the English array being sorted into alphabetical order prior to the first entry of a word. Your program should first sort the dictionary words.

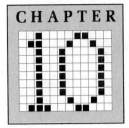

CHAPTER

Arrays of More Than One Dimension

Chapter 9 illustrated the significance and uses of one-dimensional arrays. There are, however, several kinds of problems that require arrays of more than one dimension. For example, if you want to work with a table that requires both rows and columns, a one-dimensional array will not suffice. Other programming problems require the use of a list of names; these are not conveniently written as one-dimensional arrays. Such problems can be solved using arrays of more than one dimension.

■ 10.1
Two-Dimensional Arrays

OBJECTIVES

- to declare two-dimensional arrays
- to use correct notation for two-dimensional arrays
- to create tabular output using two-dimensional arrays
- to **read** and **write** with two-dimensional arrays
- to manipulate components of two-dimensional arrays

Basic Idea and Notation

One-dimensional arrays are very useful when working with a row or column of numbers. However, suppose we want to print the table

```
1    2    3    4
2    4    6    8
3    6    9    12
```

To do this, we must access both the row and the column. Pascal accomplishes this by using *two-dimensional arrays*. This table can be produced by either of the following declarations.

```
1. VAR
      Table : ARRAY [1 .. 3, 1 .. 4] OF integer;
2. TYPE
      Matrix = ARRAY [1 .. 3, 1 .. 4] OF integer;
   VAR
      Table : Matrix;
```

It is the index—[1 .. 3, 1 .. 4]—of each of these declarations that differs from one-dimensional arrays. These declarations reserve memory that

■ to use two-dimensional arrays with procedures

can be visualized as three rows, each of which holds four variables. Thus, 12 variable locations are reserved as shown.

Table

As a second illustration of the use of two-dimensional arrays, suppose we want to print the batting statistics for a softball team of 15 players. If the statistics consist of at bats (AB), hits (H), runs (R), and runs batted in (RBI) for each player, we will work with a 15 × 4 table. Hence, a reasonable variable declaration is

```
TYPE
    Table15X4 = ARRAY [1.. 15, 1 .. 4] OF integer;
VAR
    Stats : Table15X4;
```

The reserved memory area can be visualized as

Stats

with 60 variable locations reserved.

Two-dimensional arrays are analogous to matrices in mathematics. For example, if you want to work with a 3 × 3 matrix, you can define the array type

```
Matrix3X3 = ARRAY [1 .. 3, 1 .. 3] OF integer;
```

All the mathematical properties of matrices can then be developed for matrices of this type.

Before proceeding further, let's examine another method of declaring two-dimensional arrays. Our 3 × 4 table can be thought of as three arrays each of length four, as follows:

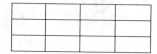

STYLE TIP

When working with charts or tables of a fixed grid size (say 15 × 4), descriptive identifiers can be

```
Chart15X4  or  Table15X4
```

If the number of rows and columns vary for different runs of the program (for example, the number of players on a team could vary from year to year), you can define a type by

```
CONST
   NumRows = 15;
   NumColumns = 4;
TYPE
   Row = 1 .. NumRows;
   Column = 1 .. NumColumns;
   TableMXN = ARRAY [Row, Column] OF integer;
VAR
   Stats : TableMXN;
```

Hence, we have a list of arrays and we can declare the table by

```
TYPE
   Row = ARRAY [1 .. 4] OF integer;
   Matrix = ARRAY [1 .. 3] OF Row;
VAR
   Table : Matrix;
```

The softball statistics can be declared by

```
CONST
   NumberOfStats = 4;
   RosterSize = 15;
TYPE
   PlayerStats = ARRAY [1 .. NumberOfStats] OF integer;
   TeamTable = ARRAY [1 .. RosterSize] OF PlayerStats;
VAR
   Stats : TeamTable;
```

In general, a two-dimensional array can be defined by

ARRAY [row index, column index] **OF** element type;
or
TYPE
   ColumnType = **ARRAY** [column index] **OF** element type;
   Table = **ARRAY** [row index] **OF** ColumnType;

SELF QUIZ 10.1   Show how the following data structure can be visualized.

```
TYPE
   Row = 1 .. 4;
   Column = 1 .. 6;
   Table = ARRAY [Row, Column] OF real;
VAR
   Chart : Table;
```

Whichever method of declaration is used, the problem now becomes one of accessing individual components of the two-dimensional array. For example, in the table

```
1   2   3    4
2   4   6    8
3   6   9   12
```

the "8" is in row two and column four. Note that both the row and column position of an element must be indicated. Therefore, in order to put an "8" in this position, we can use an assignment statement such as

```
Table[2,4] := 8;
```

This assignment statement would be used for either of the declaration forms mentioned earlier.

Next let's assign the values just given to the appropriate variables in Table by 12 assignment statements as follows:

```
Table[1,1] := 1;
Table[1,2] := 2;
Table[1,3] := 3;
Table[1,4] := 4;
Table[2,1] := 2;
Table[2,2] := 4;
Table[2,3] := 6;
Table[2,4] := 8;
Table[3,1] := 3;
Table[3,2] := 6;
Table[3,3] := 9;
Table[3,4] := 12;
```

As you can see, this is extremely tedious. Instead, we can note the relationship between the indices and the assigned values and make the row index J and the column index K. The values to be assigned are then J * K and we can use nested loops to perform these assignments as follows:

```
FOR J := 1 TO 3 DO
   FOR K := 1 TO 4 DO
      Table[J,K] := J * K;
```

Since two-dimensional arrays frequently require working with nested loops, let's examine more closely what this segment of code does. When J := 1, the loop

```
FOR K := 1 TO 4 DO
   Table[1,K] := 1 * K;
```

is executed. This performs the four assignments

```
Table[1,1] := 1 * 1;
Table[1,2] := 1 * 2;
Table[1,3] := 1 * 3;
Table[1,4] := 1 * 4;
```

and we have the memory area

Table

1	2	3	4

Similar results hold for J := 2 and J := 3 and we produce a two-dimensional array that can be visualized as

Table

1	2	3	4
2	4	6	8
3	6	9	12

The following examples will help you learn to work with and understand the notation for two-dimensional arrays.

EXAMPLE 10.1

Assume the declaration

```
TYPE
    Table5X4 = ARRAY [1 .. 5, 1 .. 4] OF integer;
VAR
    Table : Table5X4;
```

is made and consider the segment of code

```
FOR J := 1 TO 5 DO
   FOR K := 1 TO 4 DO
      Table[J,K] := J DIV K;
```

When J := 1, the loop

```
FOR K := 1 TO 4 DO
   Table[1,K] := 1 DIV K;
```

is executed. This causes the assignment statements

```
Table[1,1] := 1 DIV 1;
Table[1,2] := 1 DIV 2;
Table[1,3] := 1 DIV 3;
Table[1,4] := 1 DIV 4;
```

The contents of the memory area after that first pass through the loop are

Table

1	0	0	0

When J := 2, the assignments are

```
Table[2,1] := 2 DIV 1;
Table[2,2] := 2 DIV 2;
Table[2,3] := 2 DIV 3;
Table[2,4] := 2 DIV 4;
```

Table now has values as follows:

Table

1	0	0	0
2	1	0	0

The contents of Table after the entire outside loop is executed are

Table

1	0	0	0
2	1	0	0
3	1	1	0
4	2	1	1
5	2	1	1

■

EXAMPLE 10.2

Let's declare a two-dimensional array and write a segment of code to produce the memory area and contents depicted as follows:

2	3	4	5	6	7	8
3	4	5	6	7	8	9
4	5	6	7	8	9	10
5	6	7	8	9	10	11

An appropriate definition is

```
TYPE
    Table4X7 : ARRAY [1 .. 4, 1 .. 7] OF integer;
```

or

```
TYPE
    Table4X7 : ARRAY [1 .. 4] OF ARRAY [1 .. 7] OF integer;
VAR
    Table : Table4X7;
```

and a segment of code to produce the desired contents is

```
FOR J := 1 TO 4 DO
    FOR K := 1 TO 7 DO
        Table[J,K] := J + K;
```

■

SELF QUIZ 10.2

Consider the following two-dimensional array.

```
TYPE
    Column = ARRAY [1 .. 5] OF char;
    Table = ARRAY [1 .. 3] OF Column;
VAR
    Chart : Table;
```

Indicate the contents of Chart after the following is executed.

```
FOR J := 1 TO 3 DO
    FOR K := 1 TO 5 DO
        Chart[J,K] := chr(ord('A')+J+K-2);
```

Reading and Writing

Most problems using two-dimensional arrays require reading data from an input file into the array and writing values from the array to create some tabular form of output. For example, suppose we have our two-dimensional array for softball statistics.

```
TYPE
    Table15X4 = ARRAY [1 .. 15, 1 .. 4] OF integer;
```

```
VAR
   Stats : Table15X4;
```

If the data file named Data consists of 15 lines and each line contains statistics for one player as follows,

```
AB  H    R  RBI
┌────────────────┐■
│4   2   1   1   │   (player #1)
└────────────────┘

┌────────────────┐■
│3   1   0   1   │   (player #2)
└────────────────┘
          ·
          ·
          ·
┌────────────────┐■
│0   0   0   0   │   (player #15)
└────────────────┘
```

we can get the data from the file by reading it one line at a time for 15 lines. This is done using nested loops as follows:

```
FOR J := 1 TO 15 DO
   FOR K := 1 TO 4 DO
      read (Data, Stats[J,K]);
```

When J := 1, the loop

```
FOR K := 1 TO 4 DO
   read (Data, Stats[J,K]);
```

reads the first line of data. In a similar manner, as J assumes the values 2 through 15, the lines 2 through 15 are read. If the data are to be entered from the keyboard, this code can be modified to include

```
writeln ('Enter player stats on one line.');
writeln ('Press <RETURN> after each line.');
writeln;
writeln ('AB    H    R    RBI');
```

before the loop. The loop is then modified to

```
FOR J := 1 TO 15 DO
   BEGIN
      FOR K := 1 TO 4 DO
         read Stats[J,K]);
      readln
   END; (* of FOR loop *)
```

After reading the data into an array, some operations and/or updating will be performed and we will output the data in tabular form. For example, suppose we want to print the softball statistics in the 15 × 4 table using only three spaces for each column. We note the following:

1. Three spaces per column can be controlled by formatting the output.
2. One line of output can be generated by a **FOR** loop containing a **write** statement.

```
FOR K := 1 TO 4 DO
   write (Stats[J,K]:3);
```

3. The output buffer is dumped to the printer after each **write** loop by using **writeln.**

4. We do this for 15 lines by another loop

```
FOR J := 1 TO 15 DO
  BEGIN
    FOR K := 1 TO 4 DO
      write (Stats[J,K]:3);
    writeln
  END;
```

This last segment of code produces the desired output.

In actual practice, we will also be concerned with headings for our tables and controlling where the data occur on the page. For example, suppose we want to identify the columns of softball statistics as AB, H, R, and RBI; underline the headings; and start the output (AB) in column 25. The following segment of code accomplishes our objectives.

```
writeln (Skip:24,'AB H  R RBI');
writeln (Skip:24,'_____');
writeln;  (*  Skip a line  *)
FOR J := 1 TO 15 DO
  BEGIN
    write (Skip:22); (* Sets a tab for output,
                         skip is a blank *)
    FOR K := 1 TO 4 DO
      BEGIN
        write (Stats[J,K]:3);
        writeln (* Print the line *)
      END
  END;
```

The data file used earlier for our ballplayers causes an output of

```
AB H  R RBI

4  2  1  1
3  1  0  0
   .
   .
   .
0  0  0  0
```

SELF QUIZ 10.3 Show how the data file, Data,

| 81 93 76 100 | ■ | 98 82 73 56 | ■ | 84 95 88 70 | ■ |

can be read into the two-dimensional array declared by

```
TYPE
  Table3X4 = ARRAY [1 .. 3, 1 .. 4] OF integer;
VAR
  Score : Table3X4;
```

TABLE 10.1
Memory area

Score

98	86	100	76	95	(student #1)
72	68	65	74	81	(student #2)
85	81	91	84	83	(student #3)
76	81	72	87	80	(student #20)

Manipulating Two-Dimensional Array Components

Often we will want to work with some but not all of the components of an array. For example, suppose we have a two-dimensional array of test scores for students in a class. If there are 20 students with five scores each, an appropriate two-dimensional array can be declared as

```
TYPE
    Table20X5 = ARRAY [1 .. 20, 1 .. 5] OF integer;
VAR
    Score : Table20X5;
```

After scores are read into the array Score, we can envision the memory area as shown in Table 10.1.

When printing a table with test scores, one would normally compute several items, including total points for each student, percentage grade for each student, and average score for each test. Let's examine what is required to perform each of these computations. First, to get the total points for each student, we declare a one-dimensional array to store these values, so assume the declaration

```
TYPE
    List20 = ARRAY [1 .. 20] OF integer;
VAR
    TotalPoints : List20;
```

Since the first student's test scores are in the first row, we can write

```
TotalPoints[1] := Score[1,1] + Score[1,2] + ... + Score[1,5];
```

To compute this total for each student, we can use the loop

```
FOR J := 1 TO 20 DO
   TotalPoints[J] := Score[J,1] + Score[J,2] + ... + Score[J,5];
```

and this produces the array of totals

TotalPoints

455	TotalPoints[1]
360	TotalPoints[2]
424	TotalPoints[3]
.	.
.	.
.	.
396	TotalPoints[20]

If the two-dimensional array has several columns, we can use a loop to sum an array of numbers. We can, for instance, write a loop to sum the five test scores for the first student in our table.

```
TotalPoints[1] := 0;
FOR K := 1 TO 5 DO
   TotalPoints[1] := TotalPoints[1] + Score[1,K];
```

To do this for each student, we use a second loop.

```
FOR J := 1 TO 20 DO
   BEGIN
     TotalPoints[J] := 0;
     FOR K := 1 TO 5 DO
        TotalPoints[J] := TotalPoints [J] + Score[J,K]
   END;
```

The second task in our problem is to compute the percentage grade for each student. If we want to save these percentages, we can declare an array as follows:

```
TYPE
   Column20 = ARRAY [1 .. 20] OF real;
VAR
   Percent : Column20;
```

and include a segment of code

```
FOR J := 1 TO 20 DO
   Percent[J] := TotalPoints[J]/5;
```

The third task is to find the average score for each test. To find these numbers, we need to add all 20 scores for each test and divide the respective total by 20. We first have to find the sum of each column and we need to declare an array in which to store the averages. The declaration can be

```
TYPE
   List5 = ARRAY [1 .. 5] OF real;
VAR
   TestAv : List5;
```

We now need a loop to find the total of each column. Assuming we have an integer variable Sum declared, we can sum column one by

```
Sum := 0;
FOR J := 1 TO 20 DO
  Sum := Sum + Score[J,1];
```

TestAv[1] can now be found by

```
TestAv[1] := Sum/20;
```

To do this for each column, we use a second loop as follows:

```
FOR K := 1 TO 5 DO             (* K is the column subscript *)
  BEGIN
    Sum := 0;
    FOR J := 1 TO 20 DO        (* J is the row subscript *)
      Sum := Sum + Score[J,K];
    TestAv[K] := Sum/20
  END;
```

As a concluding example of manipulating elements of two-dimensional arrays, consider the following.

EXAMPLE 10.3

Assume we have the declarations

```
CONST
  M = 20;
  N = 50;
TYPE
  TableMXN = ARRAY [1 .. M, 1 .. N] OF integer;
  ListM = ARRAY [1 .. M] OF integer;
VAR
  Table : TableMXN;
  Max : ListM;
```

and values are read into the two-dimensional array from an input file. Let's write a segment of code to find the maximum value in each row and then store this value in the array Max. To find the maximum of row one, we can write

```
Max[1] := Table[1,1];
FOR K := 2 TO N DO
  IF Table[1,K] > Max[1] THEN
    Max[1] := Table[1,K];
```

To do this for each of the rows, we use a second loop as follows:

```
FOR J := 1 TO M DO
  BEGIN
    Max[J] := Table [J,1];
    FOR K := 2 TO N DO
      IF Table[J,K] > Max[J] THEN
        Max[J] := Table[J,K]
  END;
```

Procedures and Two-Dimensional Arrays

As we start writing programs with two-dimensional arrays, we will use procedures as before to maintain the top-down design philosophy. As with one-dimensional arrays, there are three relatively standard uses of procedures in most problems: to get the data, to manipulate the data, and to output the data. All arrays to be passed to a procedure must be declared in the **TYPE** definition section.

A NOTE OF INTEREST

Telesecurity

Increasing use of telecommunication raises the potential for security violations of computer systems. Through ingenious approaches, it is possible to gain access to major computer systems for the purposes of making free telephone calls, charging purchases to someone else's credit card number, and transferring funds to accounts in financial institutions, among others. Sometimes the perpetrators are just trying to "beat the system." Other times, there is a clear, criminal intent. In any case, security of computer systems that can be accessed by telephone is a problem which many experts are working to solve.

EXAMPLE 10.4

Western Jeans, Inc., wants a program to help them keep track of their inventory of jeans. The jeans are coded by waist size and inseam. The waist sizes are 24 to 46 and the inseams are 26 to 40. The first 23 lines of the data file contain the starting inventory; the next 23 lines contain the sales for a day. Let's write a program that will find and print the closing inventory.

A first-level pseudocode development for this program is

1. Get starting inventory
2. Get new sales
3. Update inventory
4. Print heading
5. Print closing inventory

Each of these steps uses a procedure.

Since there are 23 waist sizes and 15 inseams, we use definitions as follows:

```
CONST
   FirstWaist = 24;
   LastWaist = 46;
   FirstInseam = 26;
   LastInseam = 40;
TYPE
   WaistSizes = FirstWaist .. LastWaist;
   InseamSizes = FirstInseam .. LastInseam;
   Table = ARRAY [WaistSizes, InseamSizes] OF integer;
```

We use variables declared as follows:

```
VAR
   Inventory : Table;
   Sales : Table;
   Data : text;
```

Assuming variables are declared as needed, let's now write a procedure to get the starting inventory.

```
PROCEDURE GetData (VAR A : Table);
   VAR
      J,K : integer;
   BEGIN
      FOR J := FirstInseam TO LastInseam DO
         FOR K := FirstWaist TO LastWaist DO
            read(Data, A[J,K])
   END;
```

This procedure is called from the main program by

```
GetData (Inventory);
```

The next task is to get the sales for a day. Since this merely requires reading the next 23 lines from the data file, we do not need to write a new procedure. We call GetData again by

```
GetData (Sales);
```

We now need a procedure to update the starting inventory. This updating can be accomplished by sending both two-dimensional arrays to a procedure and then finding the respective differences of components.

```
PROCEDURE Update (VAR A:Table; B:Table);
  VAR
    J,K : integer;
  BEGIN
    FOR J := FirstInseam TO LastInseam DO
      FOR K := FirstWaist TO LastWaist DO
        A[J,K] := A[J,K] - B[J,K]
  END;
```

This is called by the statement

```
Update (Inventory, Sales);
```

The procedure for the heading is as before, so we need not write it here. Let's assume the arrays are assigned the necessary values. The output procedure is

```
PROCEDURE PrintData (Inv : Table);
  CONST
    Mark = ' !';
  VAR
    J,K : integer;
  BEGIN
    FOR J := FirstInseam TO LastInseam DO
      BEGIN
        write (J:6, Mark);
        FOR K := FirstWaist TO LastWaist DO
          write (Inv[J,K]:4);
        writeln;
        writeln (Mark:6)
      END  (*  of printing one row  *)
  END;  (*  of PROCEDURE PrintData  *)
```

This procedure is called from the main program by

```
PrintData (Inventory);
```

Once these procedures are written, the main program becomes

```
BEGIN  (*  Main program  *)
  GetData (Inventory);
  GetData (Sales);
  Update (Inventory, Sales);
  PrintHeading;
  PrintData (Inventory)
END.  (*  of main program  *)
```

Exercises 10.1   For Exercises 1–3, declare a two-dimensional array type using both the **ARRAY** [.., ..] and **ARRAY** [..] **OF ARRAY** [..] forms. Also declare a variable of the defined type.

1. A table with real number entries that shows the prices for four different drugs charged by five drug stores.
2. A table with character entries that shows the grades earned by 20 students in six courses.
3. A table with integer entries that shows the 12 quiz scores earned by 30 students in a class.

4. Write a test program to read integers into a 3 x 5 array and then print out the array components together with each row sum and each column sum.

For Exercises 5–8, sketch what is reserved in memory from the declaration. Also, state how many variables are available to the programmer.

5. VAR
```
    ShippingCost : ARRAY [1 .. 10] OF
                        ARRAY [1 .. 4] OF real;
    GradeBook : ARRAY [1 .. 35, 1 .. 6] OF integer;
```
6. VAR
```
    A : ARRAY [1 .. 3, 2 .. 6] OF integer;
```
7. TYPE
```
    Weekdays = (Mon, Tues, Wed, Thur, Fri);
    Chores = (Wash, Iron, Clean, Mow, Sweep);
VAR
    Schedule : ARRAY [Weekdays, Chores] OF boolean;
```
8. TYPE
```
    Questions = 1 .. 50;
    Answers = 1 .. 5;
    Table = ARRAY [Questions, Answers] OF char;
VAR
    AnswerSheet : Table;
```

For Exercises 9–12, assume the array A is declared as

```
VAR
    A : ARRAY [1 .. 3, 1 .. 5] OF integer;
```

Indicate the array contents produced.

9. FOR J := 1 TO 3 DO
```
     FOR K := 1 TO 5 DO
        A[J,K] := J - K;
```
11. FOR K := 1 TO 5 DO
```
      FOR J := 1 TO 3 DO
         A[J,K] := J;
```
10. FOR J := 1 TO 3 DO
```
      FOR K := 1 TO 5 DO
         A[J,K] := J;
```
12. FOR J := 3 DOWNTO 1 DO
```
      FOR K := 1 TO 5 DO
         A[J,K] := J MOD K;
```

For Exercises 13–15, let the two-dimensional array A be declared by

```
VAR
    A : ARRAY [1 .. 3, 1 .. 6] OF integer;
```

Write nested loops to cause the values to be stored in A.

13.   **A**

3	4	5	6	7	8
5	6	7	8	9	10
7	8	9	10	11	12

14.   **A**

0	0	0	0	0	0
0	0	0	0	0	0
0	0	0	0	0	0

15.   **A**

2	2	2	2	2	2
4	4	4	4	4	4
6	6	6	6	6	6

16. Declare a two-dimensional array and write a segment of code to allow you to enter two lines of data from the keyboard, each line consisting of five reals. Typical entries are

    13.2 15.1 10.3 8.2 43.6

    37.2 25.6 34.1 17.0 15.2

17. Suppose an input file contains 50 lines of data and the first 20 spaces of each line are reserved for a customer's name. The rest of the line contains other information. Declare a two-dimensional array to hold the names and write a segment of code to read the names into the array. A sample line of input is

Smith John O   268-14-1801 ▮
                          ↑
                     position 20

For Exercises 18–20, assume the declaration

```
TYPE
    Table4X5 = ARRAY [1 .. 4,1 .. 5] OF real;
VAR
    Table : Table4X5;
```

is made and values are read into Table as follows:

                   Table

−2.0	3.0	0.0	8.0	10.0
0.0	−4.0	3.0	1.0	2.0
1.0	2.0	3.0	8.0	−6.0
−4.0	1.0	4.0	6.0	82.0

Indicate the components of Table after each segment of code is executed.

```
18. FOR J := 1 TO 4 DO
        FOR K := 1 TO 5 DO
            IF J MOD K = O THEN
                A[J,K] := O
            ELSE
                A[J,K] := -1;
19. FOR J := 1 TO 4 DO
        IF A[J,1] <> O THEN
            FOR K := 1 TO 5 DO
                A[J,K] := A[J,K]/A[J,1];
```

```
20. FOR K := 1 TO 5 DO
      IF A[1,K] = 0 THEN
        FOR J := 1 TO 4 DO
          A[J,K] := 0;
```

21. Let the two-dimensional array Table be declared as in Exercises 18–20. Declare additional arrays as needed and write a segment of code for the following:

 a. Find and save the minimum of each row.
 b. Find and save the maximum of each column.
 c. Find the total of all the components.

22. Example 10.4 illustrates the use of procedures with two-dimensional arrays. For actual use, you would also need a list indicating what should be ordered to maintain the inventory. Write a procedure (assuming all declarations are made) to print a table indicating which sizes of jeans have a supply fewer than four. Do this by putting an asterisk in the cell if the supply is low or a blank if the supply is adequate.

23. Suppose you want to work with a table that has three rows and eight columns of integers.

 a. Declare an appropriate two-dimensional array that can be used with procedures.
 b. Write a procedure to replace all negative numbers with zero.
 c. Show what is needed to call this procedure from the main program.

24. If A and B are matrices of size $m \times n$, their sum $A+B$ is defined by $A+B = [a + b]_{ij}$, where a and b are corresponding components in A and B. Write a program to

 a. Read values into two matrices of size $m \times n$.
 b. Compute the sum.
 c. Print out the matrices together with the sum.

25. If A and B are matrices of sizes $m \times n$ and $n \times p$, their product is defined to be the $m \times p$ matrix AB where

$$AB = [c_{ik}], \quad c_{ik} = \sum_{j=1}^{n} a_{ij} b_{jk}$$

For example, for
$m = 2, n = 3, p = 2,$

$$\begin{bmatrix} 1 & 2 & 3 \\ 0 & 1 & -1 \end{bmatrix} \begin{bmatrix} 1 & 0 \\ 0 & 2 \\ 2 & 1 \end{bmatrix} = \begin{bmatrix} 7 & 7 \\ -2 & 1 \end{bmatrix}$$

Write a program to

 a. Read values into two matrices whose product is defined.
 b. Compute their product.
 c. Print out the matrices together with their product.

■ 10.2
Arrays of String Variables

Basic Idea and Notation

Recall from Section 9.5 that we defined string variables as packed arrays of characters. At that time, we learned that strings of the same length can be compared and strings can be printed using a single **write** or **writeln** command. A typical declaration for a name 20 characters in length is

```
TYPE
   String20 = PACKED ARRAY [1 .. 20] OF char;
VAR
   Name : String20;
```

Thus, Name can be envisioned as

Name

It is a natural extension to next consider the problem of working with an array of strings. For example, if we need a data structure for 50 names, this can be declared by

```
TYPE
   String20 = PACKED ARRAY [1 .. 20] OF char;
   NameList = ARRAY [1 .. 50] OF String20;
VAR
   Name : NameList;
```

Name can then be envisioned as

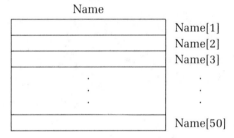

where each component of Name is a packed array.

Define and declare a data structure that can be used for a list of 200 names; each name is less than or equal to 30 characters in length.

Alphabetizing a List of Names

One standard problem faced by programmers is that of alphabetizing a list of names. For example, programs that work with class lists, bank statements, magazine subscriptions, names in a telephone book, credit card customers, and so on require alphabetizing. As indicated, Pascal uses an array of packed arrays as a data structure for such lists.

Problems that require alphabetizing names contain at least three main tasks: get the data, alphabetize the list, and print the list. Prior to writing procedures for each of these tasks, let's consider some associated problems. When getting the data, you will usually encounter one of two formats. First, data may be entered with a constant field width for each name. Each name would typically be followed by some additional data item. Thus, if each name uses 20 character positions and position 21 contains the start of numeric data, the input file might be

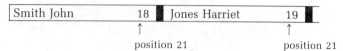

In this case, the name can be read into the appropriate component by a fixed loop. The first name can be accessed by

```
FOR K := 1 TO 20 DO
   read (Data, Name[1,K]);
```

and the second name by

```
FOR K := 1 TO 20 DO
   read (Data, Name[2,K]);
```

A second form for entering data is to use some symbol to indicate the end of a name. When the data are in this form, you must be able to recognize the symbol and fill the remaining positions with blanks. Thus, the data file is

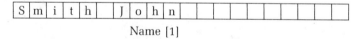

In this case, the first name can be obtained by

```
K := 1;
read (Data, Ch);
WHILE (Ch <> '*') AND (K <= 20) DO
   BEGIN
      Name[1,K] := Ch;
      K := K + 1;
      read (Data, Ch)
   END;
Length := K - 1;
FOR K := Length TO 20 DO
   Name[1,K] := ' ';
```

This process fills the remaining positions in the name with blanks. Thus, Name[1] is

| S | m | i | t | h | | J | o | h | n | | | | | | | | | | |

Name [1]

The second name in the data file is similarly read. The only change is from Name[1,K] to Name[2,K].

The next problem in getting data is determining how many lines are available. If the number of lines is known, you can use a **FOR** loop. More realistically, however, there will be an unknown number of lines and you will need the **eof** condition in a variable control loop and a counter to determine the number of names. To illustrate, assume there are an unknown number of data lines where each line contains a name in the first 20 positions. If the declaration section of a program is

```
TYPE
  String20 = PACKED ARRAY [1 .. 20] OF char;
  NameList = ARRAY [1 .. 50] OF String20;
VAR
  Name : NameList;
  Length : integer;
```

a procedure to get the data is

```
PROCEDURE GetData (VAR N : NameList;
                       VAR Ct : integer);
  VAR
    K : integer;
  BEGIN
    Ct := 0;
    reset (Data);
    WHILE NOT eof (Data) AND (Ct < 50) DO
      BEGIN
        Ct := Ct + 1;        (* Increment counter *)
        FOR K := 1 TO 20 DO (* Get a name *)
          read (Data, N[Ct,K]);
        readln (Data) (* Advance the pointer *)
      END
  END; (* of PROCEDURE GetData *)
```

This procedure is called from the main program by

```
GetData (Name, Length);
```

Let's now consider the problem of alphabetizing a list of names. If we assume the same data structure we've just seen and let Length represent the number of names, a procedure to sort the list alphabetically using the selection sort is

```
PROCEDURE Sort (VAR N : NameList; L : integer);
  VAR
    J,K,Index : integer;
    Temp : String20;
  BEGIN
    FOR J := 1 TO L-1 DO
      BEGIN
        Temp := N[J];
        Index := J;
        FOR K := J+1 TO L DO
          IF N[K] < Temp THEN
            BEGIN
              Temp := N[K];
              Index := K
            END;
        N[Index] := N[J];
        N[J] := Temp
      END
  END; (* of PROCEDURE Sort *)
```

This procedure is called from the main program by

```
Sort (Name, Length);
```

Once the list of names is sorted, you usually want to print the sorted list. A procedure to do this is

```
PROCEDURE PrintData (N : NameList; L : integer);
  VAR
    J : integer;
  BEGIN
    FOR J := 1 TO L DO
      writeln (N[J]:50)
  END; (* of PROCEDURE PrintData *)
```

This is called from the main program by

```
PrintData (Name, Length);
```

We can now use the procedures in a simple program that gets the names, sorts them, and prints them as follows:

```
BEGIN (* Main program *)
  GetData (Name, Length);
  Sort (Name, Length);
  PrintData (Name, Length)
END. (* of main program *)
```

Exercises 10.2

For Exercises 1–4, assume the declarations and definitions

```
TYPE
  String20 = PACKED ARRAY [1 .. 20] OF char;
  StateList = ARRAY [1 .. 50] OF String20;
VAR
  State : StateList;
```

are made and an alphabetical listing of the 50 states of the United States of America is contained in the data structure State. Furthermore, assume that each state name begins in position one of each component. Indicate the output for the exercise.

```
1. FOR J := 1 TO 50 DO
     IF State[J,1] = 'O' THEN
       writeln (State[J]:35);
2. FOR J := 50 DOWNTO 1 DO
     IF J MOD 5 = 0 THEN
       writeln (State[J]:35);
3. FOR J := 1 TO 50 DO
     writeln (State[J,1]:10, State [J,2]);
4. CountA := 0;
   FOR J := 1 TO 50 DO
     FOR K := 1 TO 20 DO
       IF State[J,K] = 'A' THEN
         CountA := CountA + 1;
   writeln (CountA:20);
```

5. Assume you have a sorted list of names. Write a fragment of code to inspect the list of names and print the full name of each Smith on the list.

The procedure in this section that gets names from a data file assumes the names in the data file are of fixed length and that there are an unknown number of data lines. For Exercises 6–8, modify the procedure for each situation.

6. Variable length names followed by an '*' and a known number of data lines
7. Variable length names followed by an '*' and an unknown number of data lines
8. Fixed length names (20 characters) and a known number of data lines
9. If each line of a data file contains a name followed by an age,

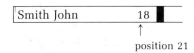

position 21

the data will be put into two arrays, one for the names and one for the ages. Show how the sorting procedure can be modified so that the array of ages keeps the same order as the array of names.

10. Write a complete program to read ten names from the keyboard, sort the names in reverse alphabetical order, and print the sorted list.

10.3 Parallel Arrays

OBJECTIVES

- to understand when parallel arrays should be used to solve a problem
- to use parallel arrays to solve a problem

There are many practical situations in which more than one type of array is required to handle the data. For example, you may wish to keep a record of names of people and their donations to a charitable organization. This requires a packed array of names and an equal length array of donations—of **real** or **integer.** Programs for these situations can use *parallel arrays*, a term used for arrays of the same length. However, most uses of parallel arrays have the added condition of different data types for the array components. Otherwise, a two-dimensional array would suffice. Generally, situations that call for two or more arrays of the same length but of different data types are situations in which parallel arrays should be used.

Using Parallel Arrays

Let's look at a typical problem that requires working with both a list of names and a list of numbers. Suppose the input file consists of 30 lines and each line contains a name in the first 20 spaces and an integer starting in space 21 that is the amount of a donation. We are to read all data into appropriate arrays, alphabetize the names, print the alphabetized list with the amount of each donation, and find the total of all donations.

STYLE TIP

Descriptive constants are especially useful when working with parallel arrays. To illustrate, in the problem just stated for 30 donors, we can define

```
CONST
    NumberOfDonors = 30;
```

and then use NumberOfDonors in subsequent definitions and loop limits.

This problem can be solved using parallel arrays for the list of names and the list of donations. Appropriate declarations are

```
CONST
    NumberOfDonors = 30;
    MaxName = 20;
```

```
TYPE
   String20 = PACKED ARRAY [1 .. MaxName] OF char;
   NameList = ARRAY [1 .. NumberOfDonors] OF String20;
   AmountList = ARRAY [1 .. NumberOfDonors] OF integer;
VAR
   Donor : NameList;
   Amount : AmountList;
   Data : text;
```

A procedure to read the data from an input file is

```
PROCEDURE GetData (VAR Name: NameList;
                        VAR Donation : AmountList);
   VAR
     J,K : integer;
   BEGIN
     reset (Data);
     FOR J := 1 TO NumberOfDonors DO
       BEGIN
         FOR K := 1 TO MaxName DO
            read (Data, Name[J,K]);
         readln (Data, Donation[J])
       END
   END; (* of PROCEDURE GetData *)
```

This procedure is called by

```
GetData (Donor, Amount);
```

After this procedure is called from the main program, the parallel arrays can be envisioned as

	Donor		Amount	
Donor[1]	Smith John		100	Amount[1]
Donor[2]	Jones Jerry		250	Amount[2]
.	.		.	.
.	.		.	.
.	.		.	.
Donor[30]	Generous George		525	Amount[30]

The next task is to alphabetize the names. However, we must be careful to keep the amount donated with the name of the donor. This can be accomplished by passing both the list of names and the list of donations to the sorting procedure and modifying the code to include exchanging the amount of donation whenever the names are exchanged. Using the procedure heading

```
PROCEDURE Sort (VAR Name : NameList;
                     VAR Donation : AmountList);
```

the code for sorting is changed from

```
IF Name[K] < Temp THEN
   BEGIN
     Temp := Name[K];
     Index := K
   END;
Name[Index] := Name[J];
Name[J] := Temp;
```

to

```
IF Name[K] < Temp THEN
   BEGIN
      Temp := Name[K];
      TempDon := Donation[K];        (* added line *)
      Index := K
   END;
 Name[Index] := Name[J];
 Donation[Index] := Donation[J];     (* added line *)
 Name[J] := Temp;
 Donation[J] := TempDon;             (* added line *)
```

The procedure for sorting the list of names and rearranging the list of donations accordingly is called by

```
Sort (Donor, Amount);
```

Our next task is to print the alphabetized list together with the donations. If Donor and Amount are sorted appropriately, we can use the following procedure to produce the desired output.

```
PROCEDURE PrintData (Name : NameList;
                     Donation : AmountList);
   VAR
     J : integer;
   BEGIN
     FOR J := 1 TO NumberOfDonors DO
        BEGIN
           write (Name[J]:40);
           writeln ('$':3, Donation[J]:5)
        END
   END; (*  of PROCEDURE PrintData  *)
```

This is called by

```
PrintData (Donor, Amount);
```

The last task this program requires is to find the total of all donations. The following **FUNCTION** performs this task.

```
FUNCTION Total (A:AmountList) : integer;
   VAR
     Sum, J : integer;
   BEGIN
     Sum : = 0;
```

```
                FOR J := 1 TO NumberOfDonors DO
                    Sum := Sum + A[J];
                    Total := Sum
                END; (*   of FUNCTION Total   *)
```

This function is called by

```
        TotalDonations := Total (Amount);
```

where TotalDonations is declared as an **integer** variable. A complete program for this problem follows.

```
PROGRAM Donations (input,output, Data);
(*******************************************************************

    This program reads data from an input file where
    each line consists of a donor name followed by the
    amount donated. Output consists of an alphabetically
    sorted list together with the amount of each donation.
    This is accomplished by using parallel arrays.
    The total amount donated is also listed.


*******************************************************************)

CONST
  NumberOfDonors = 30;
TYPE
  String20 = PACKED ARRAY [1 .. 20] OF char;
  NameList = ARRAY [1 .. NumberOfDonors] OF String20;
  AmountList = ARRAY [1 .. NumberOfDonors] OF integer;
VAR
  Amount : AmountList;         (*  An array for amounts donated   *)
  Donor : NameList;            (*  An array for donor names        *)
  TotalDonations : integer;    (*  Total amount donated            *)
  Data : text;


(*******************************************************************

               This procedure gets the data.

*******************************************************************)
PROCEDURE GetData (VAR Name : NameList; VAR Donation : AmountList);
  VAR
    J,K : integer;
  BEGIN
    reset (Data);
    FOR J := 1 TO NumberOfDonors DO
      BEGIN
        FOR K := 1 TO 20 DO
          read(Data, Name[J,K]);
        readln(Data, Donation[J])
      END
  END;      (*   of PROCEDURE GetData   *)
```

```
(*****************************************************************

    This procedure sorts the list alphabetically.
    Amounts donated are changed accordingly.

*****************************************************************)
PROCEDURE Sort (VAR Name : NameList; VAR Donation : AmountList);
  VAR
    TempName : String20;
    TempAmount : integer;
    J,K,Index : integer;
  BEGIN
    FOR J := 1 TO NumberOfDonors - 1 DO
      BEGIN
        TempName := Name[J];
        TempAmount :=  Donation[J];
        Index := J;
        FOR K := J+1 TO NumberOfDonors DO
          IF Name[K] < TempName THEN
            BEGIN
              TempName := Name[K];
              TempAmount := Donation[K];
              Index := K
            END;
        Name[Index] := Name[J];
        Donation[Index] := Donation[J];
        Name[J] := TempName;
        Donation[J] := TempAmount
      END  (*   of FOR loop   *)
  END; (*  of PROCEDURE Sort   *)


(*****************************************************************

            This procedure prints the data.

*****************************************************************)
PROCEDURE PrintData (Name : NameList; Donation : AmountList;
                      Tot : integer);
  VAR
    J : integer;
  BEGIN
    FOR J := 1 TO NumberOfDonors DO
      BEGIN
        write(Name[J]:40);
        writeln('$':3,Donation[J]:5)
      END;  (*   of printing list   *)
      writeln('_____':49);
      writeln('Total':40,'$':3,Tot:5);
      writeln; writeln
  END; (*  of PROCEDURE PrintData  *)
```

```
(******************************************************************

                This procedure prints a heading.

 ******************************************************************)
PROCEDURE PrintHeading;
  BEGIN
    writeln; writeln;
    writeln('Donor Name':33,'Donation':17);
    writeln('_____':33,'_____':17);
    writeln
  END;  (*  of PROCEDURE PrintHeading  *)


(*****************************************************************

           This function computes the total donated.

 *****************************************************************)
FUNCTION Total (A : AmountList) : integer;
  VAR
    Sum,J : integer;
  BEGIN
    Sum := 0;
    FOR J := 1 TO NumberOfDonors DO
      Sum := Sum + A[J];
    Total := Sum
  END;  (*   of FUNCTION Total   *)


(*****************************************************************

    All subprograms are written. The main program follows.

 *****************************************************************)
BEGIN    (*   Main program   *)
  GetData(Donor,Amount);
  Sort (Donor,Amount);
  TotalDonations := Total (Amount);
  PrintHeading;
  PrintData (Donor,Amount,TotalDonations)
END.   (*  of main program   *)
```

Output created from an input file of 30 lines is

```
            Donor Name        Donation
            _____        _____

            Alexander Candy   $   300
            Anderson Tony     $   375
            Banks Marj        $   375
            Born Patty        $   100
            Brown Ron         $   200
            Darnell Linda     $   275
            Erickson Thomas   $   100
            Fox William       $   300
            Francis Denise    $   350
            Generous George   $   525
            Gillette Mike     $   350
```

```
Hancock Kirk            $   500
Higgins Sam             $   300
Janson Kevin            $   200
Johnson Ed              $   350
Johnson Martha          $   400
Jones Jerry             $   250
Kelly Marvin            $   475
Kneff Susan             $   300
Lasher John             $   175
Lyon Elizabeth          $   425
Moore Robert            $   100
Muller Marjorie         $   250
Smith John              $   100
Trost Frostie           $    50
Trudo Rosemary          $   200
Weber Sharon            $   150
Williams Art            $   350
Williams Jane           $   175
Wilson Mary             $   275
                             -----
                Total  $  8275
```

Exercises 10.3

1. Which of the following are appropriate declarations for parallel arrays? Explain.

   a. TYPE
   ```
       String15 = PACKED ARRAY [1 .. 15] OF char;
       List15 = ARRAY [1 .. 15] OF real;
   VAR
       Names : ARRAY [1 .. 10] OF String15;
       Amounts : List15;
   ```
   b. TYPE
   ```
       Chart = ARRAY [1 .. 12, 1 .. 10] OF integer;
       String10 = PACKED ARRAY [1 .. 10] OF char;
       List = ARRAY [1 .. 12] OF String10;
   VAR
       Table : Chart;
       Names : List;
   ```

2. Write a test program to read names and amounts from a data file. Your program should print out both lists and the total of the amounts. Assume each line of data is similar to

   | Jones Mary   7.35 |
                      ↑
                  position 21

3. In this section you were asked to sort a list of names alphabetically and then write the sorted list together with student grades. Write a procedure to count the number of occurrences of each grade.

4. Declare appropriate arrays and write a procedure to read data from an input file where there are an unknown number of lines (but less than 100) and each line contains a name (20 spaces), an age (integer), a marital status (character), and an income (real). A typical data line is

   | Smith John   35M 28502.16 |

5. Modify the code of Exercise 4 to accommodate data entered in the data file in the following format:

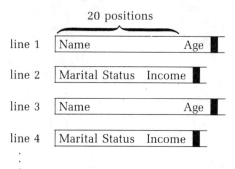

20 positions

line 1   Name   Age

line 2   Marital Status   Income

line 3   Name   Age

line 4   Marital Status   Income

6. Write a procedure to sort the arrays of Exercise 4 according to income.

■ **10.4**
Higher-Dimensional Arrays

Thus far we have worked with arrays of one and two dimensions. Arrays of three, four, or higher dimensions can also be declared and used. Pascal places no limitation on the number of dimensions of an array.

- to understand when arrays of dimensions greater than two are needed in a program
- to define and declare data structures for higher-dimensional arrays
- to use higher-dimensional arrays in a program

Declarations of Higher-Dimensional Arrays

Declarations of *higher-dimensional arrays* usually assume one of two basic forms. First, a three-dimensional array can be declared using the form

ARRAY [1 .. 3, 1 .. 4, 1 .. 5] **OF** data type;

Each dimension can vary in any of the ways used for arrays of one or two dimensions and the data type can be any standard or user-defined data type. Second, a three-dimensional array can be declared as an array of two-dimensional arrays and can be declared by

ARRAY [1 .. 3] **OF ARRAY** [1 .. 4, 1 .. 5] **OF** data type;

Each of these declarations reserves 60 locations in memory. This can be visualized as shown in Figure 10.1.

FIGURE 10.1
Three-dimensional array

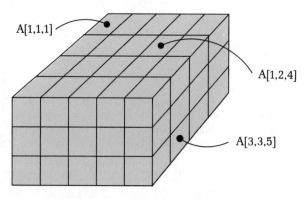

A[1,1,1]

A[1,2,4]

A[3,3,5]

An array of dimension n can be defined by

ARRAY $[1 \ldots a_1, 1 \ldots a_2, \ldots, 1 \ldots a_n]$ **OF** data type;

which reserves $a_1 * a_2 * \ldots * a_n$ locations in memory. A general definition is

ARRAY $[a_1 \ldots b_1, a_2 \ldots b_2, \ldots, a_n \ldots b_n]$ **OF** data type;

where $a_i \leq b_i$ for $1 \leq i \leq n$.

SELF QUIZ 10.5 How many memory locations are reserved when the following three-dimensional array is declared?

```
TYPE
    Block = ARRAY [-2 .. 2, 1 .. 3, 0 .. 5] OF real;
VAR
    Item : Block;
```

Declarations and uses of higher-dimensional arrays are usually facilitated by descriptive names and user-defined data types. For example, suppose we want to declare a three-dimensional array to hold the contents of a book of tables. If there are 50 pages and each page contains a table of 10 columns and 15 rows, a reasonable declaration is

```
TYPE
    Page = 1 .. 50;
    Row = 1 .. 15;
    Column = 1 .. 10;
    Book = ARRAY [Page, Row, Column] OF integer;
VAR
    Item : Book;
```

When this declaration is compared to

```
TYPE
    Book = ARRAY [1 .. 50, 1 .. 15, 1 .. 10] OF integer;
VAR
    Item : Book;
```

we realize that both arrays are identical in structure, but, in the first declaration, it is easier to see what the dimensions represent.

Accessing Components

Elements in higher-dimensional arrays are accessed and used in a manner similar to two-dimensional arrays. The difference is that in a three-dimensional array, each element needs three indices for reference. A similar result holds for other dimensions. To illustrate using this notation, recall the declaration

```
TYPE
    Page = 1 .. 50;
    Row = 1 .. 15;
    Column = 1 .. 10;
    Book = ARRAY [Page, Row, Column] OF integer;
VAR
    Item : Book;
```

If you want to assign a 10 to the item on page three, row five, column seven, the statement

```
Item [3,5,7] := 10;
```

accomplishes this. Similarly, this item can be printed by

```
write (Item [3,5,7]);
```

Using this same declaration, we can

1. Print the fourth row of page 21 with the following segment of code.

```
FOR K := 1 TO 10 DO
   write (Item [21,4,K]:5);
writeln;
```

2. Print the top row of every page with

```
FOR I := 1 TO 50 DO
   BEGIN
     FOR K := 1 TO 10 DO
        write (Item [I,1,K]:5);
     writeln
   END;
```

3. Print page 35 with

```
FOR J := 1 TO 15 DO
   BEGIN
     FOR K := 1 TO 10 DO
        write (Item [35,J,K]:5);
     writeln; writeln
   END;
```

4. Print every page that does not have a zero in the first row and the first column with

```
FOR I := 1 TO 50 DO
   IF Item [I,1,1] <> 0 THEN
     FOR J := 1 TO 15 DO
       BEGIN
         FOR K := 1 TO 10 DO
            write (Item[I,J,K]:5);
         writeln; writeln
       END;
```

SELF QUIZ 10.6   Using the three-dimensional array Item as declared, write a segment of code that prints the third column of every fifth page (pages numbered 5, 10, 15, . . . , 50).

As another illustration of the use of higher-dimensional arrays, consider the situation where the manager of a high-rise office complex wants a program to assist in keeping track of the tenants in each office. Suppose there are 20 floors, each with four wings as shown in Figure 10.2. Each wing contains five rooms.

FIGURE 10.2
High-rise floor plan

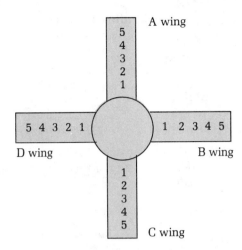

Let's first declare an appropriate array where the tenant's name can be stored (assume each name consists of 20 characters). This can be accomplished by

```
TYPE
  Floors = 1 .. 20;
  Wings = 'A' .. 'D';
  Offices = 1 .. 5;
  Name = PACKED ARRAY [1 .. 20] OF char;
  Occupant = ARRAY [Floors, Wings, Offices] OF Name;
VAR
  Tenant : Occupant;
  Floor : Floors;
  Wing : Wings;
  Office : Offices;
```

Note that this is really a four-dimensional array, since the data type name is **PACKED ARRAY.**

Now let's write a segment of code to print a list of names of all tenants on the twentieth floor. To get this list, we need to print the names for each office in each wing. Assuming a field width of 30 columns, the following code completes the desired task.

```
FOR Wing := 'A' TO 'D' DO
  FOR Office := 1 TO 5 DO
    writeln (Tenant[20, Wing, Office]:30);
```

Let's now write a segment of code to read the name of the new tenant on the third floor, B wing, room 5 from the data file, Data. Recall that character strings must be read one character at a time. Tenant [3,'B',5] is the variable name. Since this is a packed array, the code for reading is

```
FOR L := 1 TO 20 DO
  read (Data, Tenant[3,'B',5,L]);
```

Assume the string 'Unoccupied   ' is entered for each vacant office and we are to write a segment of code to list all vacant offices. This problem requires us to examine every name and print the location of the unoccupied offices. Hence, when we encounter the name 'Unoccupied ', we want to print the respective indices. This is accomplished by

```
FOR Floor := 1 TO 20 DO
   FOR Wing := 'A' TO 'D' DO
      FOR Office := 1 TO 5 DO
         IF Tenant[Floor, Wing, Office] = 'Unoccupied            THEN
            writeln (Floor:5, Wing:5, Office:5);
```

As you can see, working with higher-dimensional arrays requires very careful handling of the indices. Nested loops are frequently used for processing array elements and proper formatting of output is critical.

Exercises 10.4

In Exercises 1–4, how many memory locations are reserved in the declaration?

1. ```
   VAR
      A : ARRAY [1 .. 2, 1 .. 3, 1 .. 10] OF char;
   ```
2. ```
   VAR
      A : ARRAY [-2 .. 3] OF ARRAY[2 .. 4, 3 .. 6] OF real
   ```
3. ```
   TYPE
      Color = (Red, Black, White);
      Size = (Small, Large);
      Year = 1950 .. 1960;
   VAR
      A : ARRAY [Color, Size, Year];
   ```
4. ```
   TYPE
      String15 = PACKED ARRAY [1 .. 15] OF char;
      List10 = ARRAY [1 .. 10] OF String15;
   VAR
      A : ARRAY [1 .. 4] OF List10;
   ```

5. Write a test program to read values into an array of size 3 × 4 × 5. Assuming this represents three pages, each of which contains a 4 × 5 table, print out the table for each page together with a page number.

6. Declare a three-dimensional array that a hospital could use to keep track of the types of rooms available: private (P), semiprivate (S), and ward (W). The hospital has four floors, five wings, and 20 rooms in each wing.

For Exercises 7 and 8, consider the declaration

```
TYPE
   Pages = 1 .. 50;
   Rows = 1 .. 15;
   Columns = 1 .. 10;
   Book = ARRAY [Pages, Rows, Columns] OF integer;
VAR
   Page : Pages;
   Row : Rows;
   Column : Columns;
   Item : Book;
```

7. Write a segment of code to do each of the following:
   a. Print the fourth column of page 3.
   b. Print the top seven rows of page 46.
   c. Create a new page 30 by adding the corresponding elements of page 31 to page 30.

8. What output is produced by the following segments of code?

```
a. FOR Page := 1 TO 15 DO
      FOR Column := 1 TO 10 DO
         BEGIN
            write (Item[Page, Page, Column]:4);
            writeln; writeln
         END;
b. FOR Page := 1 TO 50 DO
      FOR Column := 1 TO 10 DO
         writeln (Item[Page, Column, Column]:(Column+4));
```

RUNNING AND DEBUGGING TIPS

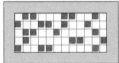

1. Use subrange types with descriptive identifiers for specifying index ranges. For example,

```
TYPE
   Page = 1 .. 50;
   Row = 1 .. 15;
   Column = 1 .. 10;
   Book = ARRAY [Page, Row, Column] OF real;
```

2. Develop and maintain a systematic method of processing nested loops. For example, students with a mathematical background will often use I, J, and K as index variables for a three-dimensional array.
3. Be careful to properly subscript multidimensional array components.
4. When reading data from a data file into a multidimensional array, use counters carefully to indicate which components are used.
5. When using an array of packed arrays as a list of strings, remember that in standard Pascal, strings must be read in one character at a time. However, strings can be written by a single **writeln** command.
6. When sorting one array in a program that uses parallel arrays, remember to make similar component exchanges in all arrays.
7. Define all data structures in the **TYPE** definition section so you do not get type mismatch errors when using subprograms.

■ **Summary**

Key Terms

two-dimensional array   higher-dimensional
parallel array   array

Key Concepts

■ Two-dimensional arrays can be declared in several ways; one descriptive method is

```
TYPE
   Chart4X6 = ARRAY [1 .. 4, 1 .. 6] OF real;
VAR
   Table : Chart4X6;
```

■ Nested loops are frequently used to **read** and **write** values in two-dimensional arrays; for example, data can be read by

```
FOR J := 1 TO 4 DO
   FOR K := 1 TO 6 DO
      read (Data, Table[J,K]);
```

- When processing the components of a single row or single column, leave the appropriate row or column index fixed and let the other index vary as a loop index; for example,

```
( sum row 3 )

Sum := 0;
FOR K := 1 TO NumOfColumns DO
   Sum := Sum + A[3,K];
```

```
( sum column 3 )

Sum := 0;
FOR J := 1 TO NumOfRows DO
   Sum := Sum + A[J,3];
```

- An array of strings in Pascal is a special case of a two-dimensional array; the data structure is an array of packed arrays and can be declared by

```
TYPE
   String20 = PACKED ARRAY [1 .. 20] OF char;
   NameList = ARRAY [1 .. 50] OF String20;
VAR
   Name : NameList;
```

- Arrays of strings (packed arrays of characters) can be alphabetized by using any valid sort.
- Three standard procedures used in programs that work with arrays of strings are (1) get the data, (2) alphabetize the array, and (3) print the alphabetized list.
- Parallel arrays are used to solve problems that require arrays of the same length that store different data types.
- A typical problem in which one would use parallel arrays involves working with a list of names and an associated list of numbers (for example, test scores).
- A typical data structure declaration for using names and scores is

```
TYPE
   String20 = PACKED ARRAY [1 .. 20] OF char;
   NameList = ARRAY [1 .. 30] OF String20;
   ScoreList = ARRAY [1 .. 30] OF integer;
VAR
   Name : NameList;
   Score : ScoreList;
```

- Data structures for solving problems can require arrays of three or more dimensions.
- A typical declaration for an array of three dimensions is

```
TYPE
   Dim1 = 1 .. 10;
   Dim2 = 1 .. 20;
   Dim3 = 1 .. 30;
   Block = ARRAY [Dim1, Dim2, Dim3] OF real;
VAR
   Item : Block;
```

In this array, a typical component is accessed by

```
Item[I,J,K]
```

■ Nested loops are frequently used when working with higher-dimensional arrays; for example, all values on the first level of array Item as just declared can be printed by

```
FOR J := 1 TO 20 DO
  BEGIN
    FOR K := 1 TO 30 DO
      BEGIN
        write (Item[1,J,K]:5:2);
        writeln
      END; (* of 1 line *)
    writeln
  END; (* of 20 lines *)
```

■ **Chapter Review Exercises**

For Exercises 1–6, using the following table

Table

5	8	12	9
4	6	1	10
11	2	7	3

indicate the value of the statement.

1. Table[3,2]   4. Table[2,1]
2. Table[1,3]   5. Table[3,3]
3. Table[3,4]   6. Table[1,4]

7. Write the necessary declarations for the table in Exercises 1–6.

8. Write a declaration for SampleTable using a **TYPE** definition in the declaration.

SampleTable

3	4	6	2	7
1	12	9	6	8

For Exercises 9–13, using SampleTable from Exercise 8, write the proper notation for the table position that contains the value listed.

9. 6   12. 12
10. 2   13. 8
11. 1

14. Suppose the contents of SampleTable (Exercise 8) are read from the following data lines.

```
3 4 6 2 7    1 12 9 6 8    ■
```

Write a fragment of code to read this data into the proper positions in the table.

15. Write a fragment of code to print SampleTable (Exercise 8) in tabular form.

16. Write a fragment of code to add the values in columns two through five in each row of SampleTable (Exercise 8) to the value in the column preceding it.

17. Write an appropriate procedure declaration and call from the main program to permit passing SampleTable (Exercise 8) to a procedure as a variable parameter.

18. Write an appropriate declaration for an array containing 50 names of up to 25 characters each.

19. Write an array declaration for a table that holds the responses to 50 multiple choice test items (letters A through E) for 100 students.

20. Write a procedure that permits input of data into the array declared in Exercise 19.

21. An array of names is stored in a table in the form

    Smith John

    Each name is 20 characters long. Write a procedure to get the names and print them in the form

    John Smith

22. Write array declarations for a list of 20 people (up to 25 characters per name), and their grade point averages (real numbers).

23. Write a fragment of code to read data into the arrays in Exercise 22. Assume each line of data consists of a name and a grade point average in the form

    ```
    Smith John* 3.89
    ```

24. Write a fragment of code to sort the arrays in Exercise 22 in order from highest GPA to lowest.

For Exercises 25–30, find any errors in the array declarations.

25. ```
TYPE
    Exercise25 : ARRAY [1 .. 20, 1 .. 30] OF integer;
```
26. ```
TYPE
    Exercise26 = ARRAY [1 .. 5, 1 .. 30] OF ArrayType;
```
27. ```
VAR
    Exercise27 : ARRAY [1 .. 5, 10 .. 20] OF integer;
```
28. ```
TYPE
    Exercise28 = PACKED ARRAY [10,20] OF char;
```
29. ```
TYPE
    Exercise29 = [1 .. 30, 1 .. 10] OF char;
```
30. ```
VAR
    Exercise30 : ARRAY [1 .. 10; -5 .. 5] OF integer;
```

31. Write **TYPE** and **ARRAY** declarations suitable for an array to hold records for a high school football team. Data consist of an opponent's name for each of ten games and a **boolean** variable; **true** indicates a win, **false** indicates a loss. Data are stored in the table for each of the last ten years.

■ Chapter Summary Program

Write a program to get a list of students' names and grades from a data file. The program should print an alphabetized list of names together with each student's grade. A first-level pseudocode development is

1. Get the data
2. Sort the names
3. Print a heading
4. Print the results

Using a procedure for each of these tasks, a complete program is

```
PROGRAM ClassList (input,output, Data);

(*********************************************************************

    This program illustrates the use of parallel arrays.
    One array is a list of student names. The other
    array is a list of grades for the students. Note
    modifications in the sort necessary for working
    with parallel arrays.

 ********************************************************************)

CONST
  ClassSize = 25;
TYPE
  String20 = PACKED ARRAY [1 .. 20] OF char;
  NameList = ARRAY [1 .. ClassSize] OF String20;
  GradeList = ARRAY [1 .. ClassSize] OF char;
VAR
  Student : NameList;  (*  Array of student names          *)
  Grade : GradeList;   (*  Array of student grades         *)
  Count : integer;     (*  Counter for number of students  *)
  Data: text;          (*  Text file for data              *)

(*   Procedure to get the data   *)

PROCEDURE GetData (VAR Name : NameList; VAR Gr : GradeList;
                   VAR Ct : integer);
  VAR
    K : integer;
  BEGIN
    reset (Data);
    Ct := 0;
    WHILE NOT eof (Data) DO
      BEGIN
        Ct := Ct + 1;
        FOR K := 1 TO 20 DO
          read(Data,Name [Ct,K]);
        readln(Data, Gr [Ct])
      END      (*   of input loop   *)
  END;     (*   of PROCEDURE GetData      *)

(*   Procedure to sort names using parallel arrays.   *)

PROCEDURE Sort (VAR Name : NameList; VAR Gr : GradeList;
                Ct : integer);
  VAR
    TempName : String20;
    TempGrade : char;
    J,K,Index : integer;
```

```
      BEGIN
        FOR J := 1 TO Ct-1 DO
          BEGIN
            TempName := Name[J];
            TempGrade := Gr[J];
            Index := J;
            FOR K := J+1 TO Ct DO
              IF Name[K] < TempName THEN
                BEGIN
                  TempName := Name[K];
                  TempGrade := Gr[K];
                  Index := K
                END;
            Name[Index] := Name[J];
            Gr[Index] := Gr[J];
            Name[J] := TempName;
            Gr[J] := TempGrade
          END
    END;      (*    of PROCEDURE Sort    *)

(*    Procedure to print a heading    *)

PROCEDURE PrintHeading;
  BEGIN
    writeln; writeln;
    writeln('Name':24,'Grade':23);
    writeln('____':24,'_____':23);
  END;      (*    of PROCEDURE PrintHeading    *)

(*    Procedure to print the list of names and grades    *)

PROCEDURE PrintData (Name : NameList; Gr : GradeList;
                     Ct : integer);
  VAR
    K : integer;
  BEGIN
    FOR K := 1 TO Ct DO
      BEGIN
        write('<':12,K:2,'>');
        writeln(Name[K]:25,Gr[K]:5)
      END;  (*    of FOR loop    *)
    writeln; writeln
  END;      (*    of PROCEDURE PrintData    *)

(*    Now start the main program    *)

BEGIN    (*  Main program    *)
  GetData(Student,Grade,Count);
  Sort(Student,Grade,Count);
  PrintHeading;
  PrintData(Student,Grade,Count)
END.  (*    of main program    *)
```

When this program is run on a sample list of names and grades, the output is

```
                  Name                      Grade
< 1>       Ashley  John                      B
< 2>       Carlson  Jennifer                 D
< 3>       Fang  Yen-Su                      A
< 4>       Jones  John                       D
< 5>       McCoy  Ann                        E
< 6>       Monahan  Gezelle                  C
< 7>       Olsen  Albert                     C
< 8>       Smith  Richard                    E
< 9>       Snyder  Martha                    A
<10>       Sullivan  Debbie                  B
<11>       Wrubel  Karla                     C
```

■ Programming Problems

1. The local high school sports boosters are conducting a fund drive to help raise money for the athletic program. As each donation is received, the person's name and amount of donation are entered on one line in a data file. Write a program to

   a. Print an alphabetized list of all donors together with their corresponding donation.
   b. Print a list of donations from high to low together with the donors' names.
   c. Compute and print the average and total of all donations.

2. Failing to meet the original goal, your local high school sports boosters (Problem 1) are at it again. For their second effort, each donor's name and donation are added as a separate line at the end of the previously sorted list. Write a program to produce lists, the sum, and average as in Problem 1. No donor's name should appear more than once in a list.

3. Mr. Lae Z. Programmer now expects you to write a program to do all record keeping for the class. For each student, consecutive lines of the data file contain the student's name, ten quiz scores, six program scores, and three examination scores. Your output should include

   a. An alphabetized list together with
      ▪ quiz total
      ▪ program total
      ▪ examination total
      ▪ total points
      ▪ percentage grade
      ▪ letter grade
   b. The overall class average
   c. A histogram depicting the grade distribution

4. The All Metro Basketball Conference consists of ten teams. The conference commissioner has created a data file in which each line contains one school's name, location, and nickname for the school team. You are to write a program to read this data and then produce three lists, each of which contains all information about the school. All lists are to be sorted alphabetically, the first by school name, the second by school location, and the third by nickname.

5. Mountain-Air Commuters, Inc., is a small airline commuter service. Each of their planes is a 30-passenger plane with a floor plan as follows:

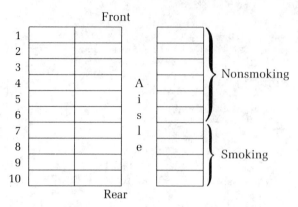

Write a program that assigns seats to passengers on a first-come, first-served basis according to the following rules:

a. Smoking and nonsmoking requests must be honored; if seats in the requested sections are all full, the customer's name should go on a waiting list for the next flight.

b. Specific seat requests should be honored next; if a requested seat is occupied, the person should be placed in the same row, if possible.

c. If a requested row is filled, the passenger should be seated as far forward as possible.

d. If all seats are filled, the passenger's name is put on a waiting list for the next flight.

Output should include a seating chart with passenger names appropriately printed and a waiting list for the next flight. Each data line (input) contains the passenger's name, smoking (S) or nonsmoking (N) designation, and seat request indicating the row and column desired.

6. Upgrade the program for Mountain-Air Commuters, Inc. (Problem 5) so it can be used for each of five daily flights. Passengers on a waiting list must be processed first. Print a seating chart for each flight.

7. Salespersons at McHenry Tool Corporation are given a monthly commission check. The commission is computed by multiplying the salesperson's gross monthly sales by the person's commission rate.

Write a program to compute a salesperson's monthly commission computed to the nearest penny. The program should prepare a list of all salespersons in descending order based on monthly commission earned (the person earning the highest commission on top). Each salesperson's commission should be printed next to his or her name. At the bottom of the list, indicate the total monthly commission (summed across all salespersons) and the average commission per salesperson. McHenry never employs more than 60 salespersons.

Any names of persons who have invalid data should be printed out separately. Data are invalid if the commission rate is not between 0.01 and 0.50, or if the gross monthly sales figure is negative.

8. In order to reduce their costs, the McHenry Tool Corporation (Problem 7) is switching from monthly to biannual commission checks. The commission is now computed by multiplying a person's commission rate by the sum of his or her gross monthly sales for a six-month period.

The McHenry Tool Corporation has asked that you develop the necessary computer program. The program should differ from Problem 7 in the following ways:

a. Each name on the output should be followed by the six figures for gross monthly sales. The columns should be labeled "January" through "June". Total six-month gross sales should be given next, followed by rate of commission, and amount of six-month commission check to the nearest penny.

b. Commission rates are based on gross six-month sales. If sales are less than $20,000, the commission rate is 3 percent. If sales are at least $20,000 but less than $40,000, the commission rate is 5 percent. If sales are at least $40,000 but less than $60,000, the commission rate is 5.5 percent. If sales are at least $60,000 but less than $80,000, the commission rate is 6 percent. If sales are at least $80,000 but less than $90,000, the commission rate is 6.5 percent. If sales are at least $90,000, the commission rate is 8 percent.

c. At the bottom of each column, the program should provide the total and the mean for that column (the column for commission rates does not require a total, only a mean).

9. The dean of a small undergraduate college has asked you to write a program to figure grade point average for an unknown number of students.

The output should be an alphabetized roster showing the sex, identification number (social security number), grade point average (rounded to three decimal places), and class status (freshman, sophomore, junior, or senior) for each student.

The data provides the name, sex (M or F), social security number (ID), and number of semesters completed. Also provided is the number of courses taken, along with the letter grade and number of credits for each course. The possible letter grades are "A" (4 points), "B" (3 points), "C" (2 points), "D" (1 point), and "E" (0 points).

Class status is determined by the number of credits as follows:

1–25 credits	Freshman
26–55 credits	Sophomore
56–85 credits	Junior
86 or more credits	Senior

10. You have just started work for the Michigan Association of Automobile Manufacturers and are asked to analyze sales data on five subcompact cars for the last six months. Your analysis should be in table form and should include the name of each make and model, a model's sales volume for each month, a model's total and average sales volume for six months, a model's total sales revenue for six months, and the total and average sales volume for each month. In addition, your output should include the total and average sales volume of all models for the entire six months and the make and model name of the car with the largest total sales revenue and the amount of that revenue.

11. You have been asked to write a program to assist with the inventory and ordering for Tite-Jeans, Inc. They manufacture three styles: straight, flair, and peg. In each style, waist sizes vary from 24 to 46 and inseams vary from 26 to 40. Write a program to

Read in the starting inventory.
Read in daily sales.

c. Print the ending inventory for each style.

d. Print order charts for each style that is low in stock (fewer than three).

e. Print an emergency order list for those that are out of stock.

12. Thomas H. Holmes and R. H. Rabe developed a Social Readjustment Rating Scale of 43 items that they feel measure the effect of stress on mental and physical health. Of those people with over 300 life-change units for the past year, almost 80 percent get sick in the near future; with 150 to 299 units, about 50 percent get sick in the near future; and with fewer than 150 units, only about 30 percent get sick in the near future.

Using the following model, write a program to read data for several individuals and produce a table listing the Life Event, Mean Value, and Personal Value for each individual. Each person should also have a total listed together with a susceptibility prediction.

Life Event	Mean Value
1. Death of spouse	100
2. Divorce	73
3. Marital separation	65
4. Jail term	63
5. Death of close family member	63
6. Personal injury or illness	53
7. Marriage	50
8. Fired at work	47
9. Marital reconciliation	45
10. Retirement	45
11. Change in health of family member	44
12. Pregnancy	40
13. Sex difficulties	39
14. Gain of new family member	39
15. Business readjustment	39
16. Change in financial state	38
17. Death of close friend	37
18. Change to different line of work	36
19. Change in number of arguments with spouse	35
20. Mortgage over $10,000	31
21. Foreclosure of mortgage or loan	30
22. Change in responsibilities at work	29
23. Son or daughter leaving home	29
24. Trouble with in-laws	29
25. Outstanding personal achievement	28
26. Spouse begins or stops work	26
27. Begin or end school	26
28. Change in living conditions	25
29. Revision of personal habits	24
30. Trouble with boss	23
31. Change in work hours or conditions	20
32. Change in residence	20
33. Change in schools	20
34. Change in recreation	19
35. Change in church activities	19
36. Change in social activities	18
37. Mortgage or lien less than $10,000	17
38. Change in sleeping habits	16

Life Event	Mean Value
39. Change in number of family get-togethers	15
40. Change in eating habits	15
41. Vacation	13
42. Christmas	12
43. Minor violations of the law	11

Reproduced by permission of Thomas H. Holmes, M.D., Professor of Psychiatry and Behavioral Sciences, University of Washington, Seattle, and Pergamon Press, Inc., in whose *Journal of Psychosomatic Research* the scale was first published.

13. A few members (total unknown, but no more than 25) at Oakland Mountain Country Club want to computerize their golf scores. Each member plays 20 games, some 18 holes and some 9 holes. Each member's name (no more than 20 characters) is written on a data card, followed by 20 scores on a second card. Each score is immediately followed by an 'E' or an 'N', indicating 18 or 9 holes, respectively.

    Write a program to read all the names and scores into two parallel two-dimensional arrays. Calculate everyone's 18-hole average. (Double the 9-hole scores before you store them in the array and treat as 18-hole scores.) Calculate how much each average is over or under par (par is 72 and should be declared as a constant). Output should be each name, average, difference from par, and scores.

14. Write a program to keep statistics for a basketball team consisting of 15 players. Statistics for each player should include shots attempted, shots made, and shooting percentage; free throws attempted, free throws made, and free throw percentage; offensive rebounds and defensive rebounds; assists; turnovers; and total points. Appropriate team totals should be listed as part of the output.

15. A magic square is a square array of positive integers such that the sum of each row, column, and diagonal is the same constant. For example,

16	3	2	13
5	10	11	8
9	6	7	12
4	15	14	1

is a magic square whose constant is 34.

    Write a program to have as input four lines of four positive integers. The program should then determine whether or not the array is a magic square.

16. Pascal's Triangle can be used to recognize coefficients of a quantity raised to a power. The rules for forming this triangle of integers are such that each row must start and end with a one, and each entry in a row is the sum of the two values diagonally above the new entry. Thus, four rows of Pascal's Triangle are

```
        1

      1   1

    1   2   1

  1   3   3   1
```

This triangle can be used as a convenient way to get the coefficients of a quantity of two terms raised to a power (binomial coefficients) by referencing the (power + 1) row. For example,

$$(a + b)^3 = 1 \times a^3 + 3a^2b + 3ab^2 + 1 \times b^3$$

where the coefficients 1, 3, 3, and 1 come from the fourth row of Pascal's Triangle.

Write a complete program to print out Pascal's Triangle for ten rows.

17. Your principal has once again come to you for help. He wants you to develop a program to maintain a list of the 20 students in your school with the highest scores on the SAT test. Input is from a text file containing the name (20 characters), and the total SAT score (verbal plus mathematical). Write a program which, when all data have been read, prints out a list of the 20 highest scores from highest to lowest, and the students' names. You may assume that no two students have the same score.

18. The transpose of a matrix (table) is a new matrix with the row and column positions reversed. That is, the transpose of matrix A, an M by N matrix is an N by M matrix, with each element, A[m,n] stored in B[n,m]. Given a 3 × 5 matrix of integers, create a matrix which is its transpose. Print both the original matrix and the new matrix.

19. Mr. Laven, the mathematics teacher at your school, wants you to write a program to help him keep his students' grades. He wants to keep track of up to 30 grades for each of up to 35 students. Your program should read grades and names from a text file, and then print the following:
   a. A table showing the names in alphabetical order and grades received by each student.
   b. An alphabetical list of students with their total points and average score.
   c. A list of averages from highest to lowest with corresponding students' names.

20. Write a program in which a person can enter data into a 5 × 7 matrix. Print the original matrix along with the average of each row and column.

21. Matrix M is symmetric if it has the same number of rows as columns, and if each element M[x,y] is equal to M[y,x]. Write a program to check a matrix entered by the user to see if it is symmetric or not.

22. The table below shows the total sales for salespeople of the Falcon Manufacturing Company.

Salesperson	Week 1	Week 2	Week 3	Week 4
Anna, Michael	30	25	45	18
Henderson, Marge	22	30	32	35
Johnson, Fred	12	17	19	15
Striker, Nancy	32	30	33	31
Ryan, Renee	22	17	28	16

The price of the product being sold is $1,985.95. Write a program which permits the input of the data above, and prints both a replica of the original table and a table showing the dollar value of sales for each individual during each week along with their total sales. Also, print the total sales for each week and the total sales for the company.

23. Your high school office wants a computerized system for finding telephone numbers of students. The program should read a list of up to 20 students and

their telephone numbers from a text file. It should permit the entry of a student's name, and then print the name and telephone number. (A binary search could be used for this.) If the name is not found, an appropriate message should be printed.

24. Write a program to permit two people to play the game of Battleship. Your program should record the ship positions, hits, misses, and ship sinkings for each player.

25. Rewrite the Battleship program (Problem 24) to have a person play against the computer.

CHAPTER 11

Records

The previous two chapters dealt extensively with the concept of a structured data type: arrays. Recall that when you declare an array, you reserve a predetermined number of variables. Each of these variables is of the same base type and can be accessed by reference to the index of an array element.

All components of an array must be of the same data type; this is a serious limitation since there are many situations in which this is not possible. For example, a bank may wish to keep a record of the name, address, telephone number, marital status, social security number, annual salary, total assets, and total liabilities of each customer. Fortunately, Pascal provides another structured data type, **RECORD**, which allows such information to be stored, accessed, and manipulated. A record contains fields, which can be of different data types. This chapter shows you how to declare records, how to access the various fields within a record, and how to work with arrays of records.

■ 11.1
**Record
Definitions**

OBJECTIVES

■ to understand the
   basic idea of

RECORD as a Structured Data Type

A *record* is a collection of *fields* that may be treated as a whole or individually. To illustrate, a record that contains fields for a customer's name, age, and annual income can be visualized as shown in Figure 11.1. This schematic representation may help you understand why a record is considered a structured data type and familiarize you with the idea of using fields in a record.

Declaring a RECORD

Let's now consider our first example of a formally declared record. Assume we want a record to contain a customer's name, age, and annual income. The following declaration can be made.

```
VAR
   Customer : RECORD
                 Name : PACKED ARRAY [1 . . 30] OF char;
                 Age : integer;
                 AnnualIncome : real
              END; (* of RECORD definition *)
```

Another method of declaring a record is to use the **TYPE** definition section to define an appropriate record type. This form is preferable because it facilitates use with subprograms. Thus, we can have

```
TYPE
   CustomerInfo = RECORD
                 Name : PACKED ARRAY [1 . . 30] OF char;
                 Age : integer;
                 AnnualIncome : real
              END; (* of RECORD definition *)
VAR
   Customer : CustomerInfo;
```

Components of a record are called fields and each field has an associated data type. The general form for defining a record data type using the **TYPE** definition section is

---

TYPE
    type identifier = **RECORD**
                        field identifier 1 : data type 1;
                        field identifier 2 : data type 2;
                             .
                             .
                             .
                      field identifier n : data type n
                    END; (* of **RECORD** definition *)

The syntax diagram for this is

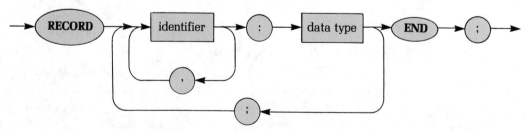

The following comments are in order concerning this form.

    1. The type identifier can be any valid identifier. It should be descriptive to enhance program readability.

FIGURE 11.1
Fields in a record

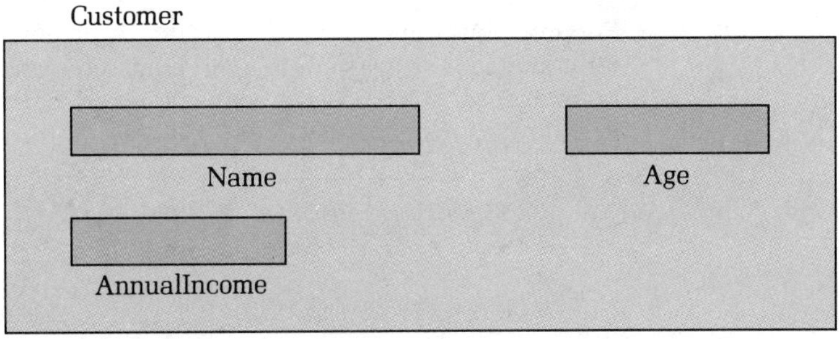

2. The reserved word **RECORD** must precede the field identifiers.
3. Each field identifier within a record must be unique. However, field identifiers in different records may use the same name. Thus,

```
FirstRecord = RECORD
                Name : PACKED ARRAY [1 .. 30] OF char;
                Age : integer
              END; (* of RECORD definition *)
```

and

```
SecondRecord = RECORD
                 Name : PACKED ARRAY [1 .. 30] OF char;
                 Age : integer;
                 IQ : integer
               END; (* of RECORD definition *)
```

can both be defined in the same program. Since this can lead to confusion, it is suggested that you avoid doing this.
4. Data types for fields can be user-defined. Thus, our earlier definitions could have been

```
TYPE
  String30 = PACKED ARRAY [1 .. 30] OF char;
  CustomerInfo = RECORD
                   Name : String30;
                   Age : integer;
                   AnnualIncome : real
                 END; (* of RECORD definition *)
VAR
  Customer : CustomerInfo;
```

5. **END;** is required to signify the end of a **RECORD** definition. This is the second instance (remember **CASE**?) in which **END** is used without a **BEGIN.**
6. Fields of the same base type can be declared together. Thus,

```
Info = RECORD
         Name : String30;
         Age, IQ : integer
       END; (* of RECORD Info *)
```

is appropriate. However, you are encouraged to list each field separately to enhance readability and reinforce the concept of fields in a record.

EXAMPLE 11.1 Suppose you want to keep a record for a student; the record is to contain a field for a student's name (Smith Jane), homeroom (127), class status (Sr), and grade point average (3.27). We can define a record and declare an appropriate variable as follows:

```
TYPE
    String30 = PACKED ARRAY [1 . . 30] OF char;
    Class = (Fr, So, Jr, Sr);

    StudentInfo = RECORD
                    Name : String30;
                    Homeroom : integer;
                    Status : Class;
                    GPA : real
                  END;  (* of RECORD definition *)
VAR
    Student : StudentInfo;
```

Illustrate the record declared in Example 11.1 and show what data might typically be used in each field.

Fields in a Record

Now that you know how to define a record, you need to examine how to access fields in a record. For our discussion, let's consider a record defined by

```
TYPE
    String30 = PACKED ARRAY [1 . . 30] OF char;

    Employee = RECORD
                    Name : String30;
                    Age : integer;
                    MaritalStatus : char;
                    Wage : real
                  END;  (* of RECORD definition *)
VAR
    Programmer : Employee;
```

Programmer can be visualized as pictured in Figure 11.2. Each field within a record is a variable and can be uniquely identified by

> record name.field name

Thus, the four field variables are

```
Programmer.Name
Programmer.Age
Programmer.MaritalStatus
Programmer.Wage
```

FIGURE 11.2
Defined fields in
Programmer

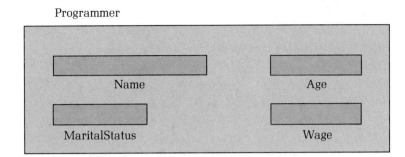

Each of these variables may be used in any manner consistent with the defined base type. To illustrate, suppose Programmer.Name and Programmer.Age are assigned values and you wish to print the names of those employees under 30 years of age. You can have a fragment of code such as

```
IF Programmer.Age < 30 THEN
    writeln (Programmer.Name:40);
```

If you wish to compute gross salary, you might have

```
read (Hours);
Gross := Hours * Programmer.Wage;
```

STYLE TIP

Use descriptive field names, appropriate subranges, and a descriptive variable name when defining records. For example, if you want a record with fields for a student's name, age, sex, and class status, you can use

```
TYPE
    String20 = PACKED ARRAY [1 . . 20] OF char;
    StudentRecord = RECORD
                        Name : String20;
                        Age : 0 . . 99;
                        Sex : (Male, Female);
                        ClassStatus : (Fr,So,Jr,Sr)
                    END;  (* of RECORD definition *)
VAR
    Student : StudentRecord;
```

The fields would then be

```
Student.Name
Student.Age
Student.Sex
Student.ClassStatus
```

and you can use program statements such as

```
IF Student.Sex = Male THEN
```
or
```
IF Student.Age < 21 THEN
```

Computer Industry Growth

In a recent article discussing growth of the computer industry, Joseph J. Kroger, president of Computer Systems Division of Sperry Corporation, stated: "Today we accept as commonplace reports of office and factory managers who respond to crucial problems uncovered by a computer programmed to read printed material with an optical scanner that picks out key words and phrases demanding immediate attention. Or of doctors who turn to computers that not only diagnose diseases with incredible accuracy but also prescribe treatment. Or of geologists who use computers to locate the exact site of valuable oil and mineral deposits.

"But exciting as those applications are,

there's little doubt that the best is yet to come. Expert systems—programs that perform at the level of human experts—utilize a process known as knowledge engineering to combine textbook learning with the insights that come only from experience, then set about working tirelessly to sort through thousands of 'if, then' rules of thumb and form a reasoned judgment. The implications for problem solving in such diverse fields as mathematics, science, and engineering are staggering.

"Combine these systems with mechanical creatures that operate independently—robots—and you've added a whole new dimension to the workplace."

SELF QUIZ 11.2   Assume a record is defined by

```
TYPE
    String20 = PACKED ARRAY [1 . . 20] OF char;
    Info = RECORD
                Name : String20;
                Age : integer
            END;  (*  of RECORD definition  *)
VAR
    Student : Info;
```

Show how a student's name can be read into the appropriate field. Assume 20 positions in the data file are used for the name.

Other Fields

Thus far, our fields have been declared in a relatively direct fashion. This is not always the case. Sometimes, when establishing the structure of a record, the data type of a field needs more development. For example, suppose you wish to declare a record for each student in a class and the record is to contain student name, class name, four test scores, ten quiz scores, final average, and letter grade. This can be visualized as shown in Figure 11.3. In this case, Test and Quiz are both arrays. Thus, a subsequent development is shown in Figure 11.4. This record can now be formally defined by

```
TYPE
    String30 = PACKED ARRAY [1 . . 30] OF char;
    String10 = PACKED ARRAY [1 . . 10] OF char;
    TestScores = ARRAY [1 . . 4] OF integer;
    QuizScores = ARRAY [1 . . 10] OF integer;
```

FIGURE 11.3
Fields in Student

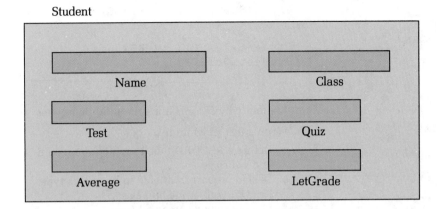

FIGURE 11.4
Fields in Student
with arrays

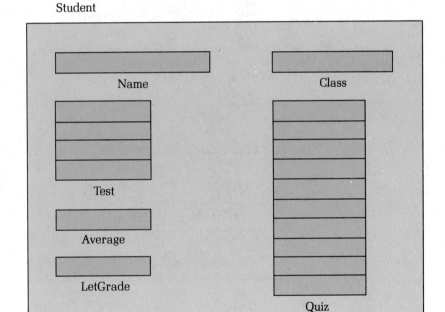

```
StudentInfo = RECORD
                 Name : String30;
                 Class : String10;
                 Test : TestScores;
                 Quiz : QuizScores;
                 Average : real;
                 LetGrade : char
              END; (* of RECORD definition *)
VAR
   Student : StudentInfo;
```

If the student associated with this record earned an 89 on the first test
and a 9 (out of 10) on the first quiz, this information can be entered by
reading the values or by assigning them appropriately. Thus, either of the
following suffice.

```
            read (Student.Test[1], Student.Quiz[1]);
or

            Student.Test[1] := 89;
            Student.Quiz[1] :=  9;
```

Exercises 11.1

1. Explain why records are structured data types.

2. Write a test program to
   a. Define a **RECORD** type in which the record contains fields for your name and your age.
   b. Declare a record variable to be of this type.
   c. Read in your name and age.
   d. Print out your name and age.

3. Discuss the similarities and differences between arrays and records as structured data types.

For Exercises 4–6, use the **TYPE** definition section to define a **RECORD** for the record illustrated. Also declare a record variable to be of the defined type.

4.   TeamMember

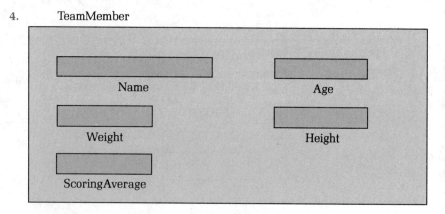

5.   Book

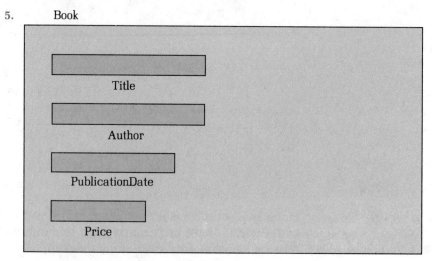

6.   Student

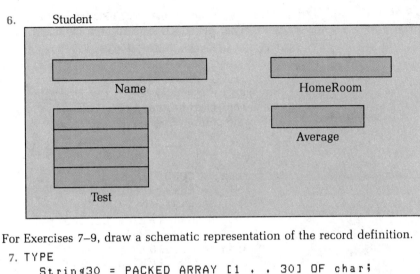

For Exercises 7–9, draw a schematic representation of the record definition.

7. TYPE
```
    String30 = PACKED ARRAY [1 . . 30] OF char;
    String11 = PACKED ARRAY [1 . . 11] OF char;
    EmployeeInfo = RECORD
                        Name : String30;
                        SSN : String11;
                        NumOfDep : integer;
                        HourlyWage : real
                     END;  (*  of RECORD definition  *)
  VAR
    Employee : EmployeeInfo;
```

8. TYPE
```
    HouseInfo = RECORD
                     Location : PACKED ARRAY [1 . . 20]
                                        OF char;
                     Age : integer;
                     NumRooms : integer;
                     NumBaths : integer;
                     BuildingType : (Brick, Frame);
                     Taxes : real;
                     Price : real
                  END;  (*  of RECORD definition  *)
  VAR
    House : HouseInfo;
```

9. TYPE
```
    String20 = PACKED ARRAY [1 . . 20] OF char;
    String30 = PACKED ARRAY [1 . . 30] OF char;
    String8 = PACKED ARRAY [1 . . 8] OF char;
    PhoneBook = RECORD
                     Name : String30;
                     Address : ARRAY [1 . . 4]
                                     OF String20;
                     PhoneNum : String8
                  END;  (*  of RECORD definition  *)
  VAR
    PhoneListing : PhoneBook;
```

For Exercises 10 and 11, use the **TYPE** definition section to define an appropriate **RECORD** type. Also declare an appropriate record variable.

10. Families in a school district: each record should contain the last name, parents' first and last names, address, number of children, and the ages of children.

11. Students in a school system: each record should contain the student's name, homeroom, classification (Fr, So, Jr, or Sr), courses being taken (at most six), and grade point average.

For Exercises 12–14, find all errors in the definitions or declarations.

12. ```
TYPE
    Info : RECORD
            Name = PACKED ARRAY [1 . . 30] OF char;
            Age : 0 . . 100
            END; (* of RECORD definition *)
```
13. ```
TYPE
    Member = RECORD
                Age : integer;
                IQ : integer
                END;  (*  of RECORD definition  *)
VAR
    Member : Member;
```
14. ```
VAR
    Member = RECORD
            Name : PACKED ARRAY [1 . . 30] OF char;
            Age : 0 . . 100;
            IQ = 50 . . 200
            END; (* of RECORD definition *)
```

In Exercises 15–26, given the record defined by

```
TYPE
    String30 = PACKED ARRAY [1 . . 30] OF char;
    Weekdays = (Mon, Tues, Wed, Thur, Fri);
    ListOfScores = ARRAY [1 . . 5] OF integer;
    Info = RECORD
            Name : String30;
            Day : Weekdays;
            Score : ListOfScores;
            Average : real
            END;  (*  of RECORD definition  *)
VAR
    Contestant : Info;
```

assume values are assigned as indicated in Figure 11.5. Indicate if the exercise is valid. If invalid, explain why.

15. ```Day := Wed;```
16. ```Contestant.Day := Wed;```
17. ```Score := 70;```
18. ```Score[3] := 70;```
19. ```Contestant.Score[3] := 70;```
20. ```Contestant[3].Score := 70;```
21. ```
FOR J := 1 TO 5 DO
    Sum := Sum + Contestant.Score[J];
```

FIGURE 11.5
Values in fields of
Contestant

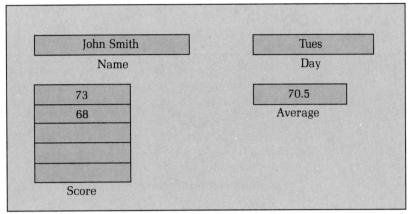

```
22. Contestant,Score[3] := Score[2];
23. Contestant,Score[3] := Contestant,Score[2] + 3;
24. Average := (Score[1] + Score[2] + Score[3])/3;
25. IF Contestant,Day < Wed THEN
        Contestant,Average := Contestant,Score[1] +
                              Contestant,Score[2];
26. writeln(Contestant,Name:40,Contestant,Average:10:2);
```

■ 11.2
Using Records

OBJECTIVES

- to use **WITH ... DO** when using records in a program
- to copy complete records
- to use a procedure to read data into a record
- to use a procedure to print data from a record

The previous section introduced you to the concept of **RECORD** as a structured data type. At this stage, you should be comfortable with this concept and be able to use the **TYPE** definition section to define such a data type. In this section, we examine methods of working with records.

WITH ... DO Using Records

Let's consider a record that contains fields for a student's name, three test scores, and test average. It can be defined by

```
TYPE
   String20 = PACKED ARRAY [1 , , 20] OF char;
   List3 = ARRAY [1 , , 3] OF integer;
   StudentRecord = RECORD
                       Name : String20;
                       Score : List3;
                       Average : real
                    END; (* of RECORD StudentRecord *)
VAR
   Student : StudentRecord;
```

and envisioned as shown in Figure 11.6. To use this record, we need to assign or read data into appropriate fields. Therefore, assume a line of data in the textfile named Data is

| Washington Joe | 79 83 94 |

FIGURE 11.6
Fields in Student

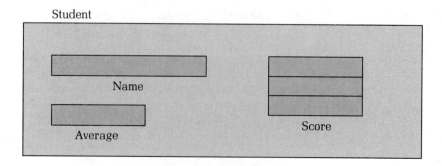

This data can be read by the fragment of code

```
FOR J := 1 TO 20 DO
  read (Data, Student.Name[J]);
FOR J := 1 TO 3 DO
  read (Data, Student.Score[J]);
readln (Data);
```

The average can be computed by

```
Student.Average := (Student.Score[1] + Student.Score[2] +
                    Student.Score[3])/3;
```

Notice that each field identifier includes the record name. Fortunately, when working with fields of a record, Pascal provides a more convenient method of referring to these fields: a **WITH** . . . **DO** statement. Using this option, the previous fragment can be rewritten as

```
WITH Student DO
  BEGIN
    FOR J := 1 TO 20 DO
      read (Data, Name[J]);
    FOR J := 1 TO 3 DO
      read (Data, Score[J]);
    readln (Data);
    Average := (Score[1] + Score[2] + Score[3])/3
  END;  (*  of WITH . . . DO  *)
```

Formally, a **WITH** . . . **DO** statement has the form

WITH record name **DO**
  BEGIN
    statement 1;
    statement 2;
    .
    .
    .
    statement *n*
  END;

where the statement used may refer to the field identifiers but do not include the record name as part of the field identifier.

As a second illustration, suppose you have a record defined as

```
TYPE
   String20 = PACKED ARRAY [1 . . 20] OF char;
   PatientInfo = RECORD
                     Name : String20;
                     Age : integer;
                     Height : integer;
                     Weight : integer;
                     Sex : char
                 END; (* of RECORD PatientInfo *)
VAR
   Patient : PatientInfo;
```

Values can be assigned to the various fields specifically by

```
Patient.Name := 'Jones Connie       ';
Patient.Age := 19;
Patient.Height := 67;
Patient.Weight := 125;
Patient.Sex := 'F';
```

or by

```
WITH Patient DO
   BEGIN
     Name := 'Jones Connie       ';
     Age := 19;
     Height := 67;
     Weight := 125;
     Sex := 'F'
   END;
```

A single **WITH** ... **DO** statement can be used with more than one record. For example, using the previous two record definitions, it is possible to write

```
WITH Student, Patient DO
   BEGIN
     Average := (Score[1] + Score[2] + Score[3])/3;
     Age := 19
   END;
```

However, when using more than one record in a single **WITH** ... **DO** statement, each field identifier should have a unique reference to exactly one of the listed records. If a field identifier is used in more than one of the records, the reference may be ambiguous and an error may result. Thus, in the preceding two records,

```
WITH Student, Patient DO
      writeln (Name);
```

is incorrect and could produce a result different from what you expect; it is not clear whether the reference is to Student.Name or Patient.Name. In some versions of Pascal, this is a compilation error. In others, it is a design error and does not produce either a run-time error or a compilation error. Thus, while you might want to print Student.Name, you would print Patient.Name instead. This is because successive identifiers used as we just have are treated as if they are nested.

Assume Patient1 and Patient2 are both records of type PatientInfo. Explain what is wrong with the following:

```
Patient1.Name := 'Smith John          ';
Patient2.Name := 'Jones Mary          ';
WITH Patient1, Patient2 DO
    Age := 21;
```

Copying Records

How can information contained in one record be transferred to another record? We need to do this when, for example, we want to sort an array of records. To illustrate how records can be copied, consider the following definitions and declarations.

```
TYPE
  InfoA = RECORD
            Field1 : integer;
            Field2 : real;
            Field3 : char
          END;  (*  of RECORD InfoA  *)

  InfoB = RECORD
            Field1 : integer;
            Field2 : real;
            Field3 : char
          END;  (*  of RECORD InfoB  *)
VAR
  Rec1, Rec2 : InfoA;
  Rec3 : InfoB;
```

The three records declared can be envisioned as shown in Figure 11.7. Now, suppose data are assigned to Rec1 by

```
WITH Rec1 DO
  BEGIN
    Field1 := 25;
    Field2 := 89.5;
    Field3 := 'M'
  END;
```

These data can be copied to the corresponding fields of Rec2 by

```
Rec2 := Rec1;
```

This single assignment statement accomplishes all the following.

```
Rec2.Field1 := Rec1.Field1;
Rec2.Field2 := Rec1.Field2;
Rec2.Field3 := Rec1.Field3;
```

It is important to note that such an assignment can only be made when the records are of identical type. For example, notice that InfoA and InfoB have the same structure but are defined as different types. In this case, if you wish to assign the values in the fields of Rec1 to the corresponding fields of Rec3, the statement

```
Rec3 := Rec1;
```

FIGURE 11.7
Copying records

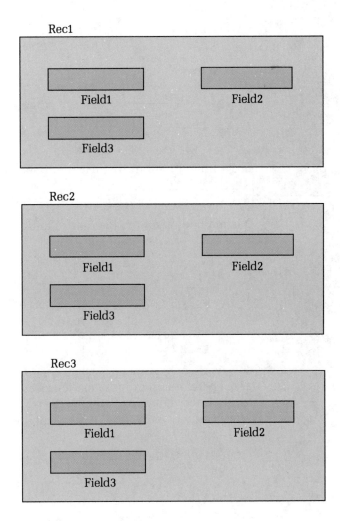

FIGURE 11.7
Copying records

produces a compilation error. Although Rec1 and Rec3 have the same structure, they are not of identical type. In this case, the information can be transferred by

```
WITH Rec3 DO
   BEGIN
      Field1 := Rec1.Field1;
      Field2 := Rec1.Field2;
      Field3 := Rec1.Field3
   END;
```

Reading Data into a Record

Once a record has been defined for a program, an early task is to get data into the record. This is usually accomplished by reading from a data file. To illustrate, assume we have a record defined by

```
TYPE
   String20 = PACKED ARRAY [1 . . 20] OF char;
```

```
PatientInfo = RECORD
                 Name : String20;
                 Age : integer;
                 Height : integer;
                 Weight : integer;
                 Sex : char
              END; (* of RECORD PatientInfo *)
VAR
      Patient : PatientInfo;
```

and a line of data in the text file, Data, is

Smith Mary	21 67 125F

One method of getting the data is to use a **WITH** ... **DO** statement in the main body of a program such as

```
BEGIN  (* Main program *)
   WITH Patient DO
      BEGIN
        FOR J := 1 TO 20 DO
           read (Data, Name[J]);
        readln (Data, Age, Height, Weight, Sex)
      END; (* of WITH . . . DO *)
```

However, good program design would have us use a procedure for this task. Therefore, in order to use a procedure, we must be careful to use the user-defined data type PatientInfo and a variable parameter in the procedure heading. With these two considerations, an appropriate procedure is

```
PROCEDURE GetData (VAR Pat : PatientInfo);
   VAR
      J : integer;
   BEGIN
      WITH Pat DO
         BEGIN
           FOR J := 1 TO 20 DO
              read (Data, Name[J]);
           readln (Data, Age, Height, Weight, Sex)
         END (* of WITH . . . DO *)
   END; (* of PROCEDURE GetData *)
```

This is called from the main program by

```
GetData (Patient);
```

As a second example of getting data for a record, suppose you are writing a program to be used to compute grades of students in a class. As part of the program, a record type can be declared as

```
CONST
   MaxName = 20;
   NumQuizzes = 10;
   NumTests = 4;
```

```
TYPE
  String20 = PACKED ARRAY [1 . . MaxName] OF char;
  QuizList = ARRAY [1 . . NumQizzes] OF integer;
  TestList = ARRAY [1 . . NumTests] OF integer;
  StudentRecord = RECORD
                    Name : String20;
                    Quiz : QuizList;
                    Test : TestList;
                    QuizTotal : integer;
                    TestAverage : real;
                    LetterGrade : 'A' . . 'E'
                  END;  (*  of RECORD StudentRecord  *)
VAR
  Student : StudentRecord;
```

If each line of data contains a student's name, ten quiz scores, and four test scores and looks like

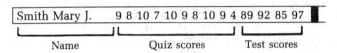

Smith Mary J.	9 8 10 7 10 9 8 10 9 4	89 92 85 97
Name	Quiz scores	Test scores

a procedure to get this data can be

```
PROCEDURE GetData (VAR Stu : StudentRecord);
  VAR
    J : integer;
  BEGIN
    WITH Stu DO
      BEGIN
        FOR J := 1 TO MaxName DO
          read (Data, Name[J]);
        FOR J := 1 TO NumQuizzes DO
          read (Data, Quiz[J]);
        FOR J := 1 TO NumTests DO
          read (Data, Test[J])
      END;  (*  of WITH . . . DO  *)
    readln
  END;  (*  of PROCEDURE GetData  *)
```

It is called from the main program by

```
GetData (Student);
```

Let's now continue this example by writing a function to compute the test average for a student. Since this average is found by using the four test scores in the record, such a function is

```
FUNCTION TestAv (T : TestList) : real;
  VAR
    J : integer;
    Sum : integer;
  BEGIN
    Sum := 0;
```

```
              FOR J := 1 TO NumTests DO
                 Sum := Sum + T[J];
              TestAv := Sum/NumTests
           END;  (*  of FUNCTION TestAv  *)
```

Since the array of test scores was the only parameter sent to the function and the average would normally be stored in the field TestAverage, this function can be called by

```
    Student.TestAverage := TestAv (Student.Test);
```

Some teachers throw out the lowest test score when computing the test average. Assume a record Student of type StudentRecord is declared and data are read into appropriate fields. Write a function to compute the test average omitting the lowest test score.

Printing Data from a Record

After information is assigned or read from a data file and appropriate calculations are made, you will want to print information from the record. Since this is frequently done in a procedure, let's assume the previous record for a student has the values illustrated in Figure 11.8. If you want the output for a student to be

```
    Name:         Smith Mary J.
    Quiz Scores:  9 8 10 7 10 9 8 10 9 10
    Quiz Total:   90
    Test Scores:  89 92 85 97
    Test Average: 90.75
    Letter Grade: A
```

a procedure to produce this is

```
PROCEDURE PrintData (Stu : StudentRecord);
   CONST
     Skip = ' ';
   VAR
     J : integer;
   BEGIN
     writeln; writeln;
     WITH Stu DO
       BEGIN
         writeln (Skip:10, 'Name:', Name:29);
         write (Skip:10, 'Quiz Scores:');
           FOR J := 1 TO 10 DO
             write (Quiz[J]:3);
           writeln;
           writeln (Skip:10, 'Quiz Total:', QuizTotal:5);
           write (Skip:10, 'Test Scores:');
           FOR J := 1 TO 4 DO
             write (Test[J]:4);
           writeln;
           writeln (Skip:10, 'Test Average:', TestAverage:6:2);
           writeln (Skip:10, 'Letter Grade:', LetterGrade:2)
       END (* of WITH . . . DO *)
   END;   (* of PROCEDURE PrintData *)
```

FIGURE 11.8
Fields with values

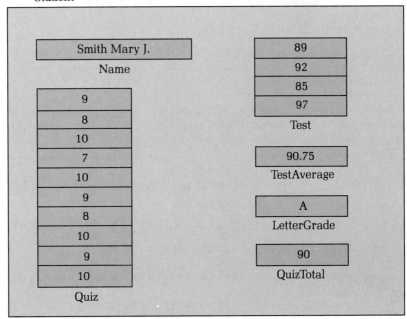

This procedure is called from the main program by

```
PrintData (Student);
```

EXAMPLE 11.2

Let's consider a short program that uses records and procedures to perform the arithmetic operation of multiplying two fractions. The fractions in the data file are in the form

1/2 3/4 ▮ 7/10 3/2 ▮

The program declares a record for each fraction and uses procedures to get the data, multiply the fractions, and print the results.

Before writing this program, let's examine appropriate record definitions and a procedure for computing the product. A definition is

```
TYPE
  RationalNumber = RECORD
                     Numerator : integer;
                     Denominator : integer
                   END; (*  of RECORD RationalNumber  *)
VAR
  X, Y, Prod : RationalNumber;
```

A procedure for computing the product is

```
PROCEDURE ComputeProduct (X1, Y1 : RationalNumber;
                          VAR Pr : RationalNumber);
BEGIN
  WITH Pr DO
    BEGIN
      Numerator := X1.Numerator * Y1.Numerator;
      Denominator := X1.Denominator * Y1.Denominator
    END (*  of WITH . . . DO  *)
END; (*  of PROCEDURE ComputeProduct  *)
```

Using Key Fields in Records

The need to search records by certain key fields is a basic and very important process. To illustrate, consider how Ted Celentino, director of PARS applications for the on-line reservation system of TWA, responded to the question: "How are reservations indexed?" He said: "By the passenger's name, flight number, and depar-

ture date. All three are needed. If a passenger forgets his or her flight number, the agent can try to find a record of it by looking through all flights to the appropriate destination at that particular travel time. It's rare that a passenger doesn't know at least a couple of pieces of information that lead to his or her record."

This procedure is called from the main program by

```
ComputeProduct (X, Y, Prod);
```

A complete program for this problem follows.

```
PROGRAM Fractions (input,output, Data);

(**************************************************************

        This program illustrates the use of records with
        procedures. In particular, procedures are used to

            1. Get the data
            2. Peform computations
            3. Print the results

        The specific task is to compute the product of two
        rational numbers.

**************************************************************)
TYPE
   RationalNumber = RECORD
                       Numerator : integer;
                       Denominator : integer
                    END;
VAR
   X,                        (*  Record for first rational number   *)
   Y,                        (*  Record for second rational number  *)
   Prod : RationalNumber;    (*  Record for product                 *)

(*      Procedure to get the data      *)
PROCEDURE GetData (VAR X1,Y1:RationalNumber);
   VAR
     Ch : char;
   BEGIN
     WITH X1 DO
       read(Data, Numerator,Ch,Denominator);
     WITH Y1 DO
       readln(Data, Numerator,Ch,Denominator)
   END;     (*   of PROCEDURE GetData   *)
```

```
(*      Procedure to compute the product      *)
PROCEDURE ComputeProduct (X1,Y1:RationalNumber;
                                VAR Pr:RationalNumber);
  BEGIN
    WITH Pr DO
      BEGIN
        Numerator := X1.Numerator * Y1.Numerator;
        Denominator := X1.Denominator * Y1.Denominator
      END     (*    of WITH . . . DO     *)
  END;      (*    of PROCEDURE ComputeProduct    *)

(*      Procedure to print the results     *)
PROCEDURE PrintResults (X1,Y1,Pr:RationalNumber);
  BEGIN
    writeln;writeln;
    writeln(X1.Numerator:13,Y1.Numerator:6,Pr.Numerator:6);
    writeln('-  *  -  =  -':25);
    writeln(X1.Denominator:13,Y1.Denominator:6,Pr.Denominator:6);
    writeln;writeln
  END;      (*    of PROCEDURE PrintResults    *)

(*    Now start the main program    *)

BEGIN     (*    Main program    *)
  reset(Data);
  WHILE NOT eof (Data) DO
    BEGIN
      GetData(X,Y);
      ComputeProduct(X,Y,Prod);
      PrintResults(X,Y,Prod)
    END      (*    of WHILE NOT eof loop    *)
END.   (*    of main program    *)
```

Given the input file

| 3/4 1/2 | | 3/2 7/10 | | 2/3 4/5 | | ■ |

the output is

```
    3       1       3
    -   *   -   =   -
    4       2       8


    3       7      21
    -   *   -   =   -
    2      10      20


    2       4       8
    -   *   -   =   -
    3       5      15
```

Exercises 11.2

For Exercises 1–5, assume a program contains the following **TYPE** definition and **VAR** declaration sections.

```
TYPE
  Info1 = RECORD
               Initial : char;
               Age : integer
             END;

  Info2 = RECORD
               Initial : char;
               Age : integer
             END;
VAR
  Cust1, Cust2 : Info1;
  Cust3, Cust4 : Info2;
```

Indicate if the statement is valid. Give an explanation for those that are invalid.

1. `Cust1 := Cust2;`
2. `Cust2 := Cust3;`
3. `Cust3 := Cust4;`
4. ```
   WITH Cust1 DO
     BEGIN
       Initial := 'W';
       Age := 21
     END;
   ```
5. ```
   WITH Cust1, Cust2 DO
     BEGIN
       Initial := 'W';
       Age := 21
     END;
   ```

6. Write a test program to see what happens when two different records with the same field name are used in a single **WITH . . . DO** statement. For example,

```
WITH Student1, Student2 DO
  Age := 21;
writeln (Student1.Age);
writeln (Student2.Age);
```

7. Assume the **TYPE** and **VAR** sections of a program include

```
TYPE
  String11 = PACKED ARRAY [1 . . 11] OF char;
  String20 = PACKED ARRAY [1 . . 20] OF char;
  Info = RECORD
             Name : String20;
             SSN : String11;
             Age : integer;
             HourlyWage : real;
             HoursWorked : real;
             Volunteer : boolean
           END;   (*  of RECORD Info  *)
VAR
  Employee1, Employee2 : Info;
```

a. Show three different methods of transferring all information from the record for Employee1 to the record for Employee2.

b. Suppose you wished to transfer all information from the record for Employee1 to the record for Employee2 except HoursWorked. Discuss different methods for doing this. Which do you feel is the most efficient?

8. Assume the **TYPE** and **VAR** sections of a program are the same as in Exercise 7. Write a procedure to be used to read information into such a record from a data file. A typical line of data is

```
Smith Jane M.        111-22-3333 25 10.50 41.5Y ▌
```

where 'Y' indicates the worker is a volunteer **(true)** and 'N' indicates the worker is not a volunteer **(false).**

9. Assume a record is declared by

```
TYPE
    String20 = PACKED ARRAY [1 . . 20] OF char;
    StudentInfo = RECORD
                    Name : String20;
                    TotalPts : 0 . . 500;
                    LetterGrade : char
                  END; (*  of RECORD StudentInfo  *)
VAR
    Student : StudentInfo;
```

Write a function to compute the student's letter grade based on cutoff levels of 90 percent, 80 percent, 70 percent, and 60 percent. Show how this function is used in a program to assign the appropriate letter grade to the appropriate field of a student's record.

10. Review Example 11.2, which was used to multiply two fractions. In a similar fashion, write procedures for

a. Dividing two fractions (watch out for zero).
b. Adding two fractions.
c. Subtracting two fractions.

11. Review Self Quiz 11.4.

a. Show how a constant in the **CONST** section can be used to generalize this to finding the best $n - 1$ of n scores.
b. Rewrite the function using a sort to sort the array of scores from high to low and then add the first three from the array.

12. Show how **PROGRAM** Fractions in Example 11.2 can be modified to check for nonzero denominators.

■ 11.3
Data Structures with Records

OBJECTIVES

■ to declare a nested record

As you have seen in the previous sections of this chapter, records are structured data types that can be used to store different kinds of information about a single customer, student, employee, event, and so on. In reality, most practical problems require being able to work with information concerning several records; for example, a list of students in a class or employees for a firm. Also, the fields in a record may be more complex than we have seen so far. In particular, it is possible to have a field of a record be another record. In this section, we examine these situations as we look at arrays of records and nested records.

- to use nested records in a program
- to declare an array of records
- to use an array of records in a program
- to sort an array of records by a field
- to use procedures for working with an array of records

Nested Records

The first concept to be examined in this section is that of *nested records*. A nested record is a record that is a field in another record. For example, suppose you are working on a program to be used by a science department and part of your work is to declare a record for a faculty member. This record is to contain fields for the person's name, room number, telephone number, and supply order. Let's assume that the supply order information is to contain the company name, a description of the item ordered, its price, and the quantity ordered. The record for each faculty member, with SupplyOrder as a record within a record, can be visualized as shown in Figure 11.9. Let's now look at how such a record can be declared. One possible method is

```
TYPE
    String20 = PACKED ARRAY [1 . . 20] OF char;
    String12 = PACKED ARRAY [1 . . 12] OF char;
    OrderInfo = RECORD
                    CompanyName : String20;
                    Item : String20;
                    ItemPrice : real;
                    Quantity : integer
                END;

    TeacherInfo = RECORD
                    Name : String20;
                    Room : integer;
                    Phone : String12;
                    SupplyOrder : OrderInfo
                END;
VAR
    Teacher : TeacherInfo;
```

FIGURE 11.9
Illustration of a nested record

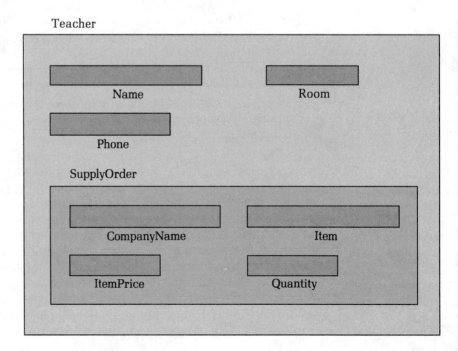

We must now consider how to access fields in the nested record. We do this by continuing our notation for field designators. Thus,

```
Teacher.Name
Teacher.Room
Teacher.Phone
```

refer to the first three fields of Teacher, and

```
Teacher.SupplyOrder.CompanyName
Teacher.SupplyOrder.Item
Teacher.SupplyOrder.ItemPrice
Teacher.SupplyOrder.Quantity
```

are used to access fields of the nested record

```
Teahcer.SupplyOrder
```

Using WITH ... DO

As expected, **WITH ... DO** can be used with nested records. Let's consider the problem of assigning data to the various fields of Teacher as previously declared. If we wish to have values assigned as in Figure 11.10, we can use the following assignment statements.

```
WITH Teacher DO
  BEGIN
    Name := 'Bland Roy R.         ';
    Room := 327;
    Phone := '800-555-1212';
    SupplyOrder.CompanyName := 'BioSupplies        ';
    SupplyOrder.Item := 'Frog               ';
    SupplyOrder.ItemPrice := 4.17;
    SupplyOrder.Quantity := 35
  END;
```

FIGURE 11.10 Values in fields of a nested record

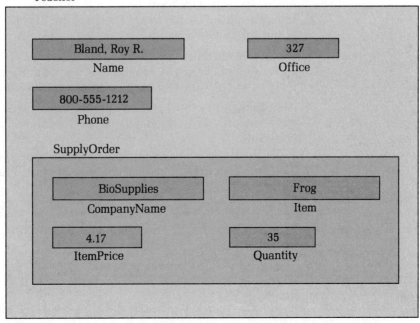

Note that the last four assignment statements all used fields in the record SupplyOrder. Thus, a **WITH ... DO** statement can be used there as follows:

```
WITH Teacher DO
  BEGIN
    Name := 'Bland Roy R.       ';
    Room := 327;
    Phone := '800-555-1212';
    WITH SupplyOrder DO
      BEGIN
        CompanyName := 'BioSupplies        ';
        Item := 'Frog                ';
        ItemPrice := 4.17;
        Quantity := 35
      END  (*  of SupplyOrder  *)
  END;  (*  of WITH Teacher DO  *)
```

There is yet a third way to accomplish our task. **WITH ... DO** can be used with both the main record name and the nested record name as follows:

```
WITH Teacher, SupplyOrder DO
  BEGIN
    Name := 'Bland Roy R.       ';
    Room := 327;
    Phone := '800-555-1212';
    CompanyName := 'BioSupplies        ';
    Item := 'Frog                ';
    ItemPrice := 4.17;
    Quantity := 35
  END;
```

Since SupplyOrder is nested within Teacher, each reference is distinctly identified and the fragment accomplishes our objective. When using nested records, you must be careful to identify fields uniquely. To illustrate, suppose Teacher1 and Teacher2 are of type TeacherInfo. Then each of the following is valid.

```
Teacher1.Name := Teacher2.Name;
Teacher1.SupplyOrder.Item := Teacher2.SupplyOrder.Item;
Teacher1.SupplyOrder := Teacher2.SupplyOrder;
```

Note that in the third statement, you are transferring the contents of an entire record. This statement is valid because both records are of type OrderInfo.

To illustrate some attempts to use inappropriate designators, assume Teacher, Teacher1, and Teacher2 are of type TeacherInfo. Consider the following inappropriate references.

```
Teacher.Item :=          ;
```

In this designator, the intermediate descriptor is missing. Thus, something like

```
Teacher.SupplyOrder.Item
```

is needed. In

```
SupplyOrder.Quantity :=          ;
```

A NOTE OF INTEREST

Information Brokers

Unlike our counterparts of a decade ago, we all have too much information. Our greatest need is not more information, but the ability to access precisely the information we need precisely when we need it. Our ability to accomplish this will be crucial to our success, whether we are employees of a major corporation, entrepreneurs, or students.

Today, a new kind of information specialist is emerging to help us manage our information needs. Called an information broker, this individual has the talents and abilities to take advantage of the latest technology while using traditional information management skills. The information broker can not only help us to identify what information we really do need, but can help us get it, interpret it, and use it. This specialist is becoming an integral part of the information age and our ability to function in it.

An information broker can deliver this information fast and precisely on target for the client's needs. After narrowly defining the client's question, the broker knows what data-base service to search, which services within that service to search, and what commands are necessary to call up that specific information.

no reference is made to which record is being accessed. A record name must be stated, such as

```
Teacher1.SupplyOrder.Quantity
```

In

```
WITH Teacher1, Teacher2 DO
   Teacher.Room := Room;
```

Room is a field in both Teacher1 and Teacher2. To correct this, something like

```
WITH Teacher1 DO
   Teacher.Room := Room;
```

is needed.

SELF QUIZ 11.5   Draw a schematic of the fields in the record Owner and list all fields.

```
TYPE
   String20 = PACKED ARRAY [1 . . 20] OF char;
   String10 = PACKED ARRAY [1 . . 10] OF char;
   PetInfo = RECORD
               Kind : String10;
               Name : String20;
               Age : integer;
               Weight : integer
            END;

   OwnerInfo = RECORD
                 Name : String20;
                 Phone : String10;
                 Pet : PetInfo
              END;

VAR
   Owner : OwnerInfo;
```

EXAMPLE 11.3   Let's write a procedure to get data from a data file for a record of type TeacherInfo with the following definitions and declarations.

```
TYPE
   String20 = PACKED ARRAY [1 . . 20] OF char;
   String12 = PACKED ARRAY [1 . . 12] OF char;
   OrderInfo = RECORD
                  CompanyName : String20;
                  Item : String20;
                  ItemPrice : real;
                  Quantity : integer
               END;

   TeacherInfo = RECORD
                   Name : String20;
                   Room : 100 . . 399;
                   Phone : String12;
                   SupplyOrder : OrderInfo
                 END;
VAR
   Teacher : TeacherInfo;
```

Assume the data for a teacher are on two lines of the data file, Data, as

(line 1) | Bland Roy R.   327 800-555-1212 |

(line 2) | BioSupplies   Frog   4.17 35 |

A procedure to obtain this data is

```
PROCEDURE GetData (VAR Teach : TeacherInfo);
   VAR
     J : integer;
     Blank : char;
   BEGIN
     WITH Teach, SupplyOrder DO
       BEGIN
         FOR J := 1 TO 20 DO
           read (Data, Name[J]);
         read (Data, Room);
         read (Blank);  (*  Move the pointer  *)
         FOR J := 1 TO 12 DO
           read (Data, Phone[J]);
         readln (Data);  (*  Go to beginning of the next line  *)

(*  Now read the second line  *)

         FOR J := 1 TO 20 DO
           read (Data, CompanyName[J]);
         FOR J := 1 TO 20 DO
           read (Data, Item[J]);
         readln (Data, ItemPrice, Quantity)
       END  (* of WITH . . . DO  *)
   END;  (*  of PROCEDURE GetData  *)
```

This procedure is called from the main program by

```
      GetData (Teacher);
```

Array of Records

Next we use structured data types to look at an *array of records*. It is easy to imagine needing a list of information about several people, events, or items. Furthermore, it is not unusual for the information about a particular person, event, or item to consist of several different data items. When this situation occurs, a record can be defined for each person, event, or item and an array of these records can be used to achieve the desired result.

For example, suppose the local high school sports boosters want you to write a program to enable them to keep track of the names and donations of its members. Assume there is a maximum of 50 members making a donation. This problem can be solved by using an array of records. Each record will have two fields: the donor's name and the amount donated. The record can be visualized as shown in Figure 11.11. We now declare an array of these records to produce the arrangement shown in Figure 11.12. The definitions and declarations needed are

```
CONST
   ClubSize = 50;
TYPE
   String20 = PACKED ARRAY [1 . . 20] OF char;
   MemberInfo = RECORD
                    Name : String20;
                    Amount : real
                END;
   DonorList = ARRAY [1 . . ClubSize] OF MemberInfo;
VAR
   Donor : DonorList;
   TempDonor : MemberInfo;
   Count : integer;
```

Before proceeding, note the following:

1. Structures are built in the **TYPE** definition section to facilitate later work with procedures and functions.
2. Each record is now an array element and can be accessed by a reference to the index. Thus, if the third member's name is Tom Jones and he donates $100.00, you can write

```
Donor[3].Name := 'Jones Tom          ';
Donor[3].Amount := 100.0;
```

FIGURE 11.11
Fields in Donor

Donor

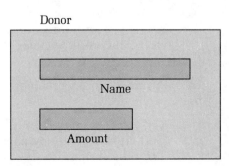

Name

Amount

FIGURE 11.12
Illustration of an
array of records

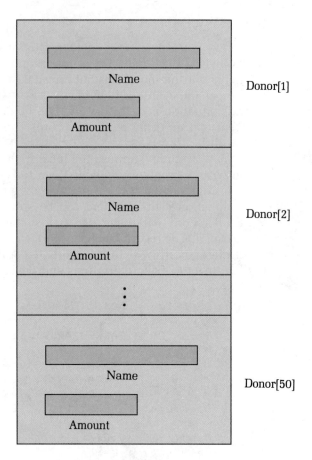

Better still, you can use **WITH** ... **DO** to get

```
WITH Donor[3] DO
   BEGIN
      Name := 'Jones Tom
      Amount := 100.0
   END;
```

3. Since records are of identical type, contents of two records can be interchanged by

```
TempDonor := Donor[1];
Donor[1] := Donor[2];
Donor[2] := TempDonor;
```

This is needed if records are to be sorted by one of their fields.

4. Be careful with syntax when using an array of records or an array as a field within a record. For example, be able to distinguish between Student[J].Average, Student.Score[K], and Student[J].Score [K].

Let's now return to the problem posed by the sports boosters. A first-level pseudocode design is

1. Get the data
2. Sort alphabetically by name
3. Print the sorted list

If we assume each line of the data file is of the form

```
Jones Tom      100.0  ▮
```

a procedure to get the data is not difficult. We have to remember, however, to count the actual number of donors read. Such a procedure is

```
PROCEDURE GetData (VAR Don : DonorList; VAR Ct : integer);
  VAR
    J : integer;
  BEGIN
    Ct := 0;
    WHILE (NOT eof (Data)) AND (Ct < ClubSize) DO
      BEGIN
        Ct := Ct + 1;  (*  Increment the counter  *)
        WITH Don[Ct] DO
          BEGIN
            FOR J := 1 TO 20 DO
              read (Data, Name[J]);
            readln (Data, Amount)
          END    (*  of WITH . . . DO  *)
      END   (*  of WHILE NOT eof *)
END;  (*  of PROCEDURE GetData  *)
```

This procedure is called from the main program by

```
GetData (Donor, Count);
```

and Count contains the actual number of donors after the procedure is
called.

The next procedure in this problem requires a sort. Recall the selection sort from Chapter 9.

```
FOR J := 1 TO N−1 DO          (*  Number of passes  *)
  BEGIN
    Temp := A[J];
    Index := J;
    FOR K := J + 1 TO N DO
      IF A[K] < Temp THEN
        BEGIN                  (*  Find smallest number  *)
          Temp := A[K];
          Index := K
        END;
    A[Index] := A[J];          (* Exchange smallest number *)
    A[J] := Temp
  END;
```

With suitable changes, the array of records can be sorted alphabetically
by

```
PROCEDURE Sort (VAR Don : DonorList; N : integer);
  VAR
    J, K, Index : integer;
    Temp : MemberInfo;
  BEGIN
    FOR J := 1 TO N-1 DO
```

```
                    BEGIN
                      Temp := Don[J];
                      Index := J;
                      FOR K := J + 1 TO N DO
                        IF Don[K].Name < Temp.Name THEN
                          BEGIN
                            Temp := Don[K];
                            Index := K
                          END;
                      Don[Index] := Don[J];
                      Don[J] := Temp
                    END   (*  of FOR loop  *)
                END;  (*  of PROCEDURE Sort  *)
```

This procedure is called from the main program by

```
     Sort (Donor, Count);
```

In this procedure, note that the sort is by only one field in the record, specifically, the donor's name

```
     IF Don[K].Name < Temp.Name THEN
```

However, when the names are exchanged, contents of the entire record are exchanged by

```
     Temp := Don[K];
```

We conclude this example by writing a procedure to print the results. If we want the output to be

```
               Local Sports Boosters
                   Donation List
          ---------------------------------------------

              Name                          Amount
              ----                          ------

          Anerice Sue                       150.00
          Compton John                      125.00
                 .                             .
                 .                             .
                 .                             .
```

a procedure to produce this is

```
PROCEDURE PrintList (Don : DonorList; N : integer);
   CONST
     Skip = ' ';
   VAR
     J : integer;
   BEGIN
     writeln; writeln;
     writeln (Skip:20, 'Local Sports Boosters');
     writeln (Skip:24, 'Donation List');
     writeln (Skip:10, '---------------------------------------------');
     writeln;
     writeln (Skip:13, 'Name', Skip:27, 'Amount');
     writeln (Skip:13, '____', Skip:27, '_____');
     writeln;

   (*  Now print the list  *)
```

```
     FOR J := 1 TO N DO
       WITH Don[J] DO
          writeln (Skip:10, Name, Amount:20:2);
     writeln; writeln
  END; (* of PROCEDURE PrintList *)
```

With these three procedures available, the main program is then

```
  BEGIN (* Main program *)
    reset (Data);
    GetData (Donor, Count);
    Sort (Donor, Count);
    PrintList (Donor, Count)
  END. (* of main program *)
```

This example is less involved than many of your problems will be, but it does illustrate an array of records, appropriate notation for fields in an array of records, sorting an array of records by using one field of the records, and using procedures with an array of records.

Searching Arrays of Records

The searching algorithms presented in Section 9.6 can be applied to arrays of records. Let's illustrate how a linear search can be used in a program. Suppose you have an array of records (sorted alphabetically) and each record contains a student's name and final average for the semester. If such an array is defined by

```
  TYPE
      .
      .
      .
     StudentInfo = RECORD
                        Name : String20;
                        Average : real
                     END;
     StudentList = ARRAY [1 . . MaxLength] OF StudentInfo;
  VAR
     Student : StudentList;
```

and StudentName contains the name of the student whose record is to be changed, and NewAv contains the value of the new average, the code for this problem is

```
  Index := 1;
  WHILE (StudentName < Student[Index].Name) AND
                                     (Index < Length) DO
     Index := Index + 1;
  IF StudentName = Student[Index].Name THEN
     Student[Index].Average := NewAv
  ELSE
     writeln (StudentName:25, ' was not found.');
```

SELF QUIZ 11.6   Assume the array of records Student is as just declared. If Mary Smith moves away, her record should be removed from the list. Write a segment of code to accomplish this task.

The following example shows how a binary search can be used to solve a problem.

EXAMPLE 11.4

A binary search can be used to delete names from a mailing list. If we assume the array of records is declared by

```
TYPE
    .
    .
    .
  ZipRange = 0 . . 99999;
  AddressInfo = RECORD
                   Street : String15;
                   City : String15;
                   State : String2;
                   Zip : ZipRange
                END;
  Customer Info = RECORD
                   Name : String20;
                   Address : AddressInfo;
                   PhoneNum : String12
                END;
  CustomerList = ARRAY [1 . . MaxLength] OF CustomerInfo;
VAR
  Customer : CustomerList;
```

and that DeleteName contains the name to be deleted (no duplicate names), we can accomplish the task by

```
    Found := false;
    First := 1;
    Last := Length;
    WHILE NOT Found AND (First <= Last) DO
      BEGIN
        Mid := (First + Last) DIV 2;
        IF DeleteName < Customer[Mid].Name THEN
          Last := Mid-1
        ELSE
          IF DeleteName > Customer[Mid].Name THEN
            First := Mid+1
          ELSE
            Found := true
      END;  (*  of binary search  *)
    IF Found THEN (*  Delete the record  *)
      BEGIN
        FOR J := Mid TO Length-1 DO
          Customer[J] := Customer [J+1];
        Length := Length-1
      END
    ELSE
      writeln (DeleteName:25, ' was not found.');
```

Exercises 11.3

1. Consider the declaration

```
TYPE
   B = RECORD
           C : real;
           D : integer
        END;

   A = RECORD
           E : boolean;
           F : B
        END;
VAR
   G : A;
```

Give a schematic representation of the record G.

For Exercises 2–11, using the declarations from Exercise 1, indicate which is a valid reference.

2. G.E
3. G.C
4. G.F.D
5. F.D
6. G.A

7. A.F.C
8. A.E
9. WITH G DO
10. WITH G, F DO
11. G.F.C

12. In the declaration in Exercise 1, why would it be incorrect to define record A before record B?

13. Write a test program that illustrates the difference between an array of records and a record with an array component.

14. Give an appropriate definition and declaration for a record that contains fields for a person's name, address, social security number, annual income, and family information. Address is a record with fields for street address, city, state abbreviation, and zip code. Family information is a record with fields for marital status (S, M, W, or D) and number of children.

15. Consider the following definitions and subsequent declarations.

```
TYPE
   String20 = PACKED ARRAY [1 . . 20] OF char;
   Mood = (Quiet, Bright, Surly);
   CurrentHealth = (Poor, Average, Good);
   PatientInfo = RECORD
                    Name : String20;
                    Status = RECORD
                                Mental : Mood;
                                Physical : CurrentHealth
                             END;  (* of RECORD Status *)
                    PastDue : boolean
                 END;  (* of RECORD PatientInfo *)
VAR
   Patient1, Patient2 : PatientInfo;
```

a. Give a schematic representation for Patient1.
b. Show how a single letter (Q, B, S) can be read from a data file and then have the appropriate value assigned to Patient1.Status.Mental.

c. Write a procedure to read a line of data and assign (if necessary) appropriate values to the various fields. A typical data line is

```
Smith Sue      BAF ▌
```

and indicates that Sue Smith's mood is bright, her health is average, and her account is not past due.

16. Declare an array of records to be used for 15 players on a basketball team. The following information is needed for each player: name, age, height, weight, scoring average, and rebounding average.

17. Declare an array of records to be used for students in a classroom (at most 40 students). Each record should contain fields for a student's name, social security number, ten quiz scores, three test scores, overall average, and letter grade.

18. Consider the following declaration of an array of records.

```
CONST
  ClassSize = 35;
TYPE
  String20 = PACKED ARRAY [1 . . 20] OF char;
  Attendance = (Excellent, Average, Poor);
  TestList = ARRAY [1 . . 4] OF integer;
  StudentInfo = RECORD
                  Name : String20;
                  Atten : Attendance;
                  Test : TestList;
                  Aver : real
                END;
  StudentList = ARRAY [1 . . ClassSize] OF StudentInfo;
VAR
  Student : StudentList;
```

a. Give a schematic representation for Student.
b. Explain what the following function accomplishes.

```
FUNCTION GuessWhat (A : StudentInfo) : real;
  VAR
    K, Sum : integer;
  BEGIN
    Sum := 0;
    FOR K := 1 TO 4 DO
      Sum := Sum + A.Test[K];
    GuessWhat := Sum/4
  END;
```

This function is called by

```
Student[J].Aver := GuessWhat (Student[J]);
```

c. Write a procedure to print out the information for one student. In this procedure, the entire word describing attendance is to be printed.

For Exercises 19–22, reconsider the problem in this section that kept a record of the name and amount donated for each member of the local high school boosters club. Expanding on that problem, write a procedure or function for each of the following.

19. Find the maximum donation and print out the amount together with the donor's name.

20. Find the sum of all donations.
21. Find the average of all donations.
22. Sort the array according to size of the donation, largest first.
23. Reconsider Example 11.4. In practice, it is quite possible that two customers have the same name. Show how you can avoid deleting the wrong name.
24. Let's work with Example 11.4 one more time. Sometimes the name and address for a customer get put on a mailing list more than once. Write a procedure to search a sorted list and remove all duplicates.
25. Consider the definitions and declarations

```
TYPE
   EmployeeInfo = RECORD
                     Name : String20;
                     Classification : String2;
                     SSN : String11;
                     HourlyRate : real
                  END;
   EmployeeList = ARRAY [1 . . MaxLength] OF EmployeeInfo;
VAR
   Employee : EmployeeList;
```

All employees with a job classification of C4 are to receive a pay raise of 7.5 percent. Write a segment of code to search the array Employee and record the new hourly rate for employees as appropriate.

26. Suppose you are using a program that contains an array of records in which each record is defined by

```
TYPE
   .
   .
   .
   CustomerInfo = RECORD
                     Name : String20;
                     AmountDue : real
                  END;
```

a. Use the bubble sort to sort (and then print) the records alphabetically.
b. Re-sort the array by the field AmountDue. Print a list ordered by Amount-Due where anyone with an amount due of more than $100 is designated with a triple asterisk (***).

■ 11.4
Record
Variants

OBJECTIVES

■ to define a record with a variant part
■ to use a record that contains a variant part

You should have noticed by now that when records are defined, each record has certain fixed fields. Since it is sometimes desirable to use a record structure in which the number and type of fields vary, Pascal allows records to be defined with a *variant part*. For example, a real estate company might want the records for their customers to contain different information depending on whether the property for sale is a house or a business. For houses, the number of bedrooms, bathrooms, and whether or not there is a fireplace should be indicated; for businesses, the number of offices and amount of possible rental income should be listed.

Defining a Variant Part

In order to define the variant part of a record, we use a form of the **CASE** statement to specify which fields should be included. Then, depending on the value of the identifier in the **CASE** part of the definition, the desired fields are listed. In the real estate example, we can have

```
TYPE
   PropertyType = (House, Business);
   Listing = RECORD
                CASE Kind : PropertyType OF
                 House     : (NumBedrms : integer;
                              NumBaths : integer;
                              Fireplace : boolean);
                 Business : (NumOffices : integer;
                             RentalIncome : integer)
             END;  (* of RECORD Listing *)
VAR
   Property : Listing;
```

Now Property is a record with a variant part. Kind is the *tag field* and, depending on the value assigned to Kind, the appropriate fields are available. If the assignment

```
Property.Kind := House;
```

is made, the record can be envisioned as shown in Figure 11.13(a). If the assignment

```
Property.Kind := Business;
```

is made, we have the record illustrated in Figure 11.13(b). In actual practice, records with variant parts usually have fixed parts also. Suppose the address and price of each property listed for sale should be included.

FIGURE 11.13
Fields in a variant record

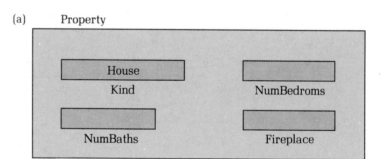

(a)   Property

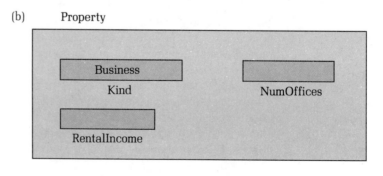

(b)   Property

Since fields for these would be defined for every record, these fields would be referred to as the *fixed part*. A complete definition is

```
TYPE
    PropertyType = (House, Business);
    String30 = PACKED ARRAY [1 .. 30] OF char;
    Listing = RECORD
                Address : String30;   ⎫ fixed
                Price : integer;       ⎬ part
                CASE Kind : PropertyType OF
                    House    : (NumBedrms : integer;    ⎫
                                NumBaths : integer;     ⎪  variant
                                Fireplace : boolean);   ⎬  part
                    Business : (NumOffices : integer;   ⎪
                                RentalIncome : integer) ⎭
            END;  (* of RECORD Listing *)
VAR
    Property : Listing;
```

The following points concerning variant parts should now be made.

1. The variant part of a record must be listed after the fixed part.
2. Only one variant part can be defined in a record.
3. The data type for the tag field must be ordinal.
4. Only one **END** is used to terminate the definition. This terminates both **CASE** and **RECORD**.

Records with variant parts are defined by a form as follows:

```
record name = RECORD
                field 1 : type;   ⎫
                field 2 : type;   ⎪
                     .            ⎬  fixed
                     .            ⎪  part
                     .            ⎪
                field n : type;   ⎭
                CASE tag field : tag type OF
                    value 1 : (field list);   ⎫
                    value 2 : (field list);   ⎪
                         .                     ⎬  variant
                         .                     ⎪  part
                         .                     ⎪
                    value m : (field list)    ⎭
            END;
```

It is possible to completely avoid the use of variant parts of a record. One can list all possible fields in the fixed part and then use them appropriately. However, this usually means that more storage is required. To illustrate, let's consider how memory is allocated. For each field in the fixed part of the previous example, an area in memory is reserved as

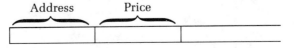

For the variant part of the record, a single area is reserved that is subsequently utilized by whichever fields are determined by the value of the tag field. In this sense, they overlap as indicated.

We close this section with an example that illustrates a definition and subsequent use of a record with a variant part.

EXAMPLE 11.5

Let's define a record to be used when working with plane geometric figures. The record should have fixed fields for the type of figure (a single character designator) and area. The variant part should have fields for information needed to compute the area. After the record is defined, write a procedure to get data from a line of the data file. Then write a function that can be used to compute the area of the plane figure.

To complete the definition of the record, let's assume we are working with at most the geometric figures circle, square, and triangle (C, S, and T, respectively). An appropriate definition is

```
TYPE
    FigureShape = (Circle, Square, Triangle);
    FIgureInfo = RECORD
                    Object : char;
                    Area : real;
                    CASE Shape : FigureShape OF
                        Circle   : (Radius : real);
                        Square   : (Side : real);
                        Triangle : (Base, Height : real)
                    END; (* of RECORD FigureInfo *)
VAR
    Figure : FigureInfo;
```

Each data line has a single character designating the kind of figure followed by appropriate information needed to compute the area. For example,

T 6.0 8.0 ▮

represents a triangle with base 6.0 and height 8.0. A procedure to get a line of data is

```
PROCEDURE GetData (VAR Fig : FigureInfo);
    BEGIN
        WITH Fig DO
            BEGIN
                read (Data, Object);
                CASE Object OF
                    'C' : BEGIN
                            Shape := Circle;
                            readln (Data, Radius)
                          END;
```

```
      'S' : BEGIN
              Shape := Square;
              readln (Data, Side)
            END;
      'T' : BEGIN
              Shape := Triangle;
              readln (Data, Base, Height)
            END
      END (*  of CASE  *)
    END (*  of WITH . . . DO  *)
  END; (*  of PROCEDURE GetData  *)
```

This is called from the main program by

```
GetData (Figure);
```

Finally, a function to compute the area is

```
FUNCTION Area (Fig : FigureInfo) : real;
  CONST
    Pi = 3.14159;
  BEGIN
    WITH Fig DO
      BEGIN
        CASE Shape OF
          Circle   : Area := Pi * Radius * Radius;
          Square   : Area := Side * Side;
          Triangle : Area := 0.5 * Base * Height
        END (*  of CASE  *)
      END (*  of WITH . . . DO  *)
  END; (*  of FUNCTION Area  *)
```

This function is called by

```
Figure.Area := Area (Figure);
```

Exercises 11.4

1. Explain how memory may be saved when records with variant parts are declared.

2. Assume a record is defined by

```
TYPE
  TagType = (One, Two);
  Info = RECORD
           Fixed : integer;
           CASE Tag : TagType OF
             One : (A,B : integer);
             Two : (X : real;
                    Ch : char)
         END;
```

and the variable declaration section of a program includes

```
VAR
  RecordCheck : Info;
```

Write a test program that allows you to examine output from the following fragment of code.

```
WITH RecordCheck DO
  BEGIN
    Fixed := 1000;
    Tag := One;
    A := 100;
    B := 500;
    writeln (Fixed:15, A:15, B:15);
    Tag := Two;
    X := 10.5;
    Ch := 'Y';
    writeln (Fixed:15, X:15:2, Ch:15);
    writeln (A:15, B:15, X:15:2, Ch:15)
  END;
```

In Exercises 3–6, find all errors in the definitions.

```
3. TYPE
     Info = RECORD
              A : real;
              CASE Tag : TagType OF
                B : (X,Y : real);
                C : (Z : boolean)
            END;
4. TYPE
     TagType = (A,B,C);
     Info = RECORD
              D : integer;
              Flag : boolean;
              CASE Tag : TagType OF
                A : (X,Y : real);
                B : (Z : real)
            END;
5. TYPE
     TagType = (A,B,C);
     Info = RECORD
              D : integer;
              Flag : boolean
              CASE Tag OF
                A : (X : real);
                B : (Y : real);
                C : (Z : real)
            END;
6. TYPE
     TagType = (A,B,C);
     Info = RECORD
              D : integer;
              CASE Tag1 : TagType OF
                A : (X : real);
                B : (Y : real);
                C : (Z : real)
              END; (*  of CASE  *)
```

```
CASE Tag2 : TagType OF
  A : (X1 : real);
  B : (Y1 : real);
  C : (Z1 : real)
END;  (*  of RECORD Info  *)
```

7. Redefine the following record without using a variant part.

```
TYPE
  Shapes = (Circle, Square, Triangle);
  FigureInfo = RECORD
                 Object : char;
                 Area : real;
                 CASE Shape : Shapes OF
                     Circle   : (Radius : real);
                     Square   : (Side : real);
                     Triangle : (Base, Height : real)
               END;
VAR
  Figure : FigureInfo;
```

8. Using the record defined in Exercise 7, indicate the names of the fields available and provide an illustration of these fields after each of the following assignments is made.

   a. Shape := Circle;
   b. Shape := Square;
   c. Shape := Triangle;

9. Redefine the record of Exercise 7 to include rectangles and parallelograms.

10. Define a record with a variant part to be used for working with various publications. For each record, there should be fields for the author, title, and date. If the publication is a book, there should be fields for the publisher and city. If the publication is an article, there should be fields for the journal name and volume number.

RUNNING AND DEBUGGING TIPS

1. Be sure to use the full field name when working with fields in a record. You may only leave off the record name when using **WITH** . . . **DO.**
2. Terminate each record definition with an **END**. This is an instance when **END** is used without a **BEGIN.**
3. Although field names in different record types can be the same, you are encouraged to use distinct names. This enhances readability and reduces the chances of making errors.
4. Be careful with syntax when using an array of records or an array as a field within a record. For example, be able to distinguish between Student[K].Average, Student.Score[J], and Student[K].Score[J].
5. When sorting records using a key field, be careful to compare only the key field and then exchange the entire record accordingly.

■ Summary

Key Terms

record	array of records	fixed part
field	variant part	
nested records	tag field	

Keywords

RECORD
WITH ... DO

Key Concepts

- A record is a structured data type that is a collection of fields; the fields may be treated as a whole or individually.
- Fields in a record can be of different data types.
- Records can be declared or defined by

> record name = **RECORD**
> > field identifier 1 : data type 1;
> > field identifier 2 : data type 2;
> >
> > .
> > .
> > .
> >
> > field identifier n: data type n
> > **END**; (* of **RECORD** definition *)

- Fields can be accessed as variables by

> record name.field identifier

- Records can be schematically represented as in Figure 11.14.
- **WITH** record name **DO** can be used instead of a specific reference to the record name with each field of a record; thus, you can have

```
WITH Student DO
   BEGIN
     Name := 'Smith John          ';
     Average := 93.4;
     Grade := 'A'
   END;
```

instead of

```
Student.Name := 'Smith John          ';
Student.Average := 93.4;
Student.Grade := 'A';
```

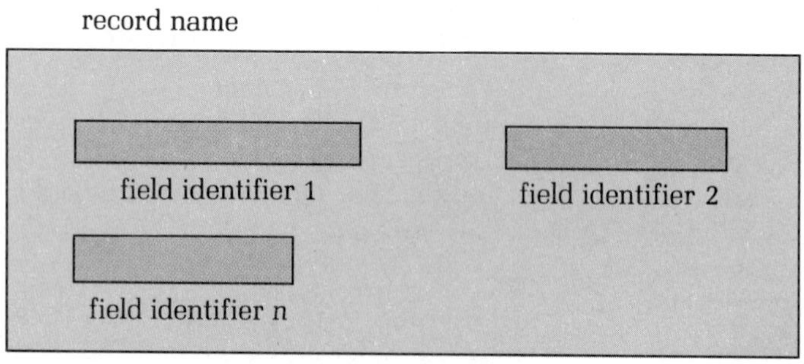

FIGURE 11.14
Fields in a record

- If two records, A and B, are of identical type, contents of all fields of one may be assigned to corresponding fields of the other by a single assignment statement such as

```
A := B;
```

- Either entire records or fields within a record can be passed to appropriate subprograms.
- A record may be used as a field in another record.
- A **WITH** ... **DO** statement may be used to access fields of nested records.
- Records may be used as components of an array.
- An array of records may be sorted by one of the fields in each record.
- Linear and binary searches can be used with arrays of records. A key field is used for the search.
- Records with variant parts list all fixed fields (if any) first and then list the variant fields using a **CASE** statement; for example,

```
TYPE
   MaritalStatus = (Married, Single, Divorced);
   String20 = PACKED ARRAY [1 , , 20] OF char;
   Info = RECORD
             Name : String20;
             CASE Status : MaritalStatus OF
                Married  : (SpouseName : String20;
                            NumKids : integer);
                Single   : (Sex : char;
                            Age : integer);
                Divorced : (NumKids : integer;
                            Age : integer;
                            Sex : char;
                            LivesAlone : boolean)
          END;    (*  of RECORD Info  *)
VAR
   Customer : Info;
```

- The **CASE** statement in a variant record declaration does not require a separate **END** statement.
- After a value is assigned to a tag field, the remaining record fields are the ones listed in the **CASE** part of the definition; for example, if we use the previous definition and we have

```
Customer.Status := Divorced;
```

the record fields are as shown in Figure 11.15.

FIGURE 11.15
Value of a tag field

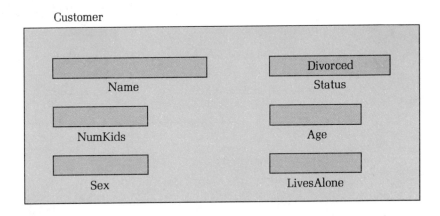

■ Chapter Review Exercises

For Exercises 1–5, use a record containing the following information.

Student name (20 characters)
Homeroom number (**integer**)
Class (2 characters)
GPA (**real**)
Lab fees paid (**boolean**)

1. Write a type and variable definition for the record.
2. Draw a schematic representation of the record.
3. Write a procedure to read data for a student into the record.
4. Revise your definition to create an array of 50 of the record as you defined it.
5. Write a procedure to print a list of the names and homerooms of the students who have not paid their fees.

For Exercises 6–17, refer to the following record defintion.

```
TYPE
  Rec1 = RECORD
           A : ARRAY [1 . . 10] OF integer;
           B : real;
           C : PACKED ARRAY [1 . . 3, 1 . . 5] OF integer
         END;  (*  of  RECORD  Rec1  *)
  Arry = ARRAY [1 . . 4] OF Rec1;
VAR
  X : Rec1;
  Y : Arry;
```

Which of the following references are appropriate?

6. X.B	12. Y[2].X[4]
7. Y.B	13. Y[3]
8. X.A[1]	14. X.C[3,4]
9. Y.A[1]	15. Y[5].B
10. X[1].B	16. Y.X.A
11. Y[1].B	17. Y.B

For Exercises 18 and 19, use a **TYPE** definition to declare the record illustrated. Also declare a record variable to be of the illustrated type.

18. AmericanLeague

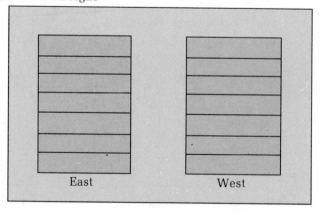

East   West

19. LanguagesLearned

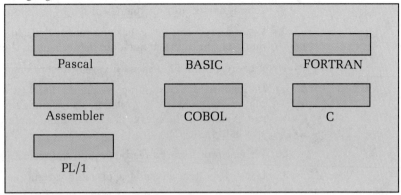

For Exercises 20–31, use the following record definitions.

```
TYPE
  A = RECORD
         B : ARRAY [1 , , 5] OF integer;
         C : boolean;
         D : PACKED ARRAY [1 , , 5, 1 , , 10] OF char
      END;

  W = RECORD
         X : integer;
         Y : ARRAY [1 , , 5] OF integer;
         Z : A
      END;
VAR
  G : A;
  H : W;
```

Which statements are appropriate?

```
20. G,C := true;
21. G,B[3] := 2;
22. read (G,D[1]);
23. H,Z,D[1,3] := 'A';
24. IF A,B[2] = 1 THEN
       write (A,B[2]);
25. H,X := H,Y[4] + H,Z,B[4];
26. writeln (H,A,D[5]);
27. IF G,D[4] = H,Z,D[4] THEN
       writeln;
28. H,B[1] := 3;
29. W,X := 3;
30. H,Z,C := true;
31. H,A,C := true;
```

Write a record that can be used to keep track of the names of the nine starters on a baseball team, their positions, and their batting averages.

33. Include the record definition in Exercise 32 in another record to also keep the school names and nicknames of ten high school baseball teams.

34. Write a procedure to check the record defined in Exercise 33 and print the name of the team having a shortstop named Mapes.

Note: Exercises 35–37 deal with variant records and may be optional for you.

35. Define a record containing the names, heights, weights, and ages of baseball players. If the player is a pitcher, also include the innings pitched and earned run average. If the player is not a pitcher, include the number of home runs and batting average.

36. Write a procedure to read data into the record defined in Exercise 35.

37. List at least two advantages of using variant records.

■ **Chapter Summary Program**

The sample program for this chapter features working with an array of records. The array is first sorted using the field containing a name. It is then sorted using the field containing a real.

Write a program to help your local high school sports boosters keep records of donors and amounts donated. The input file consists of a name (first 20 positions) and an amount donated (starting in position 21) on each line. Your program gets the data from the input file using a record for each donor. Output consists of two lists.

1. An alphabetical listing together with the amount donated
2. A listing sorted according to the amount donated

A first-level pseudocode development for this problem is

1. Get the data
2. Sort by name
3. Print the first list
4. Sort by amount
5. Print the second list

This is refined to

1. Get the data
   1.1 **WHILE NOT eof DO**
       1.1.1 get a name
       1.1.2 get the amount
2. Sort by name (use selection sort)
3. Print the first list
   3.1 print a heading
   3.2 print the names and amounts
4. Sort by amount (use selection sort)
5. Print the second list
   5.1 print a heading
   5.2 print the names and amounts

A complete program with sample output follows.

```
PROGRAM Boosters (input,output, Data);

(**************************************************************

     This program uses an array of records to process
     information for donors to the local high school sports
     boosters. Output includes two lists, one sorted
     by name and one sorted by amount donated.

 **************************************************************)
CONST
  ClubSize = 50;
TYPE
  String20 = PACKED ARRAY [1 , , 20] OF char;
  MemberInfo = RECORD
                  Name : String20;
                  Amount : real
               END;  (*   of RECORD MemberInfo   *)
  DonorList = ARRAY [1 , , ClubSize] OF MemberInfo;
VAR
  Count : integer;            (*  Counter for number of donors   *)
  Donor : DonorList;          (*  Array of records               *)
  Data : text;                (*  Data file                      *)


(**************************************************************

          This procedure gets the data.

 **************************************************************)
PROCEDURE GetData (VAR Don : DonorList; Var Ct : integer);
  VAR
    J : integer;
  BEGIN
    reset (Data);
    Ct := 0;
    WHILE (NOT eof (Data)) AND (Ct < ClubSize) DO
      BEGIN
        Ct := Ct + 1;
        WITH Don[Ct] DO
          BEGIN
            FOR J := 1 TO 20 DO
              read (Data, Name[J]);
            readln(Data, Amount)
          END    (*   of WITH , , , DO   *)
      END    (*   of WHILE NOT eof   *)
  END;    (*   of PROCEDURE GetData   *)
```

```
(****************************************************************

              This procedure sorts by name.

 ****************************************************************)
PROCEDURE SortByName (VAR Don : DonorList; N : integer);
  VAR
    J,K,Index : integer;
    Temp : MemberInfo;
  BEGIN
    FOR J := 1 TO N-1 DO
      BEGIN
        Temp := Don[J];
        Index := J;
        FOR K := J+1 TO N DO
          IF Don[K].Name < Temp.Name THEN
            BEGIN
              Temp := Don[K];
              Index := K
            END;
        Don[Index] := Don[J];
        Don[J] := Temp
      END    (*   of FOR loop   *)
  END;   (*   of PROCEDURE SortByName   *)


(****************************************************************

              This procedure sorts by amount.

 ****************************************************************)
PROCEDURE SortByAmount (VAR Don : DonorList; N : integer);
  VAR
    J,K,Index : integer;
    Temp : MemberInfo;
  BEGIN
    FOR J := 1 TO N-1 DO
      BEGIN
        Temp := Don[J];
        Index := J;
        FOR K := J+1 TO N DO
          IF Don[K].Amount > Temp.Amount THEN
            BEGIN
              Temp := Don[K];
              Index := K
            END;
        Don[Index] := Don[J];
        Don[J] := Temp
      END      (*   of FOR loop   *)
  END;     (*   of PROCEDURE SortByAmount   *)
```

```
(*****************************************************************

              This procedure prints a heading.

 *****************************************************************)
PROCEDURE PrintHeading;
  CONST
    Skip = ' ';
  BEGIN
    writeln; writeln;
    writeln(Skip:20,'Local Sports Boosters');
    writeln(Skip:24,'Donation List');
    writeln(Skip:10,'------------------------------------------');
    writeln;
    writeln(Skip:13,'Name',Skip:21,'Amount');
    writeln(Skip:13,'____',Skip:21,'_____');
    writeln
  END;        (*   of PROCEDURE PrintHeading    *)


(*****************************************************************

              This procedure prints a list.

 *****************************************************************)
PROCEDURE PrintList (Don : DonorList; N : integer);
  CONST
    Skip = ' ';
  VAR
    J : integer;
  BEGIN
    FOR J := 1 TO N DO
      WITH Don[J] DO
          writeln(Skip:10,Name,Amount:14:2);
      writeln; writeln
  END; (*   of PROCEDURE PrintList   *)


(*****************************************************************

              Begin the main program.

 *****************************************************************)
BEGIN  (*  Main program   *)
  GetData(Donor,Count);
  SortByName(Donor,Count);
  PrintHeading;
  PrintList(Donor,Count);
  SortByAmount(Donor,Count);
  PrintHeading;
  PrintList(Donor,Count)
END.    (*   of main program    *)
```

The output from this program is

```
           Local Sports Boosters
              Donation List
---------------------------------------------

       Name                        Amount

   Alexander Candy                 300.00
   Anderson Tony                   375.00
   Banks Marj                      375.00
   Born Patty                      100.00
   Brown Ron                       200.00
   Darnell Linda                   275.00
   Erickson Thomas                 100.00
   Fox William                     300.00
   Francis Denise                  350.00
   Generous George                 525.00
   Gillette Mike                   350.00
   Hancock Kirk                    500.00
   Higgins Sam                     300.00
   Janson Kevin                    200.00
   Johnson Ed                      350.00
   Johnson Martha                  400.00
   Jones Jerry                     250.00
   Kelly Marvin                    475.00
   Kneff Susan                     300.00
   Lasher John                     175.00
   Lyon Elizabeth                  425.00
   Moore Robert                    100.00
   Muller Marjorie                 250.00
   Smith John                      100.00
   Trost Frostie                    50.00
   Trudo Rosemary                  200.00
   Weber Sharon                    150.00
   Williams Art                    350.00
   Williams Jane                   175.00
   Wilson Mary                     275.00

           Local Sports Boosters
              Donation List
---------------------------------------------

       Name                        Amount

   Generous George                 525.00
   Hancock Kirk                    500.00
   Kelly Marvin                    475.00
   Lyon Elizabeth                  425.00
   Johnson Martha                  400.00
   Anderson Tony                   375.00
   Banks Marj                      375.00
   Francis Denise                  350.00
   Gillette Mike                   350.00
   Johnson Ed                      350.00
   Williams Art                    350.00
   Higgins Sam                     300.00
   Alexander Candy                 300.00
```

Kneff Susan	300.00
Fox William	300.00
Darnell Linda	275.00
Wilson Mary	275.00
Muller Marjorie	250.00
Jones Jerry	250.00
Trudo Rosemary	200.00
Brown Ron	200.00
Janson Kevin	200.00
Lasher John	175.00
Williams Jane	175.00
Weber Sharon	150.00
Erickson Thomas	100.00
Born Patty	100.00
Smith John	100.00
Moore Robert	100.00
Trost Frostie	50.00

■ Programming Problems

1. Write a program to be used by the registrar of a university. The program should get information from a data file and the data for each student should include student name, student number, classification (1 for freshman, 2 for sophomore, 3 for junior, 4 for senior, or 7 for special student), hours completed, hours taking, and grade point average.

   Output should include an alphabetical listing of all students, an alphabetical listing of students in each class, and a listing of all students ordered by grade point average.

2. Robert Day, basketball coach at Indiana College, wants you to write a program to help him analyze information about his basketball team. He wants a record for each player containing the player's name, position played, high school graduated from, height, scoring average, rebounding average, grade point average, and seasons of eligibility remaining.

   The program should read the information for each player from a data file. The output should include an alphabetized list of names together with other pertinent information, a list sorted according to scoring average, an alphabetized list of all players with a grade point average above 3.0, and an alphabetized list of high schools together with an alphabetized list of players who graduated from each school.

3. Final grades in Mr. Lae Z. Programmer's computer science class are to be computed using the following course requirements.

Requirement	Possible Points
1. Quiz scores (ten points each and the best 10 out of 12 are counted)	100 points
2. Two hourly tests	200 points
3. Eight programming assignments (25 points each)	200 points
4. Test program assignments (two at 50 points each)	100 points
5. Final examination	100 points
Total	700 points

Cutoff percentages for the grades of A, B, C, D, and E are 90 percent, 80 percent, 70 percent, and 55 percent, respectively.

Write a program to keep a record of each student's name, social security number, quiz scores (all 12), hourly examination scores, programming assignment scores, test program scores, and final examination score.

Your program should read data from an input file, compute total points for each student, calculate the letter grade, and output results. The output should be sorted by total points from high to low and include all raw data, the ten best quiz scores, total points and percentage score, and letter grade. Use procedures and functions where appropriate.

4. Write a program to input an unknown number of pairs of fractions with an operation (either +, −, *, or /) between the fractions. The program should perform the operation on the fractions or indicate that the operation is impossible. Answers should be reduced to lowest terms.

Sample Input	Sample Output
3/4 + 5/6	$\dfrac{3}{4} + \dfrac{5}{6} = \dfrac{19}{12}$
4/9 - 1/6	$\dfrac{4}{9} - \dfrac{1}{6} = \dfrac{5}{18}$
4/5 / 0/2	$\dfrac{4}{5} / \dfrac{0}{2} = \text{Impossible}$
4/3 + 7/0	$\dfrac{4}{3} + \dfrac{7}{0} = \text{Impossible}$
6/5 * 20/3	$\dfrac{6}{5} * \dfrac{20}{3} = \dfrac{8}{1} = 8$

5. Complex numbers are numbers of the form $a + bi$ where a and b are real and i represents $\sqrt{-1}$. Complex number arithmetic is defined by

Sum	$(a + bi) + (c + di) = (a + c) + (b + d)i$
Difference	$(a + bi) - (c + di) = (a - c) + (b - d)i$
Product	$(a + bi)(c + di) = (ac - bd) + (ad + bc)i$
Quotient	$(a + bi)/(c + di) = \dfrac{ac + bd}{c^2 + d^2} + \dfrac{bc - ad}{c^2 + d^2} i$

Write a program to be used to perform these calculations on two complex numbers. Each line of data consists of a single character designator (S, D, P, or Q) followed by four reals representing two complex numbers. For example, $(2 + 3i) + (5 - 2i)$ are represented by

S2 3 5 −2 █

A record should be used for each complex number. The output should be in the form $a + bi$.

6. The Readmore Public Library wants a program to keep track of the books checked out. Information for each book should be kept in a record and the

fields should include the author's name, a nonfiction designator **(boolean)**, the title, the library catalog number, and the copyright date. Each customer can check out at most ten books.

Your program should read information from a data file and print two lists alphabetized by author name, one for nonfiction and the other for fiction. A typical data line is

| Kidder Tracy | T Soul of a New Machine | 81.6044 1982 |

↑ position 21   ↑ position 52

7. Modify Problem 6 so that a daily printout is available that contains a summary of the day's transactions at the Readmore Public Library. You will need a record for each customer containing the customer's name and library card number. Be sure to make provision for books that are returned.

8. Write a program to be used to keep track of bank accounts. Define a record that includes each customer's name, account number, starting balance, transaction record, and ending balance.

The transaction record should list all deposits and withdrawals. A special message should be printed whenever there are insufficient funds for a withdrawal. When a name is read from the data file, all previous records should be searched to see if you are processing a new account. The final output for each customer should look like a typical bank statement.

9. Write a program that uses records to analyze poker hands. Each hand consists of five records (cards). Each record should have one field for the suit and one for the value. Rankings for the hands from high to low are

royal flush
straight flush
four of a kind
full house
flush
straight
three of a kind
two pair
one pair
none of the above

Your program should read data for five cards from a data file, evaluate the hand, and print out the hand together with a message indicating its value.

10. Problem 9 can be modified several ways. A first modification is to compare two different hands using only the ranking indicated. A second (more difficult) modification is to also compare hands that have the same ranking. For example, a pair of 8s is better than a pair of 7s. Extend Problem 9 to incorporate some of these modifications.

11. Divers at the Olympics are judged by seven judges. Points for each dive are awarded according to the following procedure.

a. Each judge assigns a score between 00.0 and 10.0 inclusive.
b. The high score and low score are eliminated.
c. The five remaining scores are summed and this total is multiplied by 0.6.
d. The result from c is multiplied by the degree of difficulty of the dive (0.0 to 3.0).

The first level of competition consists of 24 divers each making ten dives. Divers with the 12 highest totals advance to the finals.

Write a program to keep a record for each diver. Each record should contain information for all ten dives, the diver's name, and the total score. One round of competition consists of each diver making one dive. A typical line of data consists of the diver's name, degree of difficulty for the dive, and seven judges' scores. Part of your output should include a list of divers who advance to the finals.

12. Mrs. Crown, your computer science teacher, wishes to keep track of the maintenance record of her computers and has turned to you for help. She wants to keep track of the type of machine, its serial number (up to ten characters), the year of purchase, and a **boolean** variable indicating whether the machine is under service contract.

    Write a program which permits the entry of records, then prints a list of the machines that are under warranty and a list of those not under warranty. Both lists should be arranged in order of serial number.

13. Most microcomputer owners soon develop a large, often unorganized, library of software on several floppy disks. This is your chance to help them. Define a record containing the disk number of each disk, and a list of up to 30 program titles on each disk. Write a program to read a text file containing the information for a disk and then print an alphabetized listing of the progam titles on that disk.

14. Revise the program in Problem 13 to permit the user of the program to enter the program name desired, and have the program print the number of the disk(s) containing the program.

15. Write a program to read records containing the name, address, telephone number, and class of some of your friends. Print a list of the names of the students in the file who are in your class.

16. The Falcon Manufacturing Company wishes to keep computerized records of its telephone-order customers. They want the name, street address, city, state, and zip code for each customer. They include either a "T" if the customer is a business, or an "F" if the customer is an individual. A 30-character description of each business is also included. An individual's credit limit is in the record.

    Write a program to read the information for the customer from a text file and print a list of the information for businesses and a separate list of the information for individuals. There are no more than 50 records in the file.

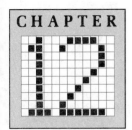
Files

In Chapter 8 you were introduced to the concept of a text file and have been using them for input since. This chapter introduces you to other kinds of files and shows how you can use them in programs.

■ 12.1
File Definition

Basic Idea and Notation

You can save information between runs of a program by using secondary storage devices such as tapes or disks (personal computers use floppy or hard disks). As a programmer, you need not be concerned with the actual physical construct of these storage devices, but you do need to know how to work with them. To oversimplify, you need to be able to get data into a program, manipulate these data, and save the data (and results) for later use. For example, if you write a program that computes grades for students in a class, you need to periodically enter data for processing. Pascal solves this problem with a structured data type **FILE.** A *file* is a data structure that consists of a sequence of components all of the same type. A **FILE** data type is defined by

> **TYPE**
>   file type = **FILE OF** data type;
>
> **VAR**
>   file name : file type;

Thus, if you wish to work with a file of integers, you define

```
TYPE
   FileOfInt = FILE OF integer;
VAR
   File1 : FileOfInt;
```

In this case, File1 is the desired file. Several comments are now in order.

1. Data entries in a file are called *components of the file.*
2. All components of a file must be of the same data type.
3. The only data type not permitted as a component of a file is another file type. This differs from arrays in that

   ARRAY [   ] **OF ARRAY** [   ] **OF** data type;

   is permitted, but

   FILE OF FILE OF data type;

   is not permitted.

Each of the following is a valid definition of a file type.

```
TYPE
    Identifier1 = FILE OF real;
    Identifier2 = FILE OF ARRAY [1 . . 20] OF integer;
    Identifier3 = FILE OF boolean;
```

Files of records are frequently used in programs. Thus, to keep a record for each student in a class, you can have the definition

```
TYPE
    String20 = PACKED ARRAY [1 . . 20] OF char;
    ExamScores = ARRAY [1 . . 4] OF integer;
    QuizScores = ARRAY [1 . . 10] OF integer;
    StudentInfo = RECORD
                      Name : String20;
                      IDNumber : 0 . . 999;
                      Exam : ExamScores;
                      Quiz : QuizScores;
                      Average : real;
                      Grade : char
                  END; (* of RECORD StudentInfo  *)
    StudentFile = FILE OF StudentInfo;
VAR
    Student : StudentFile;
```

Comparison to Arrays

Files and one-dimensional arrays have some similarities: both are structured data types and components must be of the same type. There are, however, some important differences.

1. Files permit you to store and retrieve information between runs of a program.
2. Only one component of a file is available at a time.
3. In standard versions of Pascal, files must be sequentially accessed; that is, when working with files, you start at the beginning and process the components in sequence. It is not possible (as with arrays) to access some component directly without first somehow moving through the previous components.
4. Files do not have a defined length. Once a file is defined, the number of components is limited only by your particular im-

plementation of Pascal or the physical size of the actual device such as a floppy disk. However, this is usually so large you can think of it as unbounded.

File Window and Buffer Variables

Before we get to specific work with files, we need to examine the concepts of a *file window* and a *buffer variable*. A file can be visualized as a sequence of components as follows:

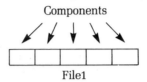

Components

File1

Only one of these components can be "seen" at a time. An imaginary window is associated with a file and values can be transferred to (or from) a component of the file only through this window. Thus, the window must be properly positioned before attempting to transmit data to or from a component.

This imaginary window, which we call a file window, has no name in Pascal. However, there is a related concept, called a buffer variable, that is the actual vehicle through which values are passed to or from the file component. When a file is declared in a program, a buffer variable is automatically declared and therefore available to the programmer. To illustrate, given the following declaration of FileA,

```
TYPE
   FileInfo = FILE OF integer;
VAR
   FileA : FileInfo;
```

the buffer variable (FileA↑) can be used in the program. The buffer variable is always the file name followed by an up arrow or, in some implementations, a caret (ˆ), but it is never declared in the variable declaration section. In general, we have

Declaration	Buffer Variable
VAR	
file name : **FILE OF** data type;	file name↑

The buffer variable is of the same data type as one component of the file. Although its use is intended for passing values to and from a file, it can be used very much like a regularly declared variable of that type. Specifically, from FileA, FileA↑ is a variable of type **integer** and statements such as

```
FileA↑ := 21;
Age := FileA↑;
GetData (FileA↑);   (where GetData is a procedure)
```

are appropriate.

Which Keyboard Should We Use?

Today's QWERTY keyboard—named for the arrangement of the first six letters in the third row—is a real killer for the novice typist and slow torture even for the 90-words-a-minute veteran. Although kinder keyboards are available (they've been around for years), this 111-year-old antique has stuck with us out of habit or ignorance, or perhaps both.

The awkward features of the QWERTY keyboard are no accident; rather, they are the result of the "anti-engineering" efforts of Christopher Latham Sholes, inventor of this keyboard. He and other typewriter inventors of the time found that, due to bearing and spring problems, rapidly hit keys often jammed. So he scrambled the locations of the most frequently used letters. The time required to reach a letter allowed the previously used letters to drop back into the type basket.

The serious drawbacks of this keyboard became apparent as Frank and Lilian Gilbreth began training speed typists for the Underwood Typewriter Company at the beginning of this century. Using special techniques (including primitive motion-picture cameras) to photograph typists' flying fingers, they discovered the following problems with the arrangement of letters on the keyboard.

● Hand motion is often unbalanced; that is, one hand types whole words and even sentences while the other sits idle. Most often it's the left hand that does the work, even though most people are right-handed. In fact, with the QWERTY keyboard, some 3,000 words in the English language must be typed with the left hand—making for slow, tiring, and error-prone typing.

● Only two of the ten most-used letters (a and s) are located in the second, or "home," row. Consequently, less than one-third of all typing occurs there. In contrast, the third row, which has four vowels (e, u, i, and o), assumes 52 percent of the typing load.

● A single finger is often called upon to type successive letters, such as ju, ft, and lo. For combinations, such as ce or my, one finger may even have to "hurdle" over the home row. This kind of movement is particularly tiring for typists, due to the distance their fingers have to travel (skilled typists' fingers have been measured to move more than 16 miles across a keyboard in eight hours).

But in 1936 August Dvorak engineered an alternative to the QWERTY keyboard. After conducting intensive studies of the human hand and the English language, he patented a new keyboard arrangement that took advantage of more natural stroking patterns. Even when subjected to a thorough computer analysis years later, this arrangement could not be significantly improved.

In the home row of Dvorak's keyboard, all

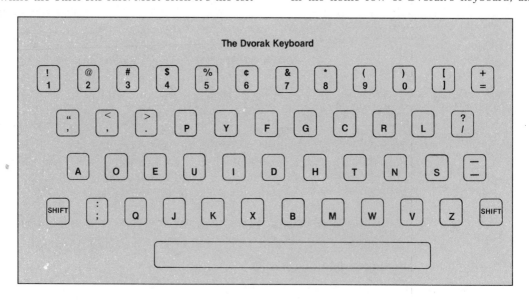

The Dvorak Keyboard

the vowels are on the left and the most frequently used consonants are on the right, making it possible for 70 percent of all typing to fall in this row. Since the consonant-vowel-consonant pattern is so common in the English language, the speedy alternating-hand stroke is built into the system. Also built in is the rolling stroke in which the hand rolls toward the center or toward the outside of the keyboard when typing common letter blends, such as *ou*, *th*, and *st*. Because of these features, most students learn the Dvorak keyboard faster than they do the QWERTY, and they type at faster speeds.

Unfortunately, until now budget constraints —if not a reluctance to learn something new— have prevented most schools from throwing out their perfectly good QWERTYs and buying all-new Dvorak typewriters. But computers have changed all that. Now students who are learning keyboarding skills on the computer have a choice. They can learn the old QWERTY method or, with just a few modifications in hardware, they can learn the Dvorak or even another keyboard. One small hardware device known as the Magic Keyboard (Southern California Research Group, P.O. Box 2231, Goleta, CA 93118), inserted into an Apple II or II Plus, allows students to select from among eight keyboards—including two for handicapped students confined to use of either hand, and one with the letters in alphabetical order. (The Magic Keyboard comes with letter and number decals that fit on existing keys to make learning the new keyboard less confusing.)

There's no doubt that learning to type on any keyboard is a slow and sometimes tedious experience. But now that computers have made the Dvorak system more accessible, it's time we minimize the frustration for our students and provide an alternative to the old QWERTY keyboard—the keyboard Mark Twain called an "ugly curiosity."

Exercises 12.1

1. Discuss the similarities between arrays and files.
2. Discuss the differences between arrays and files.

In Exercises 3–7, indicate which of the following are valid declarations of files. Give an explanation for those that are invalid. State what the component type is for those that are valid.

```
3. TYPE
      FileOfAges = FILE OF 0 . . 120;
   VAR
      AgeFile : FileOfAges;
4. TYPE
      String20 = PACKED ARRAY [1 . . 20] OF char;
      FileOfNames = ARRAY [1 . . 100] OF String20;
   VAR
      NameFile : FileOfNames;
5. TYPE
      FileA = FILE OF real;
      FileB = FILE OF FileA;
   VAR
      RealFile : FileB;
6. TYPE
      FileOfInt = FILE [1 . . 100] OF integer;
   VAR
      File1 : FileOfInt;
7. TYPE
      IntFile = FILE OF integer;
   VAR
      OldFile, NewFile, TempFile : IntFile;
```

8. Assume a program contains definition and declaration sections as listed. State which buffer variables are available and the data type of each.

```
TYPE
   FileOfAges = FILE OF 0 . . 120;
   IntFile = FILE OF integer;
   RealFile = FILE OF real;
   TruthFile = FILE OF boolean;
   List20 = ARRAY [1 . . 20] OF real;
   ListFile = FILE OF List20;
   StudentInfo = RECORD
                    Name : PACKED ARRAY [1 . . 20] of char;
                    Age : 0 . . 120
                 END;
   StudentFile = FILE OF StudentInfo;
VAR
   File1, File2 : FileOfAges;
   OldFile : StudentFile;
   NewFile : ListFile;
   TempFile : RealFile;
   TransFile : TruthFile;
   A,B,C : IntFile;
```

9. Define a file type and then declare a file to be used with records of patients for a physician. Information should include the name, address, height, weight, age, sex, and insurance company of each patient.

■ 12.2
Working with Files

Now that we have examined the concepts of files, file windows, and buffer variables, we need to see how values are transmitted to and from file components. Let's first examine the process of putting data into a file.

OBJECTIVES

- to understand the concept of opening a file
- to create a file using **write** or **put**
- to retrieve data from a file using **read** or **get**
- to understand the difference between internal and external files
- to use procedures when working with files

Creating a File

Once a file is declared in a program, entering data to the file is referred to as *writing to the file*. Before writing to a file, the file must be opened; this is done by using the standard procedure **rewrite**. Thus, if FileA is declared by

```
TYPE
   IntFile = FILE OF integer;
VAR
   FileA : IntFile;
```

then

```
rewrite (FileA);
```

opens FileA for receiving values of type **integer.** At this stage, the window is positioned at the beginning of FileA; FileA is assumed to be empty (that is, any previous values in FileA are no longer available); and values may now be stored in successive components of FileA (each value transferred is appended to the previous list of values).

Most versions of Pascal allow values to be transferred (written) to a file by assigning the desired value to the buffer variable and using the standard procedure **put** with the buffer variable as an argument. We can, for instance, store the values 10, 20, and 30 in FileA by

```
rewrite (FileA);  (*  Open for writing  *)
FileA↑ := 10;
put (FileA);
FileA↑ := 20;
put (FileA);
FileA↑ := 30;
put (FileA);
```

The **put** procedure has the effect of transferring the value of the buffer variable to the component in the window and then advancing the window to the next component. After **put** is called, the buffer variable becomes unassigned; this sequence is illustrated in Table 12.1.

TABLE 12.1
Using **put** to write to a file

Pascal Statement	Effect
rewrite (FileA);	[FileA↑ empty] [window: FileA empty cells]
FileA↑ := 10;	[FileA↑ = 10] [window: FileA empty cells]
put (FileA);	[FileA↑ empty] [window over first cell: FileA = 10, empty, empty]
FileA↑ := 20;	[FileA↑ = 20] [window: FileA = 10, empty, empty]
put (FileA);	[FileA↑ empty] [window: FileA = 10, 20, empty]
FileA↑ := 30;	[FileA↑ = 30] [window: FileA = 10, 20, empty]
put (FileA);	[FileA↑ empty] [window: FileA = 10, 20, 30, empty]

Standard Pascal also allows values to be written to a file using the procedure **write.** When this is used, the arguments for **write** are the file name followed by the desired values. Thus, the previous fragment can be

```
rewrite (FileA);  (*  Open the file  *)
write (FileA, 10, 20, 30);
```

Since some implementations permit **write** to be used only with files of type **text,** you should check to see what your implementation allows.

SELF QUIZ 12.1 Assume FileA is declared as a file with integer components. Show how the integers from 1 to 25 can be stored in the first 25 components of FileA.

The Standard Function eof

There is one additional feature associated with creating files we have not yet discussed. When a file is opened for writing, an end-of-file marker is placed at the beginning of the file. This can be thought of as the window being positioned at the end-of-file marker. When a value is transferred by **put** or **write,** the end-of-file marker is advanced to the same component position to which the window moves. The reason for this is relatively obvious. When retrieving data from a file, we need to know when we reach the end of the file. The function **eof** is used with the file name for an argument. **eof** (file name) is **true** when the window is positioned at the end-of-file marker. When writing to a file, **eof** (file name) is always **true.**

Retrieving File Data

In order to retrieve data from a file, you must first open the file for reading. This is accomplished by using the standard procedure

reset (file name);

This has the effect of repositioning the window at the beginning of the file. Furthermore, when a file is open for reading, the value of the file component in the window is automatically assigned to the buffer variable. The window can be advanced by a call to the standard procedure

get (file name);

Using the previous example of FileA with values as depicted

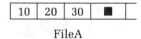

FileA

we can transfer values to the main program by

```
reset (FileA);
N1 := FileA↑;
get (FileA);
N2 := FileA↑;
get (FileA);
N3 := FileA↑;
```

Positioning of the window and transferring of values for this segment of code are illustrated in Table 12.2.

TABLE 12.2
Using **get** to read
from a file

Pascal Statement	Effect

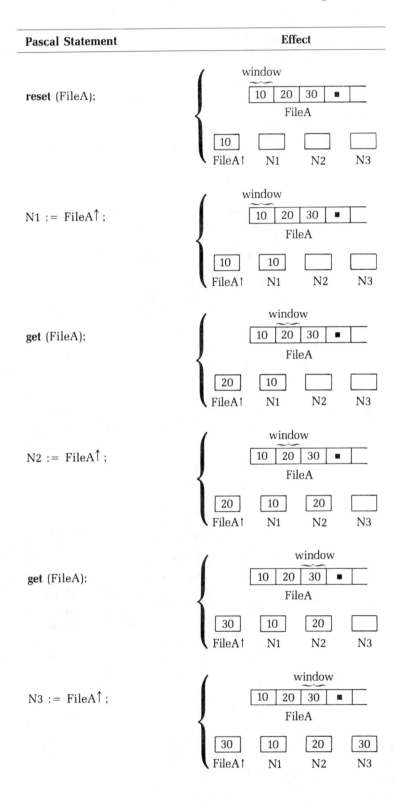

This example of retrieving data is a bit contrived since we know there are exactly three components before the end-of-file marker. A more realistic retrieval would use the **eof** function; for example,

```
reset (FileA);
WHILE NOT eof (FileA) DO
   BEGIN
      .
      .        (process FileA↑)
      .
      get (FileA)
   END;
```

The standard procedure **read** can also be used to transfer data from a file. After the file has been opened for reading, **read** can be used with the file name and variable names as arguments. Thus, either of the following can replace the previous code fragment.

```
reset (FileA);
read (FileA, N1);
read (FileA, N2);
read (FileA, N3);
```

or

```
reset (FileA);
read (FileA, N1, N2, N3);
```

SELF QUIZ 12.2 Assume that FileA is declared as a file with real components and that an unknown number of reals are stored in FileA. Write a segment of code to transfer the values into an array and determine how many values there are.

Opening Files

A file cannot be opened for writing and reading at the same time. When a file is opened for writing, it remains open for receiving values that will be appended to the file until the window is repositioned by **rewrite** or **reset,** or until the program is terminated. Thus, you may create a file and then, later in the program, add to the file without reopening it. In a similar fashion, before you first read from a file, it must be opened by **reset** (file name). You can then transfer values from the file using either **read** or **get.** You must, however, be careful to avoid the sequence

rewrite (file name);

   . put in data

reset (file name);

   . work with data

rewrite (file name);

because the second **rewrite** erases all previously entered data.

Let's now consider a short example in which we do something with each component of a file.

EXAMPLE 12.1

Suppose we have a file of reals and we want to create another file by subtracting 5.0 from each component. Assume the following definitions and declarations.

```
TYPE
   RealFile = FILE OF real;
VAR
   OldFile : RealFile;
   NewFile : RealFile;
```

We can accomplish our objective by

```
reset (OldFile);   (*  Open files  *)
rewrite (NewFile);
WHILE NOT eof (OldFile) DO
   BEGIN
     NewFile↑ := OldFile↑ - 5.0;
     put (NewFile);
     get (OldFile)
   END;
```

■

Procedures and Files

Much of the work of processing files is accomplished by using procedures. Thus, you should continue using the **TYPE** definition section for defining file types. Files can be used as arguments in a procedure call, but in the procedure heading, files must be listed as variable parameters. This requirement is implicit in the fact that you cannot assign a file variable all at once (as you can a value parameter). Any attempt to list a file as a value parameter results in an error during execution of the program.

EXAMPLE 12.2

Let's write a procedure to accomplish the task of Example 12.1.

```
PROCEDURE Subtract5 (VAR OldFl, NewFl : RealFile);
   BEGIN
     reset (OldFl);
     rewrite (NewFl);
     WHILE NOT eof (OldFl) DO
       BEGIN
         NewFl↑ := OldFl↑ - 5.0;
         put (NewFl);
         get (OldFl)
       END   (*  of WHILE . . . DO  *)
   END; (*  of PROCEDURE Subtract5  *)
```

This procedure is called from the main program by

```
Subtract5 (OldFile, NewFile);
```

Note that even though no changes are made in OldFile, it is passed as a variable parameter.

■

Internal and External Files

As we saw in Chapter 8, files used to store data in secondary storage between runs of a program are called external files. Files that are used for processing only and are not saved in secondary storage are internal files.

A NOTE OF INTEREST

Updating Data Bases

There are several problems associated with keeping data bases current and many interesting solutions and articles regarding these problems. In a recent article describing a delayed update process, Anthony I. Hinxman stated: "Record amendment is handled by 'delete-and-insert.'" He continued, explaining that "the delayed update has a number of advantages. First, the double copy of the entire database mentioned above occurs during the batch job and therefore does not cause an undesirable extension of the user's terminal session. Second,

only one database update program is necessary since the same program is used for both normal updating and transaction replay. Third, the following locking and contention problem is avoided. Suppose the update procedure U starts; it copies the database D to a temporary file D' and starts to update D'. A retrieval process R then begins and runs in parallel with U. If R is still running when U completes its update of D', a problem arises; R and D open for reading and the operating system cannot allow U to copy D' to D."

External files must be listed in the program heading in the following form.

PROGRAM name (**input, output,** external file name);

They are declared in the variable declaration section. Internal files are not listed in the program heading but are declared in the variable declaration section.

Typically, a programming problem has some external file in secondary storage that is to be updated in some form. This may require some temporary internal files to be declared for use in the program. When the program is exited, all external files are saved in secondary storage while the internal files are no longer available.

Processing Files

Before looking at a specific problem for processing files, let's consider the general problem of updating an external file. Since we eventually will **rewrite** the external file, we must be careful not to erase the original contents before they are saved and/or processed in some temporary internal file.

To close this section we consider a relatively short example of updating a file of test scores for students in a class. In the last section of this chapter, we will see a detailed treatment of processing files.

EXAMPLE 12.3

Assume we have an external file consisting of total points for each student in a class. Furthermore, assume the data file (**input**) contains test scores that are to be added (in the same order) to the previous totals to obtain new totals. A first-level pseudocode solution to this problem is

1. Copy the totals to a temporary file
2. Process the temporary file
3. Copy the temporary file to the external file

Assume the program heading is

```
PROGRAM Grades (input, output, TotalPts);
```

and the definitions and declarations are

```
TYPE
  IntFile = FILE OF integer;
VAR
  TotalPts : IntFile;
  Temp1File : IntFile;
  Temp2File : IntFile;
```

A procedure to copy the contents from one file to another is

```
PROCEDURE Copy (VAR OldFile, NewFile : IntFile);
  BEGIN
    reset (OldFile);
    rewrite (NewFile);
    WHILE NOT eof (OldFile) DO
      BEGIN
        NewFile↑ := OldFile↑;
        put (NewFile);
        get (OldFile)
      END  (*  of WHILE . . . DO  *)
  END;  (*  of PROCEDURE Copy  *)
```

This is called from the main program by

```
Copy (TotalPts, Temp1File);
```

We can now process Temp1File by adding corresponding scores from the data file. A procedure for this is

```
PROCEDURE AddScores (VAR OldFile, NewFile : IntFile);
  VAR
    NewScore : integer;
  BEGIN
    reset (OldFile);
    rewrite (NewFile);
    WHILE NOT eof (OldFile) DO
      BEGIN
        read (NewScore);   (*  Get score from data file *)
        NewFile↑ := NewScore + OldFile↑;
        put (NewFile);
        get (OldFile)
      END  (*  of WHILE . . . DO  *)
  END;  (*  of PROCEDURE AddScores  *)
```

This procedure is called from the main program by

```
AddScores (Temp1File, Temp2File);
```

At this stage, the updated scores are in Temp2File and they need to be stored in the external file TotalPts before the program is exited. This is done by another call to Copy in the main program. Thus,

```
Copy (Temp2File, TotalPts);
```

achieves the desired results. The main program is then

```
BEGIN (*    Main program  *)
  Copy (TotalPts, Temp1File);
  AddScores (Temp1File, Temp2File);
  Copy (Temp2File, TotalPts)
END.  (*  of main program  *)
```

This example obviously overlooks some significant points; for example, how do we know the scores match up, that each student's new score is added to that student's previous total? We address this issue later in the chapter.

EXAMPLE 12.4

Let's show how one file can be appended to an existing file. Assume the files are named OldFile and NewFile and the task is to append NewFile to OldFile. We use a temporary file, TempFile, for completing this task. A first-level pseudocode development for this problem is

1. Reset OldFile and NewFile
2. Open TempFile for writing
3. **WHILE NOT eof** (OldFile) **DO**
   3.1 write elements to TempFile
4. **WHILE NOT eof** (NewFile) **DO**
   4.1 write elements to TempFile
5. Copy TempFile to OldFile

Step 3 can be refined to

3. **WHILE NOT eof** (OldFile) **DO**
   3.1 write elements to TempFile
       3.1.1 assign OldFile buffer value to TempFile buffer
       3.1.2 write value to TempFile
       3.1.3 advance window of OldFile

The code for this step is

```
WHILE NOT eof (OldFile) DO
   BEGIN
      TempFile↑ := OldFile↑;
      put (TempFile);
      get (OldFile)
   END;
```

The complete code for this example is left as an exercise. ∎

Exercises 12.2

1. Explain the difference between internal files and external files.

In Exercises 2–4, write a test program to illustrate the problem.

2. What happens when you try to write to a file that has not been opened for writing?
3. What happens when you try to get data from a file that has not been reset?
4. What happens when a procedure uses a file as a value parameter?
5. Declare an appropriate file and store the positive multiples of 7 that are less than 100.
6. Explain how the file of Exercise 5 can be saved for another program to use.
7. Consider the file with integer components as shown.

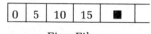

| 0 | 5 | 10 | 15 | ∎ | |

FivesFile

Write a segment of code to assign the values respectively to variables A, B, C, and D.

8. Consider the following file with component values as illustrated.

```
TYPE
   RealFile = FILE OF real;
VAR
   Prices : RealFile;
```

| 15.95 | 17.99 | 21.95 | 19.99 | ■ | |

Prices

a. Declare a new file and put values in the components that are 15 percent less than the values in components of Prices.

b. Update the values in Prices so that each value is increased by 10 percent.

9. Discuss the difference between **reset** and **rewrite.**

10. You have been asked to write a program to examine a file of integers and replace every negative number with zero. Assume IntFile is appropriately declared and contains five integer values. Why will the following segment of code not work?

```
rewrite (IntFile);
FOR J := 1 TO 5 DO
   BEGIN
      get (IntFile);
      IF IntFile↑ < 0 THEN
         IntFile↑ := 0;
      put (IntFile)
   END; (* of FOR loop *)
```

For Exercises 11–15, consider the files declared by

```
TYPE
   FileOfInt = FILE OF integer;
VAR
   File1, File2 : FileOfInt;
```

Find all errors in the exercise.

11.
```
reset (File1);
FOR J := 1 TO 5 DO
   BEGIN
      File1↑ := 10 * J;
      put (File1)
   END;
```

12.
```
rewrite (File1);
FOR J := 1 TO 5 DO
   BEGIN
      File1↑ := 10 * J;
      put (File1)
   END;
```

13.
```
rewrite (File1);
FOR J := 1 TO 5 DO
   BEGIN
      File1 := 10 * J;
      put (File1)
   END;
```

```
14. rewrite (File1);
    FOR J := 1 TO 5 DO
      File1↑ := J * 10;
15. reset (File2);
    WHILE NOT eof (File1) DO
      BEGIN
        File2↑ := File1↑;
        put (File2);
        get (File1)
      END;
16. reset (File2);
    rewrite (File1);
    WHILE NOT eof (File2) DO
      BEGIN
        File1↑ := File2↑;
        put (File1);
        get (File2)
      END;
```

For Exercises 17–19, assume the files OldFile and NewFile are declared as

```
TYPE
  IntFile = FILE OF integer;
VAR
  OldFile, NewFile : IntFile;
```

Furthermore, assume OldFile has component values as illustrated.

OldFile

Indicate the values in components of both OldFile and NewFile after each of the following segments of code.

```
17. reset (OldFile);
    rewrite (NewFile);
    WHILE NOT eof (OldFile) DO
      BEGIN
        IF OldFile↑ > 0 THEN
          BEGIN
            NewFile↑ := OldFile↑;
            put (NewFile)
          END;
        get (OldFile)
      END;
18. rewrite (OldFile);
    rewrite (NewFile);
    WHILE NOT eof (OldFile) DO
      BEGIN
        IF OldFile↑ > 0 THEN
          BEGIN
            NewFile↑ := OldFile↑;
            put (NewFile)
          END
      END;
```

19.
```
reset (OldFile);
rewrite (NewFile);
WHILE NOT eof (OldFile) DO
  BEGIN
    NewFile↑ := abs(OldFile↑);
    put (NewFile);
    get (OldFile)
  END;
rewrite (OldFile);
reset (NewFile);
WHILE NOT eof (NewFile) DO
  BEGIN
    OldFile↑ := NewFile↑;
    put (OldFile);
    get (NewFile)
  END;
```

20. Assume OldFile and NewFile are as declared in Exercises 17–19. Furthermore, assume OldFile contains the values

8	−17	0	−4	21	■	

OldFile

Indicate the output from the following segment of code and the values of the components in OldFile and NewFile.

```
reset (OldFile);
rewrite (NewFile);
WHILE NOT eof (OldFile) DO
  BEGIN
    NewFile↑ := OldFile↑;
    IF NewFile↑ < 0 THEN
      writeln (NewFile↑)
    ELSE
      put (NewFile);
      get (OldFile)
  END;
```

21. Assume you have declared three files (File1, File2, and File3) in a program such that the component type for each file is **real**. Furthermore, assume that both File1 and File2 contain an unknown number of values. Write a segment of code to transfer the corresponding sum of components from File1 and File2 into File3. Since File1 and File2 may have a different number of components, after one end-of-file is reached, you should add zeros until the next end-of-file is reached. Thus, your segment produces

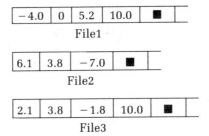

−4.0	0	5.2	10.0	■	

File1

6.1	3.8	−7.0	■	

File2

2.1	3.8	−1.8	10.0	■	

File3

22. Write a complete program that finishes the work started in Example 12.4. Your program should print out the contents of each file used and of the final file.

■ 12.3
Files with Structured Components

In actual practice, components of files are frequently some structured data type. A program might use a file of arrays or a file of records and, when such a file is desired, you declare it as an external file and then create components from a text file. Once the data are thus converted, you can access an entire array or record using **get** or **put** rather than accessing individual fields or components with **read** and **write.** The data are also saved in structured form between runs of a program. When data are stored in structured components, it is relatively easy to update and work with these files. For example, a doctor might have a file of records for patients and wish to insert or delete records of the patients, choose to examine the individual fields of each record, print an alphabetical list, or print a list of patients with unpaid bills.

Let's now examine two declarations of files with structured components. First we declare a file whose components are arrays; each array contains five integers between 0 and 10,000. Such a file can be used by a company to keep track of their inventory. For example, each array can contain information about one part as illustrated.

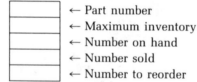

```
    ┌──────┐
    │      │   ← Part number
    ├──────┤
    │      │   ← Maximum inventory
    ├──────┤
    │      │   ← Number on hand
    ├──────┤
    │      │   ← Number sold
    ├──────┤
    │      │   ← Number to reorder
    └──────┘
```

With a file of these arrays, a program can print out a daily summary sorted by part number, print out an order list, insert arrays for new parts stocked, and delete arrays for parts no longer stocked.

Such a file can be declared by

```
TYPE
    IntRange = 0 . . 10000;
    Parts = ARRAY [1 . . 5] OF IntRange;
    PartsFile = FILE OF Parts;
VAR
    ItemInfo : PartsFile;
```

For this example, ItemInfo is an external file and the call

```
    get (ItemInfo);
```

causes ItemInfo↑ to receive the contents of an array. If the respective values are 2482, 25, 17, 8, and 16, we have

ItemInfo↑

2482	ItemInfo↑ [1]
25	ItemInfo↑ [2]
17	ItemInfo↑ [3]
8	ItemInfo↑ [4]
16	ItemInfo↑ [5]

SELF QUIZ 12.3 Using the file of arrays ItemInfo, write a procedure to print an order list. The list should contain both the part number and the number of additional parts to be ordered.

For our second illustration, suppose you are writing a program to use a file of records. Each record contains information about a student in a computer science class: in particular, the student's name, three test scores (in an array), identification number, and test average. A declaration for such a file is

```
TYPE
   String20 = PACKED ARRAY [1 . . 20] OF char;
   Scores = ARRAY [1 . . 3] OF 0 . . 100;
   StudentInfo = RECORD
                     Name : String20;
                     Score : Scores;
                     IDNumber : 0 . . 999;
                     Average : real
                 END;
   StudentFile = FILE OF StudentInfo;
VAR
   Student : StudentFile;
```

Student is a file of records that can be illustrated as shown in Figure 12.1. After Student is properly opened for reading by **reset** (Student), subsequent uses of the statement

```
get (Student);
```

cause the contents of records (after the first one) to be transferred to Student↑. The field identifiers are

```
Student↑.Name
Student↑.IDNumber
Student↑.Score
Student↑.Average
```

where Student↑.Score is an array. Components of this array are

```
Student↑.Score[1]
Student↑.Score[2]
Student↑.Score[3]
```

If you wish to compute the average for a student whose record is in the buffer, you can write

```
Sum := 0;
WITH Student↑ DO
   BEGIN
      FOR J := 1 TO 3 DO
         Sum := Sum + Score[J];
      Average := Sum/3
   END;
```

You may now want to save this computed average for later use. Unfortunately, **put** (Student) will not work because the file is open for reading rather than writing. We solve this and other problems in the remainder of this section as we investigate methods of manipulating files.

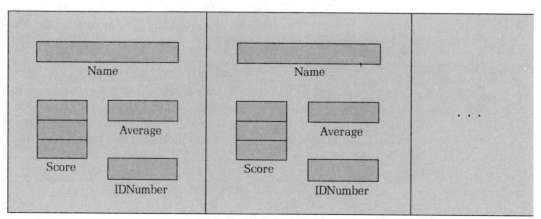

FIGURE 12.1
Student as a file of
records

Student

Assume a file of student records is declared as before and contains information for all students in a class. Write a segment of code to compute the class average for the first test.

Creating a File of Records

One of the first problems to be solved when working with files whose components are structured variables is to transfer data from some text file into the appropriate file of structured components. Once the new file is created, it can be saved in secondary storage by declaring it as an external file. To illustrate the process of creating a file of records, let's continue the example of records for students in a computer science class. Recall the definitions and subsequent declaration

```
TYPE
    String20 = PACKED ARRAY [1 . . 20] OF char;
    Scores = ARRAY [1 . . 3] OF 0 . . 100;
    StudentInfo = RECORD
                    Name : String20;
                    IDNumber : 0 . . 999;
                    Score : Scores;
                    Average : real
                  END;
    StudentFile = FILE OF StudentInfo;
VAR
    Student : StudentFile;
```

Before we can create the file of records, we need to know how data were entered in the text file named Data. For purposes of this example, assume data for each student are contained on a single line, 20 positions are used for the name, and an identification number is followed by three test scores. Thus, the data file, Data, is

| Smith John | 065 89 92 76 | Jones Mary | 021 93 97 85 | ▮ |

A procedure to create the file of records is

```
PROCEDURE CreateFile (VAR Pupil : StudentFile);
  VAR
    J : integer;
  BEGIN
    reset (Data);
    rewrite (Pupil);   (*  Open for writing  *)
    WHILE NOT eof (Data) DO
      BEGIN  (*  Get data for one record  *)
        WITH Pupil↑ DO
          BEGIN
            FOR J := 1 TO 20 DO
              read (Data, Name[J]);
            read (Data, IDNumber);
            readln (Data, Score[1], Score[2], Score[3])
          END;
        put (Pupil)   (*  Put buffer contents in file  *)
      END
  END;  (*  of PROCEDURE CreateFile  *)
```

This procedure is called from the main program by

```
CreateFile (Student);
```

After it is executed, we have the records shown in Figure 12.2.

SELF QUIZ 12.5   Illustrate the values of components and fields in Pupil and Pupil↑ during the first pass through the loop in **PROCEDURE** CreateFile.

File Manipulation

Several problems are typically involved with manipulating files and file components. Generally, a program starts with an existing file, revises it in some fashion, and then saves the revised file. Because files in standard Pascal must be accessed sequentially, this usually necessitates copying the existing external file to a temporary internal file, revising the temporary file, and copying the revised file to the external file. The existing

FIGURE 12.2
File Student with values

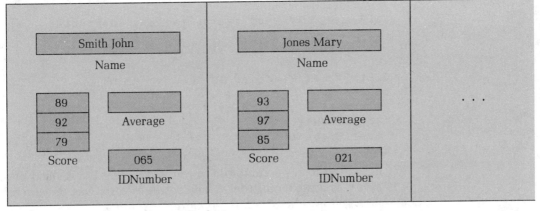

Student

external file is often referred to as the *master file.* The file containing changes to be made in the master file is called the *transaction file.*

To illustrate a simple update problem, let's consider again the problem using the file containing records for students in a computer science class. Assume that the external file is named Student. Now suppose we wish to delete a record from Student (master file) because some student moved to Australia. This problem can be solved by searching Student sequentially for the record in question. As the name in each record is examined, if the record is to be kept, it is put in a temporary file. The desired record is not transferred, thus accomplishing the update. Finally, Student is rewritten by copying the contents of the temporary file to Student.

A first-level pseudocode development is

1. Get the name to be deleted
2. Search Student for a match copying each record to TempFile
3. Copy the remainder of Student to TempFile
4. Copy TempFile to Student

Using the previous declarations and assuming that the name of the student whose record is to be deleted is read into MovedAway, step 2 can be solved by

```
(*    Open the files    *)

reset(Student);
rewrite(TempFile);
Found := false;
WHILE NOT eof(Student) AND NOT Found DO
  BEGIN
    IF Student↑.Name = MovedAway THEN
      BEGIN
        Found := true;
        get(Student)
      END
    ELSE
      BEGIN
        TempFile↑ := Student↑;
        put(TempFile);
        get(Student)
      END
  END;          (*    of search for a student name    *)

(*    Now copy the rest of student file    *)

WHILE NOT eof(Student) DO
  BEGIN
    TempFile↑ := Student↑;
    put(TempFile);
    get(Student)
  END;
```

We now need to copy TempFile to Student so that the revised master file is saved as an external file. A procedure for this was developed in Section 12.2; it is called from the main program by

```
Copy (TempFile, Student);
```

A NOTE OF INTEREST

Computer Matching: George Orwell's 1984?

Government use of computer matching received widespread publicity in 1977 when Joseph A. Califano, Jr. (then secretary of Health, Education and Welfare) announced Project Match. This plan compared computerized files of federal employees with computerized files of state welfare rolls in an attempt to eliminate fraud. Several issues have since been raised concerning the extent to which computer matching programs such at Project Match may be a threat to individual rights.

In a written debate with Richard Kusserow, John Shattuck cited the following arguments against such matching.

1. The Fourth Amendment protection against unreasonable search and seizure is violated by computer matching.
2. Presumption of innocence ceases to exist when a name appears on a "hit" list.
3. The principle underlying the Privacy Act of 1974 is not upheld.
4. Due process of law may be denied.

Speaking for computer matching, Richard Kusserow stated: "Computer matching can serve many objectives.

1. Assuring that ineligible applicants are not given costly program benefits
2. Reducing or terminating benefits for recipients who are being paid erroneously
3. Detecting fraudulent claims and deterring others from defrauding the program
4. Collecting on overpayments on defaulted loans more effectively
5. Monitoring grant and contract award processes
6. Improving program policy, procedures, and controls"

He concluded by stating: "Any computer match that does not consider privacy, fairness, and due process as among its major goals is not a good project. Well-designed computer matches are cost effective. The government's need to insure a program's integrity need not be incompatible with the individual's right to privacy and freedom from government intrusion. The point is to balance these competing interests."

As a second illustration of file manipulation, let's consider the standard problem of merging two sorted files. For example, suppose the master file is a file of records and each record contains a field for the name of a customer. Furthermore, assume this file has been sorted alphabetically by name. Now suppose an alphabetical listing of new customers is to be merged with the old file to produce a current file containing records for all customers sorted alphabetically by name.

As before, we use a temporary file to hold the full sorted list and then copy the temporary file to the master file. This can be envisioned as illustrated in Figure 12.3. The merge is not too difficult. All files are first opened. Then the initial records from MasterList and NewList are compared. The record containing the name that comes first alphabetically is transferred to TempFile and the next record is obtained from the file containing the record that was transferred. This process continues until the end of one file is reached. At that time, the remainder of the other file is copied into TempFile.

FIGURE 12.3
Merging files

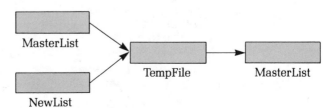

Assuming that each record has a field identified by Name, which is of type String30, and that FileType has been defined as the type for files being used, a procedure for merging is

```
PROCEDURE Merge (VAR OldMaster,NewList : FileType);
VAR
   TempFile : FileType;
BEGIN
   reset (OldMaster);
   reset (NewList);
   rewrite (TempFile);

(*   Compare top records until eof is reached   *)

   WHILE NOT eof(OldMaster) AND NOT eof(NewList) DO
     BEGIN
       IF OldMaster↑.Name < NewList↑.Name THEN
         BEGIN
           TempFile↑ := OldMaster↑;
           get(OldMaster)
         END
       ELSE
         BEGIN
           TempFile↑ := NewList↑;
           get(NewList)
         END;
       put(TempFile)
     END;

(*   Now copy the remaining names   *)

   WHILE NOT eof(OldMaster)  DO
     BEGIN
       TempFile↑ := OldMaster↑;
       put(TempFile);
       get(OldMaster)
     END;

   WHILE NOT eof(NewList) DO
     BEGIN
       TempFile↑ := NewList↑;
       put(TempFile);
       get(NewList)
     END;

(*   Now copy back to OldMaster   *)

   rewrite (OldMaster);
   reset (TempFile);
   WHILE NOT eof(TempFile) DO
     BEGIN
       OldMaster↑ := TempFile↑;
       put(OldMaster);
       get(TempFile)
     END
END;   (*   of PROCEDURE Merge   *)
```

This procedure can be called from the main program by

```
Merge (Master, NewFile);
```

A final comment is in order. It is frequently necessary to work with files of records that have been sorted according to a field of the record. Consequently, you must first be able to sort an unsorted file. In general, this is done by transferring the file components to array components, sorting the array, and transferring the sorted array components back to the file. This means that you must have some idea of how many components are in the file and declare the array length accordingly. The physical setting of a problem usually provides this information. For example, a physician will have some idea of how many patients (100, 200, or 1000) he or she sees.

Exercises 12.3

For Exercises 1–4, declare appropriate files. Fields for each record are indicated for you.

1. Patient records for a physician; include name, age, height, weight, insurance carrier, and amount owed.
2. Flight information for an airplane; include flight number, airline, arrival time, arriving from, departure time, and destination.
3. Bookstore inventory; include author, title, stock number, price, and quantity.
4. Records for a magazine subscription agency; include name and address, indicating street number, street name, city, state, and zip code.

5. Write a test program that allows you to declare a file of records, read data into the file, and print information from selected records according to the value in some key field.

6. Suppose a data file of type **text** contains information for students in a class. Each student's information uses three data lines as illustrated.

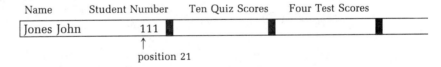

Name	Student Number	Ten Quiz Scores	Four Test Scores
Jones John	111		

↑
position 21

    a. Declare a file of records to be used to store this data.
    b. Write a procedure to create a file of records containing appropriate information from the text file.
    c. Write a procedure to sort the file alphabetically.

7. Consider the file Student declared by

```
TYPE
   String20 = PACKED ARRAY [1 . . 20] OF char;
   Scores = ARRAY [1 . . 3] OF 0 . . 100;
   StudentInfo = RECORD
                    Name : String20;
                    IDNumber : 0 . . 999;
                    Score : Scores;
                    Average : real
                 END;
   StudentFile = FILE OF StudentInfo;
VAR
   Student : StudentInfo;
```

Write a procedure for each of the following tasks. In each case, show how the procedure is called from the main program. (You may assume the file has been alphabetized.)

a. Add one record in alphabetical order.
b. Add one record to the bottom of the file.
c. Update the record of 'Smith Jane   ' by changing her score on the second test from an 82 to an 89.
d. The scores from test three are in a data file. Each line contains an identification number followed by three integer scores. Update Student to include these scores.
e. Assume all test scores are entered. Update Student by computing the test average for each student.
f. Print a list containing each student's name and test average; the list should be sorted by test average from high to low.

RUNNING AND DEBUGGING TIPS

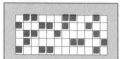

1. Be sure all files (except **input** and **output)** are properly opened for reading and writing. Remember, you must **reset** before reading from a file and **rewrite** before writing to a file.
2. You cannot execute a **rewrite-reset-rewrite** sequence when attempting to append to a file.
3. Don't try to read past the end-of-file marker. This is a common error that occurs when trying to **read** without a sufficient check for **eof.**
4. Be careful to use file names as arguments correctly when using **read, readln, write, writeln, eof,** and **eoln.**
5. List all external files in the program heading and then be sure to declare them in the variable declaration section.
6. All files listed in a procedure heading must be variable parameters.
7. Protect against working with empty files or empty lines of a text file.
8. Remember, the file buffer is undefined when **eof** (file name) is **true.**
9. Be aware of the possibility of extra blanks at the beginning or end of lines in a text file. Some implementations cause these to be inserted when creating a text file.
10. The end-of-line marker is read as a blank. Thus, when working with character data in a text file, it may appear that extra blanks are in the file. However, the **eoln** function still returns **true** when the pointer is positioned at an end-of-line marker.

■ Summary

Key Terms

file	buffer variable	transaction file
component of a file	writing to a file	
file window	master file	

Keywords

FILE
put
get

Key Concepts

- A file is a sequence of components all of the same data type; a typical declaration is

```
TYPE
   RealFile = FILE OF real;
VAR
   FileA : RealFile;
```

- In standard implementations of Pascal, files must be accessed sequentially.
- File window is a phrase commonly used to describe which component of the file is available for having data passed to or from it.
- A buffer variable is an undeclared variable that is used to transfer data to or from a file component; if the file name is FileA, then the identifier for the buffer variable is FileA↑.
- Before transferring values to a file—writing to a file—the file must be opened for writing by **rewrite** (file name); values can then be transferred from the file buffer using **put** or **write** (file name, value); for example,

```
rewrite (NewFile);
NewFile↑ := 10;
put (NewFile);
```

or

```
rewrite (NewFile);
write (NewFile, 10);
```

- Before transferring values from a file—reading from a file—the file must be opened for reading by **reset** (file name); values can then be transferred from the file by assignments from the file buffer and by using **get** (file name) or **read** (file name, variable name); for example,

```
reset (NewFile);
A := NewFile↑;
get (NewFile);
```

or

```
reset (NewFile);
read (NewFile, A);
```

- An end-of-file marker is automatically placed at the end of the file—**eof** (file name)—when a file is created.
- A file cannot be opened for reading and writing at the same time.
- When a file is declared as a parameter in a procedure heading, it must be listed as a variable parameter; for example,

```
PROCEDURE Update (VAR OldFile, NewFile : file type);
```

- External files must be listed in the program heading as well as declared in the variable declaration section; values in their components are retained in secondary storage for later use.
- Internal files are declared in the variable declaration section but are not listed in the program heading; values in components of internal files are not retained when the program is exited.
- Components of a file can be arrays; the declaration

```
VAR
   F : FILE OF ARRAY [1 . . 10] OF real;
```

FIGURE 12.4
File of arrays

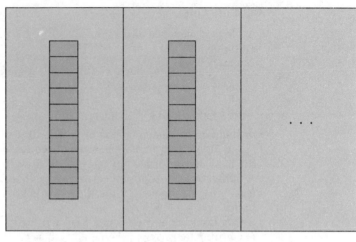

F

can be depicted as shown in Figure 12.4, where F↑ is an array and array components are denoted by F↑ [J].

- File components can also be records and can be declared by

```
TYPE
   RecType = RECORD
               Name : PACKED ARRAY [1 . . 20] OF char;
               Age : 0 . . 120;
               Sex : char
               END; (* of RECORD RecType *)
VAR
   F : FILE OF RecType;
```

and depicted as shown in Figure 12.5. In this case, the buffer variable F↑ is a record and fields can be denoted by

```
F↑.Name
F↑.Age
F↑.Sex
```

- Files with structured components frequently have to be processed and/or updated; for a file of records, you might insert or delete a record, sort the file by a field, merge two files, update each record, or produce a printed list according to some field.

FIGURE 12.5
File of records

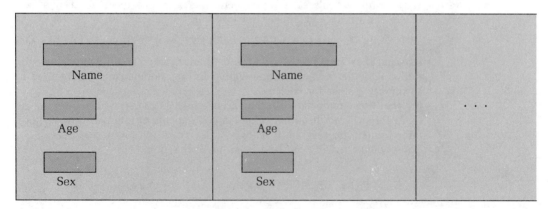

F

- When updating or otherwise processing a file, changes are normally made in a transaction (temporary) file and then copied back into the master (permanent) file.
- Since input data are generally in a text file, you need to create a file of structured components from the text file; you can then use **get** and **put** to transfer entire structures at one time.

■ **Chapter Review Exercises**

1. List three advantages of using data files in a program.

2. Explain how a sequential file is updated.

3. Explain the difference between the syntax and use of write and put statements.

For Exercises 4–8, indicate if the file definition is valid or invalid. If invalid, correct the definition or explain the error.

```
4. TYPE
     ClassFile = FILE OF ClassName;
   VAR
     File5 = ClassFile;
5. TYPE
     QuizFile = FILE OF ARRAY [1 . . 30] OF integer;
   VAR
     QuizGrades : QuizFile;
6. TYPE
     RealFile = FILE OF real;
     SecondFile = FILE OF RealFile;
   VAR
     RealNumbers : SecondFile;
7. TYPE
     String20 = PACKED ARRAY [1 . . 20] OF char;
     RealArray = ARRAY [1 . . 20] OF real;
     FileData = FILE OF String20, RealArray;
   VAR
     X : FileData;
8. TYPE
     FileData = PACKED ARRAY [1 . . 30, 1 . . 30] OF char;
     DataFile = FILE OF FileData;
   VAR
     FileVariable : DataFile;
```

9. What are some of the differences between files and arrays?

For Exercises 10–14, indicate which are correct statements. Assume all variables are properly declared.

```
10. write (FileA↑);
11. put (FileA↑);
12. ReadFile (VAR FileA↑ : DataFile);
13. FileA↑.B[7] = 4;
14. get (FileA);
```

15. Declare a record, file, and variable declarations for a file to contain the names, addresses, and telephone numbers of your classmates.

16. Write a procedure to read in a record from the file declared in Exercise 15.

17. Explain the purpose of the **rewrite** statement.

18. Write a test program to determine if your implementation of Pascal permits the use of **write** statements on other than text files.

19. Under what conditions will **eof** be **true** when reading files. When writing files?

20. List the differences between internal and external files.

21. Write an appropriate file declaration for a file containing magazine subscription information. The file contains the subscribers' names, addresses, cities, states, zip codes, and subscription expiration dates (month and year).

22. Write a procedure for Exercise 21 to print the names of those subscribers whose subscription expires this month.

23. Write an appropriate file declaration for a file that contains 100 positive integers.

24. Write a procedure to read the file declared in Exercise 23 and print the sum of the integers in the file.

25. Write a procedure to sort the components of the file in Exercise 23 into ascending order.

26. Write appropriate file and variable declarations for a file containing the names and scoring average for the members of your school's basketball team.

27. Write a procedure to print the name of the player with the highest scoring average from the file in Exercise 26.

■ Chapter Summary Program

The sample program for this chapter is a different version of the program presented at the end of Chapter 11; here a file of records is the data structure rather than an array of records. Also, we only sort and print an alphabetical listing.

A first-level pseudocode development for this problem is

1. Get the data
2. Transfer to an array for sorting
3. Sort the array by name
4. Print results
5. Save results in OldFile

A refinement of this problem is

1. Get the data
   1.1 open file for writing
   1.2 initialize counter
   1.3 **WHILE NOT eof (input) DO**
       process one line of data
2. Transfer to an array for sorting
   2.1 open file for reading
   2.2 **FOR** J := 1 **TO** NumberOfRecords **DO**
       assign record from file to array
3. Sort the array by name (use previous sorting procedure for array of records)

4. Print results
   4.1 print a heading
   4.2 print the list of names and amounts
5. Save results in OldFile
   5.1 open file for writing
   5.2 **FOR** J := 1 **TO** NumberOfRecords **DO**
       transfer a record from the array to OldFile

Since most of these steps have been previously developed, we now consider a complete program for this problem.

```
PROGRAM Boosters (input,output,Data,OldFile);
(*****************************************************************

    This program performs the same task as the Chapter
    Summary Program in Chapter 11. However, we now use
    a file of records rather than an array of records. Notice
    that an external file (OldFile) is used to save
    information between runs of the program. Another new
    feature is the method used to create a sorted file.

*****************************************************************)
CONST
  ClubSize = 50;
TYPE
  String20 = PACKED ARRAY[1 . . 20] OF char;
  MemberInfo = RECORD
                 Name : String20;
                 Amount : real
               END;  (*   of MemberInfo   *)
  DonorFile = FILE OF MemberInfo;
  DonorList = ARRAY [1 . . ClubSize] OF MemberInfo;

VAR
  NumberOfDonors : integer;   (*  Counter for number of donors  *)
  Donor,                      (*  File of records for donor     *)
  OldFile : DonorFile;        (*  External file of records      *)
  TempDonor : DonorList;      (*  Temp array for file contents  *)
  Data : text;                (*  Data file                     *)

(*****************************************************************

                 This procedure gets the data.

*****************************************************************)
PROCEDURE GetData (VAR Don : DonorFile; VAR Ct : integer);
  VAR
    J : integer;
```

```
      BEGIN
        reset(Data);
        rewrite(Don);        (*    Open for writing      *)
        Ct := 0;
        WHILE NOT eof(Data) DO
          BEGIN
            WITH Don↑ DO
              BEGIN
                FOR J := 1 TO 20 DO
                  read(Data, Name[J]);
                readln(Data, Amount)
              END;        (*    of WITH . . . DO  *)
            put(Don);  (*    Put buffer contents in file     *)
            Ct := Ct + 1
          END  (*    of WHILE NOT eof     *)
    END;  (*    of PROCEDURE GetData    *)


(*********************************************************************

        This procedure will transfer records to an array.

 *********************************************************************)
PROCEDURE WriteToArray (VAR Don : DonorFile;
                        VAR TempDon : DonorList;
                        CT : integer);

  VAR
    J : integer;
  BEGIN
    reset(Don);
    TempDon[1] := Don↑;
    FOR J := 2 TO Ct DO
      BEGIN
        get(Don);
        TempDon[J] := Don↑
      END
  END;     (*    of PROCEDURE WriteToArray    *)


(***************************************************************

        This procedure copies records to the external file
        (OldFile) for storage between runs.

 ***************************************************************)
PROCEDURE WriteToOldFile (TempDon : DonorList;
                          VAR Old : DonorFile;
                          NumDonors : integer);

  VAR
    J : integer;
  BEGIN
    rewrite (Old);
    FOR J := 1 TO NumDonors DO
      BEGIN
        Old↑ := TempDon[J];
        put(Old)
      END
  END;     (*    of PROCEDURE WriteToOldFile    *)
```

```
(***********************************************************

          This procedure sorts by name.

***************************************************************)
PROCEDURE SortByName (VAR Don : DonorList; N : integer);
  VAR
    J,K,Index : integer;
    Temp : MemberInfo;
  BEGIN
    FOR J := 1 TO N-1 DO
      BEGIN
        Temp := Don[J];
        Index := J;
        FOR K := J+1 TO N DO
          IF Don[K].Name < Temp.Name THEN
            BEGIN
              Temp := Don[K];
              Index := K
            END;
        Don[Index] := Don[J];
        Don[J] := Temp
      END     (*   of FOR loop   *)
  END;  (*   of PROCEDURE SortByName   *)


(***********************************************************

          This procedure prints a heading.

***************************************************************)
PROCEDURE PrintHeading;
  CONST
    Skip = ' ';
  BEGIN
    writeln; writeln;
    writeln(Skip:20,'Local Sports Boosters');
    writeln(Skip:24,'Donation List');
    writeln(Skip:10,'_____');
    writeln(Skip:13,'Name',Skip:21,'Amount');
    writeln(Skip:13,'____',Skip:21,'_____');
  END;         (*   of PROCEDURE PrintHeading   *)


(***********************************************************

          This procedure prints a list.

***************************************************************)
PROCEDURE PrintList (Don : DonorList; N : integer);
  CONST
    Skip = ' ';
  VAR
    J : integer;
```

```
BEGIN
  FOR J := 1 TO N DO
    WITH Don[J] DO
      writeln(Skip:10,Name,Amount:14:2);
  writeln; writeln
END;  (*  of PROCEDURE PrintList    *)


(*****************************************************************

    All procedures are now written. Begin the main program.

 *****************************************************************)

BEGIN   (*  Main program  *)
  GetData(Donor,NumberOfDonors);
  WriteToArray(Donor, TempDonor, NumberOfDonors);
  SortByName (TempDonor, NumberOfDonors);
  PrintHeading;
  PrintList (TempDonor, NumberOfDonors);
  WriteToOldFile (TempDonor, OldFile,NumberOfDonors)
END.   (*   of main program    *)
```

The output from this program is

```
                  Local Sports Boosters
                      Donation List
         --------------------------------------------
              Name                      Amount
              ----                      ------
         Alexander Candy               300.00
         Anderson Tony                 375.00
         Banks Marj                    375.00
         Born Patty                    100.00
         Brown Ron                     200.00
         Darnell Linda                 275.00
         Erickson Thomas               100.00
         Fox William                   300.00
         Francis Denise                350.00
         Generous George               525.00
         Gillette Mike                 350.00
         Hancock Kirk                  500.00
         Higgins Sam                   300.00
         Janson Kevin                  200.00
         Johnson Ed                    350.00
         Johnson Martha                400.00
         Jones Jerry                   250.00
         Kelly Marvin                  475.00
         Kneff Susan                   300.00
         Lasher John                   175.00
         Lyon Elizabeth                425.00
         Moore Robert                  100.00
         Muller Marjorie               250.00
         Smith John                    100.00
         Trost Frostie                  50.00
         Trudo Rosemary                200.00
         Weber Sharon                  150.00
```

```
Williams Art                    350.00
Williams Jane                   175.00
Wilson Mary                     275.00
```

■ Programming Problems

1. *The Pentagon* is a mathematics magazine published by Kappa Mu Epsilon, a mathematics honorary society. Write a program to be used by the business manager for the purpose of generating mailing labels. The subscribers' information should be read into a file of records. Each record should contain the subscriber's name; address, including street and street number, apartment number (if any), city, two-letter abbreviation for the state, and the zip code; and expiration information, including month and year.

   Your program should create an alphabetically sorted master file, print an alphabetical list for the office, print a mailing list sorted by zip code for bulk mailing, and denote all last issues by a special symbol.

2. The relentless Mr. Lae Z. Programmer now wants you to create a file of records for students in his computer science course. You should provide fields for the student's name, ten quiz scores, six program scores, and three examination scores. Your program should
   a. Read in the names from a text **(input)** file.
   b. Include procedures for updating quiz scores, program scores, and examination scores.
   c. Be able to update the file by adding or deleting a record.
   d. Print an alphabetized list of the data base at any given time.

3. Write a program to do part of the work of a word processor. Your program should read a text **(input)** file and print it in paragraph form. The left margin should be in column 10 and the right margin in column 72. Periods designate the end of sentences. The "*" symbol denotes a new paragraph. No word should be split between lines. Your program should save the edited file in a file of type **text.**

4. Slow-pitch softball is rapidly becoming a popular summer pastime. Assume your local community is to have a new ladies' league this year consisting of eight teams, with 15 players each. This league gets the field one night per week. They will play a double round-robin (each team plays every other team twice, resulting in 14 games). Write a program to
   a. Create a file of records (one record for each team) in which the team name is included.
   b. Print a schedule.
   c. List the teams alphabetically by team name.
   d. Print a list of players for each team.

5. The registrar at State University wants you to write a program to assist with record keeping. Your program should create a file of records. The record for each student should contain the student's name, identification number, hours completed, hours taking, and grade point average. Your program should also contain a procedure for each of the following updates.
   a. Semester-end data of hours completed and grade point average for the semester.
   b. Insert a record.
   c. Delete a record.
   d. Print a list sorted alphabetically.
   e. Print a list sorted by grade point average.

6. The local high school sports boosters (Problems 1 and 2, Chapter 10) need more help. They want you to write a program to create a file of records in which each record contains the parents' names, the children's first names (at most ten children), and the names of the sports in which the children participated.

   A typical record is shown in Figure 12.6. Your program should create a file from **input** and save it for later use, print an alphabetical list of parents' names, and print a list of the names of parents of football players.

7. A popular use of text files is for teachers to create a bank of test items and then use them to generate quizzes using some form of random generation. Write a program to allow you to create files of type **text** that contain questions for each of three chapters. Second, generate two quizzes of three questions for each of the three chapters.

8. Public service departments must always be on the lookout for those who try to abuse the system by accepting assistance from similar agencies in different geographic areas. Write a program to compare names from one county with those from another county and print all names that are on both lists.

9. Write a program to be used by flight agents at an airport (see Exercise 2, Section 12.3). Your program should use a file of records where the record for each flight contains flight number, airline, arrival time, arriving from, departure time, and destination. Your program should list incoming flights sorted by time, list departing flights sorted by time, add flights, and delete flights.

10. Congratulations! You have just been asked to write a program to assign dates for the Valentine's Day dance. Each student record contains the student's name, age, sex (M or F), and the names of three date preferences (ranked). Your program should

    a. Create a master file from the input file.
    b. Create and save alphabetically sorted files of males and females.
    c. Print a list of couples for the dance. The sexes must be opposite and the age difference may be no more than three years. Dating preferences should be in the following form.

	CAN'T MISS!	
First request	Matches	First request
	GOOD BET!	
First request	Matches	Second request
Second request	Matches	First request
	GOOD LUCK!	
	Any other matches	
	OUT OF LUCK!	
	You are not on any list	

    It's obvious (isn't it?) that a person can have at most one date for the dance.

11. Write a program to update a mailing list. Assume you have a sorted master file of records where each record contains a customer's name, address, and expiration code. Your program should allow you to input a file of new customers, sort the file, and merge the file with the master file to produce a new master.

12. Write a program to update a file of records for a library. Input is information about a book. For each book in the input file, your program should search the existing file to see if the additional book is a duplicate. If it is, change a field

FIGURE 12.6
Typical values for
fields in a record

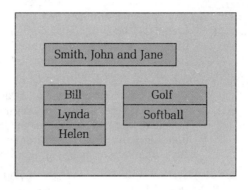

in the record to indicate that an additional copy was obtained. If it is not a
duplicate, insert the record in sequence in the file.

13. The Bakerville Manufacturing Company has to lay off all employees who
started working after a certain date. Write a program to
   a. Input a termination date.
   b. Search an alphabetical file of employee records to determine who will get
   a layoff notice.
   c. Create a file of employee records for those who are being laid off.
   d. Update the master file to contain only records of current employees.
   e. Produce two lists of those being laid off, one alphabetical and one by
   hiring date.

14. The Bakerville Manufacturing Company (Problem 13) has achieved new pros-
perity and can rehire ten employees who were recently laid off. Write a program to
   a. Search the file of previously terminated employees to find the ten with the
   most seniority.
   b. Delete these ten records from the file of employees who were laid off.
   c. Insert the ten records alphabetically into the file of current employees.
   d. Print four lists as follows:
      - Alphabetical list of current employees
      - Seniority list of current employees
      - Alphabetical list of employees who were laid off
      - Seniority list of employees who were laid off

15. The Shepherd Lions Club sponsors an annual cross-country race for area
schools. Write a program to
   a. Create a file of records for the runners: each record should contain the
   runner's name, school, identification number, and time (in a seven-char-
   acter string, such as 15:17:3).
   b. Print an alphabetical listing of all runners.
   c. Print a list of schools entered in the race.
   d. Print a list of runners in the race ordered by school name.
   e. Print the final finish order by reading the runners' numbers (order of finish) into an array, sorting the file of records according to the order of
   finish, and printing a numbered list according to the order of finish.

16. A data file consists of an unknown number of real numbers. Write a program
to read the file and print the highest value, lowest value, and average of the
numbers in the file.

17. The Falcon Manufacturing Company wants you to write an inventory file program. The file should contain a 30-character part name, an integer part number, the quantity on hand, and the price of an item. The program should permit the entry of new items into the file and the deletion of existing items. The items to be changed will be entered from the keyboard.

18. Write a program for the Falcon Manufacturing Company (Problem 17) to allow a secretary to enter an item number and a quantity, and whether it is to be added to or deleted from the stock. The program should prepare a new data file with the updated information. If the user requests to remove more items than are on hand, an appropriate warning message should be issued.

19. Write a program to read the inventory file of the Falcon Manufacturing Company (Problem 17) and then print a listing of the inventory. The program should print an asterisk (*) next to the quantity of any item of which there are fewer than 50 on hand.

20. A data file contains an alphabetized list of the secondary students in your school, and another contains an alphabetized list of the elementary students. Write a program to merge these two files and print an alphabetized list of all students in your school.

21. The Andover Telephone Company (whose motto is "We send your messages of Andover.") want a computerized directory information system. The data file should contain the customer names and telephone numbers. Your program should permit:

    a. The entry of new customers' names and telephone numbers.
    b. The deletion of existing customers' names and telephone numbers.
    c. The printing of all customers' names and their telephone numbers.
    d. The entry from the keyboard of a customer's name with the program then printing the telephone number (if found).

    Whenever customers' names and numbers are to be added or deleted, the file should be updated accordingly. You may assume there are no more than 50 customers.

22. Revise the program written to keep the grades of Mr. Laven's students (Problem 19, Chapter 10) to read the grades entered previously from a file and, when the program is complete, print the updated list of grades.

23. Revise Problem 22 from Chapter 10 to permit the sales figures to be read from a file. Also revise the program so that the information on the total dollar amount of sales for each product by each salesperson is written to a file for later use.

24. Write a program to read the total dollars sales file from Problem 23 for last month and the corresponding file for this month and print out a table showing the total sales by each salesperson for each product during the two-month period.

25. Recognizing your talents as a programmer, your principal wants you to write a program to work with a data file containing the names of the students who were absent at the start of the school day. These names are kept as 30-character packed arrays. The program should permit your principal to enter the name of a student later in the day to check to see if the student was absent at the start of the day.

26. Revise Problem 12 from Chapter 11 to permit the computer maintenance records to be kept in a file. Your program should allow the data on a machine to be changed and new machines to be added.

CHAPTER

Sets

We have thus far investigated the structured variables arrays, records, and files. These are structured because, when declared, a certain structure is reserved for subsequently holding values. In an array, a predetermined number of elements all of the same type can be held. A record contains a predetermined number of fields that can hold elements of different types. A file is somewhat like an array but the length is not predetermined and elements must be accessed sequentially.

Another structured data type available in Pascal is a set. Since the implementation of sets varies greatly from system to system, you need to check statements and examples in this chapter on your system.

■ 13.1
Declarations and Terms

OBJECTIVES

- to define a set as a data type
- to understand and use the associated terms element of a set, universal set, subset, and empty set
- to make an assignment to a set variable

Basic Idea and Notation

A *set* in Pascal is a structured data type consisting of a collection of distinct elements from an ordinal base type. Sets in Pascal are defined and used in a manner consistent with the use of sets in mathematics. A set type is defined by

```
TYPE
    type name = SET OF base type;
```

A set variable is then declared by

```
VAR
    variable name : type name;
```

■ to understand what is meant by a set constant

In a program working with characters of the alphabet, you might have

```
TYPE
   Alphabet = SET OF 'A' . . 'Z';
VAR
   Vowels, Consonants : Alphabet;
```

In a similar fashion, if your program analyzes digits and arithmetic symbols, you might have

```
TYPE
   Units = SET OF 0 . . 9;
   Symbols = SET OF '+' . . '/';  (*  Arithmetic symbols  *)
VAR
   Digits : Units;
   ArithSym : Symbols;
```

In these examples, Alphabet, Units, and Symbols are set types. Vowels, Consonants, Digits, and ArithSym are set variables.

A set can contain elements; these elements must be of the defined base type, which must be an ordinal data type. Most implementations of Pascal limit the maximum size of the base type of a set. This limit is such that a base type of **integer** is not allowed. However, base types of **char** and subranges of **integer** can usually be used.

Assignments to Sets

Once a set variable is declared, it is undefined until an assignment of values is made. The syntax for assigning is

> set name := [values];

For example, from above we can have

```
Vowels := ['A','E','I','O','U'];

Consonants := ['B' . . 'D','F' . . 'H','J' . . 'N','P' . . 'T',
               'V' . . 'Z'];

Digits := [0 . . 9];

ArithSym := ['+','-','*','/'];
```

Notice that the assigned values must be included in brackets and must be of the defined base type. Also, subranges of the base type can be used; thus,

```
   Consonants := ['B' . . 'D'];
```

is the same as

```
   Consonants := ['B','C','D'];
```

It is also possible to have set constants. Just as 4, 'H', and −56.20 are constants, [2,4,6] is a constant. In the previous example, this can be caused by

```
   Digits := [2,4,6];
```

As mentioned, sets are structured data types because, in a sense, they can be thought of as containing a list of elements. However, in listing the elements, note that each element can be listed only once and order makes no difference; thus, [2,4,6] is the same as [4,2,6].

SELF QUIZ 13.1 Define a set type and declare a set variable to be assigned a plus sign "+" and a minus "−" sign. Show how both can be assigned to the set.

Other Terminology

Once a value of the base type is assigned to a set, it is an *element of the set*. Thus, if we have

```
Digits := [2,4,6];
```

2, 4, and 6 are elements of Digits.

As in mathematics, any set that contains all possible values of the base type is called the *universal set*. In

```
Digits := [0 . . 9];
```

Digits is a universal set. It is also possible to consider a set constant as a universal set. Thus, ['A' .. 'Z'] is a universal set if the **TYPE** definition section contains

```
type name = SET OF 'A' . . 'Z';
```

If A and B have been declared as sets of the same type and all of the elements of A are also contained in B, A is a *subset* of B. If we have

```
VAR
   A, B : Units;
```

and the assignments

```
A := [1, 2, 3, 4, 5];
B := [0 . . 6];
```

are made, A is a subset of B. Note, however, that B is not a subset of A since B contains two elements (0 and 6) that are not contained in A.

The *empty set*, or *null set*, is the set containing no elements. It is denoted by [].

Note that these definitions allow for set theory results of mathematics to hold in Pascal. Some of these follow.

1. The empty set is a subset of every set.
2. If A is a subset of B and B is a subset of C, then A is a subset of C.
3. Every set (of the base type) is a subset of the universal set.

Exercises 13.1

In Exercises 1–5, find all errors in the definitions and declarations. Explain your answers.

1. ```
TYPE
   Numbers = SET OF real;
```
2. ```
TYPE
   Numbers = SET OF integer;
```
3. ```
TYPE
   Alphabet : SET OF 'A' . . 'Z';
```
4. ```
TYPE
   Alphabet = SET OF ['A' . . 'Z'];
```
5. ```
TYPE
   Conditions = (Sunny, Mild, Rainy, Windy);
   Weather = SET OF Conditions;
VAR
   TodaysWeather : Weather;
```

For Exercises 6 and 7, write test programs.

6. To discover if **char** is a permissible base type for a set.
7. To determine the limitation on the size of the base type for a set.

8. Suppose a set A is declared by

```
TYPE
   Letters = SET OF 'A' . . 'Z';
VAR
   A : Letters;
```

a. Show how A can be made to contain the letters of your name.
b. Assign the letters of Pascal to A.
c. Assuming the assignment

```
A := ['T','O','Y'];
```

list all elements and subsets of A.

For Exercises 9–15, let the sets A, B, and U be declared by

```
TYPE
   Alphabet = SET OF 'A' . . 'Z';
VAR
   A, B, U : Alphabet;
```

and the assignments

```
A := ['B', 'F', 'J' . . 'T'];
B := ['O' . . 'S'];
U := ['A' . . 'Z'];
```

be made. Indicate if the statement is **true** or **false**.

9. [] is a subset of B
10. B is an element of A
```

11. B is a subset of A
12. 'B' is an element of A
13. 'B' is a subset of A
14. A is a subset of U
15. 'O' is an element of A

For Exercises 16–21, assume A, B, and U are declared as in Exercises 9–15. Find and explain all errors in the assignment statements.

```
16. A := 'J' .. 'O';
17. U := [];
18. B := [A .. Z];
19. A := ['E', 'I', 'E', 'I', 'O'];
20. [] := ['D'];
21. B := ['A' .. 'T', 'S'];
```

For Exercises 22–25, let A be a set declared by

```
TYPE
   NumRange = 0 .. 100;
VAR
   A : SET OF NumRange;
   M,N : integer;
```

Indicate if the statement is valid or invalid. If valid, list the elements of A. If invalid, explain why.

```
22. A := [19];
23. A := 19;
24. M := 80;
    N := 40;
    A := [M + N, M MOD N, M DIV N];
25. M := 10;
    N := 2;
    A := [M, M * N, M / N];
```

For Exercises 26–29, define a set type and declare a set variable to be used.

26. Set values consist of colors of the rainbow.
27. Set values consist of class in school (Freshman, Sophomore, Junior, or Senior).
28. Set values consist of fruits.
29. Set values consist of grades for a class.

30. Explain why set is not an enumerated type.

■ 13.2
Set Operations and Relational Operators

OBJECTIVES

■ to understand the set operations union, intersection, and difference

Set Operations

Pascal provides for the set operations union, intersection, and difference where, in each case, two sets are combined to produce a single set. If A and B are sets, these operations are defined as follows:

- The *union* of A and B is A + B where A + B contains any element that is in A or that is in B.
- The *intersection* of A and B is A * B where A * B contains the elements that are in both A and B.
- The *difference* of A and B is A − B where A − B contains the elements that are in A but not in B.

to use sets with re-
lational operators

To illustrate, suppose A and B are sets that contain integer values and the
assignment statements

```
A := [1 , , 5];
B := [3 , , 9];
```

are made. The values produced by set operations follow.

Set Operation	Values
A + B	[1..9]
A * B	[3,4,5]
A - B	[1,2]

Multiple operations can be performed with sets and, when such an
expression is encountered, the same operator priority exists as with priorities for evaluating arithmetic expressions. Thus, if A and B contain the
values indicated,

$$A + B - A * B$$

produces

$$[1..5] + [3..9] - \underline{[1..5] * [3..9]}$$
$$\downarrow$$
$$\underline{[1..5] + [3..9]} - \quad [3, 4, 5]$$
$$\downarrow$$
$$\underline{[1..9]} \quad - \quad [3, 4, 5]$$
$$\downarrow$$
$$[1, 2, 6..9]$$

SELF QUIZ 13.2

Suppose A, B, and C are sets and the assignments

```
A := [-2 , , 5];
B := [0 , , 10];
C := [3 , , 20];
```

are made. Trace each step as the following expressions are evaluated.

```
A * (B + C)
A * B + A * C
```

Relational Operators

Relational operators can also be used with sets in Pascal. These operators
correspond to the normal set operators equal, not equal, subset, and superset. In each case, a **boolean** value is produced. If A and B are sets,
these operators are defined as shown in Table 13.1. Table 13.2 illustrates
boolean values associated with these expressions.

Set Membership

Membership in a set is indicated in Pascal by the reserved word **IN**. The
general form is

element **IN** set

TABLE 13.1
Set operations

Operator	Relational Expression	Definition
= (Equal)	A = B	A equals B; that is, every element in A is contained in B and every element in B is contained in A.
<> (Not equal)	A <> B	A does not equal B; that is, either A or B contains an element that is not contained in the other set.
<= (Subset)	A <= B	A is a subset of B; that is, every element of A is also contained in B.
>= (Superset)	A >= B	A is a superset of B (B is a subset of A); that is, every element of B is contained in A.

TABLE 13.2
Values of set
expressions

Set Expression	boolean Value
[1, 2, 3] <= [0 .. 10]	true
[0 .. 10] <= [1,2,3]	false
[0 .. 10] = [0 .. 5, 6 .. 10]	true
[ ] = ([1, 2] − [0 .. 10])	true
[1 .. 5] <> [1 .. 3, 4, 5]	false

This returns a value of **true** if the element is in the set and a value of **false** if it is not. To illustrate, suppose A and B are sets and the assignments

```
A := [0 . . 20];
B := [5 . . 10];
```

are made. Table 13.3 illustrates values using **IN**. Note that the last expression cannot be evaluated until priorities are assigned to the operators. Fortunately, these priorities are identical to those used for arithmetic expressions with **IN** on the same level as relational operators. They are shown in Table 13.4. Operations at each level are performed in order from left to right as they appear in an expression. Thus, the expression

80 **DIV** 20 **IN** A * B

produces

80 **DIV** 20 **IN** A * B
       ↓
   4   **IN** A * B
                   ↓
   4   **IN** [5 .. 10]
       ↓
      false

TABLE 13.3
Values of expressions
using **IN**

Expression	boolean Value
10 **IN** A	true
5 **IN** (A - B)	false
20 **IN** B	false
7 **IN** (A * B)	true
80 **DIV** 20 **IN** A * B	?

TABLE 13.4
Operator priorities
including set
operations

Priority Level	Operators
1	**NOT**
2	*, /, **MOD, DIV, AND**
3	+, −, **OR**
4	<, >, <=, >=, =, <>, **IN**

Exercises 13.2

1. When using sets in Pascal, is $>=$ the logical complement of $<=$? Give an example to illustrate your answer.

2. Let A and B be sets defined such that A := [0 .. 10] and B := [2,4,6,8,10] are valid. Write a test program to show that
   a. A + B = A
   b. A * B = B
   c. A − B = [0,1,3,5,7,9]

In Exercises 3–6, find A + B, A * B, A − B, and B − A.

3. A := [-3 .. 2,8,10]; , B := [0 .. 4, 7 .. 10];
4. A := [0,1,5 .. 10,20]; , B := [2,4,6,7 .. 11];
5. A := []; , B := [1 .. 15];
6. A := [0 .. 5, 10, 14 .. 20]; , B := [3,10,15];

For Exercises 7–14, given the following sets

    A := [0,2,4,6,8,10];
    B := [1,3,5,7,9];
    C := [0 .. 5];

indicate the values in each set.

7. A * B − C
8. A * (B − C)
9. A * (B + C)
10. A * B + A * C
11. A − B * C
12. A − (B − (A − B))
13. A * (B * C)
14. (A * B) * C

For Exercises 15–20, using sets A, B, and C with values assigned as in Exercises 7–14, indicate whether the statement is **true** or **false.**

15. A * B = []
16. C <= A + B
17. [5] <= B
18. A + B <> C
19. A − B >= []
20. (A + B = C) **OR** ([] <= B − C)

In mathematics, when X is an element of a set A, this is denoted by $X \in A$. If X is not in A, we write $X \notin A$. For Exercises 21–26, let B be a set declared by

    VAR
        B : SET OF 0 .. 10;

Examine the statements for validity and decide how Pascal handles the concept of not-an-element-of.

21. 4 **NOT IN** B
22. 4 **NOT (IN** B)
23. **NOT** 4 **IN** B
24. **NOT** (4 **IN** B)
25. 4 **IN NOT** B
26. 4 **IN** (**NOT** B)

27. Write a short program to count the number of vowels in a text file. Your program should include set types

    TYPE
        AlphaUppercase = SET OF 'A' .. 'Z';
        AlphaLowercase = SET OF 'a' .. 'z';

and set variables VowelsUppercase and VowelsLowercase declared by

```
VAR
    VowelsUppercase : AlphaUppercase;
    VowelsLowercase : AlphaLowercase;
```

■ 13.3
Using Sets

OBJECTIVES

■ to understand how
sets can be used in
a program
■ to use sets in a pro-
gram
■ to understand the
limitations of using
sets with functions
■ to use sets with
procedures

Uses for Sets

Now that we know how to declare sets, assign values to sets, and operate with sets, we need to examine some uses of sets in programs. First, however, we need to note an important limitation of sets: as with other structured variables, sets cannot be read or written directly. However, the two processes—generating a set and printing the elements of a set—are not difficult to code. To illustrate generating a set, suppose you wish to create a set and have it contain all the characters in the alphabet in a line of text. You can declare this set with

```
TYPE
    AlphaSymbols = 'A' .. 'Z';
    Symbols = SET OF AlphaSymbols;
VAR
    Alphabet : Symbols;
    SentenceChar : Symbols;
    Ch : char;
```

Code to generate the set SentenceChar is

```
Alphabet := ['A' .. 'Z'];
SentenceChar := [];
writeln ('Enter a sentence.');
WHILE NOT eoln(Data) DO
    BEGIN
        read (Data, Ch);
        IF Ch IN Alphabet THEN
            SentenceChar := SentenceChar + [Ch]
    END;
```

For many examples and the Chapter Summary Program, we assume the text file does not contain lowercase letters. A slight modification could be made to accommodate both uppercase and lowercase letters. For example, you could use both uppercase and lowercase letters by changing the set definitions to

```
TYPE
    Symbols = SET OF char;

VAR
    UppercaseAlphabet : Symbols;
    LowercaseAlphabet : Symbols;
    Alphabet: Symbols;
```

Alphabet could then be formed in the program by

```
UppercaseAlphabet := ['A' .. 'Z'];
LowercaseAlphabet := ['a' .. 'z'];
Alphabet := UppercaseAlphabet + LowercaseAlphabet;
```

The general procedure of getting values into a set is to initialize the set by assigning the empty set and use set union to add elements to the set.

The process of printing values of elements in a set is equally short. Assuming you know the data type of elements in the set, a loop can be used where the loop control variable ranges over values of this data type. Whenever a value is in the set, it is printed. To illustrate, assume the set SentenceChar now contains all the alphabetical characters from a line of text and you wish to print these characters. Since we know the data type for elements of SentenceChar is characters in 'A' .. 'Z', we can print the contained values by

```
FOR Ch := 'A' .. 'Z' DO
  IF Ch IN SentenceChar THEN
    write (Ch:2);
writeln;
```

If these two fragments of code are applied to the line of text

```
 THIS LINE (OBVIOUSLY MADE UP!) DOESN'T MAKE MUCH SENSE.
```

the output is

```
 A B C D E H I K L M N O P S T U V Y
```

SELF QUIZ 13.3

Modify the code just presented to create a set that contains all the vowels in a line of text. Print the contents of the set.

STYLE TIP

■ ■ ■ ■ ■ ■ ■

Sets with appropriate names are particularly useful for checking data. For example, a typical problem when working with dynamic variables (which are discussed in Chapter 14) is to examine an arithmetic expression for correct form. Thus, 3 + 4 is a valid expression but 3 + * 4 is not. As part of a program that analyzes such expressions, you might choose to define the following sets.

```
TYPE
  ValidDigits = SET OF '0' .. '9';
  Symbols = SET OF '(' .. '}';
VAR
  Digits : ValidDigits;
  ValidOperator : Symbols;
  LeftSymbol, RightSymbol : Symbols;
```

These sets can now be assigned values such as

```
Digits := ['0' .. '9'];
ValidOperator := ['+', '*', '-', '/'];
LeftSymbol := ['(', '[', '{'];
RightSymbol := [')', ']', '}'];
```

Now that you are familiar with how to generate elements in a set and subsequently print contents of a set, let's examine some uses for sets in programs. Specifically, let's look at using sets to replace complex **boolean** expressions, protect a program against bad data, and protect against invalid **CASE** statements.

Suppose you are writing a program to analyze responses to questions on a standard machine-scored form. If you want a certain action to take place for every response of A, B, or C, instead of

```
IF (Response='A') OR (Response='B') OR (Response='C') THEN
```

you can have

```
IF Response IN ['A','B','C'] THEN
    .
    .
    .
```

To demonstrate protecting a program against bad data, suppose you are writing a program to use a relatively large data file. Furthermore, suppose that the data are entered by operators in such a fashion that the first entry on the first line for each customer is a single-digit code. This is followed by appropriate data for the customer. To make sure the code is properly entered, you can define a set ValidSym and assign it all appropriate symbols. Your program design can be

```
read (Data, Sym);
IF Sym IN ValidSym THEN
   BEGIN
       .
       .   (action here)
       .
   END
ELSE
   (error message here)
```

Specifically, a program for printing mailing labels might require a 3, 4, or 5 to indicate the number of lines for the name and address that follow. If you are writing a program that also partially edits the data file, you can have

```
read (Data, NumLines);
IF NumLines IN [3,4,5] THEN
   BEGIN
       .
       .   (process number of lines)
       .
   END
ELSE
   (error message here)
```

EXAMPLE 13.1

Interactive programs frequently require users to enter a response if they wish to continue. For example, a message to the screen might be

```
Do you wish to continue? Y or N
```

Since users may enter either uppercase or lowercase letters, a set can be declared and used in a following program statement such as

```
IF Response IN ['Y', 'y'] THEN
    .
    .        (action for continuation here)
    .
```

```
ELSE
       .
       .        (alternate action here)
       .
```

The third use of sets is to protect against invalid **CASE** statements. This is especially appropriate for implementations that do not have an **OTHERWISE** option (as discussed in Section 5.5). To illustrate, suppose you are working with a program that uses a **CASE** statement where the selector is a letter grade assigned to students. Without sets, the statement is

```
CASE LetGrade OF
   'A' : . . .
   'B' : . . .
   'C' : . . .
   'D' : . . .
   'E' : . . .
END;  (*  of CASE  *)
```

To protect against the possibility of LetGrade being assigned a value not in the **CASE** selector list, sets can be used as follows:

```
IF LetGrade IN ['A' . . 'E'] THEN
   CASE LetGrade OF
      'A' : . . .
      'B' : . . .
      'C' : . . .
      'D' : . . .
      'E' : . . .
   END (*  of CASE  *)
ELSE
   (error message here)
```

Sets with Functions

Sets can be used with subprograms. In general, set types can be used as parameters in much the same way that arrays, records, and files are used. However, when working with functions, sets cannot be returned as values of a function because functions cannot return structured types.

To illustrate using sets with functions, let's consider two examples.

EXAMPLE 13.2

Let's write a function to determine the cardinality (size or number of elements) of a set. Assuming appropriate **TYPE** definitions, such a function can be

```
FUNCTION Cardinality (S : set type) : integer;
   VAR
      Ct : integer;
      X : base type for set;
   BEGIN
      Ct := 0;
      FOR X := initial value TO final value DO
         IF X IN S THEN
            Ct := Ct + 1;
      Cardinality := Ct
   END;
```

Time Is Cure for Computerphobia

What can make an otherwise stalwart manager break into a cold sweat, reel with dizziness, and suffer waves of nausea? The answer is not the latest version of the flu. It's the computer! As reported in a recent issue of *Executive Action Series,* published by the Bureau of Business Practice, Waterford, Connecticut, a surprising number of managers fear, distrust, and even hate the computer, some in phobic proportions.

Is there a cure for this phobia that has such a destructive effect on productivity? Time is the answer, say the experts. It takes time to overcome computerphobia. A gradual introduction to computer technology is essential. Companies that provide both private instruction to managers and the time to master simple programming have more personnel regularly using their terminals. Confidence and motivation grow as managers successfully master simple computer tasks.

This is called from the main program by

```
SetSize := Cardinality (set name);
```

SELF QUIZ 13.4

Using the set, SentenceChar, as defined at the beginning of this section, modify **FUNCTION** Cardinality so it can be used to determine the number of distinct letters in a line of text.

EXAMPLE 13.3

Let's now consider a function to find the maximum element of a set of integers. This would typically be applied to a set whose elements are in some subrange of the integers where initial value and final value are chosen to sufficiently bound the subrange. You can easily modify the function by considering the ordinals of set elements if the set does not contain integers.

```
FUNCTION MaxElement (S : set type) : base type;
   VAR
     Temp : base type;
     X : base type;
   BEGIN
     IF S = [] THEN
        writeln ('You are working with an empty set!':40)
     ELSE
        FOR X := initial value TO final value DO
           IF X IN S THEN
              Temp := X;
     MaxElement := Temp
   END; (*  of FUNCTION MaxElement  *)
```

This is called from the main program by

```
Largest := MaxElement (set name);
```

Sets with Procedures

As you recall, sets cannot be returned as values of a function. However, when a program requires a set to be returned from a subprogram, the set can be used as a variable parameter with a procedure. In this manner, sets can either be generated or modified with subprograms. The Chapter Summary Program at the end of this chapter illustrates such a use.

Exercises 13.3

1. Modify the function MaxElement used in Example 13.3 to find the character in a line of text that is latest in the alphabet. Use this function with the Chapter Summary Program presented at the end of this chapter.

2. Write a test program to create a set containing all the consonants from a line of text. Your program should also print all elements in the set.

3. Write a short program to reproduce a text file where every vowel is replaced by an asterisk.

4. Modify the code used to find all the alphabet characters in a line of text so that a complete text file can be analyzed rather than just one line.

5. Write a program to simulate arithmetic indicated in a text file. The arithmetic expression should always be of the form digit-symbol-digit (9 + 8) where all digits and symbols are given as data of type **char**. Your program should protect against bad operation symbols, bad digits (actually nondigits), and division by zero.

6. To illustrate how sets can be used to protect against invalid values for **CASE** selectors, write a short program that uses a **CASE** statement. Run it with an invalid **CASE** selector value. Change the program so the **CASE** statement is protected by using a set. Rerun the program with the same invalid selector.

7. Write a **boolean** function to analyze an integer between $-9{,}999$ and $9{,}999$ and return the value **true** if the integer contains only odd digits (1731) and **false** otherwise.

8. Write a function that returns the length of a string passed to the function as a packed array. Punctuation marks and internal blanks should add to the string length. Blanks at the beginning or end should not be added to the string length.

RUNNING AND DEBUGGING TIPS

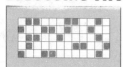

1. When defining a set type, do not use brackets in the definition; thus, the following is incorrect.

```
TYPE
    Alphabet = SET OF ['A' .. 'Z'];
```

The correct form is

```
TYPE
    Alphabet = SET OF 'A' .. 'Z';
```

2. Remember to initialize a set before using it in the program. Declaring a set does not give it a value. If your declaration is

```
VAR
    Vowels : Alphabet;
```

the program should contain

```
Vowels := ['A','E','I','O','U'];
```

3. Attempting to add an element to a set rather than a set to a set is a common error. If you wish to add 'D' to the set ['A','B','C'], you should write

```
['A','B','C'] + ['D']
```

rather than

```
['A','B','C'] + 'D'
```

This is especially a problem when the value of a variable is to be added to a set.

```
[       ] + Ch;
```

should be

```
[       ] + [Ch];
```

4. Avoid confusing arrays and array notation with sets and set notation. This is especially troublesome if you have an array of sets. In this case, you can have a statement such as

```
A[J] := [4 .. 15];
```

5. Certain operators (+, −, and *) have different meanings when used with sets.

■ Summary

Key Terms

set	subset	intersection
element of a set	empty (null) set	difference
universal set	union	

Keywords

SET   **IN**

Key Concepts

■ A set in Pascal is a structured data type that consists of distinct elements from an indicated base type; sets can be declared by

```
TYPE
   TwentiethCentury = SET OF 1900 .. 1999;
VAR
   Seventies, Eighties : TwentiethCentury;
```

■ In this definition and declaration, TwentiethCentury is a **SET** type and Seventies and Eighties are set variables.
■ Values must be assigned to a set; thus, we can have

```
Seventies := [1970 .. 1979];
Eighties := [1980 .. 1989];
```

■ When listing elements in a set, order makes no difference and each element may be listed only once.
■ Standard set operations in Pascal are defined to be consistent with set operations of mathematics; to illustrate, if

```
A := [1,2,3,4];
```

and

```
B := [3,4,5];
```

we have

Term	Expression	Value
Union	A + B	[1..5]
Intersection	A * B	[3,4]
Difference	A − B	[1,2]
	B − A	[5]

- Set membership is denoted by using the reserved word **IN.** Such an expression returns a **boolean** value; thus, if

```
A := [1,2,3,4];
```

we have

Expression	Value
2 IN A	**true**
6 IN A	**false**

- The relational operators ($<=$, $>=$, $<>$, and $=$) can be used with sets forming **boolean** expressions and returning values consistent with expected subset and set equality relationships; to illustrate, if

```
A := [1,2,3];
B := [0 , , 5];
C := [2,4];
```

we have

Expression	Value
A <= B	**true**
B <= C	**false**
B >= C	**true**
A = B	**false**
B <> C	**true**

- Priority levels for set operations are consistent with those used for arithmetic expressions; they are

Priority Level	Operation
1	**NOT**
2	*, /, **MOD, DIV, AND**
3	+, −, **OR**
4	<, >, <=, >=, <>, =, **IN**

- Sets cannot be used with **read** or **write;** however, you can generate a set by initializing the set by assigning the empty set and using set union to add elements to the set. For example, a set of characters in a text line can be generated by

```
S := [];
WHILE NOT eoln(Data) DO
  BEGIN
    read (Data, Ch);
    S := S + [Ch]
  END;
```

- This set can be printed by

```
FOR Ch := initial value TO final value DO
  IF Ch IN S THEN
    write (Ch:2);
```

- Three uses for sets in programs are to replace complex **boolean** expressions, to protect a program (or segment) from bad data, and to protect against invalid **CASE** statements.
- Sets can be used as parameters with subprograms.
- Sets cannot be returned as the value of a function.
- Sets can be generated or modified through subprograms by using variable parameters with procedures.

■ Chapter Review Exercises

1. Define a set and set variable to contain the even numbers from 2 to 20.

2. Write a procedure to read in integers and print them if they are in the set defined in Exercise 1.

For Exercises 3–11, refer to the sets below.

```
A := [1 , , 5, 9 , , 20];
B := [4 , , 12];
```

What are the elements of the following?

3. A * B
4. A + B
5. A - B
6. B - A
7. A + B - A * B
8. A * B - A + B
9. A - B + B
10. Define a set that is a subset of set A and contains four elements.
11. If set D contains [1 .. 20] as elements, what is the relationship of set D to set A?

For Exercises 12–18, indicate if the declarations are correct. If not, explain why.

12. TYPE
    TestAnswers = SET OF [1 , , 20, 'A' , , 'F'];
13. TYPE
    B = SET OF integer;
14. TYPE
    C = SET OF [1.0 , , 4.0];
15. TYPE
    D = SET OF [2, 5, 7, 12, 18, 35, 98];
16. TYPE
    LetterGrades = ['A', 'B', 'C', 'D', 'F'];
    Grades = SET OF LetterGrades;
17. TYPE
    E = SET OF [1 , , 4];
18. TYPE
    F = SET OF 1 , , 4;

19. List at least ten subsets of the set defined in Exercise 18.

20. List a superset of the set defined in Exercise 18.

21. Write a fragment of code of a set to contain the letters in the name of your school.

22. How many subsets are there of the set [1,2]?

For Exercises 23–25, refer to the sets below.

```
X = SET OF 1 .. 10;
Y = SET OF 'A' .. 'M';
```

23. What is the value of X + Y?
24. Is [] a subset of X?
25. Is [] a subset of Y?

For Exercises 26–31, using the sets from Exercises 23–25, and the following defined variables,

```
A : X;
B : Y;
```

indicate if the statements are valid. If they are not, explain why.

26. A := 1;
27. A := [1];
28. [] := A + B;
29. B := B + 'A';
30. A := A + [10];
31. A := A + [11];

For Exercises 32–35, find A + B, A * B, and A − B for the sets given.

32. A := [1, 3 .. 6, 10]; , B := [4, 5, 6, 7];
33. A := [1 .. 5, 9 .. 12]; , B := [6 .. 8];
34. A := ['A' .. 'H']; , B := ['E'];
35. A := [1 .. 5]; , B := [];

■ Chapter Summary Program

The sample program for this chapter illustrates a use of sets. In particular, a set is used as a variable parameter in a procedure. The specific problem is to write a program to determine the alphabetical characters used in a line of text. Output from the program is an echo print of the text line, a list of letters in the text, and the number of distinct letters used in the line.

A first-level pseudocode development for this problem is

1. Get the characters
2. Print the characters
3. Determine the cardinality of the set
4. Print a closing message

A refinement of this produces

1. Get the characters
   1.1 initialize set
   1.2 **WHILE NOT eoln DO**
       1.2.1 process a character
2. Print the characters
   2.1 **FOR** Ch := 'A' **TO** 'z' **DO**
       IF Ch is in the set **THEN**
           print Ch

3. Determine the cardinality of the set
   3.1   initialize counter to 0
   3.2   **FOR** Ch := 'A' **TO** 'z' **DO**
         IF Ch is in the set **THEN**
           increment counter
   3.3   assign count to function name
4. Print a closing message

Step 1.2.1 can be refined to

   1.2.1   process a character
      1.2.1.1   read a character
      1.2.1.2   write a character (echo print)
      1.2.1.3   **IF** character is in the alphabet **THEN**
           add it to the set of characters

A complete program for this problem is

```
PROGRAM SymbolCheck (input, output, Data);
(*****************************************************************

      This program is designed to illustrate working with
      sets. It reads a line of text and determines the
      number of distinct letters in that line. Output
      includes the distinct letters and the set cardinality.


******************************************************************)
CONST
  Skip = ' ';
TYPE
  AlphaSymbols = SET OF 'A' .. 'z';
VAR
  SentenceChar : AlphaSymbols;  (*  Set of possible letters  *)
  SetSize : integer;            (*  Cardinality of the set   *)
  Data : text;                  (*  Data file                *)


(*****************************************************************

      This procedure gets characters from a line of text

******************************************************************)
PROCEDURE GetLetters (VAR S:AlphaSymbols);
  VAR
    Ch : char;
    Alphabet : AlphaSymbols;
  BEGIN
    S := [];
    Alphabet := ['A' .. 'Z'] + ['a' .. 'z'];
    writeln(Skip:10,'The line of text is below:');
    write(Skip:10);
    reset(Data);
    WHILE NOT eoln (Data) DO
```

```
          BEGIN
            read(Data, Ch);
            write(Ch);      (*   Echo Print    *)
            IF Ch IN Alphabet THEN
              S := S+[Ch]
          END;  (*    of one line    *)
        writeln
      END;        (*    of PROCEDURE GetLetters    *)


(*******************************************************************

    This procedure prints elements in a set

 ******************************************************************)
PROCEDURE Print (S:AlphaSymbols);
  VAR
    Ch : char;
  BEGIN
    writeln(Skip:10,'The letters in this line are:');
    write(Skip:10);
    FOR Ch := 'A' TO 'z' DO
      IF Ch IN S THEN
        write(Ch:2);
    writeln
  END;  (*    of PROCEDURE Print    *)


(*******************************************************************

    This function counts the number of elements in a set

 ******************************************************************)
FUNCTION Cardinality (S:AlphaSymbols):integer;
  VAR
    Ct : integer;
    X : char;
  BEGIN
    Ct := 0;
    FOR X :='A' TO 'z' DO
      IF X IN S THEN
        Ct := Ct + 1;
    Cardinality := Ct
  END;  (*    of FUNCTION Cardinality    *)


(*******************************************************************

    Now start the main program

 ******************************************************************)
BEGIN   (*    Main program    *)
  GetLetters(SentenceChar);
  Print(SentenceChar);
  SetSize := Cardinality(SentenceChar);
  write(Skip:10,' There are',SetSize:5,' letters in this');
  writeln (' sentence.');
  writeln
END.    (*    of main program    *)
```

When this program is run on the line of text

```
The numbers -2, 5, 20 and symbols '?', ':' should be ignored.
```

The output is

```
The line of text is below:
The numbers -2, 5, 20 and symbols '?', ':' should be ignored.
The letters in this line are:
T a b d e g h i l m n o r s u y
There are   16 letters in this sentence.
```

■ Programming Problems

Each of the following programming problems can be solved with a program using sets. Hints are provided to indicate some of the uses; you may, of course, find others.

1. Write a program to be used to simulate a medical diagnosis. Assume the following symptoms are coded as indicated.

Symptom	Code
Headache	1
Fever	2
Sore throat	3
Cough	4
Sneeze	5
Stomach pain	6
Heart pain	7
Muscle pain	8
Nausea	9
Back pain	10
Exhaustion	11
Jaundice	12
High blood pressure	13

Furthermore, assume each of the following diseases is characterized by the symptoms as indicated.

Disease	Symptoms
Cold	1,2,3,4,5
Flu	1,2,6,8,9
Migraine	1,9
Mononucleosis	2,3,11,12
Ulcer	6,9
Arteriosclerosis	7,10,11,13
Appendicitis	2,6

Your program should accept as input a person's name and symptoms (coded) and provide a preliminary diagnosis. Sets can be used for

a. Bad data check
b. Symptoms = 1 .. 13;
   Disease = **SET OF** Symptoms;
c. Cold, Flu, Migraine, Mononucleosis, Ulcer, Arteriosclerosis, Appendicitis : Disease;

2. Write a program to serve as a simple text analyzer. Input is any text file. Output should be three histograms: one each for vowel frequency, consonant frequency, and other symbol frequency. Your program should use a set for vowels, one for consonants, and a third for other symbols.

3. Typists often complain that the standard QWERTY keyboard

Q W E R T Y U I O P

A S D F G H J K L ;

Z X C V B N M , . /

space bar

is not efficient. As you can see, many frequently used letters (E, T, N, R, and I) are not on the middle row. A new keyboard, the Maltron keyboard, has been proposed. Its design is

Q P Y C B V M U Z L

A N I S F E D T H O R ; : .

J G W K X

space bar

Write a program to analyze a text file to see how many jumps are required by each keyboard. For purposes of this program, a jump will be any valid symbol not on the middle row. Output should include the number of valid symbols read and the number of jumps for each keyboard.

4. Write a program to serve as a simple compiler for a Pascal program. Your compiler should work on a program that uses only single-letter identifiers. Your compiler should create a set of identifiers, make sure identifiers are not declared twice, make sure all identifiers on the left of an assignment are declared, and make sure there are no type mismatch errors. For purposes of your compiler program, assume as follows:

a. Variables will be declared between **VAR** and **BEGIN**; for example,

```
VAR
   X,Y : real;
   A,B,C : integer;
   M : char;
BEGIN
```

b. Each program line is a complete Pascal statement.
c. The only assignments are of the form X := Y;. Output should include the program line number and an appropriate error message for each error. Run your compiler with several short Pascal programs as text files. Compare your error list with that given in Appendix 5.

5. A number in exponential notation preceded by a plus or minus sign may have the form

Sign	Positive integer	Decimal	Positive integer	Sign	E	Exponent (three digits)

For example, $-45.302E+002$ is the number -4530.2. If the number is in standard form, it will have exactly one digit on the left side of the decimal ($-4.5302E+003$).

Write a program to read numbers in exponential form from a text file, one number per line. Your program should check to see if each number is in proper form. For those that are, print out the number as given and the number in standard form.

6. Write a program to analyze a text file for words of differing length. Your program should keep a list of all words of length one to ten. It should also count the number of words whose length exceeds ten.

   A word ends when one alphabetical character is followed by a character not in the alphabet or when an end-of-line is reached. All words start with letters (7UP is not a word). Your output should be an alphabetized list for each word length. It should also include the number of words whose length exceeds ten characters. An apostrophe does not add to the length of a word.

7. The Falcon Manufacturing Company wants a computerized system to check if a customer is approved for credit. A customer number will be entered from the keyboard, with the program printing the credit limit for the customer if credit has been approved, and "No credit" if it has not. Each line of a textfile contains a customer number and the credit limit. Valid customer numbers range from 100 to 999, and credit limits are $100, $300, $500, $1000, and unlimited credit.

8. Write a program in which you read a textfile and print out the number of times a character in the file matches a character in your name.

9. The Court Survey Corporation wishes to conduct a poll by sending questionnaires to men and women between 25 and 30 years of age living in your state or any state adjacent to it. A text file containing names, street addresses, cities and states, zip codes, and ages is to be read, with the program printing the names and addresses of those persons matching the criteria.

10. Write a program to test your ESP and that of a friend. Each of you should secretly enter ten integers between 1 and 100. Have the program check each list and print the values that are in both lists and the number of values that are in both lists.

11. Modify Problem 22 from Chapter 9 (the Wellsville Wholesale Company commission problem) to define the sales ranges as sets. Use these sets to verify input and determine the proper commission rate.

12. The Ohio Programmers' Association offices are in a large building with five wings lettered A through E. The office numbers in the wings are as follows:

Wing	Rooms
A	100–150 and 281–300
B	151–190 and 205–220
C	10– 50 and 191–204
D	1– 9 and 51– 99
E	221–280 and 301–319

Write a program for the receptionist, Miss Lovelace, so that she can enter an office number from the keyboard and then have the computer print the wing in which the office is located.

CHAPTER 14

Dynamic Variables and Data Structures

Material in the previous 13 chapters has dealt almost exclusively with *static variables*, characteristics of which include:

1. Their size (array length, for example) is fixed at compilation time.
2. A certain memory location is reserved for each variable and these locations are retained for the declared variables as long as the program or subprogram in which the variable is defined is active.
3. They are declared in a variable declaration section.
4. The structure or existence of a variable cannot be changed during a run of the program (two exceptions are the length of a file and records with variant parts).

A disadvantage of using only static variables and data structures is that the number of variables needed in a program must be predetermined. Thus, if you are working with an array and you anticipate needing a thousand locations, you would define

```
name = ARRAY [1 . . 1000] OF base type;
```

This creates two problems. You may overestimate the length of the array and use only part of it; therefore memory is wasted. Or you may underestimate the necessary array length and be unable to process all the data until the program is modified.

Fortunately, Pascal solves these problems with the use of *dynamic variables*. Some of their characteristics follow.

1. Dynamic variable types are defined in the **TYPE** section, but variables of these types are not declared in the **VAR** section.
2. Dynamic variables are created as needed and returned when not needed during the execution of a program; therefore, unneeded memory is not wasted and you are limited only by the available memory.

3. A new (and significant) technique must be developed to form a list of dynamic variables; these lists are referred to as *dynamic structures.*

4. In some instances, working with dynamic structures can be slower than working with static structures; in particular, direct access of an array element has no analogue.

5. A significantly different method of accessing values stored in dynamic variables must be developed since memory locations are not predetermined.

A complete development of dynamic variables and data structures is left to other courses in computer science. However, when finished with this chapter, you should have a reasonable understanding of dynamic variables and data structures, and be able to use them in a program. We carefully develop one type of dynamic data structure (linked list) and then introduce three others: stack, queue, and binary tree.

You may find this material somewhat difficult. If so, do not get discouraged. The reason for the increased level of difficulty is that some of the work is not as easily seen in concrete terms as the previous material. Therefore, as you work through this chapter, you are encouraged to write several short programs to help you understand concepts. You may also need to reread the chapter or particular sections to grasp the mechanics of working with dynamic variables.

■ 14.1
Pointer Variables

OBJECTIVES

- to understand the difference between the address of a memory location and the value of a memory location
- to define a pointer type
- to understand how a pointer variable is used to access a memory location
- to use a pointer variable to manipulate data in a dynamic variable
- to create and destroy dynamic variables during the execution of a program

Computer Memory

Computer memory can be envisioned as a grid depicted as in Figure 14.1. An area where a value can be stored is called a *memory location.* When a variable is declared in the variable declaration section of a program, a memory location is reserved during execution of that program block. This memory location can be accessed by a reference to the variable name and only data of the declared type can be stored there. Thus, if the declaration section is

```
VAR
    Sum : integer;
```

you can envision it as shown in Figure 14.2. If the assignment

```
Sum := 56;
```

is made, we have the arrangement shown in Figure 14.3.

Each memory location has an *address.* This is an integer value that the computer can use as a reference to the memory location. When static variables (such as Sum) are used, the address of a memory location is used indirectly by the underlying machine instruction. However, when dynamic variables are used, the address is used directly as a reference or pointer to the memory location as we shall learn.

The *value* that is the address of a memory location must be stored somewhere in memory. In Pascal, this is stored in a *pointer variable.* Designated as Ptr, a pointer variable is a variable of a predefined type that is used to contain the address of a memory location. To illustrate, assume Ptr is declared as a pointer variable. If 56 is stored in a memory location whose address is 11640, we can envision it as shown in Figure 14.4.

- to understand the difference between a pointer variable and the dynamic variable to which it refers
- to use **NIL** with pointer variables

Working with Pointer and Dynamic Variables

Pointer variables are declared by using an up arrow (↑) or caret (ˆ) in front of the type name. Thus,

```
TYPE
   Ages = 0 .. 120;
VAR
   Ptr : ↑Ages;
```

declares Ptr as a pointer variable. Ptr cannot be assigned values of type Ages; Ptr can only contain addresses of locations whose values are of type Ages.

FIGURE 14.1
Computer memory

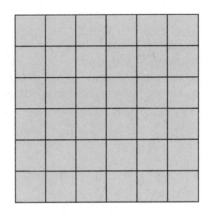

FIGURE 14.2
Variable location in memory

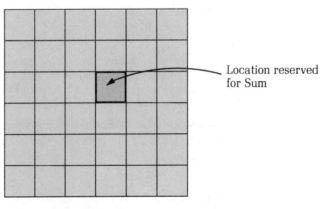

Location reserved for Sum

FIGURE 14.3
Value in variable Sum

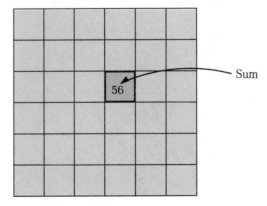

Sum

FIGURE 14.4
Relationship be-
tween pointer and
memory location

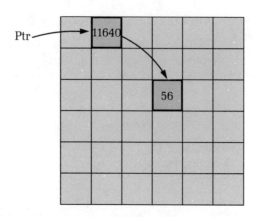

Once this declaration is made, a dynamic variable can be created. A dynamic variable, designated as Ptr↑ , is a variable accessed by a pointer variable; a dynamic variable is not declared in the declaration section of a program. Using the standard procedure **new** with a pointer variable as

```
new (Ptr);
```

creates the dynamic variable Ptr↑ . This can be illustrated by

The pointer variable followed by an up arrow (or caret) is always the identifier for a dynamic variable.

STYLE TIP
■ ■ ■ ■ ■ ■ ■

Ptr or some identifier containing Ptr (for example, DataPtr) is frequently used when declaring pointer variables. This reinforces the difference between working with a pointer variable (Ptr) and a dynamic variable (Ptr↑).

To illustrate the relationship between pointer variables and dynamic variables, assume the previous declaration and the code

```
new (Ptr);
Ptr↑ := 56;
```

This stage can be envisioned as

where Ptr contains the address of Ptr↑ .

SELF QUIZ 14.1

Assume the previous declaration of Ptr. What is wrong with the following fragment of code?

```
new (Ptr);
Ptr := 56;
```

Dynamic variables can be destroyed by using the standard procedure **dispose.** Thus, if you no longer need the value of a dynamic variable Ptr↑, then

```
dispose (Ptr);
```

causes the pointer variable Ptr to no longer contain the address for Ptr↑. In that sense, Ptr↑ does not exist because nothing is pointing to it. This location has been returned to the computer for subsequent use.

Since pointer variables contain only addresses of memory locations, they have limited use in a program. Pointer variables of the same type can only be used for assignments and comparison for equality. They cannot be used with **read, write,** or any arithmetic operation. To illustrate, assume we have the definition and declaration

```
TYPE
    Ages = 0 . . 120;
VAR
    Ptr1, Ptr2 : ↑Ages;
```

Then

```
new (Ptr1);
new (Ptr2);
```

create the dynamic variables Ptr1↑ and Ptr2↑. If the assignments

```
Ptr1↑ := 50;
Ptr2↑ := 21;
```

are made, we can envision this as

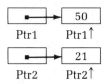

The expression Ptr1 = Ptr2 is then **false** and Ptr1 <> Ptr2 is **true.** If the assignment

```
Ptr1 := Ptr2;
```

is made, we can envision

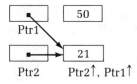

Then Ptr1 = Ptr2 is **true** and Ptr1 <> Ptr2 is **false.**

Notice that in this last illustration, 50 no longer has anything pointing to it. Thus, there is now no way to access this value. Since we did not use **dispose,** the location has not been returned for subsequent reuse. Therefore, you should be careful to use **dispose** when necessary or you could eventually run out of memory.

SELF QUIZ 14.2

Show how you can return the memory area occupied by Ptr1↑ and then cause Ptr1 and Ptr2 to both point to Ptr2↑.

Dynamic variables can be used in any context used by static variables of the same type. To illustrate, assume the previous declarations for Ptr1 and Ptr2. If appropriate values (50 and 21) are in a data file, the segment

```
new (Ptr1);
new (Ptr2);
read (Data, Ptr1↑, Ptr2↑);
writeln ('The average of', Ptr1↑:5, ' and', Ptr2↑:5,
         ' is', (Ptr1↑ + Ptr2↑)/2:6:2);
```

produces

```
The average of 50 and 21 is 35.50
```

Defining and Declaring Pointer Variables

The previous definition and declarations of pointer types and pointer variables are relatively uncomplicated; however, in actual practice, pointer types and variables are a bit more complex. For example, in the next section we define a pointer type as a record type where one of the fields in the record type is a pointer of the same type. Thus, you can have

```
TYPE
   String20 = PACKED ARRAY [1 . . 20] OF char;
   DataPtr = ↑StudentInfo;
   StudentInfo = RECORD
                   Name : String20;
                   Next : DataPtr
                 END; (* of RECORD StudentInfo *)
VAR
   Student : DataPtr;
```

Notice that DataPtr makes a reference to StudentInfo before StudentInfo is defined. StudentInfo then contains a field of type DataPtr. In this instance, Pascal makes an exception to the rule and allows something to be used before it is defined. Specifically, the following exception is permitted:

Pointer type definitions may precede definitions of their reference types. The reverse is not true. That is, a structure may not contain a field or component of a pointer type that has not yet been defined.

You will frequently want each record to point to another record. Using a record definition with one field for a pointer permits this.

A final operation with pointers should be mentioned here. The reserved word **NIL** can be assigned to a pointer variable. Thus, you can have

```
new (Student);
Student↑.Next := NIL;
```

This can be envisioned as producing

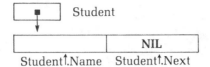

Studentↂ.Name   Studentↂ.Next

This allows pointer variables to be used in **boolean** expressions and is needed in later work. For example, if you are forming a list of dynamic variables where each dynamic variable contains a pointer variable for pointing to the next one, you can use **NIL** as a way to know when you are at the end of a list. This idea and that of pointer type definitions are fully developed in the next section.

Exercises 14.1

1. Discuss the difference between static and dynamic variables.

2. Write a test program to declare a single pointer variable whose associated dynamic variable can have values in the subrange 0 .. 50 and then

   a. Create a dynamic variable, assign the value 25, and print the value.
   b. Create another dynamic variable, assign the value 40, and print the value.

   At this stage of your program, where is the value 25 stored?

3. Illustrate the relationship between pointer variables and dynamic variables produced by

```
TYPE
   PtrType = (Red, Yellow, Blue, Green);
VAR
   Ptr1, Ptr2 : ↑PtrType;
BEGIN
   new (Ptr1);
   new (Ptr2);
   Ptr1↑ := Blue;
   Ptr2↑ := Red
END.
```

For Exercises 4–7, assume the **TYPE** and **VAR** sections are given as in Exercise 3. Find all errors.

```
4. new (Ptr2);
   Ptr2 := Yellow;
5. new (Ptr1);
   new (Ptr2);
   Ptr1↑ := Red;
   Ptr2↑ := Ptr1↑;
6. new (Ptr1);
   new (Ptr2);
   Ptr1↑ := Red;
   Ptr1↑ := Ptr2↑;
7. new (Ptr1);
   new (Ptr2);
   Ptr1↑ := Red;
   Ptr2↑ := Ptr1;
```

For Exercises 8–15, assume pointer variables are declared in the variable declaration section as

```
VAR
    RealPtr1, RealPtr2 : ↑real;
    IntPtr1, IntPtr2 : ↑integer;
    BoolPtr1, BoolPtr2 : ↑boolean;
```

Indicate if the reference is valid or invalid. Give an explanation if invalid.

8. `IntPtr1 := IntPtr1 + 1;`
9. `writeln (RealPtr2:30:2);`
10. `writeln (BoolPtr1↑:15, IntPtr1↑:15, RealPtr1↑:15:2);`
11. `IF IntPtr1 < IntPtr2 THEN`
    `writeln ('All done');`
12. `IF BoolPtr NOT NIL THEN`
    `new (BoolPtr2);`
13. `IF RealPtr1 <> RealPtr2 THEN`
    `writeln (RealPtr1↑:15:2, RealPtr2↑:15:2);`
14. `IF BoolPtr2 THEN`
    `new (BoolPtr1);`
15. `IF BoolPtr2↑ THEN`
    `new (BoolPtr1);`

16. Assume the declarations of Exercises 8–15. What output is produced from the following fragment of code?

```
new (IntPtr1);
new (IntPtr2);
new(RealPtr1);
new(BoolPtr1);
IntPtr1↑ := 95;
IntPtr2↑ := 55;
RealPtr1↑ := (IntPtr1↑ + IntPtr2↑)/2;
BoolPtr1↑ := true;
WHILE BoolPtr1↑ DO
  BEGIN
    writeln (RealPtr1↑:20:2);
    RealPtr1↑ := RealPtr1↑-5;
    IF RealPtr1↑ < 0 THEN
      BoolPtr1↑ := false
  END;
```

■ 14.2
Linked Lists

A *linked list* is a dynamic data structure and can be thought of as a list of data items where each item is linked to the next one by means of a pointer. Such a list can be envisioned as

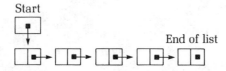

Items in a linked list are called *components* or *nodes*. These lists are used like arrays; that is, data of the same type can be stored in each node. As shown in the previous illustration, each component of a linked list can

■ to print data from a
linked list

store certain data as well as point to the next component. Consequently, a record is used for each component where one field of the record is reserved for the pointer. If names of students are to be stored in such a list, we can use the record definition from Section 14.1 as follows:

```
TYPE
    String20 = PACKED ARRAY [1 .. 20] OF char;
    DataPtr = ↑StudentInfo;
    StudentInfo = RECORD
                        Name : String20;
                        Next : DataPtr
                    END; (*  of RECORD StudentInfo  *)
```

Thus, we can envision a list of names as

When working with linked lists, the identifier Next is frequently used as the name of the field in the record that is the pointer variable. This is to remind you that you are pointing to the next record. It makes code such as

```
P := P↑.Next;
```

more meaningful.

Creating a Linked List

When creating a linked list, you need to be able to identify the first component, the relationship (pointer) between successive components, and the last component. Pointers are used to point to both the first and last component. An auxiliary pointer is also used to point to the newest component. The pointer to the first component (Start) is not changed unless a new node is added to the beginning of the list. The other pointers change as the linked list grows. When you have created such a list, the last component is usually designated by assigning **NIL** to the pointer. To illustrate, let's see how a linked list to hold five names can be formed. Using the **TYPE** definition section

```
TYPE
    String20 = PACKED ARRAY [1 .. 20] OF char;
    DataPtr = ↑StudentInfo;
    StudentInfo = RECORD
                        Name : String20;
                        Next : DataPtr
                    END; (*  of RECORD StudentInfo  *)
```

and the variable declaration section

```
VAR
    Start, Last, Ptr : DataPtr;
```

we can generate the desired list by

```
BEGIN
  new (Start);
  Ptr := Start; (*  Pointer to first component  *)
  FOR J := 1 TO 4 DO
    BEGIN
      new (Last);
      Ptr↑.Next := Last;
      Ptr := Last
    END;
  Ptr↑.Next := NIL;
```

Let's now examine what happens when this segment of code is executed.

```
new (Start);
```

causes

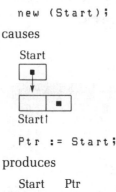

```
Ptr := Start;
```

produces

Now that we have started our list, the first pass through the **FOR** loop produces results as shown in Table 14.1. In a similar fashion, the second time through the loop causes the list to grow as shown in Table 14.2. As you can see, each pass through the body of the **FOR** loop adds one element to the linked list and causes both Ptr and Last to point to the last component of the list. After the loop is executed four times, we have

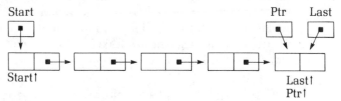

At this stage, the loop is exited and

```
Ptr↑.Next := NIL;
```

produces

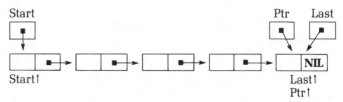

Now when we process the list, we can check the field name Next to determine when the end of the list is reached. In this sense, **NIL** is used in a manner similar to **eof** with files.

TABLE 14.1
Adding a second
node to a linked list

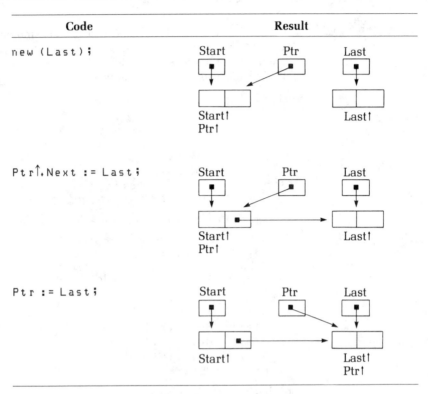

Code	Result
`new (Last);`	
`Ptr↑.Next := Last;`	
`Ptr := Last;`	

TABLE 14.2
Adding a third node
to a linked list

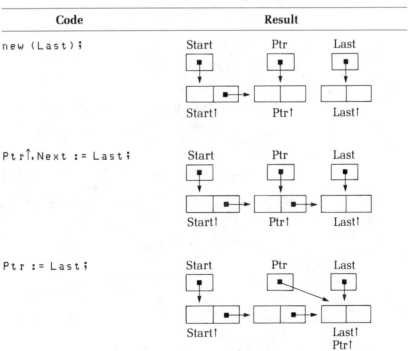

Code	Result
`new (Last);`	
`Ptr↑.Next := Last;`	
`Ptr := Last;`	

In the linked list just created, show how the code can be modified to assign a name to each record in the list.

EXAMPLE 14.1

Let's now create a linked list that can be used to simulate a deck of playing cards. We need 52 components, each of which is a record with a field for the suit (club, diamond, heart, or spade); a field for the number (1 to 13); and a field for the pointer. Such a record can be defined as

```
TYPE
   Pointer = ↑Card;
   Suits = (Club, Diamond, Heart, Spade);
   Card = RECORD
            Suit : Suits;
            Num : 1 . . 13;
            Next : Pointer
          END;  (*  of RECORD Card  *)
```

As before, we need three pointer variables; they can be declared as

```
VAR
   Start, Last, Ptr : Pointer;
```

If an ace is represented by the number 1, we can start our list by

```
BEGIN
   new (Start);
   Start↑.Suit := Club;
   Start↑.Num := 1;
   Ptr := Start;
   Last := Start;
```

This beginning is illustrated by

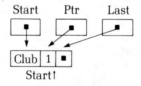

We can then generate the rest of the deck by

```
FOR J := 2 TO 52 DO
   BEGIN
      new (Last);
      IF Ptr↑.Num = 13 THEN (*  Start a new suit  *)
         BEGIN
            Last↑.Suit := succ (Ptr↑.Suit);
            Last↑.Num := 1
         END
      ELSE (*  Same suit, next number  *)
         BEGIN
            Last↑.Suit := Ptr↑.Suit;
            Last↑.Num := Ptr↑.Num + 1
         END;
      Ptr↑.Next := Last;
      Ptr := Last
   END;
Ptr↑.Next := NIL;
```

FIGURE 14.5

A linked list simulating a deck of cards

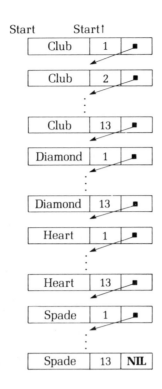

The first time through this loop we have

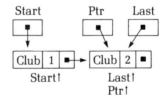

When this loop is processed all 51 times and then exited so that

```
Ptr↑.Next := NIL;
```

is executed, we have the list shown in Figure 14.5.

Printing from a Linked List

Thus far, we have seen how to create a dynamic structure and assign data to components of such a structure. We conclude this section with a look at how to print data from a linked list.

The general idea is to start with the first component in the list, print the desired information, and then move sequentially through the list until the last component **(NIL)** is reached. There are two aspects of this algorithm that need to be examined. First, the loop control depends on examining the current record for the value of **NIL** in the pointer field. If P is used to denote this field, we have

```
WHILE P <> NIL DO
  BEGIN
       .
       .
       .
  END;
```

Second, the loop increment is to assign the pointer (P) used as a loop control variable the value of the Next field of the current record. To illustrate, assume we have the definitions and declarations used previously to form a list of student names. If we declare the variable P by

```
VAR
  P : DataPtr;
```

we can then print the names by

```
BEGIN (*  Print names in list   *)
  P := Start;
  WHILE P <> NIL DO
    BEGIN
      writeln (P↑.Name:40);
      P := P↑.Next
    END
END; (*  of printing names   *)
```

SELF QUIZ 14.4   Explain why the code for printing names from a linked list works for an empty list.

In general, printing from a linked list is done with a procedure. When a procedure is used, only the external pointer (Start, in our examples) needs to be used as a parameter. An additional loop control variable (P) needs to be declared. To illustrate, a procedure to print the previous list of names is

```
PROCEDURE PrintNames (First : DataPtr);
  VAR
    P : DataPtr;
  BEGIN
    P := First;
    WHILE P <> NIL DO
      BEGIN
        writeln (P↑.Name:40);
        P := P↑.Next
      END
  END;  (*  of PROCEDURE PrintNames  *)
```

This is called from the main program by

```
PrintNames (Start);
```

Exercises 14.2

1. Discuss the differences and similarities between arrays and linked lists.

2. Write a test program to transfer an unknown number of integers from a data file into a linked list and then print the integers from the linked list.

3. Write a procedure to be used with the test program in Exercise 2 to print the integers.

4. Explain why a linked list is preferable when you are getting an unknown number of data items from a data file.   .

5. Suppose you are going to create a linked list of records where each record in the list should contain the following information about a student: name, four test scores, ten quiz scores, average, and letter grade.

   a. Define a record to be used for this purpose.
   b. What pointer type(s) and pointer variable(s) are needed?
   c. Assume the data for each student is on one line in the data file as

Smith Mary   97 98 85 90 9 8 7 10 6 9 10 8 9 7 ▮

   ▪ Show how to get the data for the first student into the first component of a linked list.
   ▪ Show how to get the data for the second student into the second component.

6. Why are three pointers (Start, Last, Ptr) used when creating a linked list?

For Exercises 7–12, consider the definitions and declarations

```
TYPE
   P = ↑Node;
   Node = RECORD
              Num : integer;
              Next : P
          END;
VAR
   A, B, C : P;
```

Show how the schematic

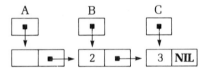

would be changed by each statement.

7. A := A↑.Next;
8. B := A;
9. C := A↑.Next;
10. B↑.Num := C↑.Num;
11. A↑.Num := B↑.Next↑.Num;
12. C↑.Next := A;

13. Using the definitions and declarations in Exercises 7–12, write one statement to change

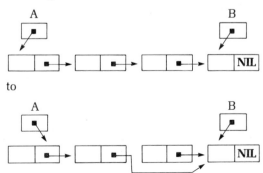

to

For Exercises 14–16, assume the definitions and declarations in Exercises 7–12 and indicate the output for each.

14.
```
new (A);
new (B);
A↑.Num := 10;
B↑.Num := 20;
B := A;
A↑.Num := 5;
writeln (A↑.Num, B↑.Num);
```

15.
```
new (C);
C↑.Num := 100;
new (B);
B↑.Num := C↑.Num MOD 8;
new (A);
A↑.Num := B↑.Num + C↑.Num;
writeln (A↑.Num, B↑.Num, C↑.Num);
```

16.
```
new (A);
new (B);
A↑.Num := 10;
A↑.Next := B;
A↑.Next↑.Num := 100;
writeln (A↑.Num, B↑.Num);
```

17. Write a function Sum to sum the integers in a linked list of integers. Show how it is called from the main program.

■ 14.3
Working with Linked Lists

OBJECTIVES

- to insert an element into a linked list
- to delete an element from a linked list
- to update an ordered linked list
- to search a linked list for an element

In this section, we examine some of the basic operations required when working with linked lists. Working with a list of integers, we see how to create a sorted list. We then update a linked list by searching it for a certain value and deleting that element from the list.

The following **TYPE** definition is used for most of this section.

```
TYPE
    DataPtr = ↑Node;
    Node = RECORD
               Num : integer;
               Next : DataPtr
           END;
```

Since most of the operations we examine will be used later, procedures are written for them.

STYLE TIP
■ ■ ■ ■ ■ ■ ■

When working with linked lists of records, Node is frequently used as the record identifier. This facilitates readability of program comments. Thus, comments such as "Get new node," "Insert a node," and "Delete a node" are meaningful.

Inserting an Element

The dynamic nature of a linked list implies that we are able to insert an element into a list. The three cases considered are inserting an element at the beginning, in the middle, and at the end.

The procedure for inserting at the beginning of a list is commonly called "Push." Before writing code for this procedure, let's examine what should be done with the nodes and pointers. If the list is illustrated by

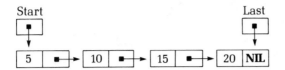

and we wish to insert

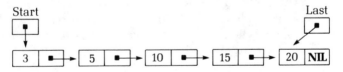

at the beginning, we need to get a new node by

```
new (P);
```

assign the appropriate value to Num

```
P↑.Num := 3;
```

and reassign the pointers to produce the desired result. After the first two steps, we have the list shown in Figure 14.6.

```
P↑.Next := Start;
```

yields the list shown in Figure 14.7. Then

```
Start := P;
```

yields

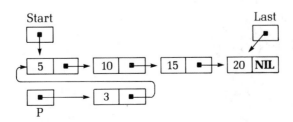

FIGURE 14.6
An assigned value in a new node

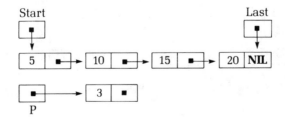

FIGURE 14.7
Assigning a pointer to the first node of a linked list

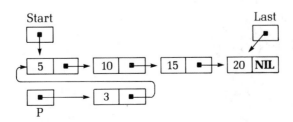

A procedure for this can now be written as

```
PROCEDURE Push (VAR St : DataPtr; NewNum : integer);
  VAR
    P : DataPtr;
  BEGIN
    new (P);              (*  Get another node       *)
    P↑.Num := NewNum;     (*  Assign the data value   *)
    P↑.Next := St;        (*  Point to the first node *)
    St := P               (*  Point to new first node *)
  END;
```

This procedure can be called from the main program by

```
Push (Start, 3);
```

A note of caution is in order. This procedure is written assuming there is an existing list with **NIL** assigned to the pointer in the final node. If this is used as the first step in creating a new list, the assignment

```
Start := NIL;
```

must be previously made.

SELF QUIZ 14.5 What happens if Push is called to start a linked list and Start has not been assigned **NIL?**

The basic idea for inserting a node somewhere in a linked list other than at the beginning or end is: get a new node, find where it belongs, and put it in the list. In order to do this, we must start at the beginning of a list and search it sequentially until we find where the new node belongs. When we next change pointers to include the new node, we must know between which pair of elements in the linked list the new node is to be inserted. Thus, if

is to be inserted in

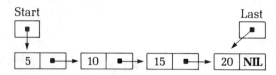

we need to know that the link

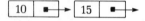

is in the list. Once this pair is identified, the pointers can be changed to produce

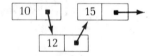

so that the new list will be

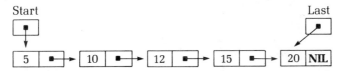

Let's now see how this can be done. We can get a new node by

```
new (P);
P↑.Num := NewNum;
```

In order to find where it belongs, we need two pointer variables to keep track of successive pairs of elements as we traverse the list. Assume Before and Ptr are appropriately declared. Then

```
Ptr := Start;
WHILE Ptr↑.Num < NewNum DO
  BEGIN
    Before := Ptr;
    Ptr := Ptr↑.Next
  END;
```

searches the list for the desired pair. (This assumes the node to be inserted is not at the end of the list.) Using the previous numbers, when this loop is completed we have the arrangement shown in Figure 14.8. We can put the new node in the list by reassigning the pointers

```
P↑.Next := Ptr;
Before↑.Next := P;
```

The list can then be envisioned as shown in Figure 14.9. When this code is written together, we have

FIGURE 14.8
Getting ready to insert a node

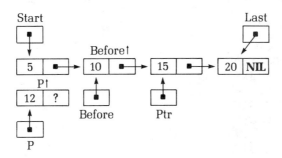

FIGURE 14.9
A new node has been inserted

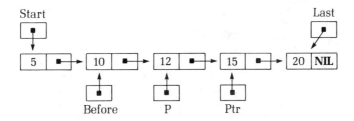

```
PROCEDURE InsertMiddle (St : DataPtr; NewNum : integer);
VAR
   P, Ptr, Before : DataPtr;
BEGIN

  (*  Get a new node  *)

   New (P);
   P↑.Num := NewNum;

  (*  Find where it belongs; assume not at end  *)

   Ptr := St;
   WHILE Ptr↑.Num < NewNum DO
     BEGIN
       Before := Ptr;
       Ptr := Ptr↑.Next
     END;

  (*  Insert the new node  *)

   P↑.Next := Ptr;
   Before↑.Next := P
END;  (*  of PROCEDURE InsertMiddle  *)
```

It can be called from the main program by

```
InsertMiddle (Start, 12);
```

The next problem to consider when inserting a node is how to insert it at the end of the list. In the previous code, when Ptr is **NIL**, a reference to Ptr↑ causes an error and thus cannot be used for inserting at the end. This problem can be solved by using a **boolean** variable Looking, initializing it to **true,** and changing the loop control to

```
WHILE (Ptr <> NIL) AND Looking DO
```

The body of the loop then becomes the **IF ... THEN ... ELSE** statement

```
IF Ptr↑.Num > NewNum THEN
   Looking := false
ELSE
   BEGIN
     Before := Ptr;
     Ptr := Ptr↑.Next
   END;
```

The loop is followed by the statement

```
P↑.Next := Ptr;
```

Thus, we have

```
new (P);
P↑.Num := NewNum;
Ptr := Start;
Looking := true;
WHILE (Ptr <> NIL) AND Looking DO
   IF Ptr↑.Num > NewNum THEN
     Looking := false
```

```
    ELSE
      BEGIN
        Before := Ptr;
        Ptr := Ptr↑.Next
      END;
  P↑.Next := Ptr;
  Before↑.Next := P;
  Last := P;
```

To see how this permits insertion at the end of a list, suppose NewNum
is 30 and the list is

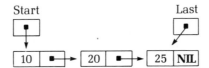

The initialization produces the list illustrated in Figure 14.10. Since Ptr
<> **NIL** and Looking is **true,** the loop is entered. Ptr↑.Num > NewNum
(10 > 30) is **false,** so the **ELSE** option is exercised to produce the list
shown in Figure 14.11. At this stage, Ptr <> **NIL** and Looking is still
true, so the loop is entered again. Ptr↑.Num > NewNum (20 > 30) is
false, so the **ELSE** option produces the list illustrated in Figure 14.12.
Since Ptr is not yet **NIL,** Ptr <> **NIL** and Looking is **true,** the loop is

FIGURE 14.10
Getting a new node
for a linked list

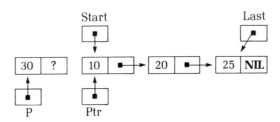

FIGURE 14.11
Positioning Before
and Ptr

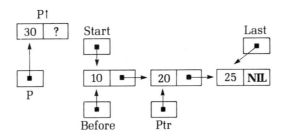

FIGURE 14.12
Moving Before and
Ptr

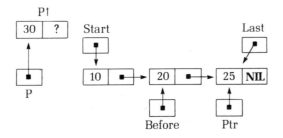

FIGURE 14.13
Before and Ptr ready
for insertion

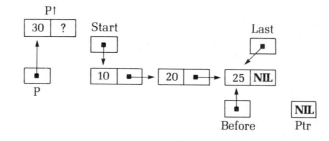

FIGURE 14.14
Insertion at end of
linked list is com-
plete

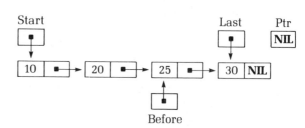

entered, Ptr↑.Num > NewNum is **false,** so the **ELSE** option produces the
list shown in Figure 14.13. Now the condition Ptr <> **NIL** is **false,** so
control is transferred to

```
P↑.Next := Ptr;
```

When this and the two lines of code following it are executed, we get the
arrangement shown in Figure 14.14.

One final comment is in order. A slight modification of this procedure
accommodates inserting at the beginning of a list. You may choose to
reserve Push for this purpose. However, if you want a single procedure
that will insert anywhere in a linked list, it is

```
PROCEDURE Insert (VAR St,Last : DataPtr; NewNum : integer);
  VAR
    P, Ptr, Before : DataPtr;
    Looking : boolean;
  BEGIN

    (*  Initialize  *)
    new (P);
    P↑.Num := NewNum;
    Before := NIL;
    Ptr := St;
    Looking := true;

    (*  Check for empty list  *)
    IF St = NIL THEN
      BEGIN
        P↑.Next := St;
        St := P
      END
    ELSE
```

```
(*  Now start the loop  *)
    WHILE (Ptr <> NIL ) AND Looking DO
      IF Ptr↑.Num > NewNum THEN
        Looking := false
      ELSE
        BEGIN
          Before := Ptr;
          Ptr := Ptr↑.Next
        END;

(*  Now move the pointers  *)
   IF Looking THEN
     Last := Ptr;
   P↑.Next := Ptr;

(*  Check for insert at beginning  *)
   IF Before = NIL THEN
     BEGIN
       P↑.Next := St;
       St := P
     END
   ELSE
     Before↑.Next := P
END; (*  of PROCEDURE Insert  *)
```

SELF QUIZ 14.6   Show why **PROCEDURE** Insert allows you to insert at the beginning of a list.

EXAMPLE 14.2   To illustrate how **PROCEDURE** Insert can be used to create a linked list of integers sorted from high to low, let's develop a short program to read integers from a data file, create a linked list sorted from high to low, and print contents of components in the linked list. A first-level pseudocode development of this is

1. Create the list
2. Print the list

Step 1 can be refined to

1. Create the list
    1.1   create the first node
    1.2   **WHILE NOT eof DO**
          insert in the list

Using procedures for inserting an element and printing the list, a program is

```
PROGRAM LinkListPrac (input,output,NumList);


(***************************************************************

    This program is a first illustration of using linked
    lists. It creates a sorted linked list from an
    unsorted data file and then prints the contents of the
    list. Procedures are used to

    1. Insert into the list
    2. Print the list


***************************************************************)
```

```
TYPE
  DataPtr = ↑Node;
  Node = RECORD
            Num : integer;
            Next : DataPtr
         END;
VAR
  Number : integer;          (*  Number to be inserted  *)
  Start,Finish : DataPtr;    (*  Pointers for the list  *)
  NumList : FILE OF integer; (*  Data file              *)


(***************************************************************

    This procedure creates a linked list sorted high to low

 ***************************************************************)
PROCEDURE Insert (VAR St,Last : DataPtr; NewNum : integer);
  VAR
    P,Ptr,Before : DataPtr;
    Looking : boolean;
  BEGIN

(*  Initialize  *)
    new(P);
    P↑.Num := NewNum;
    Before := NIL;
    Ptr := St;
    Looking := true;

(*  Now start the loop  *)
    WHILE (Ptr <> NIL) AND Looking DO
      IF Ptr↑.Num > NewNum THEN
        Looking := false
      ELSE
        BEGIN
          Before := Ptr;
          Ptr := Ptr↑.Next
        END;

(*  Now move the pointers  *)
    IF Looking THEN
      Last := Ptr;
    P↑.Next := Ptr;

(*  Check for insert at beginning  *)
    IF Before = NIL THEN
      St := P
    ELSE
      Before↑.Next := P
  END; (*  of PROCEDURE Insert  *)
```

```
(**************************************************************

     This procedure prints a linked list

 **************************************************************)
PROCEDURE PrintList (St : DataPtr);
  VAR
    P : DataPtr;
  BEGIN
    writeln; writeln;
      P := St;
    WHILE P <> NIL DO
      BEGIN
        writeln(P↑.Num);
        P := P↑.Next
      END
  END; (*  of PROCEDURE PrintList  *)

BEGIN  (*  Main program  *)

(*  Start the list  *)
  new(Start);
  reset(NumList);
  readln(NumList,Number);
  Start↑.Num := Number;
  Start↑.Next := NIL;
  new(Finish);
  Finish := Start;

(*  Now create the rest of the list  *)
  WHILE NOT eof (NumList) DO
    BEGIN
      readln(NumList,Number);
      Insert(Start,Finish,Number)
    END;
  PrintList(Start);
END.    (*  of main program  *)
```

When this program is run on the data file

| 42 | 2 | −10 | 0 | 45 | 100 | 52 | 78 | 91 | 99 | 86 | ■ |

the output is

```
-10
  0
  2
 42
 45
 52
 78
 86
 91
 99
100
```

A NOTE OF INTEREST

Using Pointers

Caution must be exercised when using pointers. Unless they are carefully described, it is easy to make a program hard to follow. Speaking to this point, Nazim H. Madhavji states: "It is often necessary to traverse deeply into the structure in order to access the required data, as can be seen in the following example, using pointers P1 and P2:

```
P1 := P2↑.IDType↑.ElementType↑.Fields . . .
```

Such 'spaghetti-like' indirections get more cumbersome as SomeType gets more complex.

Often, access paths of this kind are diagrammatically represented with no absolute certainty of their correctness." He then continues, saying: "By raising the level of description of dynamic data structures, the visibility of these structures in programmed text can be increased."

Deleting a Node

A second standard operation when working with linked lists is that of deleting a node. Let's first consider the problem of deleting the first node in a list. This process is commonly called "Pop." Before writing code for this procedure, however, let's examine what should be done with the pointers.

Deleting the first node essentially requires a reversal of the steps used when inserting a node at the beginning of a list. If the list is

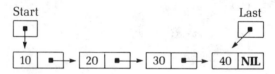

and you wish to produce

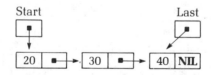

you might think that

```
Start := Start↑.Next;
```

would accomplish this. Not true. There are two problems with this method. First, you may—and probably will—want the value of some data fields returned to the main program. Thus, the appropriate fields need their values assigned to variable parameters. A second problem with this method is that the first node was not returned to the computer for subsequent reuse. Since one of the advantages of using dynamic variables is not wasting unused storage, the procedure **dispose** should be used with this node.

We can now write a procedure to delete the first node. Assuming the data value is to be returned to the main program, the procedure is

```
PROCEDURE Pop (VAR St : DataPtr; VAR NewNum : integer);
  VAR
    P : DataPtr;
  BEGIN
    P := St;                 (*  Use a temporary pointer       *)
    NewNum := P↑.Num;        (*  Return value to main program  *)
    St := St↑. Next;         (*  Move start to next node        *)
    dispose (P)              (*  Return P↑ for later use        *)
  END; (*  of PROCEDURE Pop  *)
```

The next kind of deletion we examine is when the list is searched for a certain key value and the node containing this value is to be removed from the linked list. For example, if the list contains records for customers of a company, you might want to update the list when a former customer moves away. To illustrate the process, suppose the list is

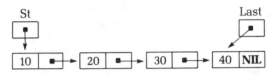

and you wish to delete

The new list is

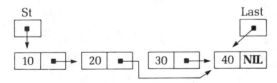

and the node deleted can be returned using **dispose** to produce

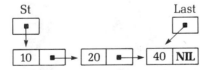

Our method of doing this uses two temporary pointers. One pointer searches the list for the specified data value and, once it is located, the second pointer points to it so we can use **dispose** to return it for subsequent use. If Before and P are the temporary pointers, the code is

```
BEGIN
  Before := St;
  WHILE Before↑.Next↑.Num <> NewNum DO
    Before := Before↑.Next;
  P := Before↑.Next;
  Before↑.Next := P↑.Next;
  dispose (P)
END;
```

Let's now see how this deletes

from the previous list.

```
Before := St;
```

yields a list as illustrated in Figure 14.15. At this stage, NewNum is 30 and Before↑.Next↑.Num is 20. Since these are not equal, the pointer Before is moved by

```
Before := Before↑.Next;
```

Thus, we have the list in Figure 14.16. Now Before↑.Next↑.Num = New-Num (30), so the **WHILE** ... **DO** loop is exited.

```
P := Before↑.Next;
```

produces the list shown in Figure 14.17.

FIGURE 14.15
Initializing
Before

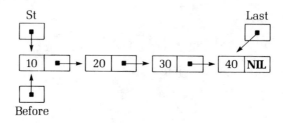

FIGURE 14.16
Positioning Before

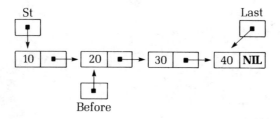

FIGURE 14.17
Positioning P

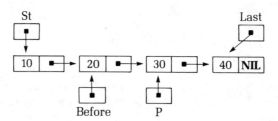

FIGURE 14.18
Reassigning a pointer

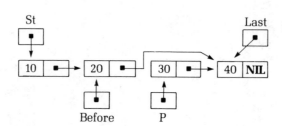

```
Before↑.Next := P↑.Next;
```

yields the list in Figure 14.18. Finally,

```
dispose (P);
```

returns the node, so we have

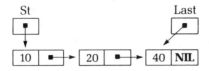

This process can be combined with deleting the first node to produce the following procedure.

```
PROCEDURE Delete (VAR St : DataPtr; NewNum : integer);
  VAR
    Before, P : DataPtr;
  BEGIN
    IF NewNum = St↑.Num THEN
      Pop (St, NewNum)
    ELSE
      BEGIN
        Before := St;
        WHILE Before↑.Next↑.Num <> NewNum DO
          Before := Before↑.Next;
        P := Before↑.Next;
        Before↑.Next := P↑.Next;
        dispose (P)
      END
  END; (*  of PROCEDURE Delete  *)
```

This procedure can now be used to delete any node from a linked list. However, it produces an error if no match is found. A modification to protect against this possibility is left as an exercise.

Exercises 14.3

1. Illustrate how **PROCEDURE** Insert works when inserting a node in the middle of a linked list.

2. Write a test program to see what happens when Ptr is **NIL** and a reference is made to Ptr↑.

3. Revise **PROCEDURE** Insert so that it calls **PROCEDURE** Push if a node is to be inserted at the beginning of a list.

4. Modify **PROCEDURE** Delete to protect against the possibility of not finding a match when the list is searched.

5. Modify **PROCEDURE** Pop so that no data value is returned when Pop is called.

6. Write a complete program to allow you to
   a. Create a linked list of records where each record contains a person's name and an amount of money donated to a local fund-raising group; the list should be sorted alphabetically.
   b. Use the linked list to print the donor names and amounts.
   c. Read a name that is to be deleted and then delete the appropriate record from the list.
   d. Print the revised list.

7. Modify **PROCEDURE** Delete to delete the *n*th node rather than a node with a particular data value. For example, you might be asked to delete the fifth node.

8. Write a procedure to copy the integers in a linked list of integers into a file of integers.

9. Write a complete program that uses a linked list to sort a file of integers. Your program should create a sorted list, print the list, and save the sorted list for later use.

■ **14.4**
Other Dynamic Data Structures

In this final section, we briefly examine some additional dynamic data structures: stacks, queues, and binary trees. The concepts behind them and their elementary use are emphasized. This section should serve as an introduction to these dynamic data structures. A suggested reading list is included for those wishing a more detailed development.

Stacks

A *stack* is a dynamic data structure in which access can only be made from one end. You can think of a stack as paper in a copying machine or plates at a salad bar. In both cases, the last one in will be the first one out; that is, you put items in, one at a time, at the top and you remove them, one at a time, from the top. This last-in, first-out order is referred to as *LIFO*; stacks are therefore often termed LIFO structures.

A stack can be envisioned as follows:

E
D
C
B
A

In this illustration, item E is considered the top element in the stack.

The two basic operations needed for working with a stack are inserting an element to create a new stack top (Push) and removing an element from the top of the stack (Pop). If a stack is represented by a linked list, Push and Pop are merely "insert at the beginning" and "delete from the beginning" as developed in Section 14.3.

To illustrate the use of a stack in a program, let's consider a program that will check an arithmetic expression to make sure that parentheses are correctly matched (nested). Our program considers

$(3 + 4 * (5 \textbf{ MOD } 3))$

to make sure that the number of left parentheses matches the number of right parentheses. A first-level pseudocode for this problem is

1. Read a character
2. **IF** it is a "(" **THEN**
   Push it onto the stack
3. **IF** it is a ")" **THEN**
   Pop the previous "("
4. Check for an empty stack

TABLE 14.3
Using a stack

Stack Before Read	Character Read	Stack After Character Processed
(empty) S	"("	[( ] ← Stack top S
[( ] S	"3", "+", "4", " ", "*", " "	[( ] ← Stack top S
[( ] S	"("	[( ] [( ] ← Stack top S
[( ] [( ] S	"5", " ", "M", "O", "D", " ", "3"	[( ] [( ] ← Stack top S
[( ] [( ] S	")"	[( ] ← Stack top S
[( ] S	")"	(empty) ← Stack top S

The growing and shrinking of the stack can be illustrated as shown in Table 14.3.

Two points need to be made. First, since the stack is represented by a linked list, the illustration can be

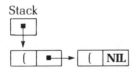

Second, before Pop is used on a stack, a check must be made to make sure the stack is not already empty. Thus, the previous procedure Pop is replaced by PopAndCheck in which a suitable error message appears if we try to pop an empty stack.

SELF QUIZ 14.7 Illustrate how the stack of parentheses grows and shrinks for the expression

$$(-3 * (2 - (3 \textbf{ MOD } 2) + (5/4)))$$

Let's now prepare code for the previous problem. The following definitions are used.

```
TYPE
  DataPtr = ↑Node;
  Node = RECORD
             Sym : char;
             Next : DataPtr
           END;
VAR
  Stack : DataPtr;
```

PROCEDURE Push is

```
PROCEDURE Push (VAR St : DataPtr; Ch : char);
  VAR
    P : DataPtr;
  BEGIN
    new (P);
    P↑.Sym := Ch;
    P↑.Next := St;
    St := P
  END; (*  of PROCEDURE Push  *)
```

PROCEDURE PopAndCheck is

```
PROCEDURE PopAndCheck (VAR St : DataPtr);
  VAR
    P : DataPtr;
  BEGIN
    IF St = NIL THEN      (*  Check for empty stack  *)
      writeln ('The parentheses are not correct.':40)
    ELSE
      BEGIN   (*  Pop the stack  *)
        P := St;
        St := St↑.Next;
        dispose (P)
      END
  END; (*  of PROCEDURE PopAndCheck  *)
```

With these two procedures, the main body of a program that examines an expression for correct use of parentheses is

```
BEGIN (*  Main program  *)
  Stack := NIL;
  WHILE NOT eoln(Data) DO
    BEGIN
      read (Data, Symbol);
      IF Symbol = "(" THEN
        Push (Stack, Symbol);
      IF Symbol = ")" THEN
        PopAndCheck (Stack)
    END;

  (*  Now check for an empty stack  *)

  IF Stack <> NIL THEN
    writeln ('The parentheses are not correct.':40)
END.  (*  of main program  *)
```

Several modifications of this short program are available and are suggested in the exercises at the end of this section.

Queues

A *queue* is a dynamic data structure in which access can be made from both ends. Elements are entered from one end (the rear) and removed from the other end (the front). This first-in, first-out order is referred to as *FIFO*; queues are termed FIFO structures. A queue is like a waiting line. Think of people standing in line to purchase tickets: each new customer enters at the rear of the line and exits from the front. A queue implemented as a linked list can be illustrated as

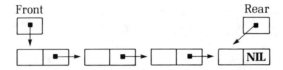

Basic operations needed for working with queues are to remove an element from the front of the list and insert an element at the rear of the list. If we use the definitions

```
TYPE
   DataPtr = ↑Node;
   Node = RECORD
              Num : integer;
              Next : DataPtr
          END;
```

we can use variables declared by

```
VAR
    Front, Rear : DataPtr;
```

when working with such a structure.

Removing an element from the front of a queue is similar to **PROCEDURE** PopAndCheck used with a stack. The only difference is that after an element is removed, if the queue is empty, Rear must be assigned the value **NIL.** A procedure for removing from the front of a queue follows. It is assumed that the value of the element removed is to be returned to the main program via a variable parameter.

```
PROCEDURE Remove (VAR First, Last : DataPtr;
                  VAR NewNum : integer);
   VAR
     P : DataPtr;
   BEGIN
     IF First = NIL THEN    (*  Check for empty queue  *)
       writeln ('The queue is empty.':40)
     ELSE
       BEGIN    (*  Pop the queue  *)
         P := First;
         First := First↑.Next;
         NewNum := P↑.Num;
         dispose (P)
       END;
     IF First = NIL THEN   (*  Set pointers for empty queue  *)
       Last := NIL
   END; (*  of PROCEDURE Remove  *)
```

This procedure is called from the main program by

```
Remove (Front, Rear, Number);
```

A procedure to insert an element at the rear of a queue (assuming there is at least one element in the queue) is similar to the procedure given in the previous section for inserting at the end of a linked list. You are asked to write the code as an exercise.

Trees

A *tree* is a dynamic data structure consisting of a special node called a *root* that points to zero or more other nodes, each of which points to zero or more other nodes, and so on. In general, a tree can be visualized as illustrated in Figure 14.19. The root of a tree is its first, or top node. *Children* are nodes pointed to by an element, a *parent* is the node that is pointing to its children, and a *leaf* is a node that has no children.

Applications for trees include compiler programs, artificial intelligence, and game-playing programs. In general, trees can be applied in programs that call for information to be stored such that it can be retrieved rapidly. As illustrated in Figure 14.19, pointers are especially appropriate for implementing a tree as a dynamic data structure. An external pointer is used to point to the root and each parent uses pointers to point to its children. A more detailed tree is illustrated in Figure 14.20.

Binary Trees. From this point on, we restrict our discussion of trees to binary trees. A *binary tree* is a tree such that each node can point to at most two children. A binary tree is illustrated in Figure 14.21.

If a binary tree is used to store integer values, a reasonable definition for the pointer type is

```
TYPE
   Pointer = ↑TreeNode;
   TreeNode = RECORD
                  Info : integer;
                  RightChild : Pointer;
                  LeftChild : Pointer
              END;
```

FIGURE 14.19
The general structure of a tree

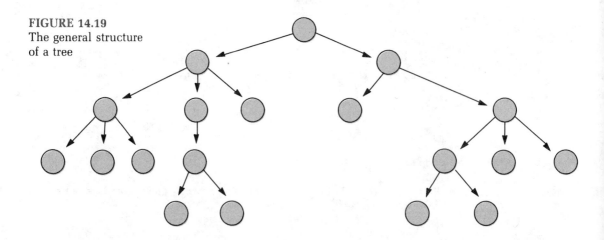

FIGURE 14.20
Using pointers to
create a tree

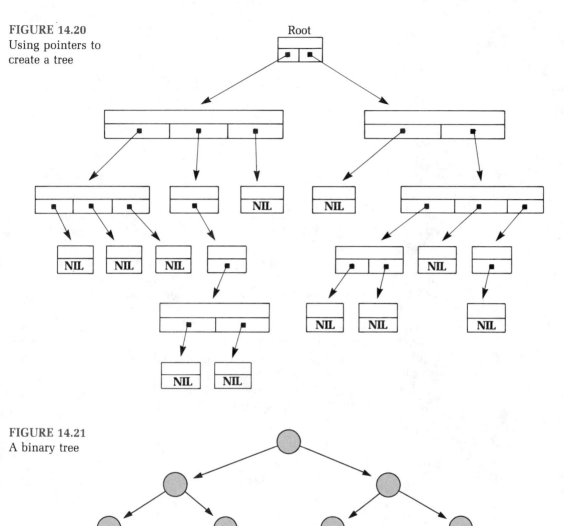

FIGURE 14.21
A binary tree

A particularly important kind of binary tree is a *binary search tree*. A binary search tree is a binary tree formed according to the following rules:

1. The information in the key field of any node is greater than the information in the key field of any node of its left child and any of its children.
2. The information in the key field of any node is less than the information in the key field of any node of its right child and any of its children. Figure 14.22 illustrates a binary search tree.

The reference to "search" is used because such trees are particularly efficient when searching for a value. To illustrate, suppose we wish to see whether or not 30 is in the tree. At each node, we check to see if the

FIGURE 14.22
A binary search tree

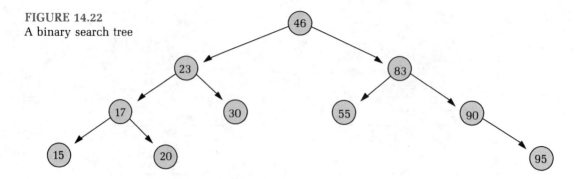

desired value has been found. If not, we determine on which side to continue looking until either a match is found or the value **NIL** is encountered. If a match is not found, we are at the appropriate node for adding the new value (creating a child). As we search for 30, we traverse the tree via the path indicated by heavier arrows as illustrated in Figure 14.23. Notice that after only two comparisons (<46, >23), the desired value is located.

Suppose we now search the tree for the value 65. The path (again indicated by heavier arrows) is shown in Figure 14.24. At this stage, the right child is **NIL** and the value has not been located. It is now relatively easy to add the new value to the tree.

Binary search trees can be used to store any data that can be ordered. For example, the registrar of a university might want to quickly access

FIGURE 14.23
Searching a tree for
the value 30

FIGURE 14.24
Searching a tree for
the value 65

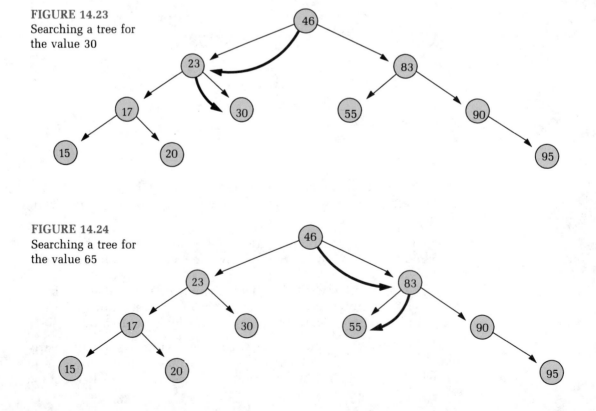

the record of a particular student. If the records are stored alphabetically by student name in a binary search tree, quick retrieval is possible.

Implementing Binary Trees. We conclude this chapter with a relatively basic implementation of binary search trees: a program to create a binary search tree from integers in a data file. We print the integers in order using a variation of the general procedure for searching a tree. The operations of inserting and deleting nodes are left as exercises.

Before developing algorithms and writing code for these implementations, we need to discuss the recursive nature of trees. (You may wish to reread Section 7.6 at this time.) When you move from one node to a right or left child, you are (in a sense) at the root of a subtree. Thus, the process of searching a tree is

1. **IF** LeftChild <> **NIL THEN**
   search left branch
2. Take desired action
3. **IF** RightChild <> **NIL THEN**
   search right branch

Steps 1 and 3 are recursive; each return to them saves values associated with the current stage together with any pending action. If the desired action is to print the values of nodes in a binary search tree, step 2 is

2. Print the value

and when this procedure is called, the result is to print an ordered list of values contained in the tree. If we use the previous definitions

```
TYPE
  Pointer =↑TreeNode;
  TreeNode = RECORD
                Info : integer;
                RightChild : Pointer;
                LeftChild : Pointer
             END;
```

a procedure for printing is

```
PROCEDURE PrintTree (Node : Pointer);
  BEGIN
    IF Node↑.LeftChild <> NIL THEN
      PrintTree (Node↑.LeftChild);
    writeln (Node↑.Info);
    IF Node↑.RightChild <> NIL THEN
      PrintTree (Node↑.RightChild)
  END; (* of PROCEDURE PrintTree *)
```

This procedure is called from the main program by

```
PrintTree (Root);
```

Notice how the recursive nature of this procedure provides a simple, efficient way to inspect the nodes of a binary search tree.

The process of creating a binary search tree is only slightly longer than that for printing. A first-level pseudocode is

1. Get a root
2. Initialize root to **NIL**

3. **WHILE NOT eof DO**
   3.1 get a number
   3.2 add a node

A recursive procedure can be used to add a node as

   3.2 add a node
      3.2.1 if the current node is **NIL,** store the value and stop
      3.2.2 if the new value is less than the current value, point
             to the left child and repeat
      3.2.3 if the new value is greater than the current value,
             point to the right child and repeat

Note that the recursive procedure to add a node adds only nodes containing distinct values. A slight modification—left as an exercise—allows duplicate values to be included. A procedure for adding a node to a binary search tree is

```
PROCEDURE AddNode (VAR Node : Pointer; Num : integer);
BEGIN
  IF Node = NIL THEN   (*  Add a new node  *)
    BEGIN
      new (Node);
      Node↑.Info := Num;
      Node↑.LeftChild := NIL;
      Node↑.RightChild := NIL
    END
  ELSE (*  Move down the tree  *)
    IF Num < Node↑.Info THEN
      AddNode (Node↑.LeftChild, Num)
    ELSE
      AddNode (Node↑.RightChild, Num)
END;  (*  of PROCEDURE AddNode  *)
```

A complete program to read unordered integers from a data file, create a binary search tree, and then print an ordered list is as follows:

```
PROGRAM TreePrac  (input,output,NumList);

(*******************************************************************

    This program illustrates working with a binary tree.
    Note the recursion used in AddNode and PrintTree.
    Input is an unordered list of integers. Output
    is a sorted list of integers that are
    printed from a binary search tree.


 *******************************************************************)

TYPE
  Pointer = ↑TreeNode:
  TreeNode = RECORD
               Info : integer;
               RightChild : Pointer;
               LeftChild : Pointer
             END;
  IntFile = FILE OF integer;
```

```
VAR
  Root : Pointer;     (*  Pointer for tree root              *)
  Number : integer;   (*  Integer read from the data file    *)
  NumList : IntFile;  (*  Data file                          *)


(********************************************************************

    Recursive procedure to add a node

 ********************************************************************)

PROCEDURE AddNode (VAR Node : Pointer; Num : integer);
  BEGIN
    IF Node = NIL THEN             (*  Add a new node  *)
      BEGIN
        new(Node);
        Node↑.Info := Num;
        Node↑.LeftChild := NIL;
        Node↑.RightChild := NIL
      END
    ELSE                           (*  Move down the list  *)
      IF Num <  Node↑.Info THEN
        AddNode(Node↑.LeftChild,Num)
      ELSE
        AddNode(Node↑.RightChild,Num)
  END;   (*  of PROCEDURE AddNode  *)



(********************************************************************

    Recursive procedure to print from a tree

 ********************************************************************)

PROCEDURE PrintTree (Node : Pointer);
  BEGIN
    IF Node↑.LeftChild <> NIL THEN
      PrintTree (Node↑.LeftChild);
    writeln(Node↑.Info);
    IF Node↑.RightChild <> NIL THEN
      PrintTree (Node↑.RightChild)
  END;   (*  of PROCEDURE PrintTree  *)

  BEGIN  (*  Main program  *)
    new(Root);
    Root := NIL;
    reset(NumList);
    WHILE NOT eof (NumList) DO
      BEGIN
        readln(NumList,Number);
        AddNode(Root,Number)
      END;
    PrintTree(Root)
  END. (*  of main program  *)
```

When this is run on the data file

the output is

```
 -5
  0
  8
 10
 16
 18
 20
 30
101
```

SELF QUIZ 14.8   Illustrate the binary search tree that is formed from integers in the data file just depicted.

Exercises 14.4

1. Using the program for checking parentheses (at the beginning of this section), illustrate how the stack grows and shrinks when the following expression is examined.

   $(5/(3 - 2 * (4 + 3) - (8$ **DIV** $2)))$

2. Write a test program to check an arithmetic expression for correct nesting of parentheses.

3. Modify the program in Exercise 2 so that several expressions may be examined; then give more descriptive error messages. Finally, include a set for the parentheses symbols "(" and ")".

4. Write a program that utilizes a stack to print a line of text in reverse order.

5. Stacks and queues can also be implemented using arrays rather than linked lists. With this in mind,

   a. Give appropriate definitions and declarations for using arrays for these data structures.
   b. Rewrite all procedures using array notation.

6. Write a procedure for inserting an element at the rear of a queue. Illustrate changes made in the linked list when such a procedure is executed.

7. Write a program that uses a stack to check an arithmetic expression for correct use of parentheses "( )," brackets "[ ]," and braces "{ }."

For Exercises 8–11, indicate which are binary search trees. Explain what is wrong with those that are not.

8.

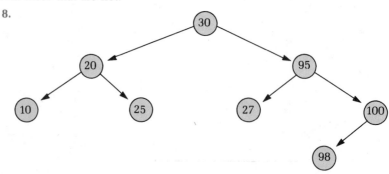

9.

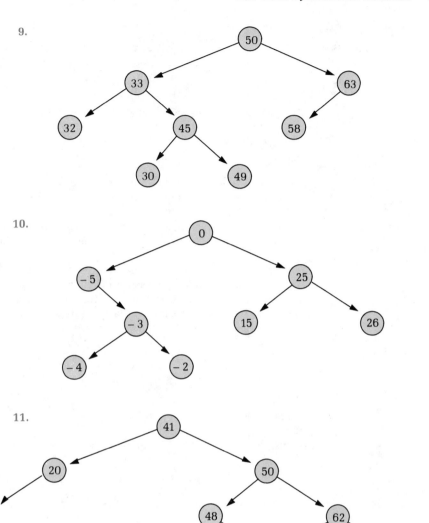

10.

11.

12. Modify **PROCEDURE** AddNode to include the possibility of having nodes equal in value.

13. Write a procedure to allow you to insert a node in a binary search tree.

14. Write a function to search a binary search tree for a given value. The function should return **true** if the value is found and **false** if it is not found.

15. Write a procedure to allow you to delete a node from a binary search tree.

16. Illustrate what binary search tree is created when **PROGRAM** TreePrac is run using the data file

| 25 | 14 | − 3 | 145 | 0 | 98 | 81 | 73 | 85 | 92 | 56 | 21 | ■ |

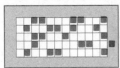

RUNNING AND DEBUGGING TIPS

1. Be careful to distinguish between a pointer and its associated dynamic variable. Thus, if Ptr is a pointer, the variable is Ptr↑ .
2. When a dynamic variable is no longer needed in a program, use **dispose** so that the memory location can be reallocated.
3. After using **dispose** with a pointer, its referenced variable is no longer available. If you use **dispose** (Ptr), then Ptr↑ does not exist.
4. Be careful not to access the referenced variable of a pointer that is **NIL.** Thus, if the asignment

   ```
   Ptr := NIL;
   ```

   is made, a reference to Ptr↑ .Info results in an error.
5. When using pointers with subprograms, be careful to pass the pointer, not the referenced variable, to the subprogram.
6. When creating dynamic data structures, be careful to initialize properly by assigning **NIL** where appropriate and keep track of pointers as your structures grow and shrink.
7. Operations with pointers require that they be of the same type. Thus, exercise caution when comparing or assigning them.
8. Values may be lost when pointers are inadvertently or prematurely reassigned. To avoid this, use as many auxiliary pointers as you wish. This is better than trying to use one pointer for two purposes.

■ Summary

Key Terms

static variable	pointer variable	root
dynamic variable	linked list	children
dynamic structure	component (node)	parent
memory location	stack	leaf
address of a memory location	LIFO	binary tree
value of a memory location	queue	binary search tree
	FIFO	
	tree	

Keywords

new
dispose
NIL

Key Concepts

- Values are stored in memory locations; each memory location has an address.
- A pointer variable is one that contains the address of a memory location; pointer variables are declared by

  ```
  TYPE
     AgeRange = 0 . . 99;
  VAR
     Ptr : ↑AgeRange;
  ```

  where the up arrow (↑) or caret (ˆ) is used before the predefined data type.
- A dynamic variable is a variable that is referenced through a pointer variable; dynamic variables can be used in the same context as any other variable of that type, and they are not declared in the variable declaration section. In the declaration

```
TYPE
   AgeRange = 0 . . 99;
VAR
   Ptr : ↑AgeRange;
```

the dynamic variable is Ptr↑ and is available after new (Ptr) is executed.
- Dynamic variables are created by

```
new Ptr;
```

and destroyed (memory area made available for subsequent reuse) by

```
dispose Ptr;
```

- Assuming the definition

```
TYPE
   AgeRange = 0 . . 99;
VAR
   Ptr : ↑AgeRange;
```

the relationship between a pointer and its associated dynamic variable is illustrated by the code

```
new (Ptr);
Ptr↑ := 21;
```

which can be envisioned as

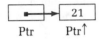

    Ptr   Ptr↑

- The only legal operations on pointer variables are assignments and comparison for equality.
- **NIL** can be assigned to a pointer variable; this is used in a **boolean** expression to detect the end of a list.
- Dynamic data structures differ from static data structures in that they are modified during the execution of the program.
- A linked list is a dynamic data structure formed by having each component contain a pointer that points to the next component; generally, each component is a record with one field reserved for the pointer.
- When creating a linked list, extra pointers are needed to keep track of the first, last, and newest component.
- When creating a linked list, the final component should have **NIL** assigned to its pointer field.
- Printing from a linked list is accomplished by starting with the first component in the list and proceeding sequentially through the list until the last component is reached; a typical procedure for printing from a linked list is

```
PROCEDURE Print (First : DataPtr);
   VAR
      P : DataPtr;
   BEGIN
      P := First;
      WHILE P <> NIL DO
         BEGIN
            writeln (P↑.field name);
            P := P↑.Next
         END
   END; (*  of PROCEDURE Print  *)
```

- Inserting a node in a linked list should consider three cases: insert at the beginning, insert in the middle, and insert at the end.
- Inserting at the beginning of a linked list is used frequently enough in later work that it is referred to as Push; one version of this is

```
PROCEDURE Push (VAR St : DataPtr; NewNum : integer);
   VAR
      P : DataPtr;
   BEGIN
      new(P);
      P↑.New := NewNum;
      P↑.Next := St;
      St := P
   END; (*  of PROCEDURE Push  *)
```

- Searching an ordered linked list to see where a new node should be inserted is accomplished by

```
Ptr := Start;
WHILE Ptr↑.Num < NewNum DO
   BEGIN
      Before := Ptr;
      Ptr := Ptr↑.Next
   END;
```

- In deleting a node from a linked list, one should be able to delete the first node or search for a particular node and then delete it.
- Deleting the first node is referred to by the procedure Pop; one version is

```
PROCEDURE Pop (VAR St : DataPtr; VAR NewNum : integer);
   VAR
      P : DataPtr;
   BEGIN
      P := St;
      NewNum := P↑.Num;
      St := St↑.Next;
      dispose (P)
   END; (*  of PROCEDURE Pop  *)
```

- When a node is deleted from a linked list, it should be returned for subsequent use; this is done by using the standard procedure **dispose**.
- A stack is a dynamic data structure where access can only be made from one end; stacks are referred to as LIFO (last-in, first-out) structures.
- A queue is a dynamic data structure where access can be made from both ends; queues are referred to as FIFO (first-in, first-out) structures.
- A tree is a dynamic data structure consisting of a special node (called a root) that points to zero or more other nodes, each of which points to zero or more other nodes, and so on. Trees are represented symbolically as

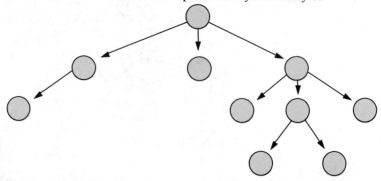

- A root is the first or top node of a tree.
- Trees are particularly useful in programs that use data that can be ordered and that need to be retrieved quickly.
- Binary trees are trees where each node points to at most two other nodes; parent, right child, and left child are terms frequently used when working with binary trees. An illustration of a binary tree is

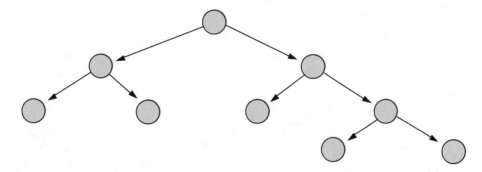

- Binary search trees are binary trees in which the information in any node is greater than the information in any node of its left child and any of its children and the information in any node is less than the information in any node of its right child and any of its children. An illustration of a typical binary search tree is

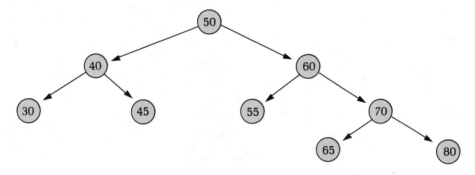

- Recursive procedures are used when working with trees; to illustrate, the values in the nodes of a binary seach tree can be printed (sequentially) with the following procedure:

```
PROCEDURE PrintTree (Node : Pointer);
  BEGIN
    IF Node↑.LeftChild <> NIL THEN
      PrintTree (Node↑.LeftChild);
    writeln (Node↑.Info);
    IF Node↑.RightChild <> NIL THEN
      PrintTree (Node↑.RightChild)
  END; (*  of PROCEDURE PrintTree  *)
```

■ **Chapter Review Exercises**

For Exercises 1–5, use the linked list

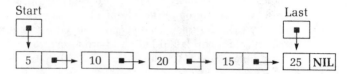

Write Pascal statements for each of the following.

1. Reorder the list so it is in an ordered sequence.
2. Have Last point to

3. Print the first value.
4. Print the last value.
5. Replace **NIL** with a pointer to the following in order to create a circular list.

For Exercises 6–10, use the linked list

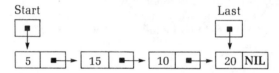

and the segment of code

```
Temp1 := Start↑.Next;
Temp2 := Start↑.Next↑.Next↑.Next;
Start↑.Next := Start↑.Next↑.Next;
Start↑.Next↑.Next := Temp1;
Start↑.Next↑.Next↑.Next := Temp2;
```

Illustrate what happens to the linked list as each statement is executed. Each statement presumes the previous code is executed.

6. ```
   new(Temp1);
   Temp1 := Start↑.Next;
   ```
7. ```
   new (Temp2);
   Temp2 := Start↑.Next↑.Next↑.Next;
   ```
8. `Start↑.Next := Start↑.Next↑.Next;`
9. `Start↑.Next↑.Next := Temp1;`
10. `Start↑.Next↑.Next↑.Next := Temp2;`
11. Assume a linked list has been formed where each node is a record defined by

```
DataPtr := ↑Info;
Info = RECORD
         Num : integer;
         Next : DataPtr
       END;
```

Write a procedure to sum the values contained in the field Num.

For Exercises 12–18, assume a binary search tree exists as illustrated.

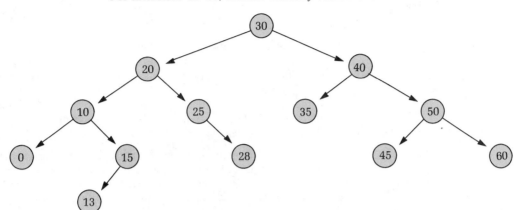

12. How would the tree be changed by inserting the node 12?
13. How would the tree be changed by inserting the node 17?
14. How would the tree be changed by inserting the node 61?
15. How would the tree be changed by inserting the node 52?
16. How would the tree look after deleting the node 15?
17. How would the tree look after deleting the node 10?
18. How would the tree look after deleting the node 45?

For Exercises 19–21, create a binary search tree assuming data are read in the indicated order.

19. 14, 20, 18, 30, 100, 3, 2, 10, 19
20. 5, 10, 15, 20, 25, 30
21. 30, 25, 20, 15, 10, 5

22. Assume each node of a binary search tree contains a three-letter word. Show how the tree looks if the following words are read (in order) as input.

son, dad, dog, cat, ski, low, mom, mow, car, sob

23. Write a segment of code to return the number of elements in a linked list.

24. Write a **boolean** function that determines whether or not a linked list is in ascending order.

■ **Programming Problems**

1. Creating an index for a textbook can be accomplished by a Pascal program that uses dynamic data structures and works with a text file. Assume that input for a program is a list of words to be included in an index. Write a program that scans the text and produces a list of page numbers indicating where each word is used in the text.

2. One of the problems faced by businesses is how best to manage their lines of customers. One method is to have a separate line for each cashier or station. Another is to have one feeder line where all customers wait and the customer at the front of the line goes to the first open station. Write a program to help a manager decide which method to use by simulating both options. Your program should allow for customers arriving at various intervals. The man-

ager wants to know the average wait in each system, average line length in each system (because of its psychological effect on customers), and the longest wait required.

3. Write a program to keep track of computer transactions on a mainframe computer. The computer can only process one job at a time. Each line of input contains a user's identification number, a starting time, and a sequence of integers representing the duration of each job.

   Assume all jobs are run on a first-come, first-served basis. Your output should include a list of identification numbers, the starting and finishing times for each job, and the average waiting time for a transaction.

4. Several previous programming problems have dealt with keeping records and computing grades for students in some class. If linked lists are used for the students' records, such a program can be used for a class of 20 students or a class of 200 students. Write a record-keeping program that utilizes linked lists. Input is from an unsorted data file. Each student's information consists of the student's name, ten quiz scores, six program scores, and three examination scores. Output should include:

   a. A list, alphabetized by student name, incorporating each student's quiz, program, and examination totals; total points; percentage grade; and letter grade
   b. Overall class average
   c. A histogram depicting the class average

5. Modify the program you developed for Readmore Public Library (Problem 6, Chapter 11) to incorporate a dynamic data structure. Use a linked list to solve the same problem.

6. Mailing lists are frequently kept in a data file sorted alphabetically by customer name. However, when they are used to generate mailing labels for a bulk mailing, they must be sorted by zip code. Write a program to input an alphabetically sorted file and produce a list of labels sorted by zip code. The data for each customer is

   a. Name
   b. Address, including street (plus number), city, two-letter abbreviation for the state, and zip code
   c. Expiration information, including the month and year

   Use a binary tree to sort by zip code. Your labels should include some special symbol for all expiring subscriptions. (See Problem 1, Chapter 12.)

■ **Suggestions for Further Reading**

1. Naps, Thomas L., and Bhagat Singh. *Introduction to Data Structures with Pascal*. St. Paul, Minn.: West Publishing Company, 1985.
2. Dale, Nell, and Susan C. Lilly. *Pascal plus Data Structures*. Lexington, Mass.: D. C. Heath and Company, 1985.
3. Singh, Bhagat, and Thomas L. Naps. *Introduction to Data Structures*. St. Paul, Minn.: West Publishing Company, 1985.
4. Tenenbaum, Aaron M., and Moshe J. Augenstein. *Data Structures Using Pascal*. Englewood Cliffs, N.J.: Prentice-Hall, Inc., 1981.

⊞ Appendixes

Appendix 1
Reserved Words

The following words have predefined meanings in standard Pascal and cannot be changed. Each of these, except **GOTO** and **Label,** has been developed in the text. These statements are discussed in Appendix 6.

AND	END	MOD	REPEAT
ARRAY	FILE	NIL	SET
BEGIN	FOR	NOT	THEN
CASE	FORWARD	OF	TO
CONST	FUNCTION	OR	TYPE
DIV	GOTO	PACKED	UNTIL
DO	IF	PROCEDURE	VAR
DOWNTO	IN	PROGRAM	WHILE
ELSE	LABEL	RECORD	WITH

Appendix 2
Predefined Identifiers

The predefined identifiers for constants, types, files, functions, and procedures are set forth in this appendix. All have predefined meanings that could (but probably should not) be changed in a program. Summary descriptions are given for the functions and procedures.

Constants	*Types*	*Files*
false	**boolean**	**input**
maxint	**char**	**output**
true	**integer**	
	real	
	text	

Functions

Function	Parameter Type	Result Type	Value Returned
abs(x)	integer real	integer real	Absolute value of x
arctan(x)	integer real	real	Arctangent of x (radians)
chr(a)	integer	char	Character with ordinal a
cos(x)	integer real	real	Cosine of x (radians)
eof(F)	file	boolean	End-of-file test for F
eoln(F)	file	boolean	End-of-line test for F
exp(x)	integer real	real real	e^x
ln(x)	integer real	real	Natural logarithm of x
odd(a)	integer	boolean	Tests for a an odd integer
ord(x)	nonreal scalar	integer	Ordinal number of x
pred(x)	nonreal scalar	same as x	Predecessor of x

Function	Parameter Type	Result Type	Value Returned
round(x)	**real**	**integer**	Rounds off x
sin(x)	**integer** **real**	**real**	Sine of x
sqr(x)	**integer** **real**	**integer** **real**	Square of x
sqrt(x)	**integer** **real**	**real**	Square root of x
succ(x)	nonreal scalar	same as x	Successor of x
trunc(x)	**real**	**integer**	Truncated value of x

Procedures:

Procedure Call	Purpose of Procedure
dispose(Ptr)	Returns variable referenced by Ptr to available space list
get(F)	Advances the file pointer for the file F and assigns the new value to F ↑
new(Ptr)	Creates a variable of the type referenced by Ptr and stores a pointer to the new variable in Ptr
pack(U, J, P)	Copies unpacked array elements from U into the packed array P; copying starts with U[J] := P[1]
page(F)	Starts printing the next line of text file F at the top of a new page
put(F)	Appends the current value of F to the file F
read(F, variable list)	Reads values from file F into indicated variables; if F is not specified, **input** is assumed
readln(F, variable list)	Executes the same as **read** and then advances the file pointer to the first position following the next end-of-line marker
reset(F)	Resets the pointer in file F to the beginning for the purpose of reading from F
rewrite(F)	Resets the pointer in file F to the beginning for the purpose of writing to F
unpack(P, U, J)	Copies packed array elements from P into the unpacked array U; copying starts with P[1] := U[J]
write(F, parameter list)	Writes values specified by parameter list to the text file F; if F is not specified, **output** is assumed
writeln(F, parameter list)	Executes the same as **write** and then places an end-of-line marker in F

⊞ Appendix 3
Syntax Diagrams

Syntax diagramming is a way to formally describe the legal syntax of language structures. Syntax diagrams show the permissible alternatives for each part of each kind of sentence and where the parts may appear. Symbolism used in the text follows.

⬭   Reserved words or terms that cannot be further defined

▭   An item that is defined by another diagram

◯   Any form of a separator

We can illustrate the use of syntax diagrams by using the English language as a model. Assume that letters cannot be further defined. A word formed by using letters from the alphabet can then be illustrated by

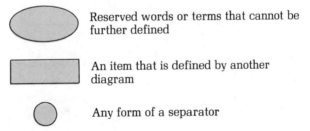

If the first letter had to be a vowel, we would have

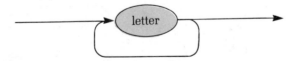

A complete sentence that ends with a period and includes the possibility of using a comma can be illustrated by

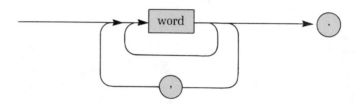

Notice that "word" has been previously defined by another diagram.

Program

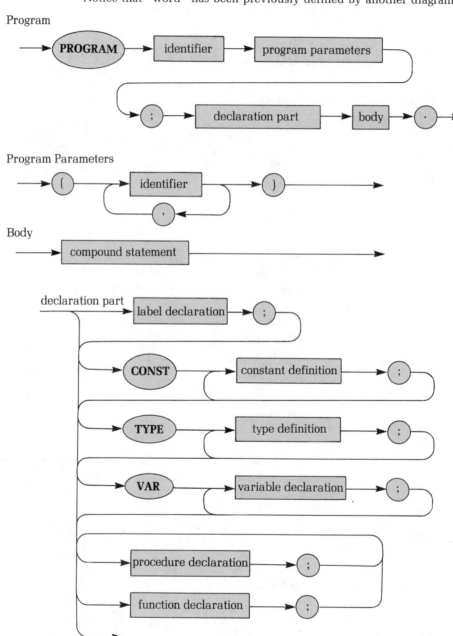

Program Parameters

Body

declaration part

Label Declaration

Constant Definition

Type Definition

Variable Declaration

Function Declaration

Procedure Declaration

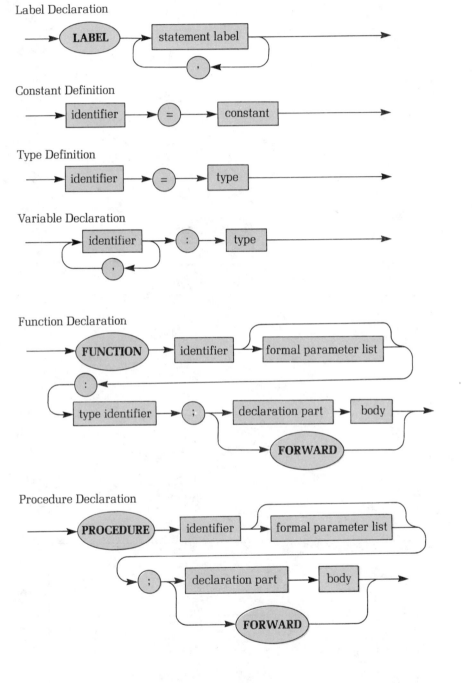

Formal Parameter List

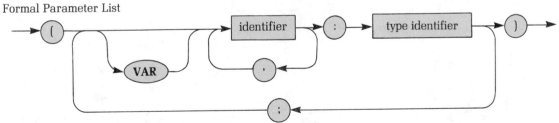

statement label

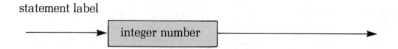

constant

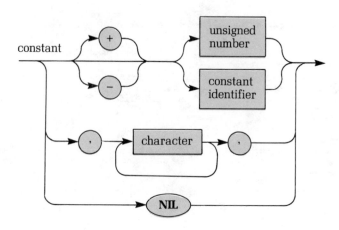

identifier

Type

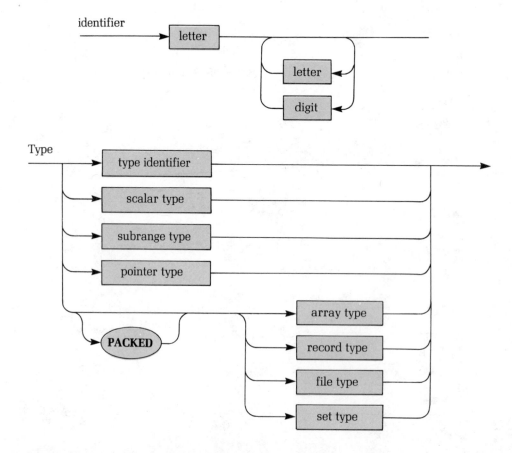

Scalar Type

Subrange Type

Pointer Type

Array Type

Record Type

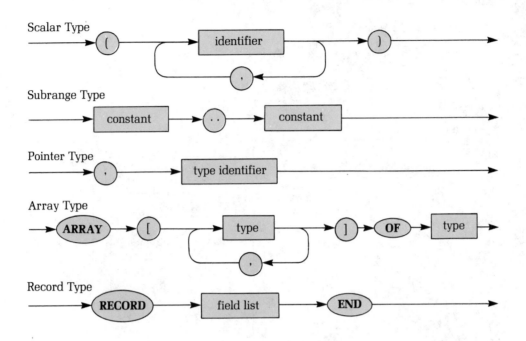

Field List

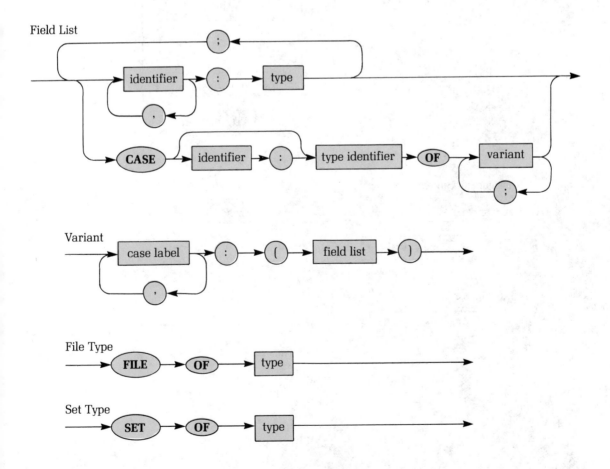

Variant

File Type

Set Type

Compound Statement

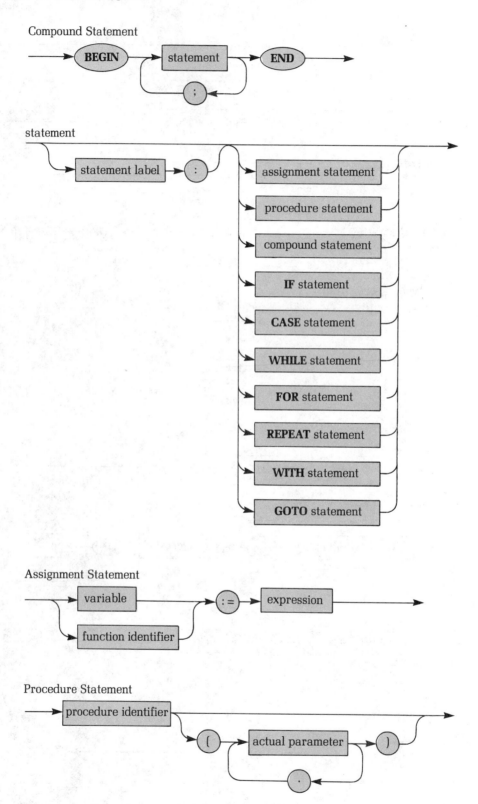

statement

Assignment Statement

Procedure Statement

IF Statement

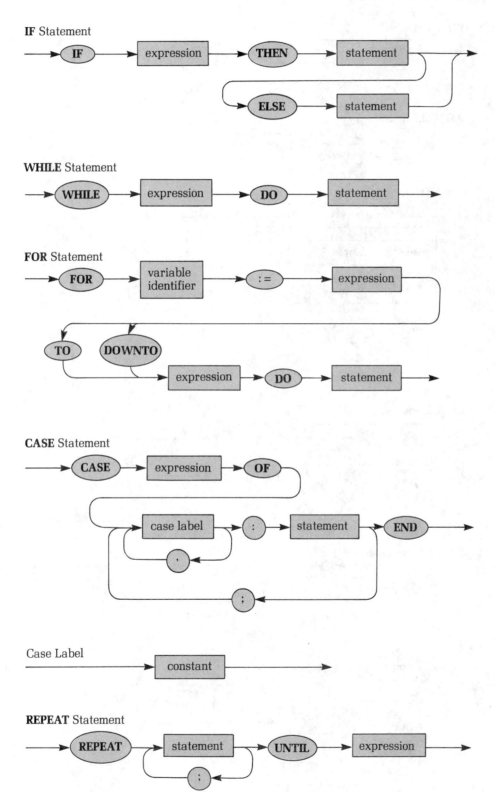

WHILE Statement

FOR Statement

CASE Statement

Case Label

REPEAT Statement

WITH Statement

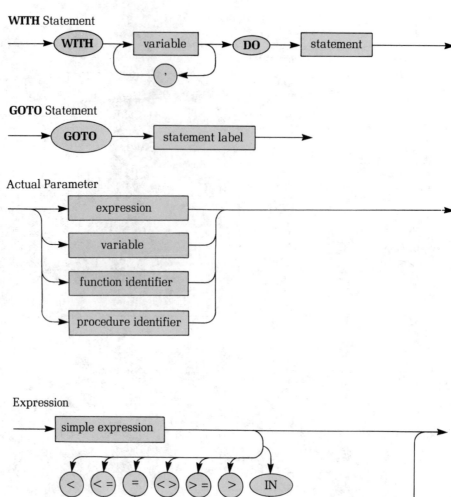

GOTO Statement

Actual Parameter

Expression

Simple Expression

Term

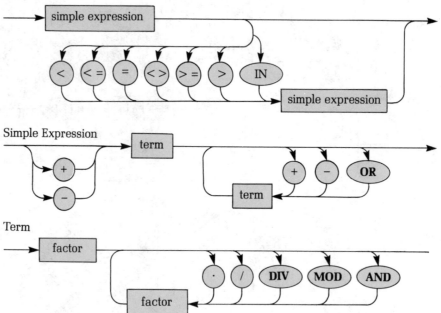

Factor

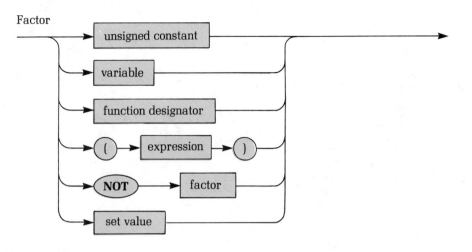

Function Designator

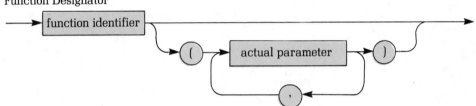

Set Value

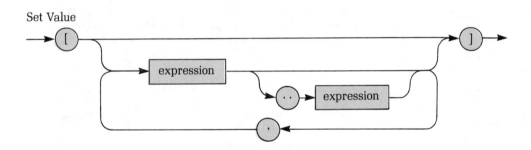

Variable

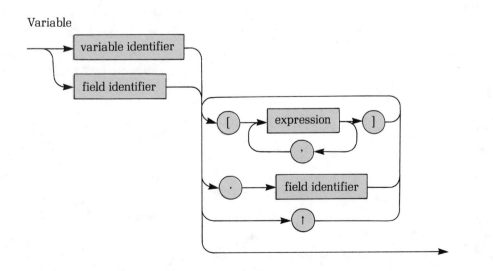

Appendix 4 Character Sets

The two tables included here show the ordering of some common character sets. Note that only printable characters are shown for each set. Ordinals without character representations either do not have standard representation, or they are associated with unprintable control characters. In each list, the blank is denoted by "b̸".

The American Standard Code for Information Interchange (ASCII)

Left Digit(s)	Right Digit									
	0	1	2	3	4	5	6	7	8	9
3			b̸	!	"	#	$	%	&	'
4	(	)	*	+	,	−	.	/	0	1
5	2	3	4	5	6	7	8	9	:	;
6	<	=	>	?	@	A	B	C	D	E
7	F	G	H	I	J	K	L	M	N	O
8	P	Q	R	S	T	U	V	W	X	Y
9	Z	[	\	]	↑	_	`	a	b	c
10	d	e	f	g	h	i	j	k	l	m
11	n	o	p	q	r	s	t	u	v	w
12	x	y	z	{	|	}	~			

*Codes 00–31 and 127 are nonprintable control characters.

The Extended Binary
Coded Decimal In-
terchange Code
(EBCDIC)

Left Digit(s)	Right Digit									
	0	**1**	**2**	**3**	**4**	**5**	**6**	**7**	**8**	**9**
6					ƀ					
7					¢	.	<	(	+	|
8	&									
9	!	$	*	)	;	¬	−	/		
10							^	,	%	−
11	>	?								
12			:	#	@	'	=	"		a
13	b	c	d	e	f	g	h	i		
14						j	k	l	m	n
15	o	p	q	r						
16			s	t	u	v	w	x	y	z
17								\	{	}
18	[	]								
19				A	B	C	D	E	F	G
20	H	I								J
21	K	L	M	N	O	P	Q	R		
22							S	T	U	V
23	W	X	Y	Z						
24	0	1	2	3	4	5	6	7	8	9

*Codes 00–63 and 250–255 are nonprintable control
characters.

⊞ Appendix 5 Compiler Error Messages

The following error messages are used by the compiler to identify compilation errors. Such errors will be identified by number with appropriate messages produced at the bottom of a compilation listing.

```
 1   ERROR IN SIMPLE TYPE.
 2   IDENTIFIER EXPECTED.
 3   'PROGRAM' EXPECTED.
 4   ')' EXPECTED.
 5   ' ' EXPECTED.
 6   UNEXPECTED SYMBOL.
 7   ERROR IN PARAMETER LIST.
 8   'OF' EXPECTED.
 9   '(' EXPECTED.
10   ERROR IN TYPE.
11   '[' EXPECTED.
12   ']' EXPECTED.
13   'END' EXPECTED.
14   ';' EXPECTED.
15   INTEGER CONSTANT EXPECTED.
16   '=' EXPECTED.
17   'BEGIN' EXPECTED.
18   ERROR IN DECLARATION PART.
19   ERROR IN FIELD-LIST.
20   ',' EXPECTED.
21   '..' EXPECTED.

40   VALUE PART ALLOWED ONLY IN MAIN PROGRAM.
41   TOO FEW VALUES SPECIFIED.
42   TOO MANY VALUES SPECIFIED.
43   VARIABLE INITIALIZED TWICE.
```

```
44    TYPE IS NEITHER ARRAY NOR RECORD.
45    REPETITION FACTOR MUST BE GREATER THAN ZERO.

50    ERROR IN CONSTANT.
51    ' =' EXPECTED.
52    'THEN' EXPECTED.
53    'UNTIL' EXPECTED.
54    'DO' EXPECTED.
55    'TO' OR 'DOWNTO' EXPECTED.
57    'FILE' EXPECTED.
58    ERROR IN FACTOR.
59    ERROR IN VARIABLE.
60    FILE TYPE IDENTIFIER EXPECTED.

101   IDENTIFIER DECLARED TWICE.
102   LOWBOUND EXCEEDS HIGHBOUND.
103   IDENTIFIER IS NOT OF APPROPRIATE CLASS.
104   IDENTIFIER NOT DECLARED.
105   SIGN NOT ALLOWED.
106   NUMBER EXPECTED.
107   INCOMPATIBLE SUBRANGE TYPES.
108   FILE NOT ALLOWED HERE.
109   TYPE MUST NOT BE REAL.
110   TAGFIELD TYPE MUST BE SCALAR OR SUBRANGE.
111   INCOMPATIBLE WITH TAGFIELD TYPE.
112   INDEX TYPE MUST NOT BE REAL.
113   INDEX TYPE MUST BE SCALAR OR SUBRANGE.
114   BASE TYPE MUST NOT BE REAL.
115   BASE TYPE MUST BE SCALAR OR SUBRANGE.
116   ERROR IN TYPE OF STANDARD PROCEDURE PARAMETER.
117   UNSATISFIED FORWARD REFERENCE.
119   FORWARD DECLARED; REPETITION OF PARAMETER LIST NOT ALLOWED.
120   FUNCTION RESULT TYPE MUST BE SCALAR, SUBRANGE, OR POINTER.
121   FILE VALUE PARAMETER NOT ALLOWED.
122   FORWARD DECLARED FUNCTION; REPETITION OF RESULT TYPE NOT
      ALLOWED.
123   MISSING RESULT TYPE IN FUNCTION DECLARATION.
124   FIXED-POINT FORMATTING ALLOWED FOR REALS ONLY.
125   ERROR IN TYPE OF STANDARD FUNCTION PARAMETER.
126   NUMBER OF PARAMETERS DOES NOT AGREE WITH DECLARATION.
127   INVALID PARAMETER SUBSTITUTION.
128   PARAMETER PROCEDURE/FUNCTION IS NOT COMPATIBLE WITH
      DECLARATION.
129   TYPE CONFLICT OF OPERANDS.
130   EXPRESSION IS NOT OF SET TYPE.
131   TESTS ON EQUALITY ALLOWED ONLY.
132   '<' AND '>' NOT ALLOWED FOR SET OPERANDS.
133   FILE COMPARISON NOT ALLOWED.
134   INVALID TYPE OF OPERAND(S).
135   TYPE OF OPERAND MUST BE BOOLEAN.
136   SET ELEMENT MUST BE SCALAR OR SUBRANGE.
137   SET ELEMENT TYPES NOT COMPATIBLE.
138   TYPE OF VARIABLE IS NOT ARRAY.
139   INDEX TYPE IS NOT COMPATIBLE WITH DECLARATION.
140   TYPE OF VARIABLE IS NOT RECORD.
```

```
141   TYPE OF VARIABLE MUST BE FILE OR POINTER.
142   INVALID PARAMETER SUBSTITUTION.
143   INVALID TYPE OF LOOP CONTROL VARIABLE.
144   INVALID TYPE OF EXPRESSION.
145   TYPE CONFLICT.
146   ASSIGNMENT OF FILES NOT ALLOWED.
147   LABEL TYPE INCOMPATIBLE WITH SELECTING EXPRESSION.
148   SUBRANGE BOUNDS MUST BE SCALAR.
149   INDEX TYPE MUST NOT BE INTEGER.
150   ASSIGNMENT TO THIS FUNCTION IS NOT ALLOWED.
151   ASSIGNMENT TO FORMAL FUNCTION IS NOT ALLOWED.
152   NO SUCH FIELD IN THIS RECORD.
155   CONTROL VARIABLE MUST NOT BE DECLARED ON AN INTERMEDIATE LEVEL.
156   MULTIDEFINED CASE LABEL.
157   RANGE OF CASE LABELS IS TOO LARGE.
158   MISSING CORRESPONDING VARIANT DECLARATION.
159   REAL OR STRING TAGFIELDS NOT ALLOWED.
160   PREVIOUS DECLARATION WAS NOT FORWARD.
161   MULTIPLE FORWARD DECLARATION.
164   SUBSTITUTION OF STANDARD PROCEDURE/FUNCTION NOT ALLOWED.
165   MULTIDEFINED LABEL.
166   MULTIDECLARED LABEL.
167   UNDECLARED LABEL.
168   UNDEFINED LABEL IN THE PREVIOUS BLOCK.
169   ERROR IN BASE SET.
170   VALUE PARAMETER EXPECTED.
172   UNDECLARED EXTERNAL FILE.
173   FORTRAN PROCEDURE OR FUNCTION EXPECTED.
174   PASCAL PROCEDURE OR FUNCTION EXPECTED.
175   MISSING FILE 'INPUT' IN PROGRAM HEADING.
176   MISSING FILE 'OUTPUT' IN PROGRAM HEADING.
177   ASSIGNMENT TO FUNCTION ALLOWED ONLY IN FUNCTION BODY.
178   MULTIDEFINED RECORD VARIANT.
179   X-OPTION OF ACTUAL PROCEDURE/FUNCTION DOES NOT MATCH
      FORMAL DECLARATION.
180   CONTROL VARIABLE MUST NOT BE FORMAL.
181   ARRAY SUBSCRIPT CALCULATION TOO COMPLICATED.
182   MAGNITUDE OF CASE LABEL IS TOO LARGE.
183   SUBRANGE OF TYPE REAL IS NOT ALLOWED.

198   ALTERNATE INPUT NOT FOUND.
199   ONLY ONE ALTERNATE INPUT MAY BE ACTIVE.

201   ERROR IN REAL CONSTANT DIGIT EXPECTED.
202   STRING CONSTANT MUST BE CONTAINED ON A SINGLE LINE.
203   INTEGER CONSTANT EXCEEDS RANGE.
204   8 OR 9 IN OCTAL NUMBER.
205   STRINGS OF LENGTH ZERO ARE NOT ALLOWED.
206   INTEGER PART OF REAL CONSTANT EXCEEDS RANGE.
207   REAL CONSTANT EXCEEDS RANGE.

250   TOO MANY NESTED SCOPES OF IDENTIFIERS.
251   TOO MANY NESTED PROCEDURES AND/OR FUNCTIONS.
255   TOO MANY ERRORS ON THIS SOURCE LINE.
256   TOO MANY EXTERNAL REFERENCES.
```

259   EXPRESSION TOO COMPLICATED.
260   TOO MANY EXIT LABELS.
261   TOO MANY LARGE VARIABLES.
262   NODE TO BE ALLOCATED IS TOO LARGE.
263   TOO MANY PROCEDURE/FUNCTION PARAMETERS.
264   TOO MANY PROCEDURES AND FUNCTIONS.

300   DIVISION BY ZERO.
302   INDEX EXPRESSION OUT OF BOUNDS.
303   VALUE TO BE ASSIGNED IS OUT OF BOUNDS.
304   ELEMENT EXPRESSION OUT OF RANGE.

350   ONLY THE LAST DIMENSION MAY BE PACKED.
351   ARRAY TYPE IDENTIFIER EXPECTED.
352   ARRAY VARIABLE EXPECTED.
353   POSITIVE INTEGER CONSTANT EXPECTED.

397   PACK AND UNPACK ARE NOT IMPLEMENTED FOR DYNAMIC ARRAYS.
398   IMPLEMENTATION RESTRICTION.

Appendix 6
GOTO Statement

In your work with computers, you may have heard of a **GOTO** statement. It is another statement in Pascal that allows a programmer to transfer control within a program. The **GOTO** statement has the effect of an immediate unconditional transfer to an indicated designation. You should not use **GOTO** statements in a Pascal program, but for the sake of completeness, you should be aware of their existence and how they work.

Early programming languages needed a branching statement; therefore, both FORTRAN and BASIC were designed using a **GOTO** statement for branching. Subsequent languages, particularly Pascal, included more sophisticated branching and looping statements. These statements led to an emphasis on structured programming, which is easier to design and read. If you are a beginning programmer and have not used the **GOTO** statement in another language, you should continue to develop your skills without including this statement. If you have already written programs in a language that uses **GOTO** statements, you should still attempt to write all Pascal programs without **GOTO** statements.

One instance in which **GOTO** statements might be appropriate is in making a quick exit from some part of the program. For example, if you are getting data from somewhere within a program and you have a check for valid data, your design could include a program segment such as

```
read data
IF (bad data) THEN
    BEGIN
        write error message
        GOTO end of program
    END
ELSE
    process data
```

With the previous admonitions against using **GOTO** statements in mind, we will now briefly examine the form, syntax, and flow of control for these statements.

GOTO statements require the use of numerically labeled statements. Thus, your program could contain

```
LABEL
   label 1,
   label 2;
      .
      .
      .

GOTO 100;
      .
      .
      .

100 : Program statement;
      .
      .
      .
```

All labels must be declared in a label declaration section that precedes the constant definition section in a program. Each label can only be used for a single program statement. The form for the label declaration section is

> **LABEL**
>   label 1,
>   label 2,
>   .
>   .
>   .
>   label n;

Correct form for a **GOTO** statement is

> **GOTO** numerical label;

where numerical label is an integer from 1 to 9999 inclusive. Declared labels are then used with appropriate statements in a program. Proper syntax for labeling a statement is

> label : program statement;

Consider the fragment

```
BEGIN
   read (Num);
   IF Num < 0 THEN
      GOTO 100
   ELSE
      Sum := Sum + Num;
         .
         .
         .

   100 : writeln ('Data include a negative number.':40)
END.
```

In this instance, when a negative number is encountered as a data item, an appropriate message is printed and the program is terminated.

GOTO statements permit you to immediately transfer out of any control structure. As stated, we recommend you avoid the use of this statement whenever possible. However, if you must use it, use it only for an immediate exit from some point in the program; never use it to construct a loop in Pascal.

▦ Appendix 7
Assertions

Special comments, called *assertions*, can be used with selection and repetition to make programs easier to read. As comments, they add nothing to the execution of the program. However, when properly formed and placed, they can aid you in developing the program and make the logic of the program easier to follow. Simply put, an assertion states what you expect to happen and when certain conditions will hold.

■ **Selection Statements**

Consider the Pascal selection statement

```
IF Num1 < Num2 THEN
   BEGIN
     Temp := Num1;
     Num1 := Num2;
     Num2 := Temp
   END;
```

The intent of this code is to have the value of Num1 be greater than or equal to Num2. We can make an assertion as follows:

```
IF Num1 < Num2 THEN
   BEGIN
     Temp := Num1;
     Num1 := Num2;
     Num2 := Temp
   END;

(*   Assertion: Num1 >= Num2 *)
```

Assertions written before particular statements are *preconditions*; those written after are *postconditions*. For example, in the previous statement, if Num1 and Num2 are both intended to be positive, we can write

```
(* Assertion: Num1 >= 0 AND Num2 >= 0 *)  ←Precondition

IF NUM1 < Num2 THEN
  BEGIN
    TEMP := Num1;
    Num1 := Num2;
    Num2 := Temp
  END;


(*  Assertion: Num1 >= Num2  *) ←Postcondition
```

In practice, you may choose to label preconditions and postconditions as the following comments illustrate.

```
(*  Precondition: Num1 >= 0 and Num2 >= 0 *)

IF Num1 < Num2 THEN
  BEGIN
    Temp := Num1;
    Num1 := Num2;
    Num2 := Temp
  END;

(* Postcondition: Num1 >= Num2 *)
```

As a second example, consider a **CASE** statement used to assign grades based on quiz scores.

```
CASE Score OF
   10       : Grade := 'A';
   9,8      : Grade := 'B';
   7,6      : Grade := 'C';
   5,4      : Grade := 'D';
   3,2,1,0 : Grade := 'E'
END;  (*  of CASE *)
```

Assertions can be used as preconditions and postconditions in the following manner.

```
(*  Precondition:   Score is an integer between 0 and 10
                     inclusively  *)
CASE Score OF
  10       : Grade := 'A';
  9,8      : Grade := 'B';
  7,6      : Grade := 'C';
  5,4      : Grade := 'D';
  3,2,1,0 : Grade := 'E'
END;  (*  of CASE *)

(*  Postcondition:  Grade has been assigned a letter grade
                     according to the scale
                     10        → A
                     8,9       → B
                     6,7       → C
                     4,5       → D
                     0,1,2,3 → E    *)
```

■ **Repetition**

Assertions can also be used with any of the loops presented in this text. In addition to preconditions and postconditions, assertions can be used to state an *invariant expression* or a *loop goal expression*.

An invariant expression is true before the loop and true after each iteration of the loop. It is typically placed at the top of a **WHILE . . . DO** or **FOR** loop and at the bottom of a **REPEAT . . . UNTIL** loop. Assertions of this type should be informative, clear statements of your intent. To illustrate, consider the loop whose task is to add all positive multiples of 5 less than or equal to 100.

```
Sum := 0;
J := 0;
WHILE J <= 19 DO
    BEGIN
      J := J + 1;
      Sum := Sum + 5 * J
    END;  (* of WHILE ... DO *)
```

An invariant expression could be a statement about the purpose of Sum. For example,

```
(*   Assertion: Sum is the sum of the first J multiples of 5.   *)
```

As an assertion in the loop, this becomes

```
Sum := 0;
J := 0;
WHILE J <= 19 DO
(*  Sum is the sum of the first J multiples of 5.   *)
    BEGIN
      J := J + 1;
      Sum := Sum + 5 * J
    END;  (* of WHILE ... DO   *)
```

Note that this assertion is true before the loop and after each execution of the loop. However, it is not true at the point in the loop after

```
J := J + 1;
```

has been executed but

```
SUM := SUM + 5 * J
```

has not been executed. This holds for all properly stated invariant assertions.

A loop goal expression is a clear statement of the purpose of the loop. It must be true immediately after the loop has been completed. To illustrate, in the previous example we have

```
Sum := 0;
J := 0;
WHILE J <= 19 DO
(*   Sum is the sum of the first
            J multiples of 5. *)    ←Invariant expression
    BEGIN
      J := J + 1;
      Sum := Sum + 5 * J
    END; (*  of WHILE ... DO  *)

(*   Sum is the sum of the first
       20 positive multiples of 5   *) ←Loop goal expression
```

Formulating assertions of these types for loops may seem like a lot of extra effort at this time. However, the long-range benefits of such statements include a direct focus on the problem to be solved, precisely stated goals to follow for the loop design, and loops that are correctly designed.

We conclude this discussion with a final example.

```
ACount := 0;
Sum := 0;
read (Score);
IF Score >= 0 THEN
   REPEAT

(*   Score >= 0   *)
      IF Score >= 90 THEN
         ACount := ACount + 1;
(*   Scores of 90 or more result in ACount
         being incremented by 1   *)

      Sum := Sum + Score;
      read (Score)
(*   Sum contains the total of positive scores
     read and ACount contains the number of
     scores read that are >= 90   *)

   UNTIL Score < 0;

(*  Assertion: 1 - Sum contains the total of positive scores
               2 - ACount contains the number of scores >= 90
               3 - A negative sentinel value has been reached in
                   the input file   *)
```

⊞ Glossary

actual parameter A variable or expression contained in a procedure or function call and passed to that procedure or function. *See also* **formal parameter.**

address Often called address of a memory location, this is an integer value that the computer can use to reference a location. *See also* **value.**

algorithm A finite sequence of effective statements that, when applied to the problem, will solve it.

argument A value or expression passed in a function or procedure call.

array A structured variable designed to handle data of the same type.

array of records An array whose component type is a record.

ASCII collating sequence The American Standard Code for Information Exchange ordering for a character set.

assembly language A computer language that allows words and symbols to be used in an unsophisticated manner to accomplish simple tasks.

assertion Special comments used with selection and repetition that state what you expect to happen and when certain conditions will hold.

assignment statement A method of putting values into memory locations.

batch input Input for a program being run in batch mode. Also called stream input.

batch mode A technique of executing the program and data from cards or a file that has been created. User interaction with the computer is not required during execution.

binary digit A digit, either 0 or 1, in the binary number system. Program instructions are stored in memory using a sequence of binary digits. Binary digits are called bits.

binary search The process of examining a middle value of a sorted array to see which half contains the value in question and halving until the value is located.

binary search tree A binary tree such that (1) the information in the key field of any node is greater than the information in the key field of any node of its left child and any of its children and (2) the information in the key field of any node is less than the information in the key field of any node of its right child and any of its children.

binary tree A tree such that each node can point to at most two children.

bit *See* **binary digit.**

block A program in Pascal can be thought of as a heading and a block. The block contains an optional declaration part and a compound statement. The block structure for a subprogram is a subblock. *See also* **subblock.**

boolean expression An expression whose value is

either true or false. *See also* **compound boolean expression** and **simple boolean expression.**

bubble sort Rearranges elements of an array until they are in either ascending or descending order. Consecutive elements are compared to move (bubble) the elements to the top or bottom accordingly during each pass. *See also* **selection sort.**

buffer variable The actual vehicle through which values are passed to or from a file component.

built-in function *See* **standard function.**

byte A sequence of bits used to encode a character in memory. *See also* **word.**

call Any reference to a subprogram by an executable statement. Also referred to as invoke.

character set The list of characters available for data and program statements. *See also* **collating sequence.**

children Nodes pointed to by an element in a tree.

code (writing) The process of writing executable statements that are part of a program to solve a problem.

collating sequence The particular order sequence for a character set used by a machine. *See also* **ASCII** and **EBCDIC.**

comment A nonexecutable statement used to make a program more readable.

compatible (type) Variables that have the same base type. A value parameter and its argument must be of compatible type. *See also* **identical (type).**

compilation error An error detected when the program is being compiled. A complete list of compilation error messages is set forth in Appendix 5. *See also* **design error, run-time error,** and **syntax error.**

compiler A computer program that automatically converts instructions in a high-level language to machine language.

component of a file One element of the file data type.

component of a linked list *See* **node.**

component of an array One element of the array data type.

compound boolean expression Refers to the complete expression when logical connectives and negation are used to generate **boolean** values. *See also* **boolean expression** and **simple boolean expression.**

compound statement Uses the reserved words **BEGIN** and **END** to make several simple statements into a single compound statement.

conditional statement A control statement that selects some particular logical path based on the value of an expression.

constant The contents of a memory location whose contents cannot be changed.

constant definition section The section where program constants are defined for subsequent use.

control structure A structure that controls the flow of execution of program statements.

counter A variable used to count the number of times some process is completed.

data Information in the form of numbers and characters.

data type *See* **type.**

debugging The process of eliminating errors or "bugs" from a program.

declaration section The section used to declare (name) all symbolic constants, data types, variables, and subprograms that are necessary to the program.

design error An error in the program that causes the output to be incorrect. *See also* **compilation error, run-time error,** and **syntax error.**

difference The difference of set A and set B is A − B where A − B contains the elements that are in A but not in B. *See also* **intersection, subset,** and **union.**

dynamic structure A data structure that may expand or contract during execution of a program.

dynamic variable Frequently designated as Ptr↑ or Ptr^, a dynamic variable is a variable accessed by a pointer variable.

EBCDIC collating sequence The Extended Binary Coded Decimal Interchange Code ordering for a character set.

echo checking A technique whereby the computer prints out values of variables and data used in a program.

effective statement A clear, unambiguous instruction that can be carried out.

element of a set A value that has been assigned to a set.

empty set A set containing no elements. Also called a null set.

end-of-file marker (eof) A special marker inserted by the machine to indicate the end of the data file. In this text it is represented by a black square (■).

end-of-line marker (eoln) A special marker inserted by the machine to indicate the end of a line in the data. In this text it is represented by a black column (█).

entrance controlled loop *See* **pretest loop.**

enumerated type *See* **user-defined data type.**

error *See* **compilation error, design error, run-time error,** and **syntax error.**

executable section Contains the statements that

cause the computer to do something. Starts with the reserved word **BEGIN** and concludes with the reserved word **END**.

executable statement The basic unit of grammar in Pascal consisting of valid identifiers, predefined identifiers, reserved words, numbers, and/or characters, together with appropriate punctuation.

execute To perform a program step-by-step.

exit controlled loop See **posttest loop**.

exponential form See **floating point**.

external file A file used to store data in secondary storage between runs of a program. See also **internal file**.

field width The phrase used to describe the number of columns used for various output. See also **formatting**.

field A component of a record.

FIFO See **queue**.

file A data structure that consists of a sequence of components all of the same type.

file window A term used in this book, though not designated by Pascal, to indicate an imaginary window through which values of a file component can be transferred.

fixed repetition loop A loop used if the number of times a segment of code needs to be repeated is known in advance. **FOR** loops are fixed repetition loops.

fixed part Fields in a record that exist for all records of a particular type. See also **variant part**.

fixed point A method of writing decimal numbers where the decimal is placed where it belongs in the number. See also **floating point**.

floating point A method for writing numbers in scientific notation to accommodate numbers that may have very large or very small values. Exactly one nonzero digit must appear on the left of the decimal. See also **fixed point**.

FOR loop A fixed repetition loop causing a fragment of code to be executed a predetermined number of times. **FOR ... TO ... DO** and **FOR ... DOWNTO ... DO** are **FOR** loops.

formal parameter A variable, declared and used in a procedure or function declaration, that is replaced by an actual parameter when the procedure or function is called.

formatting Designating the desired field width when printing integers, reals, **boolean** values, and character strings. See also **field width**.

forward reference A method by which a subprogram can call another subprogram that appears later in the declaration section.

function A subprogram used to perform a short, specific task.

function name Any valid identifier (should be descriptive) used to name a function.

global variable A variable that can be used by the main program and all subprograms in a program.

hardware Physical devices that constitute a computing system.

high-level language Any programming language that uses words and symbols to make it relatively easy to read and write a program. See also **assembly language** and **machine language**.

higher-dimensional array An array of more than two dimensions.

identical (type) Variables that are declared with the same type identifier. A variable parameter and its argument must be of identical type. See also **compatible (type)**.

identifiers Words that must be created according to a well-defined set of rules but can have any meaning subject to these rules. See also **predefined identifiers**.

index The relative position of the components of an array. Also called subscript.

index type The data type used for specifying the range for the index of an array. The index type can be any ordinal data type that specifies an initial and final value.

infinite loop A loop in which the controlling condition is not changed in such a manner to allow the loop to terminate.

input Data obtained by a program during its execution. See also **batch input** and **interactive input**.

input device A device that provides information to the computer. Typical devices are keyboards, disk drives, card readers, and tape drives. See also **I/O device** and **output device**.

integer arithmetic operations Operations allowed on data of type **integer**. This includes the operations of addition, subtraction, multiplication, **MOD**, and **DIV** to produce integer answers.

interactive input A method of getting data into the program from the keyboard. User interaction is required during execution.

internal file A file used for processing only and not saved in secondary storage. See also **external file**.

intersection The intersection of set A and set B is A * B where A * B contains the elements that are in both A and B. See also **difference, subset,** and **union**.

invoke See **call**.

I/O device Any device that allows information to

be transmitted to or from a computer. *See also* **input device** and **output device.**

iteration *See* **loops.**

keywords Either reserved words or predefined identifiers.

leaf In a tree, a node that has no children.

length (of an array) The number of components of an array.

LIFO *See* **stack.**

linked list A list of data items where each item is linked to the next one by means of a pointer.

local variable A variable that is restricted to use within a subblock of a program.

location An area in computer memory where a value can be stored.

logic error *See* **design error.**

logical connective A connective (for example, the reserved words **AND, OR)** for two **boolean** expressions.

logical operator Either logical connective **(AND, OR)** or negation **(NOT).**

loops Program statements that cause a process to be repeated. *See also* **FOR loop, REPEAT . . . UNTIL loop,** and **WHILE . . . DO loop.**

low-level language *See* **assembly language.**

machine language This language is used directly by the computer in all its calculations and processing.

main driver *See* **executable section.**

main memory Memory contained in the computer. *See also* **memory** and **secondary memory.**

mainframe Large computers typically used by major companies and universities. *See also* **microcomputer** and **minicomputer.**

master file An existing external file.

maxint The largest integer constant available to a particular system.

memory The ordered sequence of storage cells that can be accessed by address. Instructions and variables of an executing program are temporarily held here. *See also* **main memory** and **secondary memory.**

memory location A storage cell that can be accessed by address. *See also* **memory.**

merge The process of combining lists. Typically refers to files or arrays.

microcomputer A personal computer with relatively limited memory. Generally used by one person at a time. *See also* **mainframe** and **minicomputer.**

minicomputer A small version of a mainframe computer. It can be used by several people at once. *See also* **mainframe** and **microcomputer.**

mixed-mode Expressions containing data of both

integer and **real** types; the value will be given as a real and not as an integer.

modular development The process of developing an algorithm using modules. *See also* **module.**

module An independent unit that is part of a larger development. Usually a procedure or function. *See also* **modular development.**

mutual recursion When two subprograms call each other.

negation The logical operator represented by **NOT.**

nested loop A loop as one of the statements in the body of another loop.

nested record A record as a field in another record.

nested selection Any combination of selection statements within selection statements. *See also* **selection statement.**

nested subprograms Functions or procedures within functions or procedures.

node One data item in a linked list.

null set *See* **empty set.**

object program (object code) The machine code version of the source program.

open a file Preparing a file so it can be read from or written to.

ordinal data type A data type ordered in some association with the integers; each integer is the ordinal of its associated character.

output Information that is produced by a program.

output device A device that allows you to see the results of a program. Typically it is a monitor or printer. *See* **input device** and **I/O device.**

overflow In arithmetic operations, a value may be too large for the computer's memory location. A meaningless value may be assigned or an error message may result. *See also* **underflow.**

packed array An array that has had data placed in consecutive bytes.

parallel arrays Arrays of the same length but with different component data types.

parameter *See* **argument.**

parameter list A list of parameters. An actual parameter list is contained in the procedure or function call. A formal parameter list is contained in the procedure or function heading.

parent In a tree, the node that is pointing to its children.

peripheral memory *See* **secondary memory** and **memory.**

pointer variable Frequently designated as Ptr, a pointer variable is a variable that contains the address of a memory location. *See also* **address** and **dynamic variable.**

pop A procedure to delete a node from a linked list.

postcondition An assertion written after a segment of code.

posttest loop A loop where the control condition is tested after the loop is executed. **REPEAT ... UNTIL** is a posttest loop. Also called an exit controlled loop.

precondition An assertion written before a particular statement.

predefined identifier Words that have a previous definition but could have their meaning changed by the programmer. Predefined identifiers are highlighted in the text by lowercase boldface print; a list of Pascal predefined identifiers is set forth in Appendix 2.

pretest loop A loop where the control condition is tested before the loop is executed. **WHILE ... DO** is a pretest loop. Also called an entrance-controlled loop.

primary memory See **main memory** and **memory**.

procedure A subprogram designed to perform a specific task as part of a larger program. Procedures are not limited to returning a single value to the main program.

program A set of instructions that cause a computer to perform certain actions.

program heading The first statement of any Pascal program; it must contain the reserved word **PROGRAM**.

program protection A method of using selection statements to guard against unexpected results.

program walk-through The process of carefully following, using pencil and paper, steps the computer uses to solve the problem given in a program. Also called trace.

prompt A marker on the terminal screen that requests input data.

protection See **program protection**.

pseudocode A stylized half-English, half-code language written in English but suggesting Pascal code.

push A procedure for adding a node to the beginning of a linked list.

queue A dynamic data structure where elements are entered from one end and removed from the other end. Referred to as a FIFO (first-in, first-out) structure.

real arithmetic operations Operations allowed on data of type **real**. This includes addition, subtraction, multiplication, and division.

record A data structure that is a collection of fields that may be treated as a whole or that will allow you to work with individual fields.

recursion The process of a subprogram calling itself. A clearly defined stopping state must exist. Any recursive subprogram can be rewritten using iteration.

recursive step A well-defined step that leads to the stopping state in the recursive process.

recursive subprogram See **recursion**.

relational operator An operator used for comparison of data items of the same type.

REPEAT ... UNTIL loop A posttest loop examining a **boolean** expression after causing a fragment to be executed. See also **FOR loop, loops,** and **WHILE ... DO loop**.

repetition See **loops**.

reserved words Words that have predefined meanings which cannot be changed. They are highlighted in text by capital boldface print; a list of Pascal reserved words is set forth in Appendix 1.

return type The data type for a function name.

root The first or top node in a tree.

run-time error Error detected when, after compilation is completed, an error message results instead of the correct output. See also **compilation error, design error,** and **syntax error**.

scope of identifier The largest block in which the identifier is available.

secondary memory Memory contained in a peripheral device, usually a disk or magnetic tape. See also **main memory** and **memory**.

selection sort A sorting algorithm that sorts the components of an array in either ascending or descending order. This process puts the smallest or largest element in the top position and repeats the process on the remaining array components. See also **bubble sort**.

selection statement The process of executing possible alternate segments of code. Pascal selection statements are **IF ... THEN, IF ... THEN ... ELSE,** and **CASE**.

sentinel value A special value that indicates the end of a set of data or of a process.

sequential algorithm See **straight-line algorithm**.

sequential search The process of examining the first element in a list and proceeding to examine the elements in order until a match is found.

set A structured data type that consists of a collection of distinct elements from an indicated base type (which must be ordinal).

simple boolean expression An expression where two numbers or variable values are compared using a single relational operator. See also **bool-**

ean expression and **compound boolean expression.**

software Programs that make a computer do something.

sort-merge The process of repeatedly subdividing a long list, sorting shorter lists, and then merging to obtain a single sorted list.

source program A program written by a programmer. *See also* **system program.**

stack A dynamic data structure where access can only be made from one end. Referred to as a LIFO (last-in, first-out) structure.

standard function A built-in function available in most versions of Pascal.

standard identifiers *See* **predefined identifiers.**

static variable A variable whose size (for example, array length) is fixed at compilation time. A certain memory area is reserved for each variable, and these locations are retained for the declared variables as long as the program or subprogram in which the variable is defined is active.

stepwise refinement The process of repeatedly subdividing tasks into subtasks until each subtask is easily accomplished. *See also* **structured programming** and **top-down design.**

stopping state The well-defined termination of a recursive process.

straight-line algorithm Also called sequential algorithm, this algorithm consists of a sequence of simple tasks.

stream input *See* **batch input.**

string An abbreviated name for a string constant.

string constant One or more characters used as a constant in a program.

structured programming Programming that parallels a solution to a problem achieved by top-down design. *See also* **stepwise refinement** and **top-down design.**

stub progamming A no-frills, simple version of a final program.

subblock A block structure for a subprogram. *See also* **block.**

subprogram A program within a program. Procedures and functions are subprograms.

subrange The defined subset of values of an existing ordinal data type.

subscript *See* **index.**

subset Set A is a subset of set B if all the elements in A are also in B. *See also* **difference, intersection,** and **union.**

syntax The formal rules governing construction of valid statements.

syntax diagramming A method to formally describe the legal syntax of language structures. *See* **Appendix 3.**

syntax error An error in spelling, punctuation, or placement of certain key symbols in a program. *See also* **compilation error, design error,** and **run-time error.**

system program A special program used by the computer to activate the compiler, run the machine code version, and cause output to be generated. *See also* **source program.**

tag field A field used in defining variant records. Values of the tag field determine the variant record structure.

test program A short program written to provide an answer to a specific question.

text file A file of characters that is divided into lines.

top-down design A design methodology for solving a problem whereby you first state the problem and then proceed to subdivide the main task into major subtasks. Each subtask is then subdivided into smaller subtasks. This process is repeated until each remaining subtask is easily solved. *See also* **stepwise refinement** and **structured programming.**

trace *See* **program walk-through.**

transaction file A file containing changes to be made in a master file.

tree A dynamic data structure consisting of a special node (a root) that points to zero or more other nodes, each of which point to zero or more other nodes, and so on.

two-dimensional array An array where each element is accessed by a reference to a pair of indices.

two-way merge The process of merging two sorted lists.

type A formal description of the set of values that a variable can have.

underflow If a value is too small to be represented by a computer, the value is automatically replaced by zero. *See also* **overflow.**

union The union of set A and set B is A + B where A + B contains any element that is in A or that is in B. *See also* **difference, intersection,** and **subset.**

universal set Any set that contains all possible values of the base type.

unpacked array An array in which data are not in consecutive bytes.

user-defined data type A data type that is defined in the **TYPE** definition section by the programmer. Also referred to as enumerated type.

user-defined function A subprogram (function) written by the programmer to perform a specific task. Functions return one value when called.

user-friendly A phrase used to describe an interactive program with clear, easy-to-follow messages for the user.

value Often called value of a memory location. Refers to the value of the contents of a memory location. *See also* **address.**

value parameter A formal parameter that is local to a subprogram. Values of these parameters are not returned to the calling program.

variable A memory location, referenced by an identifier, whose value can be changed during a program.

variable declaration section The section of the declaration section where program variables are declared for subsequent use.

variable dictionary A listing of the meaning of variables used in a program.

variable parameter A formal parameter that is not local to a subprogram. Values of these parameters are returned to the calling program.

variant part The part of a record structure in which the number and type of fields can vary. *See also* **fixed part.**

WHILE ... DO loop A pretest loop examining a **boolean** expression before causing a fragment to be executed.

word A unit in memory consisting of one or more bytes. Words can be addressed. *See also* **byte.**

writing code The process of writing executable statements that are part of a program to solve a problem.

▦ Answers to Self Quizzes

SELF QUIZ 2.1 The problem with this statement is the word "good." It is clearly subject to interpretation. A better statement is "add all scores greater than 81."

SELF QUIZ 2.2 **1.** An identifier must begin with a letter of the alphabet.

2. Blanks are not permitted in an identifier.

3. Technically, nothing is wrong with this identifier. However, since it is so long, you must be careful to avoid an identifier such as ProgramAttempt2 in the same program.

SELF QUIZ 2.3 The only error in the **CONST** section is that December 25 must be in single quotation marks. You may think that

```
Speed = '55'
```

should be

```
Speed = 55
```

with no quotation marks around the 55. Actually, both forms are correct and which you use depends upon how Speed is to be used in the program.

```
Price = real;
```

should be

```
Price : real;
```

SELF QUIZ 2.4 **1.** 5.684391×10^{2}
    $5.684391E2$

2. 7.83×10^{-3}
    $7.83E-3$

SELF QUIZ 2.5   A trace of values in the order they are produced yields

$$8 \ \textbf{MOD} \ 3 \ - \ 15 \ * \ \underline{(5 \ + \ 1)}$$
$$\downarrow$$
$$\underline{8 \ \textbf{MOD} \ 3} \ - \ 15 \ * \ \quad 6$$
$$\downarrow$$
$$2 \qquad - \ \underline{15 \ * \quad 6}$$
$$\downarrow$$
$$\underline{2 \quad - \quad 90}$$
$$\downarrow$$
$$-88$$

SELF QUIZ 3.1   Using a line-by-line analysis, we get

Statement	Value in A	Value in B	Value in Sum
A := -8;	-8	Undefined	Undefined
B := 3;	-8	3	Undefined
Sum := A + B;	-8	3	-5
A := 3 * B;	9	3	-5
B := A;	9	9	-5
Sum := Sum + A + B;	9	9	13

SELF QUIZ 3.2   Showing the values at each successive step in the evaluation, we get

sqr(trunc(sqrt(abs(−14.5)))) =
sqr(trunc(sqrt(14.5))) =
sqr(trunc(3.807886...)) =
sqr(3.0) =
9.0

SELF QUIZ 4.1   Three semicolons are required as follows:

```
PROGRAM Sample (output);     (1)

VAR
   A : integer;              (2)

BEGIN
   A := 4;                   (3)
   writeln (A)
END.
```

SELF QUIZ 4.2   In the variable declaration section, **interger** should be **integer**. The comment following **BEGIN** should be

```
(*   Executable section   *)
```

The line

```
A = 2 * A;
```

should be

```
A := 2 * A;
```

SELF QUIZ 4.3

```
A := 5 * 3;
```

is correct.

```
B := A DIV 3;
```

is correct.

```
B := A/3;
```

is not permitted because A/3 produces a **real**. You cannot assign a **real** to an **integer** variable.

```
X := A DIV 3;
```

is correct. However, A **DIV** 3 is then stored as a **real**.

```
X := A/3;
```

is correct.

SELF QUIZ 4.4

Statement	Value of A	Value of B	Value of Temp
A := -6;	-6	Undefined	Undefined
B := 10;	-6	10	Undefined
Temp := A;	-6	10	-6
A := B;	10	10	-6
B := Temp;	10	-6	-6

SELF QUIZ 5.1

A trace of the steps in the evaluation of this expression yields

$$- \underline{3 * 4} + 5 \ >= \ 10 \ \textbf{DIV} \ 2 \ * \ (-1)$$
$$\downarrow$$
$$-12 \ + 5 \ >= \ \underline{10 \ \textbf{DIV} \ 2} \ * \ (-1)$$
$$\downarrow$$
$$-12 \ + 5 \ >= \ \underline{5 \ * \ (-1)}$$
$$\downarrow$$
$$\underline{-12 \ + 5} \ >= \ -5$$
$$\downarrow$$
$$\underline{-7 \ >= \ -5}$$
$$\downarrow$$
$$\textbf{false}$$

SELF QUIZ 5.2

Since A is zero, A <> 0 is **false.** Thus, the assignment

```
Flag := true;
```

is skipped. The next executable statement is

```
B := A + B;
```

Ending values will be

1	10	false
A	B	Flag

For better readability, this fragment should be written as

```
IF A <> 0 THEN
   Flag := true;
B := A + B;
A := 1;
```

SELF QUIZ 5.3

```
readln (Num1, Num2);
IF Num1 >= Num2 THEN
    writeln (Num1, Num2)
ELSE
    writeln (Num2, Num1);
```

SELF QUIZ 5.4

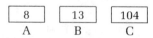

8	13	104
A	B	C

SELF QUIZ 5.5

This fragment causes the output

```
-85
```

The indenting of this fragment is misleading. Since and **ELSE** is matched with the last **IF ... THEN,** it should be written as

```
A := 15;
IF A > 0 THEN
  IF A MOD 2 = 0 THEN
      writeln (A + 100)
  ELSE
      writeln (A - 100);
```

If you want the design to be consistent with the originally written form, you can rewrite the fragment as

```
A := 15;
IF A <= 0 THEN
  writeln (A - 100)
ELSE
  IF A MOD 2 = 0 THEN
      writeln (A + 100);
```

SELF QUIZ 5.6

There are three errors in this **CASE** statement.

1. A syntax error is in line 3.

```
7,8 ; Grade := 'B';
```

should have two colons, as

```
7,8 : Grade := 'B';
```

2. The **CASE** selector 7 is used twice; one use must be eliminated.

3. There is no **END** for the statement.

A correct version is

```
CASE Score OF
    9,10  : Grade := 'A';
    7,8   : Grade := 'B';
    5,6   : Grade := 'C';
    3,4   : Grade := 'D';
    0,1,2 : Grade := 'E'
END;  (*  of CASE  *)
```

SELF QUIZ 6.1

```
writeln ('*':20);
FOR J := 1 TO 4 DO
   writeln ('*':20-J, '*':2*J);
FOR J := 1 TO 3 DO
   writeln ('*':16+J, '*':2*(4-J);
writeln ('*':20);
```

SELF QUIZ 6.2   Before printing the output, let's trace through the variable values.

J	Sum	$10+abs(J)$
Unassigned	0	Undefined
3	3	13
2	5	12
1	6	11
0	6	10
−1	5	11
−2	3	12

The output is

```
column 13
   ↓
   *
    *
   *
  *
   *
    *
         3
```

SELF QUIZ 6.3   A trace of the values produces

Count	Sum	Num
0	0	1
1	1	3
2	4	9
3	13	27
4	40	81
5	121	243

At this stage, when the condition Num < 100 is tested, it is **false** and control transfers to the writeln statements which produce the output

```
Count is    5
Sum is   121
Num is   243
```

SELF QUIZ 6.4

1	5
2	5
3	5
4	5
5	5
6	5

The last line (A = 6) is printed because the value of A in the previous loop was A = 5. Since 5 > 5 is **false,** the loop is executed one more time.

SELF QUIZ 6.5

Assuming there is at least one positive number, we have

```
readln (Num);
WHILE Num >= 0 DO
   BEGIN
      Sum := Sum + Num;
      Count := Count + 1;
      readln (Num)
   END;
```

Note that in this loop, for a negative value of Num, Sum is not changed and Count is not incremented.

SELF QUIZ 6.6

```
FOR K := 0 TO 4 DO
   BEGIN
      FOR J := 1 TO 3 DO
         write (K * J);
      writeln
   END;
```

SELF QUIZ 6.7

Count	Stop	Output
0	4	(skip a line)
1	4	1
2	4	1 2
3	4	1 2 3
4	4	All done

SELF QUIZ 7.1

This procedure skips three lines in the output.

SELF QUIZ 7.2

The **BEGIN** for the main program is misplaced. The program should be

```
PROGRAM Quiz (output);

PROCEDURE Message;
   BEGIN
      writeln ('There is an error.')
   END;

BEGIN
   Message;
   writeln ('Can you find it?')
END.
```

SELF QUIZ 7.3

1. Since the parameter list contains two reals, the procedure call must be of the form

```
Switch (X,Y);
```

where X and Y are variables of type **real.** (Switch (2.0,3.0) could also be used.) used.)

2. The two **writeln** statements first print the numbers in the original order and then print them in reverse order; thus, if X is initially 2.0 and Y is initially 3.0, we get

```
2.00            3.00
3.00            2.00
```

SELF QUIZ 7.4

```
2.00       3.00
3.00       2.00
```

Since the procedure heading has variable parameters, values are changed in the main program accordingly.

SELF QUIZ 7.5

X1 is a global variable whose scope is the entire program.
X2 is available only to **PROCEDURE** One.
X3 is available to both **PROCEDURE** Two and **PROCEDURE** TwoA.
X4 is available only to **PROCEDURE** TwoA.

SELF QUIZ 7.6

```
20
30
20
```

The assignment statement

```
A := 30;
```

in the procedure has no effect on the variable A declared in the main program.

SELF QUIZ 7.7

A reasonable function name is Average. Since three reals are received from the main program, a formal parameter list can be

```
(N1, N2, N3 : real);
```

A real is returned to the main program, so the return type should be **real.** Thus, a reasonable heading is

```
FUNCTION Average (N1, N2, N3 : real) : real;
```

SELF QUIZ 7.8

The parameter lists

```
(ND:integer; RT:char);
(RoomType, NumDays)
```

do not match. The computer tries to match ND with RoomType and there is a type mismatch error. Although the number of parameters is correct, the parameters are not in the correct order.

SELF QUIZ 7.9

Three variable parameters are needed. If we assume the main program identifiers are GasType, Amount, and Wash, a procedure can be

```
PROCEDURE GetData (VAR GT, W : char;
                   VAR Amt : real);
  VAR
    Blank : char;
  BEGIN
    readln (GT, Amt, Blank, W)
  END;
```

This is called from the main program by

```
GetData (GasType, Wash, Amount);
```

SELF QUIZ 7.10

1. is invalid.

2. is valid.

3. is valid.

4. is invalid.

5. is invalid.

SELF QUIZ 7.11

Since **FUNCTION** TotalCharge calls **FUNCTION** Tax, these are written sequentially as

```
FUNCTION Tax (RmCharge : real) : real;
  BEGIN  (*  Tax  *)
    Tax := RmCharge * TaxRate
  END;  (*  of FUNCTION Tax  *)

FUNCTION TotalCharge (NumNts : integer) : real;
  VAR
    RoomCharge, RoomTax : real;
  BEGIN  (*  TotalCharge  *)
    RoomCharge := NumNts * RoomRate;
    RoomTax := Tax (RoomCharge);
    TotalCharge := RoomCharge + RoomTax
  END;  (*  of FUNCTION TotalCharge  *)
```

SELF QUIZ 7.12

There is not a well-defined stopping state. To illustrate, if the main program contains the call

```
Recur (5);
```

the levels of recursion are

```
1.    Recur := 1 + Recur (5)
   2.    Recur := 1 + Recur (5)
      3.    Recur := 1 + Recur (5)
                 .
                 .
                 .
```

and there is nothing to terminate the process.

SELF QUIZ 8.1

This produces an infinite loop. The first data line gets printed, but when the pointer is at the first end-of-line marker,

eoln(InFile) becomes **true**. The **WHILE NOT eoln**(InFile) **DO** loop is exited. Because the pointer never gets advanced beyond this position, **eof**(InFile) never becomes **true**. This can be corrected by inserting **readln** either before or after **writeln**.

SELF QUIZ 8.2

```
TYPE
    Seasons = (Spring, Summer, Fall, Winter);

VAR
    Season : Seasons;
```

SELF QUIZ 8.3

```
TYPE
   PassRange = 70 .. 100;
   FailRange = 0 .. 69;

VAR
   PassScore : PassRange;
   FailScore : FailRange;
```

SELF QUIZ 8.4

Variable Pair	Answer	Reason
HotDay, AMTemp	Compatible	Both have **integer** base type
ColdDay, HotDay	Compatible	Both have **integer** base type
AMTemp, PMTemp	Identical	Same **TYPE** definition
ColdDay, PMTemp	Compatible	Both have **integer** base type

SELF QUIZ 8.5

Function Call	Value	Reason
ord(Yellow)	2	This ordinal comes from the base type Color
pred(Yellow)	Orange	Reference is to the base type
pred(Red)	Undefined	Red has no predecessor
succ(Indigo)	Violet	Reference is to the base type

SELF QUIZ 9.1

The array can be visualized as

```
A
┌──────┐
│      │  A[-2]
├──────┤
│      │  A[-1]
├──────┤
│      │  A[0]
├──────┤
│      │  A[1]
├──────┤
│      │  A[2]
├──────┤
│      │  A[3]
└──────┘
```

There are six variables available, each of type **real.** For example, we can have

```
A[-1] := 14.8;
```

SELF QUIZ 9.2

```
ZeroCount := 0;
FOR J := 1 TO 20 DO
   IF List[J] = 0 THEN
      ZeroCount := ZeroCount + 1;
```

SELF QUIZ 9.3

The definitions are

```
CONST
   MaxLength = 30;

TYPE
   List = ARRAY [1 .. MaxLength] OF real;
```

Since the values will normally be returned to the main program, we need a variable parameter. Thus, the procedure is

```
PROCEDURE GetData (VAR X : List);
   VAR
     J : integer;
   BEGIN
     FOR J := 1 TO MaxLength DO
       BEGIN
          writeln ('Enter a number and press <RETURN>.');
          readln (X[J])
       END
   END;
```

SELF QUIZ 9.4   Let the declarations be

```
CONST
   MaxLength = 10;

TYPE
   String = PACKED ARRAY [1 .. MaxLength] OF char;

VAR
   Name1, Name2 : String;
```

The names can be accessed by

```
FOR J := 1 TO MaxLength DO
   read (NameFile, Name1[J]);
readln; (*  Advance the pointer  *)
FOR J := 1 TO MaxLength DO
   read (NameFile, Name2[J]);
readln;
```

SELF QUIZ 9.5   No. Consider the array A with values as just indicated in text and assume you are searching for 205 (Num := 205). A trace of values produces

	First	**Last**	**Mid**	**A[Mid]**	**Found**
Before loop	1	14	Undefined	Undefined	**false**
After first pass	8	14	7	50	**false**
After second pass	8	10	11	220	**false**
After third pass	8	8	9	101	**false**

During the pass through the loop when First = 8 and Last = 10, the value is not located and Last is reassigned so that Last = 8. Then the condition First < Last is **false** and the loop is exited while Found is **false**.

SELF QUIZ 10.1   Subranges are used as data types to indicate the number of rows and columns. There are four rows and six columns. Thus, the data structure can be viewed as

Chart

SELF QUIZ 10.2   We have declared a two-dimensional array of character variables. The loop assigns a character to each array component by the line

```
Chart[J,K] := chr(ord('A')+J+K-2);
```

Thus,

```
Chart[1,1] := chr(ord('A'));
```

becomes

```
Chart [1,1] := 'A';
```

Continuing, we have the chart

A	B	C	D	E
B	C	D	E	F
C	D	E	F	G

SELF QUIZ 10.3   Since each data line can be read by

```
FOR K := 1 TO 4 DO
    read (Data,Score[J,K]);
```

a loop for reading the data file is

```
FOR J := 1 TO 3 DO
    FOR K := 1 TO 4 DO
        read (Data, Score[J,K]);
```

After this loop is executed, we have

81	93	76	100
98	82	73	56
84	95	88	70

SELF QUIZ 10.4   The appropriate structure is an array of packed arrays. One method to obtain this structure is

```
CONST
    NameLength = 30;
    NumberOfNames = 200;

TYPE
    String = PACKED ARRAY [1 .. NameLength] OF char;
    NameList = ARRAY [1 .. NumberOfNames] OF String;

VAR
    Name : NameList;
```

SELF QUIZ 10.5   The first dimension, $-2 \ldots 2$, contains five values (-2, -1, 0, 1, and 2). The second contains three values and the third six values. Thus, there are $5 * 3 * 6 = 90$ locations.

SELF QUIZ 10.6   Every third column entry will have an index of the form Item[I,J,3]. We can check for desired page numbers by the condition I **MOD** 5 = 0 where I represents the page index. With these conditions in mind, we have

```
FOR I := 1 TO 50 DO
  BEGIN
    IF I MOD 5 = 0 THEN
      FOR J := 1 TO 15 DO
        writeln (Item [I,J,3]);
    writeln
  END;
```

SELF QUIZ 11.1   The record name is Student and there are four fields as illustrated.

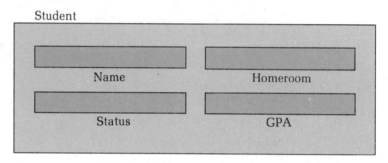

After suitable values have been assigned, we could have

Student

Smith John	127
Name	Homeroom
Fr	3.70
Status	GPA

SELF QUIZ 11.2   This is very similar to previous problems involving reading character data into a packed array. In this case, the field name is Student.Name and individual components are Student.Name[J]. Thus the name can be read by

```
FOR J := 1 TO 20 DO
  read (Data, Student.Name[J]);
```

If your implementation allows character strings to be read as strings rather than one character at a time, you can read the name by

```
read (Data, Student.Name);
```

SELF QUIZ 11.3   The statement

```
WITH Patient1, Patient2 DO
  Age := 21;
```

produces an ambiguous reference. It is not clear whether the reference is to Patient1.Age or Patient2.Age. Although many implementations would make the assignment to Patient2.Age, this is still poor code.

SELF QUIZ 11.4 The task can be accomplished by finding the smallest value and subtracting it from the total.

```
FUNCTION TestAv (T:TestList) : real;

  VAR
    Min, Sum, J : integer;

  BEGIN

  (*  Find the minimum  *)

    Min := T[1];
    FOR J := 2 TO NumTests DO
      IF T[J] < Min THEN
        Min := T[J];

  (*  Now add best three  *)

    Sum := 0;
    FOR J := 1 TO NumTests DO
      Sum := Sum + T[J];
    Sum := Sum - Min;

  (*  Now compute the average  *)

    TestAv := Sum/(NumTests-1)
  END;  (*  of FUNCTION TestAv  *)
```

SELF QUIZ 11.5 An illustration of the fields is

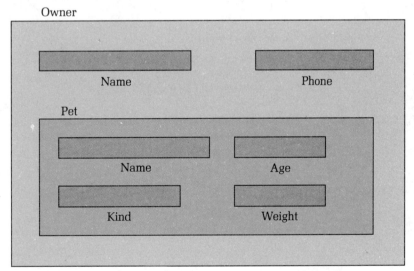

The field names are

```
Owner.Name
Owner.Phone
Owner.Pet.Name
Owner.Pet.Kind
Owner.Pet.Age
Owner.Pet.Weight
```

SELF QUIZ 11.6   A first-level pseudocode development for this task is

1. Assign the name to StudentName
2. Locate the record
3. Delete the record

Step 3 can be accomplished by merely moving all the records up one position in the array starting with the first record after the one to be deleted. The desired fragment is

```
StudentName := 'Smith Mary              ';
Index := 1;
WHILE (StudentName < Student[Index].Name) AND
                              (Index < Length) DO
   Index := Index + 1;
IF StudentName = Student[Index].Name THEN
   BEGIN
      FOR J := Index TO Length-1 DO
         Student[J] := Student [J+1];
      Length := Length - 1   (*  Change class size   *)
   END
ELSE
   writeln (StudentName:25, ' was not found.');
Length := Length - 1;  (*  Change class size   *)
```

SELF QUIZ 12.1   A **FOR** loop can be used to solve this problem. Thus, the code could be

```
rewrite (FileA);  (*  Open for writing   *)
FOR J := 1 TO 25 DO
   BEGIN
      FileA↑ := J;
      put (FileA)
   END;
```

A second method is

```
rewrite (FileA);  (*  Open for writing *)
FOR J := 1 TO 25 DO
   write (FileA, J);
```

SELF QUIZ 12.2   Obviously, an array must be declared. However, before doing so, we must have some idea of how many components are in the file. If we assume there are at most 50, a declaration is

```
CONST
   MaxLength = 50;
TYPE
   DataFile = FILE OF real;
   List = ARRAY [1 . . MaxLength] OF real;
VAR
   A : List;
   FileA : DataFile;
   Count : integer;
```

The desired code then is

```
reset (FileA);
Count := 0;
WHILE NOT eof (FileA) AND (Count < MaxLength) DO
```

```
                    BEGIN
                      Count := Count + 1;
                      A[Count] := FileA↑;
                      get (FileA)
                    END;
```

SELF QUIZ 12.3

```
PROCEDURE PrintOrder (VAR Info : PartsFile);
  BEGIN
    writeln; writeln;
    writeln ('Part Number':20, 'Order Size':20);
    writeln ('_____':20, '_____':20);
    writeln;
    reset (Info);
    WHILE NOT eof (Info) DO
      BEGIN
        writeln (Info↑[1]:20, Info↑[5]:20);
        get (Info)
      END
  END;  (*  of PROCEDURE PrintOrder  *)
```

SELF QUIZ 12.4

To solve this problem, we need to open the file for reading, add the scores for test number one, and then divide by the number of students. One method to do this is

```
Sum := 0;
Count := 0;
reset (Student);
WHILE NOT eof (Student) DO
  BEGIN
    Sum := Sum + Student↑.Score[1];
    Count := Count + 1;
    get (Student)
  END;
TestOneAv := Sum/Count;
```

SELF QUIZ 12.5

The procedure **rewrite** (Pupil) opens Pupil for writing. Any previous contents are lost. The window is positioned at the first component. We have

window

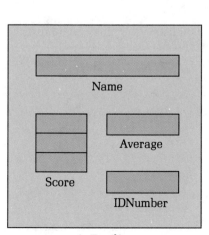

Pupil↑

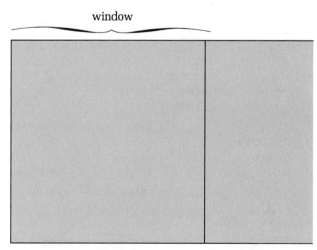

Pupil

The first time through **WITH** Pupil↑ **DO** produces

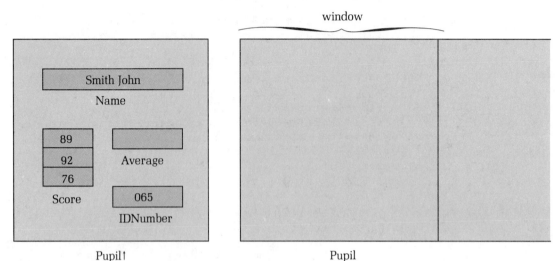

The line **put** (Pupil) results in

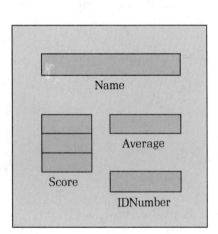
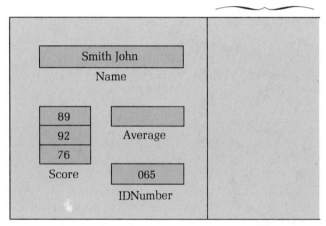

SELF QUIZ 13.1   The base type for elements of the set must include the plus and minus signs. If your implementation allows a base type of **char,** that can be used. If not, some restricted subrange is required. For now, let's assume **char** is permitted. We then have

```
TYPE
    AllSymbols = SET OF char;
```

```
VAR
    PlusMinus : AllSymbols;
```

The desired assignment in the program is then

```
PlusMinus := ['+','-'];
```

SELF QUIZ 13.2   This quiz examines one instance of a well-known result in set theory: De Morgan's Law of A ∩ (B ∪ C) = (A ∩ B) ∪ (A ∩ C). The trace of the first expression produces

$$[-2..5] * (\underline{[0..10] + [3..20]})$$
$$\downarrow$$
$$[-2..5] * \qquad [0..20]$$
$$\downarrow$$
$$[0..5]$$

The trace of the second expression produces

$$\underline{[-2..5] * [0..10]} + [-2..5] * [3..20]$$
$$\downarrow$$
$$[0..5] \qquad + \underline{[-2..5] * [3..20]}$$
$$\downarrow$$
$$[0..5] \qquad + \qquad [3,4,5]$$
$$\downarrow$$
$$[0..5]$$

SELF QUIZ 13.3   For this problem, declare a set Vowels by

```
VAR
    Vowels : AlphaSymbols;
```

This can be initialized by

```
Vowels := ['A','E','I','O','U'];
```

Assuming appropriate declarations, the set can be generated by

```
SentenceVowels := [];
WHILE NOT eoln(Data) DO
  BEGIN
    read (Data, Ch);
    IF Ch IN Vowels THEN
        SentenceVowels := SentenceVowels + [Ch]
  END;
```

The contents can be printed by

```
FOR Ch := 'A' TO 'U' DO
  IF Ch IN SentenceVowels THEN
    write (Ch:2);
writeln;
```

SELF QUIZ 13.4   Assume the segment of code set forth in the beginning of Section 13.3 has been run so that SentenceChar now contains all the letters in a line of text. Since the set type is AlphaSymbols and the element type is **char,** the function is

```
FUNCTION Cardinality (S : AlphaSymbols) : integer;
  VAR
    Ct : integer;
    X : char;
  BEGIN
    Ct := 0;
    FOR X := 'A' TO 'Z' DO
      IF X IN S THEN
          Ct := Ct + 1;
    Cardinality := Ct
  END;  (*  of FUNCTION Cardinality  *)
```

This is called from the main program by

```
SetSize := Cardinality (SentenceChar);
```

SELF QUIZ 14.1   Ptr is a pointer variable whose contents can only be the address of a memory location. This address is internally assigned when

```
new (Ptr);
```

is executed. The dynamic variable available to the program is Ptr↑. This must be used for subsequent work.

SELF QUIZ 14.2   The solution is relatively short. Assume we have

Then,

```
dispose (Ptr1);
```

produces

and

```
Ptr1 := Ptr2;
```

yields

SELF QUIZ 14.3   There are several ways this could be done. For now, let's assume there is a procedure GetName that will read a data file and get a new name. Then, the previous code could be modified to be

```
BEGIN
  new (Start);
  GetName (NewName);
  Start↑.Name := NewName;
  Ptr := Start;
  FOR J := 1 TO 4 DO
    BEGIN
      new (Last);
      GetName (NewName);
      Ptr↑.Next := Last;
      Last↑.Name := NewName;
      Ptr := Last
    END;
  Ptr↑.Next := NIL;
```

SELF QUIZ 14.4   An empty list is such that Start was **NIL.**

Start
| NIL |

In this case,

```
P := Start;
```

produces

Start   P
| NIL | | NIL |

P <> **NIL** is **false** and control is transferred to the first executable statement following the loop.

SELF QUIZ 14.5   You do not get a run-time error. However, before Push is called, you have

Start ↑

After the procedure is executed, you have

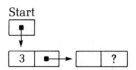

Notice that there is no end to your list. However, had Start been assigned **NIL,** you would have

SELF QUIZ 14.6   Assume we have

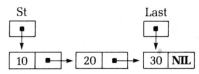

and we want to insert

The initialization produces

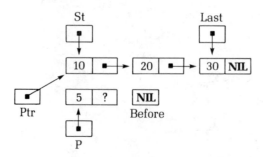

and Looking is **true.** The first time through the loop, Ptr↑.Num > NewNum is **true,** so Looking becomes **false,** and control is transferred out of the loop. Before = **NIL** is **true** and

```
P↑.Next := St;
St := P;
```

yields

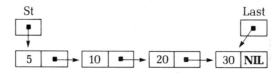

SELF QUIZ 14.7   Since the stack only changes when a parenthesis is read, we will ignore what happens when other characters are read. Originally, the stack is

Stack top

Then, as characters are read, it becomes

Character Read	New Stack
"("	$\boxed{}$ $\boxed{(}$
"("	$\boxed{(}$ $\boxed{(}$
"("	$\boxed{(}$ $\boxed{(}$ $\boxed{(}$
")"	$\boxed{(}$ $\boxed{(}$
"("	$\boxed{(}$ $\boxed{(}$ $\boxed{(}$
")"	$\boxed{(}$ $\boxed{(}$
")"	$\boxed{}$ $\boxed{(}$
")"	$\boxed{}$

SELF QUIZ 14.8   The root is the node whose value is 16.

Root
(16)

The remaining values are inserted to produce

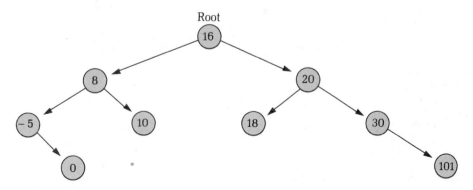

▦ Answers to Selected Exercises

This section contains answers to selected exercises from the exercise sets at the end of each section.

CHAPTER 2

Section 2.1

1. is an effective statement.

2. is not effective because you cannot determine when to perform the action.

3. is an effective statement.

4. is not effective because there is no smallest positive fraction.

5. is not effective because you cannot determine in advance which stocks will increase in value.

9.
   1. Select a topic
   2. Research the topic
   3. Outline the paper
   4. Refine the outline
   5. Write the rough draft
   6. Read and revise the rough draft
   7. Write the final paper

11.
   1. Get a list of colleges
   2. Examine criteria (programs, distance, money, and so on)
   3. Screen to a manageable number
   4. Obtain further information
   5. Make a decision

14. First-level development
   1. Get information for first employee
   2. Perform computations for first employee
   3. Print results for first employee
   4. ⎫
   5. ⎬ repeat for second employee
   6. ⎭

Second-level development
   1. Get information for first employee
      1.1 get hourly wage
      1.2 get number of hours worked
   2. Perform computations for first employee
      2.1 compute gross pay
      2.2 compute deductions
      2.3 compute net pay
   3. Print results for first employee
      3.1 print input data
      3.2 print gross pay
      3.3 print deductions
      3.4 print net pay
   4. ⎫
   5. ⎬ repeat for second employee
   6. ⎭

Third-level development
   1. Get information for first employee
      1.1 get hourly wage
      1.2 get number of hours worked

2. Perform computations for first employee
   2.1 compute gross pay
   2.2 compute deductions
      2.2.1 federal withholding
      2.2.2 state withholding
      2.2.3 social security
      2.2.4 union dues
      2.2.5 compute total deductions
   2.3 compute net pay
      2.3.1 subtract total deductions from gross
3. Print results for first employee
   3.1 print input data
      3.1.1 print hours worked
      3.1.2 print hourly wage
   3.2 print gross pay
   3.3 print deductions
      3.3.1 print federal withholding
      3.3.2 print state withholding
      3.3.3 print social security
      3.3.4 print union dues
      3.3.5 print total deductions
   3.4 print net pay
4. ⎫
5. ⎬ repeat for second employee
6. ⎭

Section 2.2

2. and 8. are invalid; an identifier cannot start with a digit.

3., 4., 6., 7., and 12. are valid identifiers.

5. is invalid. Blanks are not allowed.

9. is invalid. & is not allowed.

10. is invalid. **CONST** is a reserved word.

11. is invalid. ∗ is now allowed.

13. is invalid. Commas are not allowed.

14., 15., and 18. are valid; however, a semicolon must be used between the heading in 14. and the next line of code.

16. does not begin with the reserved word **PROGRAM.**

17. is missing an identifier for the program name.

19. and 20. use improper identifiers for the program name.

Typical constant definitions that might be used for Exercises 22–25 are

```
CONST
   Name = 'Julie Adams';
   Age = 21;
   BirthDate = 'November 10, 1964';
   Birthplace = 'Carson City, MI';
```

Section 2.3

1., 4., 5., and 7. are valid.

2. is invalid; it has a decimal.

3. is invalid; it has a comma.

6. is probably larger than **maxint**.

18. 1.73E2

19. 7.43927E11

20. $-2.3E-8$

21. 1.4768E1

22. $-5.2E0$

28. and 31. are of **integer** type.

29., 30., and 34. are **reals.**

32. and 33. are string constants.

36.
```
writeln ('Score':14);
writeln ('_____':14);
writeln (86:12);
writeln (82:12);
writeln (79:12);
```

Section 2.4

1. 11

2. -41

3. 3

4. 24

5. 126

6. 63

7. 48

8. 140

9. -2

10. 7

18. and 19. are valid, type **integer.**

20., 22., 23., 24., 25., and 26. are valid, type **real.**

21. and 27. are invalid.

CHAPTER 3

Section 3.1

1., 2., 5., 6., and 8. are valid assignment statements.

3. is invalid. A real cannot be assigned to an integer variable.

4. is invalid. An operand cannot be on the left of an assignment statement.

7. is invalid. IQ/3 is a real.

10. | 3 | | −5 |
    A   B

11. | 26 | | 31 |
    A   B

12. | −3 | | −5 |
    A   B

14.
```
Sex        M
Age        18
Height     73 inches
Weight     186.5 lbs
```

16. column 11

```
*****************************
*                           *
*    Name      Age     Sex  *
*    ----      ---     ---   *
*                           *
*    Jones     21      M     *
*                           *
*****************************
```

19.   column 10
          ↓

```
        This reviews string formatting.
When a letterAis used,
        Oops! I forgot to format.
        When a letter A is used,
        it is a string of length one.
```

Section 3.2

Note: Answers for Exercises 2–13 may vary according to the compiler used.

3. An error occurs. Since Num2 is an integer, it only reads 65 from 65.3.

5. | −20 | | 65.3 | | b̸ |
  Num2   Num3   Ch

7. | 65 | | 15.0 |
  Num2   Num3

9. | 15 | | b̸ | | 65.3 |
  Num1   Ch   Num3

11. | 15 | | 65.3 | | b̸ | | −20 |
  Num1   Num3   Ch   Num2

13. | 1̸5 3 | | 65 | | '.' |
   Num2   Num1   Ch

To determine the answers to Exercises 20–27, run the following short program on your computer and examine the output.

```
PROGRAM InputPrac (input, output);
VAR
  Num1, Num2 : integer;
  Num3 : real;
  Ch : char;
BEGIN
  readln (Num1, Num2, Ch, Num3);
  writeln (Num1:5, Num2:5, Ch:5,
           Num3:10:2)
END.
```

  c. All variables unassigned

Section 3.3

3.
```
Computer Science              Test #2
--------------------------------------

    Total points              100
    My score                   93
    Class average            82.3
```

Section 3.4

1. 15.2

2. 14

3. 0

4. 36

5. −4.5

6. −11.98

8. **a.** `sqrt(A*A+B*B)`

   b. `(-B + sqrt(B*B-4*A*C)) / (2 * A)`

16. `(round(10*X))/10.0`

24. `-4.30    4.30    -4    -4`

25. 4   (depends on character set—65 in ASCII)

26. Depends on character set

CHAPTER 4

Section 4.1

1. `Total := Test1+Test2+Test3+Test4;`

2. `Average := Total/4;`

3. `TotalIncome := Salary + Tips;`

4. `Time := Distance/Rate;`

5. `Grade := TotalPoints/6;`

6. ```
writeln (Name:20, TotalPoints:10, Grade:5);
```

7. ```
writeln (NumberAttending:5, TicketPrice:10:2,
         TotalReceipts:10:2);
```

9. ```
PROGRAM BoxVolume (output);

  CONST
    Skip = ' ';

  VAR
    Length, Width, Height, Volume : integer;

  BEGIN
    Length := 8;
    Width := 3;
    Height := 2;
    Volume := Length * Width * Height;
    writeln (Skip:10, 'Length =', Length:10);
    writeln (Skip:10, 'Width =', Width:10);
    writeln (Skip:10, 'Height =', Height:10);
    writeln;
    writeln (Skip:10, 'Volume =', Volume:10)
  END.
```

13., 14., and 15. are acceptable.

16. is not correctly stated.

17. is acceptable.

18. is valid but should have consistent comment closings.

19. should have consistent comment starts.

20 is acceptable.

## Section 4.2

1. There should be a semicolon after Y in the first line. '=' should be replaced by ':=' in the second line. The correct code is
```
X := 3 * Y;
Y := 4 - 2 * Z;
writeln (X,Y);
```

3. The added semicolons are circled for your convenience.
```
PROGRAM ExerciseThree (output);

CONST
  Name = 'Jim Jones';
  Age = 18;

VAR
  Score : integer;

BEGIN
  Score := 93;
  writeln ('Name':13, Name:15);
  writeln ('Age':12, Age:16);
  writeln ('Score':14, Score:14)
END.
```

5. The misspelled keywords (with the correct spelling) follow.

| | |
|---|---|
| PROGRRAM | (should be PROGRAM) |
| reals | (should be real) |
| chr | (should be char) |
| interger | (should be integer) |
| writln | (should be writeln) |

16. is valid.

17. is invalid. The operand (+) is on the left of an assignment statement.

18. is invalid. C has not been declared.

19. is invalid. Wage should be spelled Wages.

20. is valid.

21. is invalid. Hours has not been declared.

22. is invalid. CourseName can only be assigned a single character.

23. is invalid. A value cannot be assigned to a constant.
```

24. is invalid. A real cannot be as-
    signed to an integer.
35. Errors are circled.

```
PROGRAM Errors (output();                should be )

(*****************************************)

(*   There are at least ten errors.    $)   should be *

(*****************************************O    ) missing

VAR
  Day : char;
  Percent : realO                        ; missing
  A,B i(int;)                            ; should be : and int should be integer

BEGIN
  Day ⊝ 'M';                             should be :=
  (Percentage) := 72/10;                 Percentage should be Percent
  A := 5;
  (B) := A * 3.2;                        B cannot be assigned a real
  (writln)(A,B:20);                      should be writeln
  writeln (Day:(10:2));                  incorrect formatting
  writeln (A+B:8, Percent:8)
ENDO                                     . missing
```

Section 4.3

1.

Value of A	Value of B	Value of C
33	undefined	undefined
33	−2	undefined
28	−2	undefined
28	28	undefined
28	28	30
28	28	30
28	28	1
29	28	1

3.

Code with Errors	Corrected Code
`Max = 100.00 : real;`	`Max = 100.0;`
`A, Sum : integer`	`A, Sum : integer;`
`A := 86.0;`	`A := 86;`
`A + Sum := Sum`	`Sum := A + Sum;`
`writeln (Sum:15:2)`	`writeln (Sum:15)`

4.

Code with Errors

```
PROGRAM Compile Errors (output);
Ch := M;
B := A - 10;
writeln ('The value of A is : 20,
          A:6);
```

Corrected Code

```
PROGRAM CompileErrors (output);
Ch := 'M';
A := A - 10; (B is not declared)
writeln ('The value of A is':20,
          A:6);
```

6. The following changes would
   be needed.

   a. Underline Donations   **d.** Skip a line before total

   b. Skip a line before 100.00   **e.** Print Sum.

   c. Print dollar signs

CHAPTER 5

Section 5.1

```
1. true    true     false
                    false
```

For Exercises 3–8, only **5.** and **8.** are valid.

16. and 17. are **true.**

18. is **false.**

19. is **true.**

20. and 21. (which compare as reals) are **false.**

22. is **true.**

28.,29., and 30. are **true.**

31. and 32. are **false.**

Section 5.2

```
1. 10             5
```

2. no output

```
3.  5             B has no value
4. 10             5
5. 15             4
   15             4
6. 10             5
```

8. should be
```
IF A = 10 THEN ...
```

9. 3 < X < 10
cannot be evaluated. This should be
```
(3<X) AND (X<10)
```

10. This expression needs a **BEGIN** ... **END** to be consistent with indenting. It should be
```
IF A > 0 THEN
  BEGIN
    Count := Count + 1;
    Sum := Sum + A
  END;
```

11. IF Ch = 'A' OR 'B' THEN

should be
```
IF (Ch = 'A') OR (Ch = 'B') THEN
```

14. Yes.

21.
```
BEGIN
  readln (Num1, Num2, Num3);
  Total := Total + Num1 + Num2 + Num3;
  writeln (Num1:5, Num2:5, Num3:5);
  writeln;
  writeln (Total)
END;
```

23.
```
read (Ch1, Ch2, Ch3);
IF (Ch1 <= Ch2) AND (Ch2 <= Ch3) THEN
  writeln (Ch1, Ch2, Ch3);
```

This can also be written as
```
read (Ch1, Ch2, Ch3);
IF Ch1 <= Ch2 THEN
    IF Ch2 <= Ch3 THEN writeln (Ch1, Ch2, Ch3);
```

Section 5.3

```
1. -14           14
2.  50           25
     1           75
3.  10            5
     5            0
```

5. Since the intent appears to be a statement that counts characters other than periods, a **BEGIN** ... **END** block should be included in the **IF** ... **THEN** option.
```
IF Ch <> '.' THEN
  BEGIN
    CharCount := CharCount + 1;
    writeln (Ch)
  END
ELSE
  PeriodCount := PeriodCount + 1;
```

6. The semicolon between **END** and **ELSE** should be omitted.

7. Technically this fragment will run. However, since it appears that OldAge := OldAge + Age is to be included in the **ELSE** option, the programmer probably meant
```
ELSE
  BEGIN
    OldCount := OldCount + 1;
    OldAge := OldAge + Age
  END;
```

Section 5.4

1. X = 38.15   Y = 763.0

2. X = -21.0   Y = 21.0

3. X = 600.0   Y = 1200.0

4. X = 3000.0   Y = 9000.0

6.
```
IF Ch = 'M' THEN
   IF Sum > 1000 THEN
      X := X + 1
   ELSE
      X := X + 2
 ELSE
   IF Sum > 1000 THEN
      X := X + 3
   ELSE
      X := X + 4;
```

7.
```
read (Num);
IF Num > 0 THEN
   IF Num <= 10000 THEN
      BEGIN
         Count := Count + 1;
         Sum := Sum + Num
      END
   ELSE
      writeln ('Value out of range':27)
ELSE
   writeln ('Value out of range':27);
```

8.
```
IF A > 0 THEN
   IF B > 0 THEN
      writeln ('Both positive':22)
   ELSE
      writeln ('Some negative':22)
ELSE
   writeln ('Some negative':22);
```

9.
```
IF C <= 0 THEN
   IF A > 0 THEN
      IF B > 0 THEN
         writeln ('Option one':19)
      ELSE
         writeln ('Option two':19)
   ELSE
      writeln ('Option two':19)
ELSE
   writeln ('Option one':19);
```

14.
```
IF Average < 90 THEN
   IF Average < 80 THEN
      IF Average < 70 THEN
         IF Average < 55 THEN
            Grade := 'E'
         ELSE Grade := 'D'
      ELSE Grade := 'C'
   ELSE Grade := 'B'
ELSE Grade := 'A';
```
This could be written using sequential **IF** ... **THEN** statements. For example,

```
IF (Average <= 100) AND (Average >= 90) THEN
   Grade := 'A';
IF (Average < 90) AND (Average >= 80) THEN
   Grade := 'B';
   .
   .
   .
```

The disadvantage of this method is that each **boolean** expression of each statement will always be evaluated. This is relatively inefficient.

Section 5.5

3.
```
IF ((Age DIV 10) > 10) OR ((Age DIV 10) < 1) THEN
   writeln ('Value of age is', Age)
ELSE
   .
   .  (CASE statement here)
   .
```

10. 5   3   125

11. You have purchased   Lead Free Gasoline

12. 3   -3

13. 5   10   -5

17. Assume there is a variable ClassType. The design of the fragment to compute fees is

```
read (ClassType);
CASE ClassType OF
  'U' :
  'G' :  (list options here)
  'F' :
  'S' :
END;  (*  of CASE  *)
```

CHAPTER 6

Section 6.1

1.
```
*
  *
    *
      *
        *
          *
```

2.
```
 1 :        9
 2 :        8
 3 :        7
 4 :        6
 5 :        5
 6 :        4
 7 :        3
 8 :        2
 9 :        1
10 :        0
```

3.
```
** 2
** 3
** 4
** 5
** 6
** 7
** 8
** 9
** 10
** 11
** 12
** 13
** 14
** 15
** 16
** 17
** 18
** 19
** 20
```

4.
```
1
2
3
4
5
6
7
8
9
10
11
12
13
14
15
16
17
18
19
20
21
```

7.
```
FOR J := 1 TO 4 DO
   writeln ('*':10);
```

8.
```
FOR J := 1 TO 8 DO
   writeln ('***':J+5);
```

9.
```
writeln ('*':10);
FOR J := 1 TO 3 DO
   writeln ('*':10-J, '*':2*J);
writeln ('**** ****':14);
FOR J := 1 TO 2 DO
writeln ('***':11);
```

10. This is a "look ahead" problem that can be solved by a loop within a loop. This idea is developed in Section 6.5.

```
FOR J := 5 DOWNTO 1 DO
   BEGIN
     write (' ':(6-J); (*  Indent a line  *)
     FOR K := 1 TO (2*J-1) DO (*  Print a line  *)
       write ('*');
     writeln
   END;
```

15.
```
FOR J := 1 TO 5 DO
  write (J:3);

FOR J := 5 DOWNTO 1 DO
  write (6-J:3);
```

16.
```
FOR J := 1 TO 5 DO
  writeln ('*':J);

FOR J := 5 DOWNTO 1 DO
  writeln ('*':(6-J));
```

18.
```
FOR J := 2 TO 10 DO
  writeln (12-J:12-J);
```

20. The key loop in this program will be something like
```
FOR J := -10 TO 10 DO
  BEGIN
    Num := 5*J;
    writeln (Num:10, Num * Num:10, Num * Num * Num:10)
  END; (*  of printing the chart  *)
```

Section 6.2

3.
```
1
2
3
4
5
6
7
8
9
10
```

4.
```
1       0
2       1
3       2
4       1
5       2
```

5. 54   50

6.
```
The partial sum is    1
The partial sum is    3
The partial sum is    6
The partial sum is   10
The partial sum is   15
The count is    5
```

7.   96.00   2.00

17.
```
read (Num);
IF Num < 10000 THEN
  BEGIN
    PowerOfNum := Num;
    WHILE PowerOfNum < 10000 DO
      BEGIN
        writeln (PowerOfNum);
        PowerOfNum := PowerOfNum * Num
      END
  END;
```

Section 6.3

1. A pretest loop tests the **boolean** expression before executing the loop. A posttest loop tests the **boolean** condition after the loop has been executed.

3.
```
1       9
2       8
3       7
4       6
5       5
6       4
```

4.
```
2
4
8
16
32
64
128
```

5.
```
1
2
3
4
5
6
7
8
9
10
```

6.
```
1       0
2       1
3       2
4       1
5       2
```

16.
```
read (Num);
IF Num < 10000 THEN
  BEGIN
    PowerOfNum := Num;
    REPEAT
      writeln (PowerOfNum);
      PowerOfNum := PowerOfNum * Num
    UNTIL PowerOfNum >= 10000
  END;
```

Section 6.4

5. The loop in Exercise 4. can be rewritten in each of the following ways.

   a.
   ```
   WHILE X < 4.0 DO
      BEGIN
         writeln (X:20:2);
         X := X + 0.5
      END;
   ```
   b.
   ```
   FOR J := 1 TO 8 DO
      BEGIN
         writeln (X:20:2);
         X := X + 0.5
      END;
   ```
   c.
   ```
   FOR J := 8 DOWNTO 1 DO
      BEGIN
         writeln (X:20:2);
         X := X + 0.5
      END;
   ```

7. Since the condition $6 < 5$ is **false**, the loop will not be entered. In a **REPEAT ... UNTIL** loop, the loop body is always executed at least once before the **boolean** expression controlling the loop is evaluated.

Section 6.5

3.
```
10   12   14   16   18   20
15   18   21   24   27   30
20   24   28   32   36   40
25   30   35   40   45   50
30   36   42   48   54   60
```

5. 50 50

6.
```
FOR K := 1 TO 5 DO
   BEGIN
      write (' ':K);
      FOR J := K TO 5 DO
         write ('*');
      writeln
   END;
```

8.
```
FOR K := 1 TO 7 DO
   IF K < 5 THEN
      BEGIN
         FOR J := 1 TO 3 DO
            write ('*');
         writeln
      END
   ELSE
      BEGIN
         FOR J := 1 TO 5 DO
            write ('*');
         writeln
      END;
```

CHAPTER 7

Section 7.1

1. A procedure is a subprogram. As such it is contained within a complete program. It is headed by the reserved word **PROCEDURE** and has a semicolon after the last **END** rather than a period. A program is headed by the reserved word **PROGRAM** and has a period after the last **END.**

3.
```
PROCEDURE PrintHeading;
   CONST
      Splats = '******************************';
      Edge   = '*                            *';
      Name   = 'John J. Smith';
      Date   = 'September 15, 1986';
   BEGIN
      writeln (Skip:20, Splats);
      writeln (Skip:20, Edge);
      writeln (Skip:20 '*', Skip:5, Name, Skip:10, '*');
      writeln (Skip:20 '*', Skip:5, Date, Skip:5, '*');
      writeln (Skip:20, Edge);
      writeln (Skip:20, Splats)
   END;  (*  of PROCEDURE PrintHeading  *)
```

5. Suppose you want the heading to be

```
              R & R Produce Company
              _____

Items Purchased     Price per Item     Total per Item
_____     _____     _____
```

A procedure for this is

```
PROCEDURE PrintHeading;
   CONST
      Skip = ' ';
   BEGIN
      writeln; writeln;
      writeln (Skip:20, 'R & R Produce Company');
      writeln (Skip:20, '_____');
      writeln;
      write (Skip:3, 'Items Purchased');
      write (Skip:3, 'Price per Item');
      writeln (Skip:3, 'Total per Item');
      write (Skip:3, '_____');
      write (Skip:3, '_____');
      writeln (Skip:3, '_____');
      writeln
   END;
```

Section 7.2

3. A and B are variable parameters. X is a value parameter.

4. A and X are variable parameters. B and Ch are value parameters.

5. X, Y, and Z are variable parameters. A, B, and Ch are value parameters.

Section 7.3

7. Identifiers for this program are represented schematically by the figure at right.

9. 10
20
10
30
30

15. The main program is trying to access an identifier that is not available. The line

```
writeln (X1:20:2);
```

in the main program is inappropriate because the scope of X1 is **PROCEDURE** Sub1.

11. `Exercise11 (Num1, Num2, Letter);`

12. `PrintHeader;`

13. `FindMax (Num1, Num2, Max);`

14. `Switch (Num1, Num2);`

15. `SwitchAndTest (Num1, Num2, Flag);`

21.
```
PROCEDURE MaxAndAver (X,Y,Z:real; VAR Max,Aver:real)
  BEGIN
    Max := X;
    IF Y > Max THEN
      Max := Y;
    IF Z > Max THEN
      Max := Z;
    Aver := (X + Y + Z) / 3.0
  END;
```

PROGRAM Practice

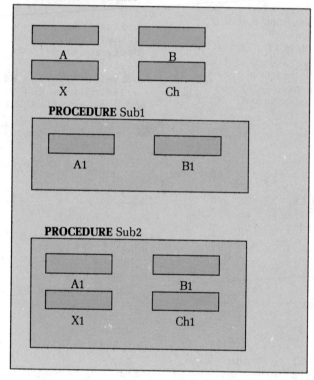

Section 7.4

3. is invalid. The data type for what will be returned to the calling program must be listed.

```
FUNCTION RoundTenth (X:real):real;
```

4. is invalid. Data types must be listed for X and Y.

5. and 6. are valid.

7. is invalid. The comma following **char** should be a semicolon.

11.
```
FUNCTION MaxOfTwo (X,Y:real):real;
  BEGIN
    IF X > Y THEN
      MaxOfTwo := X
    ELSE
      MaxOfTwo := Y
  END;
```

16.
```
FUNCTION MultOf5 (A:integer):boolean;
  BEGIN
    IF A MOD 5 = 0 THEN
      MultOf5 := true
    ELSE
      MultOf5 := false
  END;
```

19.
```
FUNCTION Factorial (N:integer):integer;
  VAR
    Fact,J : integer;
  BEGIN
    Fact := 1;
    FOR J := 1 TO N DO
      Fact := Fact * J;
    Factorial := Fact
  END;
```

21. There are several reasonably short methods of writing such a function. If we assume the main program checks for a valid symbol, one such function is

```
FUNCTION Arithmetic (Operand:char; N1,N2:integer):integer;
  BEGIN
    IF Operand = '+' THEN
      Arithmetic := N1 + N2
    ELSE
      Arithmetic := N1 * N2
  END;  (*  of FUNCTION Arithmetic  *)
```

Section 7.5

1. **a.** variable parameters   **b.** variable parameters   **c.** value parameters

3. The pseudocode design indicates procedures could be written for

1.	Initialize variables	`Initialize (Parameter list);`
2.	Print a heading	`PrintHeading;`
	3.1 get new data	`GetData (Parameter list);`
4.	Print results	`PrintResults (Parameter list);`

Until more is known about the problem, step 3.2 (perform computations) cannot be determined. However, if we assume a function (Compute) is written for this, a main program could be

```
BEGIN  (*  Main Program  *)
  Initialize (variable list);
  PrintHeading;
  Flag := true;
  Count := 0;
  WHILE Flag = true DO
    BEGIN
      GetData (variable list);
      NewValue := Compute (variable list);
      Count := Count + 1;
      IF (check condition) THEN
        Flag := false
      END;  (*  of WHILE ... DO  *)
    PrintResults (variable list)
  END.  (*  of main program  *)
```

Section 7.6

7. **FUNCTION** AddOne cannot be called from **PROCEDURE** AddTwo.

9. This is correct because **FUNCTION** AddOne has a forward reference.

11. A schematic representation is shown at right.

X, Y, and Ch can be used in all subblocks of Exercise11.

X1, Ch1, and J declared in **PROCEDURE** A can be used in all subblocks of **PROCEDURE** A but cannot be used in **PROCEDURE** B or Exercise11.

M and Y1 can be used only in **FUNCTION** Inner.

X1 and Ch2, declared in **PROCEDURE** B, can be used only in **PROCEDURE** B.

13. **a.** A schematic representation is

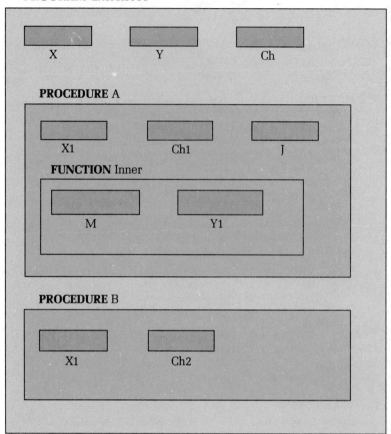

PROGRAM Exercise11

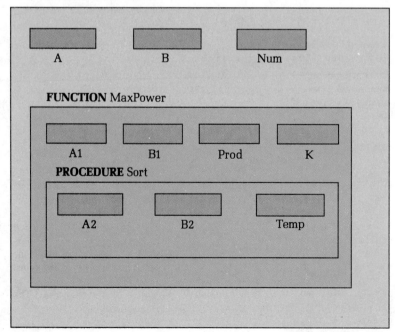

PROGRAM Exercise13

A, B, and Num are available to all blocks. A1, B1, Prod, and K are available to Max-Power and Sort. A2, B2, and Temp are available only to Sort.

b. 243

c. This function performs the task of computing A to the power of B (A^B) where A is the smaller of the two positive integers A and B.

d.
```
IF B1 = 1 THEN
   MaxPower := A1
ELSE
   MaxPower := A1 * MaxPower (A1, B1-1);
```

15. **a.** Y = 9.0
    Y = 8.0
    Y = 256.0
    Y = 1.0

19.
```
FUNCTION NthTerm (N:integer) : integer;
   BEGIN
      IF (N=1) OR (N=2) THEN
         NthTerm := 1
      ELSE
         NthTerm := NthTerm (N-1) + NthTerm (N-2)
   END;
```

CHAPTER 8

Section 8.1

3. The variable should be formatted so that the integers will be separated by blanks.

Exercises 5–21 should be checked for results on your computer due to possible compiler differences.

25.
```
PROGRAM DeleteBlanks (input, output, NoBlank);

VAR
   NoBlank : text;
   Ch : char;

BEGIN
   rewrite (NoBlank);  (* Open for writing *)
   WHILE NOT eof DO
      BEGIN
         WHILE NOT eoln DO
            BEGIN
               read (Ch);
               IF Ch <> ' ' THEN
                  write (NoBlank, Ch)
            END;  (* of WHILE NOT eoln *)
         readln;
         writeln (NoBlank)
      END  (* of WHILE NOT eof *)
END.  (* of main program *)
```

Section 8.2

3. Jane is listed in both types Names and People.

4. Red is listed twice in type Colors.

5. Parentheses are needed around the values. Thus, it should be

```
TYPE
   Letters = (A,C,E);
```

7. is valid.

8. is invalid; Tues + Wed is not defined.

9. is valid (but a poor choice).

10. and 11. are valid.

12. is invalid; you cannot **write** user-defined values.

13. is invalid; you cannot **read** user-defined ordinals.

14. is invalid; the operation Tues + 1 is not defined.

Section 8.3

1. The definition is invalid; 10 .. 1 is not a subrange of an existing ordinal data type.

2. Bases and Double are valid. Score is invalid because Second .. Home is not a subrange.

3. All definitions and declarations are valid. However, Hue := Blue is an invalid use because Blue is not in the subrange defined for Stripes.

4. The definitions are invalid because the type Days must be defined before the subrange Weekdays.

5. All definitions and delarations are valid, but

```
Score2 := Score1 + 5
```

will produce an error because the intended value (65) is not in the defined subrange.

7. Dependents usually refers to the number of single-family dependents for tax purposes. Twenty is a reasonable maximum.

8. Assuming hours worked in one week, 0 to 60 is a reasonable range.

9. The subrange was chosen for a maximum score of ten. This would vary for other maximum scores.

10. The subrange could be used if the total points were a maximum of 700. This might be used in some grading programs.

16. and 17. are compatible. The base type is ChessPieces.

18. and 21. are incompatible.

19. and 20. are compatible. The base type is **integer.**

Section 8.4

1. Oak

2. Cotton

3. 2

4. Invalid

5. 3

6. Invalid

7. 0

9. 'D'

10. 10

11. 'O'

12. Invalid; addition of characters is not defined.

13. Invalid; **pred**('K') is a character; thus, the operation, '+', is not defined.

14. 'Z'

16. ```
Weekend
Weekday
Weekday
Weekday
Weekday
Weekday
```

17. For a **WHILE** loop, you could use the **boolean** expression **WHILE** Day < Sat **DO.**

```
Day := Sun;
WHILE Day < Sat DO
  BEGIN
    .
    .  (body of loop here)
    .
  END;
```

A **FOR** loop could be controlled by the **boolean** expression

```
FOR Day := Sun TO Fri DO
  BEGIN
    .
    .  (body of loop here)
    .
  END;
```

18. This can be accomplished by using ordinal values. For example, if OrdValue has been declared, the loop could be

```
OrdValue := 0;
  REPEAT
    CASE OrdValue OF
      0        : (action here)
      1,2,3,4,5 :
    END: (* of CASE *)
    OrdValue := OrdValue + 1
  UNTIL OrdValue = 6;
```

19. The last value (Sat) is not being considered. This could be altered by using a **FOR** loop and including Sat or using a variable control loop and adding a **writeln** statement such as

```
writeln ('Weekend':20);
```

outside the loop.

22. Assume variables MonthNum and Month have been appropriately declared. A function could be

```
FUNCTION Month (MonthNum):MonthName;
  BEGIN
    CASE MonthNum OF
      1  : Month := Jan;
      2  : Month := Feb;
        .
        .
        .
      12 : Month := Dec
    END   (* of CASE *)
  END; (* of FUNCTION Month *)
```

CHAPTER 9

Section 9.1

1. `Score : ARRAY [1 .. 35] OF integer;`

2. `CarCost : ARRAY [1 .. 20] OF real;`

3. `Answer : ARRAY [1 .. 50] OF boolean;`

4. `Grade : ARRAY [1 .. 6] OF char;`

6. There is no error if Hours has been declared as a data type.

7. No error.

8. No index range has been given for the array.

9. The index range should be [1 .. 10] rather than [1 **TO** 10].

10. The index range is not appropriate; something like **ARRAY** [index range] **OF boolean** should be used.

11. [1 ... 5] should be [1 .. 5]
```

```
24. TYPE
      List = ARRAY [1 .. 100] OF 'A' .. 'Z';
    VAR
      LetterList : List;
```

```
25. TYPE                              26. TYPE
      Name = ARRAY [1 .. 30] OF char;      List = ARRAY [30 .. 59] OF real;
    VAR                                  VAR
      CompanyName : Name;                  ScoreList : List;
```

28. Money

183.25	Money[1]
10.04	Money[2]
17.32	Money[3]

29. Money

10.04	Money[1]
19.26	Money[2]
17.32	Money[3]

30. Money

19.26	Money[1]
10.04	Money[2]
2.68	Money[3]

Section 9.2

1. List

0	List[1]
0	List[2]
1	List[3]
1	List[4]
1	List[5]

2. List   Score

5	List[1]	1	Score[1]
6	List[2]	2	Score[2]
7	List[3]	2	Score[3]
8	List[4]	2	Score[4]
9	List[5]	3	Score[5]

3. Answer

false	Answer[1]
true	Answer[2]
false	Answer[3]
true	Answer[4]
false	Answer[5]
true	Answer[6]
false	Answer[7]
true	Answer[8]
false	Answer[9]
true	Answer[10]

4. The contents of this array depend on the character set being used.

6. The section counts the number of scores greater than 90.

8. TYPE
```
      ListOfLetters = ARRAY [1 .. 20] OF char;
    VAR
      Letter : ListOfLetters;
```

A **FOR** loop could be used as follows:

```
FOR J := 1 TO 20 DO
  read (Letter[J]);
```

```
10. FOR J := 1 TO Max DO
      A[J] := 0.0;
```

11. JOHN SMITH

12. SMITH, JOHN

13. HTIMS NHOJ

```
19. writeln ('Test Number', 'Score':10);
    writeln ('_____', '_____':10);
    writeln;
    FOR J := 1 TO 50 DO
      writeln ('<':4, J:2, '>', TestScore[J]:11);
```

Section 9.3

1. **a.** after one pass   after two passes

− 20
10
0
10
8
30
− 2

− 20
− 2
0
10
8
30
10

b. Three exchanges are made.

3. A high to low sort is achieved by changing

```
IF A[K] < Temp THEN
```

to

```
IF A[K] > Temp THEN
```

Section 9.4

1. is valid; it can be called by NewList (List, Aray);

2. is invalid; a semicolon is needed after Row.

3. is invalid; array declaration cannot be included in the heading.

4. is valid; it can be called by NewList (List1, List2);

5. is invalid; Column cannot be used as a variable name.

6. is invalid; array declaration cannot be included in the heading.

7. is invalid; Name is not a data type.

8. is valid; it can be called by Surnames (Name1, Name2);

9. is invalid; Name is not a data type.

10. is valid; it can be called by Table (List1, List2);

12. `PROCEDURE OldList (X:Row; Y:Column);`

13. `PROCEDURE ChangeList (X:Row; N:String20; D:Week);`

14. This call is inappropriate because the data type for A and B has not been defined in the **TYPE** section.

15. This call is inappropriate because the argument, String20, is a data type rather than a variable.

20.

List1	List2
1	0
4	0
9	0
16	0
25	0
36	0
49	0
64	0
81	0
100	0

Section 9.5

The answers for Exercises 1–6 are based on the ASCII character set.

1., 3., 4., and 6 are valid; **true.**

2. and 5. are invalid.

8. `To err is human. To forgive is not the province of the computer.`

9. `To err is human. To forgive is not the province of the computer.`
`There are 18 blanks.`

10. `   To    err   is    human.   To    forgive   is         ***************`

11. `To err is human. To forgive is not the province of the computer.`
`           .retupmoc eht fo ecnivorp eht ton si evigrof oT .namuh si rre oT`

17.
```
MCount := 0;
FOR J := 1 TO 100 DO
  IF Message [J] = 'M' THEN
    MCount := MCount + 1;
```

Section 9.6

1.
```
FOR J := 1 TO Length DO
  IF Num = A[J] THEN
    writeln (Num, ' is in position', J:5);
```

3. The value of Index in the loop can be used as a counter.

5. **a.** Num = 18

	First	Last	Mid	A[Mid]	Found
Before loop	1	5	Undefined	Undefined	**false**
After first pass	1	2	3	37	**false**
After second pass	1	2	1	18	**true**

c. Num = 76

	First	Last	Mid	A[Mid]	Found
Before loop	1	5	Undefined	Undefined	**false**
After first pass	4	5	3	37	**false**
After second pass	4	3	4	92	**false**

Since First > Last, the loop will be exited and an appropriate message should be printed.

9. Since procedures for copying and searching are already written, the main program statements for such a task could be

```
CopyToArray (filename, A); (*  A is an array  *)
SearchArray (A, Key, Position, Found);
IF Found THEN
   FOR LCV := Position TO Length DO
      A [LCV] := A[LCV + 1];
Length := Length - 1;
```

CHAPTER 10

Section 10.1

1. ```
DrugPrice : ARRAY [1 .. 4,1 .. 5] OF real;
DrugPrice : ARRAY [1 .. 4] OF ARRAY [1 .. 5] OF real;
```

2. ```
Grade : ARRAY [1 .. 20,1 .. 6] OF char;
Grade : ARRAY [1 .. 20] OF ARRAY [1 .. 6] OF char;
```

3. ```
QuizScore : ARRAY [1 .. 30,1 .. 12] OF integer;
QuizScore : ARRAY [1 .. 30] OF ARRAY [1 .. 12] OF integer;
```
```

5.   ShippingCost   GradeBook

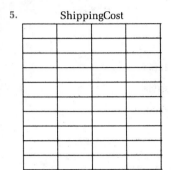

40 locations available

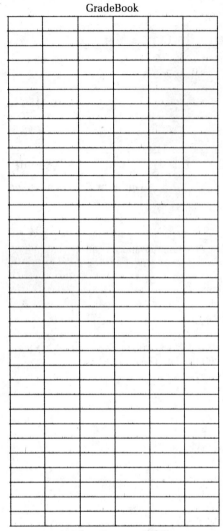

210 locations available

6.   A

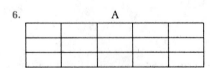

15 locations available

7.   Schedule

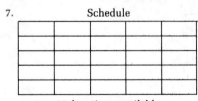

25 locations available

8.   AnswerSheet

250 locations available

13.
```
FOR  J  :=  1  TO  3  DO
     FOR  K  :=  1  TO  6  DO
          A[J,K]  :=  2 * J + K;
```

14.
```
FOR  J  :=  1  TO  3  DO
     FOR  K  :=  1  TO  6  DO
          A[J,K]  :=  0;
```

15.
```
FOR  J  :=  1  TO  3  DO
     FOR  K  :=  1  TO  6  DO
          A[J,K]  :=  2 * J;
```

```
17. TYPE
      String20 = PACKED ARRAY [1 .. 20] OF char;
      NameList = ARRAY [1 .. 50] OF String20;
    VAR
      Name: NameList;
    FOR J := 1 TO 50 DO          (*  Loop to get data  *)
      BEGIN
        FOR K := 1 TO 20 DO      (*  Read one line  *)
          read (Name[J,K]);
        readln
      END;
```

```
21. a.  FOR J := 1 TO 4 DO
          BEGIN
            MinRow[J] := Table[J,1];
            FOR K := 2 TO 5 DO
              IF Table[J,K] < MinRow[J] THEN
                MinRow[J] := Table [J,K]
          END;

    c.  Total := 0;
        FOR J := 1 TO 4 DO
          FOR K := 1 TO 5 DO
            Total := Total + Table[J,K];
```

```
23. a.  TYPE
          Table = ARRAY [1 .. 3, 1 .. 8] OF integer;

    b.  PROCEDURE Replace (VAR A : Table);
          VAR
            J,K : integer;
          BEGIN
            FOR J := 1 TO 3 DO
              FOR K := 1 TO 8 DO
                IF A[J,K] < 0 THEN
                  A[J,K] := 0
          END;  (*  of PROCEDURE Replace  *)
```

c. **PROCEDURE** Replace of **b.** could be called by

```
    Replace (Table3X5);
```

25. **a.** Reading values into A and B depends on how data are arranged in the data file.

```
    b.  FOR H := 1 TO M DO
          FOR J := 1 TO P DO
            BEGIN
              Sum := 0;
              FOR K := 1 TO N DO
                Sum := Sum + A[H,K] * B[K,J];
              C[H,J] := Sum
            END;
```

Section 10.2

1. This prints an alphabetical listing of the states whose first letter is O.

2. This prints every fifth state in reverse alphabetical order.

3. This lists the first two letters of each state.

4. This counts all occurrences of the letter A in the names of the states.

```
6. FOR J := 1 TO NumLines DO
     BEGIN
       read (Name[J,1]);
       K := 1;
       WHILE Name[J,K] <> '*' DO
         BEGIN
           K := K + 1;
           read (Name[J,K])
         END;
       Length := K;
       FOR K := Length TO 20 DO
         Name[J,K] := ' ';
       readln
     END;
```

```
8. FOR J := 1 TO NumLines DO
     BEGIN
       FOR J := 1 TO 20 DO
         read (Name[J,K]);
       readln
     END;
```

Section 10.3

1. **a.** These declarations are not appropriate because Names is an array of 10 elements while Amounts is an array of 15 elements.

   b. These are appropriate because both Table and Names represent an array of size 12 × 10.

3. Assume an array type is defined as

```
TYPE
   GradeCount = ARRAY ['A' .. 'E'] OF integer;
```

If Count is a variable of type GradeCount, the frequency of each grade can be determined by

```
FOR Ch := 'A' TO 'E' DO  (* Initialize *)
  Count[Ch] := 0;
FOR J := 1 TO ListLength DO
  CASE Grade[J] OF
    'A' : Count['A'] := Count['A'] + 1;
    'B' : Count['B'] := Count['B'] + 1;
    'C' : Count['C'] := Count['C'] + 1;
    'D' : Count['D'] := Count['D'] + 1;
    'E' : Count['E'] := Count['E'] + 1
  END; (* of CASE *)
```

Section 10.4

1. 2 * 3 * 10 = 60
2. 6 * 3 * 4 = 72
3. 3 * 2 * 11 = 66
4. 4 * 10 * 15 = 600

6.
```
TYPE
   Floor = 1 .. 4;
   Wing = 1 .. 5;
   Room = 1 .. 20;
   FloorPlan = ARRAY [Floor, Wing, Room] OF char;
VAR
   RoomType : FloorPlan;
```

CHAPTER 11

Section 11.1

7.   Employee

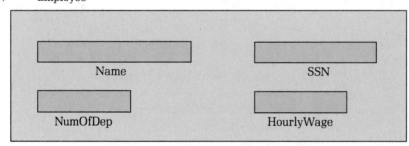

8.   House

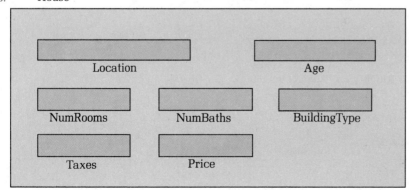

9.   PhoneListing

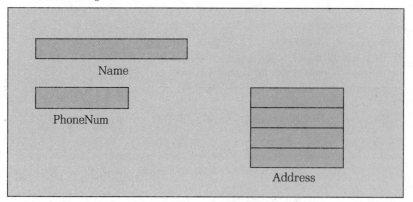

12. Info : **RECORD** should be Info = **RECORD**
    Name = **PACKED** should be Name : **PACKED**

13. Member is used as both a variable and a data type.

14. IQ = 50 .. 200 should be IQ : 50 .. 200

Section 11.2

1. is valid.

2. is invalid; Cust2 and Cust3 are not of identical type.

3. and 4. are valid.

5. is valid but demonstrates a poor practice. For better readability, you should always determine precisely which fields are being used.

7. The three different methods you could use are

```
(1)  Employee2 := Employee1;
(2)  WITH Employee2 DO
        BEGIN
          Name := Employee1.Name;
          SSN := Employee1.SSN;
          Age := Employee1.Age;
          HourlyWage := Employee1.HourlyWage;
          Volunteer := Employee1.Volunteer
        END;  (* of WITH ... DO *)

(3)  WITH Employee1 DO
        BEGIN
          Employee2.Name := Name;
          Employee2.SSN := SSN;
          Employee2.Age := Age;
          Employee2.HourlyWage := HourlyWage;
          Employee2.Volunteer := Volunteer
        END;  (* of WITH ... DO *)
```

b. Did you consider

```
WITH Employee2 DO
BEGIN
  Temp := HoursWorked;
  Employee2 := Employee1;
  HoursWorked := Temp
END;
```

```
9. FUNCTION ComputeGrade (Pts : integer) : char;
     VAR
        Percent : real;
     BEGIN
        Percent := Pts/5;  (*  Compute percent  *)
        IF Percent < 60 THEN
          Grade := 'E'
        ELSE
          IF Percent < 70 THEN
            Grade := 'D'
          ELSE
            IF Percent < 80 THEN
              Grade := 'C'
            ELSE
              IF Percent < 90 THEN
                Grade := 'B'
              ELSE
                Grade := 'A';
      ComputeGrade := Grade
     END;
```

This can be called by

```
With Student DO
   LetterGrade := ComputeGrade(TotalPts);
```

Section 11.3

1. See figure at right.
2., 4., 5., 9., 10., and 11. are valid references.
3., 6., 7., and 8. are invalid references.

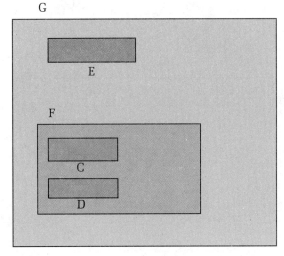

G

E

F

C

D

```
14. TYPE
      String20 = PACKED ARRAY [1 .. 20] OF char;
      Status = ('S', 'M', 'W', 'D');
      NumKids = 0 .. 15;
      FamilyRec = RECORD
                      MaritalStatus : Status;
                      Children : NumKids
                  END;  (*  of FamilyRec  *)

      AddressRec = RECORD
                      Street : String20;
                      City : String20;
                      State : PACKED ARRAY [1 .. 2] OF char;
                      ZipCode : integer
                  END;  (*  of AddressRec  *)
```

```
   CustomerInfo  = RECORD
                     Name : String20;
                     Address : AddressRec;
                     SSN : PACKED ARRAY [1 .. 11] OF char;
                     AnnualIncome : real;
                     FamilyInfo : FamilyRec
                   END;  (*  of CustomerInfo  *)

VAR
  Customer : CustomerInfo;
```

16.
```
CONST
    SquadSize = 15;

TYPE
  String20 = PACKED ARRAY [ 1 .. 20] OF char;
  AgeRange = 15 .. 25;
  HeightRange = 70 .. 100;
  WeightRange = 100 .. 300;
  PlayerInfo = RECORD
                 Name : String20;
                 Age : AgeRange;
                 Height : HeightRange;
                 Weight : WeightRange;
                 ScoringAv : real;
                 ReboundAv : real
               END;  (*  of PlayerInfo  *)
  PlayerList = ARRAY [1 .. SquadSize] OF PlayerInfo;

VAR
  Player : PlayerList;
```

18. **a.** Student

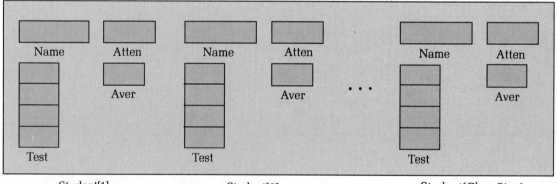

Student[1]   Student[2]   Student[ClassSize]

b. This function computes the
    test average for one student.

c. Format and headings will vary according to personal preference. However, your procedure should include

```
WITH St DO  (*  Printout for St  *)
   BEGIN
      .
      .
      .
   write ('Your attendance was ');
   CASE Atten OF
      Excellent : writeln ('excellent.');
      Average   : writeln ('average.');
      Poor      : writeln ('poor.')
   END; (*  of CASE  *)
      .
      .
      .
   END; (*  of WITH ... DO  *)
```

Section 11.4

3. The type TagType for the tag field Tag has not been defined.

4. There is no value listed for the C of the tag field.

5. There is a syntax error. A semicolon is needed between **boolean** and **CASE.** A type has not been given for the tag field. It should be

```
CASE  Tag : TagType OF
```

6. Only one variant part can be defined in a record.

8. **a.**   Figure

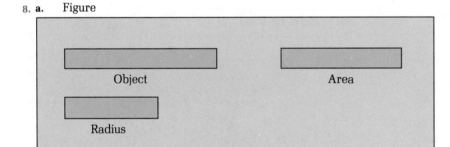

b.   Figure

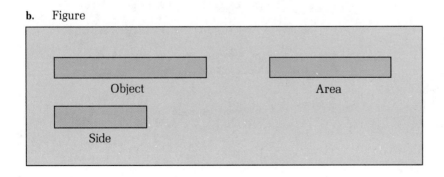

c. Figure

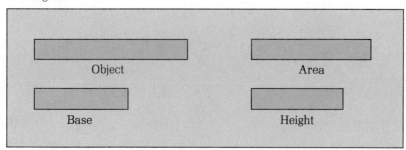

```
10. PubType = (Book, Article);
    DataRange = 1600 .. 2000;
    PublicationInfo = RECORD
                        Author : String30;
                        Title : String30;
                        Date : DataRange;
                        CASE Pub : PubType OF
                          Book    : (Publisher : String30;
                                     City : String30);
                          Article : (JournalName : String30;
                                     VolumeNumber : integer)
                        END;
```

CHAPTER 12

Section 12.1

3. is valid; the component type is an integer in the subrange 0 .. 120

4. is invalid; no file type has been defined.

5. is invalid; component type for a file cannot be another file.

6. is invalid; the expression **FILE** [1 .. 100] has no meaning.

7. is valid; the component type is **integer.**

```
9. TYPE
     String20 = PACKED ARRAY [1 .. 20] OF char;
     AddressType = ARRAY [1 .. 3] OF String20;
     SexType = (M,F);

     PatientInfo = RECORD
                     Name : String20;
                     Address : AddressType;
                     Height : 0 .. 200;
                     Weight : 0 .. 300;
                     Sex : SexType;
                     Age : 0 .. 120;
                     InsuranceCo : String20
                   END; (* of PaientInfo *)

     PatientFile = FILE OF PatientInfo;

   VAR
     Patient : PatientFile;
```

Section 12.2

```
5. TYPE
     FileType = FILE OF 0 .. 100;
   VAR
     SevenMult : FileType;
```

A fragment of code for this problem is

```
rewrite (SevenMult);  (* Open the file *)
Num := 1;
Sevens := 7;
WHILE Sevens < 100 DO
  BEGIN
    SevenMult↑ := Sevens;
    put (SevenMult);
    Num := Num + 1
    Sevens := 7 * Num;
  END; (* of WHILE ... DO *)
```

7.
```
reset (FivesFile);
A := FivesFile↑;
get (FivesFile);
B := FivesFile↑;
get (FivesFile);
C := FivesFile↑;
get (FivesFile);
D := FivesFile↑;
```

9. The **reset** procedure opens a file so that values may be read from the file. Contents of the file are not altered by this command. When **reset**(file name) is executed, the value of the first component is copied into the buffer variable.

   The **rewrite** procedure opens a file so that values may be read into the file. When **rewrite**(file name) is executed, any previous contents are lost.

11. The **reset** procedure opens the file for reading from the file, and **put** is used to write to the file. It appears that reset(File1); should have been **rewrite** (File1);

12. No errors.

13. The buffer variable is not properly written.

    ```
    File1 := 10 * J;
    ```
    should be
    ```
    File1↑ := 10 * J;
    ```

14. This loop will execute, but nothing happens. In order to put the values into File1, the loop should be

    ```
    FOR J := 1 TO 5 DO
      BEGIN
        File1↑ := J * 10;
        Put (File1)
      END;
    ```

15. The files are mixed up. It appears that the intent is to copy the contents of File1 into File2.

16. No errors. This is a correct version of a problem similar to that posed in Exercise 15.

20. The output is

    ```
    -17
    -4
    ```

    The files contain the following values.

8	−17	0	−4	21

OldFile

8	0	21

NewFile

Section 12.3

1.
```
TYPE
    String20 = PACKED ARRAY [1 .. 20] OF char;
    PatientInfo = RECORD
                    Name : String20;
                    Age : 0 .. 120;
                    Height : 0 .. 100;
                    Weight : 0 .. 350;
                    InsCompany : String20;
                    AmtDue : real
                  END; (* of RECORD PatientInfo *)
    PatientFile = FILE OF PatientInfo;
VAR
    Patient : PatientFile;
```

3.
```
TYPE
    String20 = PACKED ARRAY [1 .. 20] OF char;
    BookInfo = RECORD
                  Author : String20;
                  Title : String20;
                  StockNumber : integer;
                  Price : real;
                  Quantity : 0 .. 500
               END; (* of RECORD BookInfo *)
    BookFile = FILE OF BookInfo;
VAR
    Book : BookFile;
```

```
6. TYPE
      String20 = PACKED ARRAY [1 .. 20] OF char;
      QuizList = ARRAY [1 .. 10] OF 0 .. 10;
      TestList = ARRAY [1 .. 4] OF 0 .. 100;
      StudentRec = RECORD
                        Name : String20;
                        Number : integer;
                        Quiz : QuizList;
                        Test : TestList
                      END;  (*  of RECORD  StudentRec  *)

      StudentFile = FILE OF StudentRec;

   VAR
      Student : StudentFile;

b. PROCEDURE GetData (VAR St : StudentFile);
      VAR
         J : integer;
      BEGIN
        reset (Data);
        rewrite (St);       (*  Open St for writing  *)
        WHILE NOT eof (Data) DO
          BEGIN
            WITH St↑ DO   (*  Get data for one student  *)
              BEGIN
                FOR J := 1 TO 20 DO
                  read (Name[J]);  (*  Get a name  *)
                read (Number);      (*  Get student ID  *)
                FOR J := 1 TO 10 DO
                  read (Quiz[J]); (*  Get quiz scores  *)
                FOR J := 1 TO 4 DO
                  read (Test[J])  (*  Get test scores  *)
              END;  (*  of WITH ... DO  *)
            readln;
            put (St)  (*  Move data to file  *)
          END  (*  of WHILE NOT eof  *)
      END;  (*  of PROCEDURE GetData  *)
```

c. The basic design for this task is

1. Transfer records to an array
2. Sort the array
3. Transfer records from the array back to the file

Assuming suitable definitions and declarations have been made, a procedure for this is

```
PROCEDURE SortFile (VAR St : StudentFile);
   VAR
      Temp : StudentRec;
      J,K,Length, Index : integer;
      TempList : ARRAY [1 .. MaxSize] OF StudentRec;
   BEGIN
      J := 0;
      reset (St);
      WHILE NOT eof(St) DO  (*  Copy to array  *)
        BEGIN
          J := J + 1;
          TempList[J] := St↑;
          get (St)
        END;
      Length := J;
```

```
   (*   Now  sort  the  array   *)

     FOR  J  :=  1  TO  Length-1  DO
        BEGIN
           Temp  :=  TempList[J];
           Index  :=  J;
           FOR  K  :=  J + 1  TO  Length  DO
              IF  TempList[K].Name  <  Temp.Name  THEN
                 BEGIN
                    Temp  :=  TempList[K];
                    Index  :=  K
                 END;
           TempList[Index]  :=  TempList[J];
           TempList[J]  :=  Temp
        END;   (*   of  FOR  loop   *)

   (*   Now  copy  back  to  the  file   *)

     rewrite(St);
     FOR  J  :=  1  TO  Length  DO
        BEGIN
           St↑  :=  TempList[J];
           put  (St)
        END
  END;   (*   of  PROCEDURE  SortFile   *)
```

CHAPTER 13
Section 13.1

1. **real** is not an ordinal data type.

2. **integer** will exceed maximum size for a set.

3. : should be =.

4. Brackets should not be used.

5. No errors.

8. **a.** A := ['J', 'I', 'M'];

   b. A := ['P', 'A', 'S', 'C', 'L'];

   c. The elements are 'T', 'O', and 'Y'. The eight subsets are [], ['T'], ['O'], ['Y'], ['T','O'], ['T','Y'], ['O','Y'], ['T','O','Y']

16. Brackets are needed, as

    A := ['J' .. 'O']

17. No errors.

18. Single quotation marks are needed, as

    B := ['A' .. 'Z'];

19. 'E' and 'I' are listed more than once.

20. [] is not a set variable.

21. Since 'S' is in the subrange 'A' .. 'T', it is listed more than once.

26.
```
TYPE
   Hues = (Red,Orange,Yellow,Green,Blue,Indigo,Violet);
   RainbowSet = SET OF Hues;

VAR
   Rainbow : RainbowSet;
```

28.
```
TYPE
   SomeFruits = (Apple,Orange,Banana,Grape,Pear,Peach,
                    Strawberry);
   FruitSet = SET OF SomeFruits;

VAR
   Fruit : FruitSet;
```

Section 13.2

1. No. When A = B, both A >= B
   and A <= B are **true**.

3. A + B = [-3 ,, 4, 7 ,, 10]
   A * B = [0,1,2,8,10]
   A - B = [-3,-2,-1]
   B - A = [3,4,7,9]

5. A + B = B
   A * B = A
   A - B = A
   B - A = B

Exercises 15–20 are all **true**.

Section 13.3

```
7. FUNCTION AllOddDigits (Num : integer) : boolean;
   TYPE
      Digits = SET OF 0 .. 9;
   VAR
      EvenDigits : Digits;
      NumDigits,J,Digit : integer;
   BEGIN
      EvenDigits := [0,2,4,6,8,10];
      IF Num DIV 1000 = 0 THEN
        IF Num DIV 100 = 0 THEN
          IF Num DIV 10 = 0 THEN
             NumDigits := 1
          ELSE NumDigits := 2
        ELSE NumDigits := 3
      ELSE NumDigits := 4;
      AllOddDigits := true;
      FOR J := 1 TO NumDigits DO
        BEGIN
          Digit := abs(Num MOD 10);
          IF Digit IN EvenDigits THEN
            AllOddDigits := false;
          Num := Num DIV 10
        END  (*  of FOR loop  *)
   END;  (*  of FUNCTION AllOddDigits  *)
```

CHAPTER 14

Section 14.1

3.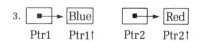

8. is invalid; IntPtr1 + 1 is not allowed.

9. is invalid; pointers cannot be
   used with **writeln.**

10. is valid.

11. is invalid; < is not a valid com-
    parison for pointers.

12. is invalid; BoolPtr **NOT NIL**
    should be BoolPtr2 <> **NIL.**

13. is valid.

14. is invalid; BoolPtr2 is not a
    boolean expression.

15. is valid.

Section 14.2

3. Assume the file name is Num.
   A procedure is then

```
PROCEDURE PrintNumbers (First : DataPtr);
   VAR
     P : DataPtr;
   BEGIN
     P := First;
     WHILE P <> NIL DO
       BEGIN
         writeln (P↑.Num);
         P : P↑.Next
       END
   END; (* of PROCEDURE PrintNumbers *)
```

and is called by

```
PrintNumbers (Start);
```

5. **a.**
```
TYPE
    String20 = PACKED ARRAY [1 .. 20] OF char;
    TestList = ARRAY [1 .. 4] OF 0 .. 100;
    QuizList = ARRAY [1 .. 10] OF 0 .. 10;
    DataPtr = ↑StudentInfo;
    StudentInfo = RECORD
                    Name : String20;
                    Test : TestList;
                    Quiz : QuizList;
                    Average : real;
                    Grade : char;
                    Next : DataPtr
                  END; (* of RECORD StudentInfo *)
VAR
    Student : DataPtr;
```

   b. The pointer variable is Student. The pointer type is DataPtr.

   c. Assume Start, Ptr, and Last have been declared to be of type DataPtr. Data for the first student can then be obtained by

```
new (Start);
Ptr := Start;
Last := Start;
WITH Start↑ DO
  BEGIN
    FOR J := 1 TO 20 DO
      read (Name[J]);
    FOR J := 1 TO 4 DO
      read (Test[J]);
    FOR J := 1 TO 10 DO
      read (Quiz[J]);
    Next := NIL
  END;
readln;
```

   Data for the second student can be obtained by

```
new (Last);
Ptr↑.Next := Last;
Ptr := Last;
WITH Last↑ DO
  BEGIN
    FOR J := 1 TO 20 DO
      read (Name[J]);
    FOR J := 1 TO 4 DO
      read (Test[J]);
    FOR J := 1 TO 10 DO
      read (Quiz[J])
  END;
readln;
Ptr↑.Next := NIL;
```

Exercise	Result

7.

8.

9.

10.

11.

12.

13. `A↑.Next↑.Next := B;`

17. Assume the linked list has been declared and values read into the field Num for each component of the list. Furthermore, assume Start is the pointer to the first node. A function for summing is then

```
FUNCTION Sum (First : DataPtr): integer;
  VAR
    Total : integer;
    P : DataPtr;
  BEGIN
    Total := 0;
    P := First;
    WHILE P <> NIL DO
      BEGIN
        Total := Total + P↑.Num;
        P := P↑.Next
      END;
    Sum := Total
  END; (* of FUNCTION Sum *)
```

Section 14.3

1. Assume the original list can be envisioned as

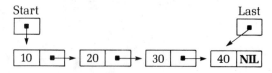

and you wish to insert 25 into the list. The initialization produces

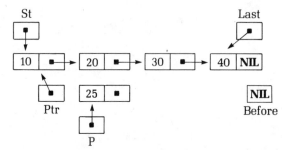

Since the loop is not empty, the **WHILE** . . . **DO** loop will be executed until we have

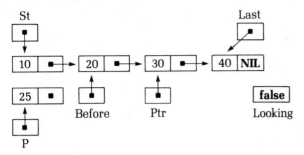

The pointers are then moved to obtain

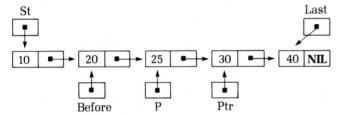

3. The new code is

```
IF Before = NIL THEN
   Push (St, NewNum)        (*  Call to Push  *)
ELSE
   Before↑.Next := P;
```

5. The heading becomes

```
PROCEDURE Pop (VAR St : DataPtr);
```

and the line

```
NewNum := P↑.Num
```

should be deleted.

7.
```
PROCEDURE Delete (VAR St:DataPtr; Position:integer);
   VAR
      Before, P : DataPtr;
   BEGIN
      IF Position = 1 THEN
         Pop (St, St↑.Num)
      ELSE
         BEGIN
            Before := St;
            FOR J := 1 TO (Position - 2) DO
               Before := Before↑.Next;
            P := Before↑.Next;
            Before↑.Next := P↑.Next;
            dispose (P)
         END    (*  of ELSE option  *)
   END; (*  of modified PROCEDURE Delete  *)
```

Section 14.4

1. Illustrating only the parentheses, you get

S

Character Read	New Stack
"("	(
"("	((
"("	(((
")"	((
"("	(((
")"	((
")"	(
")"	

5. a.
```
CONST
   MaxStack = value;

TYPE
   Stack = RECORD
              Item : ARRAY [1 .. MaxStack] OF data type;
              Top : 0 .. MaxStack
           END;

VAR
   S : Stack;
```

b. Push becomes

```
PROCEDURE Push (VAR S : Stack; X : integer);
  BEGIN
    IF S.Top = MaxStack THEN
      writeln ('Stack overflow')
    ELSE
      BEGIN
        S.Top := S.Top + 1;
        S.Item[S.Top] := X
      END
  END; (*  of PROCEDURE Push  *)
```

PopAndCheck becomes

```
PROCEDURE PopAndCheck (VAR S:Stack; VAR X:integer;
                               VAR underflow : boolean);
  BEGIN
    IF Empty(S) THEN   (*  Check for empty stack  *)
      Underflow := true
    ELSE
      BEGIN
        Underflow := false;
        X := S.Item[S.Top];
        S.Top := S.Top - 1
      END (*  of ELSE option  *)
  END; (*  of PROCEDURE PopAndCheck  *)
```

12. Change the **ELSE** option to

```
ELSE
  IF Num = Node↑.Info THEN
    writeln (Num, ' is a duplicate value.')
  ELSE
    IF Num < Node↑.Info THEN
      AddNode (Node↑.LeftChild, Num)
    ELSE
      AddNode (Node↑.RightChild, Num)
```

14.
```
FUNCTION Search (Node:Pointer; NewNum:integer) : boolean;
  VAR
    Found : boolean;
    Current : Pointer;
  BEGIN
    Current := Node;
    Found := false;
    WHILE (Current <> NIL) AND NOT Found DO
      IF Current↑.Num = NewNum THEN
        Found := true
      ELSE
      IF Current↑.Num < NewNum THEN
        Current := Current↑.RightChild
      ELSE
        Current := Current↑.LeftChild;
      Search := Found
  END; (*  of FUNCTION Search  *)
```

16.

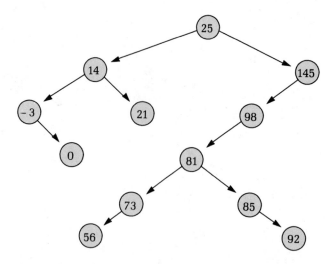

⊞ Index

Credits and Acknowledgments

PHOTOS

Figure 1.4(a): © The Photo Works. Photo Researchers.
Figure 1.4(b): © Tom McHugh. Photo Researchers.
Figure 1.5(a): © Art Stein. Photo Researchers.
Figure 1.5(b): Courtesy of IBM Corporation.

NOTES OF INTEREST

Page 5: Adapted from E. T. Bell, *Men of Mathematics*, New York: Simon & Schuster, 1937, pp. 73–89.

Page 7: Reprinted with permission from "Pascal," by T. Woteki and A. Freiden, published in the September 1983 issue of *Popular Computing* magazine. © McGraw-Hill, Inc., New York. All rights reserved.

Page 14: From William Bates, *The Computer Cookbook*, New York, Doubleday & Co., 1984–85, p. 165. Reprinted by permission of William Bates.

Page 25: From William Bates, *The Computer Cookbook*, New York, Doubleday & Co., 1984–85, p. 342. Reprinted by permission of William Bates.

Page 34: From William Bates, *The Computer Cookbook*, New York, Doubleday & Co., 1984–85, p. 255. Reprinted by permission of William Bates.

Page 61: *Communications of the ACM* 27, no. 9 (September 1984): 880. Copyright 1984, Association for Computing Machinery, Inc. Reprinted by permission of Association for Computing Machinery.

Page 64: Reprinted by permission from *Introduction to Computers with BASIC*, pp. 27–28, by Fred G. Harold. Copyright © 1984 by West Publishing Company. All rights reserved.

Page 85: Reprinted by permission from *Introduction to Computers with BASIC*, p. 203, by Fred G. Harold. Copyright © 1984 by West Publishing Company. All rights reserved.

Page 102: Reprinted by permission from *Introduction to Computers with BASIC*, p. 245, by Fred G. Harold. Copyright © 1984 by West Publishing Company. All rights reserved.

Pages 111 and 115: From J. Bentley, *Communications of the ACM* 28, no. 2 (February 1985): 139. Copyright 1985, Association for Computing Machinery, Inc. Reprinted by permission of Association for Computing Machinery.

Page 129: Adapted from E. T. Bell, *Men of Mathematics*, New York: Simon & Schuster, 1937, pp. 433–447.

Page 188: Reprinted by permission from *Introduction to Computers with BASIC*, pp. 26–27, by Fred G. Harold. Copyright © 1984 by West Publishing Company. All rights reserved.

Page 193: *Communications of the ACM* 27, no. 9 (September 1984): 886. Copyright 1984, Association for Computing Machinery, Inc. Reprinted by permission of Association for Computing Machinery.

Page 202: Reprinted by permission from *Introduction to Computers with BASIC*, pp. 24–26, by Fred G. Harold. Copyright © 1984 by West Publishing Company. All rights reserved.

Page 261: Reprinted by permission from *Introduction to Computers with BASIC*, pp. 246–249, by Fred G. Harold. Copyright © 1984 by West Publishing Company. All rights reserved.

Page 291: Adapted from Niklaus Wirth, Programming Language Design to Computer Construction, 1984 Turing Award Lecture, *Communications of the ACM*, February 1985, volume 28, no. 2.

Page 302: From Twila Slesnick, "Computer Myths We Can Live Without," *Classroom Computer Learning* 5, no. 6 (February 1985): 33. Reprinted by permission from *Classroom Computer Learning*, 2451 E. River Road, Dayton, Ohio 45439.

Page 331: From "How Girls Lose Interest: A Summary of the Research," *Classroom Computer Learning* 5, no. 8 (April/May 1985): 24. Reprinted by permission from *Classroom Computer Learning*, 2451 E. River Road, Dayton, Ohio 45439.

Page 340: From John Hamblen, "Degrees Awarded in the Computer and Information Sciences 1980–81 through 1988–89," *T. H. E. Journal* 12, no. 9 (May 1985): 66. Reprinted by permission from *T. H. E. Journal*.

Page 360: Adapted from T. R. Reid, "The Chip," *Science*, February 1985, pp. 32–41.

Page 375: From *Computer Wimp* by John Bear, Ph.D. Copyright 1983. Used with permission of Ten Speed Press. Box 7123, Berkeley, CA 94707.

Page 396: From William Bates, *The Computer Cookbook*, New York, Doubleday & Co., 1984–85, p. 180. Reprinted by permission of William Bates.

Local system notes

Local system notes

Local system notes

Local system notes